NORTHERN HUMANISM IN
EUROPEAN CONTEXT, 1469-1625

BRILL'S STUDIES IN INTELLECTUAL HISTORY

VOLUME 94

I. Portraits of Wessel Gansfort, Rudolph Agricola, Regnerus Praedinius and Ubbo Emmius in *Effigies & vitae Professorum Academiae Groningae & Omlandiae,* Groningen 1654. (Courtesy of the University Library, and the University Museum, Groningen.)

NORTHERN HUMANISM IN EUROPEAN CONTEXT, 1469-1625

From the 'Adwert Academy' to Ubbo Emmius

EDITED BY

F. AKKERMAN, A.J. VANDERJAGT AND A.H. VAN DER LAAN

BRILL

LEIDEN · BOSTON · KÖLN

1999

This book is printed on acid-free paper.

Library of Congress Cataloging-in-Publication Data

Northern humanism in European context, 1469-1625 : from the 'Adwert
    Academy' to Ubbo Emmius / edited by Fokke Akkerman,
    Arjo Vanderjagt, Adrie van der Laan.
        p. cm. — (Brill's studies in intellectual history, ISSN
    0920-8607 ; v. 94)
    Includes bibliographical references and index.
    ISBN 9004113142 (cloth : alk. paper)
    1. Latin literature, Medieval and modern—Europe, Northern—
    –History and criticism. 2. Europe, Northern—Intellectual life.
    3. Renaissance—Europe, Northern. 4. Humanists—Europe, Northern.
    I. Akkerman, Fokke.   II. Vanderjagt, Arie Johan.   III. Laan, Adrie
    van der.   IV. Series.
    PA8040.N67   1999
    144'.094'09031—dc21   99–17135
                                                                    CIP

Die Deutsche Bibliothek - CIP-Einheitsaufnahme

Northern humanism in European context, 1469-1625 : from the
'Adwert Academy' to Ubbo Emmius / ed. by Fokke Akkerman ...
– Leiden ; Boston ; Köln : Brill, 1999
    (Brill's studies in intellectual history ; Vol. 94)
    ISBN 90–04–11314–2

ISSN   0920-8607
ISBN   90 04 11314 2

PRINTED IN THE NETHERLANDS

CONTENTS

PLATES

PREFACE

In the early '80s, Fokke Akkerman and Arjo Vanderjagt embarked on a project that asked renewed attention for the interest in and love for classical scholarship and erudition of learned men in the northern Netherlands and the adjoining parts of Germany. Much work had already been done on this theme in the nineteenth and early twentieth centuries but mostly from the perspective of theology and church history. Especially important was the discovery, systematisation and research then also done by municipal and provincial archivists, and by local historians. In the third quarter of our own century Professor Edzo Waterbolk of the University of Groningen considerably extended our knowledge of the historical context of this Northern Humanism. Our own approach from the start focused on Neolatin, that is to say: on the revival of Latin literature and philology, on the history of pedagogy and didactics, and on rhetoric and philosophy, of course without excluding piety, the world of the Modern Devotion and aspects of the protestant reformation.

It was immediately obvious to us that the backbone of this project on Northern Humanism was to be the study of the four men and their circles, who have traditionally been linked to intellectual pursuits in these lands. The writer of the introduction to the *Effigies & vitae Professorum Academiae Groningae & Omlandiae*, published on the occasion of the fortieth anniversary of the foundation of the university in 1654, considers 'the triumvirate of the literary glory of Groningen': Wessel Gansfort (1419-1489), Rudolph Agricola (1444-1485) and Regnerus Praedinius (1510-1559). The fourth scholar whose work is said to be immortal is Ubbo Emmius (1547-1625), the first rector of the university. Far from being local and parochial, these learned men were in their own times well-known, even famous throughout the Low Countries, Germany and Switzerland, and in the cases of Gansfort and Agricola also in France and Italy; and Ubbo Emmius notably was highly praised by the French humanist Jacobus Thuanus (Jacques-Auguste de Thou, 1553-1617) for the first installments of his *Rerum Frisicarum Historiae*. Besides, they were members of extended groups of like-minded scholars, many of whom exchanged letters and information, thus transmitting their insights and ideas widely.

The first fruit of this project was *Rodolphus Agricola Phrisius (1444-1485). Proceedings of the International Conference at the University of Groningen 28-30 October 1985*, eds. F. Akkerman, A.J. Vanderjagt (Leiden 1988) in which the foremost scholars on Agricola and his circle presented their latest research. A second conference in 1989 put down the groundwork

for *Wessel Gansfort (1419-1489) and Northern Humanism*, eds. F. Akkerman, G.C. Huisman, A.J. Vanderjagt (Leiden 1993). Besides discussions of
Gansfort's learning, this volume has sections as well on the *Devotio moderna* and on the Northern Humanism closely connected to Agricola. It also has
important articles on Regnerus Praedinius and on the Latin correspondence
of Ubbo Emmius and of the Van Ewsums, an aristocratic family of the 'Ommelanden' of Groningen. Also included in this book is the first integral
edition of the Latin poetry of Friedrich Mormann (†1482).

The present third volume is based on the papers read at the conference on
Northern Humanism in European Context, 1469-1625, which was held at
the University of Groningen on 11-12 April 1996. Most of these papers are
included in the present book, but they were often expanded and rewritten. It
will be seen that Fokke Akkerman's contribution is far longer than the
others. The reason for this is that the two documents that he discusses are
central to debates and learned opinion on humanism and reform in sixteenth-century Groningen, and that both are exceptionally difficult to read
without the instruments here provided.

The title used for the conference of 1996 has been expanded to include a
subtitle *From the 'Adwert Academy' to Ubbo Emmius.* We have chosen to
do this in order to clarify what is meant exactly by Northern Humanism in
our context, and to dispel possible misunderstandings that this project is
about the humanism of Erasmus and his times. In the oldest letters – dating
from 1469 – that we have of Rudolph Agricola and Rudolph von Langen
first, short mention is made of a circle of early humanist scholars who were
used to meet at the Adwert monastery near Groningen. The *terminus ad
quem* is derived from Ubbo Emmius, first rector of the Academy at Groningen and arguably its last humanist, who died in 1625.

The papers printed here form a heterogeneous collection, even more so
than the ones in the Agricola and the Gansfort volumes. Their authors are
learned in many diverging areas of scholarship and they approach their subject matter from sometimes very different vantage points. The editors inter-
fered as little as possible, and they did not desire or even dare to attempt to
systematically accommodate or to unite all the ideas put forward in the individual papers. Still we carefully checked all quotations or translations from
the sources. Footnotes and bibliographical material were edited thoroughly;
references were harmonised and shortened, and a bibliography was placed at
the end of the book as in the earlier volumes. The editors are grateful to the
contributing scholars for their prompt responses to our queries and suggestions.

This volume marks the end of our project on Northern Humanism in this
form of collected essays. Of course we do not think that these books are the
final word on the renaissance of the *studia humanitatis* in the northern Low

Countries and the adjacent areas. On the contrary: we think that this work shows how much more there is to learn about this theme. It only, as it were, scratches the surface. Very much still needs to be done: texts, especially, need to be edited, commented upon and translated from the Latin. We know that there are scholars at present engaged in further research along these lines. To stimulate this kind of work was one of the initial goals of our project.

The organisation of the conference of 1996 was made possible through the generous financial support of the Royal Netherlands Academy of Arts and Sciences (KNAW), the Centre for Classical, Oriental, Medieval and Renaissance Studies (COMERS), the Faculty of Philosophy of the University of Groningen, the Stichting Groninger Universiteitsfonds, the University Administration, and the Government of the Province of Groningen, in particular the Queen's Commissioner for the Province of Groningen until recently, His Excellency H.J.L. Vonhoff.

We are grateful for the permission of several libraries to reproduce material from their collections; where appropriate below they are duly mentioned. Ms Gerda Huisman of the Rare Books Collection of the University Library and Mr Frank Smit of the University Museum of the University of Groningen provided the photographs of the seventeenth-century copperplate engravings by Steven van Lamsweerde for the dustjacket and frontispiece of this volume. The Constantijn Huygens Institute at The Hague enabled us to use their facilities for preparing the manuscript for the publisher.

Our last word of thanks is to Koninklijke Brill Publishers of Leiden and especially to Ms Gera van Bedaf and Mr Job Lisman for publishing this collection of articles in the series *Brill's Studies in Intellectual History*.

CONTRIBUTORS

Dr F. AKKERMAN, Slauerhofflaan 1, 9752 HA Haren, The Netherlands

Professor C.P.M. BURGER, Faculteit der Godgeleerdheid, Free University Amsterdam, De Boelelaan 1105, 1981 HV Amsterdam, The Netherlands

Dr J.C. BEDAUX, Keurkampstraat 24, 7415 DL Deventer, The Netherlands

Dr C.M.A. CASPERS, Liturgisch Instituut, Theological Faculty Tilburg, Academielaan 9, 5037 ET Tilburg, The Netherlands

Dr T. ELSMANN, Staats- und Universitätsbibliothek Bremen, Postfach 330160, 28331 Bremen, Germany

Ms M. GORIS, Vakgroep Nederlands, Faculteit der Letteren, Catholic University Nijmegen, Postbus 9103, 6500 HC Nijmegen, The Netherlands

Dr M.J.F.M. HOENEN, Faculteit der Wijsbegeerte, Catholic University Nijmegen, Postbus 9103, 6500 HC Nijmegen, The Netherlands

Ms P. KOOIMAN, J. Israelsstraat 82, 9718 GR Groningen, The Netherlands

Dr H.A. KROP, Faculteit der Wijsbegeerte, Erasmus University Rotterdam, Postbus 1738, 3000 DR Rotterdam, The Netherlands

Dr L.W. NAUTA, Oosterweg 12, 9892 PJ Feerwerd, The Netherlands

Dr J. PAPY, Seminarium Philologiae Humanisticae, Catholic University Leuven, Postbus 33, 3000 Leuven, Belgium

Professor E. RUMMEL, Department of History, Wilfrid Laurier University, Waterloo, Ontario, Canada N2L 3C5

Professor R.J. SCHOECK, 232 Dakota Street, Lawrence, Kansas 66046, USA

Professor A. SOTTILI, Dipartimento di studi medioevali, umanistici e rinascimentali, Università Cattolica del Sacro Cuore, Largo A. Gemelli, 1, 20123 Milan, Italy

Mr A.L. TERVOORT, 19 Shelbourne Village, Ringsend Rd, Dublin 4, Ireland

Professor A.J. VANDERJAGT, Faculteit der Wijsbegeerte, University of Groningen, A-weg 30, 9718 CW Groningen, The Netherlands

Dr A.H. VAN DER LAAN, Constantijn Huygens Instituut, Postbus 90754, 2509 LT The Hague, The Netherlands

Dr M. VAN DER POEL, Constantijn Huygens Instituut, Postbus 90754, 2509 LT The Hague, The Netherlands

Dr Z.R.W.M. VON MARTELS, Klassiek Instituut, University of Groningen, Oude Boteringestraat 23, 9712 GC Groningen, The Netherlands

Mr A.E. WALTER, MA, Fachbereich Sprach- und Literaturwissenschaft, Forschungsstelle Literatur der Frühen Neuzeit, Universität Osnabrück, Neuer Graben 19/21, 49069 Osnabrück, Germany

Professor A.G. WEILER, Hyacintlaan 4, 6860 DV Heelsum, The Netherlands

F. AKKERMAN

THE EARLY REFORMATION IN GRONINGEN.
ON TWO LATIN DISPUTATIONS[*]

In this contribution I shall report on two Latin disputations dating from the
first half of the sixteenth century. They have in common the town where
they were conceived and written, they share their spiritual, political and
intellectual background, and in their literary form, the academic disputation,
they both betray the university training of their authors. For the ideas they
propose they are certainly indebted to the discussions and beliefs of the
early German and Dutch Reformers and to the writings of Erasmus.

In my survey I shall almost entirely refrain from discussing the place
they take in the whole of the religious writing of the period, nor have I tried
to bring in more than a spark of the boundless secondary literature on the
Reformation. My analysis of these *opuscula* aims at taking my reading of
Latin texts of the humanist period of Groningen (c. 1469-c. 1625) a step
further.[1] But it is a matter of course that in reading these Groningen authors
the contents of their various writings will not be shunned.

> a. [Nicolaus Lesdorpius]: *Disputatio habita Gruningae [...] (1523)*
> b. Regnerus Praedinius: *De intercessione diuorum libellus (c. 1534)*

The participants in the so-called *Disputatio Groningensis* as well as
Praedinius were not aware of belonging to any other church than the only
one that existed in their home town, but this does not alter the fact that both
booklets can safely be reckoned to the early Reformation. Their authors or
readers had no need of labels such as Reformation, humanism or
scholasticism in fact these terms existed hardly or not at – all the time –
the only words they use are *euangelicus, bonae literae, optima studia,
liberalis* or *melior eruditio*. They propound religious beliefs and show
political attitudes, which in their time were proclaimed in many writings. It
can safely be assumed that they had read the printed books and pamphlets of

---

[*] For his ready help in correcting the English of this article I wish to thank Arjo Vanderjagt.
¹ A beginning was made by Van der Laan, Schoonbeeg and myself in *Humanistische Buch-
kultur.* See also the contributions of Kemper, and of Van der Laan and Kuik in *Wessel Gansfort
and Northern Humanism,* and further those of Schoonbeeg and myself in *Ubbo Emmius, een
Oostfries geleerde.* Far more than a beginning in Van der Laan, *Anatomie van een Taal.*

the reformers and Erasmus, which were spread all over Europe.[2] They certainly heard reports on what went on in Brabant, Flanders, Switzerland and Germany. They had learned to think and reason from the Bible only, and from some selected ancient Fathers as well. But they tried to reach conclusions of their own on the specific topics they had chosen in the context of their own environment.

Private or semi-public talks on religious, political and literary subjects had had a well-attested tradition of half a century in Groningen. Already in 1469, discussions were organised in the monastery of Aduard; the flow of written and printed letters started at about the same time,[3] later we learn about discussions between Agricola and Gansfort.[4] The dialogue *De solitudine* of Jacob Canter is a literary fiction, but it may well have drawn on common talk among town- and country people in Groningen.[5] We hear about discussions at the table of Wilhelmus Frederici, the head priest of St. Martin's church, who sometimes invited local Dominicans to discuss, 'inter pocula et prandia',[6] religious matters.[7] Albert Hardenberg tells us that Goswinus van Halen, the head of the school of the Brethren of the Common Life, wrote a number of dialogues, and with his ex-pupils he conversed by means of many letters:[8] letters are nothing but a 'sermo inter absentes', as the often quoted phrase of Cicero has it.

So both disputations that will be treated below belong to a local literary and oral tradition of long standing. Their subject matter had developed with the debate in the city and elsewhere. The two texts, therefore, do not treat questions and problems suddenly imported from abroad. Neither text enters upon a broad, many-sided religious discussion, but both concentrate on one single subject, relevant to the early Reformation, but not too directly related to delicate, dangerous questions such as those about the status of the faith,

---

[2] Some recent work on the early Reformation in the Low Countries: Duke, 'Building Heaven in Hell's Despite'; idem, *The Face of 'Popular Religious Dissent'*, Trapman, *De Summa der godliker scrifturen*; Spruyt, 'Listrius lutherizans', *idem*, 'Gerardus Listrius' Epistola theologica'; idem, 'Humanisme, Evangelisme en reformatie'; idem, *Cornelius Henrici Hoen*; Augustijn, *Erasmus*.

[3] See the letters written in Aduard and those of Liber written in Groningen and Cologne, now in Van der Laan, *Anatomie van een Taal.*

[4] We learn this from Agricola's own letters (epp. 26,27 and 41,15; see Van der Laan, *Anatomie van een Taal*, 230 and 259), from a poem by Moorman (Schoonbeeg, 'Friderici Mauri carmina', no. XVII (p. 346-7) and from Melanchthon, 'Oratio de uita Rodolphi Agricolae' (*Corp. Ref.*, 444) and 'Epistola Alardo Aemstelredamo'(Alardus, †3v).

[5] Two editions of this dialogue: Ebels-Hoving 1981 and Enenkel 1995.

[6] The phrase is here quoted from the dedication of the anonymous satire *Lamentationes Petri*, where it is said that Frederici taught his friends to discuss religious matters at dinner (*Lamentationes*, A3v).

[7] Erasmus, *Opus Epistolarum*, no. 1200; Wolfs, *Das Groninger 'Religionsgespräch'*, 41.

[8] See Gansfort, *Opera*, **5v.

of the Eucharist or the other sacraments, about the indulgences, the position of monks and monasteries, in short, to topics the open treatment of which could have endangered the social and political peace of the town or province.[9]

Though the participants in these disputes belong to the intellectual élite of the town, the town mayors and city council are not directly involved. There is no question of the discussions being a sort of trial. There is no arbitrator to decide which party won, nor notaries to guarantee an impartial report. In both disputes the initiative was taken by the upholders of the conservative view: the Dominicans in the *Disputatio Groningensis* and the 'friend' who defends the usefulness of the invocation of the saints in prayer in Praedinius's *libellus*. The status of the church and of its preaching in the town is not at stake. For all these differences with the early discussions of the Swiss and German Reformation, the term 'Religionsgespräch', which Wolfs has used for the *Disputatio Groningensis*, is perhaps less appropriate. But this remains a question of definition.[10] In other respects, Groningen shows more similarity with the 'free' towns in Germany and Switzerland than with the situation in Holland and Flanders.

Until 1536 Groningen did not belong to the Habsburg empire of Charles V; there was no Inquisition in the region. Despite the overlordship of the Duke of Guelders from 1514 till 1536, and after 1536 of the Governess in Brussels, the town managed to keep its relative independence.[11] Well into the sixties, the city council, its mayors and secretaries, its schoolteachers and town clergy maintained a cautious, relatively tolerant atmosphere that was sympathetic to religious reform. The critical, intellectual tradition of Gansfort, Agricola and the Aduard circle was continued by men such as Wilhelmus Frederici, the mighty head priest of St. Martin's church, who dominated town politics for thirty-five years (from c. 1490 till 1525), Goswinus van Halen, who lived in Groningen from 1480 till 1530, Nicolaus Lesdorpius, the headmaster of the Latin school, Hermannus Abbringhe, first priest of St. Martin's church, later dean of Drenthe, in his old age an important secretary of the town (from 1548 till 1558), Hieronymus Frederici, the son of Wilhelmus, who held several important posts in the government of the town till his death in 1558, and, last but not least, Regnerus Praedinius (1510-1559), a successor of Lesdorpius as Rector of

---

[9] Praedinius treated 'dangerous' subjects in other writings than the one investigated here, but he never published anything.

[10] On the definition of 'Religionsgespräch' see Hollerbach, *Das Religionsgespräch*, 30ff., esp. 46-7; Von Bundschuh, *Das Wormser Religionsgespräch von 1557*, 562. But in the title of his book Wolfs put the term between quotation marks.

[11] On the Duke of Guelders see the last section of Praedinius's *disputatio* here treated and n. 86. In general on the history of Groningen see *Historie van Groningen*.

the Latin school of St. Martin's church.[12] All of these men enjoyed great
prestige in the city and outside it. But, on the other hand, there was no openly proclaimed reformed congregation. The intellectual and administrative
élite tried to keep the larger population, among which Lutherans, David-
jorists and Mennonites had their adherents, away from any dramatic
upheaval.[13]

The Disputatio Groningensis *of 1523*

The text purports to be an account of a discussion on a theological theme
and a metaphysical question between three Dominican friars and four town
clerics of Groningen, which is alleged to have taken place in the House of
the Dominican friars on March 12, 1523, on the invitation of these friars.
The text was printed the same year in Zwolle by Simon Corver.[14] This early
edition is the basis of my discussion. The theological theme is that of the
kingship and priesthood of Christ, viz. the problem of his worldly and
spiritual power, and so the power of his so-called Vicars on earth, the Pope
and the Emperor. Thus the authority of the smaller local communities and
their dignitaries is also at stake. The metaphysical question concerns the
eternity of the world. Most of the speakers can be identified as existing
persons and they are called by their real names. The prior of the Dominicans
is Laurentius Laurentii, who is known as a bitter adversary of Erasmus in
Louvain.[15] Of the four town clerics, *Dominus Hermannus Aberingius
utriusque iuris doctor* and *Magister Nicolaus Lesdorpius Gymnasiarcha*
have already been mentioned above. The clergy of St. Martin's church is
backed by the two priests of Groningen, Wilhelmus Frederici and Everardus

---

[12] On Wilhelmus Frederici (Willem Frederiks) see Zuidema, *Wilhelmus Frederici*; on
Goswinus: Van Rhijn, 'Goswinus van Halen'; on Herman Abbringhe: Schuitema Meijer,
Historie van het Archief der stad Groningen, 33-7; on Hieronymus Frederici, *ibidem*, 74-5,
Mellink, 'Uit de voorgeschiedenis van de Reformatie', 146-8. See also n. 16.

[13] I repeat here the significant sentence from a city-ordinance for the clergymen of the town
(second half of the twenties?), in which they are warned not to disturb the normal ceremonies,
not to sow hatred or to introduce controversial issues in their sermons, with this restriction: 'ter
tijdt tho dattet Godt van den hemell will gheleven dat tho veranderen' (until God of Heaven
sees fit to change this). See Mellink (n. 12), 142ff.

[14] For the four subsequent printings (Basel, Adam Petri, 1523; Groningen, Hans Sas, 1614;
Groningen, Daniel Gerdes, 1744-9; Pijper, *Bibl. Ref. Neerl.* VI, 1910) see Wolfs, Anhang I.
There is no critical edition, no translation, no commentary of this important text. Jos.M.M. Her-
mans discovered another copy of the Corver printing, besides the one of the Bibl. Nat. that
Wolfs used: Berlin SBB-Pk, Dg 1592; see Hermans, *Laatmiddeleeuwse boeken in Zwolle*
(forthcoming).

[15] On Laurentius Laurentii, see *CE* II 306-7.

Jargis, both of St. Martin's church.[16] Both are present at the discussion into which they have launched their inferiors, but they do not take part in it themselves.

The text of the *Disputatio* in the Corver edition consists of three parts: 1. A letter of dedication (2¼ pages) addressed to Petrus Aquensis, a canon of Münster,[17] in which the anonymous author sets forth the aims of his edition and also the circumstances under which the talks took place. 2. The formulation of the problems, carefully arranged into one general *quaestio*, subsequently subdivided into three theses (*propositiones*), each of which is followed by two corollaries, and, finally, the metaphysical question, the *Impertinens Physicale*. This part of the text was set up by the Dominicans, and it occupies 1¼ pages. 3. The rest of the booklet is filled by the actual discussions: 18 pages, in which the four town clerics, one after the other, attack the theses of the friars and the latter try to defend them. The main role of the Dominicans seems to have been to propose the theses and to interrupt the attacks of their opponents here and there with a short remark.

The individual attackers are not allotted equal space. The longest discourse is that of *Magister Ioannes Alberti Timmermannus*,[18] who holds the floor for about eight pages, Lesdorpius gets seven pages and Aberingius two and a half. *Magister Gerhardus Pistoris* has only half a page at his disposal (in these numbers the interruptions of the Dominicans are included). On closer investigation it appears that the structure of the discussion section of the piece is as well balanced as the part of the theses. There are three substantial attacks A, B and C, and between A and B as well as between B and C there are two smaller intermezzi of a different character.[19] If we designate the *quaestio*, the theses and corollaries and the impertinent physical problem by Q, P1, P1C1, P1C2, P2, P2C1, P2C2, P3, P3C1, P3C2, IP, then the partition of the subject-matter over the speakers and over the space allotted to them is as follows:

---

[16] Abbringhe, Frederici and Jargis (see also n. 12) had studied in Italy in the late 15th century: see Tervoort in this volume, p. 227; 229; and n. 39. On Jargis see Wolfs, *Das Groninger 'Religionsgespräch'*, 54-5. Lesdorpius had been a pupil of Hegius in Deventer (see *Hamelmanns Geschichtliche Werke*, I 39). I did not find his name in any matriculation register of a university.

[17] On the learned humanist of Münster Petrus Aquensis, see Wolfs, *Das Groninger 'Religionsgespräch'*, 14-26.

[18] On Timmermannus see ibidem, 58; Hermans, *Boeken in Stad en Lande*, no. 2.1.58. He signed his books, of which the University Library of Groningen possesses a number, as Johannes Carpentarius. He studied in Cologne and/or Rostock. He died in 1527.

[19] The difference in character in intermezzo 1 is that one of the Dominicans is attacking one of their own theses, and in intermezzo 2 that the question of the eternity of the world is treated, with the help of Aristotle.

A. Aberingius attacks P1, P1C2, P1C1, P1 (2½ pages)
   Intermezzo 1: *Supprior Pittinck* of the Dominicans attacks an element of
   P3 (½ page)
B. Timmermannus attacks P3, P2C1, P2C2, P2, P3C1 (8 pages)
   Intermezzo 2: Pistoris, one of the town clerics, attacks IP and Q (½ page)
C. Lesdorpius attacks Q, P1, P2, P3C1 (7 pages)

In section C all propositions are reviewed anew by way of conclusion. This
ingenious composition makes it immediately clear that the piece, if a record
of a real discussion at all, has been vigorously adapted to literary tastes.[20] As
for the contents, it is my impression that the arguments characterize the
personalities of the speakers, as far as we know them. Abbering is the most
political of all, discussing the power of the Pope and the Emperor, as befits a
man of whom we know that he played an important role in the politics of his
town twenty five years later. Lesdorpius, the *gymnasiarcha*, is the philolo-
gist in the group, discussing words and their exact meaning. Timmermannus, priest of St. Martin's church and public notary of the town, is, so to
speak, the most 'evangelical' and 'Erasmian', and also the most practical
cleric, speaking of the central theme of the freedom of Christians, individ-
ually and as a community, organized in a municipal church, that could be
considered as a congregation.[21]

Neither Luther nor Erasmus is mentioned or quoted by name in the disputation;[22] the only modern – and controversial – author discussed, *pro* and
contra, is Reuchlin, who died in 1522, the year before the disputation was
held and printed. Texts that may have been used are the anonymous
Oeconomica christiana, of which H.G. Kleyn and J. Trapman quoted a long
passage of striking similarity,[23] and the *Epistola theologica* of Gerardus
Listrius, which brings forward some of the same arguments against the
worldly power of the Pope as the *Disputatio Groningensis*. But the tone and
manner of writing and the general purport of the texts are very different in
the *Oeconomica* as well as in the letter of Listrius. Listrius's Latin is ahead

---

[20] Wolfs does not deny the historical reality of the disputation, but is also of the opinion that
the written report is a one-sided 'Tendenzschrift' (*Das Groninger 'Religionsgespräch'*, ch. 4
and pp. 178-9).
[21] See below, e.g. the objection 14, where Groningen is explicitly mentioned.
[22] Wolfs has observed several borrowings from or references to the works of Erasmus in the
text of the *Disputatio*: see *Das Groninger 'Religionsgespräch'*, passim.
[23] Trapman, *De summa*, 45-56, is certainly right in supposing that the *Disputatio* has copied
a passage of some ten lines from the *Oeconomica*, and not the other way round, for this passage
contrasts with its environment through a higher level of its Latin. Moreover, the author of the
Disputatio has made two grammatical corrections (observed by Trapman); he also added the
words *ecclesiarum pontifices*, to fit the passage in with his own argument, and he changed *ordo
reipublicae* into *ordo publicus*, which is more in harmony with his wording elsewhere.

in the classicizing direction of that of our disputation;[24] the language of the *Oeconomica*, too, is far more copious. Therefore, the author of neither of these two texts can be considered as a possible writer of the Groningen disputation.

But before speculating on the authorship of the booklet, let us examine once more its form and contents. The main role played in the text by the town clergy, the ample treatment of their arguments – the contribution of the Dominicans is, indeed, very small – and the explicit statements of the author in the letter of dedication, make it abundantly clear that the publication aims at furthering the modern, evangelical viewpoints of the town clergy. The author has good hopes, so he tells his addressee, that before long those who still protect the old error will embrace the *euangelica philosophia*, will exchange their *theologia scholastica* for a *Paulina theologia*. And he hopes sincerely that by his publication of this report he will help the process of change 'ab Aristotele ad Paulum, a Moyse ad Christum, a lege ad gratiam, a carne ad spiritum, a seruitute ad libertatem, a metu ad hilaritatem'. The modernity of the dispute is clearly brought out by the radically biblical argumentation of the clerics of the church, and by the combination of topics brought forward by them such as the purely spiritual power of Christ; the evangelical freedom of the Christian against the Pope and the Emperor; the strictly forbidden killing of heretics; the radical pacifism; the freedom of local authorities to intervene in papal or imperial decisions and regulations, e.g. in prohibiting certain holidays or in granting dispensation from vows and oaths; the proclamation of the invalidity for modern time of the decrees of the four oldest synods of the church.

The Latin of the text does not exhibit the classical flavor and clarity of the writings of accomplished humanists of the same period such as Gerardus Geldenhauer or Gerardus Listrius. It lacks the syntactical flexibility and varied, pure vocabulary of these two authors, let alone the masterly versatility of Erasmus. Theological and philosophical jargon is not avoided. Unclassical words, or words that are very rare in pagan classical literature, occur more than once: they have their origin in the Vulgate, the Fathers or other late Latin or medieval texts, e.g. *ebuccinare, functio, inhabilis* (unfit), *succedanius, scandalisare, satellicium, circumcellio, tallia* (tax), *inabdicabiliter, chronographus, linea* (line of descent), *temporalis* (worldly), *christianismus, satrapa, synodus, libidinatio, sabbatismus, emurmurare, lectitare, beneficiatus clericus, se nuncupare c. dat.* (to devote oneself to), *graphium* (style). Words and expressions such as *pauculi, exaugeo, heus tu,*

---

[24] I base my judgement on the reading of Listrius's *Epistola theologica*, his letter to Goswinus van Halen in *Commentarioli Listrii in Dialecticen*, and his *Oratiuncula habita in coetu scholasticorum Suollensium.*

neutiquam (by no means), *bona uerba!* (mind your tongue!),[25] may have been learned from Plautus or Terence, authors the writer of the text probably read; whole passages with words such as *adfectatrix* and *interpolatrix* are borrowed from Tertullian, a Father cherished by the author.[26]

In his letter of dedication the author has done his best to write a rhetorical text, but this rhetoric displays a somewhat old-fashioned affectation: he is walking, so to speak, on stilts with curious expressions such as *vicaria scriptio* (a letter in reply), *plenario iure* (for simple *pleno iure*), *plenum phase faciant ab Aristotele ad Paulum* (they will change over fully from Aristotle to Paul).[27] Outside the introduction we read in equally pompous language: '[...] quando unica Salomonis posteritas succedania functione illi [sc. Israelitico] regno semper sit substituta' ([...] because only the direct descendants of Solomon have always been the successors in that kingship).[28]

The syntax, too, shows medievalisms: sometimes with clumsy connections frequently using *quando, quoniam,* or *quod*, taking little advantage of the possibilities of verbal forms. *Quoniam* is even, in Vulgate fashion, used to introduce direct speech. For the gerundive governed by *uenire* instead of *esse* to show purpose, see a sentence like: 'imo, nobis tum Romanus Pontifex uenit iudicandus atque arguendus, tantum abest ut illi quicquam in nos liceat'.[29]

Yet, before utterly condemning the Latin of the *Disputatio*, it should be said that, on the whole, the text does not make for difficult reading. It is mostly written in simple but good and not at all poor Latin, by someone who was certainly in touch with the classics and their modern adepts. At the end of the letter of dedication the author even indulges himself in a correct hexameter, when he tells the addressee that he, the author, has added many quotations from the Bible and other texts to the words of the speakers, for they had not had the time to draw exhaustively upon all available authorities: the speakers 'ferebant plaerique adhuc tacitos sub pectore textus' (most speakers bore still other texts tacitly in their hearts).[30] Perhaps the source from which this line welled up was Vergil, *Aeneid* 4,67: 'interea et tacitum uiuit sub pectore uulnus'.

---

[25] For 'bona uerba' see below, p. 10. The expression occurs in pagan literature in Terence, *Andria*, 204; Ovid, *Fasti*, I 71-2.

[26] Beatus Rhenanus edited in 1521 for the first time the *Opera omnia* of Tertullian in Basel (See Wolfs, *Das Groninger 'Religionsgespräch'*, 31-2).

[27] The Hebrew word *Phase* is the name of a feast, the Passover; cf. Exod. 12, 11-3.

[28] But one never can be sure that the author is not borrowing such phrases from elsewhere.

[29] This construction is frequent in medieval and Neolatin. The only occurrence I know of in a classical author is Plautus, *Miles gloriosus* 891: 'quom uenit uobis faciundum utrumque'.

[30] The hexameter begins at the syllable -*bant*.

Especially in the longer speeches of Timmermannus and Lesdorpius, passages of good Erasmian-like rhetoric occur. How well the author knew to express himself, is clear from the opening sentences of the letter of dedication:[31]

> Non ita dudum est, quod nouis subinde literis me excitaris in uicariam scriptionem. En nouus fabulator ueteri amico obstrepo! Soleo aliquoties deplorare huc prolapsam synceritatem doctrinae Euangelicae, ut nullum sit illius uestigium, quod non contaminarit haec noua nostri orbis Theologia, cuius autorem Aristotelem fecimus. Optimum certe quiddam contigerat diuo Aurelio Augustino, quod in academicorum sectam inciderit, qui ita inuestigant omnia, ut certi nihil pronuncient. Faciebatque nonnihil ad mutandos Augustini animos Ciceronis Hortensius, quod ille liber non certam aliquam sectam temere arroganterque approbarit, sed quod eos docebat audiendos philosophos, qui quam proxime accederent ad rei ueritatem, quam inuenisse philosophiae caput est. Nos his prophanis philosophis hoc certe plus sumus stupidi, plus iniqui, quod caeco nostro arbitratu statuimus, non quae habet ueritas, sed quae nostris affectibus uisa sunt optima.

> It is not so long ago now, that you exhorted me often in many letters to write to you in reply. Behold, here I assault the ears of an old friend with a new story! I am used to often deplore that the purity of the evangelical doctrine has sunken so deeply that there is no trace of it left that has not been contaminated by this new-fangled theology of our modern world, of which we have installed Aristotle as the authority. It was something excellent which befell the divine Aurelius Augustine, when he encountered the school of the Academics, who investigate all things in such a way as to pronounce nothing as certain. Also, the *Hortensius* of Cicero had not a little influence in changing Augustine's mind, for this book not without good reason or presumptively did not approve of one specific school, but taught that one should listen to those philosophers, who come as closely as possible to the truth, and to have found it is the goal of all philosophy. In this respect we are certainly more stupid and less reasonable than these pagan philosophers, that we state in our blind judgement not what the truth has, but what has appeared best to our emotions.

Who is the author of this literary composition?[32] As I observed above, Gerardus Listrius and the writer of the *Oeconomica christiana* drop out on account of their different Latin usage. Wolfs thought Goswinus van Halen a possible candidate,[33] but he, too, must be ruled out because of the learned and sophisticated character of the booklet. Goswinus had no university

---

[31] Prefaces and introductory letters of Neolatin works are often written in a far more cultivated language than the rest of the text.

[32] See Wolfs, *Das Groninger 'Religionsgespräch'*, p. 2 and n., and ch. 3.

[33] Ibidem, 45-6. It could argue for Goswinus that he, according to Hardenberg, has written several dialogues ('aliquot dialogos plenos pietatis et doctrinae') which he would have intended for Hardenberg: 'reliquit [...] ad me' (Gansfort, *Opera*, **2v). But see also the quotation of the same letter of Goswinus on p. 15.

training, and his Latin is rather poor. The *Disputatio* displays considerable
erudition, far more than can possibly be ascribed to Goswinus. In these 21½
pages I counted more than 150 quotations from the Bible, and quotations
from or references to Augustine (several works), Tertullian *(Apologeticum*
and *De praescriptione haereticorum)*, Aristotle, Philo and Annius, Jerome,
Bernard of Clairvaux, Sulpicius Severus (on St. Martin of Tours), Gregory
the Great and Reuchlin.[34] The history of the church, Erasmus, and at least
enough Greek to interpret some words (διάκονος, ἐπισκοπεῖν) belong to
his literary luggage.

The *auctores intellectuales* of the *Disputatio* are the town clerics of Groningen; the actual writer could have been one of them, and in a former publication I surmised that Timmermannus was a likely candidate.[35] But there
was little on which to base this conclusion, and now, after reading the piece
carefully for several times again, I am ready to shift my option to Magister
Nicolaus Lesdorpius. For this I have the following reasons:

1. First of all, because the author's Latin, though not of the highest quality, betrays the hand of a more or less professional student of that language;
some classical elements also suggest that the author was a schoolteacher.

2. Lesdorpius is the sharpest opponent of the Dominicans. He is the only
one who ventilates some bitter sarcasm or irony of an Erasmian type, and
also the only one to introduce his own person humorously into his sayings.
It seems natural that he, then, is also the writer of the text. His sarcasms are
the following:

a. After arguing that the priesthood was bestowed on Christ from all
eternity, Lesdorpius defines an earthly priest as someone who celebrates the
sacrifice (of the Lord). Then the *magister noster* comes out with the argument that they (the Dominicans) now have in their midst a little priest
(*sacerdotulum*), who is a priest but who has not yet offered the sacrifice.
This he shall do in four days time (at Easter). Lesdorpius finds this ridicu-
lous and answers: 'If he is a priest, who shall one day offer the sacrifice, I
also count among the priests, because I have not vowed this sacrifice'. ('[...]
quippe qui hoc sacrificium non deuouerim').[36] The *magister* warns him not
to use sacrilegious language with a 'Bona uerba' (i.e. 'Mind your tongue').
Lesdorpius's answer makes it clear that he understands the religious meaning of these words perfectly. He says in a mockingly solemn way:

---

[34] But some of these authors are quoted from other sources than their own texts; see n. 28.

[35] This guess had already been advanced by Grosheide, *Bijdragen*, 118-9. His arguments for
this choice were the length of Timmerman's contribution, and, further, the agreement of viewpoints and the quoting of Tertullian in both the letter of dedication and the words of Timmermannus. I cannot find these arguments very convincing.

[36] It can be assumed that Lesdorpius had only received minor orders. Does he mean by 'hoc
sacrificium' the crucifixion of Christ? In that case his language would be very blasphemous.

Lubens audio, daboque silentes auditus, modo magister autoritatibus grauissimis obtundat Lesdorpium. Aut certe si id nequis, pergo fabulam texere.[37]

b. Another sarcastic intervention I see in the objection 18, where the *magister noster* interprets the words 'My kingdom is not of this world' as: 'not of this world, but in this world'. Lesdorpius judges this to be a far-fetched cleverness, and answers with the stock formula, so it seems, of someone giving in in a disputation:

> Gratiam habeo; quod nesciui, te docente didici, quod sciui, te dicente non perdidi. Dextre nodum amouit theologus. Lubet et aliud inuestigare, quando in omnem nodum discutiendum Magister noster tam sit facilis.

It seems to me that it is out of the question, as Wolfs supposed, that here the *gymnasiarcha* is really agreeing with the *magister*.[38]

c. A third instance of a caustic remark and a similar introduction of his own person as earlier, can be found in the objection 19, where the *lector* argues that Christ acted as an *imperator* in driving the moneychangers out from the temple with a whip. *Gymnasiarcha*: 'Yes, with a whip, not with a sword'. So he himself, as a schoolmaster, has more right to be called the Vicar of Christ on earth than the Pope of Rome:

> Certe hac eiectione non imperatorem, sed ludimagistrum uideo egisse Christum. Igitur multo iure mihi plaudam licebit, quando ego Christi agam uicarium, idque fortassis nonnihil uerius atque monarcha Romanus pontifex, aut certe imperator, qui gladio animaduertunt si quid admissum est sceleris. Christus autem non ense proturbauit negociantes, sed flagello, ut intelligatis Christum ludimagistrum, atque pleno iure me illius uicarium, qui et ipse flagello ad meliorem mentem meos clientulos perpello.

3. It should also be noted that the text shows clear indications of a philological habit of the writer: a discussion on Reuchlin about the etymological explanation of words, including Greek and Hebrew; and, further, the author in his letter of dedication, and elsewhere, insists on the promotion of the *bonae*

---

[37] The mockery is clearly brought out by the transition from the solemn language in the third person singular ('magister [...] obtundat Lesdorpium') to the second and first person: 'Or, if you cannot, I shall continue to weave the web of my story'. (Cf. Cicero, *Ep. fam.* 9,21,1 'epistulam uero cotidianis uerbis texere solemus'.) From the last sentence it is clear that Lesdorpius was already speaking before the interruption of the magister. I do not doubt that the part spoken by Lesdorpius begins at 'Vtrum Christus benedictus ab hora natiuitatis suae' on fo. C1r. (Corver 1523; = ed. Pijper, 569), as the edition of 1614 (Sas, Groningen) indicates. Wolfs did not understand the mockery, nor the change of speakers, also because he did not investigate the overall structure of the plot. (See Wolfs, *Das Groninger 'Religionsgespräch'*, 171f., 184f.)

[38] Ibidem, 172.

litterae or *recta studia.*[39] For him, obviously, philological humanism includes religious reform, or, to put it the other way round, religious reform is a
form of literary humanism. This seems typically an attitude of a Latin headmaster in 1523. As such, Lesdorpius would make an excellent predecessor
of Praedinius and he would be an excellent parallel to Gerardus Listrius in
Zwolle:[40] a learned biblical humanist, who combines a dominating interest
in Christian scholarship with more than a smack of philological training.

4. In my earlier guess that Timmermannus was the author, the circumstance that his is the longest discourse in the disputation played a role. Perhaps, though, it is a stronger argument in favor of Lesdorpius that he is the
last speaker, who rounds off the discussions by reviewing once more all the
theses of the Dominican friars.

5. And last, but not least, it is also most likely that in the band of town
clerics it was the rector of the Latin school who should be the one to take the
pen to hand.

This hypothesis can perhaps be corroborated by a second one, viz. that the
satire *Lamentationes Petri*[41] is also from the hand of Lesdorpius. This book,
running to 84 pages of 44 lines, was edited, anonymously, like the *Disputatio*, by Simon Corver in Zwolle, and has to be dated between 16 January
and 23 September 1521. It contains a witty and bitter satire in the form of a
dialogue between a number of biblical authors and Church Fathers in heaven, directed against the mendicant orders and medieval philosophers. This
time Luther and Erasmus do play a role in the argumentation, but without
going into dogmatic questions of 'faith' etc. The arguments pleading in
favor of Lesdorpius as the author, are the following:

1. The author is extremely well informed about the Groningen intellectual and administrative élite: he praises to the sky Wilhelmus Frederici, to
whom he dedicates the book in two long letters (12 pages), and also his son
Hieronymus, further Goswinus van Halen, the head of the Frater house,
together with the house of the Brethren itself, and then a famous member of
the Canter family, named Gelmarus (i.e. Ghelmer), who was an eloquent
and learned secretary of the town from 1494 till 1520 and later.[42] It is very
natural, then, that the author himself is an inhabitant of Groningen; there is
nothing that pleads against this supposition.

---

[39] The precise terms used in the letter of dedication are: *studia optima, studia meliora, recta studia, meliores literae, literae optimae*; the term *studia humanitatis* never occurs in the *Disputatio*.

[40] And of many others, of course, e.g. Gnapheus (Willem de Volder) of The Hague.

[41] See Clemen, 'Die Lamentationes Petri'.

[42] On Canter see Ebels-Hoving 1981, 22, n. 24; Feith, *Groningse Volksalmanak* 1891, 22-4; Schuitema Meijer, *Historie van het Archief*, 28-9.

2. The learning (both its level and contents), the humanist drive, and the Latin of the *Lamentationes* are very similar to those of the *Disputatio*. I invite the reader to compare the description I gave earlier of these features in the *Disputatio*, which I wrote before I had taken cognizance of Otto Clemen's article on the *Lamentationes*, with the following quotation from this article:

> Zur allgemeinen Charakteristik des Verfassers füge ich noch hinzu: Er hat in ungewöhnlichem Masse Geist und Witz, er schreibt lebendig und fesselnd, wenn auch nicht in klassischem Latein, er ist in der Bibel, der patristischen und scholastischen Literatur und in der Kirchengeschichte wohl bewandert und vertraut mit den damals verhandelten exegetischen und dogmenhistorischen Problemen. Seiner Gesinnung nach is er Humanist.[43]

I could go further and quote similarities of the use of the Latin and very similar passages of both writings about Aristotle, the Church Fathers, the Old Testament, and about the hope of the coming to light again of the Christian texts of Antiquity, and the replacement of scholastic philosophy by the Christian, Pauline doctrine. But I won't enter into these details here.

3. Thus the conclusion is very plausible that the authors of both writings are one and the same person. That he is the rector of the Latin school, becomes practically certain from the following: After he has personified Frederici into a second Augustine, Goswinus as Gregory and Canter as Ambrose, he continues:

> Quartus qui solus desideratur Hieronymus est. Neque tamen hic deesse potuit, quem optimis linguis audio succrescere; uocabulum prudens supprimo, ne immaturior aetas insolescat.

Clemen, who also quoted these words, commented in a note: 'Ich verstehe diese geheimnisvolle Andeutung nicht'. I surmise that the quote means: a) At the moment of writing, only the fourth great figure, Jerome, the linguist among the Ancient Fathers, is still found lacking in Groningen. b) The one who ought not to be omitted in this enumeration is he, of whom I hear that he is growing up for the best languages. I suppress, however, his name, out of fear that in his immature age he becomes too proud. (Speaking is of course the author of the book, but not directly, he assumes in the satire the role of Esdras, the biblical scribe). This can only mean that a very young person is known to the author as a gifted pupil with a great talent for the languages. It is almost unavoidable, then, to suppose that the author is a

---

[43] Clemen, 'Die Lamentationes Petri', 435.

schoolteacher. Summing up the various arguments I have adduced thus far and adding one more, I conclude:

1. It is not unlikely that the author of the *Disputatio* is the *gymnasiarcha* of Groningen, Nicolaus Lesdorpius.

2. It is almost certain that the author of the *Lamentationes* is a prominent inhabitant of Groningen.

3. It is almost certain that he is a schoolteacher.

4. The similarities between the two writings make it as likely as not that one and the same biblical humanist is the author of both.

5. If the author of the *Lamentationes* were somebody else than Lesdorpius, e.g. Gerardus Listrius, then it would be very strange that besides Frederici, Goswinus and Canter, the rector of the Latin school should not have to play a part among the Groningen 'patristic' heroes. Listrius, at any rate, praises him highly in a letter to Goswinus van Halen: 'Rectorem uestrum hominem longe humanissimum eruditissimumque salutabis.'[44]

6. Lesdorpius is the best candidate for this authorship. The boy he is setting his hopes on for the future, could very well be Regnerus Praedinius, who in 1521 was eleven or twelve years old. He was in the Frater house from c. 1517 till 1526.[45] So Praedinius must have been learning Greek and Latin for some years in 1521, enough to have filled with awe his teachers. And that is why Lesdorpius predicted a future for him as a second Jerome. He went to the University of Louvain in 1526 and was 'called back', presumably by the city fathers, who may also have paid for his costs as a student, in order to assume the rectorate of the Latin school of the town in 1530, *prope adolescens* in the words of one of his later editors, Jean Crespin; so a true prodigy.[46]

There is, of course, no absolute proof for all this, but if my supposition is plausible, these are the first documents that we have on the strength of which we can judge the quality and character of the Latin school of St. Martin's in Groningen for the period between Arnold von Hildesheim and Antonius Liber in the seventies of the fifteenth century and Praedinius in the thirties, fourties and fifties of the sixteenth century. It seems, then, that the interest of the early members of the Aduard group in pagan authors and classical Neolatin style was deflected into a reform-minded, biblical (evangelical) direction in the second and third decades of the sixteenth

---

[44] *Commentarioli Listrii in Dialecticen*, Q6r.

[45] He stayed in the Frater house together with Albert Hardenberg, who was of the same age.

[46] '[...] in patriam revocatus, scholae Groningensi praeesse prope adolescens iussus est' (Crespin in his *Commentationes* 1568, Praefatio, 4v). See Postma, 'Regnerus Praedinius', 297 and n. 26.

century, without, however, losing the high, intellectual level of school training.[47] I repeat here once again the judgement of Count Enno II of Eastern
Frisia, who in a document of 1529 proclaims that he wants to set up a school
in Norden with the same regulations as those of Zwolle, Deventer or Groningen.[48] This proves that the boys of his county went to school in these
towns, and that these schools had a reputation that roused the envy of the
Count. Perhaps he understood by regulation ('Ordeninge') the combination
and cooperation of the town school and the school of the Brethren of the
Common Life, of which the latter was perhaps a sort of institute for preparing the homework for the town school.[49] Of the two leaders, Nicolaus
Lesdorpius and Goswinus Halensis, we should no longer neglect or simply
leave out Lesdorpius, as I have done in an earlier publication.[50] We now can
assume with some confidence that Lesdorpius was by far the most erudite of
the two. In 1528 Goswinus wrote to his pupil Albertus Hardenberg, then
studying in the monastery of Aduard:

> Ego libenter tibi concedo, ut multo me doctior sis, et istud libenter cuiuis con-
> cedo. Satis enim mihi est Alphabeticum manere, uerumtamen gratum adhuc est
> eruditum conuenire.[51]

> I gladly concede to you that you are far more learned than I am, and that is
> something I gladly concede to anyone. For I am content to remain just a begin-
> ner in learning, but, nevertheless, I still enjoy meeting a scholar.

It seems very unlikely that he himself had read all the authors he recommended for study to Hardenberg in the same letter.[52] The author of the *Disputatio* calls himself a *scholasticus*, his opponent in a sarcastic mood a *theo-
logus*, and his pupils playfully his *clientuli*. In the *Disputatio* he appears as a
bright, cheerful, learned humanist, who wants to draw his own conclusions
from his ardent reading of the Bible and of other Christian texts, ancient and
modern.

The *Disputatio Groningensis* perhaps does not contain many thoughts
that cannot be found in other reform-minded books and pamphlets of the
period as well, but the booklet is interesting because it expresses the reform-

---

[47] Gemma Frisius, who visited the town school of Groningen in the beginning of the 16th
century (he was born c. 1500) is said to have had an excellent training there (Suffridus Petrus,
De scriptoribus Frisiae, 158-9: 'Cumque adolescens ibi [sc. Gruningae] in literis mirum in
modum profecisset, Louanium ad grauiora studia capescenda ablegatus est.'

[48] Bartels, *Abriss einer Geschichte des Schulwesens*, 6. For the literal quotation see also my
'Onderwijs en geleerdheid', 18; and Postma, 'Regnerus Praedinius', 294, n. 15.

[49] See Postma, 'Regnerus Praedinius', 294.

[50] Akkerman, 'Onderwijs en geleerdheid', 23; cf. Postma, 'Regnerus Praedinius', 294-5.

[51] Gansfort, *Opera*, **4v. See also n. 33.

[52] Cf. Postma, 'Regnerus Praedinius', 296-7.

ist ideas of a whole intellectual élite of a quasi-independent town of moderate size that dominated a large area. It is first and foremost a political document, vigorously advocating the right of a free community to think and act for itself. It is not deep or elaborate in its theorizing, but honest and brave in starting from time-honored principles of medieval 'political theology' (the theses of the Dominicans), and in attacking them fearlessly. It is a lively and varied text, not without some touches of humor. In all these respects it contrasts sharply with the heavy stuff of such pious writings as the *Oeconomica christiana*[53] and Cornelius Hoen's *Epistola christiana admodum.*[54] In its moderate, tolerant atmosphere it contrasts as well with the more dogmatic tone of Listrius's *Epistola theologica*[55] and with the biting satire of the *Lamentationes Petri.*[56]

To conclude my discussion of the *Disputatio Groningensis*, I shall give a summary of its contents. The letter of dedication has been sufficiently characterized by the above quotations. The theses of the Dominicans could be paraphrased as follows:

Q *Quaestio generalis*: Whether Christ, since the hour of his birth, was simultaneously priest and emperor, and whether he deserved this through his passion.

P1 *Propositio 1*: The imperial power was passed on to Christ after the period of the four monarchies (see Daniël 2); this happened according to his human nature from the beginning of his birth; the power was at the same time priestly and monarchical. Thus he acquired not only the ownership of many things through a grant and by his own action, but the dominion over everything was infused into him.

    P1C1 *Corollarium 1*: For this reason the authority of both swords rests with the Roman Pontiff, Vicar of Christ on earth. The one sword is to be used by the Church, the other not by but for the Church, so that the Emperor by chance may be deposed by the authority of the Roman Pontiff.

    P1C2 *Corollarium 2*: Since Christ, by his word and by his example, taught the deepest poverty, the simple religious is not unfit for the highest monarchical dignity in worldly affairs, so that he possesses the political dominion over the entire world.

---

[53] See Trapman, *De summa*, ch. 2; Van Toorenenbergen, *Het oudste Nederlandsche verboden boek.*
[54] See Spruyt, 'Listrius lutherizans' and 'Gerardus Listrius' *Epistola Theologica'.*
[55] See Spruyt, *Cornelius Henrici Hoen.*
[56] See Clemen, 'Die *Lamentationes Petri'.*

P2 *Propositio 2*: Though Christ entrusted the general rule in worldly affairs to the Roman Pontiff, he wanted the particular rule to rest with the Emperor in such a way that nobody could prescribe anything in defiance of it. For the Emperor is better brought into power by election than by hereditary succession; consequently, he is a Vicar of Christ on earth no less than Octavian.

P2C1 *Corollarium 1*: Thus the authority of the Emperor can impose taxes, declare war, allow usury and brothels. The usury of the Jews, however, he is bound to do away from them.

P2C2 *Corollarium 2*: Because all power ought to be exercised to the honor and use of him, from whom it derives, and since every prince is a vicar of God and the Church, he is obliged to inflict appropriate punishment, even unto the death of the flesh, in the first place upon heretics, and then also upon those who manifestly commit an offence against the law of God.

P3 *Propositio 3*: Both powers bind their subjects in conscience by their laws; both free the guilty by chance by mitigating their punishment; sometimes, however, they condemn by their right him whose innocence has been proven. Nevertheless, evangelical law is not burdened by their ordinances more than Mosaic law.

P3C1 *Corollarium 1*: For this reason the Roman Pontiff has the right to grant dispensation from vows and oaths, just as he can institute canons contrary even to the determinations of scholars, whoever they are, provided that he is not acting contrary to the Scriptures or to the ordinances of the first four Councils. Still, he cannot altogether absolve the religious or those who have taken holy orders from reciting the canonical hours.

P3C2 *Corollarium 2*: Consequently, the Blessed Christ was simultaneously priest and emperor since the hour of his birth, and he deserved this through his passion.

IP *Impertinens Physicale*: Though it is inconsistent with natural law that the world had a beginning, it is nevertheless possible that it once received being, but this cannot be proven in truth. As there can be no space without body nor the reverse, there can neither be void. If, however, void is posited, even if motion were to take place in it, it would still not take place in an instant.

This much on the theses of the Dominicans. Below I shall divide the objections, continuously numbered, into the sections A, B and C as explained above. To each objection I add the *loca probantia* of the Bible or other sources. I have corrected the wrong references and added the verses to the chapters; the original text gives the chapters only.

A. *The objections of Aberingius against P1, P1C2, P1C1, P1.*
1. Since Christ is not a direct descendant of Solomon, but of Nathan, a brother of Solomon, he is not entitled to the kingship of Israel, viz. to the kingship according to his human nature. Philo and Annius.
2. Christ did not want to be either king or judge, as he made clear by his words and deeds, nor did he want his Apostles to strive ambitiously for power and rank above others. The simple religious, and every Christian, if he is a true imitator of Christ, is obliged to humility. Jn. 6.15, Lk. 12.14, Mt 20.25-28 (wrongly Mt. 17), 1 Jn. 2.6, Rom. 12.3, Phil. 2.3 (wrongly Phil. 12), 1 Pet. 5.5.
3. St. Peter was neither monarch nor prince, but a simple evangelical soldier, sent by the elders of the Church to Samaria. He did not have primacy over the other Apostles, as is clear from the fact that not he but St. James answered the questions of the Jews. Acts 8.14, 15.13ff.
4. Christ was neither priest nor emperor in our sense of these terms, but only in a spiritual way: '[...] in Christo nihil fuisse crassi, sed omnia spiritualia'. The kingdom of Christ is eternal and not of this world. Consequently, the Roman Pontiff, his Vicar, also can never be an *imperator*. The Father did not send Christ as an emperor, but as propitiator by faith in his blood. Jn. 18.36 (wrongly Jn. 6), Pss. 2.8, 81 (82).8, 8.7. Mt. 28.18, Jn. 4.24, Dan. 4.3 (3.100 Vulg.), 6.27 (6.26 Vulg.), Is. 9.6 (9.7 Vulg.), Pss. 86 (85).16, Rom. 3.25, 1 Jn. 2.2, 4.10, Is. 53.7 (wrongly Is.61). The Lector retorts with Zech. 6.12-13. Aberingius refers to the commentaries of Jerome on this text.

Intermezzo 1. The subprior Pittinck attacks an element of P3.
5. It is a gross error of the Fathers (i.e. the Dominicans) to state in general that both powers bind their subjects by their laws: what happens if the Roman Pontiff falls away from faith and becomes a heretic? In that case we have to judge and convict him. Did not St. Paul rebuke St. Peter; did not St. Paul everywhere warn against pseudo-apostles; did not St. John cry out that we should avoid the Antichrist? Gal. 2.11-14, 1 Tim. 4.1-3, 1 Jn. 4.1-3.

B. *The Objections of Timmermannus against P3, P2C1, P2C2, P2, P3C1.*
6. Neither power binds the subjects in conscience, unless it commands what Christ commands. No pontiff is allowed to add to or to remove anything from the Law of God. The Apostles affirm that they teach no inventions of their own, no human dogmas and traditions, no profane philosophy, but only the 'pura simplexque doctrina euangelica'. Just like Christ passed the Word of his Father to his disciples, so he bade them to pass his Word to us. Everywhere in the Gospel Christ utters his anger at traditions and human ordinances. Deut. 4.2, 1 Cor. 7.6, 12, 25, 2 Cor. 8.8, 10, Mk. 16.15 (but not literally), Gal. 2.7, 2 Cor.

4.5, Rom. 1.1, Mt. 15.1-9, Mk. 7.1-13, Col. 2.8, Tertullian, *De prae-scr. haer.* 6,4,3-5, Mag. Noster (Laur. Laur.): Lk. 10.16, Timm.: Mt. 5, 1 Tim. 1.12, 2 Cor. 5.20, Jn. 7.16, 12.49, 7.28 (wrongly Jn. 16), 14.10, 6.1-15).

7. The innocent are never justly condemned, because not even the most eminent prince is allowed to act against the canonical Scriptures. But the guilty may sometimes be freed from punishment. Deut. 4.2, Dan. 13.53, Acts 22.25, Prov. 8.15, Jn. 7.51, Is. 59.7, Joel 3.19, Jon. 1.14, Jn. 8.11, Aug., 'apud Marcellinum iudicem' [*PL* 33, 535-7].

8. Evangelical law is a law of freedom, which is consequently more bur-dened than the law of Moses by the ordinances of both powers. Under evangelical law we are obliged only to love each other. We pay taxes for practical reasons, not because we owe anything to a government. Evangelical law sets us free from human edicts and from the slavery of Mosaic law. The emperor is a member of the same body that we are; as a public minister he must look after the common good. If he exacts something from us for wrong and egotistic motives, we pay only because we do not want to resist the public authority, that is ordained by God, and because we do not want to disturb the public order. Under evangelical law, the authorities do not levy taxes. Rom. 13.1-7 is concerned with non-Christian princes of St. Paul's time and it ought not be applied to modern ecclesiastical authorities and Christian magistrates. Our humility in paying taxes does not cause innocence for the princes in exacting them. But Rom. 13.8 regards Christian subjects and Popes and Emperors alike. Num. 35.9-15, 1 Cor. 6.7, Jn. 8.36, Rom. 13.1-7, 8, Aug., *De civ. Dei* 5.17, Mt. 17.27.

9. The question whether a Christian is permitted to wage any war, is an-swered firmly in the negative. The doctrine of Christ and the Apostles forbids any wrath or hate or hostility, and this holds true in spite of the exceptions made by St. Augustine and St. Bernard.[57] It is even more reprehensible when Christians turn against other Christians. Even Mosaic law forbade waging war without having offered peace first. Mt. 5.40, 44, 1 Cor. 6.7, 1 Jn. 3.15, Gal. 5.13-15, 1 Cor. 12.12, Eph. 4.25, Deut. 20.10.

10. The Emperor should not allow but in practice is forced to agree to the existence of brothels, just like St. Paul felt obliged to condone a sec-ond marriage in Corinth, in order to protect the chastity of the young

---

[57] These exceptions are quoted from Erasmus, *Institutio principis Christiani*, cap. XI; see *ASD* IV-1, 215. The editor of the text, O. Herding, refers to Aug. *De civ. Dei* 4,15 and 19,7, and to Bernardus, *De laude nouae militiae* (*S. Bernardi Opera* III).

girls. But the Emperor cannot free from the resulting sin before God. Deut. 23.17-18, 1 Cor. 7.8-9, 39.

11. The most extreme form of punishment by the Church is excommunication, and this only after the guilty have first been admonished with *tolerantia*. Christ taught his followers to attack nobody and nothing with the sword. We are not allowed to judge anybody, as we can learn from the dealings of St. Paul in Corinth. Christ wanted revenge to be reserved for himself alone. Nobody ought to be pronounced a heretic as long as he is not convicted by apostolic authority of his error. The authority of Tertullian is invoked again. A quotation from *ad Titum* and other references also prove that no death penalty for heretics is ever thought of in the Bible. Christ and the Apostles often warn against false prophets, but they do not want to kill them, just as St. Martin of Tours and St. Augustine intervened on behalf of the heretics of their times. Mt. 18.15-17 (wrongly Mt. 17), 1 Cor. 5.12, 4.4-5, Rom. 12.19, Lk. 9.54-55, 1 Tim. 1.20, 2 Tim. 1.15, 2.17, Tit. 3.10, Tertullian, Sulpicius, Aug. (see above, at item 7.)

12. The imperial sword is expressly denied to the Pope and any other ecclesiastical authority. Christ taught peace, not strife. The only sword the Pope is entitled to bear, is that of the worldly power he exercises in his own territory. For the rest his task is to preach the Gospel, and when he exercises that task the Emperor has to heed. On the other hand, the Pope has to obey the Emperor as *publica potestas*, even if the Emperor levies taxes on the Pope. The immunities of churches and priest are abuses. Mt. 26.52, Jn. 14.27, Rom. 12.4-5, 13.4, 10.15, 13.1, 1 Pet. 2.13, Ambrose, *Ep.* 33.

13. The spiritual sword of excommunication is not a special right of the Pope, but is common to all people of the Church, including laymen. St. Paul did not excommunicate the lascivious Corinthian, but the Church, viz. the community that was offended; nor was St. Paul reconciled with him, but the citizens of Corinth. Timmermannus does not intend to take away from the Pope the right that Christ has given him, that is, the ministry of the Word, which he, however, shares with the Church. Difficult interpretations of Lk. 22.35-38, the basic text on the doctrine of the two swords. 2 Cor. 2.10 (wrongly 1 Cor.), Mt. 18.15, 19, 18 (wrongly Mt. 17), Lk. 22.35-38.

14. The Pope can grant dispensation from all human decisions, and, if necessary, he ought to change the institutions, including those agreed upon at the four earliest Councils; the Pope, as *episcopus*, is obliged to look after the well-being of all modern men. The decrees of the Councils were meant for other times and manners. Special reference is made to the many religious feast days and their abuses. If the Pope

proclaims feasts that threaten the peace of the flocks, then the pastors of Groningen have the full right to abolish them in the interest of the sheep that are entrusted to them. They also have the right to change the decrees of the Pope, in the same way that he can change those of the Councils. After all, there are more pastors than one! The Sabbath should serve the people, not the people the Sabbath. Ezek. 34.1-2, Nah. 3.18, Zech. 10.3, Acts 20.28, Aug. *Contra Cresconium grammaticum* 2.22, *Commonitorium ad Fortunatianum* [*PL* 33, 622-630 (esp. c.15)], *ad Probam* [*PL* 33, 493-507], *De Trinitate* 3 (prologus), *contra Donatistas* 2.3 [*PL* 43, 128-129], *ad Hieronymum Ep.* 19, *Hieronymus ad Theophilum adversus Iohannem Hierosolymitanum*, [*Decretum Gratiani*], distinct. 9, cap. Quis nesciat, distinct. 9, cap. Noli [*PL* 186, 50-51].

15. The Pope can certainly give dispensation from oaths and vows, provided that this is not to his own profit. This is true as well for the praying of the canonical hours by the religious. It is quite useless to rattle off each day a certain number of psalms and prayers. There are more important things to do in life, such as the education of the ignorant low people and the consolation of orphans and destitute widows. Christ has taught us to pray with a few words and not in the manner of the pagans with many. Mt. 6.7, Jas. 1.27.

Intermezzo 2. Pistoris attacks IP.

16. It is not against natural law that the world had a beginning. This is proven in different ways. The lector agrees with Pistoris. Aristotle, *Metaphysics* 12.7, Plato, *Timaeus* 37c-38c, *Physics* 3, Aug., *De civ. Dei* 12.14 (= 12.10).

C. *Objections of Lesdorpius against* P1, P1C1, P2, P3C1.

17. Christ, the son of God was priest not from the hour of his birth but from all eternity and in all eternity, after the order of Melchizedek. He was not anointed priest by men, but by the Father. Through his passion he did not earn priesthood for himself, but salvation for us. God has elected us in Christ from before the foundation of the world. He was our priest and we his children even before his sacrifice: 'ut pater nos praedestinauit in Christo ante mundi constitutionem (Eph. 1.4), ita et Christum nouit sacerdotem ante mundi constitutionem, cuius sacrificio saluandi erant praedestinati'. For the rest of objection 17, see above, p. 10, sub 2a. Heb. 7.1-10, 3, 16, 17, 28, Pss. 44 (45). 8, 101 (102).28, 109 (110).4, 1Cor. 1.30-31, Jn. 3.16, 1 Jn. 4.14, Eph. 1.4, Is. 9.5, Heb. 9.26 (wrongly Heb. 7), Is. 8.18 (wrongly 7), Jn. 17.11, Heb. 9.7, 11-12.

18. The monarchical dignity should be attributed to Christ's divinity, not to his humanity. He was called upon to be king, but he refused. Jn. 6.15, 8.29, 18.36.

19. Even if we were to concede that Christ succeeded to the priestly and monarchical power of the Levites and the kings of Israel, we deny that he bestowed these dignities upon any pontiff in particular. Actually, however, he bequeathed to his Apostles and through them to all of us, not an 'imperium' but a 'ministerium', by virtue of which we owe each other as 'membra' of one 'corpus', of which Christ, not the Pope is the 'caput': *care* ('sollicitudo'). This is also what words such as 'episcopus', 'diaconus', 'presbyter' actually mean. Christ has appointed all Apostles as 'ministri', not as monarchs, satraps, princes or rabbis, i.e. 'magistri nostri'. Reuchlin explained the word 'rabbi' as 'eximii magistri nostri' (our special teachers) ['rabbi' = my master]. The *magistri nostri* of our time have only one common master, they themselves are but 'ministri'. On Christ chasing the bankers from the temple, see above, p. 11, sub. 2c. 1 Cor. 3.5, 4.1, 12.12, 25, 2 Cor. 3.6, Col. 1.23, Mt. 20.25-26, 23.8, 1 Tim. 1.12, 2 Cor. 5.20, 1 Cor. 4.7, Mt. 10.1, 5, Mk. 16.15, Acts 20.28, Rom. 12.8, Col. 2.1, 2 Cor. 11.5, 1 Cor. 15.10, 9.16, 10.33, Jn. 2.13-16.

20. Christ did not give anything of a worldly power to the Apostles, but he sent them as sheep among the wolves, because he himself held no power or government over the world. Consequently, St. Peter will not be Christ's vicar on earth in worldly power, he has nothing to do with Octavian. Our Emperor should therefore govern the world according to apostolic authority, not as vicar of Christ. His government has nothing to do with theology, but it protects evangelical justice with part of his office. Rom. 13.4, 6.

21. If the Roman Pope is not allowed to establish anything new in contradiction to the four earliest Councils, he cannot claim any power outside the direct vicinity of the city of Rome, for that is against the [third] Council of Nicaea. From this we can see how badly our Fathers know their history. The [fourth] Council of Chalcedon established the primacy of the Roman bishop, but Gregory the Great rejected it. And there are other important decrees of Nicaea, e.g. concerning living together with a woman other than the mother or the sister of a cleric, and concerning the admittance to the services of priests who live in fornication, and concerning the elevation from a smaller to a larger diocese or bishop's see; and there are hundreds of customs more that time has changed.

The *magister noster* thanks Lesdorpius and the others for participating in the disputation and for the many excellent things they have taught. He invites all to a modest meal, which will be cheered by literary chat.

Regnerus Praedinius, De intercessione diuorum libellus

The second disputation under review in this article was written by a successor – perhaps the next one in function – of *Nicolaus Lesdorpius gymnasiarcha,* viz. Regnerus Praedinius, who held the post of rector of the Latin school of St. Martin's for nearly thirty years, from 1530 till his death in 1559.

Of the four celebrities of the humanist period in Groningen, Agricola, Gansfort, Praedinius and Ubbo Emmius, Regnerus Praedinius (1510-1559) is perhaps the most difficult one to understand as a figure of European significance. In the regional history of the sixteenth century he is generally considered one of the leading figures and, as a teacher, he is regarded one of the most influential men in Groningen. Remarkably, his fame is based upon rather little scholarly research. There are several reasons for this lack of work on Praedinius. Apart from a general neglect of the intellectual history of this region, there is the almost purely theological character of his writings. Moreover, his stand in the religious strife of his time could hardly meet with wholehearted sympathy in the modern scholarship of the nineteenth and the first three quarters of the twentieth century. He has nothing of an enthusiastic champion of one of the parties then active. From the very start of his career he was a convinced adherent of modern theological thought, but he remained in the Catholic Church till the end of his life. Neither believing Catholics nor Protestants of the nineteenth century could therefore claim him as an early representative. Already during and shortly after his lifetime, his fame seems almost entirely restricted to the pupils of his school. He never published any of his writings during his lifetime, and after his death, when his pupil Johannes Acronius in 1563 had finally published his theological works,[58] these *libelli* and *commentarioli* appeared to be written in difficult Latin that must have baffled any potential readers, perhaps with the exception of some of his pupils and adherents. Besides, theological debate had by then lost its character of an open discussion within the Church. So his fame remained dubious. Abel Eppens, a chronicler of Groningen in the sixteenth century, testifies to the lack of interest in Praedinius's written work: 'Want Regneri boecken worden nichtes geachtet

---

[58] Praedinius, *Opera omnia,* 1563.

dan van sijn discipelen [...]'.[59] (For the books of Regnerus are held in no esteem except by his pupils.)

Even a great man like Ubbo Emmius (1547-1625), who admired the founding fathers of intellectual life in Groningen, had not much praise to spend on the scholarship of Praedinius, who was a predecessor as the leader of St. Martin's school. In his *Rerum Frisicarum historia* he had praised for their learning Wessel Gansfort, Rudolph Agricola, Hector of Hoxwier, Gerardus Synellius, Gemma Frisius and his son Cornelius, Viglius of Zwichem (of Aytta), Joachim Hopperus and 'infiniti alii', but he had not even mentioned Praedinius.[60] One of Praedinius's pupils, Johannes Arcerius, had been annoyed at this omission, which he thought a deliberate neglect. Emmius answered him in a letter as follows:

> Regnerum uirorum e literis clarorum numero in Frisia non exemi, sed inter infinitos alios comprehendi, in quibus nonnulli, si ipsam doctrinam spectes, Regnero etiam superiores, quanquam forte eloquentes minus.[61]

> I did not take away Regnerus from the number of famous literary men in Frisia; I included him in the 'infinite others', among whom, if one considers their learning in itself, some were even superior to Regnerus, even if, perhaps, less eloquent.

Thus he makes things even worse: Regnerus lacked in Emmius's eyes a broad learning, even though he grants his somewhat meager fame as an eloquent teacher and upholder of his viewpoints.

In our collection of essays on *Wessel Gansfort and Northern Humanism*, Folkert Postma has given an excellent general introduction to Praedinius, his life, and his work as a theological thinker and as a Rector of the Latin school. I consider it an attractive obligation to continue this study of Praedinius by giving special attention to one of his *libelli* and to his Latin.

About Praedinius's use of the Latin language hardly a good word has ever been said. His faithful pupil Acronius already has it in the 'Ad Christianum Lectorem Praefatio':

---

[59] *De kroniek van Abel Eppens* (eds. Feith and Brugmans), I 337; here quoted from Bakker, 'Handschriften en boeken', I 111.

[60] Ubbo Emmius, *Rerum Frisicarum historia*, 34. All the men here mentioned by Emmius have a longer or shorter article in Suffridus Petrus's *De scriptoribus Frisiae*, but *his* treatment of Praedinius is not particularly short.

[61] Ubbo Emmius, *Briefwechsel*, I 167. The letter is dated 4 October 1598. In another letter (I 112) Emmius praised Praedinius as a very young Rector of the school: 'Et tamen scio, etiam iuuenum ministeria in Ecclesiis et Scholis saepe non inutilia esse, iisque non minus large quam adultioribus benedicere dominum. Cuius euidens exemplum Regnerus ille, qui magna cum laude quondam huic nostrae scholae praefuit.'

Non deerunt fortasse et Regneromastiges, qui Regneri nostri operam canino dente arrodentes siue stylum autoris horridum sint uocaturi, siue labores ipsius quantumuis pios ut parum frugiferos eleuaturi. Verum hos nihil moramur, homines uili potius lolio quam lautiore obsonio dignos.[62]

There will be perhaps no lack of Regnero-whips, who, with their dogsteeth gnawing at the work of our Regnerus, shall call his writing style crude, or shall make light of his efforts, pious as they may be, on the ground of being rather unfruitful. But we do not mind them, these people who deserve a worthless weed rather than a dainty dish.

The writer on Frisian history, Suffridus Petrus, not himself a pupil of Praedinius, wrote in 1593 on hearsay or simply echoing the words of Acronius:

Multa eum scripsisse intellexi, quae tamen ad manus meas hactenus non peruenerunt. Audiui scripta eius non referre gratiam, quam uiua uox habuit, eademque a Catholicis esse notata.[63]

Here the lack of grace of his written style is counterbalanced by the attractiveness of his living voice, and criticism is toned down by the alleged religious bias of his opponents.

The negative verdicts of the sixteenth century are repeated and intensified three centuries later. The only author who published a monograph on Praedinius in the nineteenth century, J.J. Diest Lorgion, wrote in 1862:

When we observe [...] that the structure of his sentences, the manner in which he connects his thoughts and arguments, often has to be called, to say the least, odd, then we characterize his style in general as long-winded and obscure. [...] The way, in which he expresses himself in his writings, makes us suspect, remembering Macauly's word 'Obscurity of expression generally springs from confusion of ideas', that his ideas, at least on theological questions, liberal as they may be, were not at all clearly developed, sharply defined nor neatly arranged.[64]

---

[62] *lolium* – darnel, a weed reputed to be harmful to the eyesight; cf. Plautus, *Miles gloriosus*, 321; Ovid, *Fasti*, I 691.

[63] Suffridus Petrus, *De scriptoribus Frisiae*, 168.

[64] 'Wanneer wij hierbij nog opmerken, dat de bouw zijner volzinnen, de wijze, waarop hij zijne gedachten en redeneringen verbindt, voor 't minst genomen dikwijls vreemd genoemd moet worden, dan mogen wij zijn stijl in 't algemeen karakteriseren als langdradig en duister. Dit is reeds door zijne tijdgenoten opgemerkt. [...] de wijze waarop hij zich in zijne geschriften uitdrukt, brengt ons, gedachtig aan Macauly's woord: [...] tot het vermoeden, dat zijne denkbeelden, althans over godgeleerde onderwerpen, hoe vrijzinnig zij ook mochten zijn, geenszins duidelijk ontwikkeld, scherp bepaald en klaar geordend waren.' (Diest Lorgion, *Verhandeling over Regnerus Praedinius*, 138).

I hope that when reading my article the reader will discover the unfairness and incorrectness of this devastating judgement, which in its turn has determined subsequent criticisms. Thus J. Lindeboom, who in 1913 wrote on Praedinius: 'He is by no means a poet, and although he does not write barbaric Latin, it is horrible and difficult to read.'[65] These words were inspired by Diest Lorgion's verdict, by Praedinius's own utterance that he had always tried to use correct Latin words (see below, p. 27), by Suffridus Petrus's report on the fate of Praedinius's successor (see below), and last but not least by an incorrect estimation of the word *horridus*, which is a technical term of Latin rhetoric and does not mean 'afschuwelijk' (horrible).

That Praedinius had no taste for poetry, is expressly stated by Suffridus Petrus, when he reported on the failure of Praedinius's immediate successor as Rector of the St. Martin's school, Gerardus Loppersum:

> For the Magistrate persuaded him [i.e. Gerardus Loppersum] through a generous salary to assume the Rectorate of the school of Groningen. But since this excellent man could not present the voice nor the body-language of Praedinius that could titillate the eyes and ears of his pupils in the way they were used to, and then also because he introduced what was a new discipline to them, viz. poetry, which Praedinius had neglected – poetry, indeed, was the only thing he lacked – his authority waned and he became a warning example, in such a way that he almost wasted away from sorrow of the heart, as he could not have any reward from his labor, and he lost all his self-esteem.[66]

This scholastic tragedy was accompanied by the sinister chorus of the jealous lower teachers (the 'hypodidascali'), who had coveted the rectorate for themselves and thus set up the pupils against their headmaster. So Gerardus Loppersum took his leave after only one year and went off to Maastricht, where he died c. 1582.

But back to Praedinius's Latin. In order to investigate the significance of its standard condemnation[67] more closely, I have chosen one of his early writings, the *De intercessione diuorum libellus*, precisely because of its early and well-established date, and because it belongs to the category of his *opuscula*, which he did not correct or expand later in his life, but which he

---

[65] 'Hij is absoluut geen dichter en schrijft een wel niet barbaristisch, maar toch afschuwelijk, moeilijk leesbaar Latijn' (Lindeboom, *Bijbelsch Humanisme*, 169).

[66] 'Magistratus eum liberali stipendio induxit ut Scholae Gruninganae gubernaculo susciperet. Sed cum uir optimus neque uocem neque motus Regneri praestaret, quae oculos et aures titillarent auditorum solito modo, introduceret deinde etiam nouam et insolitam Poetices doctrinam, quam Regnerus neglexerat, cui nihil nisi carmina deerant, euiluit ejus authoritas, et ipse in exemplum uenit, ita ut prae animi moerore pene contabuerit, cum fructum facere non posset, et existimationem omnem suam amitteret' (Suffridus Petrus, *De scriptoribus Frisiae*, 387-8).

[67] Also Van Schelven, 'Een brief van Praedinius', 54: 'Praedinius' Latijn heeft trouwens een zeer slechte reputatie'.

left unchanged, and wished to be nothing but an academic disputation of a young man.[68] It was written in the second term of three years in his service of the city as he tells us himself (see below, p. 35), when he was 'natus circiter annos uiginti quatuor'(about 24 years old),[69] and since he was born in 1509 or 1510,[70] the *De intercessione* must date from about 1534. We can be pretty sure that this essay reflects exactly the state of his Latinity when he was a young man.

Another reason for choosing *De intercessione diuorum* for my investigation is that in it Praedinius himself admits to the dubious quality of his Latin and gives an explanation for it. In fact, criticism did not begin with the 'Regneromastiges' of the sixteenth century, but with an anonymous friend who had laughed at his style and who received an answer. This friend had seen in Praedinius's earlier book *On the Christian prayer* a reason to reproach him for not having mentioned the intercession of the saints. I quote here in full the opening section of *De intercessione*, not only for the contents, but also for the Latin form:

1. Reprehendis, quamquam modeste, quod cum inscripserim Commentariolum de Precatione Christiana, tamen in eo dissimulauerim omnem mentionem de diuorum intercessione. Atque iocabundus rogas, num adeo sim offensus uocabuli abusu, ut propter fastidium eius non sustinuerim neque pro re ipsa dicere neque contra. Merito ducis in occasionem ridendi meam infelicitatem in scribendo. Nam cum ipse teneas me illud genus sermonis incon-<s>tanter sequi, quod ex consuetudine stili ultro succedat, haud tamen fere unquam praestem, quin uidear in deligendis uerbis atque coniungendis identidem superstitione commoueri. Agnosco uitium meum, neque eius me causa fallit: iuuenili istud et imperitae affectationi debetur. Etenim cum mihi prima aetate ad optima praeceptor et dux deesset, neque quicquam magis studerem quam ut in scribendo uerbis Latinis uterer, iisque inter se aliquo modo cohaerentibus, sentio nunc demum neutram uirtutem me adeptum esse

---

[68] Johannes Acronius in his *Epistola dedicatoria* (Praedinius, *Opera*, α2v.): '[...] adhuc adolescens [...] se contulit ad sacram Theologiam, et opusculum De precatione Christiana, nec diu post aliud De intercessione diuorum conscripsit, quorum illud quidem correxit et auxit, hoc uero integrum reliquit, nec aliud esse uoluit quam adolescentis Academicam disputationem'.

[69] Acronius in the heading of the 'Intercessio' (Praedinius, *Opera*, 526).

[70] The sources differ a bit on Praedinius's birth year. The text on the original tombstone (now lost), which is quoted by Suffridus Petrus (p. 168), implies a birth in 1508 or 1509; a new stone which was placed in 1810, gives as birth year 1508 (for the text, see Pathuis, *Groninger gedenkwaardigheden*, nos. 345 and 5165). But it is better to stick to Praedinius's own indications, which point to 1510 or at the earliest to 1509 (for these indications, see Praedinius, *Opera*, 198 and 491).

illo studio, sed uitium utriusque perperam affectatae, idque adeo insedisse, ut nisi diligentissime attendam, nunquam fere non admittatur.[71]

'You reproach me, though modestly, that when I entitled that commentary 'On the Christian prayer', I nevertheless omitted any mention of the intercession of the saints. And jestingly you ask me, whether I am so offended by the abuse of the word, that owing to my repugnance to it I could not bring myself to speak neither for nor against the thing itself. You are right when you seize upon my infelicitous way of writing as an opportunity for laughter. For whereas you yourself understand very well that I follow without constancy the kind of language which proceeds naturally from a regular practice of the pen, yet, I almost never succeed in avoiding the impression that in the choice and combination of words I am time and again affected by superstition. I acknowledge my fault, and the cause does not escape me: the blame for it has to be laid on my youthful and inexperienced affectation. For while in my early youth I lacked a teacher to guide me to the best, and I strove after nothing more than to use correct Latin words and such as are somehow coherent among themselves, I only now sense that I have attained neither quality through this zeal, but only the fault of both attempted in the wrong way, and that it is now so deeply rooted in me, that if I don't attend very carefully, this fault is almost never not committed.'

What is wrong with this piece of Latin? In my view it is clear and subtle and purely classical in the selection of words and syntactical features. Perhaps the reader could feel a difficulty in the sentence beginning with 'Nam cum ipse', where it is not immediately clear what the contrast or the concessive force of 'cum ipse teneas' followed by 'haud tamen' is, but it should be understood, perhaps, that things are far worse than the friend in his modest criticism had assumed. For the rest, the *consuetudo stili* – the regular practice of writing that creates fluency – and the *superstitio* – the anxious adherence to rules – are concepts that can easily be found in the rhetorical books of Cicero and Quintilian.[72] In reading this intelligent, varied Latin page of Praedinius, we immediately understand why he says that in his early youth he had lacked a teacher who could guide him to the best. Goswinus van Halen had been his guide in the school of the Brethren, Nicolaus Lesdorpius his Rector of the town school. In both cases – that is to say , if Lesdorpius is the author of the *Disputatio Groningensis* – it is easy to see

---

[71] Praedinius, *Opera*, 526.

[72] See Van der Laan, *Anatomie van een Taal*, 286, where he treats the topos of the 'stilus optimus dicendi artifex', in a note on Agricola, *Ep.* 4,13. For the *superstitio*, see Quintilian, *Inst.* 9,4,24-5.

that in Latin style Praedinius towers highly above his former schoolmasters. Praedinius's Latin is a giant step forward in the mastering of classical prose style. It follows the patterns of precisely the two authors we sensed already in the above quotation: Cicero and Quintilian. These two are also the only Latin authors mentioned among the pagans in this essay. Wherever the reader is tempted to look up a word or expression of Praedinius in the dictionary, he encounters almost invariably one or both of these two. Even in this one *libellus* there are several passages of the same high quality as the prooemium just quoted.

All the same, there is no denying the weak points. Praedinius often, though not everywhere, makes for difficult reading. Difficulties arise from complex periods; as we saw, he loves to use combinations of *cum ... tamen*, or *ut ... tamen, ut ... ita* (even though ... and yet), and then to work into these constructions other subordinate clauses with *cum* or *quod* etc. Above all, these complex structures of his syntax force the reader to read the same passage again and again, till, in the end, he almost invariably gets the satisfaction of an *Aha-Erlebnis*. Another difficulty arises from a tendency to refer to concepts or things or persons by means of pronouns or adverbs over rather long stretches of text, so that the reader must pause now and then to consider which word is referred to by *eam, istud* (*iste* is often used for *hic*), *hic, cuius, huc, quo* etc. Sometimes Praedinius uses pronouns in other cases than the nominative or the accusative of the neuter, which is not classical: e.g. *huic* – herefore; *ullo alio* – through any other thing, by any other means.

A third stumbling block on the road for the modern reader, at least in the *De intercessione*, is that Praedinius everywhere betrays his thorough training in rhetoric and dialectics. His text is steered by his technical know-how in text writing. So without knowing what a *propositio*, an *assumptio*, or a *complexio* is, what the precise function of terms such as *genus, species, causa, locus, partitio, excipere* is, the reader soon loses track of the argument. The point is that Praedinius is not a 'political' writer; he never tried, at least in his writings, to win a large audience or readership over to his standpoints by simple rhetorical means, i.e. by 'preaching', and this is what most critics of his style expect from a theologian of the sixteenth century. His texts are not persuasive, they are meant to be convincing. Twice in the *De intercessione* he expressly rejects rhetorical means in favor of philosophical strictness of reasoning: '[...] considerentur hic singulae [sc. causae], uerum ornatu rhetorico nudatae. Certius etenim res perspiciuntur omni tegumento, quod eas obscuret, remoto.'[73] It is a curious feature of all Praedinius's writ-

---

[73] Praedinius, *Opera*, 538. The other place is on p. 530, where the friend's real position is betrayed by his own renouncing rhetorical ornament: 'manifesto etenim ipsa remotio ornatus

ings, that he wrote them very carefully, and corrected and expanded on most of them later on,[74] but never published any of this, something which he had already decided not to do in his early days. In the *De intercessione* we read: 'Viuus quidem haud mihi uideor quicquam esse unquam emissurus, non solum argumenti Theologici, sed ne quidem prophani.'[75] And when during his last illness, he looked over his various *opuscula*, he intended some for posthumous publication, left others in the hands of his friends to do with them what they liked, even to publish them under their own names; and of his works 'prophani argumenti' it is said in the Praefatio by Acronius:

> Publice in Schola etiamsi fere singulis diebus quatuor integras horas praelege-ret, tamen domi nihilominus uaria alia meditatus est ac scripsit, in Platonem, Aristotelem, Demosthenem et Galenum, in Latinos Ciceronem et Quintilianum; quae, dum sanctam ueritatem perfecte non redolerent, rupit, ac multorum lachrymis Vulcano tradidit. Caeterum Theologica, quae diuinam ueritatem longe manifestius spectandam proponunt, [...] omnibus communicare uoluit.[76]

Modern commentators interpret these words as meaning that Praedinius on his deathbed rejected the pagan authors, just because they were pagan. This seems to me silly: the 'sancta ueritas', did, to Praedinius's mind, not concern the internal truth of the texts, but the scientific truth of his commentaries. They were just not ready for publication as scholarly works.[77]

The *De intercessione* is addressed to an intellectual friend, who had incited Praedinius to write an essay against the belief in the usefulness or necessity of the invocation of the saints in prayer and to do this in the form of an academic disputation. That the two friends tried to find the truth about a serious religious topic with the help of the rules of academic discussion in which they were trained, is not so strange. In one of the three letters that have been preserved of Praedinius's correspondence, it appears that there, too, two friends, or rather three, had discussed in private religious matters in the form of a regular *disputatio*.[78]

---

rhetorici prodit discrepantiam [...]' etc. Praedinius, too, shall now do the same: 'Nudam rem proponam, iis seiunctis, quae eloquentia de suo adiecit.'

[74] See n. 68.

[75] Praedinius, *Opera*, 528.

[76] Praedinius, *Opera*, α2v.

[77] The modern commentators that I mean are Lindeboom, *Bijbelsch Humanisme*, 169 and Postma, 'Regnerus Praedinius', 319. Humanists and Reformers sometimes sharply distinguished between *sanctus* and *diuus (diuinus)*. See e.g. Praedinius, 'De intercessione', *Opera*, 541 'sancti ac diui' (the living and the dead saints); so in the quoted passage 'sancta' and 'diuina ueritas' should be distinguished: the truth according to men and to God respectively. As a matter of fact, Praedinius did not throw into the flames the pagan authors, which he had taught all his life, but his own notes; the subject of 'non redolerent' are these personal annotations.

[78] The letter addressed to Francisco de Enzinas (Dryander) on 30 April 1545, published by García Pinilla, 54-9, and by Van Schelven, 54-6.

The position of the two friends in the *De intercessione diuorum* is remarkable. The friend, who lived somewhere in Germany and belonged to the German evangelical movement, had in his – now lost – letter to Praedinius, for his own part, ventured to state that the invocation of saints is a useful element of Christian prayer, and he tried to provoke Praedinius to attack this proposition. Praedinius accepted this challenge, on the condition, which the friend had suggested, that neither of the two needed to reckon with his own personal conviction – 'non habita ratione, qua sit sententia uterque nostrum'[79] – nor made any use, at least consciously, of the arguments of the German evangelicals against the intercession of the saints – 'neque sciens quidem usus argumentis scriptorum Ecclesiae Germanorum'.[80] So one could consider the whole *libellus* a purely fictional piece of academic exercise, without any religious consequence whatsoever. In reality, it is a deadly serious, thoroughly argued attack on the theory and practice of the invocation of the saints in prayer, which in Praedinius's view, is downright impiety and an insult to Christ.

The whole *libellus* takes up 21 pages of 42 (some of 41) lines each in the quarto volume of the *Opera omnia* edition of Basle 1563. It shows a careful, balanced structure. It begins and ends with an autobiographical section. The personal prooemium (28 lines) is followed by the proposition of the theme and the manner in which it will be treated (85 lines), and the personal final section (42 lines) is preceded by an epilogue (44 lines), in which the foregoing argumentation and the method of reasoning is once again summarized. The central part (613 lines) is filled by the arguments proper. Thus, the scheme for the whole is A B C B' A'.

But before summarizing the contents, I turn once more to the Latin. To illustrate its qualities and difficulties I have selected a few passages. I hope that it will become clear from these fragments that Praedinius's Latin is often clear and forceful, sometimes difficult, always elaborate, never slipshod or indifferent. Speaking for my own part, I must say that it was a pleasure, by reading the complete text several times, to discover what every single sentence and the whole argument has to say. I can accept the sixteenth-century qualification *horridus* for the style, provided that this word ('crude', 'harsh', 'uncouth') need not always have a purely negative connotation. In the sixteenth century the reality of life and thought became often too complex to be expressed by the Ciceronian smoothness of the Italian type.

---

[79] Praedinius, *Opera*, 529.
[80] Praedinius, *Opera*, 544. For Luther's attitude see Manns, 'Luther und die Heiligen'; for Zwingli see 'Von der Anrufung der Verstorbenen, die im Himmel sind'.

Cicero himself did not condemn every author who practiced, in his eyes, a *horrida oratio.*[81]

The judgement of Acronius on Praedinius's Latin style may be a bit overpraising, but it contains a more realistic insight in its qualities than later critics had to offer. The following quotation connects immediately with the passage I quoted on p. 25:

> Quam enim autor hic noster in omni genere exercitatus fuerit, illis optime perspectum est, qui multis partim annis ipsum docentem audiuere, partim ipso familiariter usi sunt. Cumque proposita materia grauissima esset, ita etiam huic sermonis stilum attemperandum esse putauit, ut et grauiter et neruose, atque pro dignitate eius tractata uideri posset. Neque uero, si inutiles quaestiones, dissidiorum syluam uidelicet, uitare studuit, propterea eius scripta parui precii censebuntur, quod uera ac solida pietas nuda ueritate contenta, controuertentes quaestiones ac subtiliora illa argumenta auersari soleat. Quod et ipse frequenter monuit seduloque in hoc Opere obseruauit, nisi quod aliquoties in locis communibus tractandis specimina obiter magnae eloquentiae appareant, quae tamen nullo modo par existit ipsi, quae in uiua eius oratione esse solet.

> For how well trained our author was in every kind [of speech], is something that those people are well aware of, who over many years heard his teaching and lived in close contact with him. Since the subject matter he intended to treat was very grave, he thought that the style of his writing ought to be adapted to it, so that it could appear to have been treated solemnly and vigorously and in accordance with its dignity. And if he strove to avoid useless questions, I mean the whole bunch of futile hairsplitting, his writings shall not for that reason be valued as of small significance, for true and unalloyed piety, that contents itself with the unadorned truth, is wont to turn away in disgust from controversial questions and abstruse arguments. This is something he himself frequently recommended and observed carefully in this work, except that from time to time when he is treating commonplaces, there incidentally appears evidence of a great eloquence, which, however, is by no means of the same level as that which he usually showed in his living oral speech.

In the following translations I purposely stay as close to the Latin as possible without losing the English meaning.

2. *It was useless for me to refute the intercession of the saints.*

Nam cum sint qui hanc intercessionem ultro condemnent, ideoque iis haud opus sit ea refutata, quanquam non omnia aeque teneant quae ad precandum conducant, ita rursus alios reperies, non illos quidem infestos religioni, neque tardos ad discendam rationem orandi neque repugnantes, adeo tamen ig-

---

[81] The Ancients sometimes associated *horrida oratio* with the rugged virtues of a former age; cf. Cicero, *Brutus*, 83; Seneca, *Ep.* 100,6; Quintilian, *Inst.* 10,1,119; cf. 2,5,21.

naros naturae istius intercessionis, ut ad mentionem huius refellendae sint
auersaturi protinus tanquam impia caetera omnia quae dicentur.[82]

'For while there are those who condemn this intercession on their own initiative, and who have therefore no need of its refutation, although they do
not grasp equally well everything that leads to effective prayer, you will find
others, I mean those who are not hostile to religion, nor slow or refractory in
learning the right method of praying, who are so ignorant of the nature of
this intercession, that at the mere mention of refuting it, they forthwith will
shrink back from anything more to be said.'

3. *There are two viewpoints, which approve of the intercession. The second
of these:*
[Dicis] Alteram uero sententiam nihilo plus detrahere gratiae Christi, quam
fiat in mutuis precibus Christianorum inter uiuos. Nam ut hi saepe flagitant
orationes plurimorum et plerunque optimorum quorumque, sic tamen, ut
omnem Patris beneuolentiam acceptam referant Christi gratiae, ita facere
hanc alteram sententiam de intercessione.[83]

'[You say] that the second viewpoint does not detract anything more from
the grace of Christ than happens in the mutual prayer of living Christians for
each other. For just as they often demand the prayers of many and mostly of
the very best, in such a way as to attribute all benevolence they have received from the Father to the grace of Christ, so, you say that in the same
way this second viewpoint does with regard to the intercession.'

4. *Two 'historical causes' advanced for the introduction of the intercession
of the saints.*
In his igitur martyrum memoriis solent haberi quasi funebres orationes, quibus exponeretur uita martyris, fides, spiritus dona, genus mortis, constantia,
suppliciorum atrocitas eaque, quae in religione Christiana uidebantur merito
laudanda esse. Noctu istud fere et ad lumina, magna tamen Christianorum
celebritate. Quorum omnium princeps causa fuit, ut reliqui ad imitationem
uirtutum tantarum concitarentur, ut Deo gratiae agerentur de tantis donis in
peremptos, ut similia ab illo ipsis uiuis orarentur, quanquam fortassis aliquid
laudis simul spectatum sit in martyribus, aut etiam pietatis in mortuos. [...]
    Sunt qui arbitrentur quosdam, cum putarent ex summis illis laudationibus
defunctos illos Deo ipsis gratiores esse, excogitasse aliquid eiusmodi intercessionis, ad similitudinem, qua superstites in hac uita precantur pro uiuis.

---

[82] Praedinius, *Opera,* 527-8.
[83] Praedinius, *Opera*, 529.

Sunt contra, qui causam duntaxat ponant in usu rerum humanarum, quod homines ardentes cupiditate impetrandi inter se, tales ad hunc allegent, qui oratur, quorum apud illum credunt gratiam maiorem esse.[84]

'In these ceremonies to commemorate the martyrs, there used to be held as it were funeral orations, in which were expounded the life of the martyr, his faith, his spiritual gifts, the kind of death he suffered, his constancy, the atrocity of his torments, and all those things which in Christian religion were rightly regarded as praiseworthy. These celebrations took place during the night, by lamplight, yet with a large attendance of the Christians. Of all this the main reason was to urge the others to imitate such great virtues, to thank God for gifts so great to the deceased, and to pray to him for similar boons for the living themselves; or perhaps at the same time something of praise was directed to the martyrs or of piety towards the dead. [...]

There are those who imagine that some people, because they think, owing to these very high praises, that those deceased are dearer to God than they themselves, have devised something like such an intercession, on the analogy of the way the survivors in this life pray for the living. There are on the other hand those who place the cause in the practice of human affairs only, because men who ardently wish to obtain anything by request from each other, send as intermediaries to him who is to be supplicated such persons as they believe to have the greatest goodwill with him.'

5. A psychological cause for the introduction of the intercession of the saints, modestia, *is also rejected.*
Non igitur potest modestia haberi talis animi demissio, quae Euangelio detrahit, illi minime consentit. Neque enim potest doceri huiusce modi aestimationem sui, quae in precando ad diuos deducit, magis conuenire ad praescriptum Euangelii, quam illam, qua se quispiam ducit scelestiorem quam ut fide queat conseruari.[85]

'Therefore such a humility of heart, that detracts from the Gospel, and is not in the least in harmony with it, cannot be regarded as modesty. For a self-esteem so low, that it brings itself down to the level of the saints in prayer, cannot be taught to be in better agreement with the lessons of the Gospel than that by which anybody considers himself criminal beyond the possibility to be saved by faith.'

---

[84] Praedinius, *Opera,* 533-4.
[85] Praedinius, *Opera,* 539.

6. *The final section: on the difficult relationship between the Duke of Guel-ders and Groningen, and between Praedinius and Groningen.*[86]

Ad extremum expostulas mecum, quod aduentum (quem etsi non studio, ta-men promisso debebam) hucusque non exoluerim. Fateor me promisisse, et quanquam potuerim proficisci, sola consilii commutatione distulisse, cuius tibi rationem breui exponam.

Mea patria, quanquam in media Frisia sit, et uerissima Frisia, tamen compulsa armis Georgii ducis Saxoniae, ante aliquot annos concessit in fi-dem ducis Geldriae, inter quem et hanc rempublicam scelestissimis quorun-dam quadruplatorum criminibus eo res euasit, ut nihil sit ad coniecturam uerisimilius, quam Principem ui demum, quando res uariis aliis modis ali-quandiu tentata non successit, aditurum imponere id iugum eamque for-mam huic reipublicae, ut in ea nec mihi expediat uiuere nec cuiquam libera-liter erudito. Sin autem Principi euentus non responderit (nam nostri non fe-rent, nisi extremis quibusque subacti), non ideo tamen minus cupio isto mo-tui discessu meo anteuertere.

Proinde exacto hoc altero triennio, in quod meam operam Senatui addixi, constitui per uos atque Heluetiam uel in Italiam uel in Galliam proficisci. Nam utro necdum satis decreui. Scio rectius atque expeditius iter esse in Galliam hinc per Brabantiam atque Flandriam, sed tecum colloqui uolo at-que deinde Erasmum uidere, non propter id modo, quod mihi de illo iampri-dem es pollicitus, sed etiam propter incredibilem uiri admirationem. Consi-lium uero est non prius huc redire, quam de eo malo fuerit decretum, sedes quidem figere post id tempus nunquam. Cuius causam aliquando tibi scripsi. Aut Louanii igitur ad extremum aut Coloniae, uti latius aliquando scripsi, cum gratias agerem tibi de conditione, quam tuo studio et beneuolentia mihi expedieras, et coram inter nos fusius consultabitur;[87] ita tamen omnia acci-pies, ut de conditione scias me prorsus non cogitare, sed omnino aut in Gal-

---

[86] In the late Middle Ages, Groningen developed into a practically independent city state that dominated a large area (the so-called Ommelanden) until 1498. From 1498-1506 Albrecht of Saxony and later his son George dominated the scene in 'Frisia', and from 1506-1514 the town recognized Count Edzard of East Frisia as its sovereign ruler. From 1514 onwards Char-les, Duke of Guelders, was the sovereign Prince of Groningen; he had, however, no military stronghold in the town. Charles was the antagonist of the growing Habsburg power. In the late twenties the relationship between Groningen and its Lord became strained for religious and financial reasons (high taxes!). The Duke threatened the town with a violent occupation, and, then, in their anxiety, the city fathers, in June 1536, surrendered the town to Charles V, but still without a Habsburg garrison within its walls. The 'Prince' Praedinius was afraid of was not Charles V, but the Duke of Guelders. See on this history *Historie van Groningen*, 173-80; and Huizinga, *Groningen onder Karel van Gelder*, esp. 85-91.

[87] We know nothing about the post the friend had offered to Praedinius, nor about the reasons why he wanted to leave his school in Groningen. Presumably it was on account of reli-gious resistance (see Postma, 'Regnerus Praedinius', 300, n. 36).

liam aut in Ialiam, neque uspiam certas sedes, dum sim coelebs.[88] Ne igitur transcurram hinc isthuc, mox rursus isthinc huc, differam, usque dum id tempus exeat, nostrum utri<que> exoptatum inter nos praesentem et sermo- nem et aspectum.

Faxint modo superi, ne interea noster Princeps aliquid commoueat, et spero hoc tempus ante exiturum, neque id uanis omnino coniecturis; ualde enim uereor, si ante discessero (quod tamen fiet, si ea Princeps perfecerit, quae uidetur cogitare), ne, qui hoc molestius ferent, ipsam causam coniiciant profectionis ante suum tempus acceleratae. Verum istud uniuersum eo ten- dit, ut quanquam promiserim me aduenturum, uideas tamen ratione fieri, cur neque hactenus uenerim, neque interea sim uenturus.[89]

'Finally, you expostulate with me that thus far I have not put into effect my plan of visiting you, which I owed, if not to my intention, at least to my promise. I confess that I promised this, and although I could have set out on my voyage, I have postponed it only because I have changed my mind, the reason for which I shall explain to you.

My home town, though lying in the heart of Frisia – indeed it is the most genuine Frisia – has passed many years ago, forced by the arms of George, Duke of Saxony, into the protection of the Duke of Guelders. Due to the slander of mischievous informers, the relationship between him and this city has worsened so far, that at a guess nothing is more likely than that the Prince, when things, after they have been tried for some time in various ways, do not yield any result, will eventually by force proceed to put our city under a yoke and a constitution, under which it is not expedient for me to live, nor for anybody with a liberal education. And if the outcome falls short of the expectations of the Prince – for our people shall not give in, unless they are forced by the most extreme measures –, I wish nonetheless to anticipate that upheaval by my departure.

So then, at the end of this second term of three years, in which I have committed myself to the service of the Senate, I have decided to travel through your country to Italy or France. To which of the two I will go, I have not yet decided. I know that the voyage from here tot France is shorter

---

[88] Eventually, Praedinius married Abele Bellingeweer; he had a son Albert, who died in 1588 (and through him a grand-daughter Elletjen Praedinius, who was married to the Syndicus of the town, Dr. Wilhelm Hammonius) and a daughter Roelina, married to Bernhard de Sighers, who died as mayor of Groningen on 24 July 1635. (See Boeles, 'St. Maartens en der A Scholen te Groningen'). To all appearances, then, Praedinius and his family were well integrated into the higher levels of town life.

[89] Praedinius visited Basel and Italy after his abdication, but returned in the same year to Groningen where he resumed his Rectorate (see Postma, 'Regnerus Praedinius', 300: a quote from Crespin's edition of Praedinius's *Commentationes*, 1568, 4v).

and easier through Brabant and Flanders, but I long to talk to you, and then to see Erasmus, not only because of what you promised me about him long ago, but also because of my incredible admiration for the man. It is my intention not to return here before these troubles have come to a conclusion. After that I shall never settle here permanently again, the reason for which I have once written to you. So, ultimately it will be Louvain or Cologne, as I once wrote you more fully, when I thanked you for the post you had arranged for me through your diligence and kindness. When I am with you, we shall discuss the matter in more detail in person. Then you will hear everything, to that effect, however, that you may know that I am not at all thinking about a post, but that I want to go to France or Italy anyway, with a fixed residence nowhere as long as I am a bachelor. Hence, in order not to run from here to there, and from there to here again, I shall postpone the moment we both long for, in which we shall see each other and talk together, till the present term ends.

The gods in heaven forbid, that in the meantime our Prince stirs up something, and I do hope, on not altogether vain grounds, that this term will end earlier than that. For I fear very much that if I leave before the end of my term – which I shall nevertheless do if the Prince carries out what he seems to have in mind – those who will take it ill may guess the real reason for my departure if hurried before the right moment. But the whole story tends to this, that, although I have promised to come, you may see that it is not without reason, that I have not come yet, nor will come in the meantime.'[90]

Summary of the contents of De intercessione diuorum libellus

I *Prooemium*
   1. The cause of this booklet; on my Latin style [see above, fragment 1]
   2. Why did I suppress any mention of the intercession in my *De precatione Christiana?*
   3. Why did I not refute it? [see fr. 2]
   4. On the dialectical method of your argumentation and on the real view-points of both of us on the intercession of the saints: you stand up for the cause of the intercession against your own conviction, and you de-

---

[90] It is interesting to compare this last fragment with the many utterings of Agricola on his position in and his feelings about Groningen. The great differences socially, politically and psychologically are also reflected in the Latin. On Agricola see my articles 'Agricola and Groningen' and 'De Neolatijnse epistolografie–Rudolf Agricola'.

mand that I, contrary to my cautious and wavering Erasmianism,[91] shall refute it. I accept the challenge.

II *The argumentation*

1. On the definition of the word *intercessio*. A classification of arguments in favor of intercession: a) The goodness of God manifests itself not only in Christ, but partially also in a saint. This argument is disputed with a reference to Galatians, ch. 5. Because you reject it also, I need not refute it any more. b) [see above, fr. 3] This is also your opinion, and it is the Church that has introduced the practice of invoking the saints in prayer.

2. You put it into words excellently, but your arguments will not do: no support can be found for them in the Bible, so you take recourse to a syllogism. You say that one has to stick to the authority of the Church. This is your major premise, and your minor premise is that the Italians, the French, the Germans, etc. have always approved of intercession. But this is a deceiving trick in your reasoning – according to Aristotle and Quintilian – in so far as your catalogue of Christian peoples is not an equivalent of the Church. The definition of 'Church' is here at stake, and according to your German evangelicals, the Church is not the assembly of Popes and bishops, who have instituted the intercession of the saints. See for this the *Confession of Augsburg*.

3. Your major term, too, is no good. Erasmus has made it clear that the opinions and decisions of Popes and Councils (the 'Church') change constantly, e.g. in the question of baptism. The Church, however it may be defined, has never made any eternal decisions. Luther, Zwingli and Bucer have distinguished between *disciplina* (viz. ceremonies, institutions) and *fides* (faith). The Church has the right to decide and to change in questions regarding the first, but in matters of faith, such as the service to God and the ordinances of the Holy Spirit, which aim at a pure life, the Bible is the only authority.

4. You ask about the origin of intercession, as if it had to be approved if a cause could not be given. Well then, I will tell you the history of its beginnings: [see above, fr. 4].

5. Now that this most important line of your defense has been stormed, I will consider the nature and significance proper of intercession. Then it appears that it conflicts: 1) with the wisdom of Christ and his love

---

[91] 'Erasmo [...] qui istam diuorum intercessionem alias non repudiat, alias etiam munit' (Praedinius, *Opera*, 528). Erasmus is mentioned four times in our *libellus*. Once Praedinius distances himself, with a reference to Erasmus, from the German evangelicals' designation of the Popes as Antichrists (*ibid.*, 531).

for his people; 2) with our love and worship towards God; 3) that it abolishes itself, because of the very reason for which it was established.

6. Did Christ not know how great the advantage of intercession was for us? Did he foresee it? If so, why did he withhold it from us? Have there been times and Christians after Christ who did not need the intercession of the saints? For example, St. Paul? Had the Apostles first to be dead? An analogy could be drawn between Christ and a man who knows how to help his best friend, but refuses to do so. The whole institution of intercession amounts to accusing Christ of a non-consummated love.

7. Was it on account of the glory of the Father that Christ did not preach the intercession of the saints, or of Christ that the Apostles kept silent about it? What, then, incited the Church to institute it? What was the reason? The reason is to obtain what one wishes, is it not? Well, for this what St. John says in ch. 14.11-14 is enough! To want more is malicious, criminal haughtiness.

8. But, so you will say, it is not my opinion that intercession gives a surer means of obtaining what we want, but that it is an easier and quicker access to God. But these are insignificant motives: God does not postpone his grants longer than his glory and our interests demand. Thus, one does not understand what prayer really is, and that is impiety! 'Quickness' and 'easiness' are contrary to God's glory and your interest. So, give up this cause.

9. I shall now forthwith treat the other 'causes' you advance, even if it is against the order of my argumentation, in which they should have occupied their proper place of refutation (*locus refutationis*). 'Modesty' as a cause of intercession is not valid; modesty does not consist of unlimited self-contempt. How could so great a self-contempt ever be a thorough argument against the Gospel, which defines salvation by faith alone without the judgement of sins? St. Paul did not think himself too low to rebuke St. Peter (see Galatians 2.11-14). Try just to imagine a man who considers himself too evil to earn salvation by God. The Gospel demands of you to pray to the Father in the name of Christ. [See above, fr. 5]

10. Another 'cause' is taken from the larger number of saints, and consequently the greater influence they exercise by praying for you. And, then, the saints are with Christ after their death and enjoy his favor. Well, I think that Christians may well be ashamed of themselves in comparison to the Jews, who, in spite of all the miseries they have suffered, and the high esteem in which they hold their patriarchs, have always stuck to the true nature of praying, viz. directly to God alone.

11. I don't deny that the advocacy of living men for each other is very useful, but you should not rush to conclusions about the saints on the analogy of the living. Analogy is a very dangerous way of reasoning, it is the source of innumerable false stories and even heresies about things in heaven, e.g. about the mystery of the holy Trinity. Not even in the story of the rich man and the poor Lazarus [Luke 16.19-31] is it said that the rich man in the realm of the dead could see or know what went on on earth. Besides, that story is at least for the greater part an allegory, told to put forth a question. About the status of the saints in heaven we know absolutely nothing. Whether they can hear us, or sense our prayers when we pray in silence, is extremely doubtful.

12. You had the good sense not to touch upon the story of St. Luke, but instead you brought up the silly invention about the saints seeing in God as in a mirror the things that happen on earth. That the saints are one with Christ does not mean a unity in knowledge or conscience. What it does mean, according to your theology, is the right to and partnership in his death and resurrection.

13. I deny that the Gospel teaches that the saints have any perception of our prayers. I deny that, if such a thing should exist, it could be known otherwise than through the spirit and the word of God. I deny that there is any acceptable reason to ask for intercession, since the certain granting of our wishes has unconditionally been promised to those prayers said in the name of Christ, and since the answer is postponed no longer than the glory of God and the interest of the prayer demands. I deny that it is out of modesty that one has recourse to the saints.

14. If it is otherwise, convince me of my error. The mediation of the saints is contrary to our love and worship of God. If you grant this, I have proved the three parts of my discourse [see no. 5 above]. The only thing to be added to the third point – viz. that intercession abolishes itself – is the total absence of it in the Scriptures. So it rests on reasoning alone, almost on a syllogism, and in such a way that the supporters do not contend that it is necessary, but only advantageous and useful, and the adversaries that it detracts from our faith in Christ and his favor with God and is contrary to a holy and pious life. Therefore the argument of the advantageous and the useful nature of intercession refutes itself.

15. If intercession is so uncertain, it is risky to use it, for the love of God must be central. One should not want to maintain the love for the Father and at the same time sell his book.

III *The epilogue*

  1. Recapitulation of the arguments. The decisions of Councils and bishops are not valid in all eternity. Intercession is in conflict with
Christ's love for us. It is very doubtful whether any such thing as the
intercession of the saints exists. The refutation has now been completed, unless you still think that the majesty of God and Christ is best
be served by the 'modesty' of descending to the invocation of the
saints. But it is not within human judgement to determine the means
through which the divine majesty is best preserved. Not every humili-
ation of ourselves can be called modesty. Analogy of the human and
divine spheres is pernicious, for they differ from each other in species
and genus. The respect of God's majesty is contained in praying to
the Father in the name of Christ, and to deviate from this is a violation
of this respect.

  2. I have done what you have asked. In future, however, I prefer to debate with you on subjects from other disciplines than theology, and if
from theology, then rather so that you uphold the views of your
church and I of mine.

  3. I shall postpone my promised visit to you till after the end of my second term of three years. [See above, fr. 6]

Postscript

One question has not yet been raised, let alone answered: Are the *Disputatio
habita Gruningae* and the *libellus* of Praedinius historical reports or literary
fictions? As for the *Disputatio*, Wolfs has made it likely that some sort of
debate between the town clerics and the Dominicans took place. Discussions
like these were quite normal; the date, the place and the actors, too, are
hardly surprising. On the other hand, the theses of the Dominicans and the
objections of the clerics are so well organized, and link up so nicely with
each other, that a pure ingenious fiction is also quite possible. Praedinius's
libellus is written as a letter to a friend. Nothing is more natural than that,
but in reading the text we do not need for a moment the real words of the
other side. A few times Praedinius quotes from or refers to the letter of the
friend, who had taken the initiative, but at other times he *imagines*
arguments that could have been brought forward by his opponent: 'you may
say [...]'. In this case, too, a pure fiction is not impossible. We must not

forget that entirely fictional dialogues and letters between and to historical persons are a normal practice in classical and renaissance literature.[92]

---

[92] Cf. e.g. Marsh, *Quattrocento Dialogue*; more literature in IJsewijn and Sacré, *Companion*, II 234ff.

F. AKKERMAN AND P. KOOIMAN

AGRICOLA MUSICAE STUDIOSUS

Rudolph Agricola's great talent for music and the degree of perfection he achieved in several branches of this art are no longer tangibly present to us. We cannot hear him play and sing, compositions from his hand have not been preserved, nor do we possess any instrument he owned. The only exception is the organ of St. Martin's Church in Groningen which preserves a considerable number of pipes that were placed in the years 1481-1482, probably under Agricola's supervision.[1] For the rest we have to content ourselves with scattered remarks in his own works and in the humanist biographies (the *vitae*) written after his death. This written reflection of his musicality is nowhere very profound, yet it is, all in all, interesting and shows an amazing diversity of accomplishments. We shall here pass in review these text passages in Latin and in translation, without too much commentary. The chronological sequence will be determined, as far as possible, by the life of Agricola. The happy thing about these sources is that they do not copy each other, nor do they overlap too much: the authors simply were ignorant of each other's writings.

Whoever has a gift for music usually shows evidence of this at an early age. Thus, we read in the biography of Goswinus van Halen, that was made up c. 1525, the following lines about the musical interests of Agricola as a child. Goswinus had known Agricola very well in Groningen. About his youth and his parents he was informed by Wilhelmus Frederici, the head priest of St. Martin's Church, who had been acquainted with Agricola's family since his early days.

> Cum Rodolphus a lacte amotus <esset> gestireque inciperet paribus colludere, harmoniam sonorum prae omnibus cepit admirari et amare quicquid ad musicam pertinebat, quo fiebat ut pulsum tintinnabulorum auide audiret et fistulas, nec ullum donum puero fistula gratius dari potuit. Sequebatur puer caecos domatim stipes colligentes, ut lyras eorum audiret, apud gregum pastores utricularios aut cornuum aut fistularum inflatores in campos sequi solitus nec ab iis diuellebatur, nisi uel metu<s> uirgarum aut extrema fames compelleret domum repetere, tanto amore ferebatur ad musicam. In aedibus sacris sola illa organa quae follibus inflantur et picturas mirabatur. [...] Cum id esset aetatis, uimina saligna excoriare solet uerno tempore et aliis temporibus, cum libros a ligno detrahere nequiret, ea

---

[1] For Agricola's involvement in the building of a new organ in St. Martin's Church, see Edskes, 'Rudolph Agricola and the organ of the *Martinikerk* in Groningen'.

in calida aqua macerabat atque ita detraxit et ex eis fistulas[2] fabricabatur easque
ad harmoniam aptabat, ut aliquando uno spiritu octo aut nouem inflaret, et
collusores pueros alios ut illi canerent ad illos sonos inuitabat.

When Rudolph had been weaned and started to want to play with other children,
he developed the greatest admiration for the harmony of sounds and a love of
anything having to do with music. Thus it came about that he eagerly listened to
the ringing of bells and to flutes, and one could not give the child a more
welcome present than a flute. As a boy he followed the blind who went from
door to door collecting alms, in order to listen to their hurdy-gurdies; among the
shepherds he used to follow bagpipers, horn or shepherd's pipe players into the
fields, nor could he be forced to leave them until either fear of the birch or
pinching hunger would drive him back home, so much did he love music. In
churches he admired only the organs and the paintings. [...] When he had the age
for it, he used to peel willow twigs in spring, and at other times, when he could
not pull the bark free from the wood, he would soak them in warm water and so
pull it off; and from the pieces of bark he made panpipes, which he tuned so that
he sometimes blew eight or nine of them with a single breath, and he would
invite other boys, his playmates, to sing to those sounds.[3]

We should set this romantic description of the years when Agricola was growing up at home and went to school, between 1444 and 1456. For the locations
we have to look in and around Baflo, where he was born and where his mother
lived, Selwerd, where his father was abbot of a Benedictine nunnery, and Groningen, where he went to school.

From his years as a student at Louvain (c. 1458-1465) we learn something
about his concern with music from another biographer, Gerard Geldenhouwer,
a text of 1536:

Musices uero ea fundamenta eiisdem annis iecit, quibus absolutam eius artis
peritiam postea superstruxit. Canebat enim uoce, flatu, pulsu.[4]

In music, too, in those same years he laid the foundation on which he later built
up his complete command of that art – for he sang, and played both wind and
string instruments.

---

[2] In this text, Goswinus used the word *fistula* four times, the Latin term for a pipe. With the
first and second *fistula* any pipe, flute or shawm is meant. The third one is a *fistula pastoralis*
(shawm or shepherd's pipe), the fourth a *fistula pani* (panpipe).

[3] The fragments of the *vitae* of Agricola are quoted from an edition that is now being
prepared by F. Akkerman (edition of the Latin texts) and R. Bremer (English translation). For
the sources of these texts, see *Rodolphus Agricola Phrisius*, 314-6, 326.

[4] Cf. Aug. *enarr. in ps.* 150, 5.6. (SL 40, 2196) 'nec praetereundum existimo quod musici
dicunt, et res ipsa manifesta est, tria esse genera sonorum; uoce, flatu, pulsu.' The same triparti-
tion in Aug. *de ordine* (SL 29, 129); *de doctr. chr.* (SL 32, 52-3); *de musica* (PL 32, 1141).

In the same *uita*, a bit further on, he writes something that we can perhaps situate in Louvain too; a place is not expressly given, but Geldenhouwer drew mostly on what he had heard about Agricola in Louvain:

> Puellas (ut hoc quoque addam) amare se nonnunquam simulabat, uerum nunquam deperiit. In harum gratiam patria lingua amatoria quaedam carmina scripsit elegantissime, quae puellis praesentibus primariisque amicis uoce et testudine[5] modulatissime canebat. Huiusmodi cantionibus animum intentiore studio grauatum interdum remittebat.

> Girls (to mention that point as well) he sometimes pretended to be in love with, but he was never truly distracted. For their sake, he wrote certain love songs in his mother tongue, very skilfully executed, which he would then sing, in the presence of the girls and of his closest friends, accompanying himself most tunefully on the lute. With this kind of song he would now and then relax his mind, weighed down by intense studying.

That he wrote amorous songs or poems in the vernacular is also told by Goswinus, but he does not mention music in this context.

The great Reformer Philipp Melanchthon chose the life of Agricola as a theme for a festive academic oration of 1539. When he introduced Agricola's wonderful pronunciation and diction of the Latin language, he also mentioned his composition of songs:

> Verum Musicae naturae ad pronunciationem et actionem aptiores sunt caeteris. Constat autem Rodolphum ita excelluisse in Musicis, multas ut cantilenas composuerit, imo ut Italis fuerit iucundior, propterea quod interdum cythara[6] luderet in conuiuiis eruditorum.

> Indeed, to people with a gift for music a good pronunciation and delivery comes more easily than to others, and it is a fact that Rudolph excelled in the field of music to such a degree that he composed many songs, and he was liked even better by the Italians because he would sometimes play the lute at the dinner parties of the learned.

With this we have arrived in Italy, where Agricola studied in Pavia from 1469 or somewhat earlier until 1475, and in Ferrara from 1475 until 1479. In the

---

[5] There is no specific Latin word for the lute, which name is derived from the Arabic *al ʿūd*, so theorists used the word *testudo* (tortoise), the Latin name for the ancient Greek lyre with a tortoise-shell resonator, because of the arched body of the lute.

[6] The terminology for stringed instruments is often ambiguous. A *cithara* could be a lute or a cittern, which name derives from the Greek κιθάρα, as well as a harp. Without a description of the instrument it is not possible to know which instrument Agricola played.

latter town he was appointed from 1 October 1475 as an organist of the ducal chapel of Ercole d'Este.[7] In a letter of 14 April 1476 (*Ep.* 10) Agricola writes:

> Ferrariae habito seruioque duci alitque me uetus haec nostra canendi in organis ineptia. [...] Habeo stipendium a principe in mensem quinque aureos; sextum quotidie expecto.[8]

> I live in Ferrara and I serve the Duke; the old folly of playing the organ keeps me alive. [...] I get a salary from the Duke of five gold pieces a month, the sixth I expect any day.

In another letter of the same period (*Ep.* 9) we learn that his friend Dietrich von Pleningen, who remained in Pavia as a student of law, had made him a present of a lute. Agricola jestingly pretends to be angry with Dietrich, and then writes:

> Expectas fortasse, ut pro cithara, quam mihi misisti, gratias agam. Ne hoc quidem, quoque magis id te benefitium perdidisse doleas: optima est.

> You expect perhaps that I am going to thank you for the lute you sent me. Even this I shall not do, and, in order that you may regret all the more the favor you bestowed on me in vain, it is excellent.

But later both brothers Von Pleningen, Dietrich and Johann, joined Agricola in Ferrara, so that in their biography (written c. 1500) they could report about Agricola's work in the service of the duke:

> [...] Ferrariam (ut uerbis suis utar) Musarum domum[9] se contulit et diui Herculis ducis et principis optimi, subtili quidem hominum aestimatori uirtutisque fautori optimo,[10] ministerio ut festis sacris ac statis organa pulsaret, uti libros Graecos coemere honestiusque uiuere posset, sese inseruit.

> [...] he betook himself to Ferrara, the home of the Muses (to use his own words), and entered the service of Ercole d'Este, the divine duke and illustrious monarch – truly a subtle judge of people as well as a most egregious patron of the talented. This service consisted in having to play the organ on regular and holy feasts, in order to be able to buy Greek books and live in a decent manner.

---

[7] Document dated 2 December 1475 and published in Vander Straeten, *La musique aux Pays-Bas avant le XIXe siècle*, VII 495. In 1475, 1476 and 1477 Agricola is mentioned as 'Rodolfo de Frisia organista'. See Lockwood, *Music in Renaissance Ferrara*, 320.

[8] The Latin quotations from Agricola's letters are here borrowed from Van der Laan, *Anatomie van een Taal*.

[9] See Geldenhouwer, *Agricolae vita*: 'Ferrariae uno ac altero anno loci amoenitate, studiosorum ac nobilium quorundam Musicorum frequentia, ipsius quoque Principis liberalitate detentus est.'

[10] *subtili ... optimo*: wrongly a dative instead of a genitive.

In the autumn of the same year 1476 it fell to the lot of Agricola, to his great honor, to inaugurate the new academic year at the university of Ferrara with a festive address. This speech, a 'laudation of philosophy and the other arts', also contains a few passages about music. First, in general, on music as such:

> Et tam uarios uagosque astrorum toto mundo recursus, uim etiam omnium potestatemque [sc. humanus animus] cognouit et natum ex tam praecipiti coelorum uertigine concentum suauiorem purioremque, quam ut crassis his auribus nostris influere possit, inuenit, quem hic quoque expressit sonis cuncta modulatione fluentibus certaque numerorum discretione dimensis.[11]

> The human mind has learned the various and wandering returning orbits of the stars in the whole of outer space, and also the force and power of them all, and it has discovered the harmony that is produced by the precipitous whirling of the heavens, which is so sweet and pure, that it cannot penetrate into our course ears and which it has expressed, here too, in sounds that flow in every kind of melody and are measured by a regular distinction of rhythms.

But when he is about to praise music as the last of the mathematical arts – after geometry, arithmetic and astronomy – he praises instead the Duke of Ferrara:

> De musica quid attinet dicere post illustrissimi principis nostri iudicium? Qui cum ipsi tantum tribuat, quantum omnes uidemus, non committam, ut uidear[12] non satis laudatum putare, quod ipse tantopere probarit. [...]; sed parcius mihi alioquin de ipsa dicendum est, etiam ob hoc fortasse, ne ipse placere mihi studiisque meis mollius uidear esse blanditus.

> What is the sense of praising music, after the judgement of our illustrious Prince? Since he places so much value on it, as we all see, I do not dare to raise the suspicion of thinking that that has not been praised enough, what he has so much approved. [...] But apart from this, perhaps I have to be more restrained in my utterance on this subject also for this reason, lest I seem to have flattered myself and my pursuits too much.

The next passage, taken from the Von Pleningen-*vita* again, may possibly be located in Ferrara as well:

> Et cum animum suum lectione fatigatum relaxare uellet, ad haec quoque diuerticula sese transferre solebat, quo tempestiua intermissione esset ad studia uegetior: aliquando namque fidibus citharaue[13] <canebat> et inter cantandum pulsa-

---

[11] This fragment and the next one are quoted from Agricola, *Lucubrationes*, 154.

[12] Alardus mistakenly reads *uideat*.

[13] *fidibus citharaue*: a hendiadys; cf. Vergil, *Aeneid* 6, 119-20 '[...] Orpheus/ Threicia fretus cithara fidibusque canoris.'

bat; interdum sonabat tibiis;[14] organa denique tam pulsabat egregie, ut omnes saeculi sui potuisset ad certamen prouocasse. Cantor quoque fuit eximius et non indulcis, praecipue cum uoce cantaret media. Et nisi morte immatura raptus fuisset, librum de musica, quemadmodum instituerat, scripsisset. Nullum enim genus nullaue ratio musices homini doctissimo fuit incognita.

And when he wanted to relax his mind, tired with reading, he also used to address himself to the following amusements, so as to be fresher for his studies thanks to a timely break: to wit, sometimes he played the lute, and plucked it as he sang; at other times he played the shawm; finally, he was such an excellent organ-player that he might have challenged any of his contemporaries to a contest. And he was an exceptional and not unmellifluous singer too, particularly when singing in the middle register of the voice. Yes, had he not been cut off by an untimely death, he would have written a book on music, as he had planned, for no kind or manner of music was unknown to this very learned man.

The latter general pronouncement on Agricola's musicality we find in similar words in the well-known adage 'Quid cani et balneo' of Erasmus, in the 1508 version: 'Nulla pars musices, quam non exactissime calleret.' (There was no branch of music that he had not most scrupulously mastered.)[15]

With Jacobus Barbirianus (Jacob Barbireau), *magister choralium* (choir-master) at Our Lady's Church in Antwerp, Agricola entertained a close friend-ship that was based upon their mutual love for music and humanist learning. Three ample letters from Agricola to Barbireau have been preserved.[16] Of music, however, they scarcely speak. Most of the contents are concerned with the world of humanist letters, into which Agricola wishes to introduce his younger friend. Once, in a letter of 27 March 1482, Agricola complains to Barbireau about the sterile artistic and intellectual climate of Groningen, where he had been living again since 1479 or 1480, after his long stay in Italy:

Meae Musae non tacent solum, sed prorsus obmutescunt. Ideo neque uel unum uersum, posteaquam Antuerpia decessi, feci neque uel cano uel psallo aut ullam partem illius studii attingo, ut uidear aliquando mihi meipsum perdidisse.

My Muses are not just silent, they are totally struck dumb. So I haven't composed even a single verse since leaving Antwerp, nor do I sing and play anymore; I do not touch any branch of that art, so that it seems sometimes as if I have lost my own self.

---

[14] *Tibiae* (shin-bone) is the name of the ancient Roman wind instrument consisting of a pair of double-reed pipes, comparable with the Greek αὐλοί. *Tibia* is the term Tinctoris (*De inventione et usu musicae*, c. 1486) used for the shawm.

[15] *Adagium* 339 (*ASD* II-1, 439).

[16] See Kooiman, 'The letters of Agricola to Barbirianus'; Kooiman, 'The biography of Jacob Barbireau'.

And later, in a letter of 7 June 1484 (*Ep.* 38), when he has just moved to Heidelberg, he makes the following request of Barbireau:

> Oro te, mitte ad me aliquid ex iis quae ad canendum composuisti, sed quod accuratum sit et cum laude ostendi uelis. Habemus et hic cantores, apud quos crebram mentionem tui facio. Eorum magister nouem et duodecim etiam uocibus canendos modulos componit, sed nihil suorum audiui quod tribus aut quatuor uocibus caneretur, quod magnopere placeret mihi. Nec ego tamen animum meum iudicii loco pono; potest enim fieri, ut meliora sint quam ego possim intelligere.

> Please send me some of what you have composed for singing, something composed with care, that you would like to have performed and praised. We have singers here, too, and I often mention your name to them. Their master composes vocal works for nine and even for twelve voices, but of his work for three or four voices I have heard nothing which pleases me much. But I should not like to present my taste as the judge. After all, it is possible that they are better than I can understand.

The master here referred to is Johannes von Soest, who from 1472 onwards was choirmaster at the court of Elector Friedrich I of the Palatinate, who was succeeded in 1476 by Philipp. His musical compositions are not extant.

Our last quotations have their origin in the North again, and they are about Groningen. The first is taken from a booklet of Cornelius Kempius about Frisia and the Frisians, that was printed in 1588 in Cologne. Kempius had already said that Agricola 'applied himself earnestly to music and painting.'[17] He then continues:

> Hic organum propria manu,[18] miro uocalium concentu grataque auribus melodia suauem [*sic*], in aedibus sacris Diui Martini Groningae construxit, ut profecto nihil amoenius nihilque uoluptuosius audiri possit, in qua[19] tota ferme consistit harmonia neque ulla lyra consonantiorem reddere posset sonum. Extant praeterea eiusdem uiri quidam uersiculi, mira quadam suauitate, quatuor uocum modulamina, in formam Rithmicam redacti, quos Agricola saepe cantillare solebat. Circumferuntur multa a dicto Agricola composita cantica, patria sermone ad nos reseruata, quae passim apud multos in Ciuitate Groningana in magno precio habentur, et quatuor uocum modulamine cantillantur.

> He built with his own hands an organ in St. Martin's Church in Groningen, of such a miraculous harmony in the voices, so melodious, such a delight to the ears, that nothing sweeter or more pleasant can be heard, and above all harmony consists in this. No lyre could produce a more euphonious consonance. Besides, there are still extant from the same man certain little songs of a miraculous

---

[17] '[...] Hebraeae etiam linguae postremo cognitionem habuit, et Musicae et picturae quoque apprime studiosus fuit, omnemque fidium modulationem callebat [...].'

[18] Cf. Psalm 151 'Manus meae fecerunt organum et digiti mei aptauerunt psalterium.'

[19] *in qua*: perhaps *in quo* should be read.

sweetness for four voices and brought into a rhythmic form, which Agricola
would often sing. Many of the songs composed by the aforementioned Agricola
still circulate; they have come down to us in the vernacular, and they are
everywhere in the city of Groningen greatly appreciated; they are sung in four
parts.

So far Kempius. He is the first one to write that Agricola himself personally
built the organ in St. Martin's Church in Groningen. This may not be true in
the literal sense, but it can also be read on the cartouche of the organ: OPVS
RODOLPHI AGRICOLAE. We will end this little catalogue of textual *testimonia*
to Agricola as a musician with the complete text of this cartouche, which dates
from 1691:

OPVS RODOLPHI AGRICOLAE, / ANTE ANNOS CCXII PATRIAE / HVIVS CIVITATIS SYN-
DICI; / SEMEL ITERVMQ. AVCTVM, / AC DENVO VETVSTATE ET INERTI. / REFECTIONE
CORRVPTVM; / COSS. ET SEN. G., OB GRATAM / MEMORIAM CIVIS SVI, / IMMORTALI-
TATE DIGNISSIMI, / INTEGRITATI PRISTINAE / RESTITVI CVRAVERVNT / EX S.C. ANN.
AER. XP. CIƆIƆCXCI.[20]

This work of Rudolph Agricola, 212 years ago syndic of this, his home town,
repeatedly expanded, and then again spoiled by old age and inexpert restoration,
has now been restored to its former integrity by order of the Mayors and Council
of Groningen, in thankful commemoration of their citizen, most worthy of
immortality. This has been done on the strength of a decision of the Senate in the
year of the Christian Era 1691.

[20] A photograph of this cartouche in *Rodolphus Agricola Phrisius*, 115.

II. Maximilian I with his musicians. Woodcut by Hans Burgkmair from *Der Weisskunig* (1505-1516). In the centre a harpist. On the left an organist and behind him four singers and a cornet player. On the right a clavichord player. On the table: viol, flute, recorders, cornet, and crumhorn. On the floor: kettledrum, tabor, drumsticks, sackbut, lute case, tromba marina, viol. (Österreichische National-bibliothek, Vienna)

J.C. BEDAUX

ALEXANDER HEGIUS ALS DICHTER

In meinem Beitrag[1] berichte ich zuerst über einige neue oder weniger bekannte biographische Fakten des Alexander Hegius. Diese beziehen sich auf sein Geburtsjahr, seine Ankunft in Deventer und seinen Tod. Dann werde ich eingehen auf die allgemeine Würdigung von Hegius, unter besonderer Berücksichtigung seiner Dichtkunst, die an Hand eines seiner Gedichte (*Carmen in vitia*) erläutert wird.

In seinem Beitrag für die Festschrift des Emmericher Gymnasiums schreibt der Osnabrücker Domprälat Beckschäfer 1932, er erinnere sich, daß bei einem Jubiläum seiner Schule vor fünfzig Jahren Alexander Hegius auf die Weise des 'Gaudeamus igitur' wie folgt geehrt wurde:

> Velut luna domina
> Siderum minorum
> Praefulgebat inclitus
> Alexander Hegius,
> Dux grammaticorum.[2]

> (Sowie der Mond der Meister der kleineren Sterne ist, so überstrahlte der berühmte Alexander Hegius, Fürst der Grammatiker, alle.)

Es ist nicht ausgeschlossen, daß im Jahre 1998 in Deventer ein ähnliches Lied erklingen wird, denn dann sind es fünfhundert Jahre her, daß Alexander Hegius in dieser Stadt starb. Am 27. Dezember 1498 wurde er in der Lebuinuskirche bestattet. Noch am selben Tag ging der Magistrat – auf eine etwas merkwürdige Weise (siehe weiter unten) – auf die Suche nach einem Nachfolger. Dieses Gedächtnisjahr bietet eine gute Gelegenheit dem 'Altvater des deutschen Humanismus', wie Reichling Hegius genannt hat,[3] besonders in Deventer Aufmerksamkeit zu widmen.

Ich beschäftige mich zur Zeit mit der Vorbereitung einer Ausgabe der Gedichte von Hegius, der eine biographische Skizze vorausgehen wird. Hierin werde ich versuchen alle Zeugnisse über sein Leben und die wichtig-

---

[1] Für ihre Hilfe bei der deutschen Bearbeitung habe ich meinen Freunden A.W.E. van der Vleuten und O. Burghardt viel zu verdanken.
[2] Beckschäfer, 'Alexander Hegius', 67.
[3] Reichling, *Johannes Murmellius*, 5.

sten Zitate seiner Rezensenten und Kritiker zusammenzustellen.[4] Deshalb werde ich mich hier nicht allzu ausführlich mit den biographischen Fragen beschäftigen. Im *Verfasserlexikon* der *Deutschen Literatur des Mittelalters* bietet Worstbrock eine vorzügliche Übersicht,[5] während Van Leijenhorst in den *Contemporaries of Erasmus* einen kurzen, guten Überblick geschrieben hat.[6] Auf drei neue oder noch nicht lange bekannte biographische Fakten will ich aber eingehen. Sie beziehen sich auf Hegius' Geburtsjahr und -ort, seine Ankunft in Deventer und seinen Tod.

Biographische Fakten

Das Geburtsjahr

Die Forschung von Worstbrock hat ergeben, daß Hegius nicht im Jahre 1433, sondern so gut wie sicher 1439 oder 1440 geboren wurde (ich neige dazu 1439 zu bevorzugen) und daß er außerdem nicht aus Heek, sondern aus Burgsteinfurt stammt. Diese Fakten gründete Worstbrock auf die Matrikel der Rostocker Universität, wo Hegius von 1457 bis 1463 urkundlich nachweisbar ist.[7]

Die Ankunft in Deventer

In seiner Studie über das Geburtsjahr von Erasmus hat mein Amtsvorgänger Koch behauptet, Hegius sei früher als 1483 nach Deventer gekommen.[8] Er gründete seine Auffassung auf das Sterbedatum des Amtsvorgängers von Hegius, Peter van Spairwoude, der zwischen September 1481 und Februar 1482 starb. Als 'Peter Scholmeyster' wurde er im Mitgliedsverzeichnis der Sankt Jacob-Bruderschaft verzeichnet. Es stellt sich aber heraus, daß Hegius einen anderen Vorgänger gehabt hat: 'Johan scholemeyster', der 1482 als Mitglied derselben Bruderschaft erwähnt wird. Offensichtlich hat Koch diesen Namen übersehen. Im selben Verzeichnis begegnet man im Jahr 1479 der Erwähnung 'meyster Sander'. Koch hat daraus geschlossen, daß sich Hegius vielleicht schon damals in Deventer niedergelassen hätte.[9] Diese

---

[4] Inzwischen als Dissertation erschienen: Bedaux, *Hegius poeta*.
[5] Worstbrock, 'Hegius, Alexander'.
[6] Van Leijenhorst, 'Alexander Hegius'.
[7] Worstbrock, 'Zur Biographie des Alexander Hegius'.
[8] Koch, *The year of Erasmus' birth*, 28-37.
[9] Koch, *Zwarte kunst in de Bisschopstraat*, 59. Das Register der Sankt Jacob-Bruderschaft befindet sich beim Stadsarchief Deventer.

Erwähnung ist aber unverkennbar von einer anderen, späteren Hand geschrieben. Meiner Meinung nach ist es daher sehr unwahrscheinlich daß
Hegius früher als 1483 nach Deventer gekommen ist.

Der Tod

Die Deventer Stadtrechnung von 1498 enthält eine merkwürdige Nachricht:

> Item op den dach vors[eid] Ernst onse bode gegaen myt onsen scriften na
> Utrecht an meister Johan van Diepholt omme meister Johan van Breda onser
> stat medicus totter scolen te helpen in stede zeliger meister Sander ende wairt
> meister Johan van Diepholt onser bode to Apeldorn te gemuete gekomen is.[10]

> (An dem genannten Tag [27. Dezember] ist ebenfalls unser Amtsbote Ernst
> mit unseren Schriftstücken nach Utrecht gegangen [mit der Bitte] an Meister
> Johan van Diepholt, Meister Johan van Breda, unserem Stadtarzt, an der Schu-
> le zu helfen statt des seligen Meisters Sander. Und Meister Johan van Diepholt
> begegnete unserem Amtsboten in Apeldoorn.)

Es stellt sich also heraus daß schon am Beerdigungstag der Stadtarzt Johan
van Breda an der Lateinschule lehrte und daß Johan van Diepholt gerne
kommen wollte. Der Amtsbote traf ihn schon in Apeldoorn, nur fünfzehn
Kilometer von Deventer entfernt. In der Geschichte der Lateinschule von
Deventer sind die Namen Johan van Diepholt und Johan van Breda nirgendwo nachweisbar. Überdies ist es sonderbar, daß nicht einer der Kollegen von
Hegius als stellvertretender Rektor auftrat. Laut Johannes Butzbach war
jedenfalls im Jahre 1500 Johannes Oostendorp sein Nachfolger.[11]
    Daß doch etwas Ungewöhnliches vor sich gegangen sein muß, läßt uns
auch ein Brief vermuten, den Jacobus Faber, der Textbesorger der *Carmina*
und *Dialogi* von Hegius, am 8. Mai 1499 an seinen Bruder Andreas schrieb.
Faber spricht dort über das 'fatum triste et lugubre' von Hegius, dessen Tod
ihn mit großem Schmerz erfüllt habe. Er fährt dann fort:

> Dignus enim (ni fallor) qui de hostibus illis grave insectantibus triumphasse
> ducatur. Propter quod autem epicedion rude, quod ei defuncto excogitavi,
> docebit pleraque quibus miratur praestringens. [...] Qui eum in vita noverunt,
> quo pacto ultimum hominis finem assequutum abnuant non video.[12]

> (Denn wenn ich mich nicht irre, verdient er es als Sieger über seine Feinde be-
> trachtet zu werden, die ihn stark bedrängten. Darum wird jetzt ein unbeholfe-

---

[10] Gemeentelijke Archiefdienst Deventer, Stadsrekening 1498 II, 5v.
[11] Butzbach, *Odeporicon*, III 14 (ed. Beriger, 300).
[12] Faber, *Panegijricon in Jesu Christi triumphum*, [Av]v-[Avi]r.

nes Lobgedicht, das ich nach seinem Tode gemacht habe, die meisten Sachen behandeln, um die er bewundert wurde. [...] Ich sehe nicht auf welche Weise die Leute, die ihn während seines Lebens gekannt haben, verneinen daß er das höchste Ziel für einen Menschen erreicht hat.)

Aus diesen Stellen ergibt sich, daß nicht jedermann Hegius gleichermaßen wohlgesinnt war. Was sich aber genau abgespielt hat, ist nicht mehr festzustellen. Es fragt sich übrigens, ob eine Beziehung besteht zwischen den Mitteilungen von Faber und der Nachricht in der Stadtrechnung von Deventer.

Hegius der Dichter

Wenn man die Veröffentlichungen über Hegius liest, die in den vergangenen Jahrhunderten erschienen sind, fällt auf, daß die biographischen Daten weitaus die meiste Aufmerksamkeit auf sich ziehen. Für seine Arbeiten als Schulrektor und seine Bedeutung für den Humanismus besteht dagegen weniger Interesse. Das gilt um so mehr für seine Schriften, die 1503, also postum, herausgegeben wurden.[13]

Es ist nicht einfach ein ausgewogenes, nuanciertes Urteil über die Bedeutung von Hegius zu geben. Über seine Aktivitäten als Rektor und Dozent ist wenig bekannt, und harte Kriterien um seine didaktischen Leistungen zu messen fehlen. Es würde zu weit führen die Blüte der Lateinschule von Deventer lediglich Hegius zuzuschreiben. Auch vor seiner Ankunft in Deventer erfreute sich die Schule einer großen Bekanntheit, denn Erasmus ist sowieso früher als Hegius nach Deventer gekommen (laut Vredeveld entweder im Herbst 1477 oder Ostern 1478).[14] Wir dürfen annehmen, daß die Modernisierung des Unterrichts das wichtigste Verdienst von Hegius ist. Er hat dabei eine stimulierende und begeisternde Rolle gespielt. Die Einführung des Griechischen, das Hegius in Emmerich von Agricola gelernt hatte, stellt davon einen ganz wesentlichen Teil dar. Weil Erasmus im Frühjahr 1484 Deventer verlassen hat und dort, wie er selber sagt, mit dem Griechischen bekannt wurde,[15] muß Hegius nicht lange nach seiner Ankunft mit dieser Erneuerung angefangen haben. Die Deventer Lateinschule war in dieser Hinsicht eine der ersten im nördlichen Europa.

Wahrscheinlich hat Hegius als Person mit seinen tiefreligiösen und stren-

---

[13] Hegius, *Carmina* (Nijhoff und Kronenberg I 375, nr 1041); Hegius, *Dialogi* (Nijhoff und Kronenberg I 375-6, nr 1042).

[14] Vredeveld, 'The Ages of Erasmus', 803.

[15] Erasmus, *Adagia* 339 (*ASD* II-1, 440, 814-5): '[Hegius] qui ludum aliquando celebrem oppidi Daventriensis moderabatur, in quo nos olim admodum pueri utriusque linguae didicimus elementa.'

gen moralischen Auffassungen, die sich besonders in seinen Gedichten zeigen, in seiner Umgebung starke Beachtung gefunden. Der Einfluß der Devotio Moderna ist dabei unverkennbar. Seine Lebensweise war stark asketisch. Unterkunft bekam er bei dem Drucker Richard Pafraet, der in einem Brief von Agricola an Hegius als 'hospes tuus' erwähnt wird.[16] Eine Bestätigung dieser Nachricht finden wir bei Butzbach in dessen *Auctarium*, der uns auch weiter informiert über den Tod und die Bestattung von Hegius.[17]

Ebenfalls laut Butzbach arbeitete Hegius nachts mit einem Kerzenstumpf in der Hand um nicht einzuschlafen.[18] Sehr treffend sagt Erasmus in seinen *Adagia*:

> in quo unum illud vel Momus ipse calumniari fortasse potuisset, quod famae plus aequo negligens nullam posteritatis haberet rationem.[19]

> (daß man Hegius nur eine Sache vorwerfen kann, nämlich daß er sich weniger um seinen Ruhm gekümmert habe als er hätte tun sollen, und daß er keine Rücksicht auf seine Nachkommen genommen habe.)

Daneben sehen wir, daß die Anerkennung für Hegius als Dichter nicht eindeutig positiv ist. Die Literatur aus den ersten Jahrhunderten nach Hegius' Tod ist mit Ausnahme von dem, was Erasmus in vorgerücktem Alter schreibt, ein fortwährender und wenig kritischer Lobgesang. Die Bedeutung von Hegius für den Humanismus fußt einerseits auf seinen humanistischen Freunden (unter ihnen vor allem Agricola), andererseits auf der großen Zahl der Schüler, die in der weiteren Entwicklung des Humanismus in den Niederlanden und Deutschland eine wichtige Rolle gespielt hat.

Von einem echten Interesse für Hegius als Dichter ist erst die Rede seit 1852, dem Jahr in dem ein Artikel des Deventerer Pfarrers und Bibliothekars Molhuysen erschien.[20] Besonders dank einer deutschen Bearbeitung aus dem Jahre 1861 bekam dieser Beitrag weite Bekanntheit.[21] Molhuysen betrachtete sich als nicht zuständig die literarischen und poetischen Verdienste

---

[16] Der Brief (Nr 43) ist abgedruckt in Hegius, *Carmina*, [Aiv]v-[Av]v; bei Krafft und Crecelius, 'Beiträge zur Geschichte des Humanismus in Rheinland und Westfalen', 7-9; und bei Van der Laan, *Anatomie van een Taal*, 259-60.

[17] Butzbach, *Auctarium*, in Krafft/Crecelius, 'Mittheilungen über Alexander Hegius', 240.

[18] Butzbach, *Macrostroma* XI (Universitätsbibliothek Bonn, Hs. S 358, 94r-v): 'Alexander item Heygius candele ardentis frustum in manu tenere solebat, cum inter lucubrationes paulisper somno cogeretur, ut, quando rursus ad studium evigilare vellet, adustionem lucerne ad manum perciperet.' (Ebenso pflegte Alexander Hegius, wenn er während seiner nächtlichen Arbeiten eine Zeitlang durch Schlaf gequält wurde, ein Stümpfchen einer brennenden Kerze in seiner Hand zu halten, um, sobald er zum Studieren aufwachen wollte, das Brennen des Lichtes an seiner Hand zu fühlen.)

[19] Erasmus, *Adagia* 339 (*ASD* II-1, 440, 817-9).

[20] Molhuysen, 'Alexander Hegius'.

[21] Troß, 'Alexander Hegius'.

zu beurteilen. Seines Erachtens schließen die Gedichte einen großen geistlichen Wert in sich ein:

> Über den literarischen und poetischen Werth dieser Stücke maßen wir uns kein
> Urtheil an, aber von dem Geiste, der darin weht, hegen wir hohe Achtung. [...]
> jemehr man den Dichter versteht, desto mehr gewinnt man ihn, seiner reinen
> Ansichten und seiner gesunden Moral wegen, lieb.[22]

Auffallend ist, daß nach Molhuysen viele andere zu einem ähnlichen Urteil
gekommen sind. Negative Bemerkungen über die Dichtkunst von Hegius
werden kompensiert durch die 'ungekünstelte Einfachheit und den aus ihnen
hervorleuchtenden tiefreligiösen Sinn', wie Reichling gesagt hat.[23] In diesem Sinne äußern sich auch Wiese, Ellinger, Bömer und Van Rhijn.[24] Wenig wohlgesinnt lautet das Urteil von Bot und Reedijk. Bot charakterisiert
das Lateinische von Hegius als sehr ungelenkig.[25] Laut Reedijk waren die
Gedichte 'quite suitable for recitation in the presence of a lively crowd of
healthy boys, but they are hardly literary masterpieces of a nature to inflame
a young heart with a burning love of poetry.'[26] Dagegen ist es auffallend,
daß sich das junge Herz von Erasmus 1489 so lobend über die Dichtkunst
seines Meisters äußert:

> Qui tanta elegantia veterum exprimit dicendi stylum, ut, si desit carmini titu-
> lus, in autore facile erraveris.[27]

> (der mit einer solchen Genauigkeit die Sprechweise des Altertums handhabe,
> daß, wenn der Titel eines Gedichtes fehlt, man sich in dem Autor schnell irren
> kann.)

Am 29. Juli 1503 ließ Jacobus Faber, ein Schüler von Hegius, eine Ausgabe
der *Carmina* bei Pafraet erscheinen. Den Gedichten geht ein Brief von Faber
an Erasmus voran, dem er diese Edition widmet.[28] Am Ende dieser Ausgabe
weist Faber darauf hin, daß trotz einer 'diligens inquisitio' Gedichte seiner
Aufmerksamkeit entgangen sein könnten. Das gilt jedenfalls für ein Gedicht
von Hegius an Theodericus Ulsenius.[29] Faber sammelte für seine Ausgabe

---

[22] Zitat aus Troß, 'Alexander Hegius', 354.
[23] Reichling, 'Beiträge zur Charakteristik der Humanisten', 294-5.
[24] Wiese, *Der Pädagoge Alexander Hegius*, 18; Ellinger, *Geschichte der neulateinischen Literatur Deutschlands*, 392; Bömer, 'Alexander Hegius', 358; Van Rhijn, *Studiën over Wessel
Gansfort*, 146.
[25] Bot, *Humanisme en onderwijs in Nederland*, 30-1.
[26] Reedijk, *The poems of Desiderius Erasmus*, 47.
[27] Erasmus, *Opus epistularum*, I 106 (ep. 23, 61-2).
[28] Erasmus, *Opus epistularum*, I 384-8 (ep. 174).
[29] Santing, *Geneeskunde en humanisme*, 41.

38 Gedichte von Hegius. Er versah sie einzeln mit einer kurzen Erläuterung, in der er auch das Metrum erwähnte. Am Ende fügte er drei eigene Gedichte hinzu, unter anderem 'ne paginae vacantes relique iacerent' (um keine Seiten leer zu lassen).[30]

Das ganze Oeuvre umfaßt 1382 Verse. Die Länge der Gedichte variiert zwischen 2 und 106 Zeilen. Von den 39 Gedichten haben 17 ein religiöses Thema. Sie behandeln unter anderem Geburt, Leiden und Auferstehung Jesu. Fünf sind Maria gewidmet. Dreizehn Gedichte sind stark moralisch gefärbt, bekämpfen Sünden und Untugenden oder fordern zur Redlichkeit auf. Eine Diversität an Themen kommt in den übrigen neun zum Ausdruck, so beispielsweise über den Nutzen des Griechischen (Carmen 22).

Es erscheint mir sinnvoll an Hand eines der Gedichte auf die poetischen Qualitäten von Hegius einzugehen. Als Beispiel habe ich Carmen 10 gewählt, in dem Hegius gegen die Sünden ('in vitia') wettert.[31]

In vitia

Heu vita paucis degitur mortalibus
Foelix et exors criminum; quotus abnuit
Iam quisque pulchra posthabere turpibus?
Nemo beatus turpium sibi conscius.
5   Nec cura libertatis usquam cernitur.
In servitutem quisque semet asserit,
Cum letifera facit imperata daemonum.
Admissa servum culpa pectus efficit.
Quot quisque viciis pectora sua dedidit,
10   Tot cogitur iussa miserandus exequi,
Hoc turpior quo pluribus se sub‹di›dit.
Servire multis sortis est miserrimae.
Oblectat hunc congesta vis pecuniae,
Cui nil satis quantumlibet paraverit.
15   Nec admovet loculis manum tumentibus,
Servet magis oculis miser nomismata.
Testatur hic celi deum, cum peierat,
Credens eum curare nil mortalia,
Nec pertimescit aere salvo infamiam.
20   Deum negat quisquis per illum peierat.
Hic ora porrigit capistro feminae,
Quam si videt iussis madere fletibus,
Ultro venit supplexque fit dominae suae.
Nemo beatus dediticius Cypridis.
25   Res est voluptas omnium blandissima.

---

[30] Jacobus Faber, in Hegius, *Carmina*, [Eviii]r.
[31] Hegius, *Carmina*, [Bi]v-[Bii]v.

Si cui tenaces hec manus iniecerit,
Non ille sarcina facile levabitur,
Simul ore frenos illius receperit.
Qui querit hec quot imperet mortalibus,
30   Cur nosse vult, quot vere volucres concinant
Aut quot sereno sidera niteant polo?
Regnum, voluptas, iam patet late tuum.
Turpia Tartarei qui regis iussa facessit,
Quamvis sit locuples, est, mihi crede, miser.
35   Si faciat que mandavit regnator Olympi,
Moribus est dives, sit licet aeris inops.

Gegen die Sünde

(1) Ach, nur wenige Sterbliche verbringen ihr Leben glücklich und frei von Freveltaten! Wie wenige Leute weigern sich noch das Schöne hinter das Schändliche zu stellen! Niemand ist glücklich, der sich häßlicher Sachen bewußt ist.

(5) Nirgendwo sieht man die Sorge um die Freiheit. Jeder begibt sich in Sklaverei, wenn er die verderblichen Befehle der Teufel ausführt. Eine Übertretung begehen macht das Innere zum Sklaven.

Jeder, der sein Inneres vielen Untugenden ausgeliefert hat, ist beklagenswert; (10) er wird gezwungen ebensovielen Befehlen zu folgen, und ist um so schändlicher, je mehr er sich den Untugenden unterwirft. Vieler Sachen Sklave zu sein gehört zu einem unglücklichen Schicksal.

Eine gesammelte Menge Geld macht ihm Vergnügen, der nie zufrieden ist, wieviel er sich auch verschafft hat. (15) Und er streckt seine Hand nicht nach den übervollen Geldkisten aus. Möge der Unglückliche die Geldstücke mehr mit seinen Augen aufbewahren.

Er ruft, während er einen Meineid schwört, den Gott des Himmels als Zeugen an, weil er glaubt, dieser kümmere sich nicht um irdische Sachen. Und solange sein Geld sicher ist, hat er keine Angst um einen schlechten Leumund. (20) Wer auf Gott einen Meineid schwört, leugnet ihn.

Ein anderer verstrickt sich in das Netz einer Frau. Wenn er sie Krokodilstränen weinen sieht, kommt er aus eigenem Antrieb auf sie zu und wird kniefällig vor seiner Gebieterin. Niemand ist glücklich, der ganz der Venus unterworfen ist.

(25) Genuß ist von allem das am meisten Verführerische. Wenn dieser mit seinen festhaltenden Händen jemanden gegriffen hat, wird jener nicht leicht von der Last befreit werden, sobald er in seinen Mund die Zügel des Genusses bekommen hat.

Wer fragt, über wieviele Sterbliche der Genuß herrscht, (30) warum wünscht der zu wissen wieviele Vögel im Frühling singen oder wieviele

Sterne am klaren Himmel glänzen? Genuß, dein Reich erstreckt sich schon
weit aus.

Wer die schändlichen Aufträge des Königs der Unterwelt ausführt, ist,
glaub mir, unglücklich, wie reich er auch sein möge. Wenn er das täte, was
der Herrscher über den Olymp aufgetragen hat, ist er reich an guten Sitten,
obwohl er finanziell bedürftig ist.

Kommentar

Metrum

Hegius hat dieses Gedicht in einem jambischen Trimeter geschrieben.
Dieses Metrum trifft man bei ihm sonst nirgendwo. Die letzten vier Zeilen
bestehen aus elegischen Disticha. Eine solche Kombination finden wir in
zwölf anderen Gedichten vor. In Zeile elf fehlt in der Deventerer Edition
eine Silbe. Deshalb ist *subdit* in *subdidit* korrigiert.[32]

Wortgebrauch und Inhalt

Die Wortwahl dieses Gedichtes macht einen mühsamen, wenig geschmeidi-
gen Eindruck, den man auch von den übrigen Carmina bekommt. Der Wort-
schatz von Hegius ist überdies beschränkt. Das zeigt sich in der ziemlich
großen Anzahl der Wiederholungen von Wörtern (*turpis* in 3, 4, 11 und 33,
quisque in 3, 6 und 9, *peierat* in 17 und 20, und *quot* in 29, 30 und 31).
Daneben begegnet man hier wie in den anderen Gedichten vielen Allitera-
tionen (in 3 *pulchra posthabere*, 5 *cura cernitur*, 9 *quot quisque*, 12 *servire
sortis*, 18 *credens curare*, 29 *quaerit quot*, 31 *sereno sidera* und 33 *turpia
Tartarei*). Ein auffallendes Beispiel von Paronomasia ist die Wiederholung
loculis oculis (15-16). Das Wort *dediticius* (24) findet man nicht bei klassischen Dichtern; *Cypris* als Bezeichnung für Venus ist in der klassischen
lateinischen Literatur nirgendwo anzutreffen. In der neulateinischen Dichtung wird es öfters benutzt.

In den meisten moralischen Gedichten erscheint eine Aufzählung der
'verkehrten Beispiele', hier in den Versen 14-24. Das Gleichnis mit den
Mengen von Sternen (29-31) trifft man in zwei anderen Gedichten (Carmen
6, *In habendi amorem*, 35-36 und Carmen 15, *De stulticiis mortalium*, 5-8)
wieder.

---

[32] Diese Emendation hat mir dr F. Akkerman während der Conferenz vorgeschlagen, wofür
ich ihm sehr herzlich danke.

Zitate

In dem Gedicht kommt nur ein Zitat vor, nämlich in Vers 21, das aus Iuvenal (Satire 6, 43) entlehnt ist: 'iam porrigit ora capistro'. Hegius gebraucht dieses Zitat auch in 15, 56: 'sua porrigit ora capistro'. Das Wort 'capistrum' erscheint auch bei Erasmus, Carmen 103, 13 (ed. Vredeveld = ed. Reedijk 5): 'Victa dedo tuis stultissimus ora capistris.' Erasmus zitiert hier Vergil, *Georgica* 3, 188 'inque vicem det mollibus ora capistris.' Er hat dieses Gedicht um 1489 geschrieben und ist vielleicht von Hegius beeinflußt worden. Jedenfalls wußte er sich 1521 dieses Gedichtes zu erinnern, denn Zeile 12 hat er in *De contemptu mundi* zitiert: 'Porro, ut scite noster scripsit Hegius: Servire multis sortis est miserrimae'.[33] Dresden weist in seinem Kommentar auf eine Stelle kurz vor dem Hegius-Zitat hin (684-685: 'Iam tibi quot vitia sunt, tot dominis parendum est quidem teterrimis, improbissimis, saevissimis.') Hier haben laut Dresden die Zeilen 9 und 10 des vorliegenden Gedichtes ('Quot quisque viciis pectora sua dedidit, tot cogitur iussa miserandus exsequi') Erasmus vielleicht zu seiner Formulierung inspiriert. Es kann nicht mehr als eine Vermutung sein, die jedenfalls darauf hindeutet, wieviele lateinische Texte Erasmus bekannt waren.

In dem Gedicht sind sechs Stellen vorhanden, in denen von Einflüssen lateinischer Autoren die Rede ist, ohne daß es sich um echte Zitate handelt:
- Die Redewendung 'iussa [...] exsequi' (10) ist vielleicht beeinflußt von Vergil, *Aeneis* 4, 396 'iussa tamen divum exsequitur.'
- Die Zeile 22-23 sind deutlich beeinflußt von Terenz, *Eunuchus* 67-70 'Quae verba ea una mehercle falsa lacrimula,/ quam oculos terendo misere vix vi expresserit,/ restinguet, et te ultro accusabit, et dabis/ ultro ei supplicium.'
- In Zeile 25 'voluptas blandissima': *blanda voluptas* ist bei Ovid, *Fasti* 4, 99 zu finden: 'Quid genus omne creat volucrum, nisi blanda voluptas?' *Blanda voluptas* erscheint auch dreimal bei Lukrez am Ende der Zeile (2, 966; 4, 1263; 5, 178).
- Der Ausdruck 'iussa facessit' (33) wird seit Vergil, *Aeneis* 4, 295 'imperio laeti parent et iussa facessunt' häufig am Ende des Hexameters gebraucht.
- Ebenso ist 'regnator Olympi' (35) seit Vergil, *Aeneis* 2, 779 'aut ille sinit superi regnator Olympi' wiederholt anzutreffen.
- Der Ausdruck 'aeris inops' trifft man auch bei Iuvenal 7, 61: 'paupertas atque aeris inops.'

Wie sich mir in meinen Untersuchungen gezeigt hat, stößt man in den

---

[33] Erasmus, *De contemptu mundi* (*ASD* V-1, 66, 714-5).

Gedichten von Hegius nur auf wenige Zitate klassischer Autoren. Sie sind
überdies nicht gleichmäßig über das ganze Oeuvre verbreitet. Besonders in
den monostichischen religiösen Gedichten finden sie sich sehr wenig. Klassischen Reminiszenzen begegnet man frequenter. Das vorliegende Gedicht
ist in dieser Hinsicht gewiß beispielhaft.

Dem Vorhergehenden ist zu entnehmen, daß Alexander Hegius bestimmt
kein großer Dichter gewesen ist. Vermutlich haben seine Gedichte als Un-
terrichtsmaterial gedient. Dies könnte man aus Bemerkungen von Faber und
Erasmus schließen. Faber sagt in seinem Widmungsbrief an Erasmus: 'carmina gravissima, quae quotannis, ut moris est, dedit'[34] (sehr ernsthafte Gedichte, die er jährlich traditionsgemäß vortrug). Und Erasmus sagt in seinem
Compendium vitae: 'Post aliquoties audivit Hegium, sed non nisi festis quibus legebat omnibus.'[35] (Dann hörte er ziemlich häufig Hegius, aber nur an
Festtagen, an denen er allen vorlas.) Hegius ist meines Erachtens nicht als
ein echter Vertreter des Humanismus, sondern als eine Übergangsgestalt zu
betrachten, die am Anfang der langen Entwicklung der lateinischen Dichtkunst innerhalb des 'Northern Humanism' steht.

[34] Erasmus, *Opus epistularum*, I 386 (ep. 174, 58).
[35] Erasmus, *Compendium vitae*, in *Opus epistularum*, I 48, 39-40.

C.P.M. BURGER

IST, WER DEN RECHTEN ZUNGENSCHLAG BEHERRSCHT, AUCH SCHON EIN HUMANIST? NIKOLAUS BLANCKAERT (ALEXANDER CANDIDUS) O. CARM. (†1555)

Der Kölner Theologieprofessor aus dem Karmelitenorden Nikolaus Blanck-aert alias Alexander Candidus hat bisher nur in geringem Maße die Aufmerk-samkeit der Reformationsforscher erringen können. Es ist auch nicht verwun-derlich, daß er nicht bekannter geworden ist. Er steht beispielsweise im Schat-ten seines Kollegen Johann Gropper und seines bedeutenderen Ordensbruders, Provinzials und Kölner Kollegen Eberhard Billick. Aber auch als minder be-deutender Gelehrter verdient er Interesse. Können doch gerade seine Schriften dazu beitragen, Klarheit darüber zu gewinnen, welche humanistische Bildung ein eher durchschnittlicher Kölner Theologe in der Mitte des 16. Jahrhunderts besaß und wie er sich verhielt, wenn ihm heidnische Antike und christliches Gedankengut zu kollidieren schienen.[1] Ich beginne mit einem kurzen Überblick über Blanckaerts Biographie und seine uns überlieferten Schriften.

Blanckaerts Leben und Wirken im Überblick

Die Angaben zur Biographie des Nikolaus Blanckaert in Nachschlagewerken und in der Sekundärliteratur differieren nicht wenig.[2] Er stammte vermutlich aus Gent. In Utrecht trat er in den Karmelitenorden ein. Von 1523 bis 1530 studierte er zunächst die Artes, dann Theologie am Generalstudium des Or-dens in Köln.[3] Die humanistische Terminologie und Gewandtheit im Aus-

---

[1] Vgl. IJsewijn, 'The Coming of Humanism to the Low Countries', 276: 'This coexistence of humanism and scholasticism in one place and sometimes, as an inevitable consequence, in one person is characteristic of northern Europe [...].' Zur Rezeption der Kirchenväter in der Schrift des Blanckaert gegen Calvin vgl. Burger, 'Der Kölner Karmelit Nikolaus Blanckaert'.

[2] Den zuverlässigsten Eindruck machen die Angaben von Lickteig, *The German Carmelites at the medieval universities*, 268. Man vergleiche aber etwa miteinander Postina, *Der Karmelit Eberhard Billick*; Böse, 'Alexander Blanckaert'; Starin, 'Candidus (Blankaert)'; Mesters, 'Candi-dus, Alexander'; Raczek, 'Candidus (Blanckart), Alexander'.

[3] In Köln hatte der Karmelitenorden seit 1294 ein Generalstudium, vgl. Lickteig, *The German Carmelites at the medieval universities*, Karte IV nach S. 192. Ausführlicher unterrichtet über dessen Geschichte der Abschnitt 'Het studium generale te Keulen' in Lansink, *Studie en onderwijs in de Nederduitse provincie van de karmelieten*, 115-26. 1391 wurde das studium generale der Universität Köln inkorporiert (116). Dennoch wurde auch ein eigener Studienbetrieb aufrecht erhalten (119-21). Blanckaert ist als 'fr. Alex. de Gandavo, o. Carm.; theol.; i. et s.; 24' in die

64 C.P.M. BURGER

druck, die uns in den Schriften begegnen, die hier dargestellt werden sollen, dürfte er sich in diesen sieben Jahren angeeignet haben, und zwar wohl bereits als Artist, nicht erst als Theologe. Er latinisierte seinen Nachnamen 'Blanckaert' in 'Candidus' und nannte sich 'Alexander' statt 'Nikolaus'. Freilich begegnen auch Mischformen zwischen dem Tauf- und dem latinisierten Namen. So heißt es auf dem Titelblatt der maßgeblich von ihm durchgesehenen Bibelübersetzung 'Duer B. Alexander Blanckart/Carmelit'. Nach Abschluß des Studiums dozierte er zunächst als Lektor in Geldern.[4] Eine ihm angebotene Stelle in Trier trat er nicht an. Vielmehr lehrte er von 1533 an als *baccalaureus biblicus* in Köln.[5] Von 1534 an unterrichtete er als *lector principalis* in Utrecht. 1540 oder 1541 wurde er Prior des Utrechter Karmeliterklosters und (zugleich oder erst 1542) Pfarrer der St. Nikolauskirche.[6] Dieser wiederholte Wechsel zwischen Tätigkeiten in Utrecht und in Köln war damals gerade für einen Karmeliter nichts Außergewöhnliches. Das Bistum Utrecht war Kölner Suffragan-Bistum und die niederdeutsche Provinz des Karmelitenordens umfaßte Klöster im Nordwesten des Heiligen Römischen Reiches Deutscher Nation, aber auch in Gebieten wie Utrecht, die Karl V. seinen habsburgischen Erblanden angliederte. 1544 entsandte das Provinzialkapitel des Karmelitenordens Blanckaert als *magister studentium* ans Kölner Ordensstudium.[7] 1546 nahm er als Notar seines Provinzials Eberhard Billick am Regensburger Religionsgespräch teil.[8] Die Kölner theologische Fakultät erteilte ihm die Aufgabe, gemeinsam mit Johannes Spengel und weiteren Mitarbeitern eine für Altgläubige akzeptable Revision der von dem Antwerpener Drucker Wilhelm Vorsterman 1531 gedruckten, 1546 verbotenen flämischen Bibelübersetzung vorzunehmen. Eile war geboten, wollte doch die theologische Fakultät der Universität Leuven (Louvain, Löwen) auf der Basis ihrer Neuausgabe der *Biblia Vulgata* (November 1547) ebenfalls eine orthodoxe flämische Übersetzung auf den Markt bringen.[9] Die Kölner hatten Erfolg, im Dezember 1547 konnte ihre Überset-

---

Matrikel eingetragen worden. Er rangiert als sechzehnter Student unter dem Rektorat des Johannes de Busco[ducis] im April 1533 (*Die Matrikel der Universität Köln*, II 919).

[4] Vgl. Lickteig, *The German Carmelites at the medieval universities*, 300: 'Alexander Blanckaert [...] had been [...] the new lector at Geldern.'

[5] Vgl. Lickteig, *The German Carmelites at the medieval universities*, 268 mit Anm. 651.

[6] Die Angaben in den verschiedenen Nachschlagewerken widersprechen einander. Nach Mesters, 'Candidus, Alexander', hätte Blanckaert 1529 bis 1540 zunächst in Utrecht, danach in Köln Theologie doziert. Als überholt gelten kann die Behauptung von Rosier, Blanckaert sei von 1529 bis 1540 'Professor in de theologie' in Utrecht gewesen (Rosier, *Biographisch en bibliographisch overzicht van de vroomheid in de nederlandse Carmel*, 74).

[7] Das geschah gegen den Wunsch des Bischofs von Utrecht, Georg von Egmond, vgl. Postina, *Der Karmelit Eberhard Billick*, 152.

[8] Vgl. Postina, *Der Karmelit Eberhard Billick*, 86, Anm. 1.

[9] Meinem Kollegen A.A. den Hollander, der 1997 eine Dissertation über die niederländischen Bibelübersetzungen zwischen 1522 und 1545 vorgelegt hat, verdanke ich den Hinweis auf den vorzüglichen Aufsatz von Gilmont, 'Deux traductions concurrentes de l'Ecriture Sainte.' Dieser

zung gedruckt werden,[10] während die der Leuvener Konkurrenten erst im September 1548 bei dem Leuvener Drucker Bartholomaeus van Grave erscheinen konnte. 1550 wurde Blanckaert zum Doktor der Theologie promoviert und als stellvertretender Regens des Generalstudiums der Karmeliten ins Kollegium der Kölner Theologieprofessoren aufgenommen.[11] Freilich bezahlte ihn – wie diejenigen Professoren an der Artes-Fakultät, die im Geiste des Humanismus wirken sollten – die Stadt Köln. Er lehrte nicht an einer Burse, und das schwächte seine Position.[12] Im Mai des Jahres seiner Promotion, 1550, konnte er die Vorworte zu zwei Schriften unterzeichnen, die er für lateinkundige Priester, Klerikermönche und gebildete Laien geschrieben hatte. Er faßte die beiden Schriften zu einem Büchlein zusammen und ließ sie im Jahr 1551 bei demselben Kölner Drucker Caspar [Jasper] von Gennep drucken, der 1547 die Bibelrevision verlegt hatte, an deren Zustandekommen er federführend beteiligt gewesen war.[13] In der ersten Schrift bekämpft

Aufsatz korrigiert die Angaben in der älteren Arbeit von Vogel, 'Europäische Bibeldrucke des 15. und 16. Jahrhunderts in den Volkssprachen', 65, und übertrifft, was Blanckaerts Leistung betrifft, an Präzision auch die Angaben in der durch Broeyer besorgten Neuauflage des Werks von De Bruin, *De Statenbijbel en zijn voorgangers*, 137-41. Gilmonts Schilderung des Wettlaufs zwischen den miteinander konkurrierenden Bearbeitern Nicolas van Winghe (Leuven) und Nikolaus Blanckaert (Köln) einerseits, den Druckern Bartholomaeus van Grave (Leuven) und Caspar von Gennep (Köln) andererseits, schließlich des Ansinnens der Kölner theologischen Fakultät an die Löwener theologische Fakultät, ihre Übersetzung, immerhin ein Konkurrenzvorhaben, dogmatisch zu prüfen (140), liest sich für Liebhaber wie ein Kriminalroman.

[10] 'Die Bibel/ we//derom met grooter nersti//cheit ouersien [...]. Duer B. Alexander Blanckart.' Beispielsweise vorhanden in den Universitätsbibliotheken der Vrije Universiteit Amsterdam (Signatur: Oude drukken, XC. 05048) und der Universiteit Utrecht.

[11] Vgl. Lickteig, *The German Carmelites at the medieval universities*, 268-9 mit Anm. 655.

[12] Zur Verankerung von Professuren in einer Burse vgl. unten bei Anm. 37.

[13] Der Titel der ersten Schrift lautet *Iudicium Iohannis Calvini de Sanctorum reliquiis: collatum cum Orthodoxorum sanctae Ecclesiae Catholicae Patrum sententia*. Sie umfaßt im Druck die ff. A2r-D7v. Die zweite Schrift ist auf dem (nicht foliierten) Titelblatt des Büchleins überschrieben: *Item Oratio de Retributione Iustorum statim a morte*. Sie nimmt im Druck die ff. D8r-G4v ein. Offenbar plante Blanckaert ursprünglich, eine weitere Ansprache zu diesem Thema drucken zu lassen. Heißt es doch im Unterschied zum Titelblatt unmittelbar vor Beginn des Textes: *Oratio prima de Retributione Iustorum* (D8v). Auch im Widmungsbrief an den Kölner Patrizier Konstantin Ließkirchen vom 27.5.1550 schreibt Blanckaert: 'Orationem hanc *primam* de Retributione Iustorum' und stellt, falls seine Schrift Anklang finde, den Druck weiterer Ansprachen in Aussicht, die er bereits auf seinem Amboß schmiede (D8r). Eine zweite Schrift Blanckaerts zu diesem Thema habe ich jedoch nirgends verzeichnet gefunden. – Beide Schriften sind zusammen gedruckt worden: sie werden nicht nur beide auf dem Titelblatt genannt, sondern auf dem letzten Blatt der ersten Schrift (D7v) erleichtert auch die erste Silbe des Widmungsbriefs zur zweiten Schrift als Kustode einem Vorleser das Weiterlesen. Die Foliierung läuft durch. Auch an dieser Stelle danke ich der Bayerischen Staatsbibliothek in München, die mir freundlicherweise einen Mikrofilm hat anfertigen lassen (Signatur: Polem. 2820/1). Auf Blanckaerts Schrift aufmerksam gemacht hat mich deren Erwähnung in dem Aufsatz meines verehrten Lehrers Oberman, 'The Pursuit of Happiness', 260 und 278, Anm. 80. – Die Titel der beiden Predigten, die Blanckaert in Bologna hielt (siehe dazu Anm. 15), zweier Ansprachen aus Anlaß von Synoden in Utrecht, der *Oratio de Retributione Iustorum* und den Fundort eines Briefs, nicht aber den Titel der ersten Schrift, die hier dargestellt wird, vermerkt Rosier, *Biographisch en bibliografisch*

Blanckaert die lateinische Übersetzung einer französischen Schrift Calvins, die die Verehrung der Reliquien scheinbar von Mißbräuchen zu reinigen, in Wirklichkeit aber zu untergraben versucht, in der zweiten tritt er dafür ein, daß die Heiligen sofort nach ihrem Tod in den Himmel kommen und nicht erst nach dem Jüngsten Tage. 1551 sandte die Statthalterin der Niederlande, Karls V. Schwester Maria, die Witwe des Königs von Ungarn,[14] Blanckaert als ihren Vertreter zur zweiten Sitzungsperiode des Konzils von Trient.[15] Seine bedeutenderen Kollegen Johann Gropper und Eberhard Billick vertraten dort die Stadt Köln und die Kölner Universität. Zweimal war Blanckaert Dekan der theologischen Fakultät, 1551/52 und 1554/55.[16] Er starb am 31.12.1555.

Der Charakter von Blanckaerts Schriften

Die Widmungsbriefe zu den beiden Schriften sind datiert auf den 15. Mai und auf den 27. Mai 1550.[17] Es sind von Blanckaert zu wenige Werke bewahrt, als daß wir beurteilen könnten, ob er für beide Schriften auf fremden oder eigenen Vorarbeiten hat aufbauen können. Ein Vergleich mit Billicks Schriften zeigt, daß Blanckaert weniger Kirchenväter zitiert als dieser. Ungewiß bleibt, ob man aus den Datierungen der Vorworte schließen darf, daß Blanckaert die zweite Schrift in nur zwölf Tagen geschrieben hat. Wenn er sich tatsächlich

overzicht van de vroomheid in de nederlandse Carmel, 74 und 75. Zu ergänzen sind die Angaben von Lickteig, *The German Carmelites at the medieval universities*, 269, Anm. 660.

[14] Die Frömmigkeit der Habsburgerin Maria im Konflikt zwischen ihren Pflichten und ihren Neigungen schildert Spruyt, 'Verdacht van Lutherse sympathieën'. Ausführlicher in englischer Sprache: Ders., 'En bruit d'estre bonne luteriene'.

[15] Vgl. Postina, *Der Karmelit Eberhard Billick*, 118; Lickteig, *The German Carmelites at the medieval universities*, 269, der auf Cod. Vat. Lat. 6208, 41r, verweist. Der Vorsitzende des Geheimen Rats Viglius van Aytta hatte Blanckaert vorgeschlagen. Zu diesem Staatsmann und Humanisten vgl. Postma, *Viglius van Aytta*. Postma arbeitet an einer Studie über Viglius' spätere Jahre. Blanckaerts Name fehlt in der Aufzählung der deutschen und niederländischen Theologen, die an dieser Sitzungsperiode teilnahmen, bei Jedin, 'Die deutschen Teilnehmer am Trienter Konzil', 251-3. Vielleicht erklärt sich das daraus, daß die drei Kölner Theologen in den Verzeichnissen der Teilnehmer am Trienter Konzil nicht als Abgesandte der Universität, sondern stets nur als Begleiter ihrer Bischöfe vermerkt wurden, wie Postina vermerkt (*Der Karmelit Eberhard Billick*, 122, Anm. 4). Blanckaert wurde die ehrenvolle Aufgabe zuteil, am 25.10. und am 24.12.1551 vor den in Bologna versammelten Konzilsvätern zu predigen. Weiterführende Literatur hierzu nennt Lickteig, *The German Carmelites at the medieval universities*, 269, Anm. 662. Von den dort genannten Werken war für mich nicht zugänglich: Gabriel a Virgine Carmeli, 'Die Karmeliten auf dem Konzil von Trient', *Ephemerides Carmeliticae*, 4 (1950), 291-359.

[16] Vgl. Lickteig, *The German Carmelites at the medieval universities*, 232, Anm. 359.

[17] Blanckaert, *Iudicium* (A4v, an Johannes von Hüls, den Abt des Zisterzienserklosters Camp): 'Reverendo in Christo Patri et Domino, Domino Iohanni ab Hulss, Insignis Monasterii Campensis Abbati uigilantissimo' und *De retributione iustorum* (D8r, an den Kölner Patrizier Konstantin Ließkirchen): 'Nobili, Generoso et Erudito D. Constantino, ex Veteri Familia LiessKirchen, Patritio Coloniensi'.

nur wenig Zeit genommen hat, dann ist es nicht erstaunlich, daß beide Schriften weder besonders originell noch besonders profund sind. Interesse erregen sie vielmehr eben als Gelegenheitswerke eines eher durchschnittlichen Hochschullehrers, dem man eine gewisse humanistische Schulung zubilligen darf. Gerade dadurch liefern sie einen Beitrag zu einer präziseren Bestimmung dessen, wie ein solcher minder bedeutender Gelehrter in der Mitte des 16. Jahrhunderts scholastische Theologie und humanistische Schulung in sich vereinigte und wo seiner Meinung nach ein Punkt erreicht war, an dem eine Entscheidung zwischen beiden fallen mußte. Im Druck nehmen beide Schriften zusammen 106 Seiten im Quartformat ein. Die erste Schrift bekämpft die lateinische Übersetzung von Johannes Calvins volkssprachlichem Werkchen gegen die Reliquien. Blanckaert zitiert deren Titel verkürzt als 'Iudicium de Admonitione reliquiarum'.[18] Seine zweite Schrift verteidigt die Ansicht, daß Heilige alsbald nach ihrem Tode in den Himmel kommen und dort Fürbitte für die noch lebenden Gläubigen leisten, nicht erst nach dem Jüngsten Tage. Gedruckt hat das Büchlein, wie gesagt, Caspar [Jasper] von Gennep. Die erste Schrift widmet Blanckaert Johannes V. Ingenray von Hüls, Abt des bedeutenden Zisterzienserklosters Camp im Rheinland, die zweite dem Kölner Patrizier Konstantin Ließkirchen. Die beiden Widmungsbriefe machen deutlich, daß Blanckaert Verbindungen zu dem Abt des ältesten Zisterzienserklosters Deutschlands[19] und zu einem Kölner Patrizier hatte oder herzustellen suchte. Faßt man den Drucker und die Adressaten der beiden Widmungsbriefe näher ins Auge, so würde man heute sagen, Blanckaert habe sich bemüht, in ein effizientes 'Netzwerk' verläßlicher altgläubiger An-

---

[18] *Ioannis Calvini admonitio.* Auch an dieser Stelle möchte ich der Hauptbibliothek der Franckeschen Stiftungen, Halle, vielmals für die Anfertigung eines Mikrofilms des dort vorhandenen Exemplars der Schrift danken (Sign. ULB Fr, 54 J 16). – Calvins volkssprachliche Streitschrift *Advertissement tresvtile* (*Bibliotheca Calviniana*, Nr. 43/2) stammt von 1543. Sie ist bequem zugänglich in: 'Jean Calvin. Three French Treatises', 12-6; 47-97. Diese Edition weist in einem textkritischen Apparat Varianten verschiedener Drucke nach. Nachweise zitierter Quellen und einige Erläuterungen enthält die Ausgabe 'La vraie piété', 153-61; 163-202. – Hollweg hat 1909 Blanckaerts Schrift kurz erwähnt in seinem Aufsatz 'Calvins Beziehungen zu den Rheinlanden', 178-80. Herrn Kollegen Hansgeorg Molitor (Düsseldorf) danke ich für den Hinweis auf diesen Aufsatz wie für die Freundlichkeit, sich bei dem Leiter der Handschriftenabteilung und der Abteilung Frühe Drucke der Universitätsbibliothek Düsseldorf, Herrn Kollegen Heinz Finger, zu erkundigen, ob ein Exemplar der lateinischen Übersetzung von Calvins Schrift heute noch dort nachweisbar sei, leider mit negativem Ergebnis. Herr Kollege Winrich Löhr (Bonn, nun Cambridge) war so liebenswürdig, in der Universitätsbibliothek Bonn und in der Bibliothek der Erzdiezese Köln nach Calvins Schrift zu suchen: auch diese Suche hatte keinen Erfolg. Das Exemplar von Calvins Schrift, das Blanckaert benutzt hat, muß also als verschollen gelten.
[19] Zu Johannes von Hüls, Abt des Zisterzienserklosters Camp 1529-63, vgl. Dicks, *Die Abtei Camp am Niederrhein*, 432-41. Ein 'Joh. Huls' ist ohne nähere Kennzeichnung als siebzehnter Student unter dem Rektorat des Arnoldus de Dammone im April 1531 in die Matrikel der Universität eingetragen worden. Ein 'Const. Lijskyrch' wurde in Köln im Juni 1530 als siebenundzwanzigster Student unter dem Rektorat des Hermannus Keutenbruer immatrikuliert (*Die Matrikel der Universität Köln*, II 907).

gehöriger der sozialen Elite aufgenommen zu werden oder es aufzubauen. Blanckaert schreibt wie die meisten altgläubigen Theologen, die reformatorische Einflüsse bekämpfen, nicht in der Sprache des Volkes, sondern lateinisch,[20] und er widmet seine Schriften Männern der gesellschaftlichen Elite, die, nach seinen Worten zu schließen, im Kampf gegen reformatorische Bemühungen des Erzbischofs Hermann von Wied ihre verläßliche Altgläubigkeit bewiesen haben. Nimmt man seine Aussagen über das 'einfache Volk' hinzu, zu dem er sich, wiewohl er Bettelmönch ist, als Hochschullehrer mit einer gewissen humanistischen Schulung ganz offensichtlich nicht rechnet, so wird deutlich, daß er sich zu der in Gesellschaft und altgläubiger Kirche führenden Schicht zählt.

Ich skizziere nun zunächst in aller Kürze den Forschungsstand zur Akzeptanz humanistischer Studien in den Bettelorden und zur Lage der Kölner theologischen Fakultät in der Mitte des 16. Jahrhunderts, um dann Nikolaus Blanckaert in diesen Rahmen einzuordnen.

Humanistische Studien bei Karmeliten

Wichtige Grundlagen für jeden, der sich mit der Schnittfläche zwischen Humanismus und Scholastik in den Bettelorden beschäftigt, haben Paul Oskar Kristeller[21] und Kaspar Elm gelegt. Seit sie deutlich gemacht haben, welche Rolle Bettelordensklöster für die Förderung humanistischer Studien gespielt haben, wird wesentlich differenzierter geurteilt als vor dem Erscheinen ihrer Arbeiten. Kaspar Elm skizziert auf der Grundlage seiner souveränen Kenntnis spätmittelalterlicher Ordensgeschichte den Rahmen für die Beziehungen von Ordensangehörigen zum Humanismus. Er warnt einerseits davor, generalisierend davon zu sprechen, humanistische Studien seien jemals in 'den' Bettelorden rundheraus akzeptiert gewesen.[22] Gerade auch im Karmelitenorden hätten manche einflußreiche Obere gegen Kontakte mit der humanistischen Bewegung geeifert und auf Beibehaltung der *vita eremitica* angedrungen.[23] Es habe 'Furcht vor dem Neuen' gegeben, 'vor neuen Bildungsinhalten und

---

[20] Vgl. zu den unterschiedlichen Zielgruppen der Protestanten und der Altgläubigen im Meinungskampf der Reformationszeit die Aussagen von Edwards, 'Catholic Controversial Literature', 191: 'Catholics, in contrast, may have been addressing a smaller audience of what we might term 'opinion leaders' such as clerics, councilors, and rulers'; 196: 'Cologne's presses are producing almost exclusively for a learned elite (85% of their production is in Latin)'. Edwards konstatiert 'a deep Catholic suspicion about addressing theological tracts to laity' (203).

[21] Kristeller, 'The contribution of religious orders to Renaissance thought and learning'.

[22] Elm, *Mendikanten und Humanisten*, nun in: Elm, *Vitasfratrum*, 263-84; hier 268.

[23] Vgl. op. cit., 265 und 266 mit Anm. 25.

Wertvorstellungen, durch die Selbstheiligung und Gotteslob, kurzum Ordens-
leben und monastische Spiritualität gefährdet zu sein schienen.'[24] Andererseits
hätten 'seit der Mitte des 15. Jahrhunderts' manche Gruppen in den Bettelorden, zugespitzt formuliert, 'allen Widerstand gegen das Studium der antiken
Autoren aufgegeben und eine aktive Rolle in der Rezeption und Pflege des
antiken Erbes übernommen [...].'[25] Die Art der Beschäftigung mit den *studia
humanitatis* sei also nicht ausschließlich von der jeweiligen Ordensspiritualität
geprägt, sondern stelle sich als eine Art von Synthese zwischen der geistigen
Eigenart einer monastischen Gemeinschaft zu einer bestimmten Zeit an einem
bestimmten Ort und der konkreten politischen und sozialen Situation dar.[26]

Blanckaert ist keineswegs der einzige Karmelit seiner Epoche mit
humanistischen Interessen. Schon ein halbes Jahrhundert vor ihm vereinbarte
der Karmelit Arnold van Bosch (Bostius, †1499) Ordenszugehörigkeit und
Sympathien für Humanisten offenbar ohne Spannungen miteinander. Wie
Blanckaert stammte er aus Gent. Er unterhielt Kontakte mit hervorragenden
Humanisten seiner Zeit. Geht man die Namen der Freunde durch, die er 1497
dazu anregte, in einem Wettstreit Gedichte auf die Eltern Marias, Anna und
Joachim, zu schreiben, dann wird deutlich, daß es nicht möglich ist, hier eine
Grenze zwischen Mönchen und Humanisten zu ziehen.[27] Arnold van Bosch
versuchte auch Konrad Celtis dazu zu bewegen, ein Epigramm auf das Werk
De Laudibus ordinis Fratrum Carmelitarum des Abts Trithemius zu schrei-
ben.[28] In einem Brief gratuliert er einem Mitbruder dazu, die Freundschaft des
Trithemius erworben zu haben. Aus diesem Brief geht auch hervor, daß Ar-
nold van Bosch Sebastian Brant dazu bewegen wollte, einen Lobpreis auf den
Karmel zu verfassen.[29]

Zu apodiktisch scheint mir im Vergleich zu Elms sorgfältigen Erwägungen
denn auch das Urteil des Karmeliten Zimmerman zu sein, nach 1528 gebe es
im Karmelitenorden keine Repräsentanten des Humanismus mehr.[30] Ich ver-

---

[24] Op. cit., 266 mit Anm. 32.
[25] Op cit., 268.
[26] Vgl. op. cit., 284.
[27] Vgl. Massaut, *Josse Clichtove*, I 261-7; 326. Massaut formuliert an anderer Stelle (261):
'moines pieux et humanistes [...] un monde d'amateurs de poésie et de bonne latinité, mais dési-
reux de mettre les lettres restaurées au service de la dévotion.'
[28] Vgl. dazu den Brief des Bostius an Celtis vom 23.10.1496 (Celtis, *Der Briefwechsel*, 219).
[29] Vgl. dazu den Brief des Bostius an seinen Ordensbruder Johannes Paleonydorus (De
Aquaveteri, De veteri limpha, Oudewater, Outwater) aus Gent vom 20.5.1496: 'Gaudeo te tam
doctissimorum optimorumque virorum Abbatis Tritemii et Rogeri Sycambri aliorumque non
minus noticiam quam amiciciam nactum, teque eis in sacrarum litterarum cultu collaborare. [...]
Pollicitus est Sebastianus Brant Basiliensis, vtriusque iuris doctor, elegantissimi stili mea ad-
hortatione opus de laude nostre religionis conditurum. Adhorteris eciam vt faciat.' (Allen, 'Letters
of Arnold Bostius', 228; 229).
[30] Zimmerman, 'Les Carmes Humanistes', 20: 'Après 1528, les représentants de l'humanisme
dans l'Ordre avaient entièrement disparu.' Herrn Dr. Lansink vom 'Nederlands Carmelitaans In-

weise zur Begründung meines Widerspruchs auf den Karmeliten Adrianus
Hecquetius (1510 oder 1515-1580). Er gehörte wie der Humanist Petrus Nannius (Pieter Nanninck, 1496-1557), Professor für Latein am Collegium Trilingue in Louvain, der fünfzehn oder neunzehn Jahre älter war als er, zu den
Schützlingen des Bischofs von Arras, Antoine Perrenot de Granvelle (1517-
1586). Von der Bewunderung des Karmeliten für den Humanisten zeugen er-
haltene Briefe beider aneinander aus dem Jahre 1552 und ein Gedicht des
Hecquetius, das den Tod des Nannius betrauert.[31]

*Die Haltung der theologischen Fakultät der Kölner Universität gegenüber
humanistischen Bestrebungen in der Mitte des 16. Jahrhunderts*

Die Auseinandersetzungen der Kölner theologischen Fakultät mit Reuchlin
und die 'Dunkelmännerbriefe' haben die Aufmerksamkeit mancher Forscher
so sehr auf die Kölner Dominikaner konzentriert, daß ihnen die Angehörigen
anderer Orden und die Weltgeistlichen neben diesen als unbedeutend erschienen. Daran ist für unsere Frage nach dem Verhältnis zwischen Humanisten
und scholastischen Theologen so viel richtig, daß der Dominikaner Hoogstraeten (um 1465-1527) an der theologischen Fakultät der Kölner Universität im
ersten Viertel des 16. Jahrhunderts den Mittelpunkt des Widerstandes gegen
die humanistische Bewegung bildete.[32] Schaut man allein auf Hoogstraeten
und andere Dominikaner, so kann man tatsächlich zu der Einschätzung gelan-
gen, die theologische Fakultät der Kölner Universität sei damals eine Hoch-
burg reaktionärer scholastischer Theologie gewesen. Doch ist es nicht angebracht, allein die Dominikaner als in Köln einflußreiche Bettelordenstheolo-
gen zu betrachten und einseitig ihren Widerstand gegen humanistische Bestrebungen ins Auge zu fassen. Sehr abgewogen beurteilt Meuthen in seiner Kölner Universitätsgeschichte die Bedeutung der Dominikaner innerhalb der Kölner theologischen Fakultät:

> Liegt es uns fern, die Bedeutung des Ordens für die Kölner Universität zu
> bagatellisieren, so sei doch mit Nachdruck betont, daß auch er nur eine
> Komponente zu dem insgesamt viel reichhaltigeren Ensemble geistiger Kräfte
> beitrug.[33]

---

stituut', dem Verfasser der oben in Anm. 3 genannten Arbeit, danke ich herzlich dafür, daß er mir
sowohl die Studie von Zimmerman als auch eine ungedruckt gebliebene Abschlußarbeit (docto-
raalscriptie) zugänglich gemacht hat: H. van Veen, *Carmelieten en humanisten: de geschiedenis
van een verwijdering* (An der Universität Groningen vorgelegt am 8.6.1977.)
[31] Vgl. De Smet, 'A Sixteenth-Century Carmelite at Louvain'.
[32] Vgl. zu Hoogstraeten nun Peterse, *Jacobus Hoogstraeten gegen Johannes Reuchlin*.
[33] Meuthen, *Kölner Universitätsgeschichte*, 158.

Zutreffender als die auf die Dominikaner zugespitzte Sichtweise, die Meuthen kritisiert, ist die Periodisierung, die James Mehl als Herausgeber eines Sammelbandes zum Humanismus in Köln vornimmt. Er untersucht in erster Linie humanistische Bestrebungen zur Erneuerung des universitären Curriculums an der Kölner Universität und unterscheidet drei Stadien der Auseinandersetzung: Zunächst, am Ende des 15. Jahrhunderts, eine Phase der begeisterten Rezeption humanistischer Impulse, dann ein zweites Stadium, in dem politische und religiöse Kontroversen eine Reform des universitären Curriculums an der Kölner Universität in den Hintergrund drängten, und ein drittes Stadium, in dem die Jesuiten erfolgreich humanistische Curricula durchsetzten.[34]

Diese schrittweise Akzeptanz humanistischer Erneuerung des Curriculums mußte, wie Meuthen aufweist, gegen erhebliche Widerstände durchgesetzt werden. Die Kölner Universität verschloß sich zunächst der Erneuerung des Curriculums nach humanistischen Maßstäben. Zwei Versuche in den Jahren 1523 und 1525, das Curriculum nach humanistischen Vorstellungen umzugestalten, hatten wenig Erfolg.[35] Beeinträchtigte schon diese Verweigerung die Anziehungskraft der Universität, so schadete auch die reformatorische Bewegung der Universität, die altgläubig blieb, erheblich. Am Ende der zwanziger Jahre des 16. Jahrhunderts ließen die Einschreibungen von Studenten und das Einkommen der Universität nach. Im Gegensatz zu ihrer Blütezeit im 15. Jahrhundert vermochte sie nur noch Studenten aus altgläubig gebliebenen Gebieten Nordwestdeutschlands anzuziehen. An diesem wichtigen Bollwerk der Altgläubigen in den geistigen Auseinandersetzungen der Reformation sank die Zahl der Studierenden rapide. Um den Erfordernissen der Zeit zu entsprechen, ordnete der Kölner Stadtrat im Jahre 1550 eine Universitätsreform an. An der Artes-Fakultät wurden drei humanistische Professuren eingerichtet.[36] Erich Meuthen relativiert deren Geltung freilich: den Inhabern dieser drei Professuren sei wenig Geltung beschieden gewesen, weil ihre Lehrstühle nicht in Bursen integriert waren. In die Bursen aber hatte sich der Unterricht der Artes-Fakultät immer mehr verlagert.[37] Um die Attraktivität der theologischen Fakultät zu verstärken, wurden deren Professoren dazu verpflichtet, Exegese zu treiben. Die Stadt Köln, die im Jahre 1517 die Zahl der von ihr besoldeten Professoren erheblich reduziert hatte, griff 1550 für kurze Zeit wieder tiefer in die Tasche. Für die theologische Fakultät bezahlte sie zeitweise sechs Professoren.[38] Die Bereitschaft, sich diese Fakultät etwas

---

[34] *Humanismus in Köln*. Dieses Werk von Mehl war mir nicht zugänglich. Ich referiere nach der Rezension von Haude, hier 449.

[35] Vgl. Haude (wie Anm. 34), 450.

[36] Vgl. Eckert, 'Köln II. Universität', 303, Zeilen 22-7.

[37] Vgl. Meuthen, 'Die Artesfakultät der alten Kölner Universität', 379; 383; 392: die Artesfakultät 'Summe ihrer Bursen'.

[38] Vgl. Meuthen, *Kölner Universitätsgeschichte*, 292.

kosten zu lassen,[39] war freilich von kurzer Dauer. Schon 1552 reduzierte Köln seinen Beitrag wieder auf die Bezahlung von nur noch zwei theologischen Professuren. Statt sich auf die Zahlung fester Gehälter zu verpflichten, finanzierte die Stadt Köln zeitweise lieber eine Zulage: Der Karmelit Blanckaert, um den es uns hier geht, erhielt nun doppeltes Gehalt, vierzig Taler statt zwanzig. Dafür sollte er eine zusätzliche Vorlesung halten, und zwar über die kontroverstheologisch zentrale Frage des Altarsakraments.[40] Eine Aufstellung des Provinzialkapitels der Karmeliten des Jahres 1552, welche Stipendien verfügbar waren, nennt auch Blanckaert.[41] Die Rolle des Kölner Stadtrats in der Auseinandersetzung um die Erneuerung der universitären Curricula nach humanistischen Vorstellungen bedarf noch weiterer Untersuchung. Charles Nauert und James Mehl beurteilen sie unterschiedlich.[42]

Zitate aus Schriften der Kirchenväter bei den Kölner Karmeliten Billick und Blanckaert

In den Bemühungen der Kölner theologischen Fakultät, attraktiv zu bleiben, spielen die Karmeliten eine wichtige Rolle. In seiner Kölner Universitätsgeschichte bescheinigt ihnen Erich Meuthen, daß sie die Krisen besser meisterten als die anderen in Köln vertretenen Bettelorden, unter anderem dank einer überlegten Ordenspolitik.[43] Als Erzbischof Hermann von Wied den Reformator Martin Bucer nach Bonn holt, um eine Reform des Erzstifts einzuleiten, muß Blanckaerts Ordensbruder und Vorgesetzter Eberhard Billick nicht auf scholastische Autoritäten zurückgreifen, deren Geltung erschüttert ist, sondern ist in der Lage, diesen Gegner mit dessen eigenen Waffen zu bekämpfen. Mit Hilfe zahlreicher Zitate aus Schriften von einundzwanzig Theologen von Irenaeus bis Anselm von Canterbury argumentiert er gegen Bucer.[44] Er muß in den patristischen Schriften gut beschlagen gewesen sein, wenn er nicht einfach ein gutes Florilegium benutzt.

Auch Nikolaus Blanckaert führt eine Fülle patristischer Zitate an. Zwar verfügt er nicht über die Breite von Billicks Wissen. Manche der von ihm an-

---

[39] Die Besoldung von Theologieprofessoren der Mendikanten war verhältnismäßig niedrig. Zimmerman ('Les Carmes Humanistes', 21) verweist auf die exorbitanten Differenzen zwischen den Gehältern von Professoren aus den Bettelorden (30-40 Florinen) und denen von Juristen, die bis zu 3000 Florinen verdienten.

[40] Meuthen, *Kölner Universitätsgeschichte*, 495, Anm. 214, verweist dafür auf H. Keussen, *Regesten und Auszüge zur Geschichte der Universität Köln 1388-1559* (Köln 1918), Nr. 3502.

[41] 'Bursa nova procurata per R.M. Alexandrum Candidum 18 flor.' (Lansink, *Studie en onderwijs in de Nederduitse provincie van de karmelieten*, Beilage 4, 349).

[42] Vgl. Haude (wie Anm. 34), 451.

[43] Meuthen, *Kölner Universitätsgeschichte*, 272.

[44] Vgl. Fabisch, 'Eberhard Billick', 109.

geführten Kirchenvätertexte gehören zum Standardrepertoire wie beispielsweise die Aussagen des Hieronymus über die Märtyrerverehrung in dessen
Schrift gegen Vigilantius, der Lobpreis der Märtyrerreliquien von Johannes
Chrysostomus und der Auszug aus einem Brief Gregors des Großen, mit dem
dieser der Kaiserin die Bitte um die Reliquien der Apostel Petrus und Paulus
abschlägt. Andere Zitate aber sind minder geläufig. Freilich setzt sich Blanckaert nicht intensiv inhaltlich mit seinen Gegnern auseinander. Er beschränkt
sich darauf, Zitate aus Schriften der Kirchenväter auszuwählen, diese aneinan-
derzureihen und jeweils am Rand zustimmende oder tadelnde Bemerkungen
abdrucken zu lassen.

Nikolaus Blanckaert – gewiß ein scholastischer Theologe, aber auch ein
Humanist?

Blanckaert wirkt als altgläubiger Hochschullehrer der Theologie an der insgesamt konservativen Kölner theologischen Fakultät. Aber das berechtigt noch
nicht ohne weiteres dazu, ihn als scholastischen Theologen und nur als solchen zu bezeichnen. Erfüllt er nicht auch die Bedingungen, um zu Recht ein
'Humanist' genannt werden zu dürfen? Je nachdem, wie man 'Humanist sein'
definiert, wird man auf diese Frage ganz verschieden antworten.
    Erika Rummel fordert in ihrem Aufsatz 'Et cum theologo bella poeta gerit'
ganz zu Recht klare Definitionen, wenn man zum Zwecke der Klassifizierung
scholastische Theologen und Humanisten voneinander unterscheiden will. An
dieser Stelle definiert sie als einen scholastischen Theologen den, der die dia-
lektische Methode einsetzt und Zitate aus Werken mittelalterlicher Theologen
anführt. Als einen Humanisten sieht sie im Unterschied dazu hier denjenigen
an, der sich der philologischen Methode bedient und klassische und patris-
tische Autoren zitiert.[45] Wollte man sich auf diese Definitionen beschränken,
so verdiente Blanckaert gewiß ein Humanist genannt zu werden. Denn er
argumentiert mit Bibelzitaten und zitiert einen Kirchenvätertext nach dem
anderen. Dagegen beruft er sich nicht auf einen einzigen scholastischen Theologen. Im Zusammenhang seiner Argumentation dafür, daß die Heiligen schon
jetzt im Himmel für die Gläubigen eintreten, referiert er, daß Paulus im Ephe-
serbrief einen Psalmvers abgewandelt zitiert.[46] Ausdrücklich wendet er sich

---

[45] Vgl. Rummel, 'Et cum theologo bella poeta gerit', 718.
[46] Blanckaert, *De retributione iustorum* (F3v/F4r): 'Lege uersic.[ulum] psal.[mi] 67 [,19]: 'As-
cendisti in altum, accepisti captiuitatem, accepisti dona in hominibus', siue, ut citat locum istum
apostolus Paulus ad Ephesi[os] 4 [,8.10]: 'Ascendens in altum, captiuam duxit captiuitatem, dedit
dona hominibus. [...] Qui descendit, ipse est qui ascendit super omnes coelos.'' Anstelle von 'accepisti captiuitatem' steht in (modernen Ausgaben) der Vulgata lediglich 'cepisti captiuitatem'. In
Blanckaerts Vorlage wird wohl 'ac cepisti' gestanden haben. Denn in der für Altgläubige be-

gegen Menschen, die Kritik am geltenden Kanon des Neuen Testaments zu
üben wagen, die nach seinen Worten mit der gleichen 'Leichtigkeit oder vielmehr Leichtfertigkeit' die Apokalypse des heiligen Johannes ablehnten wie
den zweiten Brief des Apostels Petrus.[47] Er verspricht, er wolle Bibelzitate,
die seiner eigenen Position zu widersprechen schienen, später erläutern.[48]
Meist freilich begnügt er sich mit einer Aneinanderreihung von *dicta probantia* für seine eigene Ansicht.

Es läßt sich auch sonst noch manches dafür anführen, Blanckaert einen
Humanisten zu nennen. Nicht umsonst latinisiert er seinen Namen Nikolaus
Blanckaert zu 'Alexander Candidus'. Wie es manchen Humanisten eigen ist,
setzt er sich vom einfachen Volk ab als von der *plebs*, der *plebecula*, dem
popellus. Solche Äußerungen über das 'einfache Volk' finden sich gehäuft auf
der Rückseite des nicht paginierten Titelblatts seiner beiden in einem Bänd-
chen vereinigten Schriften. Er stellt dort mehrere Motti voran und gibt diesen
(außer dem ersten) nochmals Überschriften. Der gemeinsame Tenor ist, daß
das einfache Volk die Priester um ihren Reichtum beneide und daß deren
Schandtaten es feindlich stimmten:

> Ob tua probra tibi plebs est inimica sacerdos,
> Ob pia facta fauens fiet amica tibi.

> *Virulenta plebeculae contra sacerdotes inuidia:*
> Inspiciunt oculis inopes bona divitis aegris,
> Invidiaeque gravem produnt per murmura morbum.

> *Odium popelli in Sacrificos:*
> Sit licet innumeris putris plebecula morbis,
> In peccata tamen Mystarum despuit atrox.

---

stimmten Revision der Bibelübersetzung, die Blanckaert maßgeblich mit verantwortete (siehe
Anm. 10), lautet die Übersetzung von Psalm 67, 19: 'Ghi zijt in de hoochte geclommen/ enn hebt
die geuangenisse geuangen/ gy hebt gauen ontfangen in die menschen.' Eph. 4, 8.10 lauten dort
so: 'Om hooch climmende/ heeft hy die geuangenisse geuangen geleyt/ ende heuet den menschen
gauen gegeuen/ [...] Dhy ghene dye nedergeclommen is/ dat is dye selfde/ dye oock op ghe-
clommen is bouen alle hemelen/ op dat hy alle dinck veruellen soude.'
   [47] Blanckaert, *De retributione iustorum* (E6v): 'Vbi nolo eos audire qui eadem facilitate imo
leuitate rejiciunt Apocalypsim D. Ioannis, qua secundam Apostoli Petri.'
   [48] Blanckaert, *De retributione iustorum* (E6r): 'Quae et similia loca cum nostris asscrtionibus
in speciem dissidentia postea conciliabimus.'

Multi hoc tempore bonis Ecclesiasticis inhiant:
Templorum dotes iam turba famelica captat,
Non secus atque ferox ambit ovile lupus.[49]

Aussagen über das einfache Volk kommen auch im Text seiner Schrift vor. So schreibt Blanckaert beispielsweise, Calvin habe sich bewußt der französischen Sprache bedient, um das 'ungelehrte, einfache, unvernünftige Volk [*vulgus*]' zu vergiften.[50]

Blanckaert schreibt gewandt Latein und kennt eine ganze Reihe der unter Humanisten geläufigen Termini. In seinen beiden Schriften spricht er nicht von Priestern *(sacerdotes),* sondern von Einleitern in einen Gottesdienst, von 'Hierophanten'. Wenn er den Gegnern der Reliquienverehrung vorwirft, sie wollten die Reliquien entweder einäschern oder in Vergessenheit bringen, dann bezeichnet er diese zweite Möglichkeit, die Reliquien dem Vergessen anheimzugeben, als 'in den Fluß Lethe werfen'.[51] Im besten humanistischen Stil nennt er Kardinal Jacopo Sadoleto 'unseren Sadoleto'.[52] Ihm ist vertraut, daß Apelles als der größte Maler der Antike galt: Schon Hieronymus habe in seiner Polemik gegen Vigilantius die Argumente Calvins so vorzüglich widerlegt, daß nicht einmal die Zeichenkunst eines Apelles dem noch einen Strich würde hinzufügen können, behauptet er.[53] Wenn er von der Unterwelt redet, gebraucht er ebenfalls klassische Terminologie: Der erste Märtyrer Stephanus habe Gott gebeten, seinen Geist nicht in den *Orkus* oder in den finsteren *Tartarus* eingehen zu lassen, sondern in Jesu Hände.[54] Alle, die seiner Wertschätzung der Reliquienverehrung nicht beipflichten, ziehen sich nach seiner

---

[49] Wen die darauf folgende Warnung vor dem Glücksspiel betrifft, wird nicht recht deutlich:
Ad Petrellum suum E. de assiduo lusu fugiendo:
Tempora qui multo perdit puer aurea lusu,
Non facit ille lucri dulceis sibi perditus arteis.
Bonus uitae finis assidue petendus a Deo:
Peruigil & supplex precibus feruentibus ora,
Vt bonus obtingat post haec tibi tempora FINIS.
[50] Blanckaert, *Iudicium* (B4v): 'quo facilius (quod ego credo) indocti, simplicis, et imprudentis uulgi animis uirus suum insinuaret.'
[51] Blanckaert, *Iudicium* (A3v): 'diuorum uenerationem sublatam cuperent, et eorum reliquias aut in cineres redactas, aut in amnem laethaeum proiectas.'
[52] Blanckaert, *Iudicium*, ep. dedicatoria (A4r): 'audio uirum [Calvinum] magna apud suos esse et autoritate et aestimatione (ut quem eruditissimo Sadoleto nostro non sunt ueriti opponere) [...].'
[53] Blanckaert, *Iudicium* (B4r): 'qui in Vigilantio Caluinum tam graphice nobis expressit, ut ne Appelles quidem ipse lineam superadderet.' Von Apelles aus Kolophon, einem griechischen Maler der 2. Hälfte des 4. Jahrhunderts, dem allein Alexander der Große erlaubt haben soll, ihn zu malen, wurde im Altertum wiederholt behauptet, er sei der größte Maler überhaupt. Vgl. dazu beispielsweise Quintilian, *De institutione oratoria* XII, sowie zum Bild des Apelles im 16. Jh. Robert Stephanus, *Thesaurus linguae latinae*, s.v. 'Apelles'.
[54] Blanckaert, *De retributione iustorum* (E1v/2r): 'Beatus Stephanus protomartyr Christi [...] precabaturque Spiritum suum non quidem demitti ad orcum siue ad obscura tartara [...].'

Auffassung das Urteil zu, in Selbstsucht befangen zu sein, in *philautia*.[55] Von Gott spricht er als vom *Deus Optimus Maximus*, von den Folgen der Ursünde als von einer *Andria malorum*.[56]

Alle Register humanistischer Rhetorik, die ihm zu Gebote stehen, zieht Blanckaert im Widmungsbrief der ersten Schrift an den Abt Johannes von Hüls:

> Quod iudicium, quae censura est Ioannis Caluini, in eo libello cui De Admonitione reliquiarum titulum fecit. Quem cum cepissem legere, arridebat mihi prima (quod aiunt) fronte uiri consilium, et probabatur institutum, qui cuperet nobiscum ueras et germanas reliquias a suppositítiis et adulterinis repurgatas. Porro cum in progressu lectionis non subolerem modo, sed quasi caeca manu palparem, hoc ipsius esse studium, huc destinari subdolos suos conatus, eo tendere sua molimina, ut Diuorum reliquiae, cultus, ueneratio, prorsus tollantur et pessundentur: Non arbitratus sum ego officium esse ciuis Christianae Reipublicae,[57] ad tam praesens malum et ciuium suorum exitium, aut conniuere aut conticere. Nam audio uirum magna apud suos esse et auctoritate et aestimatione (ut quem eruditissimo Sadoleto nostro non sunt ueriti opponere) et nostrorum quoque prurientes aures uerborum suorum lenociniis demulcere. Quo fit, ut ab illo magis metuendum sit, quia duplici nomine nostris posset imponere, ad eloquentiam accedente etiam autoritate.[58]

---

[55] Blanckaert, *Iudicium* (D7v): 'ille satis seipsum arguet philautiae, temeritatis, et ignorantiae, ne dicam infidelitatis.' *Philautia* ist Neolatein.

[56] Blanckaert, *De retributione iustorum* (D8v): 'Deum Opt.[imum] Max.[imum] [...].' 'Peccatum vero primum hominis [...] mortem, et cum ea andriam malorum inuexit.' Blanckaert spielt an auf das Lustspiel des Menander über ein Mädchen aus Andros, das Terenz nachdichtete. Die Ausgabe des lateinischen Texts in Straßburg um 1470 und die deutsche Übersetzung in Straßburg 1499 belegen die Aufmerksamkeit, die dies Lustspiel im deutschen Sprachraum schon geraume Zeit vor Blanckaerts Schrift gefunden hatte.

[57] Blanckaert dürfte einerseits das Erzstift Köln meinen, wenn er sich als 'ciuis Christianae Reipublicae' bezeichnet, andererseits im Anschluß an Augustinus auch die 'civitas Dei' im Gegensatz zur 'civitas diaboli'. Spricht er doch wenig später im Widmungsbrief davon, daß er mitten unter den Bürgern des 'Christlichen Reiches' sicher kämpfe (A4v: 'inter medios ciues Christianae Reipublicae securus pugno'). Nicht zugänglich war mir leider die maschinenschriftlich vorliegende Straßburger Habilitationsschrift, auf die mich Herr Kollege Hansgeorg Molitor (Düsseldorf) freundlicherweise hinwies: Gérald Chaix, *De la cité chrétienne à la métropole catholique. Vie religieuse et conscience civique à Cologne au XVIe siècle* (Straßburg 1994).

[58] 'Dies sind das Urteil und die Einschätzung des Johannes Calvin in seinem Büchlein, dem er den Titel 'Ermahnung über die Reliquien' gab. Als ich es zu lesen begann, sagte mir sein Plan auf den ersten Anschein, wie man so sagt, zu, und ich billigte sein Vorhaben, weil er wie wir auch zu wünschen schien, daß eine Reinigung der wahren und echten Reliquien von den untergeschobenen und verfälschten stattfinde. Als ich aber weiter las, da witterte ich nicht bloß, sondern da tastete ich gleichsam blind mit der Hand, sein Wirken gehe dahin, seine listigen Bestrebungen richteten sich darauf, seine Bemühungen gingen dahin, der Heiligen [*Diuorum*] Reliquien, Dienst, Verehrung völlig aufzuheben und zu ruinieren: Da hielt ich es für mit den Pflichten eines Bürgers des Christlichen Gemeinwesens nicht vereinbar, angesichts eines so offenkundigen Übels, das den Bürgern Verderben bringen konnte, Augen oder Mund geschlossen zu halten. Höre ich doch, der Mann genieße bei den Seinen große Autorität und Wertschätzung, so daß sie sich nicht scheuten, ihn unserem höchst gelehrten Sadoleto gegenüberzustellen, und auch die lüsternen Ohren der Unsren streiche er mit den Schmeicheleien seiner Worte. Desto mehr ist von ihm zu befürchten, doppelt

Humanistische Stilmittel beherrscht Blanckaert, daran kann kein Zweifel sein. Doch macht ihn sein humanistischer Zungenschlag auch schon zum Humanisten? Bemühen sich doch von 1530 an nicht allein Humanisten, sondern auch scholastische Theologen, klassisches Latein zu schreiben.[59] Meint man also überhaupt zu einer Entscheidung kommen zu sollen, meint man bestimmen zu sollen, wo denn eigentlich Blanckaerts Herz schlägt, so kann kaum seine Gewandtheit im Ausdruck allein den Durchschlag geben. Es gibt ja in der Mitte des 16. Jahrhunderts durchaus auch andere Menschen, deren eigentliche Liebe der scholastischen Theologie gilt, die durch Klassiker-Zitate mit mehr oder weniger Erfolg zeigen wollen, daß sie imstande sind, auch auf dem Feld der humanistischen Konkurrenten Lorbeeren zu erringen,[60] ja das Argumentieren mit humanistischen Slogans kann damals geradezu irreführend werden.[61] Maßgeblich dafür, ob Blanckaert ein Humanist genannt zu werden verdient, muß wohl sein, wofür er sich im Falle eines Konflikts zwischen scholastischer Theologie und humanistischer Schulung entscheidet.[62]

In Blanckaerts Schriften finden sich Hinweise auf zwei solche Konflikte. Es geht dabei um seine Einstellung gegenüber Calvin und gegenüber Cicero.

kann er die Unseren hintergehen, weil zur Beredsamkeit auch noch Autorität hinzutritt.' Blanckaert, *Iudicium*, ep. dedicatoria (A3v/A4r).

[59] Vgl. Rummel, *The Humanist-Scholastic Debate*, 11: 'After 1530 especially, style becomes meaningless as an indicator, because classicizing Latin was increasingly becoming the norm in scholarly writing.' Mit Blanckaert vergleichbar durch die auch bei ihnen zu beobachtende Synthese von gut altgläubiger theologischer Position und humanistischer Schulung sind die etwa gleichzeitigen französischen Prediger Jean Le Gaigny (1495-1549), Bibliothekar des Königs von Frankreich und Kanzler der Universität, Claude Guilliaud (1493-1551), Kanoniker und theologischer Lehrer an der Kathedrale von Autun, Etienne Paris (1495-1561), Dominikaner-Provinzial und Weihbischof von Rouen und Orléans, François Le Picart (1504-56), Kanoniker und Dekan von St.-Germain l'Auxerrois. Vgl. dazu Taylor, 'The Influence of Humanism.' Kennzeichnend sind etwa Urteile wie: 'Gaigny used humanistic techniques to buttress Catholic doctrine' (123); 'Simplicity of form, admiration for learning, and openness to new ideas coexisted with the rather unhumanistic ability to preside and preach at the burning of a heretic' (über Guilliaud, 124); 'Paris's homilies bear the unmistakable imprint of humanism, and the elegance of his style is something new in French popular preaching' (125); 'Le Picart exemplifies, in my view, the humanistic non-humanist [...] his attitude toward humanism reveals a deep ambivalence. Too often he had observed the humanistic association with Protestantism [...]' (132). Meinem Kollegen Wim Janse aus Leiden danke ich für den Hinweis auf diesen Aufsatz, der nach Abschluß meines Manuskripts erschien.

[60] Vgl. Rummel, *The Humanist-Scholastic Debate*, 13: 'Thus we find scholastics quoting classical authors to show that they were not as innocent of the New Learning as their opponents depicted them; and humanists using syllogisms to prove that they too knew how to use dialectical reasoning [...] More often than not, however, cross-over attempts remain amateurish and the 'impostor' is promptly unmasked by the opponent.'

[61] Vgl. Rummel, *The Humanist-Scholastic Debate*, 13: 'More confusing is the appropriation – or rather misappropriation – of humanistic slogans by scholastics during a period of internal reform that took place in the early sixteenth century.'

[62] Man vergleiche etwa Rummel, *The Humanist-Scholastic Debate*, 14: 'Thus the cultural affiliation of a writer should be determined by means of probing his attitude and searching for a consistent pattern and sustained views.'

Blanckaert betrachtet Calvin einerseits als einen beredten Mann. Das emp-
fiehlt ihn. Bei seinen Anhängern genießt er große Autorität und Wertschätzung.[63] Er kann einschmeichelnd formulieren, er ist so beredt, daß seine Anhänger sich nicht scheuen, ihn 'unserem' hochgelehrten Sadoleto entgegen-
zustellen.[64] Als Gelehrter ist Calvin hoch zu schätzen. Er könnte Erhebliches
leisten, wenn er nur gut altgläubig wäre. Doch so gut sein Latein auch sein
mag, der Mann ist ein Ketzer.

> Daß [Calvin] in der lateinischen Sprache erfahren ist, bezeugen die sehr vielen
> Arbeiten, die er Nachtstunden abgerungen hat, in solchem Maße, daß ich den
> Verlust eines vom Glück so begünstigten Geistes betrauere, der, hätte er sich den
> wahren, christlichen Gegenständen zugewandt, ohne Zweifel in Herrlichkeit
> unsterblich geworden wäre, während er nun wahrscheinlich in ewiger Schande
> sein wird.[65]

Als Angehöriger der Gemeinschaft der Freunde humanistischer Studien, der er
auch sein will, betrauert Blanckaert, daß Calvin sich außerhalb des Christlichen Gemeinwesens gestellt hat, zu dem er sich in erster Linie rechnet.

In der zweiten Schrift, die in seinem Büchlein enthalten ist, der *Oratio
[prima] de Retributione Iustorum [statim a morte]*, führt Blanckaert gleich
nach Zitaten aus Augustinus und Chrysostomus zwar Ciceros Schrift *Somnium Scipionis* als Beleg dafür an, daß die Seelen gleich nach dem Tode des
Leibes gen Himmel fahren:

> Denn es ist auch durch Übereinstimmung der heidnischen Philosophen ganz
> allgemein akzeptiert, daß die Seelen tüchtiger sterblicher Menschen, die die
> Götter aus dem Körper hier gleichsam als aus ihrem Kerker hervorgerufen
> haben, sofort nach dem Tode gen Himmel ziehen. Das zeigte der ältere Scipio
> dem jüngeren laut Cicero wie in einem Traum.[66]

Es folgt ein Zitat aus Ciceros *Somnium Scipionis* von 14 Zeilen im Druck.
Andererseits aber qualifiziert Blanckaert gleich darauf Cicero als einen gottlosen Autor ab:

---

[63] Blanckaert, *Iudicium* (A4r), siehe Zitat bei Anm. 58.

[64] Blanckaert, *Iudicium* (A4r, wie oben bei den Anm.en 52 und 58).

[65] Blanckaert, *Iudicium* (B4v): 'Nam linguae Latine peritum esse testantur plurima [!] eius lucubrationes, ita ut doleam tam foelicis ingenii iacturam, quod si ad res ueras et Christianas se con-
tulisset, haud dubium immortale futurum erat in gloria, quod fortasse aeternum erit cum ignominia.'

[66] Blanckaert, *De retributione iustorum* (E3v/E4r): 'Est enim etiam gentilium philosophorum
consensu receptissimum, animas mortalium et fortium virorum, quas dii hinc e corpore uelut ex
carcere euocarunt, statim a morte in coelum abire. Quod uelut per somnium apud Ciceronem Seni-
or Iuniori Scipioni indicauit.'

Ich könnte dazu noch mehr anführen sowohl aus Cicero als aus Platon und aus den übrigen Philosophen, um die Seligkeit der Seelen der Heiligen zu verteidigen, was nicht wenig zur Sache beitragen würde. Doch die Rücksicht auf mein Vorhaben und auf mein Fach ruft mich anderswohin. Als einer, der die christliche Lehre durch Beweise stützt, will ich Zeugnisse von *Christen* heranziehen, damit nicht die Meinung von Gottlosen [*infideles*], der Aussage von Glaubenden [*credentes*] und Gläubigen [*fideles*] beigemischt, das Licht der evangelischen Wahrheit eher verdunkle als erhelle.[67]

Wiewohl er humanistisches Latein schreibt, will er doch nicht den Eindruck erwecken, in erster Linie ein Vertreter der *bonae litterae* zu sein. Erika Rummel hat die hier formulierte Befürchtung treffend als 'fear of pagan contamination' bezeichnet.[68]

Diese bewußte Stellungnahme beweist meiner Ansicht nach deutlich, daß Nikolaus Blanckaert zwar ein humanistisch geschulter scholastischer Theologe ist, aber im Fall eines Konflikts zwischen paganer und christlicher Sicht des Menschen keine pagane humanistische Anthropologie vertritt. In Nikolaus Blanckaert behält der scholastische Theologe dann die Oberhand, wenn es zu einem Wertkonflikt kommt. In dem Augenblick, in dem Blanckaert sich entscheiden muß, ob er in erster Linie ein Bürger des Christlichen Gemeinwesens oder des Reiches der Gelehrten sein möchte, macht er klar, wo seine Präferenzen liegen. Auch für ihn treffen die Beobachtungen von Cornelis Augustijn zu, daß 'das Verhältnis zwischen Christentum und Antike der neuralgische Punkt' ist, an dem sich entscheidet, ob jemand als Humanist bezeichnet werden darf,[69] und daß von Bedeutung ist, wie jemand sich selbst versteht.[70] So richtig Cicero nach Blanckaerts Meinung auch formulieren mag, er vermag eben doch nichts Entscheidendes dazu beizutragen, die 'evangelische Wahrheit' zu erweisen. Blanckaert wählt auch nicht die Möglichkeit, Cicero zuzubilligen, er habe durch seine Schrift auf das in Christus kommende Reich Gottes vorbereitet.[71]

---

[67] Blanckaert, *De retributione iustorum* (E4r): 'Possem huc plura adducere ex eodem Cicerone et Platone caeterisque Philosophis pro tuenda Sanctarum animarum foelicitate, quaeque ad rem non parum facerent, sed alio me uocat instituti et professionis meae ratio: quique Christianum dogma astruo, Christianorum testimoniis uti uolui, ne infidelium opinio credentium et fidelium sententiae permixta, Euangelicae ueritatis lucem obscuraret potius quam illustraret.'

[68] Rummel, 'Et cum theologo bella poeta gerit', 720.

[69] Vgl Augustijn, 'Calvin und der Humanismus', 129: 'Kernpunkt des Humanismus ist m. E. eher die Frage: Was haben Christentum und Antike, *sacrae litterae* und *bonae litterae*, mit einander zu tun? Gibt es überhaupt ein Verhältnis zwischen beiden, oder stehen beide unversöhnt nebeneinander?'

[70] Augustijn, 'Humanisten auf dem Scheideweg zwischen Luther und Erasmus', 157: 'Wie hat der Betreffende sich selber gesehen, empfunden? In welchen Verhältnissen sah er die eigene Arbeit, welche Freunde und Feinde hatte er, wer war gegebenenfalls sein Leitbild?'

[71] Vgl. Augustijn, 'Calvin und der Humanismus', 141: 'Demgegenüber steht das Geschichtsbild der ganzen humanistischen Bewegung, nach dem Gott in der Antike zumindest eine Vorberei-

Ich formuliere abschließend, welche Kriterien meiner Meinung nach geeignet sind, festzustellen, ob ein scholastischer Theologe der Mitte des 16. Jahrhunderts zugleich rundheraus ein Humanist genannt zu werden verdient.

Ich halte es nicht für zureichend, von seiner Kenntnis der Werke antiker Autoren auszugehen. Setzte man ausschließlich dies Kriterium ein, dann müßte man schon *den* im Unterschied zu scholastischen Theologen einen Humanisten nennen, dessen Kenntnis und Verwendung der Werke antiker Autoren diejenige übersteigt, die auch schon bei scholastischen Autoren üblich war. Von einem Humanisten erwarte ich nicht bloß eine gewisse Kenntnis, sondern auch eine bestimmte Einstellung.

Ich halte es auch nicht für zureichend, von der Methode auszugehen, die ein solcher Autor gebraucht. Ginge man von der verwendeten Methode als dem entscheidenden Kriterium aus, so könnte man *den* einen Humanisten nennen, der sich eine bestimmte philologische Fertigkeit angeeignet hat und der sie zum besseren Verständnis biblischer Texte und Kirchenvätertexte gebraucht.

Für angemessener halte ich es vielmehr, die Wertschätzung antiker heidnischer Philosophen (in unserem Falle Ciceros) und gewandten humanistischen Formulierens (in unserem Falle Calvins) im Verhältnis zur 'evangelischen Wahrheit' zum Maßstab zu machen. Geht man so vor, dann muß man auch selbst zu werten versuchen: welche Rolle spielt die Wertschätzung der antiken heidnischen Autoren und humanistischer Gelehrsamkeit im Verhältnis zum sonstigen Bezugssystem des Autors? Ich plädiere damit für eine inhaltliche Füllung des Begriffs 'Humanist', die eine bestimmte Wertschätzung der nicht-christlichen Antike einschließt.

Die Theologie des Nikolaus Blanckaert, soweit eine eigene Theologie in seinen knappen eigenen Beiträgen erkennbar wird, scheint mir nicht in diesem Sinne humanistisch geprägt zu sein. Weder sein latinisierter Name noch auch die termini, die er humanistischem Sprachgebrauch entleiht, weder seine Kirchenväterzitate noch seine Ansätze zu philologischer Methode, weder sein gepflegtes Latein und seine gewandte Rhetorik noch sein Zitat aus Cicero machen Nikolaus Blanckaert zum Humanisten. Zu Recht fehlt meiner Meinung nach sein Name in den beiden gehaltvollen Aufsätzen von Kristeller[72] und IJsewijn,[73] die die Forschung entscheidend gefördert haben. Der Hochschullehrer aus dem Karmelitenorden zieht eine scharfe Trennungslinie zwischen heidnischen oder ketzerischen Autoren einerseits, christlichen Autoren andererseits. Wer aber der heidnischen Antike nicht einmal eine irgendwie

tung auf das in Christus kommende Reich Gottes gegeben hat, meistens aber die Antike einen eigenständigen Platz im Walten Gottes über die Welt empfängt.'

[72] Kristeller, 'The contribution of religious orders to Renaissance thought and learning'.
[73] IJsewijn, 'The Coming of Humanism to the Low Countries'.

vorbereitende Rolle auf dem Weg zum Heil zuerkennt, den kann man meiner Meinung nach nicht zu Recht einen Humanisten nennen.

C.M.A. CASPERS

MAGISTER CONSENSUS. WESSEL GANSFORT (1419-1489) UND DIE GEISTLICHE KOMMUNION[*]

In der Geschichtsschreibung über die Abendmahlsauffassungen innerhalb der Reformation ist Wessel Gansfort immer mehr zu einem 'Schemen' geworden. Die Auffassung, Wessel sei auf diesem Gebiet für Luther, der für ihn große Bewunderung hatte, ein Inspirator gewesen, ist schon seit Jahrzehnten überholt; ebenso die Auffassung, er habe Zwingli dazu gebracht, die Einsetzungsworte 'hoc est corpus meum' zu interpretieren als 'hoc significat corpus meum'.[1] Dagegen ist Wessels Festhalten an der Transsubstantiationslehre weit entfernt von Zwinglis Charakterisierung dieser Lehre als bäurisch, lächerlich und ehrfurchtslos.[2] Und wurde Wessel am Anfang der achziger Jahre wegen seiner Auffassung über die geistliche Kommunion noch als (Mit-)Wegbereiter der Abendmahlsauffassung der Wiedertäufer betrachtet,[3] so wurde er in späteren Studien auch auf diesem Gebiet als Repräsentant spätmittelalterlichen Gedankengutes gekennzeichnet.[4]

Dieser Beitrag, dessen Titel der gerade gegebenen Zusammenfassung zu widerstreiten scheint, besteht aus vier Teilen. Zunächst will ich näher auf das spätmittelalterliche Gedankengut eingehen, vor allem auf die Stellung, die die Auffassungen über das Sakrament der Eucharistie darin einnahmen. Nach einigen Nuancierungen möchte ich dann aufs Neue Wessels Stellung innerhalb des genannten Gedankengutes aufzeigen: Geht Wessel darin restlos auf, oder kann doch etwas über eine gewisse Eigenständigkeit, evtl. etwas 'Richtungweisendes' in seinen Auffassungen gesagt werden? Ausgangspunkt hierfür ist sein Kommentar zum Vater Unser und zur darin enthaltenen Bitte um Brot. Vor diesem Hintergrund möchte ich Wessels Auffassungen dann noch sowohl zur protestantischen als auch zur

---

[*] Aus dem Niederländischen von Gabriele Merks-Leinen, M.A.

[1] Vgl. Van Rhijn, *Wessel Gansfort*, 230-63, wo einerseits ein direkter Einfluß von Wessel auf Luther bereits geleugnet wird (vgl. bes. 247), andererseits Wessels Auffassung von der geistlichen Kommunion noch als Quelle der Inspiration für das spätere Abendmahlsverständnis Zwinglis angesehen wird (vgl. bes. 261-3).

[2] Zwingli, 'De vera et falsa religione' (März 1525) in *Sämtliche Werke*, 590-912, bes. 787; Kist, 'Nog iets over den Nederlandschen oorsprong der zoogenaamde Zwingliaansche Avondmaalsleer', bes. 393-5.

[3] Voolstra, *Het woord is vlees geworden*, 89.

[4] Neben Beiträgen anderer Autoren vgl. bes. Augustijn, 'Wessel Gansfort's rise to celebrity'; vgl. auch Janse, *Albert Hardenberg als Theologe*, 278-83.

katholischen Spiritualität in den Niederlanden des 16. Jahrhunderts in Beziehung setzen.

Die eucharistische Frömmigkeit im Spätmittelalter

Bereits am Anfang des dreizehnten Jahrhunderts entstand innerhalb der westlichen Christenheit, vor allem in Kreisen frommer Frauen, eine Frömmigkeit, bei der die Person Jesu Christi, so wie sie im Sakrament der Eucharistie als gegenwärtig erfahren wurde, zentral stand. Die überlieferten Vitae vieler dieser Frauen, als auch ihre selbst verfaßten Bekenntnisse, zeigen, daß sich ihr Streben vor allem auf die Vereinigung der individuellen Seele mit Christus mit Hilfe des Sakramentes richtete. In vielen dieser Schriften wurde dankbar von den durch scholastische Autoren formulierten Auffassungen über die *praesentia realis* Gebrauch gemacht. Für diese frommen Frauen und ihre Geistesverwandten und für viele nach ihnen war die Kommunion die beste Art, sich während des irdischen Lebens schon auf irgendeine Weise mit Christus zu vereinigen.

Diese im Laufe des 13. Jahrhunderts voll entfaltete Spiritualität war ihrem Wesen nach eine Fortsetzung der ein Jahrhundert vorher aufgekommenen Spiritualität der Zisterzienser, als deren geistlicher Vater, sicher in Bezug auf die Eucharistie, Wilhelm von St.-Thierry betrachtet werden kann. Von Bedeutung waren vor allem die Implikationen seiner Interpretation, bzw. die innerhalb seines Umkreises, von einigen Äußerungen des Kirchenvaters Augustinus. Es geht hier um die Worte aus seinem 25. Traktat über das Johannesevangelium: 'Utquid paras dentes et ventrem? Crede et manducasti'[5] und aus den Confessiones die Worte: 'Cibus sum grandium; cresce, et manducabis me. Nec tu me in te mutabis, sicut cibum carnis tuae; sed tu mutaberis in me'.[6] Natürlich hatte man zur Zeit von Wilhelm schon jahrhundertelang über Augustinus' Worte nachgedacht, aber niemand vor ihm verknüpfte diese Worte so eng mit der von ihm vertretenen geistliche Kommunion. Darunter verstand Wilhelm eine geistliche Vereinigung mit Christus, die zwar durch das Sakrament der Eucharistie ermöglicht wird, die aber unabhängig von Liturgie, Zeit und Ort, geschehen kann und wofür das Verzehren der Hostie nicht wesentlich ist.[7]

Im Gegensatz zu dem, was die Geschichtsschreibung behauptet, blieb die geistliche Kommunion nicht auf Menschen mit einem religiösen 'Status'

---

[5] Zu Joh. 6, 28-30, vgl. Augustinus, *In Iohannis Evangelium Tractatus 124*, 254.

[6] *Confessionum libri*, 103-4; vgl. Caspers, *De eucharistische vroomheid*, 24 (n. 59).

[7] Wilhelm von St.-Thierry, *Meditaties*, 10, 119-21; vgl. Macy, *The Theologies of the Eucharist*, 96-8.

beschränkt.[8] Schon in der ersten Hälfte des 13. Jahrhunderts war die geistliche Kommunion, nach den Statuten des damaligen Bistums Cambrai, in die pastorale Praxis dieses Bistums integriert,[9] kurz danach im Bistum Lüttich, später, im 13. und 14. Jahrhundert, in den anderen Bistümern der westlichen Kirche.[10]

Mit durch den Platz, den dieses Sakrament in dieser Zeit für die Sterbestunde erhielt, genauer bei der Spendung des Viaticum ('Wegzehrung'),[11] galt es für das Empfinden der damaligen Christenheit als das 'Sakrament der Sakramente', oder einfach als 'das Sakrament'. Denselben Ehrentitel erhielt es von den Lehrmeistern der Kirche: Zwar ging von allen sieben von Christus eingesetzten Sakramenten die Gnadenwirkung aus, in einem aber, der Eucharistie, war Er auch selbst gegenwärtig.[12]

Neben der geistlichen Kommunion gab es noch die sogenannte sakramentale Kommunion, die durch den Genuß einer konsekrierten Hostie gekennzeichnet wurde. Je nach der Form unterschied man sogar drei verschiedene Arten des Kommunizierens:

a) die rein geistliche Kommunion;

b) die sowohl geistliche als auch sakramentale Kommunion;

c) die rein sakramentale Kommunion (sacramentum tantum).[13]

Der Intention nach gab es allerdings nur zwei Arten des Kommunizierens: die würdige Kommunion, die immer auch zugleich geistliche Kommunion ist (a und b), und die unwürdige Kommunion, die nur sakramental ist (c). Wenn man unwürdig kommunizierte, d.h. die Hostie genoß, ohne dabei in der geforderten geistlichen Verfassung zu sein, so 'ißt man sich' – nach den Worten von 1. Kor. 11, 29 – 'das Gericht'.

Wegen der großen mit ihr verbundenen Gefahr ('Gericht', d.h. 'ewige Verdammnis') war die sakramentale Kommunion im Spätmittelalter nie populär.[14] Der häufige Genuß der konsekrierten Hostie – ein- oder zweimal im Monat – war denen vorbehalten, die sich durch einen vorbildlichen Lebenswandel auszeichneten. Umgekehrt wünschten die, die so vorbildlich erscheinen wollten, dies auch gerne durch eine häufige sakramentale Kommunion

---

[8] Schlette, *Die Lehre von der geistlichen Kommunion*, 214; Caspers, *De eucharistische vroomheid*, 95-6.

[9] *Les statuts synodaux français du XIIIe siècle*, 42.

[10] Caspers, *De eucharistische vroomheid*, 95-9.

[11] Caspers, *De eucharistische vroomheid*, 79-87.

[12] Kinn, *The Pre-Eminence of the Eucharist among the Sacraments*.

[13] Diese dreifache Unterscheidung machte als erster Anselmus von Laon (†1117); vgl. Geiselmann, *Die Eucharistielehre der Vorscholastiker*, 437; *Catechismus Romanus*, 269-70; Troelstra, *Stof en methode der catechese*, 290-1.

[14] Vgl. Ripelin von Stratsburg, *Compendium totius theologicae veritatis*, 353; Dirc von Delft, *Tafel van den Kersten Ghelove*, 453; Caspers, *De eucharistische vroomheid*, 207.

zu illustrieren, was ihnen nicht selten das Odium der Scheinheiligkeit ein-
brachte.[15]

Über die wirkliche Gegenwart, die verschiedenen Arten zu kommunizieren, die Bedeutung dieses Sakramentes für die Vereinigung der Seele der
Gläubigen mit Christus und für das Erlangen des Ewigen Lebens gab es in
der Zeit vom 13. bis zum 15. Jahrhundert innerhalb der westlichen Kirche
einen breiten Konsens.[16] In Unterricht und Predigt wurden stark die
Bedingungen betont, die alle erfüllen mußten, um würdig kommunizieren zu
können: dem wahren Glauben und vor allem der kirchlichen Lehre über die
wirkliche Gegenwart anhängen; ein reines Gewissen haben, was bedeutete,
daß man rechtzeitig zur Beichte zu gehen hatte; und einen geistlichen Hunger oder 'minne' zu verspüren, um sich mit Hilfe des Sakramentes mit
Christus zu vereinigen.

Um diesen Bedingungen zu genügen – und dies galt sicher für die sakramentale Kommunion, zu der man seit dem IV. Laterankonzil verpflichtet
war zum Beweis der Zugehörigkeit zur sichtbaren Kirche[17] – mußten die
Gläubigen sich gründlich vorbereiten. Im allgemeinen galt das Überdenken
oder sogar Miterleben des Leidens Christi als beste Vorbereitung. Nicht
selten empfingen die, die bekannt waren für ihre Hinwendung zum Sakrament und später als 'eucharistische Heilige' berühmt wurden – wie z.B. in
den Niederlanden Liduina von Schiedam – die Stigmata.[18] Die unzähligen
Kunstwerke, die sich auf Aspekte des Leidens oder auf das Leiden Christi
beziehen und die uns aus dem Spätmittelalter erhalten geblieben sind, zeugen von der damaligen Christenheit als von einem *orbis eucharisticus*.[19]

Das beabsichtigte Ergebnis all' dieser Bemühungen waren die 'Früchte
der Eucharistie'. Diese Früchte wurden in sog. 'Früchtenreihen', aber auch
in anderen Schriften auf vielfältige Weise aufgezählt, in wechselnder Rei-
henfolge und Zahl.[20] Die bekanntesten Reihen, wie z.B. die, die den Namen
des Bischofs Guiard de Laon von Cambrai tragen, zählten, inspiriert durch

---

[15] Caspers, *De eucharistische vroomheid*, 220-1 (über Ruusbroec und Dirc van Delft).

[16] Burr, *Eucharistic Presence and Conversion*, 8-15. Macy, *The Theologies of the Eucharist*,
139-40, zeigt allerdings, daß Theologen des 12. Jahrhunderts und spätere, obwohl im allgemeinen sich dieses Konsenses sehr bewußt, sehr verschiedene Arbeitsweisen anwendeten.

[17] *Decrees of the Ecumenical Councils*, 245 ('Omnis utriusque sexus'). Im Spätmittelalter
galt für Laien viermal im Jahr als ein akzeptiertes Maximum für den Empfang der sakramentalen Kommunion: an Ostern, Pfingsten, Weihnachten, und Allerheiligen, später auch an Fron-
leichnam, vgl. Browe, *Die häufige Kommunion im Mittelalter*, 3-44; Caspers, *De eucharistische vroomheid*, 47.

[18] Die Stigmata der Liduina werden übrigens in ihren ältesten *vitae* noch nicht genannt, vgl.
Caspers, *De eucharistische vroomheid*, 247.

[19] Vgl. Caspers, 'Het laatmiddeleeuwse passiebeeld'.

[20] Caspers, *De eucharistische vroomheid*, 192; vgl. *Katechismus der katholischen Kirche*,
381-4 (Nr. 1391-1401): 'Die Früchte der Kommunion'.

den in Off. 22, 2 beschriebenen Lebensbaum, zwölf Früchte. Guiard unterscheidet die folgenden, z.T. inhaltlich einander überlappenden, Früchte:[21] Gesundheit und Reinheit der Seele (durch Sünden wird die Seele verwundet, durch das Sakrament wird sie wieder geheilt); Befreiung von (Sünden)-schuld; Schutz gegen Versuchungen; Reinigung von falschen Gedanken und Begierden; das Zurückgewinnen von Dingen, die der Seele verloren gegangen waren; Stärkung des Herzens der Gläubigen, sodaß diese besser imstande sind, den Versuchungen zu widerstehen; Veränderung in 'bessere Dinge': während gewöhnliche Speise sich im Körper dessen, der sie ißt, verändert, verändert sich der, der diese geistliche Nahrung ißt, selbst (vgl. den oben genannten Abschnitt aus den *Confessiones* des Augustinus); neues Leben für die Seele; Ausgerichtetsein auf den Willen Gottes und nicht auf das Verlangen der Sinne; Aufnahme in die 'Bruderschaft vom Hl. Geist'; ein reines und unbeschwertes Herz; eine gute Vorbereitung auf das Ewige Leben.

Zusammenfassend kann man die Frömmigkeit, die mit dem Konsens über die Eucharistie zusammenhing, charakterisieren als 'innerliches Vorbereiten auf die Kommunion, und innerliches Vollziehen und Verarbeiten der Kommunion'. Diese Charakterisierung widerspricht der in der Geschichte immer wiederholten Rede, daß die eucharistische Frömmigkeit im Spätmittelalter sich sozusagen auf das Anschauen der konsekrierten Hostie beschränkte, wobei dieser Tätigkeit allerlei magische Effekte zugeschrieben wurden (die sog. 'Augenkommunion').[22] Diese hartnäckig sich haltende Überlieferung wird oft an die ebenso unrechte und in kirchengeschichtlichen Handbüchern noch immer manifeste Auffassung gekoppelt, im Spätmittelalter habe man der Kommunion eine sog. *ex opere operato*-Wirkung zuerkannt, bzw. eine automatische heilsame Wirkung.

Zwar wirkten den scholastischen Theologen zufolge alle sieben Sakramente *ex opere operato* – d.h. daß ihre Gnadenwirkung ausschließlich vom Willen Gottes und Seiner Liebe zum Menschen abhing, und nicht von den Verdiensten derer, die ein Sakrament spendeten oder empfingen – aber das hieß nicht, daß sie davon ausgingen, daß ein Sakrament für jeden dieselbe Wirkung hatte. Im Gegenteil, ihren Auffassungen nach verlieh Gott Seine Gnade immer auf eine Weise, die zur Person der Empfänger paßte. In Bezug auf das Sakrament der Eucharistie impliziert dies, daß der Transsubstantiation in der Messe ein *ex opere operato*-Charakter zuerkannt wurde (die Veränderung der Opfergaben geschah ungeachtet dem Stand der Sünde, in dem sich der Zelebrant oder die anwesenden Gläubigen befanden), der

---

[21] Caspers, *De eucharistische vroomheid*, 193-5.
[22] Caspers, *De eucharistische vroomheid*, 217; 271-2; idem, 'The Western Church during the late Middle Ages', bes. 84 und 96.

Teilnahme an diesem Sakrament, der Kommunion allerdings ein *ex opere operantis*-Charakter (wohl abhängig vom Stand der Sünde des Zelebranten, bzw. Kommunikanten).[23]

Einige Nuancierungen

Wenn es auch, wie gesagt, einen Konsens gab, so kann ein Phänomen, das einen so wichtigen Platz im Leben so vieler einnahm, natürlich unmöglich eine 'Einheitswurst' genannt werden. Selbstverständlich gab es Abstufungen und deshalb müßen Nuancierungen angebracht werden. Im allgemeinen kann man behaupten, daß in der Frömmigkeitsliteratur, die in der Periode des späten Mittelalters verfaßt wurde, in Bezug auf Kleriker, Ordensfrauen und 'betrachtende' Laien viel Wert auf die unmittelbare Begegnung der individuellen Gläubigen mit Gott mit Hilfe des Sakraments gelegt wurde und weniger auf die Vermittler-Rolle des Priester-Zelebranten und (*ipso facto*) die institutionelle Kirche. Für die 'gewöhnlichen' Gläubigen lag der Schwerpunkt genau auf der anderen Seite: In den für diese Gruppe zusammengestellten Predigten und Unterweisungen ist der Aspekt der Begegnung zwar noch feststellbar, die Betonung liegt aber auf der endgültigen Vereinigung der Seele mit Christus nach dem irdischen Leben; eine Vereinigung, die man der Kirche und ihren Priestern, den Vermittlern des Sakramentes, verdankt.[24]

Wichtig für das Thema dieses Beitrags sind auch zwei Fragen, die sich denen sozusagen von selbst stellten, die sich auf betrachtende Weise mit dem Sakrament beschäftigten.

a) Die mit den beinahe endlosen allegorischen Erklärungen der Schrift Vertrauten standen irgendwann fast unvermeidlich vor der Frage, ob die Worte 'hoc est corpus meum' dasselbe bedeuteten wie 'hoc significat corpus meum' (vgl. oben über Zwingli).

b) Wenn die sakramentale Kommunion mit so vielen Risiken verbunden ist, warum soll man sie dann nicht ganz lassen?

Der ersten Frage begegnen wir z.B. in der neunten *distinctio* (über das Sakrament des Leibes und Blutes Christi) der Beispielesammlung *Dialogus miraculorum*, die der Zisterzienser Cäsarius von Heisterbach zwischen 1219 und 1223 zusammengestellt hat. In einem der Beispiele, die von der

---

[23] Thomas Aquinas, *Summa Theologica XXIX*, 493-8; 518-9; idem, *Summa Theologica XXX*, 532; Schillebeeckx, 'Sacrament', bes. 4190 und 4199; idem, *De sacramentele heilseconomie*, 639-63; Caspers, *De eucharistische vroomheid*, 31-2 (n. 93); 272-3 (vor allem n. 11).

[24] Caspers, *De eucharistische vroomheid*, 224-7; vgl. Macy, *The Theologies of the Eucharist*, 127.

würdigen Kommunion handeln, gesteht ein gelehrter Kanoniker der Kölner Andreaskirche in bestürzender Weise ein, daß er beim Feiern seiner Messen immer davon ausgegangen war, daß nach der Konsekration der Leib und das Blut Christi nur auf symbolische Weise gegenwärtig seien (*signum et repraesentatio*). Cäsarius will mit diesem Beispiel deutlich machen, daß es sich hier zwar um eine ketzerische Vorstellung handelt, daß diese aber guten Glaubens bei diesem Kanoniker entstanden war und daß Gelehrtheit offensichtlich nicht vor Irrtümern schützt.[25] Erst das hartnäckige Festhalten an einer symbolischen Sakramentenauffassung, auch noch nachdem man auf die orthodoxe 'metabolische' Auffassung der Kirche verwiesen wurde, machten Individuen und Gruppen zu Dissidenten.[26]

Auch die zweite Frage behandelt Cäsarius in der genannten *distinctio*.[27] In dem 'Dialog' zwischen Novize und Mönch stellt der erste die Frage, warum so selten kommuniziert wird. Nach Meinung des Mönchs ziehen manche sich aus Demut zurück, weil sie sich selbst für unwürdig erachten; andere sind zu gleichgültig oder wagen es wegen einer sündigen Vergangenheit nicht, zur Kommunion zu gehen. Dann erzählt er über einige Erscheinungen (der Maria, bzw. des Christuskindes) bei einem Laienbruder, die deutlich machen sollen, daß die eigene Unwürdigkeit nicht als Entschuldigungsgrund dafür gebraucht werden darf, die sakramentale Kommunion zu unterlassen. Streng genommen ist ja niemand würdig genug, um unbeschwert zu kommunizieren, aber man sollte es doch aus dem Bewußtsein heraus tun, daß Gottes Liebe größer ist als Seine Strenge.[28] Auch in den Predigten des 15. Jahrhunderts wurde darauf hingewiesen, daß niemand es aus falschem Sündenbewußtsein unterlassen darf, (sakramental) zu kommunizieren,[29] und daß umgekehrt niemand denken darf, daß er die Würdigkeit zu kommunizieren eigenem Verdienst zurechnen könne. 'Denn hätte ein Mensch vierzig hundert tausend Jahre lang jeden Tag Buße getan und gute Werke, dann wäre er noch nicht würdig, den Leib unseres Herrn Jesus Christus zu empfangen, der wahrhaftig Gott und Mensch ist.'[30]

---

[25] Caesarius Heisterbacensis, *Dialogus Miraculorum II*, 209-10; Caspers, *De eucharistische vroomheid*, 149-50.

[26] Vgl. Spruyt, 'Laat-middeleeuwse ketterijen en de vroege hervorming in de Nederlanden'.

[27] Vgl. bzgl. des 12. Jahrhunderts, Macy, *The Theologies of the Eucharist*, 128.

[28] *Dialogus Miraculorum*, 197-9; Caspers, *De eucharistische vroomheid*, 147-8.

[29] Caspers, *De eucharistische vroomheid*, 173.

[30] Johannes van Namen, 'Een capittel van onderscheyde weder het beter es als men ten heileghen sacramente gaen sal grote sueticheit hebbe oft niet'. *Hier beghint een sympel voer redene vanden navolghenden boeke. Men sal weten dat in desen boeke staen xli sermoenen beghinnende vander heiligher glorioser maghet sinte Katherinen ende alsoe vervolghende diaeromme na dat die daghe volghen* (Gent, Universiteitsbibliotheek, Hs. 902, 178v-179r; Zitat auf 179r); Caspers, *De eucharistische vroomheid*, 175. Vgl. Molenaar, *Werken van de Heilige Geertruid van Helfta*, 272-3 (*De heraut van de goddelijke liefde* 3, 18).

Auch diese Beispiele aus der Exempel- und Frömmigkeitsliteratur passen gut zu dem, was große Theologen über die zwar gefährliche, wohl aber unersetzliche sakramentale Kommunion sagen.[31] Zweifellos war die angesehendste Schrift, in der erklärt wurde, daß es besser sei, die sakramentale Kommunion aus Liebe zu Gott zu empfangen als sie aus Furcht vor Ihm zu unterlassen, der Traktat *Esurientes implevit bonis* aus dem *Collectorium super Magnificat* des bedeutendsten kirchlichen Autors, den das 15. Jahrhundert kannte, des Johannes Gerson.[32] Eine vorbildliche Rezeption dieses Traktats finden wir in einer um 1435 anonym verfaßten mittelalterlichen (westflämischen) Schrift, die von ihrem Herausgeber, D.A. Stracke, den Titel *Devote samenspraak over de veelvuldige Communie* ('Demütiges Zwiegespräch über die häufige Kommunion') erhalten hat.[33] In diesem 'Zwiegespräch' führt eine 'demütige Tochter' ein Gespräch mit ihrem Beichtvater über die Vor- und Nachteile der häufigen sakramentalen Kommunion. Die Tochter äußert eine Reihe Beschwerden, die man gegen diese Art zu kommunizieren hegen könnte, die ihr Beichtvater jedoch systematisch widerlegt. Die Tochter leitet das Kernstück des Dialogs ein, indem sie darauf beharrt, es sei gefährlicher, zur Kommunion zu gehen, als es nicht zu tun. Wenn die jährliche (Oster)kommunion nicht eine Verpflichtung wäre, würde sie auch diese unterlassen. Der Beichtvater meint hingegen, daß Furcht ein schlechter Ratgeber sei, und daß, wer so denkt wie seine geistliche Tochter, Gott beleidige, weil er nicht auf Seine Barmherzigkeit vertraue. Über diese Schrift sei deutlichkeitshalber angemerkt, daß sie sich nicht an ein großes (sprich: Laien-) Publikum wendet, sondern an die, die zu einem bestimmten 'Stand' (hier: zu den Ordensfrauen) gehören.[34]

Wessel Gansfort über geistliche und sakramentale Kommunion

Im 14. und 15. Jahrhundert brachte man in zahlreichen Kommentaren zum Vater Unser die Brotbitte in Beziehung zur würdigen (normalerweise ausschließlich geistlichen) Kommunion.[35] So auch bei Wessel Gansfort in

---

[31] Z.B. Thomas Aquinas, *Summa Theologica XXX*, 233-4 (q. 80, art. 4, ad quartum).

[32] Gerson, *Oeuvres complètes*, VIII 376-455.

[33] *Devote samenspraak over de veelvuldige Communie*; zur Sprache gebracht u.a. durch Nouwens, *De veelvuldige H. Communie in geestelijke literatuur der Nederlanden*, 23.

[34] Vgl. auch Caspers, *De eucharistische vroomheid*, 221-2.

[35] Vgl. Bock, *Die Brotbitte des Vaterunsers*, 291. Einige mittelniederländische Autoren: Gheraert Appelmans (um 1300; vgl. Reypens, 'Gheraert Appelmans' glose op het Vaderons', bes. 96-101); der unbekannte Autor von 'Ene corte glose opt pater noster' (um 1350; vgl. *Middeleeuwsche Glose op het Pater en Ave*, 27); Dirc Coelde van Münster (†1515; vgl. Drees, *Der Christenspiegel des Dietrich Kolde von Münster*, 185; Caspers, *De eucharistische vroomheid*, 187-8).

seinem *Tractatus de oratione et modo orandi*. Während andere Autoren normalerweise die rein geistliche Kommunion und die sakramentale Kommunion (falls würdig empfangen) als das 'tägliche Brot' ansehen, stellt Wessel
in seinem Kommentar zur Brotbitte die geistliche und die sakramentale
Kommunion als Gegensätze dar (siehe Abb. III):[36]

– Die sakramentale Kommunion bringt ohne die geistliche keine Frucht
und führt dann sogar zum Tod (natürlich mit Verweis auf 1. Kor. 11); die
geistliche Kommunion dagegen ist immer fruchtbar und führt zum Leben.

– Die sakramentale Kommunion ist an Ort und Zeit gebunden und nur
bestimmten Personen erlaubt. Die geistliche Kommunion hat mit dem reinen
Glauben zu tun, der aus dem Herzen kommt, und kann immer und überall
vollzogen werden, unabhängig von Alter, Geschlecht oder Herkunft.

– Kurz: Die erste ist oft schädlich, die zweite immer heilsam.

Auf den ersten Blick scheint hier nicht viel los zu sein: Wessels Vorliebe für
die geistliche Kommunion, die er übrigens auch in seinem Traktat über die
Messe äußert,[37] kommt völlig mit der diesbezüglichen Sicht von Wilhelm
von St.-Thierry überein. Wessels Vorliebe für bestimmte Termini, wie das
'Wiederkäuen' der geistlichen Nahrung, stimmt sogar so sehr mit der Terminologie, die Wilhelm in einigen seiner *meditationes* gebraucht, überein

---

[36] Es wurde die folgende Ausgabe benutzt: Gansfort, *Tractatus de oratione et modo orandi*,
in der Bibliothek der Theologischen Fakultät Tilburg vorhanden (sign. PRE 107). Der Kommentar zur Brotbitte, in zehn *capitula* eingeteilt, nimmt die ff. [lxviii]r-[lxxvi]r ein; von
Bedeutung ist hier vor allem [lxxiii]v (=[lxxi]v)-[lxxii]v: 'Capitulum sextum. Quod nedum
spiritualiter manducatur caro filii hominis commemoratione credentis, sed et sacramentalis
manducatio non solum infructuosa, sed ad mortem est sine spirituali manducatione'. Die Gegenüberstellung von geistlicher und sakramentaler Kommunion ist am deutlichsten ausgearbei-
tet in dem Abschnitt [lxxii]v: 'Interest autem inter sacramentalem et spiritualem manducatio-
nem, quod illa sine ista infructuosa, imo ad mortem est, contra preceptum domini, hoc quocienscumque feceritis in mei memoriam facietis. Et Paulus. Quocienscumque panem hunc man-
ducabitis et calicem domini bibetis, mortem domini annunciabitis. Et non diiudicans corpus
domini, ad iudicium manducat. Et qui manducat indigne, reus erit corporis et sanguinis, non
diiudicans corpus domini. Spiritualis autem manducatio semper fructuosa est et ad vitam. Est
quoque spiritualis communio, et communio pietatis, aliquanto fecundior sacramentali, saltem in
hoc quod manducat et bibit. Illa quantum est in laicis manducat solum, nisi quia felici haustu
suppletur pace pietatis. Illa tempori et loco alligata, certis tantum personis permissa, formam
servare cogitur. Haec de corde puro fide non ficta, nullum genus respuit, omni loco, omni tempore commoda est. Illa sepe damnosa, haec semper salutaris.' Vgl. Van Rhijn, *Wessel Gansfort*,
213-4; Augustijn, 'Wessel Gansfort's rise to celebrity', 3-6 (über die 'officina Corveriana');
Spruyt, 'Wessel Gansfort and Cornelis Hoen's *Epistola christiana*', bes. 134; Caspers, *De eucharistische vroomheid*, 218-9.

[37] Spruyt, 'Wessel Gansfort and Cornelis Hoen's *Epistola christiana*', 134-5; Visser,
'Among the good teachers', bes. 148-9; Janse, *Albert Hardenberg als Theologe*, 274-8.

DE ORATIONE

irritamenta caritatis,incentiua caritatis, oblectameta fome
ta & alimenta.Panis aut propofitionis integru & fummum
amoris eft fpeculu,eleuatu in montibus, vt omnes uideant,
ut nemo fit qui fe abfcondat a calore eius.Mercenarij abu
dant pane.Sed quibus labor fuor merces & fruct amare.
Vero pane uerbi dei reficitur,quifquis uere dicere poteft,
Q dulcia faucibus meis eloquia tua,fuper mel ori meo.Et
in alio loco,Dulciora fuper mel & fauum.Similiter ex crea
turis reficitur,quem de ita delectat in creatura fua ut dicat,
Delectafti me dne in factura tua. Sed eft refectio fup oem
refectione, ex carne ueft ien te uerbu & condente uniuerfos
thefauros grae fapientiae iudicij & iufticiae dei,cui ex amore
dni Iefu fuper mel & fauum dulcia funt aeloquia dni Iefu,
exempla dni Iefu & mifteria dni Iefu, qui non folu credit
defyderat fitit fperat confidit expectat, fed amat & amore
languet. Intereft aut inter facramentalem & fpualem ma
ducatione, quod illa fine ifta infructuofa, imo ad mortem
eft,contra pceptu dni,hoc quocienscuq feceritis in mei me
moriam facietis.Et Paulus.Quociescuq pane huc mandu
cabitis & calice dni bibetis,morte dni annunciabitis.Et no
diiudicans corpus dni,ad iudicium manducat.Et qui man
ducat indigne,reus erit corporis & fanguinis, no diiudicas
corpus dni. Spualis aut maducatio femper fructuofa eft &
ad uitam. Eft quoq fpualis comunio,& comunio pietatis,
aliquanto fecundior facramentali,faltem in hoc q manducat
& bibit. Illa quantu eft in laicis manducat folu,nifi quia fe
lici hauftu fuppletur pace pietatis. Illa tempori & loco alli
gata,certis tantu perfonis permiffa,formam feruare cogitur.
Haec de corde puro fide non ficta,nullam aetatem, nullum
fexum,nullum genus refpuit,omni loco,omni tpe comoda
eft. Illa fepe damnofa,haec femper falutaris.

¶ Quod idem qui panis caro a beftijs laniata ac per hoc immuda
iudicata,ficut comemoratione reficit,fic eu quoq p quo offertur
a peccatis hoftia pro peccato abfoluit. Ca.VII

III. Wessel Gansfort, *Tractatus D. VVESSELI GRONINGENSIS De Oratione & modo orandi cum luculentissima Dominicae orationis explanatione,* Zwolle: Officina Corveriana, c. 1520-1522, fol. [lxxii]v (Bibliothek der Theologischen Fakultät Tilburg, PRE 107)

daß nicht ausgeschlossen werden darf, daß ersterer mit dem Werk des zuletzt genannten bekannt war.[38]

Auch andere Dinge, über die Wessel sich in seinem Kommentar zum Vater Unser verbreitet, wie z.B. die Betonung der leiblichen Gegenwart Christi
im Sakrament und der Betrachtung des Leidens Christi als beste Vorbereitung auf die Vereinigung mit Ihm, stimmen mit dem überein, was oben als
spätmittelalterliche Sakramentenauffassung skizziert wurde.[39]

Bei näherer Betrachtung jedoch mag gerade seine starke Geringschät-
zung der sakramentalen Kommunion Befremden hervorrufen, und zwar um-
so mehr als Wessel doch selbst ein Rezipient des Werkes von Gerson war.[40]
Auch im Vergleich mit den Autoren des 15. Jahrhunderts aus dem Kreis der
Devotio moderna nimmt Wessel eine Sonderstellung ein. Mit Ausnahme
vielleicht von Wessels jüngerem Freund, Jan Mombaer, hatte sich innerhalb
dieses Milieus – im Sinne von Gerson und des oben behandelten Zwiege-
sprächs – die Auffassung verbreitet, daß es besser sei, aus Liebe zu Christus
sakramental zu kommunizieren, als sie aus Furcht vor Ihm zu unterlassen.[41]
Namentlich durch römisch-katholische Kirchenhistoriker – die entweder die
Spiritualität der Devotio moderna als repräsentativ für alle damaligen Gläubigen einschätzen oder aber die Kommunionpraxis des 20. Jahrhunderts bereits im Spätmittelalter aufweisen zu können glauben – wird Wessel deshalb
ein zu extremer Standpunkt vorgeworfen.[42]

---

[38] Vgl. z.B.: Wilhelm von St.-Thierry, *Meditativae orationes*, vor allem 237 ('meditatio X').
Vgl. Persijn, *Wessel Gansfort: De oratione dominica in een dietse bewerking*, 61; 149 ('weder-
cauwen'). Vgl. auch die jetzt intrigierende Bemerkung von Oberman, der behauptet, daß Wessel mit seiner *ruminatio* auf originale Weise arbeitet und hiermit größere Tiefen erreicht als
frühere Devoten wie z.B. Geert Grote und Thomas a Kempis: Oberman, 'Wessel Gansfort:
Magister contradictionis', bes. 121.

[39] Bemerkenswert ist, daß Wessel in dem in n. 36 wiedergegebenen Abschnitt auch die
Unvollkommenheit der rituellen Form der sakramentalen Kommunion für Laien andeutet,
nämlich den Genuß nur des Brotes, nicht das Trinken des Weins. Auch kirchliche Autoren vor
ihm bringen diese Unvollkommenheit zur Sprache, wobei sie als Entschuldigung für die
Kommunion unter nur einer Gestalt immer auf die Praxis der Kirche hinweisen: Wegen der
dem Sakrament zukommenden Ehrerbietung ist es – wegen des Risikos, Wein zu verschütten –
nicht angebracht, das Kirchenvolk aus dem Becher trinken zu lassen. Vgl. z.B. Gerson, *Oeuvres
complètes*, X 55-68.

[40] Augustijn, 'Wessel Gansfort's rise to celebrity', 8.

[41] Vgl. Gerrits, *Inter Timorem et Spem*, 227-30.

[42] Franz, *Die Messe im deutschen Mittelalter*, 27-8; Axters, *Geschiedenis van de vroomheid
in de Nederlanden*, 402; Post, *The Modern Devotion*, 542; vor allem Smits van Waesberghe,
'Iets over leer en praktijk van de Geestelijke Communie in de Middeleeuwen', bes. 183-4.

Spätere Generationen: Wessel doch Erblasser?

a) Für eine breite Rezeption von Wessels Traktat über das Vater Unser im katholischen Bereich gibt es keine Hinweise. A.J. Persijn, der die mittelniederländische Bearbeitung von *De oratione et modo orandi* herausgegeben hat, hat nicht mehr als drei Mitteilungen (zu denen auch der von ihm herausgegebene Text selbst gehört) über ein Interesse an dieser Schrift bei der Generation nach Wessel, und dies ausschließlich innerhalb des Kreises der Devotio moderna.[43]

Es ist nicht unwahrscheinlich, daß für Katholiken das Lesen dieser Schrift, ebenso wie des gesamten Werkes von Wessel, sehr schnell tabu war. Vor allem weil ein Teil des Werkes einen Empfehlungsbrief von Luther und eine von Antonius de Castro verfaßte Schrift gegen Wessels Auffassung vom Ablaß enthielt, prunkte das Werk des Groningers schon gleich nach seinem ersten Erscheinen zwischen 1520 und 1522 auf den katholischen *Indices librorum prohibitorum*.[44]

Schon der mittelniederländische Text, der von Persijn beschrieben wird als eine um 1500 verfaßte Abschrift eines östlichen, möglicherweise aus Overijssel stammenden Originals,[45] ist eine Bearbeitung, in der so manche der polemischen Äußerungen Wessels nicht mehr zu finden sind. Auffallend gut paßt dazu, daß bei der Behandlung der Brotbitte gerade die Abschnitte, in denen geistliche und sakramentale Kommunion miteinander verglichen werden, im mittelniederländischen Text völlig fehlen.[46] Obwohl auch die angepaßte Übersetzung der Brotbitte eine durch und durch eucharistische Bedeutung verleiht, hat das fast völlige Fehlen expliziter Hinweise auf Termini wie Kommunion und Eucharistie dem Herausgeber des 20. Jahrhunderts Sand in die Augen gestreut und ihm die Bemerkung entlockt, daß 'Wessel eigentlich nirgendwo die Brotbitte direkt in Verbindung bringt mit der Eucharistie'![47] Falls dieser mittelniederländischen Bearbeitung ein be-

---

[43] Persijn, *Wessel Gansfort: De oratione dominica in een dietse bewerking*, 34-6. Vgl. Augustijn, 'Wessel Gansfort's rise to celebrity', 3.

[44] Vgl. *Die indices librorum prohibitorum des sechzehnten Jahrhunderts*, 10: am 3.11.1526 verfaßt John Veysey, Bischof von Exeter, eine Liste verbotener Bücher, darunter auch *De oratione* und andere Schriften Wessels. Über die Empfehlung Luthers: Augustijn, 'Wessel Gansfort's rise to celebrity', 9. Über die Schrift De Castros, schon 1490 verfaßt, aber erst öffentlich bekannt nach der Ausgabe von 1520-2, vgl. Paulus, *Geschichte des Ablasses am Ausgange des Mittelalters*, 529. Für eine Ausgabe, vgl. Van Rhijn, *Impugnatorium M. Antonii de Castro*.

[45] Persijn, *Wessel Gansfort: De oratione dominica in een dietse bewerking*, 12; 76-7.

[46] Vgl. op. cit., 144-5. Im mittelniederländischen Text sind neben vielen kleineren Abschnitten auch *capitula* aus dem ursprünglichen lateinischen Text nicht übernommen; namentlich der Abschnitt zwischen [lxix]v und [lxxv]r aus dem Druck des 16. Jahrhunderts fehlt vollständig im mittelniederländischen Text.

[47] Persijn, *Wessel Gansfort: De oratione dominica in een dietse bewerking*, 57; 59.

deutender exemplarischer Wert zuerkannt werden darf, dann war Wessels Auffassung über Eucharistie und Kommunion sogar in seinem eigenen Kreis von Bewunderern schnell 'wegzensuriert'.

Doch ist hiermit noch nicht das letzte Wort gesagt. In seiner Studie über die häufige Kommunion stellt der niederländische Kirchenhistoriker Jac. Nouwens fest, daß, trotz wichtiger, vor allem aus Südeuropa stammender, theologisch motivierter Ansätze zur Förderung der häufigen Kommunion auch unter Laien, im 16. Jahrhundert geistliche Autoren sowohl aus den Nord- als auch aus den Süd-Niederlanden zugunsten der geistlichen Kommunion dieser Neuerung gegenüber auffallend abgeneigt waren. Als Beispiel nennt Nouwens u.a. Ludolphus Nicolai van Zwolle (*Die Declaratie vander Missen*, 1554 und 1568 herausgegeben), Broeder Cornelis (*De seven Sacramenten wtgeleyt ende openbaerlyck te Brugghe ghepreect*, 1556 und 1566 herausgegeben; siehe Abb. IV), Franciscus Amelry (*Cleen traectaetkin van de waerde des helich sacraments/ ende preparatie oft beredinghe tot dien om dat waerdeghelick te ontfanghene*, 1548, 1551, 1552 und 1564 herausgegeben) und Frans Vervoort (*Het Boeck vanden heylighen Sacramente*, 1556 herausgegeben). Immer wieder aufs Neue empfehlen sie die geistliche Kommunion; die wenigen Male, daß für die sakramentale Kommunion ein gutes Wort eingelegt wird, geschieht dies im Hinblick auf Kommunikanten, die zu einem bestimmten 'Stand' gehören.[48] Allen voran könnte noch der anti-reformatorische Priester-Humanist Alardus von Amsterdam genannt werden, der sich in seinem *Parasceve* (von 1532) als ein scharfer Verfechter der täglichen, rein geistlichen Kommunion erweist.[49] Dem Niederländer Michael ab Isselt zufolge, der 1586 auf seinen Aufenthalt während der vergangenen Jahre in Löwen, Amersfoort, Zwolle und Amsterdam zurückblickte, stand es um die Sache der häufigen Kommunion, 35 Jahre nach dem Konzil von Trient, noch schlecht. In diesem Teil der Welt, so Ab Isselt, ist man mehr daran gewöhnt, über die Art des Sakramentes zu disputieren, statt daß man sich auf seine Früchte durch das Mittel der sakramentalen Kommunion verlegt.[50]

Insgesamt scheint Wessel mit seiner Kommunion-Auffassung innerhalb des Kreises, nämlich der Devotio moderna, mit der er normalerweise assoziiert wird, ein Aussenseiter zu sein, ansonsten aber innerhalb einer viel breiteren Tradition zu stehen, die bis weit nach Trient weiterbestehen wird.

---

[48] Nouwens, *De veelvuldige H. Communie in geestelijke literatuur der Nederlanden*, 18-34.

[49] Kölker, *Alardus Aemstelredamus en Cornelius Crocus*, 242-3; Caspers, *De eucharistische vroomheid*, 219.

[50] Nouwens, *De veelvuldige H. Communie in geestelijke literatuur der Nederlanden*, 35; Vermaseren, *De katholieke Nederlandse geschiedschrijving*, 32-4; Kölker, *Alardus Aemstelredamus en Cornelius Crocus*, 72; 75.

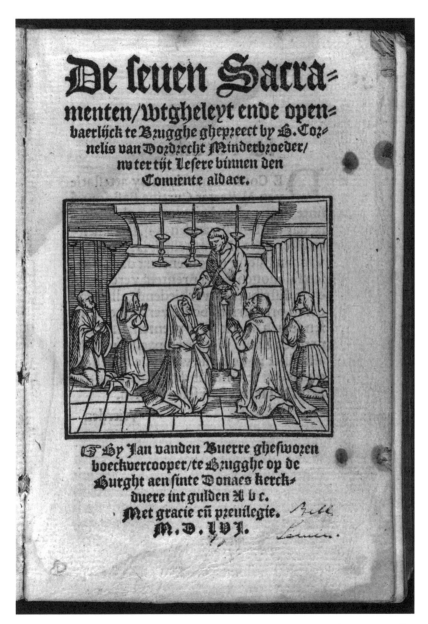

IV. Titelblatt von *De Seven Sacramenten, Wtgheleyt en de openbaerlijck te Brugghe ghepreect by B. Cornelis van Dordrecht* [...], Brugge: Jan vanden Buerre, 1556 (Bibl. der Theologischen Fakultät Tilburg, TFH-A 11.903)

b) Kann nach alledem noch etwas über Wessel als Erblasser der Reformation gesagt werden? Am Anfang dieses Beitrags wurde bereits gesagt, daß in der neueren Geschichtsschreibung diese Person, zumindest als geistlicher Autor, immer mehr auf einen 'Mittelalterlichen' reduziert worden ist. In dem 1993 erschienenen Sammelband aus Anlaß der Gedächtnisfeier zu Wessels 500. Todesjahr 1989 in Groningen legitimiert Oberman das wissenschaftliche Interesse für den Groninger dadurch, daß Wessels Auffassung über die geistliche Kommunion und sein möglicher Einfluß auf Luther und Zwingli nur einen – in der Geschichtsschreibung überbelichteten – Nebenzweig des Ganzen, innerhalb dessen seine Person betrachtet und belichtet werden muß, bildet. Als Hauptzweige dieses Ganzen nennt Oberman: die *via moderna*, die *devotio moderna* und die erste Phase der Renaissance nördlich der Alpen.[51] Diese Erweiterung des Interesses für Wessel scheint gerade im richtigen Augenblick zu kommen; denn was Oberman noch einen Nebenzweig nennt, ist faktisch ja schon wegbeschnitten. So scheint nur noch der Ruhm übrigzubleiben, den Wessel Luther und dem Faktum zu verdanken hat, daß dessen Empfehlung für die Nachkommenschaft erhalten blieb, da sie 1522 in die Ausgabe einiger Briefe Wessels aufgenommen wurde.[52] Eine *recommandatio*, die der große Reformator vielleicht nicht geschrieben hat, weil er durch das Werk eines 'Vorläufers' inspiriert worden wäre, sondern weil er sich einsam in seinen Beschlüssen fühlte, die so weitgehende Folgen für die westliche Kirche haben würde.[53]

Doch ist auch hiermit das letzte Wort noch nicht gesprochen. Bis zum heutigen Tag wissen wir noch sehr wenig über die Kommuniongewohnheiten innerhalb der protestantischen Kirchen in den Niederlanden (und anderswo) während des 16. und 17. Jahrhunderts. Wir wissen wohl, daß hier allgemein galt, daß die Kommunion gründlich und durch die nötige Gewissenserforschung vorbereitet werden mußte und daß lange Zeit nur maximal viermal im Jahr die Kommunion empfangen wurde: genauso wie im Spätmittelalter an Weihnachten, Ostern und Pfingsten, anders als im Mittelalter nicht am 1. November, sondern am 31. Oktober. Auch wissen wir, daß nicht alle zur Kommunion zugelassen wurden und daß es ein bekanntes Phänomen war, das Abendmahl zu meiden, weil man sich nicht für würdig hielt. Und auch, daß die, die zur Kommunion gingen, wußten, daß sie gewarnt waren; denn auch für sie galten die Worte des Paulus: 'Wer unwürdig ißt und trinkt, ißt und trinkt sich selbst das Gericht'![54] Nicht nur stimmten nach

---

[51] Oberman, 'Wessel Gansfort: *Magister contradictionis*', 121; vgl. 110.
[52] Vgl. n. 44; Augustijn, 'Wessel Gansfort's rise to celebrity', 9-21.
[53] Zu diesem 'psychologischen' Argument, vgl. Van Rhijn, *Wessel Gansfort*, 233.
[54] Barger, *Ons Kerkboek*, 235-49; Van Deursen, *Bavianen en slijkgeuzen*, 196-200; Luth, 'Communion in the Churches of the Dutch Reformation', bes. 103-5 und 108-9; Van Beelen, *Doet dit tot Mijn Gedachtenis*, 48; 53.

der Trennung der Wege die Kommuniongewohnheiten innerhalb des westlichen Christentums noch lange Zeit überein, sondern auch die protestantische (hier namentlich die calvinistische) Abendmahlstheologie hatte im 16.
Jahrhundert noch einen langen Weg vor sich. Zu Recht hat man festgestellt,
daß Calvins Auffassung von der Kommunion als geistliche Vereinigung des
individuellen Gläubigen mit Christus, *corporaliter* gegenwärtig, katholische
Grundzüge trägt.[55] Auch in diese reformierte (calvinistische) Tradition kann
man Wessel daher einfügen.

Kurz gesagt: Wessel paßt ohne Schwierigkeiten in eine Tradition, die im
Spätmittelalter schon einige Jahrhunderte lang bestand, in eine katholische
Tradition des 16., teilweise sogar des 17. Jahrhunderts, die im Bereich des
Kommunionempfangs und -erlebens dem Trienter Konzil gegenüber abge-
neigt war, und in eine protestantische Tradition. Diese Situierung ist nicht
durch grobe Verallgemeinerungen erzielt, sondern im Gegenteil mit dem
Blick auf das, was wesentlich als das Wichtigste betrachtet wurde in der
Glaubenserfahrung innerhalb der drei genannten Traditionen.

So wird aus Wessel Gansfort, dem *magister contradictionis*, jedenfalls
was seine Auffassung über die Kommunion angeht, der *magister consensus*.[56] In der Geschichtsschreibung haben Autoren verschiedener Signatur
Wessel als Geistesverwandten abwechselnd umarmt und wieder von sich
gestoßen. Entgegen der Aussage in den von ihnen selbst gemachten Voraus-
setzungen waren sie sich zu wenig bewußt, daß ihr Bezugsrahmen in bedeu-
tendem Maße bestimmt war durch theologische Entwicklungen nach dem
16. Jahrhundert. Wenn man Wessel Gansfort skizziert als *magister consensus*, wird deutlich, daß er als Exponent des 'spätmittelalterlichen Gedankengutes' doch Erblasser genannt werden kann, sowohl für die Reformation als
auch die katholische Kirche, vielleicht mehr für die erste als für die zweite.[57]

Zum Schluß. In den letzten zehn Jahren neigen Kirchenhistoriker dazu, die
Devotio moderna nicht mehr als eine von anderen Gruppen getrennte Gruppe zu betrachten. Auch finden sie es nicht mehr adäquat, einen möglichen
direkten Einfluß der Devotio moderna auf spätere Denominationen aufzu-
zeigen.[58] Auf der Ebene der Kommunion-Auffassungen und -Gewohnheiten
und was damit zusammenhängt – nicht zuletzt die Vorstellung von sich
selbst! – bildeten vor allem die Devoten des 15. Jahrhunderts ganz deutlich

---

[55] Vgl. z.B. Brink, 'Thomas en Calvijn tezamen ter communie'.
[56] Zur Bezeichnung *magister contradictionis*, die Wessel von einigen Geschichtsschreibern
erhalten hat, vgl. Van Rhijn, *Wessel Gansfort*, Bijlage B, xxxvii.
[57] Vgl. in Bezug auf das noch immer bestehende Problem der Abendmahlsvermeidung und
den Verweis auf seinen 'mittelalterlichen' Ursprung: *De deelname aan het Avondmaal*, 10-2;
Ambt en avondmaalsmijding, 34-40; Van Beelen, *Doet dit tot Mijn Gedachtenis*, 25-31.
[58] Neben Beiträgen anderer Autoren vgl. Jelsma, 'Doorwerking van de Moderne Devotie'.

eine Elite, die sich stark von der Masse unterscheiden wollte. Sie können durchaus in eine besondere, 'elitäre' Tradition eingeordnet werden. Diese hat dieselben Wurzeln wie die Tradition zu der Wessel gehörte, stand aber zu jener in einem gespannten Verhältnis. In dieser 'elitären' Tradition unterschieden Frauen und Männer sich durch ihren besonderen 'Stand'. Sie schätzten sich selbst als gut genug ein, um unbeschwerten Herzens häufig sakramental zu kommunizieren: manchmal zur Bewunderung, manchmal zum Spott des gemeinen Volkes. Lange nachdem man schon nicht mehr von modernen Devoten sprach, sollte die durch sie vertretene häufige Kommunion durch andere, neue 'gemeine' Völker übernommen werden.

T. ELSMANN

DAS BREMER *GYMNASIUM ILLUSTRE* UND SEINE VORLÄUFER IN
IHRER BEDEUTUNG FÜR DEN RAMISMUS IN DEUTSCHLAND
(1560-1630)

Jede Beschäftigung mit dem Ramismus sieht sich bis heute mit einer Reihe
von Urteilen resp. Vorurteilen konfrontiert, seien sie zeitgenössischer oder
wissenschaftsgeschichtlicher Natur. Erinnert sei nur an das viel zitierte und
im konfessionellen Zeitalter verhängnisvolle *dictum* des kursächsischen
Rates Erich Volkmar von Berlepsch (†1589) "Der Ramismus ist ein gradus
ad Calvinismum",[1] eine in ihrer Pauschalität entstellende, aber rhetorisch
geschickte Äquivalenz. Ist die Motivation für diese Äußerung im wesentlichen in der konfessionellen Frontstellung zwischen Calvinisten und Luthe-
ranern zu suchen, so überrascht die vehemente Verurteilung durch Thomas
Erastus (1524-1583), des zwinglianisch-reformierten Rektors der Universität Heidelberg, der Petrus Ramus als 'Pest aller Wissenschaft' diffamierte
und zugleich dessen Berufung nach Heidelberg verhinderte.[2] Bleibt schließlich noch Justus Lipsius (1547-1606) ins Feld zu führen, der 1583 in einem
Brief an Paulus Busius (1531-1594) in Delft ein von Aristoteles bestimmtes
Curriculum entwarf und Petrus Ramus (Pierre de la Ramée, 1515-1572) nur
unter Vorbehalten zu den zu lesenden Autoren rechnete.[3]

Kaum weniger gravierend sind aktuelle Einschätzungen: Der Ramismus
sei eine philosophische 'Modeströmung' ohne abgeschlossenes Gesamtsys-
tem, die relativ rasch im siebzehnten Jahrhundert im Zuge der protestantischen Aristotelesrenaissance[4] zum Scheitern verurteilt war und sich selbst
im reformierten Bekenntnisbereich nicht in Gänze durchzusetzen vermochte.[5] Manche dieser Anwürfe relativieren sich, versuchen wir den Ramismus
als wissenschaftshistorisches Phänomen zu verorten. In Genese und Verbreitung ist er ohne Antischolastik sowie ohne Konfessionalisierung im
sechzehnten Jahrhundert und der damit verbundenen Neugestaltung des

---

[1] Die zeitgenössischen Urteile bei Moltmann, 'Zur Bedeutung des Petrus Ramus', passim.
[2] Vgl. Hautz, *Geschichte der Universität Heidelberg*, II 55ff.
[3] Lipsius an Paulus Busius in *Epistolae*, I 436-40, bes. 440: "At iuventus nostra a me hoc
audiat: Nunquam ille magnus erit, cui Ramus est magnus." Deutsche Übersetzung bei Garin,
Geschichte und Dokumente der abendländischen Pädagogik, II 294-7; vgl. auch Justus Lipsius
an Issac Causobonus (22.8.1590) in *Epistolae*, III 295-6.
[4] Zur Stellung von Aristoteles in der philosophischen Ausbildung vgl. Freedman, 'Aristotle
and the Content of Philosophy Instruction' (Literatur).
[5] Vgl. Ong, *Ramus*, passim; Ong, 'Ramus, Peter'; Menk, *Die Hohe Schule Herborn*, 203ff.

Bildungswesens nicht zu verstehen. Antischolastisch ist der Ramismus zunächst in seiner Entstehungsphase, Hauptstoßrichtung ist der Aristotelismus. Petrus Ramus geriet während seines Studiums in Paris in den Streit zwischen neuaristotelischen Averroisten und den Platonismus der florentinischen Akademie. Die oft gescholtene und meist überzeichnete Frontstellung von Ramus gegen Aristoteles ist tatsächlich eine Reaktion gegen die Scholastik. Sie führte bei Ramus aber eben nicht zur Rückbesinnung oder zur Transformation des Aristotelismus im Sinne der Reformation, sondern zum Versuch eines Neuansatzes. Wenn dieser Neuansatz aus der heutigen Sicht gelegentlich als gescheitert beschrieben wird, so werden die Maßstäbe verkannt. Der Ramismus stand mit dem Aristotelismus gegen d i e methodisch-philosophische Grundrichtung, die wie wohl keine andere das abendländische Denken beeinflußt hatte. Zudem war der Ramismus mit seiner starken konfessionellen Komponente ohnehin stark auf den reformierten Bekenntnisbereich eingeschränkt, ohne diesen tatsächlich dominieren zu können. Als zu einflußreich erwies sich der Aristotelismus calvinistischer Prägung, wie er von Theodor Beza (1519-1605) in Genf ausging, und philippistischer Prägung, wie er von Philipp Melanchthon (1497-1560) geformt wurde.

Trotz dieses, auf den ersten Blick ernüchternden Ergebnisses bleibt festzuhalten, daß der Ramismus als eine genuin calvinistisch geprägte Denkhaltung seit der Mitte des sechzehnten Jahrhunderts an Einfluß gewann. Warum aber, berücksichtigt man die oft zitierte Unvollständigkeit und Unzulänglichkeit des Systems, wenn wir überhaupt von einem solchen sprechen können? Gelegentlich wurde eine individuelle Erklärung gegeben: Ramus sei aufgrund seines gewaltsamen Todes in der Bartholomaeusnacht in die Rolle eines Märtyrers gerückt worden, dessen Lehren dadurch aber zugleich zusätzliche Autorität gewannen.[6] Ohne diese (psychologische) Erklärung von der Hand weisen zu wollen, scheint es sinnvoller, die Rezeptionsgründe in den inhaltlichen Aussagen zu suchen.

Der Ramismus ist ein Teil einer humanistischen Grundströmung, die im sechzehnten Jahrhundert versucht, die Artes-Fakultäten im Sinne der neuen Geisteshaltung zu reformieren. Für Ramus sind Dialektik und Rhetorik, orientiert an Cicero und Quintilian, die analytisch-empirischen Leitwissenschaften zur gründlichen Denkschulung, ausgerichtet auf die Rhetorik,[7] die wiederum bestimmender Faktor in der konfessionellen Auseinandersetzung wird. Konfessionalität u n d Sprachbeherrschung prägen im Verbund ein humanistisches Menschenbild ramistischer Prägung, die Sprache rückt in das Zentrum von Denken und Philosophie. Um zu diesem Ziel hinzuführen, ent-

---

[6] Vgl. Menk, *Die Hohe Schule Herborn*, 204.
[7] Zur Entwicklung vgl. Barner, *Barockrhetorik*, 246ff.

wickelten Ramus und sein bekannter Schüler Talaeus (Omer Talon, 1510-
1562) eine Reihe von Lehrbüchern, die durch Einfachheit und Übersicht-
lichkeit bestechen und durch Methoden der Visualisierung an Plastizität
gewinnen. Das gilt für die sprachlichen und philosophisch-methodischen
Werke ebenso wie für die naturwissenschaftlichen. Insgesamt gesehen
haben wir es, pointiert gesagt, in vielen Punkten eher mit einem pädago-
gisch-didaktischen, denn mit einem grundlegenden philosophischen Neuansatz zu tun, der in Strukturierung und Visualisierung vieles antizipiert, was
Johann Amos Comenius (1592-1670)[8] und Wolfgang Ratke (1571-1635) im
siebzehnten Jahrhundert formulieren sollten.[9] Das gilt auch für die Propagie-
rung der Muttersprache; erinnert sei an die französische Grammatik von
1562 oder die *Dialectique* von 1555, die das Französische auch zur Wissen-
schaftssprache machte. So betrachtet, ist Ramus eher neben Juan Luis Vives
(1492-1540), Johannes Sturm (1507-1589) und Melanchthon, also in die
Reihe prägender Didaktiker, zu stellen. Hier scheint, aus der Retrospektive,
die eigentliche Bedeutung des Ramismus zu liegen, in einer methodisch-
didaktischen Neuorientierung, deren Einfluß und Bedeutung nicht zu unter-
schätzen ist.[10]
Die Zeugnisse dieses *a priori* postulierten Einflusses sind vielschichtig
und dokumentieren sich in Drucken ramistischer Schriften, in ihrer schulischen Rezeption, nachweisbar z. B. durch Lektionsindices und Dissertatio-
nen bzw. Disputationen, sowie in der Fortentwicklung des ramistischen Systems bzw. in der kritischen Auseinandersetzung mit ihm. Walter Ong, dem
wir nach wie vor die maßgebliche Studie über Pierre de la Ramée und seine
Lehre verdanken,[11] hat zum letztgenannten Punkt Kategorien wie Ramisten,
Anti-Ramisten, Semi-Ramisten und Synkretisten, d. h. sog. Aristotelo-
Ramisten und Philippo-Ramisten eingeführt. An der Praktikabilität und
Aussagekraft dieser Schemata ist in letzter Zeit wiederholt Kritik geübt
worden,[12] da sich tatsächlich eine kontinuierliche, deckungsgleiche Entspre-
chung der Termini in zeitgenössischen Texten nicht durchgängig finden
läßt. Von dieser Frage abgesehen, gibt die Mehrzahl der Schriften, die sich
in der einen oder anderen Weise mit Ramus auseinandersetzen, einen deutli-
chen Hinweis auf das vornehmliche Wirkungsfeld des Ramismus. Es handelt sich zu großen Teilen um schulische Lehrwerke, um Kompendien, kleine Tafelwerke, eklektische Lehrbücher, z.T. komparatistisch zwischen Ra-

---

[8] Zur Verbindung von Comenius und dem Ramismus, vgl. Menk, 'Kalvinismus und Pädagogik'; Menk, 'Johann Amos Comenius und die Hohe Schule Herborn'.
[9] Den didaktischen Aspekt betonen u. a. Hooykaas, *Humanisme, science et réforme*, 29ff.;
Menk, *Die Hohe Schule Herborn*, 203ff.; und Ong, *Ramus*, 149ff.
[10] Zum allgemeinen Hintergrund, vgl. Böhme, *Wirkungsgeschichte des Humanismus*.
[11] Ong, *Ramus*.
[12] Vgl. Freedman, 'The Diffusion of the Writings of Petrus Ramus', 99f. und passim.

mismus und Melanchthonismus ausgerichtet. Großangelegte philosophische
Entwürfe finden sich hier kaum, vielleicht allein vom Umfang her abgesehen von den weitgreifenden Enzyklopädien des siebzehnten Jahrhunderts,
die sich Ramus methodisch verpflichtet fühlten. Das verdeutlicht einmal
mehr die pädagogisch-didaktische Dimension. Diese läßt sich wesentlich
durch einen mühsamen, aber aussagekräftigen methodischen Ansatz historisch nachvollziehen – er besteht in der Analyse von schulischen Curricula,
von Lektionsindices, von Vorlesungsankündigungen, gekoppelt mit der
quantitativen und qualitativen Analyse der Verbreitung von ramistischen
Lehrbüchern, in erster Linie der Dialektik und der Rhetorik von Talon.
Während Walter Ong bereits 1958 den zweiten Schritt durchgeführt und der
Forschung damit reiches Material an die Hand gegeben hatte,[13] hat den
ersteren Joseph Freedman 1993 in *Renaissance Quarterly*, im Anschluß an
eine größere Studie über den von Ong als Ramisten bezeichneten Steinfurter
Philosophen Clemens Timpler (1563/64–1624),[14] in bezug auf den Zeitraum
von 1570 bis 1630 unternommen.[15] Fassen wir beide Untersuchungen zusammen, so lassen sich einige inhaltliche Punkte zunächst festhalten: 1. Hinsichtlich der Quantität der Drucklegungen ist Deutschland bevorzugter Ver-
breitungsort in Europa, gefolgt von der Schweiz, Großbritannien, Frankreich
und den Niederlanden; 2. Bei näherer Analyse zeigt sich, daß seit 1580 die
Anzahl der ramistischen Drucke steigt, um zur Jahrhundertwende die höchste Dichte zu erlangen. Nach 1630 erfolgt ein unvermittelter Abschwung,
die Nachfrage nach ramistischen Werken sinkt offenbar rapide. Es läge
nahe, angesichts der enormen Drucktätigkeit, Deutschland zum 'Zentrum'
des Ramismus zu erklären. Es steht jedoch zu bedenken, daß wir z. B. mit
der Druckerdynastie Wechel, die besonders stark Schriften von Ramus in
den Druck brachte, eine Offizin vor uns haben, die nicht für einen regiona-
len oder nationalen, sondern gesamteuropäischen Markt produzierte.[16] Somit
entfällt auch die durchgängige Gleichsetzung von Druckort und Ort der
Rezeption, z. B. in Form der Aufnahme in schulische Curricula. Weiterhin
ist festzustellen, daß unter den Druckorten auch eine Reihe von nicht-calvi-
nistischen, d. h. lutherischen zu finden ist – ein offensichtliches Indiz für die
Unbeständigkeit der simplen Gleichsetzung von Ramismus und Calvinismus. Das Bild vervollständigt sich, nehmen wir Freedmans Ergebnisse hinzu. Danach zeigen die verfügbaren Zeugnisse, daß der Ramismus auf der
universitären Ebene scheiterte, bevorzugt in den Universitäten scholastischer Tradition. Hingegen sind Ansätze zur Rezeption in den lutherischen

---

[13] Vgl. Ong, *Ramus and Talon Inventory*.
[14] Freedman, *European Academic Philosophy*.
[15] Freedman, 'The Diffusion of the Writings of Petrus Ramus'.
[16] Vgl. die Nachweise bei Evans, *The Wechel Presses*.

Universitäten Rinteln und Gießen überliefert, aber in Straßburg blieb er hingegen wirkungslos, trotz der Nähe zu Sturm.[17] Als Grund dieser Verweigerung ist einerseits die aristotelische Prägung zu nennen,[18] andererseits die Struktur des Curriculums der Artes-Fakultät. Wie bereits angesprochen, bezogen sich Ramus' Schriften nur auf Teile des breiten Spektrums der philosophischen Teildisziplinen, besonders auf Teile, die weniger den Fakultäten als der universitär-propaedeutischen Bildung zuzuordnen sind.[19] Die Domäne des Ramismus lag in den Lateinschulen, überwiegend reformierte, aber auch lutherische, in den reformierten Hohen Schulen, den Gymnasien und Paedagogien. Zu nennen sind beispielhaft Bremen, Herborn, Kassel, Steinfurt, Wesel und Zerbst als reformierte sowie Braunschweig, Korbach, Lemgo, Marburg und Stadthagen als lutherische Bildungsanstalten. Diese Nennungen bedeuten nicht, daß tatsächlich durchgängig eine ramistische Prägung im Unterricht festzustellen ist. Das liegt natürlich an der jeweiligen Überlieferungslage etwa von Lektionsverzeichnissen, aber auch an der fälschlichen Vorstellung, daß Bildungsinstitutionen, vergleichbar einen festen konfessionellen Verortung, ebenso einer festen philosophisch-methodischen Grundhaltung zuzuordnen sind. Herborn, die 1584 gegründete reformierte Hohe Schule, scheint hier, neben schweizerischen Universitäten und Schulen, eine Ausnahme in Deutschland zu sein. Die beiden ersten Generationen von Professoren, also Wilhelm Zepper (1550-1607), Johann Althusius (1566-1638) und Johann Piscator (1546-1625) einerseits, Matthias Martinius (1572-1630) und Johann Heinrich Alstedt (1588-1638) andererseits, waren eindeutig vom Ramismus geprägt. Zwar wurde nach außen hin eine Gleichberechtigung von Ramismus und Aristotelismus melanchthonischer Interpretation dokumentiert, tatsächlich aber blieb die Anstalt dem Ramismus verpflichtet. In umgekehrter Richtung ist vergleichbares in Groningen feststellbar. Die Statuten der Akademie und deren Fortschreibungen legten sich eindeutig auf das aristotelische Lehrsystem fest.[20] Dennoch scheint der Ramismus nicht spurlos an Groningen

---

[17] Zu Straßburg maßgeblich Schindling, *Humanistische Hochschule und freie Reichsstadt*.

[18] In Zusammenhang mit der zeitgenössischen Auseinandersetzung mit dem Ramismus soll hier zumindest auf ein Manuskript hingewiesen werden, das seit dem Zweiten Weltkriege der Forschung nicht mehr zu Verfügung stand. Es handelt sich dabei um ein Manuskript des in Altdorf lehrenden Philippus Scherbius (1553-1603) *adversus P. Rami dialecticam commentarius*, das 1646 durch den Ankauf der Sammlung von Melchior Goldast von Haiminsfeld (1576-1635) in die damalige Bremer Bibliothek gelangte, während des Zweiten Wetkrieges ausgelagert wurde, als verschollen galt und jetzt, im Zuge der Restituierung von kriegsbedingten Beutebeständen aus Georgien, wieder in den Besitz der heutigen Staats- und Universitätsbibliothek Bremen (Signatur msb 0068) zurückgekehrt ist.

[19] Vgl. dazu umfassend Freedman, 'Philosophy Instruction'.

[20] Vgl. zur Philosophie in Groningen Vanderjagt, 'Filosofie tussen humanisme en eclecticisme'; Sassen, '350 jaren wijsgerig onderwijs te Groningen'; Dibon, *La philosophie néerlandaise au siècle d'or*, 164-93. Die *Leges* von 1615 und deren Fortschreibungen von 1619, 1621 und

vorbeigegangen zu sein. Ubbo Emmius (1547-1624) selbst schreibt in seinem Schulprogramm von 1591 für die Lateinschule Ramus u n d Melanchthon vor,[21] mit Hermann Ravensperger (1586-1625)[22] wurde ein Professor
nach Groningen berufen, der dezidierter Ramist war. Lediglich an der friesi-
schen Akademie in Franeker scheint der Ramismus einen weitergehenden
Einfluß gehabt zu haben.[23] Die Herborner Zeugnisse beziehen sich durch-
weg auf die letzten Dezennien des sechzehnten Jahrhunderts, mit Sicherheit
muß es aber frühere Zeugnisse der schulischen Rezeption in Deutschland
geben, zu eng waren die Kontakte zu den deutschen Reformierten. Wir
kennen Belege aus den 1570er Jahren (Paedagogeum Marburg 1574; Korbach 1578), indes scheint der westdeutsche Raum Einfallstor für den Ramismus gewesen zu sein, zumal eine oberrheinische Rezeption scheiterte, da
Sturm in Straßburg weder Ramus als Person noch seine Lehre durchzusetzen vermochte. Im westlichen Deutschland sind Düsseldorf, Dortmund
und Duisburg als Pflanzstätten anzuführen.[24] Von Duisburg aus führen um
1560 Verbindungen in den Norden, konkret nach Bremen und in der Person
des Flamen Johannes Molanus.

Molanus wurde um 1510 in Nieuwekerk bei Ypern geboren.[25] Nach dem
Studium in Löwen und der wegen der Hinwendung zur Reformation er-
zwungenen Zwangsexilierung nach Emden, gelangte Molanus um 1553
nach Bremen, als Lehrer an der 1528 gegründeten Lateinschule, zugleich
mit der Möglichkeit ausgestattet, einen privaten Schülerkonvikt zu unterhal-
ten. Molanus nahm Heimstatt in einem Gemeinwesen, das sich in einem
Stadium schwerster konfessioneller Konflikte befand, die zwischen Anhängern Luthers, Sympathisanten einer melanchthonischen Linie und Zwinglia-
nern ausgebrochen waren. Molanus tendierte in die anti-lutherische Richtung, ohne daß er in dieser Opposition auf eine eindeutige Linie festzulegen
wäre. Als verhängnisvoll erwies sich die Nähe zum Domprediger Albert
Rizaeus Hardenberg (ca. 1510-1574), des Führers der innerstädtischen
Opposition. Dessen zunehmende Isolierung durch eine von außen gestützte,
lutherische Reaktion ließ Molanus' Stellung ins Wanken bringen. Als Aus-

---

1622 benennen ausdrücklich Aristoteles als Maßgabe; vgl. Groningen, Rijksarchief, *Archief van den Senaat*, Nr. 46.2-3.

[21] Dazu ausführlich Elsmann, 'Ubbo Emmius: Inhalt und Ziel des Unterrichts', 190; 197.

[22] Vgl. *Effigies et vitae professorum academiae Groningae et Omlandiae*, 61-2; Grün, 'Die theologische Fakultät der Hohen Schule Herborn', 70-2.

[23] Vgl. Van Berkel, 'Franeker als centrum van ramisme'; Elsmann, 'Ein unbekannter *Ordo lectionum et horarum*', 31-2.

[24] Vgl. Menk, *Die Hohe Schule Herborn*, 209, passim; Waddington, *Pierre Ramus*, passim.

[25] Zum folgenden Elsmann, 'Hardenberg und Molanus in Bremen', passim (Literatur); Moltmann, 'Zur Bedeutung des Petrus Ramus', passim; idem, *Christoph Pezel*, 29ff.

weg erwies sich im März oder April 1559 ein Ruf an das Gymnasium in
Duisburg. Die Überlieferung aus dieser Zeit ist in Form von Briefen recht
gut, allein äußert sich Molanus nicht zu den Inhalten des Unterrichts. Der
Aufenthalt in Duisburg war nur eine kurze Episode: zum einen scheiterte
das Duisburger Schulprojekt, zum anderen hatte sich in Bremen eine philip-
pistische, kryptocalvinistische Linie durchgesetzt. Resultat war die Rückbe-
rufung von Molanus nach Bremen und seine Ernennung zum Rektor der
Bremer Lateinschule im Jahre 1563. Möglicherweise machte Molanus gerade während des Duisburger Exils Bekanntschaft mit dem Ramismus. Wir
kennen einen Brief von Molanus an Ramus, ein Teil der bedeutenden humanistischen Briefsammlung der Staats- und Universitätsbibliothek Bremen,[26]
vom Februar 1570, in dem er berichtet, bereits seit sechs Jahren die ramistische Dialektik zu lehren.[27] Mit dem Datum 1564 haben wir damit ein
frühes Zeugnis der nachweisbaren schulischen Rezeption ramistischen Denkens vor uns. Das bedeutet nichts weniger, als die Abwendung von der aris-
totelisch-melanchthonischen Bildung, die von Wittenberg aus die meisten
protestantischen Schulen und Universitäten dominierte. Abwendung heißt
nicht Abkehr! Die vorhandenen Lektionsindices belegen 1566 die erstmali-
ge Nennung von Ramus als Leitfaden zur Analyse von Reden Ciceros (*secunda classis*),[28] 1568 die Rezeption der Dialektik (*secunda classis*)[29] und
1576/77 die Aufnahme der Rhetorik Talons,[30] ausgerichtet auf eine Schule
mit Klassen von *Secunda* bis *Sexta* bzw. *Septima* oder *Octava*. Parallel dazu
finden sich aber auch Lehrwerke Melanchthons, allerdings wesentlich bezogen auf die Sprachaneignung, sowie von Aristoteles, etwa die Ethik und die
Schrift *De anima* in melanchthonischer Auslegung, eben Felder, zu denen
kein ramistisches Lehrwerk vorlag. Molanus deutet damit schon früh eine
nicht nur für Bremen wesentlich bestimmende selektiv-eklektische Rezeption an. Die Alternative war hier nicht Aristoteles/Melanchthon o d e r
Ramus, sondern die Entwicklung ging in Richtung Aristoteles/Melanchthon
u n d Ramus. Molanus hat die Präferenz für Ramus auf den Feldern Dialektik und Rhetorik verschiedentlich begründet.[31] Er hielt die melanchthonischen Regelwerke schlichtweg für überholt, die ramistische Methode sei die
klarere. Deren Empirismus biete besseres Rüstzeug in der konfessionellen

---

[26] Die Erschließung dieses umfangreichen Briefkorpus wird z. Zt. durch Mittel der Deutschen Forschungsgemeinschaft finanziert.
[27] Staats- und Universitätsbibliothek Bremen, msa 0007/204 (Abschrift in: msa 0012/171).
[28] *Brevis index lectionum [...] 1566* (Wolfenbüttel, Herzog August Bibliothek).
[29] *Brevis artium et lectionum index [...] (1568)* (Bremen, Staats- und Univ.-bibliothek).
[30] *Hibernae lectiones [...] Anno novissimi temporis 1576* (Bremen, Staats- und Universitätsbibliothek, msa 0007/269).
[31] Dazu etwa: Bremen, Staats- und Universitätsbibliothek, msa 0007/189; msa 0007/310;
msa 0010/142.

Auseinandersetzung, bevorzugt mit den Widersprüchen des Luthertums, d.h. in erster Linie bezogen auf die Konflikte um das Abendmahl!

1584, ein Jahr nach dem Tode von Molanus, wurde die *schola Bremensis* um eine akademisch-propaedeutische Klasse, die *Prima*, erweitert, die die Fakultätswissenschaften beinhaltete, ohne jedoch nach Fakultäten gegliedert zu sein.[32] Tatsächlich scheint Ramus unter den Nachfolgern von Molanus zunächst eine eher randständige Rolle gespielt zu haben. 1589 übernimmt Melanchthon die Dominanz in Rhetorik und Dialektik,[33] 1590 hatte sich zumindest die talaeische Rhetorik wieder ihren Platz gesichert.[34] Vergleichbar geht 1596/97[35] der aus Rostock gekommene Rektor Nathan Chytraeus (1543-1598) vor, der in der Dialektik Melanchthon, in der Rhetorik aber Talon favorisiert.[36] Die Unbeständigkeit in der philosophisch-methodischen Orientierung ist nicht ungewöhnlich, sie belegt zugleich die große individuelle Gestaltungsmöglichkeit der einzelnen Rektoren.

Der eigentliche, in methodischer Hinsicht, Epigone von Molanus ist der zu Beginn des 17. Jahrhunderts nach Bremen gekommene Andreas Widmarius (1552-1621),[37] Vater des späteren Groninger Professors Abdias Widmarius (1591-1668).[38] Er ist der konsequenteste Ramist, der eine für Jahrzehnte gültige Grundstruktur schief, die aber zugleich von einem komplizierten, inhaltsschweren Anforderungskanon überwuchert wurde. Widmarius' Rektorat wird – den Urteilen von Zeitgenossen folgend – als unglücklich bezeichnet. Er habe die Schüler überfordert und als Nicht-Theologe versucht, die Schule von kirchlichem Einfluß fernzuhalten; tatsächlich wurde er 1610 zwangsweise versetzt. Er verkörpert in seiner Person die tendenzielle Abkehr weg von einer philippistisch-melanchthonischen Richtung, hin zum – auch methodisch konsequenten – Calvinismus.[39] Er konstruiert eine klare inhaltliche Trennlinie zwischen *Prima*, zweigeteilter *Secunda* und den übrigen Klassen. Während in den Klassen unterhalb von *Prima* und *Secunda* für Dialektik und Rhetorik n u r Ramus und Talaeus verwendet werden, ändert sich dies hinsichtlich der daran anschließenden Klassen. Hier wird die Rhetorik anhand von Aristoteles, Melanchthon u n d Talaeus unterrich-

---

[32] Zur Geschichte der Bremer Schule und des *Gymnasium Illustre* vgl. die Hinweise (Literatur) bei Elsmann, 'Hardenberg und Molanus in Bremen'; idem, 'Humanismus in Bremen', 83ff.; idem, 'Reformierte Stadt und humanistische Schule', 72ff.; idem, 'Humanismus, Schule, Buchdruck und Antikenrezeption', 214ff.

[33] *Index artium & lectionum [...] 1589* (Bremen, Staats- und Universitätsbibliothek).

[34] *Index artium et lectionum [...] 1590* (Bremen, Staats- und Universitätsbibliothek).

[35] *Lectiones hibernae Scholae Bremanae [...] 1596/97* (Rostock, Universitätsbibliothek).

[36] Vgl. Elsmann, 'Reformierte Stadt und humanistische Schule'.

[37] Vgl. Rotermund, *Lexikon aller Gelehrten*, II 252-3.

[38] Vgl. *Effigies et vitae professorum academiae Groningae et Omlandiae*, 164-97.

[39] Zum folgenden als Quellengrundlagen: ΕΝΔΕΙΞΙΣ *Scholae Bremanae* (1600) und *Elenchus Gymnasii Bremani* [1606] (beide Bremen, Staats- und Universitätsbibliothek).

tet. Überhaupt geht Widmarius besonders in der *Prima* recht eigenständige Wege. Für die Ethik gilt Aristoteles als Maßgabe, für die Geometrie Euklid in Behandlung mit dem gleichnamigen Traktat und Kommentar von Petrus Ramus. Zugleich wird die Dialektik anhand von Aristoteles, Melanchthon und Ramus, ebenso Rhetorik anhand von Aristoteles, Melanchthon und Ramus vermittelt. Damit wird in der Separation die inhaltliche Maßgabe für die Zeit nach 1610 gesetzt.

Unter Matthias Martinius wird in diesem Jahr die *Prima* durch eine *schola publica* mit vier Fakultäten ersetzt, damit wird die Bremer Lateinschule zu einem universitätsähnlichen, reformierten *Gymnasium Illustre*. Obgleich vom Herborner Ramismus geprägt, verlangt Martinius für die Artes-Fakultät Ramus und Aristoteles,[40] die Lehrbücher von Ramus und Talaeus dominieren hingegen im untergeordneten *Paedagogeum*, der *schola privata*. Das gilt für Dialektik und Rhetorik, aber abgeschwächt auch für die bremischen griechischen und lateinischen Schulgrammatiken, in deren Vorreden Melanchthon und Ramus als Leitfäden benannt werden. 1619 bzw. 1625 werden Dialektik und Rhetorik von Ramus bzw. Talaeus in Bremen gedruckt,[41] ein Lektionsindex von 1636/37 belegt beide nochmals für die *Secunda*,[42] aber bereits 1638/39 – nach dem Tode von Martinius – ist der Bruch nachvollziehbar. Im einzig noch bekannten Exemplar dieses Lektionsverzeichnisses sind bei den Angaben *Dialectica Rami simpliciter explicata* und *Rhetorica integra Talaei* von Hand die Namen gestrichen.[43] Damit wird der Bremer Befund nicht nur zu einem der frühesten Zeugnisse der Rezeption ramistischen Gedankengutes im schulischen Rahmen in Deutschland, sondern zugleich zu einem wichtigen Indiz für die nachlassende Attraktivität in den 1630er Jahren. An die Stelle der talaeischen Redekunst und der ramistischen Dialektik treten jetzt von Mitgliedern des Schulkollegiums verfaßte Kombinationen aus Lehrbuch und Florilegienkollektion, als neuer methodischer Ansatz löst Comenius in Bremen Ramus ab.

Die allgemeine Rezeptionsbreite des ramistischen Schrifttums sinkt, auch ausweislich der Druckverteilung, rasch. Der Ramismus gerät in eine philosophisch-methodische Zangenbewegung zwischen protestantischer Aristotelesrenaissance und dem aufkommenden Cartesianismus, der in Bremen und der neu gegründeten Universität Duisburg schnell greift, während er in Herborn scheitert. Als rezente Philosophierichtung lebte der Ramismus zu einem Gutteil von der persönlichen Faszination des Begründers. Eine ramisti-

---

[40] Vgl. dazu das Gutachten von Martinius hinsichtlich der Struktur des bremischen *Gymnasium Illustre* (Bremen, Staatsarchiv).

[41] Ong, *Ramus and Talon Inventory*, no. 150; 680.

[42] *Index lectionum et exercitationum [...] 1636/37* (Bremen, Staatsarchiv).

[43] *Index lectionum et exercitationum [...] 1638/39* (Bremen, Staatsarchiv).

sche Schule, also Anhänger, die noch intensiv zu Lebzeiten Ramus zuge-
neigt waren, ist nur in Ansätzen erkennbar. Dennoch ist festzuhalten, daß
der Ramismus – sei er gescheitert oder nicht – als Teil einer bestimmenden
Neuorientierung des sechzehnten Jahrhunderts nicht wegzudenken ist. Er
gewinnt an Bedeutung weniger als isolierter Ansatz, als vielmehr als Glied
in einer Kette dieser Neuorientierungen. Daß er offensichtlich gerade in
Bremen rasch Fuß faßte, kann mit persönlichen Neigungen von Molanus
erklärt werden, ist aber auch als Indiz innovativer Modifikationen zu deuten,
wie sie im sechzehnten Jahrhundert im Zuge der konfessionellen Neube-
stimmung das bremische Schulwesen bestimmten, dessen treibende Kraft
für die reformierte *res publica litteraria* bisher unterschätzt wurde.

M. GORIS AND L.W. NAUTA

THE STUDY OF BOETHIUS'S *CONSOLATIO* IN THE LOW COUNTRIES AROUND 1500: THE *GHENT BOETHIUS* (1485) AND THE COMMENTARY BY AGRICOLA/MURMELLIUS (1514)[*]

Boethius's *De consolatione philosophiae* was unquestionably one of the most influential books of the Middle Ages and Renaissance, and that for a variety of reasons. Its combination of Stoic morality and Platonic metaphysics and its discussions of various crucial philosophical issues guaranteed a wide audience among literate people. Moreover, its prosimetric style in which the dialogue between Boethius and Lady Philosophy is couched was much appreciated by all kinds of medieval readers, and attracted many imitators. While the cult of Boethius as a martyr for the Christian faith may have been limited, his death in the prison of the Arian Gothic king Theodoric at Pavia was as effective for his popularity as Ayatollah Khomeini's fatwah for that of Salman Rushdie.

The *Consolatio* is almost unique in the sense that it continued to be translated and studied from the eighth century through the Renaissance and thereafter, and hence that it attracted readers from such diverse social ranks such as kings, nobility, clerics, monks, and laymen. Hundreds of Latin manuscripts, translations into various vernacular languages, and no fewer than sixty printed editions before 1500 bear witness to its enormous popularity.[1]

As one might expect with such a classic, its reputation depended to a large extent on the cultural and intellectual preoccupations of its readers. Thus, it could be provided with overtly Platonic, Aristotelian or Christian-devotional interpretations, and of course most of the time was interpreted in a mixture of these ways.[2]

In the fifteenth century, new ways of reading old texts began to be developed in the Low Countries under the influence of the humanist movement, and one can find several different approaches to the *Consolatio* within that

[*] Research for this article was funded by the *Netherlands Organisation for Scientific Research* (NWO). We would like to thank John North and Robert Black for their stylistic suggestions.
[1] In this article all references to the *Consolatio* are to text and translation of the Loeb edition. On Boethian manuscripts, see *Codices Boethiani*; and Troncarelli, *Boethiana Aetas*. Essential reading on various aspects of Boethius and his influence is Courcelle, *La Consolation de Philosophie*; and the essays in *Boethius: His Life, Thought and Influence*. Chadwick, *Boethius,* is a good introduction into Boethius's life and works.

[2] See *The Medieval Boethius*; Minnis, *Chaucer's Boece*; *Boethius in the Middle Ages*. For a later, Cartesian reading of the *Consolatio*, see Nauta, 'Platonic and Cartesian Philosophy'.

same period. On the one hand, Boethius's *Consolatio* was part of a boom in consolation literature, 'Trostliteratur'. As is well known, at this time a great number of texts, mostly of a compilatory character, appeared with the aim of consoling and instructing their readers by offering remedies against the precariousness and hardship of earthly existence. Some of these texts stressed catechetical and practical lessons such as confession, penance and virtuousness. Other texts laid emphasis on reason (*ratio*) as man's principal guide for this life and the preparation for the next life.[3] But what most texts had in common was a stress on man's own, individual responsibility for casting out sins and, with the help of God, attaining moral perfection. Readers of these texts were often found in religious circles, especially those of the Modern Devotion. In this context, it comes as no surprise that readers of Boethius's *Consolatio* focused mainly on its moral-theological implications. A striking example of Boethius's popularity among the Modern Devotion is the circle at Zwolle where the *Domus Parva* had fifty copies of 'Boecius' in stock, and several editions appeared in Deventer and Zwolle.[4]

On the other hand, during this same period the *Consolatio* was also read through humanist eyes, with a focus on philological, rhetorical and historical issues. Printed editions flowed in their dozens from the presses – for example, seven within fifteen years in Venice – and humanist attention to the *Consolatio* resulted in the first scholarly editions of the early sixteenth century. Most of these early printed books, however, continued to give the faulty medieval vulgate text of the *Consolatio*, sometimes accompanied by the commentary of Pseudo-Aquinas, a German product of the late fifteenth century, which was printed as much as ridiculed by the humanists.[5]

It is not our intention – nor is it feasible here – to discuss these different approaches in much detail. Moreover, given the fact that the *Consolatio* was read and studied by students in grammar schools, by monks in the cloisters, and by clerks in their houses, and that it was often translated into the vernacular, it is difficult to differentiate very clearly between these various approaches. Our aim is therefore a more modest one: by discussing two responses to Boethius's *Consolatio*, we hope to show something of its

---

[3] For an account of this consolation literature in the Low Countries, see Pleij, *Nederlandse literatuur van de late middeleeuwen*; Mertens, 'Ter Inleiding'; Mertens's contribution to *Boethius in the Middle Ages*; Auer, *Johannes von Dambach und die Trostbücher*.

[4] Wierda, *De Sarijs-handschriften*, 160. It is not clear whether the '½ c boecij libros' refer to printed books or manuscripts. Moreover, the popular Ps-Boethius's *De disciplina scolarium* was perhaps included in this number.

[5] Obertello, *Severino Boezio*, II 13-15 and 23-33 for a list of Latin editions. For the medieval vulgate text of the *Consolatio*, see Kottler, 'The Vulgate Tradition of the *Consolatio*'. The Ps-Thomas commentary may be found in Aquinas, *Opera* (Parma 1869), xxiv; and in *Opera* (Paris 1879), xxxii. For the mocking of this 'medieval' text by humanists, see the remarks by Cally in *PL* 63, 550D ff.

varied 'Nachleben' at about this time in the Low Countries. Both works may be said to reflect the intellectual and cultural preoccupations of the time. As representative of the 'late-medieval' reading of the *Consolatio*, we shall be looking at the so-called *Ghent Boethius*, a bilingual work, which has the further advantage of bringing the role and importance of the vernacular into the picture. As an illustration of a 'humanist' interpretation, we take the commentary by the Dutch scholar Murmellius (incorporating material from Agricola), a work that has received hardly any attention so far. By taking these two works, we do not mean to suggest that there were no other orientations around 1500, nor that the late-medieval and humanist interpretations followed each other in simple succession and had nothing in common. Late-scholasticism and humanism are, of course, not monolithic and homogeneous movements. Our contribution may be considered as a further illustration of that point.

The Ghent Boethius

The incunable

Our example of the 'late medieval' interpretation of the *Consolatio* is the so-called *Ghent Boethius*, and because it has only been discussed in publications in Dutch, it is expedient first to give an idea of this work. It has come down to us in an impressive incunable, printed by Arend de Keysere in 1485 in Ghent.[6] Over fifty copies of this incunable have survived. In size it is a large folio, with 360 leaves, set in Gothic type of two different sizes. It contains the complete Latin text of the *Consolatio*, a Middle Dutch translation in verse and prose and an extensive commentary – probably the most extensive commentary ever composed on the *Consolatio*. A prologue and a table of contents complete this huge work.

The translation and commentary were written somewhere between 1444 and 1477, but probably closer to 1444.[7] In the incunable the text of the *Con-*

---

[6] Our discussion is based on the incunable of The Hague, KB, 171 A 2. On the history of the printing of the *Ghent Boethius*, see Machiels, *Meester Arend de Keysere*. At the University of Nijmegen an edition is in progress: book 1 is being edited by Wilma Wissink, book 2 by Mariken Goris. The rest must await funding.

[7] See Hoek, *De Middelnederlandse vertalingen*, 36-38 for a discussion of the date. The *terminus post quem* is based on a passage in III pr. 5 (the commentator describes the death in 1444 of Wladislaw III of Poland). For his *terminus ante quem* of 1477, Hoek assumed that the Ghent commentator would have used the Mansion translation if it had already appeared (it was published in 1477). For more on this, see Goris and Wissink's contribution to *Boethius in the Middle Ages*.

solatio is divided into short sections; each section is followed by its Middle Dutch translation and the commentary related to that section (see Plate V).

Unfortunately, we do not have the autograph of this *Ghent Boethius* nor any other handwritten copy of the text, and this raises a series of pertinent questions: was the 'Vorlage' the autograph or a copy? When were translation and commentary composed? Did the manuscript have the full Latin text as well? Further, there is hardly any evidence pointing to the identity of the man behind this huge work, although he was probably connected with Saint-Verelde in Ghent, as seems to be suggested in the prologue.[8] Neither do we know much about the aims and objectives of the translator/commentator, nor whether they concurred with those of the printer Arend de Keysere, since there may have been a large gap in time between the manuscript and the printed version. Still, the prologue offers some clues as to why the Ghent commentator had set himself to such a Herculean task. As *captatio benevolentiae* he writes the following:

> Biddende eenen ygheliken die den selven bouc horen of lesen sal, dat hine ten besten sinne betrecken wille. [...] Nochtans ic en twifele niet dat so wie desen bouc punctelic overleist ende studiert, hij salre in vinden begrepen als boven: harde goede, noodsakelike, oorborlike ende ghestichtighe leeringhe an ziele ende live.[9]

The author's principal source is the Latin commentary of Renier of St-Truiden, written at the end of the fourteenth century, of which long passages are translated by the Ghent commentator.[10] There are other parts, however, that do not find an equivalent in Renier's commentary, but how 'authentic' these are, or whether they are translations of other commentaries, is still uncertain at this stage of research.

---

[8] 'So heb ic tot elcx nutscap ende profite den allereersten bouc van deser translacie, met mijnder hand ghecorrigiert, te Sente Verelde te Ghend in de librarie doen legghen, daer jeghen dat een yghelick duutghescrifte daer af sal prouven moghen' (in paraphrase: 'that is why I have put, to everyone's profit, the first book of my revised translation in the library of St. Pharaildis in Ghent, so that everyone is able to read this manuscript'); *Ghent Boethius*, a3rb (transcription from Wissink's edition in prep.).

[9] a3rb (transcription from Wissink's edition in prep.). In paraphrase: 'Praying for everyone who will hear or read this book, in order that he will extract the meaning in a most profitable way [...]. But I do not doubt that anyone who reads and studies this book carefully, will find good, necessary, useful and devotional instructions for the soul and for life.'

[10] A striking difference between the two, however, is Renier's very scholastic structure, which is not taken over (or only in very simplified form) by the commentator of the *Ghent Boethius*. See Hoek, *De Middelnederlandse vertalingen*, 194-6, and in more detail Angenent, 'Het Gentse Boethiuscommentaar'.

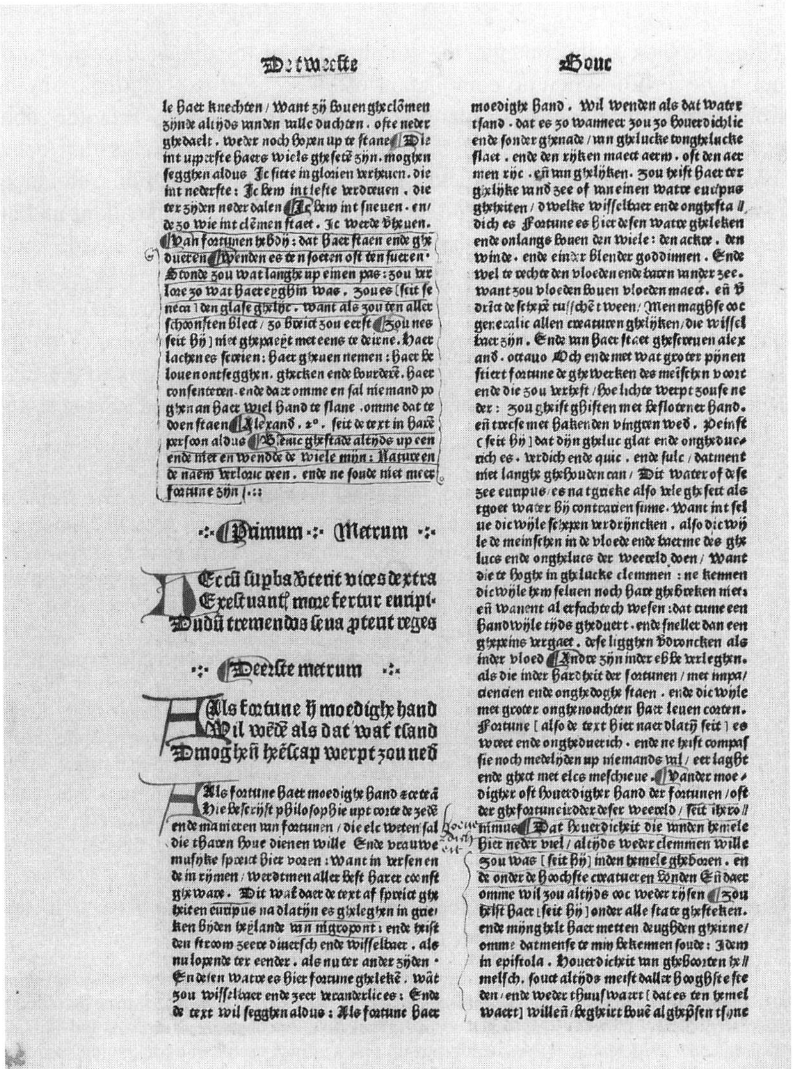

Dat tweeste

le haer knechten / want zij houen ghecl̄omen
zijnde altijds vanden valle duchten . ofte neder
ghedaelt . weder noch hopen up te stane. Die
int upperste haers wiels ghesete zijn . moghen
segghen aldus Ic sitte in glorien verheuen . die
int nederste : Ic bem int leste verdreuen . die
ter zijden neder dalen Ic bem int sneuen . en/
de zo wie int cl̄emen staet . Ic werde verheuen.
Van fortunen hebdij : dat haer staen ende ghe
dueren wenden es ten soeten oft ten sueren .
Stonde zou wat langhe up einen pas : zou ver
lore zo wat haer eyghin was . Zou es [seit se
neca] den glase ghelijc . want als zou ten aller
schoonsten bleet / zo breict zou eerst Zou nes
seit hij] niet ghepaeyt met eens te deirne . Haer
lachen es screien : haer gheuen nemen : haer be
louen ontsegghen . ghecken ende bourderē . haer
consenteren . ende daer omme en sal niemand po
ghen an haer wiel hand te slane . omme dat te
doen staen Alexand . 2° . seit de text in harē
persoon aldus Bemic ghestade altijds up een
ende niet en wende de wiele mijn : Nature en
de naem verlore ic ween . ende ne soude niet meer
fortune zijn [.::

.:. Primum .:. Metrum .:.

Hec cū supba verterit vices dextra
Exestuantis more fertur euripi.
Dudū tremendos seua pterit reges

.:. Deerste metrum .:.

Als fortune hare moedighe hand
Wil wēdē als dat wat tsand
Dmoghen heerscap werpt zou neer

Als fortune haer moedighe hand ꝛc̄ te ā
Hie bescrijft philosophie upt corte de zedē
ende manieren van fortunen / die elc weten sal
die thaven houe dienen wille Ende vrauwe
musijke spreict hier voren : Want in versen en
de in rijmen / werdtmen aller best harer coonst
ghewaer . Dit wat daer de text af spreict ghe
heiten euripus na dlatijn es ghelegen in grie/
ken bijden heylande van nigropont : ende heist
den stroom zeere diuersch ende wisselbaer . als
nu lopende ter eender . als nu ter ander zijden .
Ende desen water es hier fortune ghelekē . wāt
zou wisselbaer ende zeer veranderlic es : Ende
de text wil segghen aldus : Als fortune haer

Boec

moedighe hand . Wil wenden als dat water
tsand . dat es zo wanneer zou zo houerdichlic
ende sonder ghenade / van ghelucke tongheluck
slaet . ende den rijken maect aerm . oft den aer
men rijc . eñ van ghelijken . Zou heist haer ter
ghelijke vand zee of van einen water euripus
gheheiten / dwelke wisselbaer ende onghesta//
dich es Fortune es hier desen water ghelekent
ende onlangs houen den wiele : den ackere . den
winde . ende einer blender goddinnen . Ende
wel te rechte den vloeden ende baren vander zee.
want zou vloeden houen vloeden maect . eñ v
drict de schepē tusschē t ween / Men magh se oec
generalic allen creaturen ghelijken / die wissel
baer zijn . Ende van haer staet ghescreuen alex
and . octauo Och ende met wat groter pijnen
stiert fortune de ghewerken des meinschen voort
ende die zou verheft / hoe lichte werpt zouse ne
der : zou gheift ghiften met beslotener hand .
eñ treckse met haken den vinghren wed . Peinst
[seit hij] dat dijn ghelue glat ende onghedue/
rich es . verdich ende quic . ende sulc / datment
niet langhe ghehouden can / Dit water of dese
zee euripus / es na tgrieke also vele ghe seit als
tgoet water bij contrarien sinne . Want int sel
ue dic wijle schepen verdrijncken . also dic wij
le de meinschen in de vloede ende baerme des ghe
lucs ende onghelucs der weereld doen / Want
die te hoghe in ghelucke clemmen : ne kennen
dic wijle hem seluen noch haer ghebreken niet .
eñ wanent al ersachtech wesen : dat cume een
handwijle tijds gheduert . ende sneller dan een
ghepeins vergaet . dese ligghen verdroncken als
inder vloed Andre zijn inder ebbe verleghen.
als die inder hardheit der fortunen / met impa/
cientien ende onghedoghe staen . ende dic wijle
met groter onghenouchten haer leuen corten.
Fortune [also de text hier naer dlatijn seit] es
wreet ende onghedurich . ende ne heift compas
sie noch medelijden up niemands val / eer laghe
ende ghect met elcs meschieue . Vander moe/
digher oft houerdigher hand der fortunen / oft
der ghefortuneirder deser weereld / seit ihero//
nimus Dat houerdicheit die vanden hemele
hier neder viel / altijds weder clemmen wille
Zou was [seit hij] inden hemele gheboren . en
de onder de hoochste creaturen vonden Eñ daer
omme wil zou altijds oec weder rijsen Zou
heist haer [seit hij] onder alle state ghesteken.
ende mijnghelt haer metten deughden gheirne/
omme datmense te min bekennen soude : Idem
in epistola . Houerdicheit van gheboorten he//
melsch . souct altijds meist dallerhooghste ste
den / ende weder thuuswaert [dat es ten hemel
waert] willeñ / begheirt bouē al ghepijsen t sijne

V. *Ghent Boethius*, fol. glv (Royal Library, The Hague, 171 A 2)

Quotations

When we look at its contents, the commentary of the *Ghent Boethius* turns
out to be an idiosyncratic compilation of all sorts of explanations ranging
from textual analysis to elucidations of topics that are only remotely concerned with the actual text of the *Consolatio*. The ingredients that occur
most regularly are summaries and paraphrases of the translation, references
to other passages in the *Ghent Boethius*, quotations, and explanations and interpretations. Thus, the commentary is a valuable source for a wide spec-
trum of issues and themes.[11]

The author has a strong preference for moralizing and stressing devotional and religious aspects, as is clear from the range and choice of quotations. For instance, in Book Two where Lady Philosophy refers to the fick-
leness of Lady Fortune, quotations are given from Ovid, Seneca and
Chrysostom:

> Ende Ovidius seit: So moet hij van alle ghelucke derven, zo wie meint of
> waent datmen van einigher dijnc na haer beghin jugieren sal. Of Philosophie
> segghen wilde: De meinsche die gheluckich waent wesen, es wijs of zot. Es hij
> zot, zo nes hij gheinsins gheluckich. Want also Seneca seit: Dleven der onwij-
> ser ende der ignoranten es als een ymage ende beilde vander dood. Es ooc de
> meinsche wijs, zo zal hij dhende mercken ende dbejeghenen dat hem toecom-
> men mach. Het es dan grote wijsheit dhende wel merken ende oversien eer
> men einich dijnc beghint, want al heift dbeghin een goet behaghen, dhende
> moet nochtens de laste draghen. [...] Daer omme seit wel de wijse man: Over-
> dijnct de uterste ende de leste dijnghen, ende du en suls niet sondeghe in
> eewicheden. Of hij segghen wilde: Zo wie up zijnen sterfdach merct wattij
> werdt ter dood ende waer hij ten hende henen moet, die sal hem billics van
> mesdoene wachten. Vier uterste dijnghen zijnt, als Crisostimus seit, de dood,
> doordeil, dhelle ende tparadijs, daer ic eldre wat af ghescreven hebbe.[12]

Obviously, all quotations relate to the question of how to live well, and

---

[11] On the Ghent commentary in general, see Goris, 'Boethius' *De consolatione philosophiae*'
and Hoek, *Middelnederlandse vertalingen*. Discussions of individual passages may be found in
Gerritsen, 'Dese fabule es elken toegescreven' (about the Orpheus metre, III m. 12) and Wissink,
'Dolinghe der consciencien' (about conscience in I pr. 4). On the scholastic background, see Hoenen's contribution to *Boethius in the Middle Ages*.

[12] II pr. 1 = f8rb-f8vb. In paraphrase: 'Ovid says: he who thinks that he can judge something on
the basis of its beginning, will remain without luck. So Lady Philosophy says: the person who
thinks himself happy, is wise or foolish. When he is foolish, he cannot be happy, as Seneca says:
life of the ignorant is an image of death. When he is wise, he will recognize the end, and see what
is coming to him. It is very wise to know the end before one starts with something. For every
beginning is a delight; the end, however, carries the weight. [...] That is why the wise man says:
Consider last things and you will not sin in eternity. As if he wanted to say: He who recognizes, on
his day of death, what death means and where he is to go to, will be protected against sin. The four
ultimate conditions are, as Chrysostom says, death, jugdment, hell and heaven.'

amount to a simple, moral instruction: Look before you leap. Thus, Lady Fortune's fickle character is used as the occasion for digressions on the end of one's life – but for no other purpose, since in the long passage that follows she is not mentioned again. Apparently, this is the kind of 'ghestichtige leeringhe' (devotional-religious instruction) that the *Ghent Boethius* wanted to inculcate; an explanation of Boethius's text was not the only aim he had in mind.

Sometimes the quotations in the *Ghent Boethius* form a cluster around a particular theme. They may very well be translations of florilegia, but exact sources have not yet been found. Here again, the connection with the text of the *Consolatio* is often tenuous: just one word from the *Consolatio* can give rise to a dozen quotations that hardly have anything in common with Boethius's own argument. It seems, therefore, that the quotations are not just quotations but that they are used as a vehicle for interpretations of the *Consolatio*, and reflect the commentator's wider aims. In the third prose of Book Two, for instance, Lady Philosophy hands the floor to Boethius ('dabimus tibi dicendi locum'). In the commentary on this passage the author gives many quotations that concern the merits of silence in contrast with speaking, such as 'who is silent, takes care for his soul' and Solomon's saying 'the fool says what he knows, the wise man keeps silence.'[13] Also in the poem where the subject is the building of one's house of life 'on a low, rock base' (II m. 4), the Ghent commentator does not comment on the wise man's munificent rest, 'smiling at all the anger of the skies', but he takes avarice as the central issue:

> Den zande moghen de ghierighe wel gheleken zijn, want hoe dicwijle datment beghiet, het schijnt nochtan altijds doore of droghe. Aldus eist vanden ghierighen man, want al ghecreghe hij ein ganse weereld, zijne begheirten bleven altijds wan. Seneca *Epistola viij.* seit dat ghiericheit so vele te schaerper, zo de hope van hebben meerder es. Of: Zo de meinsche rijker valt, zo hij hongherigher ende duustigher werdt na tgoed. Augustinus .12. *De civitate Dei*: Ghiericheit nes tghebrec sel selvers noch des gouds niet, maer der zielen diese qualic begheirt of mint, achterlatende gherechticheit diemen boven alle rijcheit gheiren zoude.[14]

---

[13] *Ghent Boethius*, h1rb-h1vb.

[14] *Ghent Boethius*, i7rb (this is only a small part of this part of the commentary on avarice). In paraphrase: 'The sand is like a miser, because however much water it gets, it always seems dry. So is the miser: when he has got the whole world, his desire is still insatiable. Seneca (*Epistola* 8) says that avarice is stronger as the hope of getting more is stronger. Or: the richer a man is, the more hungry for goods he becomes. [...] Augustine (*De civitate dei*, 12): Avarice is not the lack of silver and gold, but the soul that wrongly loves it, neglecting justice that should be loved above all wealth.'

Other clusters of quotations focus on concepts such as pride, humility, patience, misery. Together they give us an idea of the character of the Ghent commentary. Their aim is to offer the reader guidelines indicating how to live well, and how to prepare one's life for the Final Judgement.

Christianization

This use of quotations may already be seen as a christianization of Boethius's work. A more direct type of christianization – one example should suffice here – may be found in Book Two, where Lady Philosophy admonishes Boethius not to give up hope 'when the anchors still hold firm which ensure that neither present consolation nor future hope shall be wanting.'[15] In the commentary on this passage, the image of the anchors is explained not as a common symbol of hope, but as hope in God, anchored in heaven: hope in God with faith, virtue and good deeds is the anchor that guides men's spiritual ship. But the Ghent commentator does more; he lashes out at non-Christians. When he speaks about what one can expect after death, he refers to 'the dirty dog Mohammed':

> Daer sal, seit hij, een yghelic heurer met wiven ende met maeghden ende met boelen sijne ghenouchte vrij antiere moghen, daer sonder men niet salich wesen mochte. Want alle solaes te vergheefs wesen soude, moeste men daer sghebruucs van vrauwen derven. Dus blijket emmer dat dese vuyle hond Machomet eenegherande beestelijke salichte na dit leven stelt, als in etene, in drijnkene ende int oncuusche weerc.[16]

Mohammed's promising prospect for the afterlife is, of course, as the Ghent commentator is not slow to point out, a false representation of the Last Supper. The supreme salvation is in the rational part of the soul, and has nothing to do with carnal pleasures.

Latinity

All this suggests that the *Ghent Boethius* is only quite loosely connected with the *Consolatio*-text itself, but that is not the case. In the first place, the

---

[15] Translation of Tester (Loeb), 193.

[16] i5rb. In paraphrase: 'Mohammed says that one is free to enjoy women there, otherwise one will not be happy. All misery would be without purpose, if one had to forgo the pleasure of women there. As always, the dirty dog Mohammed holds out a beastly happiness after this life, with food, drink and vileness.'

Ghent commentator is a competent translator who tried to translate the *Consolatio* as precisely as he could. In the prologue he explains his method of translating the metres of the *Consolatio*:

> Ende de prosen zijn na onser ghemeender tale ghestelt, maer de rijmen ende de versen bij meerderen compasse van coonsten ghemaect. Ende haren stilen ne bem ic niet connen ghevolghen, maer hebbe wat van gheliken ghetale van versen den sin der van up tcurtste besloten, om dat zij so vele te lichter onthoudeliker ende beter om lesen werden. Ende hebbe also vele vander substancien der inne betrocken alse ic hebbe gheconnen, maer niet al den sin, overmids dat alle de Dietsche versen voorscreven up .vij. .viij. .ix. of .x. sillaben ten hooghsten ghesloten zijn ende de Latijnsche al meest wat langher vallen.[17]

Thus, as the Ghent translator/commentator explains, he could not preserve the metrical variety of the Latin metres, but translated them using no more lines than the Latin original, and no more than ten syllables a line, retaining as much of the original contents as possible.[18] Because of the rules he imposes on himself, he was not always able to translate the complete substance of the argument of the Latin metre. (He usually translates the missing parts in the commentary, where he gives the complete text by means of paraphrase.) His commitment to the Latin text is evident in the prose parts of the *Consolatio* too: he translates *verbum e verbo* in such a strict way, that his translation follows the Latin source even in word order, choice of words and idiom. Compare, for instance, 'cum ipsum hominem velox hora dissoluat' with 'als dicwile den mensch selve de haestighe wile verslaet', and 'cum te matris utero natura produxit' with 'als dij uter moeders buuc nature brochte'. In Middle Dutch prose, the position of subject and object are generally in reverse order. This way of translating makes the Middle Dutch of the Ghent translator highly idiosyncratic, and raises the question whether his translation could easily be read and understood by fifteenth-century readers.

In the commentary, attention is also paid to the grammar of the Latin original. The Ghent commentator explains grammatical constructions, unusual words and technical terms, and often etymologizes. He elucidates, for instance, words such as 'missilia' ('money that one used to throw at parties among young people'), gives the proper meaning of a word and the more precise meaning of a passage, and has remarks on the text of the *Consolatio* itself such as: 'some texts have *aditu*, it would be better to read *adito*'. These remarks need not, however, be original to the Ghent commentator;

---

[17] a3rb. Transcription from Wissink's edition in preparation.
[18] On the translation of the metres, see Goris, 'Het metrum in de gedichten'.

frequently, they are taken from the work of Renier of St-Truiden.

From our short discussion so far, the position of the *Ghent Boethius* within the late-medieval tradition of Boethius turns out to be a complicated one, and it cannot be brought solely under the heading of devotional-religious literature. The translation betrays a remarkable knowledge of the intricacies of Boethius's Latin, as Hoek has shown by comparing it with other medieval translations (Vilt, Von Kastl, Jean de Meun, Pseudo-de Meun, Chaucer, Mansion).[19] This is not the place to review Hoek's conclusions, but in general it can be said that the translation is a good and reliable one. The fact, however, that explanations of various linguistic phenomena occur does not warrant the conclusion that the Ghent translator exhibits traits of a humanist frame of mind; they were the stock trade of the commentary tradition. Its devotional, catechetical and practical-religious overtones rather point to a different sphere, although it is hard to identify the audience that the Ghent commentator would have liked to address. It may have been a mixed readership of members of the Chapter of Saint-Verelde in Ghent and other clerks, as well as laymen.[20] Further, his extensive use of the scholastic commentary of Renier of St-Truiden has been documented by Angenent.[21] All this suggests a late-medieval context for this fifteenth-century work rather than a humanist one.

Murmellius

When we now come to the Latin commentary that the humanist Johannes Murmellius (1480-1517) published in 1514, we seem to be in a far different world from that of the *Ghent Boethius*. Murmellius's name is today no longer a household name, even among Neo-Latinists, but in his own time and long afterwards he had a wide reputation as humanist, author of pedagogical works, editor of classical and contemporary texts, and as poet.[22] His editions and works, mostly intended for use in schools to replace the medieval school texts, continued to be printed and studied long after his

[19] Hoek, *Middelnederlandse vertalingen*, 111-93.

[20] Wissink, 'Dolinghe der consciencien', 337-41; and Pleij, *Nederlandse literatuur*, 158-91. Most of the owners' inscriptions are from the 16th century and later, and suggest a mixed audience of monks and (wealthy) laymen. Unfortunately, they do not tell us anything about the circulation of the *Ghent Boethius* in the late 15th century; cf. Machiels, 'De Boekdrukkunst te Gent'.

[21] Angenent, 'Het Gentse Boethiuscommentaar'.

[22] On Murmellius's life, see Reichling, *Johannes Murmellius*; the article in *NNBW* I, 1348-51 (by Van der Velden); Van Gelder, *Geschiedenis der Latijnsche School te Alkmaar*, 39-45; 90-108; 149-55; Nauwelaerts, 'Johannes Murmellius', with a chronological list of Murmellius's writings (228-33).

death, even till the end of the eighteenth century. When he died at the age of thirty-seven, he had written or composed more than twenty-five school-books, nine collection of poems and epigrams, and a complete list of his works would probably include more than fifty titles. Although not a humanist of the rank of Valla, Agricola or Erasmus, he was an important supporter of humanist ideals in the North.

His Latin primer *Pappa puerorum* was by far his most succesful work, but without doubt his commentary on Boethius is his best, and has rightly been called 'a creditable piece of philological scholarship'.[23] Yet to this day, little attention has been paid to it. In the context of this contribution, we shall discuss only a few salient points which illustrate the change that had come about in interpreting and reading the *Consolatio*, when compared with the late-medieval *Ghent Boethius*.

The Boethius Commentary

As a young schoolmaster Murmellius had already read the *Consolatio* with his pupils and he had published an edition of the text in 1511, when he came forward with his scholarly commentary (Deventer 1514; see Plate VI (over-leaf) for the Cologne 1516 reprint).[24] The work is dedicated to his former master Rudolph of Langen, and apart from his own preface, Murmellius in-cludes introductory material from other humanists (Nicholas Crescius, James of Bologna, Augustino Dati). Their common intention was, as ap-pears from the prefaces, to rescue Boethius's text from the corruptions and impurities of the medieval tradition, and to replace the often silly glosses from late medieval commentaries (esp. that of Pseudo-Aquinas) by humanist ones.[25]

A more important and more interesting insertion in his commentary is a series of glosses and notes on the *Consolatio* by Rudolph Agricola, who had died in 1485. Murmellius tells us that, when he was twenty years old and had begun teaching in Münster, these 'enarrationes autographas' fell into his

---

[23] *CE* II 471; cf. Nauwelaerts, 'Johannes Murmellius', 213: 'het filologisch meesterwerk'. The few pages devoted to the work are: D'Elia, 'Il commento di Giovanni Murmellius' (a note on the famous III m. 9); and Herding, 'Probleme des frühen Humanismus', esp. 368-74.

[24] The work was reprinted several times (e.g. Cologne 1516; Cologne 1535; Basel 1570, and in *PL* 63, 869A-1074A). All quotations in this article refer to *PL* 63, giving only the number of the columns in *PL*. Reichling, *Johannes Murmellius*, 92 note 3, notes that Murmellius as a young master already read the *Consolatio* with his pupils, as appears from a letter of Rudolph of Langen to Murmellius in 1501.

[25] *PL* 63, 869-78; cf. Herding, 'Probleme des frühen Humanismus', 370; cf. note 5.

VI. Murmellius's commentary on Boethius's *De consolatione philosophiae*, Cologne 1516, fol. [Ei]v (University Library, Groningen)

Liber primus   Foliū.xxiiij.

Hⁿ Ec vbi ɔtinuato doloꝛe ꝺlatraui. illa vultu placido nihilꝗ   Pꝛosa qnta.
meis queſtibꝰ mota. P. Cum te inquit meſtū lachꝛymantem
ꝼ vidiſſem .illico miſerum exulemꝗ cognoui . Sed ꝗ id lōgin
quū eſſꝫ exiliū.niſi tua pꝛodidiſſꝫ oꝛo neſciebá. Sꝫ tu ꝗ pꝛocul a
patria nō ꝗdē pulſus es.ſed aberraſti.At ſi pulſum exiſtimari ma
uis.te potius ipe ꝑpuliſti. Nā id ꝗdē ꝣ te nūꝗ cuiꝗ fas fuiſſet.
Si eñi cuius oꝛiūdus ſis patrie reminiſcaris.nō vti Atheniēſium
quondam multitudinis imꝑio regis. αλλα εισ βασιλευσ
εστιρεισ κοιραγοσ. qui frequentia ciuiū nō ꝛepulſione letaſ.
Cuius agi frenis atꝫ obtēꝑerare iuſticie ſumma libertas eſt. An ig
noꝛas illā tue ciuitatis antiquiſſimā legēꞇqua ſancitū eſt ei ius ex,
ulare nō eſſe. ꝗſquis in ea ſede fundare maluerit. Nā ꝗ vallo 'eꝰ ac
munimine ɔtinef.nullus metꝰ eſt ne exul eē mereat. At ꝗſꝗs inha
bitare eā velle deſierit.pariter deſinit etiā mereri. Itaꝗ nō taꝫ me lo
ci huꝰ quā tua facies mouet. Nec bibliothece potius cōptos ebo
re ac vitro parietes ꝗ tue mētis ſedē reꝗro. Jn ꝗ non libꝛos.ſed id
qð libꝛis pciū facit.libꝛoꝛ quōdā meoꝛ ſentētias collocaui. Et tu
ꝗdē ꝣ tuis in cōe bonū meritꝫ vera ꝗdē.ſ.ꝑ multitudine geſtoꝛum
tibi pauca dixiſti.De obiectoꝛ ꝗdē tibi vſ honeſtate vel falſitate.
cūctis nota memoꝛaſti.De ſceleribꝰ fraudibuſꝗ delatoꝛ recte tu ꝗ
dem ſtrictim attingēdū putaſti. ꝙ ea melꝰ vtriuſꝗ recognoſcētis
omnia vulgi oꝛe celebꝛenꞇ. Jncrepuiſti etiam vehementer iniuſti ſa
ctū ſenatꝰ.ꝣ noſtra etiā criminatōe doluiſti.leſeꝗ opinionis dam
na fleuiſti Poſtremo aduerſus foꝛtunā doloꝛ incāduit.ɔqueſtuſꝗ
nō equa meritis pmia pēſari. Jn extremo muſe ſeuictis.vt ꝗ celum
terras quoꝗ pax regeret vota poſuiſti.Sed qñ pluriꝰ tibi affe
ctuum tumultus incubuit. diuerſumꝗ te doloꝛ. ira.meoꝛ.diſtra
hunt vti nūc mentis es.nōdum te validioꝛa remedia contingūt.
Itaꝗ leuioꝛibꝰ pauliſper vtemur.vt que in tumoꝛem perturbatio
nibꝰ influctibꝰ induruerūt.ad acrioꝛis vim medicaminis recipiē
dam.tactu blandioꝛe moleſcant

          E ij.

VI. Murmellius's commentary on Boethius's *De consolatione philosophiae*, Cologne 1516, fol. Eii]r (University Library, Groningen)

hands.[26] From Murmellius's account it appears that Agricola had been asked for help in explaining Boethius's text by his friend Lambertus of Groningen, a doctor of medicine, who had received his degree in Ferrara, with Agricola as a witness (December 22, 1478). Agricola, however, did not get far with it, and the only part of the *Consolatio* for which we have his notes is metre 4 to prose 6 of Book One. Lambertus had shown these notes to Murmellius (probably on a visit to Münster). It seems that on his sudden departure Lambertus took the autograph with him but not before Murmellius had made a transcript himself. Murmellius recognized their value and decided to incorporate Agricola's notes in his own commentary, 'lest they did not wither away any longer in my *dactylotheca*', giving full credit to their author. In our discussion, we shall not distinguish too strictly between Murmellius's commentary and Agricola's small but significant contribution, since their approach and explanations are of the same character.[27]

We shall briefly look at three themes: the method employed in the commentary, the Latinity of the *Consolatio*, and the general attitude towards Boethius and his work.

Structure

One of the first striking points to note when reading Murmellius's work is the structure of the commentary. There are hardly any divisions of the text in *divisiones*, *partitiones* and so forth (let alone *quaestiones*), which are prominent features of the (late-)medieval Latin commentaries; only an occasional *sequitur* reminds one of the medieval commentary idiom. Each prose or metre begins with a short introduction to that particular section, after which an elucidation of words and phrases follows. This is a conspicuous simplification when compared to the methods employed in older commentaries. In the Boethius commentary by Murmellius's predecessor Badius Ascensius, this simplification of structure – what Paul Gerhard Schmidt has called 'Sinn für Ökonomie' – is apparent as well, and may reflect the fact 'daß sie gegenüber dem Text kein Eigenleben entwickeln, sondern ganz auf eine dienende Funktion beschränkt sind', as he writes on Badius Ascensius's

---

[26] For Murmellius's account, see 908D-909C. There also seems a connection with Cologne and particularly the Albertists in the protracted and enigmatic story of the publication of Agricola's *De inventione dialectica*, that is in the person of Pompeius Occo, who studied in the Bursa Laurentiana in 1504-5. His uncle Adolf Occo, to whom Agricola bequeathed his works and manuscripts on his death in 1485, in turn had bequeathed these to his nephew Pompeius in 1503. See Tewes, *Die Bursen der Kölner Artisten-Fakultät*, 711 and notes with bibliography.

[27] Only once does Murmellius take issue with Agricola, and rightly so, because there 'dignitatem' (not: 'indignitatem') is the correct reading (931D, on I pr. 4, line 135).

commentaries.[28]

Another point worth noting here is the unequal share of attention allotted to each of the five books of the *Consolatio*. The first three books get far more attention than the last two (more philosophical) books. From his programme of teaching in the summer of 1511 we know that Murmellius planned to read with his pupils the first two books only.[29] Concentration on only the first part of a work has, of course, always been common practice in teaching, but Murmellius's case is a rather extreme one: in Migne's *Patrologia Latina*, Book One covers some sixty-five columns, Book Two thirty-nine, Book Three fifty-one, Book Four nineteen, and Book Five only nine. Apparently, Murmellius had a limited interest in such philosophical issues as the metaphysical status of evil and the reconciliation of divine providence and freedom of the will. He was happy to direct the reader to Lorenzo Valla's *De libero arbitrio*, and to leave the question open whether Boethius, as Valla had argued, had obscured rather than solved the problem of free will (1072C).

Latinity

Murmellius is much more interested in the language than in the philosophy of the *Consolatio* and, consequently, his notes and clarifications focus mainly on grammar, syntax, figures of speech, meaning of words, spelling, other linguistic phenomena and formal aspects of argumentation. In places, this leads on to textual criticism, and the emendation of readings found in the medieval manuscripts. We shall give a few examples.

In metre 4 (line 11) of Book One, where Boethius speaks about 'cruel tyrants (*saevos tyrannos*) raging with no real power', Murmellius writes that one should read 'feros' and not 'saevos', a reading which Rudolph of Langen had seen in 'quodam exemplari' twelve years earlier when he had been consulted by Murmellius (913B). Rudolph of Langen is also credited with the reading 'excitantis' instead of 'exagitantis' (I m. 4, line 6), which can be read in 'exemplaribus depravatis' but which is supposed to be unmetrical (913A). And in the same metre (line 2), Agricola wants us to read 'dedit' instead of 'egit' which 'many copies have' (910C). (Ironically, the most recent editor of the *Consolatio*, Bieler, has opted for the readings rejected by these three humanists.) In the next prose part, Agricola emends

---

[28] Schmidt, 'Jodocus Badius Ascensius als Kommentator', 69.
[29] Nauwelaerts, 'Johannes Murmellius', 219.

(correctly) 'percussi sumus' to 'perculsi sumus', quoting Tacitus to strengthen his case (920B).

A gloss of a different kind is given to the word 'barbarorum' (917D). Here Agricola explains that the Greeks were wont to divide the whole human race into two categories: Greek and non-Greek, i.e. *barbari*. After the Greeks, Italians used the word to denote people devoid of 'humanitas et eruditio', and now Christians have appropriated the term to refer to non-Christians ('gentiles'). Formal aspects of argumentation are identified as in '*Nonne igitur bonum censes*] Syllogismus est tertii primae figurae modi' (1058C on IV pr. 7, line 17).

Etymologies are given, often taking into account a Greek origin, as in: '*Caminus*] Α καίομαι, quod est ardeo, dicitur' (911B); or '*Sirenes*] Graece scribitur Σειρὴν. Falluntur igitur qui per υ scribunt. Nec a σύρω, id est traho, sed vel a σείω, vel (quod magis probant) ἀπὸ τῆς σειρᾶς derivatur' (893D). When Boethius's diction reveals his debt to the Greek, this is noted too, as in 'notas insigniti frontibus' (branded on the forehead; I pr. 4, line 65): 'Figura loquendi Graeca', Agricola comments, for 'notis' would have been more correct (921A). 'Nihil puduit' in the same passage is a 'locutio Graecanica' (921C). 'Decretum' is glossed as corresponding with Greek δόγμα, 'quod indocti pro doctrina accipiunt' (924B).

In Cologne, Murmellius had learned Greek from Joannes Caesarius, a former pupil of Lefèvre d'Etaples, and by the time he came to write his Boethius commentary he had acquired sufficient knowledge of the language to allow him to teach it to his pupils. This enabled him to print (for the first time) the Greek quotations in the *Consolatio* in Greek characters, and to explain them with the aid of Caesarius and his friend Joannes Aedicollius.[30] Not surprisingly, the Ghent translator had still had to rely exclusively on Latin paraphrases of the Greek quotations.

Sometimes Boethius is criticized for his Latin. Living as he did in the early sixth century, he did not always meet the standards of classical Latinity, and certainly not the humanists' ideal (or idea) of pure, classical Latin. His images and metaphors are sometimes not to the taste of his humanists commentators. When Boethius writes, for example, 'compta colore' (bedecked in false colours; I m. 5, line 38), Agricola criticizes him: Boethius ought rather to have written 'tincta colore' (939D). Likewise, 'locari in sententia' (holding to an opinion; I pr. 6, line 16) is called a 'frigida et seg-

---

[30] See e.g. 918C-D; 932A; 957B; 1056A. Murmellius writes about the Greek expression ὄνος πρὸς λύραν (i.e. an ass hearing the sound of a lyre; I pr. 4, line 2) that Agricola had written it in 'Latinis litteris, forsitan eo quod is [i.e. Lambertus] cujus usui scriberet Graeca nesciret' (918C), but it is not clear whether all Greek quotations in Agricola's notes were written in Roman letters. Since Agricola's notes were written at the request of his friend Lambertus, who was his fellow student in Ferrara, it is possible that the notes date from Agricola's student days there.

nis translatio' (948D). On the other hand, Boethius is sometimes defended against the far more severe criticisms of Lorenzo Valla, who had launched an attack on his philosophy and particularly his Latin, abounding as it did in ungrammatical substantives such as *summum, bonum, unum* and *ens*.[31] Although Valla had famously called Boethius the 'last of the Romans, first of the scholastics', it was especially the second part of this tag that summed up what Valla thought of him in the field of language, namely that with Boethius, and largely because of him, Latin had deviated from its classical (Ciceronian) path and deteriorated with the ages. This concern for a return to classical Latin was shared by Agricola. To give an example: 'Affectus', Agricola writes, is what the Greeks call πάθος, and what moderns, ignorant of the Latin spoken by Cicero and other classical authors, incorrectly call 'passio' (943A). Murmellius repeats the point later on (950A-B), but generally takes no heed of Valla's appeal to replace substantives such as *summum, bonum* and the like for *res*. At one place, he refers to Valla's *De vero falsoque bono* (book 3), but adds that here the great Valla was 'driven by too great a desire for quibbling and hairsplitting' (nimia cavillandi libidine percitus; 1047B-D).[32]

These examples (which can be multiplied *ad infinitum*) will hardly surprise the reader of Renaissance editions of classical texts, but together with the impressive array of Greek, Latin, ancient and contemporary sources that Murmellius draws upon, they warrant, we think, the conclusion that his edition is indeed a creditable piece of philological scholarship. It may very well have been the first scholarly edition of the *Consolatio*, certainly more sophisticated than that of Badius Ascensius of 1498, who had already started to move away from the medieval 'interpretatio Christiana'.[33]

A last point which, for the sake of convenience, may be noted under the heading of Latinity is the fact that Murmellius is not much interested in natural science, while his medieval predecessors could easily fill a page or two in explaining Boethius's allusions to comets, planets, stars and such natural phenomena as winds, tides, thunder, and so forth.

---

[31] Valla's views on Boethius's style, see e.g. Gaeta, *Lorenzo Valla*.

[32] Cf. 986C: '*Summum*] Bonum summum, rem summam, bonorum finem'. (Possibly under the influence of Valla?)

[33] *Commentum duplex in Boetium de consolatione philosophiae*, Lugduni 1498 (= Ps-Aquinas and Badius Ascensius), praefatio. Cf. Courcelle, *La Consolation de Philosophie*, 331-2; Herding, 'Probleme des frühen Humanismus', 352 note 31, where Murmellius is quoted as saying that Badius Ascensius 'tardiusculis ingeniis totum se accommodat'. On the other hand, Ascensius often quotes Lorenzo Valla's *Elegantiae*, which reflects his linguistic (esp. grammatical) orientation. See Schmidt, 'Jodocus Badius Ascensius als Kommentator', esp. 66.

General attitude to Boethius

Boethius was recognized throughout the Middle Ages as a Christian author, but at the same time it was realized that Christianity was conspicuously absent from the *Consolatio*. Hence, the urge was always felt of defending Boethius from critics (such as Bovo of Corvey, c. 900) who associated him with the pagan Platonists. In his Boethius commentary, published in 1498, Badius Ascensius, however, had rejected the 'interpretatio Christiana' of the *Consolatio* without feeling that he thereby jeopardized its status as a morally edifying classic.[34]

This de-christianization of the *Consolatio* became possible, of course, only when a wider knowledge of Boethius's time, culture and its pagan background began to be acquired. Like Badius Ascensius, Agricola and Murmellius felt that a sound interpretation of the *Consolatio* must take Platonic philosophy into account, without denying the fact that Boethius was a Christian. As Agricola writes: 'Boethius was not only a Christian, but also a follower of the old Academy of Plato' (946C). At times, however, even Murmellius cannot refrain from giving passages a Christian twist, for example where Boethius writes about the many (*multos*) who 'have sought the enjoyment of happiness not simply through death but even through pain and suffering'. Murmellius glosses 'multos' with: 'Non Stoicos, neque Cynicos, sed magis Christianos martyres accipe' (968D on II pr. 4, lines 97-101).[35] The allusions in the text to Neoplatonic doctrines such as the pre-existence of the soul, knowledge as recollection, the creation of the World Soul and the eternity of the world, are elucidated by ample quotations from, for example, Plato's *Timaeus* ('pulcherrimum librum', 1023A) and Macrobius's *On the Dream of Scipio*. Such typically humanist notions as the immortality of the soul and the divine origin of man's soul are emphasized.[36] The regular occurrence, however, of phrases like 'ex Platonis doctrina', 'ut Platoni placet' and 'ut Platoni visum est' must make it clear that Murmellius, knowing that Boethius was more of a Platonist than an Aristotelian ('magis sit Platonicus quam Aristotelicus'; 1066C), cannot always share Boethius's Platonism: the notion of the soul's preexistence and learning as anamnèsis is rejected as 'vanissimum'; Plato is said to use 'summa et incredibili eloquentia' and the authority of Augustine is invoked to refute the

---

[34] Schmidt, 'Jodocus Badius Ascensius als Kommentator', 67-8.

[35] Cf. 992A (on II m. 8, line 22). Murmellius does not gloss the other passage, where Boethius, according to many medieval commentators, was alluding to Christian martyrs (IV pr. 6, line 154) – an example of Christian interpretation that Badius Ascensius had rejected (*Commentum duplex in Boetium*, ad loc.).

[36] E.g. on III m. 2: 'Unde probat hominis originem coelestem esse, et a summo bono profectam' (997C).

'Platonicum dogma'.[37]

Another aspect of Murmellius's interpretation is the apparent absence of a desire to read more behind the text than is in fact there (which is not to say that the humanists did not have their own programme in interpreting classical texts). The medieval bent for allegorization is discarded, leaving thereby more room for humanist interest in philological and historical matters. Thus, the Orpheus myth at the end of Book 3, as well as other mythological passages, are dealt with in a cursory way and are not treated as *integumenta*, that is coverings of more profound (Christian) meanings.[38] In this context, there is an interesting remark by Agricola, who notes that Boethius's pervasive use of medical metaphors, such as milder and stronger medicines to cure the patient, turns the *Consolatio* almost into 'allegoria' (943B). It is clear that this emphasis on the literal sense has a different ring from that in medieval hermeneutics. For medieval scholars the *Consolatio* could be read at several levels, and the term 'allegoria' was especially used for denoting the deeper meanings (plural) of, for example, the Orpheus fable and the myth of the creation of the world in the Platonic hymn in Book 3, m. 9. The most that Murmellius will allow by way of a figural sense, on the other hand, is the hardly surprising reading of Lady Philosophy as 'recta ratio' and Boethius as a 'homo fortunae adversitatibus afflictus' (889B).

Conclusion

In this paper we have looked at two very different works, the *Ghent Boethius* and the commentary by Murmellius (with notes by Agricola). Within the limits of our contribution, it has been neither possible nor feasible to discuss other texts, but even from this limited material we are able to draw a few conclusions. As should be expected, continuity and innovation can be observed in the study of the *Consolatio* around 1500. The *Ghent Boethius* seems to be a product of late-medieval religious culture, and the interpretation is therefore couched in devotional and religious terms. Boethius is

---

[37] See resp. 1036A-B; 1037A-B; 1036B. We cannot therefore fully agree with D'Elia, who suggested (without much discussion) that Murmellius '[s]equendo questa precisa linea ermeneutica di convergenza del carme boeziano [i.e. III metre 9] con la dottrina biblico-patristica [...] è indotto a minimizzare la concezione dell' anima del mondo e della preesistenza delle anime' ('Il commento di Giovanni Murmellius', 453). On the history of these Platonic notions, see Nauta, 'The Preexistence of the Soul in Medieval Thought'.

[38] Murmellius refers to the standard medieval interpretation (initiated by William of Conches) as 'Quam [sc. fabulam] quidem sic interpretantur: Orpheus uxorem habuit Eurydicen [...]', and briefly summarizes it ('Est autem Eurydice humana anima [...]'; 1039B-C).

treated as an Everyman, and his imprisonment and fallen state function as a mirror in which late-medieval men and women could see reflected their own post-lapsarian condition reflected. The impersonal return of the soul to the One in Boethius's Neoplatonic world view is easily interpreted in late-medieval terms of personal devotion and mystical unification of man with God. The Ghent Commentary, moreover, reflects a typical feature of many medieval commentaries: it has the size and almost the character of an encyclopedia, packed as it is with an enormous amount of learning and hundreds of quotations.

The commentary by Murmellius and Agricola, on the other hand, entirely lacks encyclopedic character. The emphasis here is on the language of the *Consolatio*, its imagery, its sources and parallels in other classical works, and the background of the political upheavals of Boethius's time. They certainly do not ignore the moral-pedagogical dimension of the work, but there is hardly any exploration of that dimension, unlike the *Ghent Boethius*. The text is pressed into service as an aid to the study of the language of a late-classical text. Rather than offering a devotional and religious interpretation, they recognize the complexity of Boethius's culture in which Neoplatonism and Christianity could form one intellectual amalgam. The appropriation of classical sources, including Greek ones, is vastly different from the clusters of quotations from Augustine, Ambrose, Chrysostom, Bernard of Clairvaux, Bonaventure and so forth, that the *Ghent Boethius* offers as a means to inculcate devotional-moral instructions.

The differences between the two works, however, should not blind us to the fact that there are also similarities to be noticed, which – when put into a broader, historical context – illustrate the multicoloured and complicated transition from late-medieval scholasticism to humanism. This is too broad an issue to broach here, but a few remarks are in order. First, the literary genre of the commentary was not abandoned by the northern humanists, but was taken as a vital vehicle for teaching the classics and the Latin language.[39] Besides, although its character changed over the years, many of its ingredients, such as grammatical explanations, paraphrases, etymologies, synonyms of words and the like, remained standard elements. In this respect, the difference between the *Ghent Boethius* and Murmellius's commentary is one of degree rather than of kind.

The Dutch translation of the Ghent translator is characterized by a sound

---

[39] Kemnerus, for example, who was rector of the Latin school in Münster (under whom Murmellius was conrector), wrote commentaries on medieval text books such as Alexander de Villa Dei's *Doctrinale* and Peter Hispanus's *Summulae logicales* for his students. This was the rule rather than the exception. In general, see *Der Kommentar in der Renaissance*; Kristeller, *Medieval Aspects of Renaissance Learning*.

grasp of the complexities of Boethius's Latin. As Hoek has shown, it can bear favourable comparison with other medieval translations.[40] His translation was clearly done from the Latin original without the aid of another vernacular translation as intermediary (as in the case of his predecessor in Dutch, Jacob Vilt, who used a French translation, or Chaucer, who used Jean de Meun's *Li Livres de Confort*). It was no longer a paraphrase (as in the Old-French tradition), but an attempt to render the Latin as correctly and faithfully as possible. Another indication of its high quality is the fact that it was taken as a model by the Dutch humanist Dirck Volckertszoon Coornhert, who published his first translation of the *Consolatio* in 1557.[41]

Although, as we have seen, the objectives of the two Boethius scholars are different, on a higher level they were both concerned with the well-being of their pupils and readers. Murmellius's oeuvre is imbued with the desire to improve his pupils' knowledge of Latin in order that they may be morally better persons.[42] His aims are as pedagogical as those of the Ghent commentator, but less aimed at piety and devotion than the latter. To quote Herding's paraphrase of Murmellius's programmatic statement in his *Enchiridion Scholasticorum* (1505): 'Am Ende möge sich jeder Mensch erinnern, daß er dazu geboren ist, um sich durch gutes und ehrenhaftes Leben und durch die Bewahrung des göttlichen Gesetzes den Weg zum Himmel zu bahnen. *Quod si litteras noverit, facillime effecturus est!*' Murmellius, underlining the high sentential value of the *Consolatio*, often exclaims: 'Pulchra verissimaque conclusio' (964A), 'Pulchra exclamatio' (981B), 'Sententia est notissima' (1008A), 'Vetus adagium est' (1021B) and so forth, and he provides strings of quotations to illustrate moral lesson such as 'nobody is free from care in this life' (966B-C), 'he who is silent and speaks at the appropriate time, is wise' (986A-B). Here too, the distance between the world of the Ghent commentator and the adagium culture of Murmellius, who recommends Pseudo-Cato's *Disticha Catonis* and Pseudo-Seneca's *De quatuor virtutibus* for moral education, does not seem that far, and illustrates what Schmidt has called the 'langandauernden Lösungsprozeß vom Mittelalter'.[43]

But here the similarities end. What is conspicuously absent from Murmellius is the effort to provide the *Consolatio* with an 'interpretatio Christiana'. Indeed, Murmellius and Agricola viewed medieval allegorization and christianization rather as impediments standing in the way of a proper understanding of the *Consolatio*. Thus, their sense of 'understanding a text'

---

[40] Hoek, *Middelnederlandse vertalingen*, esp. 113ff and 190-3.
[41] Cf. Gerritsen, 'Coornhert and Boethius'.
[42] See Herding, 'Probleme des frühen Humanismus', 356-8 (also for the following quotation).
[43] Schmidt, 'Jodocus Badius Ascensius als Kommentator', 69.

seems to be different from the *Ghent Boethius*'s. In this they show themselves to possess what Panofsky has called 'a focused perspective'. 'The Middle Ages', Panofsky wrote in his book *Renaissance and Renascences in Western Art*, 'had left Antiquity unburied and alternately galvanized and exorcised its corpse. The Renaissance stood weeping at its grave and tried to resurrect its soul. And in one fatally auspicious moment it succeeded.'[44] Although most of us have no wish to subscribe to that last conclusion, it is evident that the changing interpretations of the *Consolatio* form an apt illustration of the new and important contributions of the northern humanists to a resurrection of their version of 'the soul of Antiquity'.

---

[44] Panofsky, *Renaissance and Renascences*, 113.

M.J.F.M. HOENEN

AT THE CROSSROADS OF SCHOLASTICISM AND NORTHERN HUMANISM*

The late medieval and early modern periods experienced change in a variety of fields: economics, religion, theology, and philosophy. These changes have been studied in many articles and book publications, most recently in the two-volume *Handbook of European History 1400-1600*.[1] Some of the most interesting studies have shown – if we restrict ourselves to the transition from scholasticism to humanism – that scholasticism already bears humanist elements and that conversely humanism still carries with it scholastic attributes, an observation which *mutatis mutandis* also applies to many other changing areas of the period.[2] The distinction, then, between scholasticism and humanism is not as strict as some of the standard works of intellectual history would have it. This is hardly surprising. Historical reality is always more complex than human concepts can express. To meet this complexity, the transition from scholasticism to humanism needs to be studied again and again, when new questions suggest themselves, and in the light of newly revealed or neglected scholastic sources. Only then can we begin to understand the complexities of intellectual history as it evolved in the late medieval and early modern period.[3]

For my part I would like to investigate the similarities and differences between scholasticism and northern humanism based on some interesting scholastic source materials, that in my view deserve closer attention and study. It is my contention that these materials shed new light on the relationship between scholasticism and humanism. Before starting the investigation, however, the following methodological remark needs to be made, because the structure of the inquiry is guided by it. I consider neither scholasticism nor northern humanism as self-contained units.[4] They each embrace a great

* Research for this paper was funded by the Netherlands Organization for Scientific Research (NWO). I thank Inigo Bocken, Lodi Nauta, Harold J. Cook and Faye Getz for their helpful suggestions.
[1] *Handbook of European History, 1400-1600.* See also with extensive bibliography Meuthen, *Das 15. Jahrhundert.*
[2] See among others the classic studies of Gilson, *La philosophie au Moyen Age*, 741-53 (Le retour des lettres en France), and Kristeller, *Medieval Aspects of Renaissance Learning.*
[3] Cf. Saccaro, *Französischer Humanismus des 14. und 15. Jahrhunderts*, 7.
[4] On the characteristics of northern humanism, its differences from Italian humanism, especially its focus on religious questions and its penetration into the universities, see Nauert, *Humanism and*

many different and sometimes conflicting aspects, which together result in what we call in shortened form 'scholasticism' and 'northern humanism'. These aspects do not always imply each other or form a necessary or exclusive unity.[5]

I will therefore not take scholasticism or northern humanism as a whole, but consider only a number of different aspects, which will be studied according to their own separate development. At the end of the investigation, these different aspects will be brought together, to see whether they still match the traditional concept of the distinction between scholasticism and northern humanism. I have selected the following items for study here: 1. the style and format of the treatises, 2. the language used, 3. the sources which are employed, and 4. the subjects under discussion. The emphasis will be on the scholastic sources, yet I will single out those developments which, though still belonging to the scholastic tradition, already manifest some characteristics of northern humanism. As will become apparent from this study, the transition from scholasticism to northern humanism began early and was much more gradual than one is at first glance inclined to believe, at least if we consider the different aspects separately. The final rupture between the two came only then, when the four different aspects of style, language, sources, and subject matters pointed in one direction and hence were able to reinforce each other and to intensify, a constellation which happened about the end of the fifteenth century. By then, the dominant intellectual culture changed substantially and urged the historians to speak of a new period in intellectual history, the humanist era.[6]

Style and format of the treatises

Since the thirteenth century, at the universities and *studia* of the religious orders, a style of reasoning emerges that has become characteristic of scholasticism and which indeed can be said to have given scholasticism its proper name. This style is largely determined by the educational and institutional

---

the Culture of Renaissance Europe, 95-163, with an annotated bibliography on 222-6. For a description of scholasticism and its method, see De Rijk, *La philosophie au Moyen Age*, 82-105.

[5] Both scholasticism and northern humanism, for example, embody the conflict between tradition and renewal, each in its own way. In scholasticism that conflict is manifested in the many commentaries on set texts, whereas in humanism it is materialized in the debate over *Latinitas*, as exemplified by the many texts on this issue, such as Erasmus's *Ciceronianus* (*ASD* I-2, 581-710). On the Ciceronian controversy, see Copenhaver and Schmitt, *Renaissance Philosophy*, 206-9.

[6] This is not to say that scholasticism disappears. It remained partially alive at the universities, which by rigidity of their educational programs had a tendency to conservatism and thus impeded overall humanist influence.

settings and it manifests itself in two forms: that of the commentary and that of the disputation.[7] Already in antiquity, important works were explained and commented upon in a regularized fashion, as is exemplified by the many Greek commentaries on Plato and Aristotle.[8] It is this habit of elucidating key texts that continued into the Middle Ages. A clear example of the early medieval traditions are the commentaries on Boethius's *Consolatio*, the earliest of which dates from the ninth century.[9] As part of the twelfth-century renaissance, as is well-known, the Latin West absorbed a great number of new Greek and Arab sources, thereby stimulating new commentary traditions, which became part of the newly-established university system.[10] Soon glosses and commentaries on the *Sentences* of Peter Lombard became standard works and the first commentaries on the newly recovered works of Aristotle appeared.[11] These commentaries were not occasional pieces, but they were written as part of the educational system: they were the starting point for discussion and the means by which intellectual knowledge was passed on to the younger generation.[12]

It goes without saying that the flurry of commentaries and the fact that knowledge was developed and transmitted almost exclusively by these commentaries, had an enormous impact on the formal structure of scholastic thinking. I will single out four features:

1. There is a rigorous arrangement of and a strict connection between the subjects under discussion, which is determined not by the subject matter itself or by contemporary interests, but by the text that is commented upon. In the commentaries on Peter Lombard, problems concerning the nature of God are always treated in the first book, whereas those concerning human beings are discussed in the second.[13]

---

[7] See Kenny and Pinborg, 'Medieval Philosophical Literature'; Schönberger, *Was ist Scholastik*, 52-102.

[8] For the Greek commentaries on Plato, see *The Greek Commentaries on Plato's Phaedo*, 7-20. For commentaries on Aristotle, see the 'General Introduction' by Sorabji in Philoponus, *Against Aristotle*, 1-17 (with a list of the commentaries edited in the Berlin edition).

[9] On these commentaries, see Courcelle, *La Consolation de Philosophie*.

[10] On the twelfth century renaissance, see among others *A History of Twelfth-Century Western Philosophy*; and *Aufbruch, Wandel, Erneuerung*.

[11] The glosses and commentaries on Peter are discussed in Colish, 'From the Sentence Collection to the Sentence Commentary'. For information on the reception of Aristotle see De Libera, *La philosophie médiévale*, 358-67.

[12] Not only in the Latin, but also in the vernacular tradition, translations, glosses, and commentaries played an important role in education, as is exemplified by the vernacular reception of Boethius's *De consolatione*. For a recent review of the field, see Kaylor, *The Medieval Consolation of Philosophy*.

[13] An outline of the chapters of the *Sententiae* of Peter Lombard is given in Lombardus, *Sententiae in IV libris distinctae*, 5-53. On the theology of Peter Lombard, see Colish, *Peter Lombard*.

2. Also, there is a certain restriction as to the subjects that are treated: not only the organization and ordering, but also the themes are fixed by the text under consideration. In every commentary, the same problems are discussed.[14] As we will see further on, in the *quaestiones quodlibetales* these two restrictions are eliminated. But even so, in their circulated form, they follow the structure of the set texts.

3. These two points, the invariable structure and the fixed subjects, stimulate the rise of theological and philosophical schools, which although they may and do represent conflicting currents of thoughts, are part of a large coordinating tradition, as the same texts and the same subjects are discussed over a period that covers several intellectual generations.[15]

4. Finally there is a continuing unity as far as terminology and concepts are concerned, that rests on the source texts that are commented upon. This too provokes uniformity of intellectual style and motivates the emergence of related intellectual traditions, which in spite of their diversity all bear the characteristics of scholasticism.

The disputation, the second literary genre typical of scholasticism, is much more freely structured.[16] Its format is largely dominated by developments in medieval logic, especially since the end of the thirteenth century. The emphasis is on the logical structure of the argument. The reasoning becomes separated in distinct statements (*conclusiones*), each of which are demonstrated syllogistically.[17] Also the development of the obligations-literature, which studies the rules of different sorts of dialectical disputation, played an important role in the structuring and formalization of the scholastic debates, especially those of the fourteenth century.[18]

---

[14] Cf. e.g. the *Sentences* commentaries of the second half of the 13th and the early 14th centuries (Bonaventure, Thomas Aquinas, Richard de Mediavilla, Giles of Rome, John Quidort, Hervaeus Natalis). The same applies to the commentaries on Aristotle at the university of Paris in the mid-14th century, as is documented in the list of questions published in Marshall, 'Parisian Psychology in the Mid-Fourteenth Century'. Also it should be taken into account that there was an institutional separation of philosophy and theology at the university of Paris: members of the Arts faculty were not allowed to discuss theological problems. See *Chartularium Universitatis Parisiensis I*, n. 441, 499f. (1272).

[15] On the medieval schools of thought, see Courtenay, *Schools and Scholars in Fourteenth-Century England*; Kaluza, *Les querelles doctrinales à Paris*; and *Philosophy and Learning. Universities in the Middle Ages*, esp. 247-386 (Late medieval universities: School formation and school conflict).

[16] On the disputation, see the contributions of Bazan and Wippel in *Les genres littéraires dans les sources théologiques et philosophiques médiévales*, 31-49 and 67-84; and Weijers, 'L'enseignement du *trivium* à la Faculté des arts de Paris'.

[17] An example of this is provided by the disputation between Pierre Roger and Francis of Mayronis as it survived in their *principia*. See Barbet, *François de Meyronnes–Pierre Roger*, esp. 39-49, which gives the structure of the dispute.

[18] On the medieval game of obligation, see the contributions of Stump and Spade in *The Cambridge History of Later Medieval Philosophy* (1982), 315-41.

The nature of subjects that are treated in these debates depends on the type of disputation, of which there are several. The *quaestiones quodlibetales* have a much looser subject matter than the *quaestiones disputatae* or the *quaestiones vacantiales*, which in the theological faculty are often structured according to the *Sentences* of Peter Lombard.[19] Yet also the much looser *quaestiones quodlibetales*, which theoretically could cover any subject that had contemporary interest, in their circulated form are mostly organized as the *quaestiones disputatae* or *quaestiones vacantiales*, thus witnessing medieval concern for method and order.[20]

This form of scholasticism, as it expressed itself in the commentary and disputation, accounts for developments during the second half of the thirteenth and the first two decades of the fourteenth century, both on the Continent (Paris) and in England (Oxford and Cambridge). If attention were fixed only to developments on the Continent, one might be inclined to think that the traditional form of scholasticism as described here continued until the beginning of the sixteenth century. One may refer to the many commentaries on Aristotle, the *Sentences* commentaries of John Capreolus, Denys the Carthusian and John Tartaretus, as well as to the notebooks with disputations from the second half of the fifteenth century.[21] Against this background, the works of the humanists are completely different in style and subject: they appear less traditional, are more freely composed, and have not a logical, but a rhetorical line of reasoning.

If this traditional picture of the scholastic period were complete and exhaustive, then indeed there was a remarkable change between scholasticism and humanism. However, it is not complete. It applies largely to the Continent, but not to fourteenth- and fifteenth-century England. If we consider scholasticism as it developed at the university of Oxford, things appear differently and are more in line with the above mentioned characteristics of humanist writings.

---

[19] For the *quaestiones quodlibetales* and *quaestiones disputatae*, see the literature in n. 16 above. A collection of *quaestiones vacantiales* that were held in 1465 and 1466 at the university of Cologne has been preserved in Eichstätt, Universitätsbibliothek, Cod. st 688. I discussed one of its questions in my 'Tradition and Renewal'.

[20] Cf. Thomas of Sutton, *Quodlibeta*, especially Sutton's remarks at the beginning of each *Quodlibet*, at 3, 155, 339, and 495. The commentary and the disputation not only exist separately, but also together. This is the case in the so-called question-commentaries. In these treatises, elements of the disputation are incorporated in the structure of the commentary. Examples are the commentaries on Aristotle by Buridan and Marsilius of Inghen and the commentaries on Lombard by Gregory of Rimini and again Marsilius of Inghen.

[21] On these notebooks, see Löhr, *Die theologischen Disputationen an der Universität Köln*; and Shank, *'Unless You Believe You Shall Not Understand'*, 205-19.

In the following I will point out a few aspects of this remarkable development, which begins in the 1320s at Oxford with a shift in the nature and arrangement of traditional scholastic treatises.

1. The number of *quaestiones quodlibetales* decreases since the 1320s and only fifteen years later, after 1335, they disappear almost entirely. With this, one of the two typical scholastic genres, the disputation, becomes notably rare.[22]

2. Also with regard to the commentaries on the *Sentences* there is a change. In contrast to what happened on the Continent, the English commentaries and especially those read at Oxford became much more independent of the text of Peter Lombard. Emphasis is on the first of the four books, which gets most of the attention.[23] Also there is a change in the arrangement of the topics that are discussed. Robert Holcot deals with the problem of divine foreknowledge not in the first book, where the divine attributes are usually discussed, but in the second book as part of the theory of creation.[24] This means that the original structure of the text that is commented upon is left behind and that the author follows his own ambition and design. The distance between the commentary and its principal source is growing, which means that the nature of these commentaries has been changed as compared to that of the previous period: there is a shift away from the commentary on a traditional source to a more or less independent work, written only with loose reference to that source.

3. In the following period, after about 1350, other literary forms are preferred, as a result of which the *Sentences* commentary almost completely disappears as a genre. A clear example is John Wyclif, who in all probability incorporated the materials from his lectures on the *Sentences* in his *Summa de ente*, a work with an entirely different structure.[25] The style of other philosophical and theological treatises changes as well. A growing number of works are devoted to a single subject, dealing with current matters of debate. Again the works of Wyclif are a case in point. His *De veritate sacrae scripturae* criticizes contemporary 'sophistic' exegesis of the Scripture and his *Summa de ente* discusses topics that dominated late medieval thinking, such as the divine attributes, the problem of time, and theory of the univer-

---

[22] See with references to the sources Courtenay, *Schools and Scholars in Fourteenth-Century England*, 45; 251f.

[23] This development is studied in op. cit., 252-8.

[24] Holcot, *In quatuor libros Sententiarum quaestiones*, II q. 2; and *Seeing the Future Clearly*, which contains on 112-195 a critical edition of the pertinent question.

[25] On the structure of the *Summa de ente* and its relationship to the commentary of the *Sentences*, see Robson, *Wyclif and the Oxford Schools*, 115-40; Catto, 'Wyclif and Wycliffism at Oxford', esp. 179.

sals, almost independent of any set text and with a clearly personal spirit and ambition.[26]

4. Not only the treatises, but also the nature of theology changes. Since the second half of the fourteenth century, speculative and metaphysically based theology gradually gave way to a more practically orientated style. This change is documented by the growing number of commentaries on Scripture, in which those parts of Scripture are most commonly dealt with that have a liturgical and thus a practical significance.[27]

5. Finally, at the end of the century there is also a shift in the public to whom the philosophical and theological treatises are addressed. They are no longer produced solely for an academic audience, but also for laymen, those who have had little or no academic training, and they are written more and more in the vernacular.[28] The works of Reginald Pecock are an impressive example of this development, especially his *Repressor*, a vernacular treatise in which Lollard's attitude towards Scripture is heavily criticized.[29]

Considering these issues, it is clear that a number of specific aspects of scholasticism were transformed in the fourteenth century: the style, the format and the language of the treatises. Yet the works which document these changes are still part of the scholastic tradition. The theory of universals as put forward by Wyclif, which according to his own statement is the cornerstone of his reading of Scripture, can only be understood as part of medieval scholastic developments.[30] And the same applies to the syllogism and the 'doom of reason', the foundations of the thinking of Reginald Pecock.[31]

If we now consider the northern humanists, we find that they react against the traditional form of the scholastic treatise and that they choose a form which corresponds to the style and format of the writings mentioned above.[32] I will limit myself to a discussion of two authors, Wessel Gansfort and Desiderius Erasmus, both significant exponents of northern humanism, but what will be said can easily be applied to other writers as well.

---

[26] Wyclif, *De veritate Sacrae Scripturae*; cf. Catto, 'Wyclif and Wycliffism at Oxford', 209. For a discussion of the theories of the *Summa de ente*: Robson, *Wyclif and the Oxford Schools*, 141-95.

[27] For references to source materials, see Catto, 'Wyclif and Wycliffism at Oxford'; Catto, 'Theology after Wycliffism' (with examples).

[28] On this development, see Courtenay, *Schools and Scholars in Fourteenth-Century England*, 355; 356-80.

[29] A printed edition of this work is available in Pecock, *The Repressor of Overmuch Blaming of the Clergy*.

[30] Wyclif, *Determinatio contra Kylingham Carmelitam*, esp. 453. Wyclif's theory of universals is dicussed by Spade in Wyclif, *On Universals (Tractatus de universalibus)*, vii-xlvii. For a recent history of the problem of universals, see De Libera, *La querelle des universaux*.

[31] An introduction into the thinking of Pecock is Green, *Bishop Reginald Recock*.

[32] A recent study on the discussions between scholasticism and humanism is Rummel, *The Humanist-Scholastic Debate*. See also Overfield, *Humanism and Scholasticism in Late Medieval Germany*.

The writings of Wessel Gansfort, as they are published in the edition of 1614, are a good example of theologically inspired northern humanism. They do not include commentaries on set texts such as those of Aristotle or Peter Lombard nor on any *quaestiones disputatae* or *quaestiones quodlibetales*. Also the lost writings, which are known only by title, do not seem to be of a scholastic nature.[33]

Although Wessel Gansfort treats traditional subjects that are also discussed by scholastic authors, such as the Pater Noster, the Incarnation, and the Eucharist, his way of handling them is free and not dominated by traditional rules. Also, his style of reasoning and his vocabulary is not scholastic. He rarely uses the syllogism and his argumentation is not logical but rather essayistic and expository, as in the writings of Wyclif and Pecock.[34]

This line continues in the case of Erasmus. His enormous oeuvre is strongly influenced by classical authors and the Greek and Latin Fathers. Compared to scholastic literature, it is designed more freely, the subjects discussed are not determined by set texts, the intended public is not academic, and he uses sources that are not part of the university curriculum.[35] In his writings, he emphasizes the practical rather than the theoretical significance of his subjects, as is exemplified in his *Enchiridion militis christiani* and still more clearly in his polemic writings on the free will, *De libero arbitrio* and the *Hyperaspistes*, a topic that caused scholastic writers to engage in elaborate semantic distinctions, which are absent in his works.[36]

It is clear from the above that there are a number of similarities in style and format between John Wyclif and Reginald Pecock, and Wessel Gansfort and Erasmus. The typical features of the commentary and the *quaestiones*, which characterized scholasticism since the thirteenth century, are no longer visible in their works. Yet, these similarities should not make us blind to the differences, as they are also significant. The language of Wyclif and Pecock is different from that of Wessel and Erasmus. In their phrases, the syntax is still dominated by medieval scholastic Latin. The writings of Wyclif and Pecock in this respect belong to a different era. This means that by limiting ourselves to the format of the treatises, the initial question about the transition from scholasticism to humanism cannot properly be solved. We have to consider a second aspect, that of the language.

---

[33] Gansfort, *Opera* (with a list of his works on f. ***6). On the extant and lost writings of Wessel, see Van Rhijn, *Wessel Gansfort*, LI-LXX (bijlage C). Further editions of his works are listed in *Wessel Gansfort and Northern Humanism*, 395f. (Bibliography).

[34] For a discussion of the thought of Wessel, see the volumes mentioned in the previous note.

[35] On Erasmus, see with a bibliography the study of Augustijn, *Erasmus*.

[36] These writings are extensively discussed in the study of Augustijn and printed in *LB* V 1-66 (*Enchiridion*); IX 1215-48 (*De libero arbitrio*); X 1249-1336 (*Hyperaspistes*).

The language

One of the most striking characteristics of humanism is its renewed attention to language. This expresses itself in different ways, for example in highlighting rhetoric as a substitute for scholastic logic and also in the pursuit of a new Latin style.[37] This last item is important for our investigation. Humanism is averse to scholastic Latin and seeks classical latinity, an ambition that is expressed by humanist Ciceronianism.[38] For many humanists, Cicero was the model of right and proper Latin, with regard to his vocabulary, his style, and the spiritual attitude which emanated from his writings. This phenomenon is carefully immortalized in the person of Nosoponus in the *Ciceronianus* of Erasmus.[39] It is not new. Already in Latin antiquity, language and culture were measured according to the rules of Cicero. In the Renaissance, however, Latin style and culture were used as weapons against scholasticism, from which humanists sought to distinguish themselves with the most basic means for human communication: the spoken and written language.

If one compares scholastic and humanist Latin, there is a difference as to sources of vocabulary. What the authors of classical antiquity did for the stock of words used by the humanists, the Latin translations of Aristotle, Avicenna, and Averroes did for that of the scholastics. As a result of an intensive reading of these sources, elements of vocabulary and the syntax were absorbed. The following examples illustrate the growth of Latin philosophical terminology in scholasticism based on the reading of the new translations: 'certitudo' for essence, 'intentio' for concept, and 'esse diminutum' for the intelligible object of thinking or being found in the mind – all these terms were used to express concepts in Arabic sources and received different meanings than they had had before as a consequence of that use.[40] Also, idiomatic expressions were taken over from the new translations of Arabic texts, such as 'redeamus et dicimus', 'intelligas igitur' and 'ex hoc accipe', phrases that are not used in classical or early medieval Latin.[41]

Not only the sources, but also the educational framework put its stamp on the scholastic language. In many fourteenth- and fifteenth-century treatises,

---

[37] On humanist rhetoric and Latin style, see Jensen, 'The Humanist Reform of Latin and Latin Teaching'; Mack, 'Humanist Rhetoric and Dialectic'; Murphy, *Renaissance Eloquence*; Vasoli, *La dialettica e la retorica dell' Umanesimo*.

[38] A bibliography on Ciceronianism s.v. in *Historisches Wörterbuch der Rhetorik*, II 225-47.

[39] See note 4 above.

[40] See Goichon, *Lexique de la langue philosophique d'Ibn Sina (Avicenne)*, n. 171 (haqiqa, *certitudo*); n. 468 (ma'na, *intentio*); and Maurer, '*Ens Diminutum*'.

[41] These expressions are frequently used in the Latin translations of the works of Avicenna and the *Liber de causis*. The Latin translations of the works of Avicenna are now available in the series *Avicenna Latinus* (Leiden 1968-). For the Latin translation of the *Liber de causis*, see Pattin, 'Le Liber de causis. Édition'.

one comes across clauses beginning with 'arguo', 'distinguo', and 'sed dice-res', which have their origin in the scholastic disputation and are rather strange and uncommon to classical ears.

Moreover, since the thirteenth century the syntax of Latin philosophical and theological treatises becomes plain and unsophisticated. The word order is guided by that of spoken language: the sentences became shorter and words that belonged together were put together and not dispersed for aesthetic reasons. *What* is said is more important than *how* it is said. The Latin of twelfth-century authors such as John of Salisbury and Alan of Lille is more complicated than that of thirteenth-century university teachers like Bonaventure and Thomas Aquinas.[42]

Yet, these two characteristics – the use of words alien to classical Latin and the simplified syntax – do not completely explain scholastic Latin. In the second half of the fourteenth century, for example, there is a remarkable change in the language used at the universities. In the writings of some authors, the vocabulary becomes more poetic and the syntax becomes more complicated than in other contemporary sources, which still use the tradi-tional scholastic style from the thirteenth and early fourteenth centuries. The writings of Peter Ceffons of Clairvaux are an interesting case in point here. Even in traditional scholastic writings such as the commentary on the *Sen-tences*, he shows a remarkably humanist attitude. In the opening lectures of the commentary, the *principia*, he quotes many classical sources and writes literary and poetic Latin.[43] In the *Tractatus trium libellorum* he distinguishes between the rhetorical Latin he normally writes and the scholastic Latin of the doctors that is required for the treatise, excusing himself for using the latter.[44]

In the fifteenth century this development continues and increases in inten-sity. I give three examples: 1. The written language becomes more elaborate, as is testified by the growing use of doublets. In at least one case it is pos-sible to trace back the introduction of this stylistic phenomenon. In the edit-ion of the *Problemata* of Heymericus de Campo, there are a great number of doublets. This edition was printed in 1496 in Cologne by John Landen.[45] In the manuscripts, however, which go back to the original text that was

---

[42] Cf. e.g. John of Salisbury, *Policraticus*, or the works collected in *Alain de Lille. Textes Inédits*.

[43] Trapp, 'Peter Ceffons of Clairvaux'.

[44] Troyes, cod. 930, 79r (as quoted in Trapp, 'Peter Ceffons of Clairvaux', 112): "Depositis etiam coloratis rhetoricae sermonibus et stellato Latino, verborum ornatibus, dictaminis amictibus phalera-tis, ut paululum cedat Quintilianus cum Sidonio et quiescat rhetorica Tulliana, utar communi stilo doctorum theologiae eorumque dum describunt quaestiones [...]."

[45] Heymericus de Campo, *Problemata inter Albertum Magnum et Sanctum Thomam*.

published in 1428, their number is far less.[46] The editor, John Landen, adjusted his edition of the text to the taste of the medieval Latin reader. Where the manuscripts read 'per illustrationem intellectus agentis', the printed edition has 'per illustrationem et lumen intellectus agentis'. And where the manuscripts already use a doublet 'a causa gustus et nutritionis', the printed version adds a second one 'a causa vel cura gustus et nutritionis'.[47]

One can only speculate about the reasons why these doublets occur in philosophical texts. In any case, it makes clear that according to the author or editor, the essence of what he likes to say cannot adequately be expressed by the meaning of a single word, an attitude that fits perfectly with the growing influence of realism over nominalism in Paris and other universities, such as Cologne where the *Tractatus problematicus* was written and printed.[48] According to nominalism, the meaning is imposed on the word by the user of the language. Therefore, words always refer to what is meant. According to realism, however, words refer to a world that exists independently of the speaker. If reality is too complex to be covered by a single word, then more words are used. Yet, whether or not there is a true connection between the occurrences of these doublets and the rise of realism cannot be decided here and must wait for another occasion.

2. The written phrases became much larger. Again, the writings of Heymericus de Campo, but also those of Denys the Carthusian may serve as an example. If we use modern punctuation as a standard, phrases containing more than 200 words are not uncommon.[49] This is at odds with the length of the clauses in late thirteenth- or early fourteenth-century writings of Giles of Rome, William of Ockham, Walter Chatton, or Adam Wodeham. Their average is only about 10 to 15% of what we can find in fifteenth-century authors.

3. In connection with the length of phrases there is an additional point that needs our attention: in the fifteenth century, syntax again became as complex as it was in the twelfth century. For a modern reader, it is hardly possible to have a clear understanding of the writings of Heymericus de

---

[46] The dating of the *Problemata* is according to Meersseman, *Geschichte des Albertismus*, 24. For a list of the manuscripts of the treatise that survived, see Burie, 'Proeve tot inventarisatie van de in handschrift of in druk bewaarde werken van de Leuvense theologieprofessoren', esp. 222f.

[47] I checked Heymericus de Campo, *Problemata inter Albertum Magnum et Sanctum Thomam*, problema 13, 41v, against Colmar, Bibliothèque Municipale, cod. 59 (190); Prague, Bibliotheca publica atque universitatis, cod. 914; Vatican City, Bibliotheca Apostolica Vaticana, cod. lat. 11585; and Eichstätt, Universitätsbibliothek, cod. st 685.

[48] On this development see Tewes, *Die Bursen der Kölner Artisten-Fakultät*; and Kaluza, 'La crise des années 1474-1482: L'interdiction du Nominalisme par Louis XI'.

[49] See Denys's *Epistola de cursu puerorum* and Heymeric's *Determinatio super peregrinatione multorum iuvenum* edited in my 'Denys the Carthusian and Heymeric de Campo on the Pilgrimages of Children to Mont-Saint-Michel'.

Campo without first making a grammatical analysis.[50] The structure of the sentences is too complex. There is nothing left of the clear-cut language of thirteenth- and fourteenth-century scholastic treatises, which so much resembled actual speech. This development took place at the level of the written, not of the spoken language, as can be ascertained by considering the *quaestiones vacantiales* that took place during the summer vacations at the University of Cologne.[51] These disputations have been recorded in students' notebooks of the late fifteenth century. By studying these notes, it becomes clear that the Latin of the question title and of the syllogistic demonstration, which both were prepared in advance, is much more difficult and elaborate than that of those parts that report the actual oral discussion. In the question title and the demonstration, words are dispersed for stylistic reasons. The phraseology of the oral discussion, however, is plain and straightforward. To make the contrast clear, I will give an example. One of the question titles goes as follows:[52] *Utrum Christus, qui in primo suae conceptionis instanti sibi et nobis meruit nostrosque defectus assumens sua nos acerbissima liberavit passione.* This is a well-phrased sentence. Yet the discussion opens in a different way: *Arguitur: liberum arbitrium est potentia, ut videmus ponere. Respondit quod liberum arbitrium nec est pura potentia, nec purus habitus, sed est potentia simul cum habitu.* This again is the kind of Latin which stems from the thirteenth and fourteenth centuries, distinguishing itself by its frugality and spareness.

If we consider these developments in late medieval scholastic Latin, it is clear that scholastic writers have ambitions which are comparable to those of humanist authors. Yet, in scholasticism there is no pursuit of *latinitas*. The emphasis is mainly on the content and not on the form, with the exceptions we have mentioned. The rhetorical aspect fails in most cases. The logical structure of the reasoning, not the art of effective language use is dominant in scholastic discourse.

The sources

As was pointed out earlier, the urge for *latinitas* was stimulated by a renewed introduction to the writings of classical antiquity, especially Cicero. The

---

[50] Meersseman, *Geschichte des Albertismus*, 109. See also the partial edition of the *Alphabetum* in Kaluza, 'La voix creatrice de dieu'.

[51] See note 18 above.

[52] Eichstätt, Universitätsbibliothek, cod. st 688, 264r.

new sources therefore played an important role in the creation of humanism.[53]

This desire for new sources may be seen as a glaring contrast in comparison to the earlier period, scholasticism. Yet, in this case things are more complicated as well. What develops into humanism is the search for the sources of knowledge which began in the early twelfth century, when the Latin West, because of an increasing prosperity, could open its mind to Greek and Arabic thinking. It is on the basis of these Greek and Arabic sources that scholasticism expanded, just as humanism could flourish because of the rediscovery of sources from classical antiquity.[54] The question is not *whether* contemporary scholars were open for new sources, but rather for *which* sources.

As concerns scholasticism, the search for new sources did not break off after the twelfth century nor did scholastic authors close their minds to the ideas of pagan and non-Christian authors which later were studied by humanists.[55] This scholastic knowledge of pagan sources is documented in the writings of Albert the Great, which show remarkable use of non-Christian authors. In his *De natura et orgine intellectus* the following authors and schools are named:[56] *Academicorum schola, Aegyptii, Anaxagoras, Apuleius, Athalus, Bragmanorum schola, Caecina, Chaldaei philosophi, Democritus, Empedocles, Epicurei, Epicurus, Hermes Termegistus, Hesiodus, Metrodorus, Macrobius, Platonici, Plotinus philosophus, Pythagoras, Socrates, Solon Atheniensis, Speusippus,* and *Stoici.* This list speaks for itself. A number of these sources afterwards played an important role in Renaissance thinking, especially Hermes Trismegistus, Plato, and Plotinus.[57]

This fascination with pagan sources continued in the writings of Meister Eckhart, who often refers to the 'heidnische meister', and in authors like Dietrich of Freiberg and Berthold of Moosburg.[58] Not only the writings of the *corpus hermeticum,* but also the newly-translated works of Proklos were held in high esteem. Between 1323 and the beginning of the 1360s Berthold

---

[53] See Reeve, 'Classical Scholarship'; Reynolds and Wilson, *Scribes and Scholars*, 122-63.

[54] Cf. Copenhaver and Schmitt, *Renaissance Philosophy*, 4f.

[55] On the humanist interest in pagan sources, see Nauert, *Humanism and the Culture of Renaissance Europe*, 62 and 203. Cf. also Wind, *Pagan Mysteries in the Renaissance*.

[56] Albertus Magnus, *De natura et origine animae*, 322-6 (index auctorum and index rerum). See also Sturlese, 'Proclo ed Ermete in Germania da Alberto Magno a Bertoldo di Moosburg'. It should be noted, however, that most knowledge of these pagan works was based on secondary sources (Aristotle and his Greek and Arabic commentators that were available in Latin).

[57] Cf. Hankins, *Plato in the Italian Renaissance*, Index. See also Robb, *Neoplatonism of the Italian Renaissance*.

[58] See Eckhart, *Traktate*, 589 (index s.v. 'heidnische[r] meister'); Dietrich of Freiberg, *Opera omnia*, IV 367f. (index); and Berthold of Moosburg, *Expositio super Elementationem theologicam Procli, 184-211: De animabus* (tabula auctoritatum).

of Moosburg wrote an extensive commentary on the *Elementatio theologica* and Proklos is also quoted in the *De causa dei* of Thomas Bradwardine, together with many other non-Christian authors.[59] In the fifteenth century the impact of pagan philosophy was still growing, in the writings of Heymericus de Campo and Nicolas of Cusa, among others.[60] All these men were in search of a universal form of knowledge that encompassed both philosophy and theology, which they thought could also be found in the writings of pagan or pre-Christian authors, since they, not illuminated by revelation, found truth by human reason alone, an ideal which had followers in renaissance humanism.

There is also a second return to the sources in scholasticism, which is more difficult to see for us, as we very often identify scholasticism with the thinking of thirteenth-century authors such as Bonaventure and Thomas Aquinas and skip an important development of the early and mid-fourteenth century. The reason for this shortcut is easy to explain: in the fifteenth century, there is a remarkable return to thirteenth-century ways of thinking. Yet, this should not make us blind to the fact that there is no continuous line from thirteenth-century scholasticism to its fifteenth-century form. The impact of thirteenth-century authors was not always the same. In the period form 1290 to 1370, theologians like Alexander of Hales, Bonaventure, and Thomas are quoted, to be sure, but they do not yet have the prominent place that they would receive later on in the fifteenth century. In the 1370s, however, there is a change. Perhaps because of the imbroglio of the Schism, contemporary authors were no longer quoted in theological literature and also there was a return to the sources of the twelfth and thirteenth centuries. Marsilius of Inghen is a good example. In his commentary on the *Sentences*, read in the early 1390s in Heidelberg, almost no theologians writing after 1370 are quoted by name. His main sources date from the twelfth to the mid-fourteenth century. The same holds true for the *Sentences* commentary of John Capreolus (written 1409-1432). He mentioned practically no theologian of the second half of the fourteenth century, with the exception of John de Ripa, who worked at Paris in the 1350s.[61]

This return to the sources of the twelfth and thirteenth century (which is also documented in the library of Marsilius, which he bequeathed to the uni-

---

[59] Berthold of Moosburg, *Expositio super Elementationem theologicam Procli. Prologus. Propositiones 1-13*, xli (dating). On Bradwardine, see Molland, 'Addressing Ancient Authority'; and *Abendländische Mystik im Mittelalter*, 227.

[60] Colomer, *Nikolaus von Kues und Raimund Llull*, 9-39, esp. 16 n. 72 (Heymericus de Campo); and Moffitt Watts, *Nicolaus Cusanus*, index.

[61] For furher details and source materials, see my *Marsilius of Inghen. Divine Knowledge in Late Medieval Thought*, 19-22.

versity of Heidelberg)[62] goes hand-in-hand with a change in theological methodology and style. Many authors reacted against the use of logical tools in theology as it flourished in the mid-fourteenth century. They preferred a less-ambitious and less technical form of theology: not the analysis of theological reasoning, but the collection of important *auctoritates*, which helped to penetrate the mysteries of faith.[63] Theology thus became eclectic, as can be seen in the many works of Denys the Carthusian.[64] In this conversion of theology towards a 'scientia pietatis', authors like Richard of St. Victor, Bernard of Clairvaux, Bonaventure, and Thomas Aquinas play an important role.[65] There is a return to the past, caused by the need to reinvigorate theological discourse. The same quest, yet expressed differently, is also dominant in authors of the Christian northern humanist tradition. Wessel Gansfort, although inspired by contemporary philosophical and theological debates, hardly quoted any contemporary author. His writings have the same eclectic arrangement and pious design characteristic of many late-medieval scholastic treatises.

The subject matter

My final point concerns the subject matter of scholastic and humanist treatises. A few relevant points have already been touched upon in the foregoing sections. We can therefore be brief here.

If one studies the bibliographies of renaissance humanist authors, there are two items that repeatedly occur: practical philosophical and theological subjects, and discussions of the human intellect.[66] Both items are treated in the works of Wessel Gansfort, where they are intimately connected.

In recent literature the turn towards practical philosophy and theology and the emphasis on matters of the human intellect have been considered as characteristic of renaissance humanism as opposed to scholasticism, with its speculative theology and its emphasis on ontology.[67] Yet, a closer examination

---

[62] The library of Marsilius is studied in Walz, 'Marsilius von Inghen als Schreiber und Büchersammler'.

[63] On this change in theology, see the interesting remarks in Kaluza, 'Les sciences et leurs langages', esp. 223-55.

[64] His works are edited in Dionysius Carthusiensis, *Opera omnia*. See also idem, *Opera Selecta*.

[65] The expression 'scientia pietatis' is used by Marsilius of Inghen in his commentary on the *Sentences*. See n. 69 below.

[66] Cf. the bibliographical data collected in *The Cambridge History of Renaissance Philosophy*, 805-41 and 842-68; and the bibliographical list of humanist published as Appendix B in Kristeller, *Medieval Aspects of Renaissance Learning*, 126-58.

[67] See e.g. Gerl, *Einführung in die Philosophie der Renaissance*.

of scholastic sources shows that this distinction needs reconsideration. I will offer three observations.

1. The stress on practical matters in theology can be found already in the second half of the fourteenth century and remained, at least on the Continent, a part of scholasticism. This becomes manifest if we consider the late medieval commentaries on the *Sentences*. In the fourteenth century, it is the first book, which deals with the divine nature, which is the most important. In the fifteenth century, however, it is the fourth, which treats the sacraments and clearly has practical relevance.[68] Also the transition from speculative theology to theology as *scientia pietatis*, which also took place in the commentaries on the *Sentences*, testifies this development.[69]

2. It is also important to realize that by the time of the Schism, academics became involved in matters which were not strictly confined to the traditional lecture hall. They were occupied with church politics, gave advice on matters of worldly politics and were engaged in the battle against popular heresy. This had its effect on the literature which was produced by academics. Examples are the many treatises on church politics, which because of the enduring Schism not only served an academic but also a practical need, and the works against the heresy of Hussitism, which was both an ecclesiastical and a political threat. The manner in which these problems were treated was still in the tradition of speculative scholasticism. Yet the subject matter and the intention of the author were clearly practical.[70]

3. Also in the debate about the nature of the human intellect, humanism continued a discussion that had already started in scholasticism, or to put it another way, in scholasticism there was already a movement away from ontology towards psychology. In his *Quaestiones parisienses*, delivered in the early fourteenth century, Meister Eckhart argued that the essence of the first principle of reality is better defined by the term 'knowing' than by that of 'being'. Only that which is higher than being, namely knowing, can be the cause of being.[71] Eckhart on this point criticized the ontology of Thomas Aquinas, who identified in God being itself (*ipsum esse*) as well as knowing (*intelligere*).[72]

Also in the human sphere, Eckhart attributed a central role to the intellect and its proper activity: 'knowing'. The human intellect in its thinking can deny

---

[68] The medieval commentaries on the Sentences are listed in Stegmüller, *Repertorium commenta-riorum in Sententias Petri Lombardi.*

[69] Braakhuis and Hoenen, 'Marsilius of Inghen: a Dutch Philosopher and Theologian', esp. 9-11.

[70] Meuthen, *Das 15. Jahrhundert*, 147-55; and my 'Academics and Intellectual Life in the Low Countries'. See also for the changing positions of intellectuals, Shank, *'Unless You Believe You Shall Not Understand'.*

[71] Eckhart, *Parisian Questions and Prologues*, 43-50.

[72] For a discussion of the two positions, see Imbach, *'Deus est intelligere'.*

created being and thus open itself to divine illumination and have direct knowledge of the God.[73] This line of reasoning goes back to the Arabic commentaries on Aristotle and was developed in the Latin West in the works of Albert the Great.[74] Again in opposition to Thomas Aquinas, Dietrich of Freiberg asserted the active intellect to be an image of God which by its own essence could know both itself and the rest of reality. Consequently it could be both the subject and object of all possible knowledge.[75] This line of thinking was taken over in the fifteenth century by a number of Albertist authors, still in opposition to Thomas Aquinas, and it became an important current of thought at late medieval universities, which is documented in the writings of Heymericus de Campo, John of Mechelen, Denys the Carthusian, and also of Wessel Gansfort.[76] The human mind could, by a pure intellectual reflection on his own essence, without knowledge from the senses, attain wisdom of the first principles of reality. This view is put forward by Heymericus de Campo, the most important protagonist of the Albertist theory of intellect, with the means of traditional scholasticism, that is, in a discussion about the true reading of Aristotle's theory of intellect.[77] Yet between the lines of this traditional approach, a whole new concept of philosophical knowledge emerges: Heymericus attempted to discover reality by reflecting on human thought and thereby he postulated the autonomy of the human mind, an idea that was to become the cornerstone of modern philosophy.

Taken together, these three items show again that characteristic elements of humanism have their roots in scholasticism and that the distinction between the two is not as clear-cut as some of the literature would have it.

Conclusion

In the introduction, the period under consideration was characterized as one of transition, which in any case holds true for the items we have studied. If we now try to bring the results of our investigation together under one heading, we might say that the time and nature of the transition is different for each of the items: style, language, sources, and subject matter. The change of style begins in the early 1320s in England, while the Latin language becomes more elaborate only in the second half of the fourteenth

---

[73] See the sermon *Quasi stella matutina*, transl. in Eckhart, *Sermons and Treatises*, II 149-56 (sermon 67).

[74] De Libera, *Albert le Grand et la philosophie*, 251-66.

[75] Mojsisch, *Die Theorie des Intellekts bei Dietrich von Freiberg*.

[76] I discussed this development in my 'Albertistae, thomistae und nominales'; and my 'Heymeric van de Velde (†1460) und die Geschichte des Albertismus'.

[77] Heymericus de Campo, *Problemata inter Albertum Magnum et Sanctum Thomam*, 40r-44v.

century. As far as the sources are concerned, the search for new materials continued on from the twelfth century. And finally, the subject matter that interests humanist authors goes back in part at least to the beginning of the fourteenth century and the urge for practical matters in theology was clearly visible from the 1370s. The exact history of these transitions is difficult to determine. They are independent, although related to each other. The style, language and subject matter are conditioned by the sources, while conversely the search for the sources and consequently, style and language, is determined by the subject matter.

It is therefore true that new sources played a role in the transition from scholasticism to humanism, as it is often stated. Yet these sources were not discovered by chance. The search for these sources met a specific cultural and intellectual need, which was not only induced by an aversion to scholasticism, but also manifested the same eagerness for new knowledge found in scholasticism as well, yet in a different setting. Humanism developed out of the intellectual pursuits of the foregoing period, which were, to be sure, not undifferentiated, but multiform.

This situation is thus comparable to the already-mentioned discovery of Aristotelian sources in the twelfth century. Initially, the philosophical sciences did not develop because of the discovery of the works of Aristotle, but rather because of the development of the philosophical sciences these sources were discovered. Yet, in its turn, the discovery of the works of Aristotle did eventually change the style of the sciences irreversibly. The neoplatonic axiomatic ideal of the twelfth century is fundamentally different from the Aristotelian model of the *Analytica posteriora* as followed in the thirteenth century. This means that the same universal quest for knowledge did divide into two different forms of science as a result of the impact of distinct sources.

The same applies to the transition from scholasticism to humanism. The developments in the field of style, language, and the quest for new sources in the fourteenth and fifteenth centuries did create an environment in which the texts of Greek and Roman antiquity could create a whole new cultural landscape, which in its fundamental quest was not different from that of scholasticism, as is clear from the foregoing investigation. Scholasticism and humanism were both motivated by the pursuit of knowledge, which in the course of history is always pursued in differing ways.

H.A. KROP

NORTHERN HUMANISM AND PHILOSOPHY:
HUMANIST THEORY AND SCHOLASTIC PRACTICE[*]

Johannes Huninga, one of the two recently-appointed professors of philosophy at the new university of Groningen, delivered his inaugural oration on August 24, 1614.[1] In the first part of it he thanked God and the Estates of the Province, those 'terrestrial gods', for the good they had done by founding a university. The second part of the oration is also laudatory, dealing with the Frisians in general, and in particular with the principal town of the province, Groningen. The fertility of the soil of Friesland had made possible the erection of beautiful cities, castles and churches. The virtue of its inhabitants, their steadfastness and love of liberty, had made the Frisian people the first of all the tribes of Germany. It was only right that their delegates, Verritus and Malorix, should have been acclaimed by the people of Rome, and treated as their equals by those rulers of the world.[2] These northern parts were also the cradle of many other peoples, such as the Franks and the English.

According to Huninga, Frisia is also the dwelling-place of the sciences. The province was one of the first in this part of Europe to be converted to Christianity, and from that time onwards it has been a seminary and nursery, sending scholars out to all the regions of the earth.[3] The foundation of the university of Groningen should be seen as the logical outcome of this tradition of learning, which Huninga carefully reconstructs. The thirteenth-century Parisian doctor of theology Emo of Wierum, author of a Frisian chronicle, is the first to be named, and he is followed by others representing the different faculties of the university. This tradition culminates in Wessel Gansfort and Rudolph Agricola. Praedinius, the third of the famous sequence of Groningen humanists, is left somewhat in the background.[4] Wessel

---

[*] Gratefully I acknowledge my debt to prof. M.J. Petry, who put this paper into English.

[1] Published, with the oration of the theologian H. Ravensperger, under the title *Orationes ad inaugurationem academiae illustrium ordinum Groningae et Omlandiae habitae*. For the biography of the Groningen professors: Boeles, 'Levensschetsen der Groninger hoogleeraren'.

[2] *Orationes ad inaugurationem*, Oratio altera, c3v. Huninga's remark is based on *Annales* 13, 54. Tacitus, of course, in no way regarded the Frisians as the equals of the Romans.

[3] *Orationes ad inaugurationem*, c4v.

[4] After Ubbo Emmius's 'Natales academiae' in the *Effigies et vitae professorum academiae Groningae et Omlandiae* there are biographies of Gansfort (16 pp.), Agricola (10 pp.) and Praedinius (3 pp.), and the theologian Ravensperger, who spoke one day before Huninga, considered them as equally important. Directing himself to the Estates and the citizens of Groningen, he

Gansfort, nicknamed 'the light of the world', was aware of the decay of
religion, and dared to defy the pope and his followers openly. It was he who
really prepared the Reformation. The philosopher Agricola cleaned out the
slough of errors and idolatry and revived true philosophy and theology.
They were as two 'illustrious soldiers, clad in their gowns, fighting vigorously against the forces of superstition and ignorance.'[5] They are truly
brilliant representatives of theology and philosophy. By an overview of their
careers, Huninga is able to show that the Reformation and humanism are
essentially one and the same, since a pure knowledge of God is only possible once one has broken away from both scholasticism and the Church of
Rome. This view is subsequently put forward in the works of quite a number
of Protestant humanists – French theologians such as Antoine de Chandieu
and Lambert Daneau, the Franeker Hebraic scholar Sixtus Amama, the
Leiden professors of philosophy Adriaan Heereboord and Georg Hornius.[6]

Huninga's oration is a typical expression of Renaissance patriotism. Perhaps the best-known example of this genre is provided by Goropius Beca-
nus, who in the two thousand folio-pages of his *Origines Antwerpianae* tried
to demonstrate that the language spoken in Antwerp was also that spoken in
Paradise. Huninga's history of Frisian learning also gives evidence of the

---

urges them to ask God, who gave them those holy and learned men, to give them in the future
'Wesselos, Rudolphos, et Praedinios' (b4r).

[5] *Orationes ad inaugurationem*, Oratio altera, d2r: 'veros togatae militiae milites contra su-
perstitionum et ignorantiae tela fortissime dimicantes.'

[6] De Chandieu, *Locus de verbo Dei scripto adversus humanas traditiones*, 6-8. According to
Chandieu, Daneau, Heereboord and Hornius, the principal error of scholasticism is the mixture
of theology and philosophy and 'the darkening of truth by vain subtleties', that is to say the too
technical language of medieval logic. For Daneau, see the preface of his commentary on the
first book of Peter Lombard's Sentences published in 1580 and discussed by Fatio, *Méthode et
théologie*, 118-30. For Amama, see his 'De barbarie oratio' of 1626 included in his *Anti-Barbarus biblicus*; in the preface he states: 'ego omnes scholasticos [...] inter barbaros pono' (b5r). In
the introduction of his address he ranks the German reformers Luther and Melanchthon and the
humanists Erasmus and Reuchlin together. They not only purified religion but also medicine,
law and philosophy, which had been deformed by the negligence of the languages, 'divinam illam philosophiam, ut non amplius ingeniorum cos et lima, sed crudelis potius ingeniorum car-
nificina fuerit' (c1r). Amama's peculiar version of agressive protestant humanism is discussed
by Van Rooden, *Constantijn L'Empereur*, 74-80. For Heereboord, see his inaugural address
held February 9, 1641, printed in his 'Epistola ad curatores' and included in his *Meletemata*, 2-
6. 'Impertiit Germaniam hoc lumine primus Rodolpus Agricola [...] qui [...] adversus receptum
philosophandi modum Socratica dixit libertate. Exinde plures purgando Augiae isti stabulo [sc.
the impious philosophy of scholasticism] manus auxiliares admovere; prae ceteris Hollandiae
nostrae ac totius orbis decus miraculum Desiderius Erasmus, Martinus Lutherus, Philippus Melanchthon, primi apud religionis simul ac philosophiae restauratores' (5). He condemns on the
same page the technical language of scholasticism as follows: 'Hi nobis tot quidditates, entita-
tes, haecceitates vel ecceitates et quae non verborum monstra nihil rerum significantia procude-
re, quibus speciosissimam philosophiae ac theologiae faciem turpiter dehonestarunt.' For Hornius, see chapter 6 of his *Historiae philosophicae libri VII* and my 'Georg Hornius als historicus van de filosofie'.

theory of philosophy he shared with his colleagues. This can only be reconstructed indirectly, since the address of Huninga's colleague, William Makdowell, who as professor of philosophy spoke about the use and excellence of philosophy, has been lost.[7] The surviving documentation, which gives the gist of the argument in a programmatic form and dates from the very first years of the university, allows us to get some impression of their views. In the first section of this paper, the concept of philosophy that prevailed among the earliest professors of the subject at Groningen will be outlined, and three particular aspects will be distinguished.

In a stimulating paper on the early years of the university of Groningen, professor Vanderjagt has pointed out that with respect to the function and aim of the discipline, the actual teaching of the subject rapidly diverged from the ideas of the founding fathers.[8] The documentation of what was taught, especially the disputations, shows a continuity with 'scholasticism'. For some time during the sixteenth and seventeenth centuries, 'scholasticism' and 'humanism' went together in the universities of the Republic. During the first half of the seventeenth century a 'humanist' conception of philosophy found its adherents among professors of the subject, while at the same time 'scholastic' methods remained in use in the teaching.

This thesis may seem self-contradictory, for until quite recently 'scholasticism' and 'humanism' have been associated with a set of mutually exclusive philosophical views and values. Scholars such as Gilson and Grabmann interpreted 'scholasticism' in a doctrinal way, stressing its theological nature and its emphasis on the synthesizing of faith and reason.[9] Yet, according to L.M. de Rijk, scholasticism is not a philosophy or a theology but a method, which he characterizes as 'a way of analyzing problems which in research and teaching recurrently applies a system of concepts, distinctions, definitions, analyses of propositions, techniques of argument and methods of disputation, derived from [...] logic.'[10] In this sense scholasticism originated in the schools of France and Germany just after the beginning of the millennium, and it was 'fully developed by the fourteenth and fifteenth centuries, when it possessed a complete range of logical techniques, especially those of terminist logic.'[11] It is against this scholasticism that the humanists

---

[7] Ubbo Emmius, 'Natales academiae', 7. For Makdowell see Dibon, *L'Enseignement philosophique*, 170-4.

[8] Vanderjagt, 'Filosofie tussen humanisme en eclecticisme', 39.

[9] De Rijk, *Middeleeuwse wijsbegeerte*, ch. 1.6 and 4.1.

[10] De Rijk, *Middeleeuwse wijsbegeerte*, 110. With respect to different forms of scholasticism such as Reformed, Lutheran, Spanish, Cartesian, Baroque etc., Leinsle, *Einführung in die scholastische Theologie*, 9, points out that 'Eine Definition des 'Wesens' von Scholastik ist nicht möglich.'

[11] Op. cit., 114. Cf. Rummel, *The Humanist-Scholastic Debate*, 11-12: 'A better criterion to distinguish humanists from scholastics is their methodology. Champions of scholasticism favor

reacted from the fifteenth century onwards; they emphasized its abstruse vocabulary, its incomprehensible subtleties, its delight in sophistical dispute and its empty and lifeless obscurity.[12] The humanist attack on medieval logic, the core of scholasticism, was successful.[13] Scholasticism, however, did not completely disappear in the sixteenth century. Some aspects survived well into the seventeenth century.[14]

Philosophy at Groningen prior to 1625

Ceremonial orations and official documents provide us with insight into the ideas prevailing in the university during the first years of its existence. It is worth noting that philosophy was regarded as the survival of an ancient wisdom, a so-called *prisca theologia*.[15] In many humanist authors the notion of man's having once been in possession of a perfect knowledge of reality

syllogisms and other forms of inference familiar from dialectical textbooks. Their disquisitions are usually tightly structured and often arranged in numbered points or caption paragraphs. [...] Humanists, by contrast, opted for more informal presentations. [...] Humanists tended instead to use rhetorical devices – similes, metaphors, historical examples – to give their works the characteristics of essays or orations.'

[12] For these characteristic humanist judgements upon scholasticsm see Voetius, 'De scholastica theologia'. Although this influential Utrecht theologian is usually associated with scholasticism (see *De scholastieke Voetius*, 22-24), it should be noted that he distinguishes between three senses of 'theologia scholastica'. *Latissime* it is every theology taught to others; *late* it means theology taught in European schools; and *stricte* it is the theology which uses the *Sentences* and the *Summa theologiae* as its starting point. The 'form' of scholasticism in the last sense is 'elenctiva seu quaestionaria' and it 'fancied quaestiones and quodlibeta with respect to the text commentated.' Garin, 'Aux origines de la scolastique', 182-3, equally points out that the humanist critique of scholasticism is primarily a critique of the form of the argumentation, not of its content.

[13] After 1530 the writing of commentaries on medieval logical treatises came to an abrupt end, see Ashworth, 'Traditional Logic', 153; idem, *Language and Logic*; and idem, 'Changes in Logic Textbooks', 76. In the last publication Ashworth shows that even sixteenth-century Spanish 'scholastic' logicians left out a good deal of medieval logic.

[14] According to Kristeller, 'humanism' does not imply a philosophical point of view nor a conception of the world. See e.g. his 'The scholar and his public in the late Middle Ages and the Renaissance', 5: 'Humanistic literature likewise includes textbooks, commentaries and treatises, which are nevertheless distinct in content and style from the scholastic ones, and to those we must add the oration, the letter, the dialogue and the translation.' The difference between the scholastic and humanist method becomes evident by comparing Danaeus's *In Petri Lombardi librum primum Sententiarum* with any medieval scholastic commentary. Instead of a sequence of *quaestiones*, Danaeus quotes the text of Lombard in full, structuring the text with notes in the margin. At the end of every distinction philological comments are added; for example, in defining the subject-matter of theology Lombard quotes Augustine's: 'omnis doctrina res vel rerum est vel signorum, sed res etiam per signa discuntur.' Danaeus comments that Augustine did not write *etiam*, which is even against his intentions (op. cit., 12). Danaeus's principal concern is to show that Lombard misquoted the patres and corrupted their clear Latin.

[15] Malusa, 'Introduzione, sezione prima'.

resulting from his seeing God face to face was a living one. Such an original wisdom had been lost, but as far as this was possible philosophers had retained their primitive purity, and they could recover at least some part of this pristine theology. This notion may have been the background to the typically humanist succession of Frisian scholars outlined by Huninga.

The theologian Herman Ravensperger had held his inaugural oration one day before Huninga. It was divided into three parts: in the first he provided an etymological explanation of the words 'school' and 'academy', in the second and third he analyzed the history and use of schools and academies. The origin of public education was the Fall, which consigned the 'miserable mortals, and more particularly their souls' to profound ignorance. Nevertheless, the sparks of the divine image remaining after the Fall made humanity aware that academic learning can overcome this evil in one way or another.[16] Although many profane historians describe the history of the various schools, our most certain source is Holy Writ, which never contradicts itself. The first schoolmasters were the Levites. God entrusted them with forty cities, in which they founded academies and colleges to guard the purity of the old religion and the liberal arts. In the New Testament we read that Christ, the supreme schoolmaster of mankind, did not suppress the traditional synagogues and schools which taught youth the principles of the arts and the languages. He Himself founded a theological school for his disciples.

At the end of his oration, Ravensperger compares the new academy of Groningen with Paradise. The university embodies the recollection of the earthly paradise, for 'God planted the earthly paradise by the Word of his power, and he clothed it with all manner of plants, and among other trees the tree of life and the tree of the knowledge of good and evil.'[17] Four rivers irrigated the dwelling-place of the first men, which they had to leave on account of their aversion to God. It was, however, God's will that in the schools 'a kind of Paradise' remained visible.[18] Ravensperger goes on to maintain that He also provided the academies with a tree of life and a tree of

---

[16] *Orationes ad inaugurationem*, a3v-a4r: 'Diabolus [...] ausus est [...] calumniari interdictum divinum de non usurpanda arbore scientiae boni et mali, cumque infelicissimi mortalium ab illo capitalissimo hoste in fraudem ac lapsum inducerentur, poenas sibi exitiales et pernitiales, et praecipue animo, hoc est illustri imaginis divinae sedi, densissimam caliginem, inscitiam et inscientiam suo ipsorum jumento attraxerunt. Hisce malis cum miserum genus humanum aliquo pacto mederi satageret et id per doctrinam scholasticam quam commodissime fieri posse vel divino monitu vel scintillularum et reliquiarum imaginis divinae post lapsum ductu sentiret, opinor omnino negari non posse, quin paulatim scholastici, id est docentium ac discentium coetus, frequentati fuerint.'
[17] *Orationes ad inaugurationem*, b2v-b3r: 'Paradisum terrestrem Deus verbo potentiae suae plantaverat et omnis generis plantis, interque caeteras arboribus vitae et scientiae boni malique convestiverat, et quatuor pulcherrimis maximisque fluviis irrigaverat.'
[18] *Orationes ad inaugurationem*, b3r: 'speciem Paradisi.'

the knowledge of good and evil, thus leading the pious to life by teaching them to distinguish between truth and falsity. He feeds the schools with the four rivers of philosophy, theology, medicine and law.

> The inhabitants of this Paradise will finally reach that heavenly Paradise and Academy, where instructed by God himself, who will be all in all, we shall have insight with the utmost delight into all the mysteries which elude our intellect in this vale of tears.[19]

According to Ravensperger, therefore, real knowledge and philosophy are the result of knowing God as the creator of the universe.

This image of Paradise involves a view of the relation between philosophy and theology different from that of scholasticism. Since the thirteenth century, scholastic scholars were increasingly inclined to draw a formal distinction between theology and philosophy. Thomas Aquinas, for example, states that although theology and philosophy have the same object, they consider it differently, namely by the light of revelation and by the light of the natural intellect.[20] Humanist philosophers were less inclined to make this distinction. Scholars often quoted the Tübingen professor Jacob Schengk (1511-1587): 'According to my judgement, the churches will only be quiet and peaceful if the true philosophers dedicate themselves to theology and theologians piously philosophize.'[21] Both Emmius and Ravensperger considered pagan philosophy as a prefiguration of Christian theology. According to them there is a continuity and not a break between the philosophy of antiquity and Christian doctrine, for pagan philosophers said many true things about the divine origin of reality. This is apparent in the observation that 'Plato, the theologian-philosopher of the pagans, rightly called such a cult, expressing itself in golden temples, a flattery, and not a worship of the divinity.'[22] Ravensperger contrasts the pagan temple of Diana and the first temple of Solomon, in all their finery and vain appearance, with the true spiritual temple of the Gospel and true wisdom. He admits, however, that this knowledge was at least partly possessed by the pagans. According to Emmius the view of the ancients on the end of life and on knowledge was correct: 'Should we think otherwise, if these philosophers, who were

[19] Ibidem: 'Hujus Paradisi cultores [...] tandem pervenient in Paradisum et Academiam illam caelestem, in qua, quae intelligentiam nostram in hac miseriarum valle fugerunt, summa voluptate omnia percipiemus mysteria, docente nos ipso Deo, qui erit omnia in omnibus.'

[20] *Summa theologiae* I q. 1 a. 1.

[21] Makdowell, *Oratio de quadruplici nodo philosophico*, a3r; and Hornius, *Historiae philosophicae libri VII*, 3 (preface). See also Voetius, *Gymnasii Ultrajectini inauguratio*, g1v (ed. and transl. by A. de Groot, Kampen 1978, 40).

[22] *Templi Academici, quod est Groningae* [...] *ΚΑΘΙΕΡΩΣΙΣ* (Groningen 1616), a4r.

ignorant of the Faith and the Christian religion, judged rightly?'[23]

The second aspect of the conception of philosophy that prevailed in the minds of the founders and the first professors is its Stoic division of philosophy. Although in his description of the genesis of the university Emmius pointed out that the Estates had decided that Aristotle should be followed in the teaching of philosophy, the Eternal Edict that established the university divided philosophy into logic, physics and ethics.[24] Such a division of philosophy is endorsed in Ravensperger's oration. As a humanist, Ravensperger regarded grammar as fundamental to knowledge, since without reading and writing we are unable to acquire knowledge of any texts, either holy or secular. He considers mathematics to be just as elementary as the art of reading and writing, and he quotes Plato's observation that arithmetic and geometry are the wings of the soul flying towards knowledge. The second group of disciplines includes music, the languages, in particular those with which the name of Christ was written on the cross, and history. The last science in this group provides us with a theatre of the world 'in which all things worthy of remembrance are to be seen.' The third group consists of rhetoric and logic. These are essentially the same, since discourse is nothing but spoken reason. Ravensperger establishes their fundamental status by presenting man as the microcosm.

> We all know that God according to his infinite wisdom and goodness collected abundantly all whatsoever is encompassed within the wide and extensive reach of this universe in human nature, so that human intellect is able fully to represent all things within it. And so, what the sun is to the world at large, reason and speech is to man.[25]

The last theoretical science discussed by Ravensperger is physics, which provides us with knowledge of the God-given nature of all animate and inanimate things. According to the apostle Paul, this science provided the pagans with the means to know God.[26] The practical sciences are then discussed: medicine, law, moral philosophy and theology. Ethics teaches us the supreme good in this life, the behaviour of the father in the household, and it makes clear the laws and foundations of cities. It makes towns pros-

---

[23] *Oratio* (held on the occasion of his demise from the rectorate) (Groningen 1616), b3v.

[24] 'Natales academiae', 4 and 5.

[25] *Orationes ad inaugurationem*, b1r: 'Novimus omnes [...] Deum intra hominis naturam pro infinita sua sapientia et bonitate plena [...] manu congessisse, quicquid hic mundus vastissimo et capacissimo suo ambitu comprehendit, ita ut plane nihil sit, quod ille non cumulate in se queat repraesentare. At enim quod huic amplissimo mundo sol est, id homini ipsi ratio est atque oratio.'

[26] Ravensperger refers to Paul's *Epistle to the Romans* 1, 20.

perous, civilized and peaceful.[27] The ultimate science is theology, which is concerned with the Creator and Guide of all in heaven and on earth. It is essentially a practical science, however, for it makes clear to us the diseases of the soul, and directs us from the depth of evil to the supreme good. Ravensperger divides philosophy into dialectic, physics and ethics. This Stoic classification of philosophy was influential throughout the Renaissance, and it had been put forward by Agricola in his oration *In Praise of Philosophy*.[28] This meant that in the universities of the northern Netherlands, metaphysics tended to be excluded from the official curriculum.[29]

The final aspect of this conception of philosophy is that it is a practical science. Humanists usually required that in all schools public education should lead on not only to erudition but also to ethical soundness. Emmius, for example, takes the aim of the new university, dedicated as it was to Christ, to be the acquirement of virtue and piety by the students. In founding the university, results are sought for, not simply erudition. Learning without social relevance is like a sword in the hands of a lunatic. The most important virtue to be acquired by the students is the ability to obey, for only those who from boyhood on know discipline are able to guide the church and the state. This was why public education flourished in Sparta and Persia. Moreover, teachers have not only to instruct, but also to guide, form, punish and correct their students. According to Emmius, therefore, academic liberty is not licence since 'we are the servants of the law, so that we could be truly free.'[30]

It is therefore evident to Ravensperger that the school has a social function. As proof he quotes Erasmus's statement in his *Anti-barbarians* to the effect that the welfare of the state depends on three things: a well-instructed prince, public orators and schoolmasters.[31] The model of the authors of the Eternal Edict was the Spanish king Alfonso the Wise of Aragon 'who did not take pleasure in a life of leisure and retirement', for he was also a philosopher. His example was to make clear to both the magistrates of Groningen and the newly-appointed professors that politics is impossible without

---

[27] Ravensperger refers to a well-known text of Cicero from *Tusculan Disputations* 5,5-6 (also quoted by Scanderus in his Deventer inaugural address discussed later on).

[28] 'In laudem philosophiae et reliquarum artium oratio', in Agricola, *Lucubrationes*, 144-59; for a Latin text and a French translation, see *Rodolphe Agricola, Ecrits sur la dialectique et l'humanisme*, 46-67.

[29] That is to say in Leiden and Groningen, see Dibon, *L'Enseignement philosophique*, 9 ff. (Leiden); 166 nt 9, and 168 (Groningen). In Franeker the *Statuta Academiae* of March 30, 1586 prescribed only lectures in rhetoric, logic and 'the rest of philosophy' (130).

[30] *Oratio*, b3r: 'Servi legum sumus, ut vere liberi esse possimus.'

[31] *Orationes ad inaugurationem*, a2v. The text is Erasmus, *Antibarbari* (ASD I-1), 53.

philosophy, and that philosophy is useless if it has no social relevance.[32]

This requirement of practical consequences for philosophy had an explicit Stoic variation. According to Makdowell, the true philosopher should be free from human ambition in respect of wealth and honour. Persons who aspire to social success and want to take possession of the resources of nature directly have an aversion to philosophy. They think that only Galen, that is to say medicine, provides them with wealth, and only Justinian, that is to say law, with honour.

> By the immortal Gods! Is their's a miserable life, or do they possess a pitiful treasure who are not vexed by the desire to acquire more external goods, and have no fear of losing them? Are not persons who restrain their insatiable desires more truly the rulers than those who, as the poet says, would connect Libya with distant Spain?[33]

Makdowell cites the Eternal Edict as setting the students the example of the Spanish kings Alfonso the Wise and Alfonso the Noble, who preferred to renounce their earthly powers rather than refrain from the study of philosophy. Only by controlling his emotions can a philosopher acquire self-sufficiency and tranquillity of mind. For, does not such a man possess the real goods 'which accompany the owner from his ship that has been wrecked? Are they not real, which are as near as possible to the Idea of the Good?'[34] Philosophy makes possible the achievement of the real Good, for it extinguishes the desire for all earthly goods, by making clear their transitoriness. By restraining his emotions, the philosopher is able to master fortune and become a real king. These 'royal' aspirations, however, should be seen in the context of the social position of the philosopher in seventeenth-century academic life. In general, the salaries of professors of philosophy were considerably lower than those of their colleagues in the other faculties, indicating that in the academic institutions of the Early Modern Period philosophy retained its traditional propedeutic status.

---

[32] 'Natales academiae', 5. Makdowell in his address of 1616 (*Oratio de quadruplici nodo philosophico*, a3v) refers to two Spanish kings: 'Alphonsos illos Castellae Aragoniaeque duos amplissimo se regno exui malle accepimus quam philosophiae studio privari.'

[33] Ibidem: 'An per Deos immortales ea vita egena est, an iis curta supellex, qui neque augendi cupiditate neque amittendi metu cruciantur? Nunquid latius regnant avidum domando spiritum, ut ait poeta, quam ‹si› Lybiam remotis Gadibus jungerent?' The poet Makdowell refers to is Horace and the text quoted is *Carmina* 2, 2, 9-11.

[34] Ibidem: 'Haeccine vera bona quae fracta navi simul cum domino enatant? Haeccine vera bona quae ad ideam boni quam proxime accedunt?'

Philosophy after 1625

In Groningen, the development of the conception of philosophy during the first few years after 1625 is difficult to trace, since no inaugural orations or prefaces to manuals earlier than 1640 have been preserved.[35] Since the Stoic-humanist conception of philosophy prevailed at other Dutch universities, however, it is probably reasonable to assume that it also retained its influence in Groningen. In order to illustrate the pervasiveness of late-humanist ideas on philosophy, two examples from other universities will be discussed. The first is the recently discovered inaugural oration of the Deventer professor of philosophy, David Scanderus, held at the opening of the Deventer Athenaeum on February 16, 1630.[36] Like Huninga, he begins by praising Deventer as an ancient dwelling-place of wisdom. Ever since it offered Willebrord, Boniface and Lebuinus a safe haven, it has been the patroness of the faith and of civilization. It provided Rudolph Agricola and Erasmus with the necessary means for driving away the darkness of ignorance from Germany and even from the whole world. The second part of Scanderus's oration discusses the use of philosophy. He quotes Cicero's statement: 'All are convinced of the fact that the arts which form part of human culture are linked together, having something in common which connects them as forms of knowledge.'[37] There may be some who deny that philosophy is indispensable to law and politics. The invalidation of this last attitude is the principal aim of Scanderus's discourse. According to him, a state is favoured 'if philosophers rule or princes are philosophers.'[38] A ruler is the determinating principle of the people – if he is good, they too are likely to be good, for it is by means of philosophy that he guides his people to virtue and happiness. 'For, it is philosophy that steeps the corrupted souls in a divine fluid, and immersed in it they proceed from evil to good, from ferocity to humanity, from vice to virtue.'[39] Philosophy, therefore, is not only a form of theoretical knowledge. Scanderus waxes eloquent on the sterility and subtlety of medieval philosophy, and in particular of its logic:

---

[35] The first inaugural oration preserved is Schoock's, who was appointed in 1640.

[36] *Oratio inauguralis de philosophiae et politicae coniugio* (Deventer 1630). The only copy is in the Rijksarchief of Arnhem; a Dutch translation by this author is found in *Deventer denkers*, 167-85. About Scanderus see De Haan, 'Geschiedenis van het wijsgerig onderwijs te Deventer', 37-9.

[37] *Oratio inauguralis*, a2r. The text is from *Pro Archia* 2.

[38] Ibidem: 'quando vel philosophi dominantur vel reges philosophantur'.

[39] *Oratio inauguralis*, a2v: 'illa enim est quae pravis hominum mentibus divinum illum liquorem instillat, quo imbutae eae a pravitate ad bonitatem, a feritate ad humanitatem, a vitio ad virtutem [...] transeunt.'

Such philosophers erred grossly in thinking that the divine doctrine consists only of words, and only prospers with tying and untying the artificial knots of syllogisms, and solving the perplexing problems of the sophists which often would have silenced even an Oedipus. Whoever fancies such an art to be philosophy takes blocks of wood for the forest, and mistakes words for virtue.[40]

Scanderus, therefore, supports the humanist charge against scholastic philosophy, taking it to be only interested in words and not in the things themselves.

True philosophy is a medicine for curing the soul, since it does not consist of empty words which leave the soul untouched, but guides the soul to virtue:

Instead of fear it raises courage, instead of lust shame, instead of gluttony frugality, instead of dissipation economy, instead of avarice liberality, instead of ambition modesty, instead of arrogance humility, instead of narrowness generosity, instead of irascibility leniency, instead of moroseness courtesy, and finally instead of cruelty humanity.[41]

After this characteristically Stoic catalogue of virtues, Scanderus picks out Alexander the Great as the example of a philosopher-king. He pictures the situation in the Macedonian empire after the death of his father Philip. The treasury was exhausted and Alexander had only a small army of less than 30,000 foot-men and 4,000 horsemen at his disposal. Yet he dared to attack Persia, for he had far greater means at his disposal: generosity, prudence, modesty, courage and wisdom.[42] Scanderus's example was well chosen, for his audience certainly would have compared Alexander's enterprise with the war of the small Dutch Republic against the Spanish empire.

Scanderus realized that to most members of the audience the ideal of the philosopher-king did not apply. However, he pointed out that even to them philosophy was of practical importance, since it enabled them to endure the

---

[40] Ibidem: 'Errant enim et errant graviter qui divinam disciplinam in verbis tantum consistere opinantur [...], quae tantum vigeat in texendis et retexendis artificiosis syllogismorum nodis, in solvendis intricatis Sophistarum griphis, ad quos saepe ipse obmutesceret Oedipus; talem quandam qui sibi imaginantur philosophiam, nae illi ut lucum ligna, sic virtutem putant esse verba.'

[41] *Oratio inauguralis*, a3r: 'Vera et immutabilis recte philosophantium regula haec est, ut sic in omnibus legendis et discendis, agendis et omittendis quisque versetur, ut proficiat veritati et charitati. Veri philosophi schola non est inanium litium et otiosarum contentionum sentina, sed medicina quaedam officina. [...] Ejus igitur oratio non est tantum inane quoddam verborum lenocinium aut vana λογομαχία, quae [...] animum autem nil afficiat [...]. Pro timiditate fortitudinem; pro libidine pudicitiam; pro ingluvie frugalitatem; pro prodigalitate parcimoniam; pro avaritia liberalitatem; pro ambitione modestiam; pro superbia humilitatem; pro pusillanimitate animi magnitudinem; pro iracundia mansuetudinem; pro morositate comitatem; pro feritate denique humanitatem inducit.'

[42] *Oratio inauguralis*, br-v.

vicissitudes of fortune. In view of the variability of things and the changeability of life, man should provide himself with arms against fortune. Such arms could only be provided by the director of all things and the master of fate.[43] Philosophy teaches us to enjoy prosperity with moderation and to endure misfortune with dignity. It is also the science of things divine and human, and teaches us to distinguish between the two. Philosophy concerns itself with this first kind of things and honours them. It despises and neglects the last kind. Thus, a philosopher does not change his attitude when fortune turns a different face to him.[44] Since he is free of all earthly desires, he will use his eagle-wings, if one tries to enchain him, and he then 'returns to the dwelling-place of his master, flying aloft to God.'[45]

At the end of his oration, Scanderus returns to the fundamental notion of the unity of knowledge. He compares the higher disciplines without philosophy to the universe without the sun, to a body without a soul, to an army without a commander, to a state without law:

> The world without the sun is not a world but an unformed abyss of darkness, a body without a soul is a putrid corpse, an army without its commander is an unmighty mob: thus a state without philosophy and laws is not a community of right-living men, but a band of robbers and tramps.[46]

Scanderus concludes his discourse by quoting the well-known passage in Cicero's *Tusculan disputations,* in which philosophy is praised as a guide to life and to the founding of cities, as that which generates humanity and civilization. According to Scanderus, therefore, philosophy is undoubtedly of practical use and of direct relevance to daily life and to politics. Although Scanderus does not touch on all aspects of the conception of philosophy outlined above, his ideas are certainly similar to those of the professors at

---

[43] *Oratio inauguralis*, b3v.

[44] *Oratio inauguralis*, b4r: 'Id vero quis? nisi illa rerum omnium moderatrix et fortunae domina philosophia facit, quae duo haec docet: prosperitate modeste uti et calamitatem honeste ferre. Quippe divinarum et humanarum rerum est scientia: novit ergo quae sint res divinae, scit quae sint humanae. Illas sectatur et suspicit, has negligit et despicit. Hinc quamcumque fortuna obvertat faciem, ad omnem ejus ictum philosophus eundem servat vultum.' This text is followed by a parade of philosophical heroes of Antiquity: Stilpo, Archimedes, Zeno, Diogenes and Socrates. Stoic imperturbability is also glorified in Barlaeus's *Mercator sapiens*. According to Barlaeus, philosophy teaches the merchant 'ne nimium appetat'. If his debtors fail, his ships are swallowed by the sea, or if his bookkeeper makes a mess of his accounts, he is consoled by philosophy who taught him to despise all things except virtue. The wise man is good, because he is self-sufficient; *Mercator sapiens*, 33-36.

[45] *Oratio inauguralis*, b4v: 'ad patroni sui domum se recipit, ad Deum evolat.'

[46] *Oratio inauguralis*, b4v-cr: 'Mundus sine sole non est mundus, sed deformis tenebrarum abyssus; corpus sine anima non est ‹nisi› putridum cadaver, exercitus sine duce invalida turba: sine philosophia et legibus respublica non hominum recte viventium societas, sed praedonum et erronum quaedam colluvies.'

Groningen.

The second oration to be discussed is *Of True Philosophy* by Arnoldus Senguerd, delivered at his inauguration on May 15, 1648. Senguerd came from Utrecht to Amsterdam as the successor of Barlaeus. He sees the world created by God as a perfect machine. In this world man is placed as a kind of terrestrial God.[47] Man surpasses all animals by his reason, and he is impelled by his innate desire to know, more especially in so far as learning raises some of mankind above ordinary people. In all walks of life, there are individuals who possess the sparks and flames of this ardent zeal – the *gymnosophists* in India, for example, the *magi* in Persia, the *druids* in Gaul. In spite of the unity of truth, however, there are many divergent opinions between philosophers. The reason for this is the 'obscurity of reality, the blindness of our intellect, the vehemence of our emotions.'[48] How is true philosophy to be obtained, in what way must we proceed? The answer, according to Senguerd, is through the acquisition of virtue.[49] The most important virtue is piety, which is necessary if we are to know God properly. Philosophy is the science of all things, and such knowledge is only possible if one knows God, the highest object and the source of all things. 'So, the wise man or the philosopher should occupy himself in particular with knowing God.'[50] Revelation is necessary to the true worship of God, but although philosophy is based on natural reason alone, it is able to wean us from false gods and to demonstrate that God is the provident Creator of all things. The second virtue indispensable to the true philosopher is humility. Humility leads to self-knowledge, and he who knows himself 'sees what he was, nothing; he considers what he is, the plaything of time and fortune; he foresees what he will be, food for worms.'[51] The third virtue is humanity, that is to say civilized and refined behaviour. Rabbi Hillel, who never became angry when he was asked a stupid question, is adduced as an example of a wise man with this virtue. He remained friendly even when he was provoked by someone who was to get a reward of forty guilders on being able to annoy him. The fourth of Senguerd's virtues is tranquility of mind – for the end of philosophy, the knowledge of truth and a good will, cannot be attained by anyone disturbed by his emotions.[52]

---

[47] *De vero philosopho*, 3-4. Dibon, *L'Enseignement philosophique*, 241-4, discusses this address.

[48] *De vero philosopho*, 5.

[49] *De vero philosopho*, 6-7.

[50] *De vero philosopho*, 7: 'sapientis igitur sive philosophi est praecipue in cognitione Dei occupari.'

[51] *De vero philosopho*, 11: 'videt quid fuerit: nihil scilicet; considerat quid sit: temporis spolium, fortunae luxus; praevidit quid futurus sit: esca vermium.'

[52] *De vero philosopho*, 14.

The true philosopher acquires knowledge by discipline and experience. Teaching is the beginning of all arts. The teacher may be living or dead: we can learn from books.[53] This is why Cato read during the debates in the Senate, why the emperor Theodosius read at night when the affairs of state were not troubling him, why the Spanish king Alfonso chose a book as a weapon. Direct contact between teacher and pupil, however, is also important, because the spoken word, the facial expression, the gestures and the attitude of the master engrave lessons on the mind of the pupil better than silent reading does. Instruction should, however, be supplemented by experience. The book of nature is to be opened by the philosopher; he must see things with his own eyes. Experience of truth finally sets at rest man's ardent desire for knowledge.[54] Instructed by his mentors and trained by experience, the true philosopher will be of great use to society. It is apparent that Senguerd's oration, as outlined above, fits in well with the humanist theory of philosophy. Philosophical erudition should be directly relevant to our daily life and to society.

Humanist theory and practice

Those institutions of higher education which were either reformed or founded on the basis of humanist ideals retained the principal teaching methods of scholasticism, the lecture and the disputation.[55] In general, humanist scholars did not object to the disputation. Ubbo Emmius, for example, regarded it the most important element in the instruction given in the higher classes of the Latin school. Heereboord defended it as being indispensable to the teaching of philosophy, for

> disputation is the sieve and as it where the whetstone of truth; it enhances the mind, it sharpens judgement [...]. As fire bursts forth from the striking of two flints, so truth arises from disputations [...]. Several eyes see more than one

---

[53] *De vero philosopho*, 17: 'a sapientibus liber vocatum vas plenum sapientiae, putaeus acquae vivae, hortus plenus fructibus, pratum fluens floribus, principium intelligentiae, fundamentum memoriae.'

[54] *De vero philosopho*, 23-24: 'in perspecta veritate acquiescit animus discendi cupidus.' Dibon calls attention to the open Aristotelianism of Senguerd and his notion of human progress. Senguerd indeed acknowledges the importance of inventions such as the compass, the art of printing and gunpowder, but he does compare nature with the mysteries of Eleusis. The common man sees only the vivid colours of the outside, while the philosopher penetrates deeper into its secrets. There are no indications that Senguerd considered human history to be the history of technological progress.

[55] Leinsle, *Einführung in die scholastische Theologie*, 264; Dibon, *L'Enseignement philosophique*, 42; Tholuck, *Das akademische Leben*, I 241; Fraenkel, *De l'écriture à la dispute*.

eye; iron is sharpened by iron; man by other men.[56]

At Leiden, the first university founded in the new Republic and home to such humanist luminaries as Scaliger and Lipsius, disputations were held from the very outset.[57]

Nevertheless, the character of disputations was changed by humanism. Dibon has pointed out that the seventeenth-century disputation was reformed so as to satisfy the demands of humanism. Its technical language was purified, and not only Aristotle but all classical texts were used as proof of an argument. In logic, moreover, two disputational techniques are distinguished – attacking someone's thesis by constructing an argument the conclusion of which is the negation of the thesis, and asking questions so that the defendant of the thesis is led to contradict himself. The former may be called the argument and the latter the questioning technique. The medieval *ars obligatoria* is an example of the questioning method, while in the seventeenth century the method of argument was applied.[58] A second major difference between the medieval disputations and early modern ones is that in the seventeenth century the printed disputation usually consists of a list of theses, sometimes but not always accompanied by arguments for and against. The subject matter is not usually formulated in the question form. A rare exception in the collection of Groningen disputations preserved in the University Library is Huninga's *Political Disputation – Various Questions* of 1619, which contains eight questions. The argument of the answer is printed in italics, and references are given. These differences between medieval and early-modern disputational techniques are not important, however, but the similarities are. Both used authoritative texts as their point of departure, and they presupposed that truth could be obtained by harmonizing conflicting texts and authoritative opinions.[59]

---

[56] *Sermo de ratione philosophice disputandi* (Leiden 1648), 29. The text continues: 'Si veritas omnis ex se nota est [...], nulla opus foret disputatione. Homo est animal κοινονικῶν vitamque degit in mutua conversatione.' See Verbeek, 'Descartes and Some Cartesians', 188; and Emmius, *Programma bij de aanvaarding van het rectoraat*, 14.

[57] Ahsmann, *Collegia en colleges.*

[58] Angelelli, 'Techniques of Disputation', 801-2. For a description of the factual proceedings, see Geulincx, 'Tractatus de officio disputantium'.

[59] De Rijk, *Middeleeuwse wijsbegeerte*, 112-4 and 124-6. According to De Rijk, medieval philosophers had no blind belief in an authoritative text, but a text was regarded as a proper guide towards truth. This applies to the seventeenth century as well. According to the Utrecht professor H. Reneri, it goes without saying that in the lectures an authoritative text is commented upon. In his inaugural address 'De lectionibus et excercitiis philosophicis', *Illustris Gymnasii Ultrajectini inauguratio*, zv-z3v, he prefers Aristotle, because his philosophy is based on lifelong experience and corroborated by the experience of other scholars in the centuries after his death. Sassen's comments in *Henricus Renerius*, 22, that he prefers 'scholastic' authority above his own research suggest an antithesis which in the Middle Ages and the 17th century did not exist.

Disputations are almost our only source with respect to the teaching of philosophy. Two hundred and sixty-four of the disputations held in Groningen between 1614 and 1666 have been preserved.[60] This number increases from 22 in the first decade, to 145 in the fifties. After 1665 these numbers fall sharply.[61] Here are the numbers of philosophical disputations, and their subject:

	Philosophy	Logic	Natural Philosophy	Ethics	Metaphysics
1614	2	1	2	15	2
1625	3	4	1	26	1
1635		1	2	10	
1645	2	20	45	45	17
1655		22	32	10	2
1665			1	1	
1675	1		1		
1685			1		3
1695			3		2

The first striking difference between theory and practice is that in spite of the requirement of direct relevance, the students had to be thoroughly conversant with a very precise philosophical terminology, which, as Scanderus observes, is only 'of use in solving problems too complicated even for an Oedipus.' In 1620 Makdowell presided over a disputation concerned with efficient causes. Adrianus Simonides, the respondent, demonstrated his competence in using distinctions such as those between the 'cause in itself' and the 'accidental cause', the 'principal' and the 'instrumental cause', the 'moral' and 'physical cause', as well as between a necessary cause and a free agent. Four years later, Warmold Ackema had no problem in defining ethics through the use of medieval theories of science together with the terminology of subject, object, and the central and ancillary aspects of a science (*materia circa quam* and *ex qua*).[62] Another example is provided by a disputation defended by Gerard Mildius, also dating from 1624. Here one comes across terms such as the 'instrumental habit', a 'tendency to form', a 'first act, real and complete being in itself', 'indifferent matter' and a 'for-

[60] This is the number given by the catalogue of Van der Woude at the Library of the university of Amsterdam.

[61] These figures correspond with those in Deventer, see the diagram at the end of Van Sluis, 'Bibliografie van Deventer disputaties', 224.

[62] Makdowell, *Disputatio secunda de definitione ethicae, ad usum ad praxin accomodata* (R. Warmoldus Ackema; Groningen 1624). This disputation is part of a sequence of eleven.

mal concept of being'.[63] In understanding such terms, familiarity with the works of Aristotle is not sufficient; one also has to have a certain insight into medieval theories. It is quite evident, therefore, that in the teaching of philosophy students were made familiar with medieval scholastic texts. In disputations dating from the first years of the university, the authors actually mention medieval scholastics such as Avicenna, Averroes, Duns Scotus and Thomas Aquinas.

A second major difference between theory and practice is that from the very beginning metaphysics was dealt with in the classroom, and in two early disputations it is even included in their title.[64] In these disputations reference is made to the tradition of metaphysical thinking developed in the writings of Avicenna, Duns Scotus and Suárez. Quite unlike Aristotle and Thomas Aquinas, these philosophers treated metaphysics as a transcendental science of being as such. We may form a coherent concept of this object and refer to it by means of an unambiguous term.[65] According to this theory, metaphysics is quite distinct from physics. In Groningen, traces of such a concept are found in Mildius's disputation, inasmuch as he regards the real being common to both God and creatures as the object of metaphysics.

In his article on philosophy in Groningen prior to 1625, Vanderjagt maintains that after the disappearance of the first generation of professors the 'humanistic ideals' were no longer maintained, and that the broad pedagogical conception of philosophy which stressed its practical nature was replaced by the more professional ideals of the scientific specialist.[66] One of his arguments is based on the fact that the main subject-matter of the surviving disputations is of an ethical nature. We might well ask whether this is a reliable inference. Only twenty-two disputations have survived for the period between 1614-1625, and they probably constitute only a small part of all the disputations held. Those for which Makdowell was responsible in 1616, for example, preceded by his address concerning the four impediments to the study of philosophy, have now been lost. Indeed, fifteen of these certainly discuss ethical themes, but eleven are part of a continuously numbered course which has survived as a whole. They cannot, therefore, be used to prove the predominance of practical philosophy in philosophical teaching as a whole.

Another argument for questioning this inference can be derived from a

---

[63] Makdowell, *Positiones miscellaneae philosophicae* (R. Gerardus Mildius; Groningen 1624).

[64] Makdowell, *Discursus metaphysicus de substantia spirituali infinita et finita* (R. Martinus Joannis); and *Quaestiones aliquot illustres metaphysicae de causis* (R. Fredericus ab Oesbroeck; Groningen 1624).

[65] The best introduction in this tradition is Honnefelder, *Scientia transcendens*.

[66] 'Filosofie tussen humanisme en eclecticisme', 43-4.

cursory comparison with Leiden. Dibon analysed the disputations from the period 1597-1606, which are now contained in five collections, arranged according to their subject-matter.[67] Although about half discuss logical themes, and about a third natural philosophy, twenty-two of the three hundred and twelve deal with a metaphysical theme. In the twenty years prior to 1614, therefore, and in spite of the official regulations, metaphysics was a regular teaching subject at Leiden. The technical terms used in the early disputations, moreover, indicate that in the teaching of philosophy the acquisition of a specialized knowledge was emphasized. In a physical disputation defended in 1614, for example, one finds such terms as: actuality as such (*actus simpliciter*), primary substantial actuality (*actus primus substantialis*), primary accidental actuality (*actus primus accidentarius*), secondary actuality, and the power of change (*vis alterandi*).[68]

A striking difference between medieval disputations and early modern ones is the importance attached to etymology. For, 'words give us an easy access to the inner nature of things, since they are as it were their picture and mark of identification.'[69] These etymological considerations concerning the terms, which precede their definition, are a typically humanist aspect of the otherwise scholastic genre of the early-modern disputation. It is now a commonplace that the seventeenth century saw a revival of Aristotelianism. C.B. Schmitt's research into Renaissance Aristotelianism urges us to prudence, however, for it appears that Aristotle was by no means neglected by philosophers of the humanist period. This survey of what we know of the teaching of philosophy at these Dutch universities suggests that this may also have been the case in respect of scholasticism.

---

[67] Dibon, *L'Enseignement philosophique*, 28-32.

[68] G. Jaccheaus, *Disputatio physica de anima in genere* (R. Abrahamus Lounaeus; Leiden 1614).

[69] M. Pasor, *Disputatio ethica de liberalitate et magnificentia* (R. Hayo Tjassens; Groningen 1647). Other examples from 1646 are M. Pasor, *Disputatio theologica practica de conscientia* (R. J. Clauberg); and Schoock's *Disputatio philosophica expendens an intellectus brutis attribui possit* (R. Henricus a Reede); *Disputatio physica de glacie* (R. Bernhardus Vriesen); *Disputatio physica de hyeme* (R. Joannes Bertlingh); *Disputatio physica de acqua* (R. Christophorus Wittichius); and *Disputatio physica de nive* (R. Arnoldus a Stralen).

J. PAPY

THE RECEPTION OF AGRICOLA'S *DE INVENTIONE DIALECTICA* IN THE TEACHING OF LOGIC AT THE LOUVAIN FACULTY OF ARTS IN THE EARLY SIXTEENTH CENTURY

On 14 October 1535 an anonymous compilation of commentaries on Aristotle's *Organon* was printed in Louvain by Servaas van Sassen. The entire initiative was developed and sponsored by the Louvain faculty of arts and – according to the historian Joannes Molanus – left in the care of master Johannes Stannifex (Jean Stainier/Estainier) of Gosselies, *legens in Porco*.[1] For various reasons the faculty wished to offer its *baccalaurei* at the beginning of the new academic year 1535 a uniform and coherent syllabus on the dialectical works of Aristotle. This work, which is so far unstudied, is important for the history of the Louvain faculty of arts and its teaching of logic for more than one reason.

First of all, of these *Commentaria in Isagogen Porphyrii, et in omnes libros de dialectica Aristotelis*, which are known to have been republished in 1547; 1553 and 1568, only one copy of the edition of 1535 has been preserved. This unique – and annotated – copy of the *editio princeps* is presently held by the university library of Courtrai and was the property of Egidius van Landeghem, nephew of Jan de Hondt (1486-1571), canon of Courtrai.[2] The fact that only this copy is extant is probably the reason why Paquot – and in his footsteps De Wulf – does not consider the work as published,[3] why later, in the repertories by Wilhelm Risse and Charles Lohr, it is invariably dated in 1547 and why today it is still not mentioned in the standard bibliography of Aristotle's editions by

---

[1] *Molanus sur l'histoire de la ville de Louvain*, I 600. Following this Andreas, *Bibliotheca Belgica*, 566; Vernulaeus, *Academia Lovaniensis*, 167; De Vocht, *Foundation and Rise of the Collegium trilingue*, IV 104.

[2] For a brief description, see *Catalogus van de bibliotheek van Jan de Hondt*, 48-50, nr. 2. The first owner of this copy was Egidius van Landeghem (matriculated at Louvain on 30 August 1537; cf. *Matricule de l'Université de Louvain*, IV 165), student at the Pedagogy the Burcht (Castrum) in the years 1537-8. On the endpage one can read: *Sum Egidij Landeghem in Castro artium Theatro longe florentissimo a[nn]o D[omi]ni 1538* and at the printed date *M.D.XXXV*, which was completed by Van Landeghem *M.D.XXXVII mense septembri*; on the first page is written in his hand: *Ita est Egidius Landeghem Die Santo Paulo In Castro anno D[omi]ni 1537*. Afterwards the work was in possession of the canon of Courtrai, Jan de Hondt (?). Later on it ended up in the collegiate church of Courtrai, whence it passed to the church of Saint-Martin. The work is also described in the exhibition catalogue *Van Vicus Artium tot nieuwbouw*, 62, nr. 112.

[3] Paquot, *Mémoires*, III 622; De Wulf, *Histoire de la philosophie scolastique*, 322.

Cranz.[4] Also Peter Mack hesitates to claim that the work was published as early as 1535, and therefore he bases his conclusions on the edition of 1568.[5]

This new dating puts the work in a new perspective within the history of the teaching of logic. One hundred years ago Carl Prantl had already calculated that every year between 1480 and 1520 some fifteen tracts on logic were published and that consequently every university with any name at all had published its own companion.[6] The initiative of the Louvain faculty of arts is therefore not original but seems to be a late offshoot of this tradition. On the other hand, the Louvain compilation is the work of a number of authors who each contributed the part for which they were most qualified. Because of this origin[7] and the anonymous collection of authors, the Louvain companion strikes the eye as an unbalanced mixture of contributions, some inspired by scholasticism, and others revealing typically humanist tendencies.

Thirdly, a study of the content of the work allows us to define which new stock of ideas from the humanist movement was absorbed in the basic teaching of the baccalaureat students at the Louvain faculty of arts. Apparently this period is a turning point. The well-known tensions between humanists of the Collegium Trilingue (founded in 1517) and the faculty of theology seem to appear as well at the faculty of arts. In this sense our contribution is intended to fill a gap in the historical research regarding the curriculum at the early university of Louvain. Whereas it was previously the *communis opinio* that until the Cartesian revolution the *Alma Mater* of Louvain offered merely scholastic education,[8] we now have ample evidence at our disposal to reconsider these views.

---

[4] Risse, *Die Logik der Neuzeit*, 32-4; Risse, *Bibliographia Logica*, 59 s.v. *Lovanienses*; Lohr, 'Renaissance Latin Aristotle Commentaries', 544 s.v. *Lovanienses*; Lohr, *Latin Aristotle Commentaries*, 227; Lohr, 'Latin Aristotle Commentaries Supplement', 161-8; Cranz and Schmitt, *A Bibliography of Aristotle Editions*.

[5] Mack, *Renaissance Argument*, 269-70 and 295 (n. 70). His conclusion that 'It seems very likely that *De inventione dialectica* was taught in Louvain in the late 1520s and early 1530s' (pp. 269-70) must be nuanced. Mack has no knowledge of the appearance of the *Auctarium* in 1537, in which Agricola has a larger presence.

[6] Prantl, *Geschichte der Logik*, IV 173.

[7] An example of a similar cooperative initiative is the important edition of the *Commentarii Collegii Conimbricensis in Quatuor Libros de Coelo, Meteorologicos, Parva Naturalia, et Ethica Aristotelis* (Lugduni 1608) of the jesuit college of Coimbra. These commentaries on the Aristotelian corpus came into being in the years 1592-1605 and were conceived after the model of the scholastic *quaestio*; they were reprinted several times in the 17th century; cf. Lawn, *The Rise and Decline of the scholastic 'Quaestio Disputata'*, 129-30; and Murdoch, 'From the medieval to the Renaissance Aristotle', 164-74.

[8] Cf. Van Pamel, *Echo's van een wetenschappelijke revolutie*.

Humanist Thought in the Commentarii Lovanienses

The faculty of Louvain introduces its commentary as new. It is obvious that this is a relative notion. A commentary on Aristotle's Organon dated 1535 is *a priori* influenced by a centuries-old tradition and a Louvain commentary is moreover bound by the statutes of the university and has to respect certain scholastic masters.[9] First of all, therefore, the faculty faced the problem of balancing old and new.

The question remains then whether the chief editor, Johannes Stannifex, and his collaborators realised their goal. It is clear from the notes in its margins that the *Commentarii Lovanienses* fit in with the Louvain tradition as developed by the founders of the university and their immediate successors at the beginning of the fifteenth century. Their dictata were handed round, *solenni more*, from year to year and then from generation to generation. In the university statutes and the *Acta Facultatis* we can read the names not only of those who were recommended or even required masters of the scholastic tradition, but also of those who were forbidden.[10] Certain names were excluded during the early years of the university: Buridan and his pupil Marsilius van Inghen, Ockham and the nominalists in general and John Wyclif.[11] In Louvain the discrepancies were apparently less complicated than in Paris, where various medieval trends were embedded in the tradition of certain colleges. The four Pedagogies of the Louvain faculty of arts, however, do not show such a diversity: the faculty remained in control and directed the complete corps of professors in one and the same direction.

First, this can be deduced from the predominant presence of the authorized or recommended masters in the *Commentarii Lovanienses*: primarily Thomas Aquinas and Albertus Magnus, and then Averroës, Aegidius Romanus and Joannes Duns Scotus.[12] Secondly, the single record of 'Guilielmus Occanus, nominalium antesignanus, qui teste Marco Antonio Sabellico floruit temporibus Ioannis vigesimi primi Papae, circiter annum salutis 1334' shows that Ockham

---

[9] Paquet, 'Statuts de la Faculté des Arts de Louvain', 190-1.

[10] Cf. *Molanus sur l'histoire de la ville de Louvain*, 582-6, about the doctrines forbidden by the faculty of arts in 1427, 1447 and 1512.

[11] Cf. Weiler, 'Les relations entre l'Université de Louvain et l'Université de Cologne', 60-1. From Martinus Dorpius's *Apologia* to Menardus Mannius it appears that it was already stipulated by the first statutes of the faculty of arts that no-one was allowed to teach at the university unless he had taken an oath that he would never teach the doctrines of Buridan, Marsilius, Ockham or their followers (De Vocht, *Monumenta Humanistica Lovaniensia*, 104).

[12] Duns Scotus is only mentioned six times: in the commentary on the *Isagoge* (p. 2), *Praedicamenta* (p. 94 and 125), *Definitiones* (p. 188), *Analytica priora* (p. 356), *Analytica posteriora* (p. 462). Scotus was allowed at Louvain by a decision of 1446.

was a stranger in Louvain and remained as such in the commentaries of 1535.[13] Moreover, the nominalists are excluded, as we learn from the first page of the Louvain commentary.[14]

Apart from this traditional element, the *Commentarii Lovanienses* also contain modernizations, in particular, an increasing recourse to the antique tradition. However, we should first explain where the difference between the *veteres* and *neoterici/ recentiores* actually lies,[15] since the great masters of the thirteenth century such as Albertus Magnus, Thomas Aquinas, Aegidius Romanus and Robert Grosseteste are situated in both categories. All those who come after the great masters of scholasticism up to the contemporary authors of the Louvain commentaries are mentioned as *recentiores* or *neoterici*; the *veteres* on the other hand, go from Aristotle's direct commentators to the Commentator himself, Averroës.[16] According to the humanists, this gave the term an erroneous extension and represented the problems in a wrong way. The Arabs had altered Aristotle's text and ideas and belonged to some in-between category. According to them, it was unacceptable to claim a return to the 'ancients' and at the same time to leave the territory of Greek-Roman antiquity. Apart from this, the humanists could not but applaud the new program of the logic professors: ancient authors like Themistius, Boethius, but also Alexander of Aphrodisias,

---

[13] The distinction between admitted and forbidden authorities is not totally coherent in the Louvain commentary. The faculty recommended *magistri* that were never mentioned in the *Commentarii Lovanienses*: Alexander of Hales, Bonaventure, Willem of Auxerre, Daraud, Henry of Ghent, Petrus Paludanus. On the other hand, Gilbert de la Porrée is mentioned seven times in the commentary on the *Praedicamenta* and Robert Grosseteste 21 times in the *Analytica posteriora*, while Molanus did not come across their names in the *Acta Facultatis*.

[14] Cf. *Commentarii Lovanienses*, pp. 1-2: 'Sola haec universalia signa agnoscunt illi, qui a nominum maiori cura nominales vulgo appellantur, ad nomina referentes fere cuncta, quae a Porphyrio, Aristotele et caeteris, in logicis traduntur. Arbitrantur hi, universalia signa nihil aliud significare, quam omnia et singula singularia sua conjunctim. Quorum sententiam, quod non satis consentanea sit priscis illis scriptoribus, et magnis probatis [...] prosequi non intendimus'. De Wulf, *Histoire de la philosophie scolastique*, 154, thinks just the opposite: 'La philosophie professée à Louvain se sut pas affranchir de ces entraves de l'occamisme'. De Wulf is referring to Molanus, but his opposition is only one of appearance: De Wulf's 'occamism' is synonymous with 'formalism'.

[15] Surprisingly enough one can also find the term *iuniores* instead of *recentiores* or *neoterici* (e.g. in the commentary on *Peri Hermenias*, p. 260, l. 23 and p. 268, l. 30-1), but in the margin the term *neoterici* is reiterated in a hand written note.

[16] The *neoterici* are distinguished from the high scholastic period (p. 593; 612; 635; 637; 675; 867; *Auctarium*, 6; 26). Sometimes the periods of the commentators are divided into three: 'triplex de relative oppositorum natura opinio', in which Thomas Aquinas, Boethius and his followers, and the *neoterici* are meant respectively (p. 157). Further specifications on p. 376: 'Haec autem est Iacobi Fabri caeterorumque neotericorum expositio. Alteram sequuntur plures quam suis in commentariis tradidit Albertus' and p. 497: 'Caeterum huius loci duae sunt expositiones [...] Albertus, Divus Thomas, Egidius Romanus, et pene tota neotericorum caterva post Robertum Lincolnensem [...] Haec fere Divi Thomae verba sunt [...] id quod apertissime scribit Commentator [...] Sed de hac priori expositione satis. Alii [...] Huic expositioni omnino consentit Themistius'.

Augustine and the writings of pseudo-Augustine were restored in a meaningful manner.

If we accurately interpret the term *recentes* in the title of the *Commentarii Lovanienses*, it refers to contemporary commentators as well as to the interpreters who immediately preceded them. In this respect we can mention the name Jerôme de Hangest (†1538) amongst the names of the frequently used authorities of the *Commentarii Lovanienses*. His *Problemata logicalia*, published in 1504 and 1516 is one of the most difficult works of the Paris Collège de Montaigu.[17] The commentator on the *Praedicamenta*, however, has not cited Jerôme de Hangest for his clever attitudes but for a coincidental remark about the *habitus*.[18] Modernism was not a priority for the commentators of Louvain.

Of the three companions with a humanist slant, i.e. the *Compendium de formis ratiocinandi* by Johannes Argyropulos[19] and the *Dialectica* by Angelo Poliziano (1454-1494) and Giorgio Valla (1447-1500), only the *Dialectica* by Poliziano is known by the Louvain commentators. The commentator on book two of the *De interpretatione* refers to him twice as an authority on the question of the authenticity of Aristotle's tracts: 'Liber Peri hermenias apud Aristotelem unicus et continuus est ac indivisus (teste etiam in sua dialectica Politiano); a posterioribus tamen quos nunc scholae sequuntur, non incommode in duo volumina dissecatur' (p. 252) and 'Quamvis plerique, ut tradit Politianus, hunc ultimum tractatum seu caput, crediderunt non esse Aristotelis ob difficultatem nimiam eorum quae hic tractantur' (p. 285). Nevertheless, the contact with Poliziano's tract is rather superficial: in addition to the two stated critical remarks, the commentator on the *Analytica priora* (2,4) borrowed a technical term from Poliziano without using it further: 'In huius literae exordio, duos proponit Philosophus deductionis modos, quae Graecis ἀπαγογὴ dicitur, et quam Politianus nuncupat avocationem' (p. 421).

Deeper affinities between the *Commentarii Lovanienses* and the Italian humanists should thus be attributed to intermediary humanists of the North like Rudolph Agricola and Jacques Lefèvre d'Etaples (Jacobus Faber Stapulensis; c.

---

[17] Cf. *CE* II 163-4; Renaudet, *Préréforme et Humanisme à Paris*, 648; Farge, *Biographical Register of Paris Doctors of Theology*, nr. 234; Guerlac, *Juan Luis Vives*, 20-3. Prantl, *Geschichte der Logik*, IV 262, gives some excerpts.

[18] Cf. p. 119: 'Quibusdam nihilominus placet, nullos esse veros in corpore habitus, sed tantum per frequentes huiusmodi operationes, tolli quaedam corporis impedimenta exercendarum talium operationum'; *in margine*: Hieronymus Hangestus. This is an example of a commentary which started apparently as a marginal note and of which the full text was filled in later on.

[19] Argyropulos's companion was only printed in 1964 (Vasoli, *La dialettica e la retorica dell'Umanesimo*, 106, n. 9), but left several traces in the companion of his pupil Poliziano. At Louvain, only the translation by Argyropulos of Aristotle's *Categories, De interpretatione* and *Analytica priora-posteriora* was known (cf. *Commentarii Lovanienses*, p. 538, 541, 557, 562, 565, 586, 729); of Giorgio Valla just his *Geometria* (cf. *Commentarii Lovanienses*, p. 422).

1460-1536).[20] The latter is one of the most cited *neoterici* in the *Commentarii Lovanienses*. Indeed, the ample use of citations from or references to Lefèvre in all of the commentaries is remarkable. With the exception of the inserted tracts *De divisione et de definitionibus* (pp. 181-96) and *De hypotheticis syllogismis* (pp. 434-42), tracts which are too short to draw negative conclusions, all commentators made use of the work of the Parisian humanist. This does not mean, however, that Lefèvre could persuade everybody of all his views.

More important within the scope of this work is the attack of the Louvain professors on Lorenzo Valla (1407-1457). 'If only he could have made the distinction in the question 'interrogatio per quid',[21] he would have refrained from attacking Aristotle in such a brutal manner'. In this way the young students at the Louvain faculty of arts in 1535, dealing with the second chapter of Porphyrius's *Isagoge*, became acquainted with the existence of one of the first humanists who criticized Aristotle. Further on in this commentary on the *Analytica priora*, the Louvain professor reminds us of the name Valla while discussing Aristotle 51b25ff. He claims again that Valla, whose work he seems to have gone over thoroughly, made the same mistake as those ancient Greek philosophers who are countered by Aristotle in exactly this passage.[22] He quotes Valla elaborately. An additional note in the margin (1538-1539) (p. 292) on the commentary on the *Analytica priora* (1,1) about the *propositiones particulares* shows, moreover, that in Louvain, apart from the printed commentaries, questions raised by Valla were also treated in the courses. But for the professor of

---

[20] Vasoli, *La dialettica e la retorica dell'Umanesimo*, 183-213.

[21] Cf. *Commentarii Lovanienses*, p. 12: 'Uno modo, ut inquirat totam ac completam rei substantiam seu quidditatem, quomodo hic non accipitur. Nam id soli competit definitioni essentiali. Aliter, ut non totam quaerat substantiam, sed eius partem, non quamlibet, sed quare per modum materiae seu substantiae, non qualitatis, se habet, et in hunc sensum hic accipitur. Hanc distinctionem si intellexisset Valla, non adeo procaciter Aristotelem, Porphyrium et omnem fere philosophorum turbam falsitatis arguisset'. We are dealing here with the 'definitio generis'. Phrissemius encountered the same objection in his commentary on Agricola (1,5; 15r), but he admits that he is not able to refute it.

[22] Cf. *Commentarii Lovanienses*, p. 377: 'Porro ne quis ex superioribus in errorem lapsus arbitretur dictas propositiones omnino diversas esse, ita ut illis nihil sit commune, ostendit ibi, Habent autem praedictae propositiones etc. [=Arist. 51b25ff.] quem inter se habent ordinem, quaeque aut alias inferant, aut ex aliis inferantur, et quae non, idem faciens in affirmativis et negativis propositionibus, constantibus ex terminis privative oppositis: quales erant inaequale et aequale, quibus est usus. Aut quia antiqui pro eisdem habebant contradictorie et privative opposita, ut pro eodem inaequale et non aequale. In qua sententia esse videtur et Laurentius Valla 32. capite 2 libri de inventione Dialectica. In nonnullis tamen (inquit) quidem arguti homines, publicos mores ac leges emendare conantur ostentandi ingenii gratia, si ingeniosum est falsum esse cum adiectivo compositum, et idem adiectivum simplex cum adverbio negativo: ut omnis homo est iniustus, et omnis homo est non iustus etc. In quo se aut ignorare usum loquendi indicant, aut illum velle corrumpere etc.'

Egidius Van Landeghem at the Pedagogy of the Burcht these matters were apparently of lesser importance.[23]

The reduction of the induction to the syllogism, discussed in *Analytica priora* 2,2, reminds the commentator of Valla's criticism of the formula 'et sic de aliis'.[24] This criticism appears later in the *Topica* commentary, but there the commentator only uses Phrissemius's commentary instead of directly referring to Valla's *Dialecticae disputationes* (3,16). This passage concerns us because in its margin we find a handwritten note 'In omni bona argumentatione ipsum antecedens includit consequens. Vide apud Commentatorem ipsius Agricole' (p. 418). This illustrates that Van Landeghem's professor did not just stick to Aristotle's text, but that he also told his students about Phrissemius's commentary on Agricola (sc. 2,14; f. 141-8), which, also in this respect was used and assimilated by the commentator on the *Topica* I-II (pp. 634-7). This leads us to the question of the assimilation of Agricola's ideas in the teaching at Louvain.

Assimilation of Humanist Thought

Lisa Jardine has claimed in no uncertain terms: 'It is becoming increasingly clear that despite a certain inertia in the statutes, humanist texts began to be studied in art courses throughout Northern Europe in the early decades of the sixteenth century, as study of book inventories of students, commonplace books, and teachers' lecture notes proves'.[25]

An examination of the sources of the *Commentarii Lovanienses* could shed light on the Louvain practice. Admittedly this is a dangerous criterium when it has to serve as *argumentum e silentio*, but the *Summulae logicales* by Petrus Hispanus are in this case an obvious and indisputable example. Petrus Hispanus's companion was required in Louvain from the first statutes onwards,[26] but it is completely missing in the one thousand pages of the *Commentarii Lovanienses* of 1535. It is impossible to assume that all commentators forgot it accidentally. In addition, the tract about the *Divisiones* and *Definitiones* should have included a reference to the *Summulae logicales*. Or had Petrus Hispanus disappeared from the Louvain arts environment by 1535? A handwritten note

---

[23] Cf. *Commentarii Lovanienses*, p. 292, *nota in margine*: 'Solet hic moveri questio utrum hec propositio sit utilis: quilibet homo currit. Laurentius Valla asserit hanc esse particularem et hac ratione, quia 'quilibet' significat 'aliquis qui libet'. Nos tamen non usque adeo superstitiose dicimus eam esse utilem'.

[24] Cf. *Commentarii Lovanienses*, p. 418.

[25] Cf. Jardine, 'Humanism and the Teaching of Logic', 805, n. 40.

[26] Cf. *Molanus sur l'histoire de la ville de Louvain*, I 588; Reusens, 'Statuts primitifs de la Faculté des Arts de Louvain', 176-7; Van Belle, *De Fakulteit van de Artes te Leuven*, 217.

on the first endpaper at the end of the edition of 1535 mentions him as such: 'Petrus Hispanus et eius commentatores dant huiusmodi argumentationes: Semper valet consequentia a privativo ad contradictorium et sequitur: Johannes est cecus, ergo Johannes est non videns'. We therefore have to assume that Stannifex and his team – just like Juan Luis Vives in his *In pseudodialecticos* of 1520[27] – ostracised Petrus Hispanus and chose the humanist path by replacing the *Summulae* by their own tract *De divisione et de definitionibus*.[28]

The aforementioned criterium of the use of sources reveals itself even more obviously when pronounced contrasts can be pointed out as in the case of the *De inventione dialectica* (1479) by Rudolph Agricola. Referring to the *Commentarii Lovanienses*, Risse discovered that Agricola had already entered the Louvain scholastic stronghold.[29] Indeed, all commentators quote Agricola at least once, with the exception of the commentator of the *Analytica posteriora* I and the *Topica* III-VIII. In the commentaries on the *Analytica posteriora* I and II the diversity in sources does not lead us to presume two authors, of whom one opposes and the other favours Agricola. It is more likely that the (one) commentator on the *Analytica posteriora* read Agricola's *De inventione dialectica* but did not find any common ground with Aristotle's first book and only assimilated Agricola's criticism of Aristotle from the beginning of the second book onwards.[30]

We also notice that Agricola is not simply shut out from the Louvain stronghold since certain Louvain dialecticians enter into a serious discussion with Agricola. The crux of this debate is found in the *Topica*. The difficulties Stannifex faced as chief editor of the *Topica* have to be related to the content of the *Topica* itself, where positions in favour of or against Agricola are inevitable. On the basis of the preface, Stannifex can be considered as pro: he quotes Agricola twice and reuses passages of the commentator on the *Topica* I-II which originate from Phrissemius's notes to Agricola. We have to differentiate, though, because one can distinguish various categories in the Louvain arts

<hr/>

[27] Guerlac, *Juan Luis Vives*, 3-9; 22-4; 71-9; Vives, *In pseudodialecticos*, 15-8; 61-3; Noreña, 'Agricola, Vives and the Low Countries', 116; Lawn, *The Rise and Decline of the scholastic 'Quaestio Disputata'*, 117-20; Mundt, 'Rudolf Agricolas *De inventione dialectica'*, 91-3. On the attitude towards the logic of Peter of Spain of the professors of the Collège de Montaigu at Paris, where Vives studied, see González, *Joan Lluís Vives*, 127-59.

[28] The Louvain faculty of arts is not the only one; in 1531 Agricola's *De inventione dialectica* was also used by progressive professors at the university of Tübingen. At Cambridge it was stipulated by the statutes of 1535 that the medieval companions were to be replaced by Agricola's. Cf. Heath, 'Logical Grammar, grammatical Logic and Humanism', 63; Jardine, 'The Place of dialectic teaching', 31-62; Jardine, 'Humanism and Dialectic in sixteenth-century Cambridge', 147; Jardine, 'Lorenzo Valla and the intellectual origins of humanist dialectic', 147; Mack, *Renaissance Argument*, 291-2.

[29] Risse, *Die Logik der Neuzeit*, 32.

[30] The commentator, like all the others, cites Agricola after the annotated edition of J. M. Phrissemius, professor at the Cologne faculty of arts (Cologne, F. Birckmann, 1523, 1527 and 1528).

milieu of those days. Those who stick only to Agricola, like Alardus of Amsterdam,[31] do not play any role within the faculty and hardly get through to the Collegium Trilingue, a milieu in which they should have found a response.[32] Those who can be rated among the moderate are the followers of the Cologne professor Johannes Matthias Phrissemius, and his edition is the only one that is used for the *Commentarii Lovanienses*. Phrissemius was a determined opponent of Petrus Hispanus, as is evident from the fierce invective in his introduction. The use of Phrissemius's edition in Louvain[33] clearly explains why Petrus Hispanus was excluded from the curriculum. Unlike Risse,[34] Phrissemius's contemporaries did not consider him to be the only truly orthodox commentator on Agricola.[35]

The Louvain commentator on *Topica* I-II on the other hand readily agrees with Phrissemius when he criticizes Agricola and opts for Aristotle. He is the only one who takes the 'third' kind of induction into account as introduced by Phrissemius (pp. 634-5) when discussing Agricola, *De inventione dialectica* 2,14. After quoting Agricola (1,3) and Phrissemius's explanation, the commentator points out (p. 648):

> Haec tua sunt mi Phrisseni, quibus et Rodolphi explicas sententiam, et quicquid ab ipso dictum est in dicentis caput reiicis. Neque enim qui vel invito Rodolpho frequentius Peripateticae sectae partes tueris, hoc loco indicas, quid in hac re secundum Aristotelis sententiam dicendum esse censes, ob id fortassis, ne ex Aristotele depromenda forent, quae velut ex diametro cum Rodolphi sententia pugnarent. Caeterum sive tuo, sive Agricolae nomine illa scripseris.

Without doubting Agricola's influence in Louvain, we must take a close look at the distinctions between the different tendencies. We would be inclined to rate Phrissemius, the commentator of *Topica* I-II and the author of the *Auctarium* as

---

[31] See on Alardus's one-sided view on Agricola's *De inventione dialectica*, Grafton and Jardine, *From Humanism to the Humanities*, 135-6.

[32] De Vocht, *Foundation and Rise of the Collegium trilingue*, I 156-7; Mack, *Renaissance Argument*, 260-2.

[33] In the *Commentarii Lovanienses* no trace is to be indicated of Bartholomeus Latomus's popular and often reprinted summary of Agricola's *De inventione dialectica*, the *Epitome Commentariorum Dialecticae Inventionis Rodolphi Agricolae*, published at Cologne in 1530 after Phrissemius's edition. On Latomus's position in his *Epitome* and intermediary function between Phrissemius and Ramus, see Ong, *Ramus*, 126-30.

[34] Cf. Risse, *Die Logik der Neuzeit*, 22.

[35] According to Erasmus, Phrissemius betrayed Agricola's ideas because he diluted them with many superfluous additions, some of which were sometimes unpleasant. See Erasmus's letter to Haio Hermannus of 20 March 1528 (*Opus epistolarum* VII 368, ep. 1978): 'Opus de Inuentione Rhetorica quidam onerauit commentariis, iuuenis, ut apparet, nec indoctus nec infacundus; sed insunt multa πάρεργα, quaedam etiam odiosiora iuueniliterque destomachata. Malim scholia docta et ad rem facientia. Ni tot oneribus essem oppressus, non grauarer hanc suscipere prouinciam; adeo faueo Rodolphi memoriae.'

moderate followers of Agricola, although the latter two may be one and the
same person and would dispute our classification. They might, for instance,
argue that Phrissemius considered Agricola a 'Latin Plutarch', philosopher and
rhetor, while to them, Agricola was merely a rhetor who meddled with dialectics.[36] They would have called themselves peripatetici and their language would
not have differed much from the commentator on the *Analytica priora* (p. 428)
who, after quoting Agricola (2,18) with regard to the enthymeme, makes the
following remark: 'Quam varie incerteque utantur hoc nomine et consimilibus
diversi rhetores, non magnopere refert nostra, quibus Aristotelis insequi vestigia
propositum est ac praefinitum'. Logic specialists keep their distance from
specialists in rhetoric, but sometimes this distance is so small and so hard to
discern that Risse – legitimately – tries to group them with the term 'Rhetoridia-
lektiker'.[37]

The question might be put, of course, whether Aristotle's *Topica*, as it was
severely criticized in Agricola's *De inventione dialectica*, was still valuable for
education. Certain Louvain professors believed that Agricola's criticism was a
definitive deathblow for Aristotle's tract, others believed in a compromise,
whereas a few hoped for a complete revival. Phrissemius expressed the opinion
of the first group: he noted 'sex causas [...] propter quas topica Aristotelis minus
videantur satis facere studiosis' (9v). The commentator on *Topica* I-II points out
in his commentary that Aristotle's *Topica* can be followed till the end of book
II. The main reason why students disliked the *Topica* was according to him the
third reason, 'quod locos neque describat neque in certum aliquem cogat nume-
rum'.[38] The others could reply to this that the version which was obligatory in
Louvain did indeed work with numbered *loci* (32 in book two; 59 plus 7 and 9
in book three; 73 in book four) and that each had its own name so that the commentaries and the notes in the margin could easily be matched with the text and
as such facilitated its usage. In reality this turned out differently: the commentator becomes tired of the cross-references and finally gets confused: on p. 674 he
refers to *locus* 14 'a contrariis immediatis', but he means *locus* 12 'ab antece-
dentibus et consequentibus' or *locus* 13 'ab antecedentium et consequentium
multitudine'. In fact, from *locus* 4 'ab instantia' onwards he loses the conviction
which is so necessary for a pedagogue. Typical is the disillusioned proposal he
gives his students (p. 656):

> Caeterum cur hunc locum hic tradiderit Philosophus, et non potius capite supe-
> riori, cum illi sit pene idem, quemadmodum habet littera, nos latet. Quod si
> quis huius et aliorum quamplurimorum causam animo duxerit, caveat ne som-

---

[36] As Phrissemius wrote to Alardus in his introductory letter of his edition.
[37] See for example Risse, *Die Logik der Neuzeit*, 54.
[38] Cf. *Auctarium*, 2.

nia ridiculaque pro causis inveniat, inventaque in apertum temere proferat.

Perhaps he thinks in reality about the six cases of *instantia* without textual numbering with which book two ends (pp. 688-9). But the commentator is obviously irritated by the hundreds of *loci* he still has to deal with, so he abandons his boring job of commentator and gives his own *locus* to his students.[39]

The Auctarium *and Agricola*

The *Auctarium*, which in 1535 filled the two quires [Oo] and [Pp] with 32 pages, has not been preserved. Of the second edition, published in September 1537, only a few copies have reached us: they each contain six quires signed [Aaa] to [FFf] which are not numbered.[40]

The first edition of the *Auctarium* probably contained only a synoptic table of the 29 dialectic *loci* and a clarification about each topos. The second edition, on the other hand, is a basic dialectical companion meant for continued education. It is not only meant for the *artistae*, but also for the *grammatici* (*ad iudicandum de scriptis autorum*), the *oratores* and all other students. This is consistent with the wish of Agricola and the humanists after him: a *Topics* which is more accessible and usable than Aristotle's. Therefore, we believe that Risse is too superficial when he argues that the *Auctarium* merely offers Agricola's theory with just a few different details.[41] The author of the *Auctarium* certainly quotes Agricola on nearly every page, and sometimes a few times on one page. From the beginning Agricola has the same footing as the great dialecticians who followed Aristotle like Themistius, Cicero and Boethius. He is showered with praise[42] and his *De inventione dialectica* is recommended as an outstanding companion.[43] Aristotle's *Topica* are no longer the basis of teaching. In the *Auctarium* Agricola's tract is considered the essential document, a brief and clear teaching tool,[44] because we can even read (p. 35): 'Hic Aristotelem sequimur'. Louvain teaching willfully disregarded the most

---

[39] Vives also was irritated by the 'subtilia instantia'; see e.g. Guerlac, *Juan Luis Vives*, 81-3.

[40] Cf. Nijhoff and Kronenberg III, nr. 4181. The handwritten annotations in the Antwerp copy are also by Egidius van Landeghem. Probably this *Auctarium* was removed in later years (1914-8?) from the copy of Courtrai. In any case, it was sold to the Antwerp City Library by the antiquarian and collector E. Van Hoof from Melsele in November 1958, where it is kept under the number C 180055/29a. Another copy, which has not been annotated, is kept at Brussels, Royal Library, under the number II, 90166C/LP. The pagination starting from the title page is ours.

[41] Cf. Risse, *Die Logik der Neuzeit*, 35.

[42] Cf. *Auctarium*, 10 ('luculenter et speciose'); 14 ('gravissima oratione'); 28 ('eleganter'); 41 ('ex Cicerone, Aristotele, Rodolpho quique plures eiusdem notae sunt auctores').

[43] As it was the case at the university of Cambridge, see n. 28.

[44] Cf. *Auctarium*, 3: 'Suppressis [...] plaerisque abstrusioribus a rudium tyronum captu alienis'.

difficult part of the *dialectica*, i.e. the *inventio*. It resolutely put an end to sterile disputes concerning the shadow of a donkey[45] and opted for a practical slant: all obscure points are eliminated so as not to divert the beginners from the main point. They are only supplied with known examples.[46] Here we clearly hear the echo of Agricola's criticism of Aristotle and the way in which the latter was taught: the youngsters want a different teaching method and what they cannot find in Aristotle they should at least like to hear from their tutors.[47] The author of the *Auctarium* is nevertheless not completely honest as far as his promises are concerned. The title leads us to believe that he also offers a method 'in tractandis affectibus', as treated in the third book of Agricola's *De inventione dialectica*.[48] As a matter of fact, the author perhaps purposely has not assimilated the third book of Agricola in his *Auctarium* and he does not breathe a word about the *affectus*. In this respect, the credulous buyer of the *Auctarium* is left in the dark.

However, the author of the *Auctarium* does not want to be counted as one of the absolute followers of Agricola and he dissociates himself fundamentally from the 'sectatores Rodolphi'. He disagrees with Agricola's views on the primordial concepts of the *quaestio* and the *problema* (pp. 3-4), on the reduction of the *probabilia* to dialectic syllogisms (p. 12), and on the difference between *transsumptio* and *interpretatio* which Agricola wanted to neutralize (p. 60). He is especially opposed to the rejection of the maxims: he will not disregard them (p. 3) and, after some five pages of theory (pp. 16-20), he indicates the difference between maxims and axioms. In no way he wants to exclude the maxims as if they belong to the *iudicium*, he wants rather to situate them within the *inventio*, also named the topos 'differentia maxima'. He rejects the possible criticism that these maxims would be invented for educational reasons: they are truly Aristotelian since they can be directly deduced from his *Topica*.[49] He also rejects Agricola's division (1,4) between internal and external *loci*.[50] He resolutely returns to the tradition of Cicero, Boethius and Themistius. Together with Boethius he allows for three *loci* (*a coniugatu, a casibus, a divisione*) as constituants of the category 'loci medii'. He follows Boethius as well in the division in internal and external *loci* and adopts his hierarchy by lifting the

---

[45] Cf. *Auctarium*, 9: 'De asini umbra'; 49: 'Nobis enim nec libet, nec vacat omnium cavillationibus satisfacere'.

[46] Cf. *Auctarium*, 3: 'Familiaria potissimum exempla proponemus'.

[47] The first sentence of the *Auctarium* promises already (p. 2): 'ut copia mediocris et ordo accuratior praestet, quicquid iuventus nostra, sive ab Aristotele, sive potius a suis praeceptoribus desiderare possit'.

[48] On Agricola's theory on affects, see Mack, *Renaissance Argument*, 207-12.

[49] Cf. Green-Pedersen, *The Tradition of the Topics*, 60-5.

[50] Agricola, *De inventione dialectica* (ed. Phrissemius 1528) gives also a 'tabula divisionis locorum', which is also represented in Vasoli, *La dialettica e la retorica dell'Umanesimo*, 256-7, n. 13.

'locus substantiae' and the one of simultaneity onto a higher level. Also the internal, external and middle *loci* are raised in the hierarchy; on top we get the *locus* 'maxima and differentia maximarum'. His knowledge of Boethius was not, therefore, as in Agricola, influenced by the view of Cicero, but he went back to a direct reading of Boethius's *De differentiis topicis* (pp. 16-21).[51] In addition, after the publication of the first edition of the *Auctarium*, its author seems to have been criticised by the supporters of a division of the *loci*, so much loved by the 'rhetori-dialectici'.[52] The result is visible in the second edition: an elaborate justification for the system used in this text and a scrupulous description of each minimal difference from Agricola (pp. 21-2). He is evidently convinced that everbody will believe that he distances himself from Aristotle. The latter seems to derive all 'dialectical *loci*' from maxims[53] while he bases his subdivision of *loci* on three universal *loci*, also called 'differentiae maximarum',[54] which can be transformed to three means of affinity between the 'terminus inferens' and the 'terminus illatus'.[55] He is consequently happy to observe that in Themistius, Cicero, Quintilian, Boethius or Agricola the maxims do not figure under the *loci* but under their 'differentiae'. Now he can add weight to his thesis with Agricola's sentence about the nature of the *loci*, which according to Agricola, depends on the affinity between the proposed argument and the demonstrable issue.[56] He can imply that he does not break with the highest tradition and that Agricola in spite of everything principally agrees with this tradition. It fits in with his ultimate goal, a 'discors concordia rerum'.[57] And this was also, although less explicitly, the aim of the commentator of *Topica* I-II. For this reason it is possible to assign both commentaries to one and the same author.

---

[51] Especially *PL* 64, 1186 and 1196A (summary of Themistius by Boethius).

[52] Cf. Vasoli, *La dialettica e la retorica dell'Umanesimo*, 256.

[53] Cf. *Auctarium*, 20: 'Certe Aristoteles videri potest maximas esse prosecutus'.

[54] Cf. *Auctarium*, 20: 'Nobis contra visum est, locorum accipere distributionem, ex locis differentiis maximarum propositionum'.

[55] This doctrine is not original, because it is linked – by chance? – with an analogous doctrine from Vincent de Beauvais's *Speculum doctrinale* 3, 46 (ed. Douai 1624, 246B). This justification of his Aristotelian classification is for our author of current interest, for Vives had rejected it because it was based upon metaphysical principles as *genus, species* and *differentia* (cf. Vives, *De disciplinis*, ed. Basel 1555, I 379). Vives is nowhere mentioned by name by the *Commentarii Lovanienses* because he was prohibited. In this case, however, one might think of a reaction to Vives's objections: the author is trying to leave the metaphysical grounds and to call only upon logical bases for his classification of 'dialectical loci'.

[56] Cf. *Auctarium*, 20: 'Naturam loci pendere ex argumenti proposci cognatione, et quadam (ut Rodolphus ait) societate cum re probanda'. Reference to Agricola, *De inventione dialectica* 1,2: 'omnia, quae vel pro re quaque vel contra dicuntur, cohaerere et esse cum ea quadam (ut ita dicam) naturae societate coniuncta'.

[57] Cf. *Auctarium*, 22. Similar thought on p. 17: 'in concordiam reduci posse' and p. 56: 'ut in consentionem quandam ista componamus. Apparet sententia nostri Aristotelis recipienda, sed ita, ut ne a reliquis discedere videamur'.

Pro Agricola, against Demochares

In the last resort, Stannifex found a collaborator who wanted to take care of the remaining part of the *Topica*. Contrasting sharply with the commentator of *Topica* I-II and the author of the *Auctarium*, this commentator does not take a particular standpoint with regard to traditional dialectics or the influential ideas of Agricola; he simply pretends that Agricola does not exist and consequently never quotes him. Already from the second page onwards he takes Antonius Demochares as his guide: 'Huic responsum sit ex cuiusdam et eruditi et elegantis sententia [...]', where he finishes a quote of thirteen lines (pp. 692-3).

The commentary of Demochares – the grecized name of Antoine de Mouchy – was published in Paris in 1535 by the printing business of Simon de Colines: *Antonii Democharis Ressonei Pernecessarium in octo libros Topicorum Aristotelis Hypomnema, quo tota disserendi vis in omne problema ingeniose demonstratur, cum recta contextus distinctione, ad phrasim Graecam bona fide innumeris sordibus repurgati.*[58] Consequently, the Louvain commentator had little time to assimilate everything in his own commentary, as it had to be printed before September. This is evident in his contribution: print and editorial work are of lower quality than the rest of the *Commentarii Lovanienses*.[59]

The influence, however, of Demochares on the Louvain commentator of Topica III-VIII can hardly be exaggerated. More than ten percent of the commentary is virtually a literal copy or summary of Demochares's superfluous prose;[60] and for his methodology and point of view the commentator drew his inspiration from Demochares as well. The self-confidence of the young professor of the Parisian Collège de Bourgogne, who with this work made his first appearance in the world of philosophy, is clear but at the same time also understandable. Since the beginning of the thirties, the Parisian university saw with disappointment the aversion for Aristotle's *Topica* in favour of Agricola's dialectics:[61] Demochares devoted himself to a complete rehabilitation of Aristotle.

[58] Cf. Adams, *Catalogue of Books*, I nr. 1881; Renouard, *Bibliographie des éditions de Simon de Colines*, 245-6, for a description of the printing. Erroneously, Renouard dates the letter of dedication to Charles de Villers, bishop of Beauvais, to 1 January 1534; in fact, the text gives: 'XIIII Calendas Ianuarias, Anno a partu virginis 1534', which means a later dating on 19 December in (!) the year 1534.

[59] Many initials have not been printed, even though space has been left for them; some of the chapters are nothing more than a simple title.

[60] There are c. 215 lines of literal citations; adding the citations without a source raises this number to c. 487 lines. The pages of the *Topica* III-VIII (690-828) are normally filled with 47 lines, but several pages contain titles that take up much space.

[61] Risse, *Die Logik der Neuzeit*, 41 suggests that Johannes Sturmius is mainly responsible for Agricola's success at Paris (Mack, *Renaissance Argument*, 265-6). According to Risse, Sturmius had been deeply influenced by his stay with the Jesuits at Liège. Sturmius's time at Louvain between his stay in Liège and Paris is also of great importance. Consequently, it may be argued that the Collegium Trilingue was the most active centre to propagate Agricola's ideas and that it

And this is not the only reason why to our Louvain commentator he was a valuable source. For each paragraph of Aristotle, Demochares gave a Latin translation, verified against the translations of Boethius, Argyropoulos and Jacques Lefèvre d'Etaples and the ancient Greek text. Moreover, he sometimes gave excerpts from the four Greek manuscripts he had consulted to show that his text of the *Topica* was the most reliable ever published. Demochares's commentary also went back on the oldest tradition: the tradition of Alexander of Aphrodisias, Themistius, Porphyrius, Syrianus, Philoponus, Ammonius, Simplicius and Psellus. The Latin Middle Ages have not – according to Demochares in his preface – produced a contribution to Aristotelian dialectics worth mentioning. Great names from scholasticism are hardly mentioned;[62] Demochares points an accusing finger at the followers of Petrus Hispanus.[63]

Still Demochares does not often carry on controversies in his commentary and – with the exception of Valla and Agricola – he attacks his opponents without mentioning their names.[64] His refutations are generally short and polite and he even admits that literature owes a lot to Agricola and other humanists.[65] The most glorious and, at the same time, discrete tribute which Demochares bestows on Agricola is certainly the concordance (after book two of the *Topica*) he gives between the *loci* of Aristotle, Themistius, Cicero and Agricola. Meant as a counterpart to similar concordances in the editions of Agricola, it shows that many students started their studies of dialectics with Agricola. Instead of wasting his time with sterile polemics, Demochares repeatedly underscores the excellence of the tract about the *Topica*.[66]

---

influenced Sturmius – who studied there under Goclenius and Rescius and spent four years of his youth at Louvain – in a more profound way (De Vocht, *Foundation and Rise of the Collegium trilingue*, II 579-90; IV 212, n. 1). Risse's opinion suggests that Sturmius's stay in Paris was of overwhelming importance. In this way, the personal role of Phrissemius and his editors for the propagation of Agricola's ideas at Paris before 1530 is underestimated. For Paris editions before 1530, see Mack, *Renaissance Argument*, 267, and for Sturmius's dependence on Agricola's dialectical work, see Gilman, 'From Dialectics to Poetics', 421-6.

[62] Only Thomas Aquinas (159r) and – indirectly – Robert Holkot and William Ockham (148r) are mentioned.

[63] In his preface, he is aiming at the Parisian master John Mair (1467/9-1550) and his school: 'Illi infestissimi omnis literaturae hostes, et continui totius purioris disciplinae osores, quibus tantum nugae, deliriae et (plane dicam) castra Hispanica arrident, qui nunquam in meliores traditiones desinunt conspirare'. On Mair and his school, see Renaudet, *Préréforme et Humanisme à Paris*, passim; González, *Joan Lluís Vives*, 144-59; Murdoch, 'From the medieval to the Renaissance Aristotle', 164-7; and Broadie, *The Circle of John Mair*.

[64] Valla on 175v, 232r, 237r, 283r; Agricola explicitly on 19v, 21r, 22v, 160r, 272v-273r, 289r-v and implicitly on 5r, 6r-7r, 177v, 212v-213r. Vives is most probably meant on 14v in the reference to the man who wanted to exclude the dialectics from the *artes*.

[65] See e.g. 160r: 'Rodolphus Agricola, vir sane multae eruditionis'; 289r: 'Scimus Agricolam (ut agnoscamus eos a quibus profecimus) and 213r: 'etsi doctissimi viri, cui multa debent bonae litterae, quas ab inferis magno animi ardore, et pertinaci studio revocavit'.

[66] Cf. 291r.

These details about Demochares's companion are necessary to outline clearly the Louvain tactics vis-à-vis Agricola. The publication of Demochares's commentary undoubtedly encouraged some people to hope that the dark clouds gathering over Aristotle's *Topica* had been driven away. Nevertheless Demochares's work knew little success, perhaps because it was prolix and too vague. As we learn from the handwritten notes, the Louvain commentator of *Topica* III-VIII, imitating Demochares, also received little attention from the professor of the Pedagogy of the Burcht, where Egidius van Landeghem studied in 1537-1538. The *Auctarium* was studied in depth but the commentary on *Topica* III-VIII was simply skipped except for the pages 822-823 (8,13), where the *petitio principii* was treated.

This observation is important for the position of moderate 'rhetori-dialectics' in Louvain, even though it is based on the indications of merely one student, one professor and one Pedagogy. More clarifying in this respect is the fact that the first edition of the *Auctarium* – sold together with the *Commentarii* – was out of print in 1537. As many copies of this small companion were sold in two years as were sold of the complete commentaries in twelve years: the first republication of the *Commentarii Lovanienses* only came on the market in 1547, integrating the *Auctarium* within the paging.

Conclusion

The *Commentarii Lovanienses* should be placed within the context of the printing business of the Louvain faculty of arts. The following scheme might be kept in mind:

1522: *Physica* and psychological tracts of Aristotle in Latin,[67]
1523: commentary on the *Physica*,
1525: Organon of Aristotle in Latin,
1532: *Organon* of Aristotle in the Latin translation of Argyropulus,
1535: commentary on the *Organon* with *Auctarium*,
1537: republication of the *Auctarium*,
1547: republication of the commentary on the *Organon* with *Auctarium*
1547: republication of the commentary on the *Physica*
1553: republication of the commentary on the *Organon* with *Auctarium*,
1568: republication of the commentary on the *Organon* with *Auctarium*.

[67] Nijhoff and Kronenberg, I nr. 138: the title page is dated 1522, the colophon Januari 1523. See also Van Iseghem, *Biographie de Thierry Martens*, 324-6, nr. 183.

First, it should be pointed out that the faculty did not take such great pains to invest in this project without reason. The enterprise was certainly calculated according to its economic validity. This is not only clear from the fact that the *Auctarium* was printed separately in 1537 and that students could easily slide it into the commentaries. More important is the fact that the faculty saw to it that the voluminous and costly companion was actually used. However, the solidarity visible on such occasions should not be seen merely as inspired by pedagogic concerns. The cooperation on the production and publication of the commentaries had tightened other bonds between the professors concerned. Only collective promotion could recuperate the costs of printing and allowed for the payment of the printer and his cooperators or correctors.

In addition it should be realized that this anonymous and collective edition, which actually limits the academic freedom of the professors, is unique in time and genre. To explain this phenomenon, the motives on the title page as well as Stannifex's preface should be taken into consideration: pedagogic uniformity, saving of time and a sovereign remedy for Christian education in the struggle of the Counter-Reformation. Also the hypothesis with regard to economic motives is no isolated fact. It cannot be denied that for the members of the faculty of arts the motive of competition counted as well. Those who read the preface closely can find a pejorative attitude towards the so-called 'rhetoristes'. This does not mean that these 'rhetoristes' should be seen as imaginary or distant enemies, but as concrete competitors who are not mere sojourners in Louvain but are in the faculty of arts itself: the professors of the Collegium Trilingue.

The situation that was created by the foundation of the Collegium Trilingue in the years 1520-1540 is specific. On the one hand the Collegium was part of the faculty of arts, but on the other hand it was not integrated in it institutionally or ideologically. In the same way as this had caused tensions with the faculty of theology, one can find amongst the professors of the faculty of arts and other Pedagogies an attitude of distrust and rivalry. The tense atmosphere of the years 1520-1530 was maybe less marked in the following decade, but it still to a large degree influenced the collective attitude of the faculty of arts. The publication of a collective commentary on Aristotle and the efforts to maintain its monopoly position cannot be seen as a neutral action inspired merely by pedagogic and economic reasons. It should rather be considered as an offensive move of the Louvain faculty of arts against the Collegium Trilingue. This offensive was obviously motivated by the increase of the number of students in the Collegium Trilingue.[68] This increase was especially spectacular with regard

---

[68] De Vocht, *Foundation and Rise of the Collegium trilingue*, IV 50-1, mentions the measure of 1539, by which the faculty proposed to pay the double for the contribution for Charles V, on condition that the rector of the university does not allow a student to be inscribed only for the

to language instruction[69] and consequently it undermined the comfortable position of the old Pedagogies, as the arts education gave the only possible entry to
the study of medicine, law and theology.

On the other side we see a similar strategy. At the beginning of the academic
year in September 1538, Alardus of Amsterdam dedicated his new edition of
Agricola to Goclenius, holder of the chair in Latin at the Collegium Trilingue.
In his dedicatory letter Alardus is contemptuous about academics who remain
attached to their traditional dialectics, 'quamvis barbara, quamvis ἀπροσδι–
όνυσα, quae in Academiis traduntur dialectica, ut quae olim ipse Rodolphus
Lovanij didicit'.[70] Agricola's tract clarified this science and made it more efficient and useful for other sciences.

In this particular context the decision of the faculty of arts to record her
dictata in print and to bring uniformity to its commentaries on Aristotle is a
clear stand. The faculty held on to its old teaching methods and the traditional
shape of the commentaries on Aristotle. If in certain rare places it gave a new
look to these commentaries by slightly adapting them to new tendencies, it preserved the essence of the antique heritage. The faculty would also maintain this
position in later editions of 1547, 1553 and 1568. In addition it continued its
debating exercices and it emphasized – against the criticism of Vives and others
– the importance of these *disputationes.* They even wanted to extend them.

In the same way, the Louvain commentaries confirm the general conclusions
of E.J. Ashworth: 'Writings purely in the medieval tradition ceased abruptly
after 1530, at least outside Spain; but some parts of the medieval contribution to
logic continued to be included in at least some textbooks. The new interests of
rhetorical humanism, the emphasis on the topics, on strategies for plausible
argumentation, on methods of organizing discourse, on the use of literary
examples, had a great influence on the classroom [...]'.[71] Although theoretically
the faculty had defined its position in 1535 and therefore defined which course
to take, in practice it did not exclude side-roads. Petrus Hispanus was replaced
by Boethius; the study of the *Topica* predominated. Certain professors gradually
followed the new direction of the 'rhetori-dialectici'[72] of the Collegium

---

courses of the Collegium Trilingue. While the faculty of theology contributed 15 Rhineguilders, the
faculty of civil and canon law 20 and of medicine 10, the faculty of arts offered 100 Rhineguilders!

[69] De Vocht, *Foundation and Rise of the Collegium trilingue*, II 347. Goclenius wrote to
Erasmus on 10 May 1528 that the auditorium in the Collegium Trilingue had become once again
too small and that he was forced to double his courses (*Opus epistolarum*, ep. 1994a; De Vocht,
Foundation and Rise of the Collegium trilingue, III 13-4). As a consequence of this growing success, Goclenius decided to enlarge the building during the summer of 1530 (op. cit. III 14).

[70] Alardus's letter to Goclenius in Alardus's edition of Agricola's *De inventione dialectica*, a2r-
a4v; passage cited on a3r.

[71] Cf. Ashworth, *Changes in Logic Textbooks*, 76.

[72] The opposition *rhetores-philosophi* appears from the preface of Stannifex, but also comes to
the surface at several places in the *Commentarii*. See e.g. the commentary on the *Analytica priora*

Trilingue. So, the hybrid character of the *Commentarii Lovanienses* reflects the pivotal position of the Louvain faculty on the eve of Erasmus's death.

(p. 428): 'Quare non possumus accedere illorum sententiae, quibus (ut narrat Rodolphus) persuasum est, Aristotelem non discrevisse formam argumentandi a ratiocinatione seu syllogismo enthymema, sed certo tantum rerum genere constare voluisse, ut sit ex verisimilibus et signis. Quam varie incerteque utantur hoc nomine et consimilibus diversi rhetores, non magnopere refert nostra, quibus Aristotelis insequi vestigia propositum est ac praefinitum'; reference is to Agricola, *De inventione dialectica* 2,18.

E. RUMMEL

HUMANISM AND THE REFORMATION: WAS THE CONFLICT BETWEEN ERASMUS AND LUTHER PARADIGMATIC?

There is considerable disagreement among modern scholars about the historical significance of the conflict between Erasmus and Luther. Some have seen
it as a landmark defining the relationship between humanism and the Reformation, 'opening an unbridgeable gulf' between the two movements, as Wilhelm Maurer put it. Others have deflated or even denied Erasmus's role as a
catalyst in the process.[1] In this paper I would like to reopen the question, in
the hope of casting further light on the matter. For this purpose I shall first
examine what I see as principal elements shaping Erasmus's attitude toward
the Reformation: his epistemology and his professional commitment. Secondly, I shall consider whether these elements are merely 'Erasmian', that is,
represent his personal attitude toward Luther and the Reformation, or have a
broader currency and can be labelled 'humanist'.

First, then, let me examine Erasmus's epistemology, taking my departure
from Luther's well-known observation that he himself was a 'Stoic asserter',
while Erasmus was a 'Sceptic doubter'.[2] The sceptic procedure involves arguing on both sides of a question and, if no logical answer emerges, suspending
judgment. This, at any rate, is the method of the sceptic hardliners, the Pyrrho-
nists. The qualified scepticism of the New Academy circumvents the difficulties arising from *epoche* by proceeding to judgment on the basis of probability. Erasmus cannot be regarded as a sceptic in either of those senses, at
least not in his search for doctrinal certainty and when dealing with articles of
faith. He does begin by arguing on both sides; and if a clear answer does not
emerge, he pauses to reflect on the logical impasse; like the New Academi-
cians, he then proceeds to judgment. This judgment, however, is not based on
probability but on authority and consensus. He defines articles of faith
accordingly. They are based, he says in his *Apologia ad monachos Hispanos*,
on 'unequivocal scriptural passages (that is, authority) and commonly accepted creeds or universal synods' (that is, consensus). In the *Detectio praestigi-
arum* he supplies a similar definition. An article of faith is 'that which the
Catholic Church holds without controversy and by a large consensus, such as

---

[1] 'Der Abgrund ist unüberbrückbar aufgerissen' (Maurer, 'Melanchthon als Humanist'). For a
summary of recent literature on the subject see Augustijn, 'Humanisten auf dem Scheideweg zwischen Luther und Erasmus'.
[2] See below, note 11.

the doctrines expressly stated in Holy Scripture and in the apostles's creed, to which may be added the decrees of councils properly constituted and following due process'.[3]

We refer to Erasmus as a Christian Humanist to distinguish his brand of humanism from more secular ones; similarly, we should refer to Erasmus's scepticism as Christian Scepticism to distinguish his brand from the classical antecedents. When he uses the sceptic methodology but in the end admits scriptural or ecclesiastical authority and the consensus of the faithful as criteria of judgment, he is clearly modifying a pagan philosophy to bring it in line with Christian thought. Erasmus's Christian Scepticism played a crucial role in shaping his attitude toward Luther and the reformers.

It is well-known that Erasmus initially gave qualified support to Luther. He praised his moral integrity, his gospel spirit, and, as late as 1519, Luther's willingness 'to submit himself to the judgment of the apostolic See and entrust himself to the judgment of the universities'.[4] By 1521 Erasmus had changed his tune in response to the fact that Luther was now openly defying authority. He had been excommunicated and was under the imperial ban. In a lengthy letter to his friend Justus Jonas, Erasmus admits that he and others had been mistaken in their opinion of Luther, 'for we readily believe what we strongly wish to be true; and people thought a man had arisen who was unspotted by all this world's desires and would be able to apply some remedy to these great evils'. Instead Luther had poured forth an unchristian torrent of abuse and was rupturing the unity of the Church.[5]

Erasmus's change of direction was, however, not as sudden as alleged by some of his critics. From the very beginning Erasmus had carefully qualified his support. He consistently expressed misgivings about Luther's radicalism which, he feared, would result in discord. By the end of 1520, Erasmus began highlighting these misgivings. He now claimed that his discreet warnings to Luther advising him to be more moderate showed that he had anticipated or recognized early on that the movement would lead to schism. Writing to Pope Leo X, for example, Erasmus claimed that he 'was almost the first person to detect the risk that the affair might issue in public strife'. In a contemporary letter to Cardinal Campeggi, he made similar claims. 'I feared that so much freedom of speech would end in civil strife'. Again he made claims for his farsightedness: 'I was the first person to condemn Luther's books, at least to the extent that they seemed to envisage public disturbance, which I have always consistently abhorred'.[6]

---

[3] *LB* IX, 1091C; *ASD* IX-1, 258.
[4] *CWE*, ep. 1033, 127-8.
[5] *CWE*, ep. 1202, 202-10.
[6] *CWE*, epp. 1143, 23; 1167, 202-3; 439-41.

Historians usually interpret the sentiments expressed here as apologetic. They see in them an effort on Erasmus's part to cover his tracks and avoid the danger of being associated with a declared heretic. Others regard Erasmus's fear of a public disturbance or schism an aspect of his pacifism. A third group put his emphasis on unity into the context of his ecclesiology.[7] These considerations may have played a role, but Erasmus's epistemology should be our first point of reference and it provides a more coherent and satisfactory explanation for his attitude toward the reformers. In my opinion, Erasmus abhorred religious strife, not because he loved peace (he was quite contentious in intellectual matters), but because he regarded consensus as an essential criterion of doctrinal truth. Schism posed a threat to the Christian Sceptic's decision-making process. If papal authority was questioned in principle, if long-standing traditions were abandoned, if consensus was destroyed, the Christian Sceptic was arrested at the stage of *epoche* and paralyzed in his actions.

It has been pointed out that Erasmus's controversy with Luther over the question of free will illustrates Erasmus's decision-making process.[8] The *Diatribe on Free Will*, especially, is a methodological showcase, a demonstration how one should approach and settle doctrinal questions. Erasmus calls his work a *collatio*, a comparison. He compiles evidence on both sides of the question, listing scriptural passages for and against the concept of free will. However, this process leads to probability rather than to certainty,[9] and in these circumstances Erasmus the sceptic would have liked to suspend judgment, but as a Christian Sceptic he had to press on. Thus his well-known declaration: 'I have so little fondness for assertions that I would readily join the ranks of the sceptics, if it were permitted by the inviolable authority of Scripture and the decrees of the Church'.[10] Here we see the Christian Sceptic pause to reflect on the impossibility of reaching a rational decision, then listen for the authoritative voice of the Church.

Luther perfectly understood the import of this demonstration. In his reply he contrasted Erasmus's reluctance to pass judgment with his own willingness to make assertions. It is in this context that Luther, using classical terms of reference, identified himself as a stoic, Erasmus as a sceptic. He believed that sceptics must be banished from Christianity; what was needed were 'asserters twice as unyielding as the stoics themselves'. He insisted that assertions were a quintessential Christian mode of speaking: 'This is how a Christian will speak. [...] I will not only consistently adhere to and assert sacred writings

---

[7] For recent discussions, see Dickens, *Erasmus the Reformer*, 115-47 ('The Lutheran Tragedy'); Augustijn, *Erasmus*, 119-33 ('The Luther Question'); Pabel, 'The Peaceful People of Christ'.
[8] For recent discussions and literature, see Augustijn, *Erasmus*, 134-45; Boyle, *Rhetoric and Reform*, esp. 122-31.
[9] Cf. *LB* IX, 1251C; 1242A.
[10] *LB* IX, 1215D.

everywhere and in all its parts, but I also wish to be as certain as possible in things that are not vital and that lie outside of Scripture. For what is more miserable than uncertainty'; and conversely he criticizes Erasmus for wanting 'to compare everything, affirm nothing'.[11]

It is significant that Erasmus does not reject the label 'sceptic' in the *Hyperaspistes*, his response to Luther. Rather he clarifies the term. Sceptics, he says, care about the truth, but do not jump to conclusions, 'do not offer facile definitions and fight for their opinions tooth and claw'. Sceptics 'accept as a probability what another accepts as certainty'. But – and this is important to note – Erasmus does not leave it at that. The definition 'the sceptic accepts as a probability what another accepts as certainty' applies to the Academic Sceptic. Erasmus's Christian Sceptic is able to overcome the limitations of human reason and convert probability into certainty by using authority and consensus as criteria of the truth. Erasmus therefore continues: 'I specifically exempt (from uncertainty) [...] what has been revealed in Sacred Scripture and what has been handed down by the authority of the Church'. He returns to the two criteria, authority and consensus, in the conclusion of his argument: Doctrine is based on scriptural authority and 'the decrees of the Church, especially those that were published at general councils and are confirmed by the consensus of the Christian people'.[12]

Consensus becomes for Erasmus the touchstone of true religion and, conversely, discord the characteristic mark of false doctrine – and this is to be understood not merely as a strategic position or as an aspect of his pacifism or his ecclesiology but as a cornerstone of his epistemology. He makes this point with increasing frequency in references to the reformers. In the dialogue *Explanatio Symboli* (1533) the catechumen asks how he may recognize the authentic voice of the Church among the many sects that claim to be the only genuine interpreters of the Word of God. Erasmus provides this answer: 'There are many indications [...] but the foremost is the authority of the ancient synods approved by the lasting consensus of so many centuries and nations'.[13] In the same vein, Erasmus declares repeatedly that he cannot join the reformers because they do not manifest the tell-tale consensus. 'If I could convince myself that you are all following the genuine Gospel, I would already be in your camp. But the dissensions among you clearly show that this is not the case,' he writes in the *Epistola ad fratres inferioris Germaniae*. In a letter to Conradus Pellicanus he uses similar arguments: 'I refuse to depart from the public verdict and the consensus of the Church and am not convinced

---

[11] Luther, *The Bondage of the Will*, 106-8.
[12] *LB* X, 1258B-1262B.
[13] *LB* V, 1171F-72A.

by a dissenting opinion. You are fighting among yourselves'.[14] The Lutherans, he noted sarcastically, were a *disgregata congregatio* and a *dissecta secta*, a disintegregated congregation, a dissected sect.[15] He also returns to the crucial difference between his own approach and that of the reformers, their stoic assertions and his own scepticism: 'What they call certain, I consider doubtful. [...] No blame adheres to careful and sober inquiry into specific points, what is dangerous is the commitment to one point of view, which once it occupies the mind, takes away true judgment'.[16] It must be stressed, however, that being doubtful, keeping an open mind, and making inquiry are only interim processes for Erasmus. If they do not lead to a logical conclusion, judgment, as we have seen, must be based on authority and consensus.

The evidence I have cited so far indicates that Erasmus's epistemology shaped his attitude toward the Reformation. I now turn to the question: is this type of scepticism merely 'Erasmian' or can we generalize and say that it is humanist? Some historians, notably Paul Oskar Kristeller, have asserted that humanism cannot be identified with any philosophical system. Rather it is a 'cultural and educational program' with 'literary preoccupations'. Humanism, according to this school of thought, should be associated with the rhetorical rather than the philosophical tradition. As philosophers, says Kristeller, the humanists 'seem to lack not only originality, but also coherence, method, and substance'. At best, they express 'interesting opinions'.[17]

Not all scholars are as categorical as Kristeller, but studies examining the relationship between humanism and classical schools of philosophy usually focus on Aristotelianism (the humanist critique of) and Platonism (the humanist revival of). Discussions of scepticism often remain on the periphery. The reason for the relative marginalization of scepticism in surveys of Renaissance humanism is the tendency to concentrate on formal connections. Scholars focus on the formal transmitters of the sceptic tradition, noting, for example, the paucity of references to Cicero's *Academica* or the lack of citations from Sextus Empiricus before the end of the fifteenth century.[18] It might be more profitable, however, to concentrate on other, informal expressions of a sceptic frame of mind, such as the popularity of the open-ended dialogue in humanist writings, or the interest in the literary scepticism of Lucian. We must be on the lookout for crypto-scepticism because there was after all a risk in professing an open interest. Scepticism, unlike Platonism or Aristotelianism, had not been Christianized. Indeed it was perceived as

---

[14] *ASD* IX-1, 418; *CWE*, ep. 1644, 15-7.

[15] *LB* X, 1268E.

[16] *ASD* IX-1, 419; 330.

[17] Kristeller, *Renaissance Thought*, 10-1.

[18] For recent literature, see Jardine, 'Humanist logic', 173-98; Popkin, 'Theories of knowledge', 678-84.

essentially incompatible with or inimical to Christian philosophy, and sceptics were therefore routinely labelled 'absurd' or 'atheists'. Erasmus himself did not escape being called an atheist, although his modified scepticism represents an attempt to Christianize a classical philosophy.[19]

Can we then label Erasmus's position 'humanist'? It is not without a humanist context. It builds on Lorenzo Valla's rejection of the dogmatism of the Aristotelians of his time; it builds on Rudolf Agricola's doubt in the validity or sufficiency of proof based on formal syllogism. It feeds on the literary scepticism of Lucian, who had already been discovered as a kindred soul by Italian humanists like Leon Battista Alberti or Giovanni Pontano in the fifteenth century and who saw another vogue among the Northern humanists in the sixteenth century. The prefaces of humanist editors and imitators of Lucian, like Pirckheimer or Eobanus Hessus or Erasmus himself, express approval of his scepticism, and praise or adopt his criticism of intellectual pretensions.[20] But Erasmus's Christian scepticism feeds on another source as well: the mystical dimension of the Devotio Moderna, its emphasis on the limitations of human knowledge, its concept of a *docta pietas*, an intellectual curiosity that is circumscribed by awe for the divine and a recognition of the impotence of human reason. Erasmus's Christian scepticism thus combines two traditions, the classical and the Christian, a combination that is representative of humanism, and more particularly, of Northern Humanism. It is therefore not unreasonable to call Erasmus's epistemology 'humanist'.

However, in labelling ideas 'humanist' we must distinguish between those that reflect the humanist tradition and the roots of the movement and those that foreshadow its future development and provide direction. Erasmus's ideas have humanist roots, but it is questionable whether they provide a model for the future. There is no evidence that Erasmus's brand of scepticism had many followers. Scepticism remained an important facet of humanist thought, but it took other forms. It continued as an element of anti-Aristotelianism in the circle of Petrus Ramus and in the works of Francisco Sánchez; it was a recurrent theme also in religious controversies, as in Castellio's opposition to Calvin's dogmatism; it forms a subtext in the occult philosophy of Agrippa of Nettesheim where it is transformed into an argument against rationalism; and it surfaces in the essays of Montaigne, who suggests that we accept custom and tradition while awaiting divine enlightenment. None of these uses of scepticism, however, contain specifically Erasmian notions. The protagonists I mentioned substitute plausibility for certainty (Castellio) or limit certainty to

---

[19] The Spaniard Luis Carvajal called Erasmus an 'atheist [...] like Lucian'; cf. Rummel, *Erasmus and His Catholic Critics*, II 101.

[20] For a discussion of humanist uses of Lucian and recent literature on the subject, see Rummel, *The Humanist-Scholastic Debate*, 24-7.

the intuitive apprehension of individual points (Sánchez), or advocate reliance on faith in view of the impotence of human reason. There may be a vague kinship, but there is no precise fit between these forms of scepticism and Erasmus's Christian Scepticism, which uses a combination of scriptural authority and consensus as criteria of doctrinal truth. Thus we can merely say that Erasmus's scepticism represents facets of the humanist past but does not project its future.

I now turn to my second consideration: Erasmus's professional commitment, as it affected his relationship with Luther and the reformers. Erasmus was by inclination a humanist rather than a theologian. The labels 'Lutheran' and 'Erasmian' are suggestive in themselves. One is a confessional label attesting to Luther's leadership as a theologian; the other is a cultural label, attesting to Erasmus's leadership as a man of letters. Erasmus reinforces this distinction, when he insists that he 'has as much in common with Luther as the cuckoo with the nightingale'. Translating this simile for us, he asks the pointed question: 'What can liberal studies have in common with matters of religious faith?' – a question that suggests a difference in professional commitments along the lines of humanism and theology.[21] Such protestations were necessary because many of Erasmus's contemporaries put him and Luther into one category. 'Either Erasmus lutheranizes or Luther erasmianizes' was a popular saying.[22] It encapsulates a perception that was, for some time, shared by both Catholics and reformers. The papal legate Girolamo Aleandro, for example, called Erasmus the 'director of the Lutheran tragedy'. In the other camp, Conradus Pellicanus, one of the Basle reformers, declared that Erasmus and Luther were saying the same thing, except that Luther 'uses stronger terms and speaks more candidly'. And the Strasbourg reformer Martin Bucer stated categorically that 'Erasmus and Luther agree in everything.'[23]

Erasmus strenuously denied this association. He posed the programmatic question 'What can liberal studies have in common with matters of religious faith?' reacting to the failure of his contemporaries to distinguish between his own and Luther's ideas, or more generally between humanists and reformers. In objecting to this muddling of issues, Erasmus often expressed concern for the fate of the humanities; he feared that humanism would be made a scapegoat in the process. Erasmus's statements on the subject come in two variants. Some put the blame for the confusion on reactionary Catholic theologians, others on the reformers. Both parties stood to gain from linking the two

---

[21] *LB* IX, 519F-520A; *CWE*, ep. 1033, 228-9 (Latin text in Erasmus, *Opus epistolarum*, ep. 1033, 208: *quid rei bonis studiis cum fidei negotio*). Hereafter the Latin text will be cited as in this edition.

[22] *LB* IX, 519F.

[23] *ASD* IX-1, 236; Bucer, *Correspondance*, ep. 3, 54-5.

causes. Erasmus therefore suggests that there is a conspiracy, 'a conspiracy of fanatics' (as he told Cardinal Campeggi, referring to Catholic critics). When Luther's writings appeared, 'their spirits rose at once: here was a weapon put in their hands, with which they could finish off the tongues and the humanities' by confusing matters and 'including under one label things by nature quite distinct'.[24] He repeats this message over and over again. The humanities had nothing in common with the Reformation, but theologians saw the Lutheran affair as 'an opening to suppress [...] humane studies', he said. 'Those people [...] have long resented the new blossoming of the humanities and the ancient tongues, and the revival of the authors of Antiquity [...]. When Luther's books had appeared, as though this gave them a handle, they began to tie up the ancient tongues and the humanities (with Lutheranism).'[25]

The Catholic theologians were not the only culprits in Erasmus's eyes; he also blamed the reformers for drawing the humanities into the dispute. They were 'piling on both liberal studies and myself a massive load of unpopularity,' he lamented. Elsewhere he exclaims: 'What a burden of unpopularity Luther has put on the humanities [...] he involves everyone he can in his business'.[26] Erasmus himself insisted that the two causes be kept separate. Indeed, the humanists had no reason to engage themselves on Luther's behalf. After all, Erasmus says, 'Luther is not so far advanced in the knowledge of the tongues or of elegant scholarship to provide supporters of such studies with any interest in his case'.[27] In all of these cases Erasmus speaks as a man committed to the cause of humanism.

At this point it will be useful to ask: was Erasmus an alarmist? Was the confusion over the two movements as pervasive as he suggests, and was it intentional? Evidence shows that the confusion was indeed widespread. It is striking to note how often writers indiscriminately grouped together Reuchlin, Lefèvre, Erasmus, and Luther, and how often they drew parallels between cases which from our modern vantage point are quite distinct. I have already quoted the tag 'Either Erasmus lutheranizes or Luther erasmianizes,' which expresses a popular conception; another epigrammatic phrase cited by several writers refers to Lefèvre, Reuchlin, Erasmus, and Luther as the four precursors of Antichrist.[28] This saying represents the position of reactionary Catholics. In the other camp, however, Willibald Pirckheimer made the same connection. He saw attacks on Erasmus as just another instance of theologians defaming humanists and put Erasmus into a lineup that included Reuchlin, Lefèvre, and

---

[24] *CWE*, ep. 1167, 30-1; 88-92; 106-7.
[25] *CWE*, epp. 980, 8; 1033, 215-26.
[26] *CWE*, epp. 1185, 22-3; 1186, 1-2.
[27] *CWE*, ep. 1167, 113-4.
[28] *Correspondance des Réformateurs dans les pays de langue française*, I 72; and a variant on the theme, *CWE*, ep. 1192, 29-33.

Luther.[29] Similarly, an anonymous dialogue sympathetic to Luther, entitled *Gesprech des apostolicums, angelica und anderer spezerei der apotheken*, has one character state that the church routinely persecutes pious learned men. He, too, lists as examples Reuchlin, Luther, and Erasmus.[30] Indeed, the Louvain theologian Frans Titelmans makes the blanket statement: 'All the most eminent representatives of the humanities have become captains and leaders of the heretics'.[31] It is clear therefore that this confusion existed and is not an Erasmian construct, but it is not entirely clear whether it was deliberate and a conspiracy, as Erasmus claimed. It is true that Erasmus is not the only one who makes this claim, but the conspiracy theory seems to be emanating from the Erasmian circle and to be largely confined to it.[32]

The confusion over humanists and reformers was not universal, however. Some people clearly distinguished between the two movements and, what is significant in our context, they clearly identified Erasmus as a spokesman of humanism. We have Melanchthon's famous *iudicium* that Luther was committed to 'true, evangelical, Christian preaching', whereas Erasmus merely taught 'good manners and civility', *boni mores et civilitas*, a phrase that evokes the cultural parameters of humanism.[33] Ulrich von Hutten was another one, who did not labour under the mistaken notion that Erasmus's and Luther's interests were interchangeable. He acknowledged the prevailing confusion in a letter to Erasmus. There is a perception, he said, that 'you are the fountain-head of the [...] present troubles. They think you showed us the way, you taught us, [...] you are the man on whom the rest of us depends. Of course this isn't true'. The Reformation did not depend on Erasmus. Hutten goes on to plead with Erasmus not to stand in Luther's way because, if the Reformation succeeded, 'liberal studies too will flourish and the humanities will be held in honour'.[34] Hutten's statement is significant for two reasons: its attempt to link the two causes, not conceptually (for he is quite aware of their distinct character) but politically. Perhaps this does not amount to a conspiracy, but it does indicate an agenda. Secondly Hutten's statement is significant in our context because it clearly addresses Erasmus as a representative of humanism. Hutten assumes that Erasmus's prime concern is the fate of the humanities,

---

[29] *CWE*, ep. 1095, 82-95.

[30] *Satiren und Pasquillen aus der Reformationszeit*, 49.

[31] Titelmans, *Collationes quinque super epistolam ad Romanos*, [Eiii]r.

[32] Cf. e.g. Beatus Rhenanus in *Epistolae aliquot eruditorum virorum*, 41; the conspiracy of the theologians against the humanists is the general subject of the satires *Theologists in Council* (English text in Rummel, *Scheming Papists and Lutheran Fools*, 55-71) and the *Letters of Obscure Men* (English text in *On the Eve of the Reformation*). Both satires appeared anonymously, but the reputed authors, Crotus Rubeanus, Ulrich von Hutten, and Hermann Buschius belonged to the Erasmian circle.

[33] Melanchthon, *Opera*, XX 701.

[34] *CWE*, ep. 1161, 18-21; 46-7.

not the fate of the Reformation. He therefore sees a risk of his turning against Luther to protect the interests of the humanists.

Luther's statements similarly indicate that he thought Erasmus's principal talent lay in the field of humanism and that he could make no further contribution to the cause of the Reformation. In 1523 he wrote to Oecolampadius: 'Erasmus has accomplished what he was ordained to do: he has introduced the knowledge of languages and has called us away from sacrilegious studies.' He repeats these sentiments in a letter to Erasmus in April 1524. He does not deny Erasmus's merits as a humanist. 'That learning flourishes through you and wins the day, thus opening the way to the genuine study of the Bible, is a thing the whole world simply cannot deny.' But Erasmus has clearly reached his limits. And 'if you cannot contribute anything else, remain a spectator.'[35]

As for Erasmus, he gives us the impression that he would have liked nothing better than to stay on the sidelines of a dispute that was theological. He in turn asked not to be drawn into Luther's affairs: 'Do not bring my friends's names into what you write in an unpleasant way [...] your enemies seek every opportunity to make us unpopular'. The words 'my friends' and 'us' designate 'the authors of the new learning' who are the subject of conspiracies everywhere.[36]

In the late twenties a new theme appears in Erasmus's letters, which has a bearing on the question of the relationship between humanism and the Reformation. Whereas earlier on he had depicted Catholic theologians as the principal enemies of humanism, who wished to link the two causes to be able to destroy them both, he now found the reformers equally hostile to the New Learning. Hutten, as we have seen, suggested a win-win scenario. The humanities would benefit from a victory of the reformers. This did not come to pass, according to Erasmus. In 1528 he wrote to Pirckheimer: 'Wherever Lutheranism reigns, letters perish'. In the same vein he wrote to Nicholas Varius: 'I hate those evangelicals for many reasons, but especially because on account of them humanist studies are neglected everywhere, grow insipid, lie prostrate, and perish'.[37] In his letter to the Strasbourg ministers in 1530 he defends and reiterates this sentiment: 'So far I have heard of no one in your sect who has acquired a knowledge of letters'. In the Lutheran camp, he was willing to except Melanchthon from this censure. He was, however, the lone exception. Those whose purpose it was to link the humanities with Lutheranism used him as an example, but 'the majority of Luther's champions know neither Greek nor Latin'.[38] Even among those who had studied the biblical

---

[35] Luther, *Briefwechsel*, III 96; *CWE*, ep. 1443, 15-9.
[36] *CWE*, ep. 1127A, 77-82; 60-1.
[37] Erasmus, *Opus epistolarum*, epp. 1977, 40-1; 1973, 13-5.
[38] *ASD* IX-1, 344; 396.

languages, he saw 'no one who studied literature or cared to study it' he wrote to Bucer.[39] It is notable that Erasmus distinguishes between studying the biblical languages to acquire certain technical, philological skills from studying languages to appreciate literature. The former does not make a man cultured, it does not make him a humanist. 'Language studies by themselves do not add up to erudition', Erasmus writes.[40] This type of criticism, which attacks the reformers on cultural rather than doctrinal grounds, once again reveals Erasmus speaking as a humanist and as a man determined to make a clear distinction between the objectives of the two movements.

We now turn to the question of impact. Were Erasmus's efforts to disentangle the cause of humanism from that of the Reformation successful? Did they set up a model of thought? We may say that Erasmus was correct in noting an existing confusion of issues, but it does not appear that his conspiracy theory took root outside a circle of close friends. He was correct also in his observation that philology was coopted by reformed theologians and used as a tool of interpretation, but he was unduly harsh in his assessment of their educational programme. There is some indication that his judgment was shared by other humanists, for example, by Eobanus Hessus, who laments the fact that the gains made by the humanists are being lost in the turmoil of the Reformation, and who calls Protestant preachers 'boors without learning', 'blathering demagogues', 'ignorant of all knowledge'.[41] However, it cannot be demonstrated that Erasmus's influence was a key factor in shaping this notion or that it developed into a larger theme.

In the final analysis Erasmus failed to capitalize on his position as the leading humanist in Northern Europe, to galvanize the humanists into a party of his own, and to deliver them *en masse* to the reformers or conversely draw them away. This failure contributed to a dwindling of his reputation, a process that began in the mid-twenties and by the second half of the sixteenth century had reduced him from a leading intellectual to a model of style.

To sum up my findings: I focused my investigation on two defining issues: Erasmus's epistemology and his professional commitment. His epistemology is characterized by a Christian scepticism, as I proposed to call it, which uses authority and consensus as criteria of doctrinal truth. The need to maintain and safeguard these criteria kept Erasmus out of the reformers's camp. Professionally, Erasmus was committed to humanism, and this led him to combat any efforts to link the movement with the Reformation, an association he regarded as detrimental to the humanist cause. Neither his epistemology nor his ideolo-

---

[39] Erasmus, *Opus epistolarum*, ep. 2615, 427-9.
[40] *ASD* IX-1, 344.
[41] Hessus, *Dialogi tres*, [Civ]v; [Di]r.

gy, however, had a large following. Clearly he was not cast in the role of a Moses leading the humanists out of the confessional wilderness.

It is legitimate to depict Erasmus as a representative of humanism, but one must distinguish between ideas reflecting the humanist past and ideas foreshadowing its future. As I see it, Erasmus's position can be traced backward on a time line, but it cannot clearly be traced forward.

What Cornelis Augustijn has said of Erasmus's influence on posterity in general applies to this case in particular. Augustijn wrote that Erasmus's ideas were not adopted in their entirety ('es handelt sich nicht um integrale Übernahme von erasmischem Ideengut'), but his ideas strike a chord in the reader ('es findet ein Wiedererkennen statt').[42] Erasmus, then, did not succeed in setting up a paradigm in the strict sense of the word, but he did ask paradigmatic questions, that is, questions that every humanist had to confront. In some of his readers he created a resonance; in others he merely stimulated thought. This kind of influence, however, is too fine to be caught in the coarser web of historiography.

---

[42] In the German version, Augustijn, *Erasmus von Rotterdam: Leben-Werk-Wirkung* (Munich 1986), 176; in the English version, Augustijn, *Erasmus*, 200.

R. J. SCHOECK

THE GEOGRAPHY OF ERASMUS

All travellers are not necessarily wise; if that were so, then all travelling sales-
men would be the wisest of men, and as a former night-clerk in a large hotel I
know that is not so. But Erasmus of Rotterdam was wise as well as being
much travelled, and it is not surprising that he took great interest in
geography, and that for him geography was intimately connected with other
fields of learning. To a young correspondent he wrote in 1518: 'History will
mean more to you if you have a taste of geography first.'[1] The importance of
geography in Erasmus's writings can readily be seen in other letters, as well as
in the *Adagia, Colloquia,* and notably in his paraphrases and commentaries on
Scripture, particularly the *Acts of the Apostles.*[2]

What do we have in detail? I calculated that there were more than 3,000
place-name references in Erasmus's writings; but I have been steadily adding
to my notebooks, and that number is far short of the full count. By the time
my monograph on Erasmus's geography is completed, I expect to have about
5,000 references. They divide for convenience into classical references,
Biblical references, and references to his contemporary world; and there are,
very roughly, the same numbers in each of these three divisions.

What does this large number of geographical references tell us about
Erasmus, and by extension the world of humanism? We learn that geography
indeed mattered greatly for his understanding of events, and for his study of
history. He often alludes to the places from which his correspondent writes –
and let us recall that there are extant more than 3,000 letters with more than
1900 people mentioned in his correspondence[3] – and some of his letters are
itineraries of his own travels. He frequently weaves place-references into his
letters, the *Adagia* and *Colloquia,* as well as other writings. A consideration of
Erasmus's place-references *tout ensemble* will give the modern reader an
awareness of how extensive and how detailed his geographical knowledge
was, both for his own times and historically; we can then appreciate how
informed a sense of his physical world he possessed. That world embraced the
ancient world, Biblical as well as classical, thus covering the full sweep from
the Middle East to the Atlantic, and from Africa to the northernmost parts of

---

[1] *CWE* 5, 275 (ep. 760).
[2] I am grateful to Robert D. Sider for permitting me to read the manuscript of his translation
of Erasmus's Paraphrase on the Acts of the Apostles (*CWE* 50).
[3] *CWE* 1, ix-xi.

Europe. As for his contemporary world, the range of his knowledge of places is most impressive, for he expected his regular correspondents to provide him with all kinds of news, of the fighting that might be going on, and of dynastic as well as scholarly activities.

To be sure, there are some mistakes in details, but very few. In September 1522 Erasmus visited his friend Johann Botzheim in Constance, and – having fallen ill – remained with him three weeks. The Dutchman fell quite in love with his house and the setting of Constance. At some length he expressed his admiration of the house and the charm of its location:

> Constance is dominated by a wonderful great lake, which stretches both far and wide for many miles and at the same time loses none of its beauty. Its attractions are increased by the forest-clad hills prominent in all directions, some distant and some near at hand. For at that point, as though wearied by its rocky headlong passage through the Alps, the Rhine seems to have found an agreeable resting-place to recuperate in, through the middle of which it makes its gentle progress; at Constance it gathers again into its proper channel and therewith resumes its own name – though the lake as a whole has always preferred to take its name from the city, being the lake of Constance now but in the old days the lake of Bregenz, as long as Bregenz was the name of the city which is now called Constance.[4]

Of course Bregenz is a city at the other end of the lake, located in Austria; and this may have been merely a slip of the pen on Erasmus's part.[5] Still, Erasmus had been ill, and the confusion of Bregenz and Constance may have been a genuine misconception on his part. Even more than the place-name reference, this letter has special importance for demonstrating Erasmus's capacity to respond to natural beauty (something we also learn from his poetry), though doubtless he rarely had the time, or occasion, or audience, to write about the beauties of nature. At another time he wrote about visiting with John Colet a monastery in the north of England, and he confused the west and east coasts of England. Such confusion is readily excusable as a *lapsus memoriae*, like his occasional mix-ups of brothers, or of the names of spouses, which are not unknown to us all even with fewer than 1900 people to keep straight.

In his prolific commentaries and paraphrases on Scripture, Erasmus occasionally erred as well, yet he did not hesitate to correct earlier mistakes. Thus, in the first commenting on Bethany it was noted as the place of the Ascension (in the first Paraphrase on Acts); in a 1522 addition to the commentary on Acts 1:12, Erasmus correctly explained that Bethany was on the slope of the Mount of Olives; but this involved redefining the length of a Sabbath Day's

---

[4] *CWE* 9, 379-80 (ep. 1342).
[5] Schoeck, *Erasmus of Europe*, 286.

journey to accomodate the allusion in the text, and this Erasmus did. Geography often involved the etymology of place-names; thus in spite of acknowledging in 1522 that Jerome thought the word *Akeldama* Aramaic (in the annotation on Acts 1:19, *Aceldemach*), Erasmus continued to regard the word as Hebrew and so annotated it in the 1527 commentary on 1:19 *et notum factum est* – a token of Erasmus's refusal to accept authority unchallenged.

Yet hostile critics were eager to seize upon not only errors but possible errors. Thus Sepúlveda, a learned Spanish theologian and later the official chronicler and chaplain of Charles V, accused Erasmus of inaccuracies in geographical and historical facts. Epistle 3096 from Sepúlveda to Erasmus (from Rome, February 13, 1536) seems to have been occasioned, as Allen notes, by the 1535 edition of Erasmus's New Testament; but their disagreements had been going on for some time. Earlier Erasmus had written the Spaniard from Fribourg on July 3, 1534, in a letter that is a confession from the aging humanist: 'in locis et historia crebro lapsus sum' – an honest confession to be taken, I suggest, in the spirit of St Augustine's *Retractationes*. But in point of fact Erasmus also notes to Sepúlveda that the placing of Rhegium is now correct, and that Constantinople had already been correctly placed in Thracia.[6] He adds that he does not know whether his friend and associate Goclenius, a noted humanist, will have added anything since.

Erasmus was fond of maps, although this question is all but unstudied.[7] In the colloquy called 'A Fish Diet' Erasmus writes in some detail:

> Recently I saw a painting, on a very large canvas, of the whole world. From it I learned how small a portion of the world wholeheartedly and sincerely professes Christianity: part of western Europe, of course; then another part towards the north; a third stretching far away to the south; Poland seemed to be as far as the fourth part went, towards the east. The rest of the world contains either barbarians, not so very different from brutes, or schismatics or heretics, or both.[8]

In this and other colloquies it must be kept in mind that each speaker in a colloquy is a character in a dramatic piece, and it is not always a simple matter to distinguish Erasmus's own considered judgments from those intended to give dramatic or local color. The speaker of the quoted passage is a butcher, not a theologian or geographer. The painting does not seem to have been identified, though Erasmus's allusion to it clearly indicates that it was not one in his possession. The colloquy 'A Fish Diet' was first printed in the edition of February

---

[6] Erasmus, *Opus epistolarum*, XI 13.
[7] The study by De Smet ('Erasme et la cartographie') of Erasmus's edition of Ptolemy is notable, but it does not examine maps. That remains a largely unstudied question.
[8] *CWE* 40, 686.

1526, which suggests Basel connections. We do know, by the way, that a map of Switzerland was in his possession.[9]

Erasmus was richly familiar with all of the classical geographers. There is much on geography in Pliny's *Naturalis Historia*, and we find Erasmus drawing upon that work (3,2) for details on the bays of Europe; e.g. see *Adagia* 1,2,43, where this knowledge is dexterously worked into an essay on *Tricae; apinae*, 'Stuff and nonsense', or, as we would say, trivial pursuits. Even more importantly, we know that Erasmus edited the *Geographia* of Ptolemy (printed at Basel, 1533), which was the first edition of the Greek text. Although Allen carefully notes that 'neither the title-page nor the contents suggest that Erasmus had anything to do with the editing',[10] more recent scholarship has demonstrated that this was not the case, and in fact Erasmus made corrections in the text. In his preface Erasmus speaks of the importance of Ptolemy as the first to work with latitudes and longitudes, and he mentions Marinus of Tyre (fl. c. 120 A.D.), whose work on geography is known to us only through Ptolemy. Much of the new sciences was then distrusted, attacked or condemned by Vatican authorities, as by Protestant leaders, as is well known; and the 'official' stand of the Church against Galileo comes well after the period of Erasmian humanism. But even during the lifetime of Erasmus, Nicolaus Copernicus (1473-1543) was making contributions to the history of geography, and he can be said to have developed out of ancient, mathematical astronomy.[11] A link between Erasmus and Copernicus is to be found in the figure of Celio Calcagnini of Ferrara (1479-1541), a humanist and diplomat who also contributed to mathematical and astronomical studies. Calcagnini's treatise *Quod caelum stet, terra moveatur* is a notable precursor of Copernicus's *De revolutionibus*. Erasmus, Calcagnini, Copernicus: all learned humanists who saw the rightness of integrating astronomy and geography with the humanities.

Not surprisingly, then, Erasmus was interested in cosmography. In the colloquy 'A Problem' (*Problema*, 1533), Erasmus gave evidence of that interest:

> If some god bored straight through the middle of the earth – through the centre perpendicularly to the antipodes, as cosmographers are wont to do when representing the position of the whole earth with wooden globes – then, if you threw a stone into the hole, how far would it be carried?[12]

---

[9] Erasmus, *Opus epistolarum*, XI 271.

[10] Erasmus, *Opus epistolarum*, X 148.

[11] Copernicus was actively making cartographic measurements, and his understanding of geography was enlarged further in the work of Rheticus, especially the *Chorographia* of 1541.

[12] *CWE* 40, 1060.

Not surprisingly, Erasmus's explanations in the colloquy are thoroughly Aristotelian.

Astronomy too was an interest. In a copy of the *Institutiones Astronomicae* of Joachim Sterck of Ringelberghe (published at Basel, 1528), there is the second of two epigrams in praise of the *Institutiones*. Joachim or Jan Sterck was the first president of the Collegium Trilingue in Louvain and a Flemish humanist with whom Erasmus had worked closely. Two of Erasmus's poems (118-119) are epigrams in praise of the *Institutiones* of Sterck, and although Cornelis Reedijk, the editor of Erasmus's poems, asserts that '[Erasmus's] lines have only the vaguest connection with the actual contents of the books',[13] that is by no means unusual and in no way precludes Erasmus's full understanding of the astronomical nature of Sterck's writings. We have already noted that the figure of Calcagnini was another connection with the world of astronomers, and his key text *Quod caelum stet, terra moveatur* defends the notion of the rotation of the earth on its axis from a philosophical approach.

What is amazing in the wealth of place-name references is the grasp of detail by Erasmus, so much of which must have been held in memory, although there were classical and patristic treatises (such as the *Onomasticon* of Eusebius, and Jerome's *De situ et nominibus locorum Hebraicorum*), and he must have made use of commonplace books. But what is even more impressive is that all of the knowledge and wisdom of geography, cosmography and astronomy were bound together for Erasmus, as they were for Dante. Cosmography naturally leads one to thoughts of the infinite, and in *Adagia* 1,8,59 'You join thread with thread' (*Linum lino nectis*) there is just such a reaching from the known world of sun an stars to the infinite:

> Aristotle in the third book of the *Physics*, in a discussion of the infinite, where he prefers Parmenides' opinion to that of Melissus (for Melissus had held that the universe as a whole was infinite, while Parmenides said it was finite, equidistant from the centre), says 'For it is impossible that the infinite should be connected with the universe as a whole, just as thread is with thread.'[14]

'Connexa sunt studia humanitatis', Coluccio Salutati declared; and for that circle of Erasmus, Glareanus, Calcagnini, and Sterck, the world of geography and astronomy was also to be connected, even if by thread with thread.

[13] Reedijk, *Poems of Erasmus*, 340.
[14] *CWE* 32, 158 (I, viii, 59).

Conclusions

In one of the exciting new fields of study that have been seeded and have flourished between traditional disciplines, cognitive mapping has told us much about the ways in which an age-old and fundamental need to know more about the world around us is experienced and developed in the individual. Cognitive mapping 'is an abstraction covering those cognitive or mental abilities that enable us to collect, store, recall, and manipulate information about the spatial environment'[15] – it is a more scientific investigation of what we all know as a sense of place. For we all have cognitive maps in our heads, though we may not have had a term or label for them.

One's sense of identity is closely related to a sense of place, as can be seen in the historic phenomenon of changing or renaming places. Anyone from Erasmus's part of Europe, then or now, experiences the disorientation (or at least bilingual split) in shifting from place-names for the same city from Flemish to French (Leuven to Louvain), or French to German (Sélestat to Schlettstadt) – or dealing with a place-name that exists simultaneously in somewhat different form in three languages in Switzerland: Bâle, Basel, Basle.

By the end of his long and productive life Erasmus thought of himself as *homo europaeus* rather than simply Dutch, or French, or German: a citizen of the world. Yet until he was well past twenty-five he had never left the Low Countries, those flat lands with rivers and canals everywhere around him, where he would be used to the flatness of the horizon and the merging of trees and grass and water with the sky. But travel he did, and travellers like liars must have good memories to keep their stories straight.[16]

What all of this tells us about the mind of Erasmus and his work-habits reinforces what we have learned elsewhere in his writings: that geography mattered greatly for his understanding of events and of the making and writing of history, and for the understanding of man's condition. We find too that his prodigious memory served him well, even though it was not infallible.

And what does all of this tell us about the humanism of his age? That it was linked with the realities of history we have known, for humanism has always been anchored in history at the very moment that it is also deeply concerned with the present. There were other humanists to whom we might

---

[15] Downs and Stea, *Maps in Minds*, 6.

[16] In another essay I intend to write on the maps in the mind of Erasmus, and there to take up such questions as geographical identity, homesickness, and the like. Since the writing and presentation of this paper, a most useful study has appeared by Bejczy, 'Erasmus becomes a Netherlander', with its eminently sound conclusion: 'A Hollander by birth and a Brabantine by circumstance, Erasmus was a Netherlander par excellence.'

turn to support these generalisations. One prime example is the above-mentioned Henricus Glareanus (so named because he came from Glarus, Switzerland – his dates are 1488 to 1563), who was a valued member of the Basel school of humanists and after a somewhat nomadic career settled down in Freiburg, where he was noted as a teacher of poetry, having himself been named poet laureate by Maximilian I at Cologne in 1512. In 1510 Glareanus published a map of the world that was based on an earlier map (now lost) by the humanist cosmographer Martin Waldseemüller. That map, Fritz Büsser has written, 'not only presented the eastern coast-line of America with reasonable accuracy and correct nomenclature, but also exhibited remarkably exact latitudes and longitudes': we cannot sneer at the geography of the early sixteenth century. In 1527 Glareanus published (at Basel) his *De geographia,* which can be described as a mathematical-physical description of Asia, Africa, and Europe. His *Descriptio Helvetiae* (published at Basel in 1515) is a careful geographical description of the Swiss Confederacy region by region, presenting Helvetia as the summit and centre of Europe, with its snow-covered mountains sending forth rivers to all four directions,

> like Olympus [Büsser writes glowingly], like a paradise from which flow the streams of the world [with the four rivers, Thur, Limmat, Reuss, and Aare] as a basic grid for the presentation of four regions, each with its separate characteristics.[17]

His *Panegyricum* of 1514 is a poetic eulogy of the thirteen Swiss cantons that 'uses the example of individual cantons to describe the grandeur and free spirit, the awe-inspiring scenery, and the cultural achievements of his fatherland.'[18] Glareanus also edited classical authors, wrote on music and arithmetic, and in his later Freiburg years was notable as a layman supporting the Catholic reformers. This friend, admirer and disciple of Erasmus is a notable example of the marriage of humanism and geography, along with other parts of the liberal arts. Glareanus, as I have said, was one prime example, but there were other humanists who studied geography, such as Georgius Joachim Rheticus (1514-1576), who studied with Myconius at Basel and then later, in 1541, published his influential *Chorographia* (at Wittenberg), so important in spurring Copernicus to complete his *De Revolutionibus,* and Copernicus had made an effort to found a humanist university in Poland, we recall.

---

[17] *CE* 2, 107.
[18] Ibidem.

We may mention here Konrad Peutinger of Augsburg, who collected Roman maps (the celebrated *Tabula Peutingeriana*, a Roman road-map, is from his estate); the son of a wealthy merchant in Augsburg, Peutinger associated with Ermolao Barbaro in Padua, with Felippo Beroaldo in Bologna, and with Pico della Mirandola and Angelo Poliziano in Florence. And there were still others who studied and edited the ancient geographers. Melanchthon, one remembers, made an unsuccessful attempt to provide a map of Palestine as an illustration for Luther's translation of the New Testament.[19]

It must be recognized that of course there were many kinds of ignorance of geography, one of which has been detailed by Elisabeth Wåghäll.[20] But equally it must be recognized that there was a powerful stream of interest in geography that produced the celebrated ethnography of Montaigne, to use Peter Burke's term,[21] and across the Channel the many-volumed account of voyages by Richard Hakluyt, with the keen popular interest shown in the drama and poetry of the Elizabethan period (as detailed by R.R. Cawley). That fascinating brother-in-law of Thomas More, John Rastell, was an early but by no means an isolated example of keen geographical interest early in the sixteenth century. By the seventeenth century there is a veritable flood of great map-makers, and an imaginative flowering in the many-sided geographical interests of John Milton.

Geography, I urge, should be a necessary element in our studies of the humanism of the Renaissance and Reformation, and for our study of Erasmus it is vital.

---

[19] Brecht, *Martin Luther*, II 54.
[20] 'The Ignorance of Geography. Example Georg Wickram' (paper given at the Central Renaissance Conference, April 1992).
[21] Burke, *Montaigne*, 44.

A. SOTTILI

JURISTEN UND HUMANISTEN: RUDOLF AGRICOLA
AN DER UNIVERSITÄT PAVIA

Im Rahmen der Kulturbeziehungen zwischen Italien und den burgundischen Staaten hat die Universität Pavia eine Rolle gespielt, die wahrscheinlich noch nicht ausreichend hervorgehoben und untersucht worden ist. An der Universität Pavia sind in der zweiten Hälfte des 15. Jahrhunderts verhältnismäßig viele Studenten in der Jurisprudenz ausgebildet worden, die nach der Rückkehr in ihre burgundische Heimat politische Führungsposten innegehabt haben. In den Jahren 1473-1474, als der Brügger Paul de Baenst Juristenrektor in Pavia war,[1] haben innerhalb von wenigen Monaten drei künftige Mitglieder des großen Rates promoviert, nämlich Arnould de Lalaing, Jean Haneton und Josse Quevin.[2] Es ist ferner jedem bekannt, daß Paul de Baenst Präsident des Rates von Flandern wurde.[3] Die in Frage kommenden Jahre waren auch für die Entfaltung des Humanismus von großer Bedeutung. Es bleibt den Rechtshistorikern vorbehalten, zu klären, inwieweit der Pavia-Aufenthalt der erwähnten Juristen die Rezeption des römischen Rechts in der juristischen Praxis des großen Rates beeinflußt hat. Den Historikern des mitteleuropäischen Kulturlebens hingegen sind Leben und Wirken des Humanisten Rudolf Agricola so vertraut, daß es für die Untersuchung und die Diskussion neuerer Details aus der Zeit von 1468-1475, die er in Pavia verbracht hat, keiner besonderen Rechtfertigung bedarf.[4]

Der Biographie des Johannes von Plieningen zufolge kam Rudolf Agricola nach Pavia, als er 24 Jahre alt war. Da er nach der gleichen Quelle im Jahr 1444 geboren wurde, war es im Jahr des Herrn 1468, als der Friese in Italien auftauchte.[5] F.J. Worstbrock vermutet, Agricola sei in Begleitung des Antonius Liber nach Pavia gereist.[6] Über Pavia äußert sich Johannes von Plieningen, der die Stadt und seine Universität sehr gut kannte,[7] mit Begeis-

---

[1] Sottili, 'Rettori e vicerettori'; idem, 'Le contestate elezioni rettorali'.
[2] Sottili, *Lauree pavesi*, s.v. Josse Quevin hat eigentlich kurz, nachdem Baensts Rektoratszeit abgelaufen war, in bürgerlichem Recht promoviert. Für Lalaing, Haneton und Quevin: Kerckhoffs-De Hey, *De Grote Raad en zijn functionarissen*, 85; 90; 116-7.
[3] Karagiannis, *De functionarissen bij de Raad van Vlaanderen*, 69-72.
[4] Ausführlich über Agricola: *Rodolphus Agricola Phrisius*; *Rudolf Agricola 1444-1485*.
[5] Straube, 'Die Agricola-Biographie des Johannes von Plieningen', 14; 16.
[6] Worstbrock, 'Liber'.
[7] Er ist in Pavia am 14 Juli 1473 studienhalber eingetroffen: Adelmann, *Dietrich von Plieningen*, 17.

terung, indem er es ein 'litteratorum emporium clarissimum' nennt.[8] Auch Agricola behielt Pavia in sehr guter Erinnerung, nachdem er nach Ferrara übergesiedelt war. Im August 1476, als er seit mehreren Monaten in Ferrara weilte, um sich den humanistischen Studien und insbesondere der Erlernung der Griechischen Sprache zu widmen, schrieb er an Johannes von Plieningen im Kontext eines Briefs, der den Freund überzeugen sollte, ebenfalls die Universität zu wechseln: 'cunctaque vos Papie meliora, uberiora letioraque relicturos'.[9] Das sind jedoch eher allgemeine Redewendungen. Konkreter äußert sich Agricola im Brief vom 23. Dezember 1476 an Johannes von Dalberg,[10] der nach einer Abwesenheit aus Italien von mehr als einem Jahr wieder im Lande war. Dalberg steht vor der Entscheidung, wo er seine Studien fortführen soll, die er in Pavia begonnen hatte. Zur Wahl standen anscheinend Pavia, Padua und Ferrara. Dalberg entschied sich für Padua, obwohl Agricola ihm davon abgeraten hatte. Padua sei nämlich wegen der Roheit der dort lebenden Menschen bekannt. Diese Stadt besitze keineswegs den Reiz Pavias, die Lebensart sei nicht so angenehm und Dalberg werde dort nicht mit dem Ansehen rechnen können, das er in Pavia genoß, wo er Juristenrektor gewesen war.[11] Als Agricola auf Ferrara zu sprechen kommt, erlaubt er sich zuerst einen Scherz. Hoffentlich handelt es sich tatsächlich um einen Scherz, weil zu viel Vertrautheit mit Mädchen zweifelhafter Lebensführung sich nicht für einen Geistlichen wie Dalberg anschickt.[12] Ferrara sei also voller Mädchen wie die Felicinae und die Magdalenae, die Agricola und Dalberg in Pavia kennengelernt hatten.[13] Alle Straßen und alle

---

[8] Straube, 'Die Agricola-Biographie des Johannes von Plieningen', 16. Zur pavesischen Juristenschule: Massetto, 'La cultura giuridica civilista'. Zum literarischen Kulturleben in Pavia während des 15. Jahrhunderts: Marchi, 'La cultura letteraria a Pavia'; Cavagna, 'Questo mondo è pien di vento'.

[9] Leibenguth and Seidel, 'Die Korrespondenz Rudolf Agricolas', 206-7. Zur Übersiedlung Agricolas nach Ferrara mit dem Zweck, sich in das Studium der griechischen Sprache zu vertiefen: IJsewijn, 'Gli studi greci di Rodolfo Agricola', 28-9.

[10] Leibenguth and Seidel, 'Die Korrespondenz Rudolf Agricolas', 209-10.

[11] Dalberg ist als pavesischer Juristenrektor in den Promotionsurkunden nachgewiesen: 21.10.1474, Lizentiatur in Bürgerrecht des Josse Quevin; 10.6.1475, Lizentiatur und Doktorat *in utroque* des Heinrich Schertlin; Lizentiatur und Doktorat *in utroque* des Battista Sfondrati; 21.7.1475, Lizentiatur und Doktorat *in utroque* des Giovanni Agostino Beccaria: Sottili, *Lauree pavesi*, 382. Die Dokumentation ist m.E. sehr lückenhaft. Zu Dalberg: Walter, 'Johannes von Dalberg und der Humanismus'.

[12] Es ist nicht bekannt, wo Dalberg die Tonsur erhalten hat: Walter, 'Johannes von Dalberg und der Humanismus', 153, Anm. 14. Die vier niederen Weihen erhielt er am 21.12.1474 in Pavia: Sottili, 'Notizie per il soggiorno', 83-4.

[13] Das Bordell befand sich in Pavia in der Straße zu den 'tre Marie', wie aus dem folgenden Brief des in Pavia residierenden herzoglichen Referendars Francesco Pozzobonello ersichtlich wird: 'Illustrissimi Principes et excellentissimi Domini Domini mey metuendi. Per debito mio et etiam per discarico del officio aviso vostre Excellentie che facendo exercire li dacii (Hs. dacicii) de la bolatura del vino da minuto de questa cità (in) una taberna situata in una contrata dove se dice a le tre Marie de essa citade, ne la quale taberna habitava certe meretrice facendo

Häuser seien voll davon. Es gibt aber noch Größeres und Wunderbareres als dies, aber Agricola wagt einem Geistlichen so etwas kaum zu erzählen.[14]

Nach dem Scherz kommt Agricola zum Kern des Problems: 'Studiorum quidem non ea diligentia neque magnitudo quae Papiae; ea tamen quae Plinii praecipue sequuntur, id est humaniores litteras, vel coelum ipsum hoc loco alere mihi videtur'. In Ferrara ist zwar die Gründlichkeit und die Bedeutung der Studien nicht so hoch wie in Pavia; das jedoch, was Johannes und Dietrich von Plieningen in erster Linie betreiben, nämlich die humanistischen Wissenschaften, scheint in Ferrara schon vom Klima bzw. von den Sternen her begünstigt zu werden.[15] Der eigentliche Vorteil, den Ferrara den Studenten Pavia gegenüber bietet, sind die humanistischen Studien, ansonsten ist die Universität Pavia weit überlegen, weil in Pavia besser unterrichtet und fleißiger studiert wurde. Das scheint mir Agricola zum Ausdruck bringen zu wollen, als er Pavia wegen der 'diligentia studiorum' hochlobt. Mit dem Wort 'magnitudo' bezeichnet Agricola wahrscheinlich das üppige Lehrangebot, das die Universität Pavia charakterisierte, und ferner alle anderen Ausdrucksformen des akademischen Lebens, die wie die 'disputationes' die eigentliche Lehrtätigkeit begleiteten.[16]

el loro officio como è solito fare in simili lochi, ho inteso e fato chiaro essere comisso una grande insolencia per certi scolari Galici et Germanici tre nocte continue cum coraze et arme ofensibile non obstante che dicte meretrice servano ad caduno cum soy dinari, non di meno, adendo mala malis motu temerario tre nocte continue li è stado zitato per terra la porta, li ugii et fenestre de le camere cercando cum grando impeto se li era alcuni de la familia del potestà e comisario de questa città cum grande minaze dicendo de taliarli a peze, e per dicti daciari hano facto grande rechiamo denante a mi de dicto insulto etiam alegando loro volere fare retracione et haver restauro de esso dacio per non potere fare exercire esso dacio pacifice per le predicte insolencie, m'è parso per fare mio debito etiam per interesse de vostre illustrissime Signorie darne aviso a quelo supplicando se degnano fare tale provisione come sono certo quele farano per evitare ogni scandolo posa intervenire, sia exemplo ad altri, cun ciò sia che etiam da quatro giorni in qua s'è ritrovato una nocte una grande compagnia de essi scolari armati et hano insultata la familia de esso potestà, la quale, se subito non se fuseno retrati in la rocheta del ponte de Ticino, sarebeno stati mali. A vostre illustrissime Signorie piaza farle quele provisione meglio li parirà ad ciò non intervenga pegio. A le quale humilmente sempre cum fede e devocione me recomando. Datum Papie die XI Februarii 1479. Earundem Dominationum vestrarum fidelissimus servitor Franciscus de Putheobonelo Papie referendarius.' Auf der Rückseite die Adresse. Im Brief wird die permanente Spannung offensichtlich, die in Pavia zwischen herzoglicher Polizei und Studenten immer bestanden hat. Die Verwaltung hielt das Vorhandensein von Prostituierten in einer Universitätsstadt für selbstverständlich. Anscheinend liehen diese Prostituierten Studenten und anderen Leuten Geld.

[14] 'Est hic videre non omnibus vicis solum, sed fere omnibus domibus Felicinas et Magdalenas, sed etiam, quamquam te audiente dicere vix audeam, maiora mirabilioraque istis.' Prostitutionsstraße in Ferrara war die 'Via delle Volte': Adelmann, *Dietrich von Plieningen*, 17-8, Anm. 5.

[15] Einiges zu diesem Thema: Piacente, 'Battista Guarini'. Der ganze Band ist von großer Bedeutung für die Geschichte der Universität Ferrara.

[16] Im akademischen Jahr 1472-3 verzeichnet das Vorlesungsverzeichnis folgende Lehrveranstaltungen: *Decretum* (Amicinus de Bozulis, Jacobus Gualla, Bartholomeus de Aliprandis), *Lectura ordinaria iuris canonici* (Hieronymus de Mangiariis, Christophorus de Butigellis, Jo-

Ursprünglich war aber Agricola nach Italien gekommen, um auf traditionelle Weise zu studieren. 'Primis annis iuris civilis auditor fuit', in den ersten Jahren seines Italienaufenthalts hat er Zivilrecht gehört, wohl mehr, um dem Wunsch der Eltern zu entsprechen als aus persönlichem Interesse, wie Johannes von Plieningen betont.[17] Wie dem auch sei, Agricola ist Student des römischen Rechts gewesen und dies jahrelang. Diese unbestreitbare Tatsache rechtfertigt die Frage, welche Professoren des Zivilrechts Agricola gehört bzw. hat hören können. Die Namen der Professoren, die an der Universität Pavia während Agricolas Aufenthalt in dieser Stadt gelehrt haben, sind so gut wie vollständig überliefert. Mir sind die Vorlesungsverzeichnisse der folgenden akademischen Jahre bekannt, die teilweise im Staatsarchiv Pavia[18] und zum Teil im Staatsarchiv Mailand aufbewahrt werden: 1468-69, 1469-70, 1471-72, 1472-73, 1473-74, 1474-75.[19] Sieht man vom akademischen Jahr 1470-71 ab, sind uns die Namen aller Professoren bekannt, die Agricola hat hören können. Der Verlust der Professorenliste für das akademische Jahr 1470-71 ist leicht zu verschmerzen, weil Agricola in jenen Monaten anscheinend nicht in Pavia weilte, wie seine aus Selwerd datierten Briefe an Rudolf von Langen (26. Oktober 1470?) und Anton Vrije (Selwerd? 5. Februar 1471)[20] beweisen, und die Inhaber der wichtigsten zivilrechtlichen Lehrstühle in der Zeit zwischen 1469 und 1472 die gleichen geblieben sind.

Die Rechtswissenschaft stand in Pavia hoch im Kurs, weshalb es nicht müßig ist, die Namen der Koryphäen der pavesischen Bürgerrechtswissenschaft in den zwei erwähnten Jahren aufzuzählen. Die 'Lectura ordinaria iuris civilis de mane' hatten Johannes de Grassis, Johannes de Putheo und Ambrosius de Oppizonibus im akademischen Jahr 1469-70 mit jeweils 950,

hannes Antonius de Sancto Georgio), *Lectura Sexti et Clementinarum* (Stephanus Costa, Matheus de Curte, Georgius Nata), *Lectura extraordinaria iuris canonici* (Christophorus de Piscariis, Thomenus de Gambarana), *Lectura festorum iuris canonici* (Petrus Antonius de Martinengho, Gabriel Gambarellus), *Lectura iuris civilis ordinaria de mane* (Johannes de Putheo, Ambrosius de Oppizonibus, Lucas de Grassis), *Lectura iuris civilis extraordinaria de sero* (Hieronymus de Tortis, Lancellotus de Desio), *Lectura extraordinaria ordinariorum* (Philippus de Astariis, Jacobus de Mangiariis, Aymus de Romagnano, Johannes Antonius Zasius), *Lectura Institutionum* (Jason de Mayno, Petrus de Grassis, Franciscus de Ozeno, Christophorus de Albaritiis), *Lectura iuris civilis festorum* (Antonius Oldoninus, der auch über die 'Libri pheudorum' lesen soll, Johannes Petrus de Comite), *Lectura ultramontanorum* (Johannes de Colonia), *Lectura notarie* (Ubertus de Mangano). Wenn ich richtig gezählt habe, haben 1472-3 in Pavia dreißig Professoren die juristischen Fächer unterrichtet. Das zitierte Vorlesungsverzeichnis ist aufbewahrt in Pavia, Archivio di Stato, *Acta Studii Ticinensis*, 22, 155r-156r.

[17] Straube, 'Die Agricola-Biographie des Johannes von Plieningen', 16. Literarische Quelle zu dieser Stelle der Agricola-Biographie ist Agricolas Lebensbeschreibung des Petrarca: Akkerman, 'Rudolf Agricola, een humanistenleven', 36.

[18] Vgl. Anm. 16.

[19] *Studi. Parte antica*, 390.

[20] *Rodolphus Agricola Phrisius*, 321.

400 und 170 Gulden inne. Die 'Lectura extraordinaria iuris civilis de sero' hatten im gleichen akademischen Jahre Lucas de Grassis, Hyeronimus de Tortis und Lancilotus de Desio mit jeweils 600, 800 und 200 Gulden inne.[21] Die Benennung 'Lectura ordinaria' und 'Lectura extraordinaria' impliziert keine Rangordnung . Sie war lediglich die Folge der gleichnamigen Teilung der Bücher des *Corpus iuris* in 'libri ordinarii' und 'libri extraordinarii'.[22] Damit ersichtlich wird, welche akademische und soziale Stellung die er-wähnten Gehälter für die Spitzenjuristen zur Folge hatten, sei darauf hinge-wiesen, daß Jacobus de Mangiariis, der bestbezahlte Professor für 'Instituti-ones',[23] für den Einführungskurs ins Zivilrecht, sich mit 50 Gulden begnü-gen mußte. Was dann die Professoren für Moralphilosophie der medizi-nisch-artistischen Fakultät angeht,[24] so wurden sie noch erheblich schlechter belohnt, weil ihr Gehalt 12 Gulden betrug. Gemeint sind immer die Jahres-gehälter. Johannes Grassus, der bestbezahlte Zivilrechtler,[25] bekam ein Gehalt, das neunzehnmal höher als jenes des bestbezahlten Professors für 'Institutiones' und einundsiebzigmal höher als dasjenige seines Kollegen war, der Moralphilosophie dozierte. Moralphilosophie soll angeblich das be-deutendste philosophische Fach für die Humanisten gewesen sein.[26] Anges-ichts dieser Gehälter bin ich sowohl hinsichtlich der Bedeutung der Moral-

---

[21] Mailand, Archivio di Stato, *Studi. Parte antica*, 390 (2). Zur Familie Opizzoni: Allegri, *La feudalità tortonese*. Wichtiges zur Familie und zu Professor Ambrosius in den beide betreffenden 'Schede Marozzi' in der Stadtbibliothek Pavia: Zaffignani, 'Lo schedario nobiliare Marozzi', 352. Zu Ambrosius: Maiocchi, *La Chiesa e il Convento di San Tommaso*, 79-80; idem, *Ticinensia*, 64; Buzás, 'Die Bibliothek des Ingolstädter Professors Dr. Wolfgang Peysser', 83. Über Hieronymus de Tortis kenne ich eine sehr reiche archivalische Dokumenta-tion, die in diesem Zusammenhang nicht aufgeführt werden kann. Man vgl. jedoch: Mariani, 'La laurea in leggi di Giason del Mayno', 241; Kisch, *Die Anfänge der juristischen Fakultät*, 133-4; Ganda, 'Origine della Biblioteca dei giureconsulti milanesi', 232. Zu Lancilotus de Desio: Mazzacane, 'Lancellotto Decio', 560-1.

[22] Belloni, *Professori giuristi a Padova*, 77-9.

[23] Herrmann, *Albrecht von Eyb*, 59; Pellegrin, *La biliothèque des Visconti et des Sforza*, 393; Autenrieth, *Die Handschriften der ehemaligen Hofbibliothek Stuttgart*, 126-7; Buzás, 'Die Bibliothek des Ingolstädter Professors Dr. Wolfgang Peysser', 83; Albertini Ottolenghi, 'La Biblioteca dei Visconti e degli Sforza', 12; Cerrini, 'Libri dei Visconti Sforza', 258. Für die Mailänder Verwaltung war die 'Lectura Institutionum' sehr wichtig, wie der Senat in einem Brief an Herzog Galeazzo Maria Sforza betont: 'Consyderato sono alcune altre lecture che hanno molto tenue salario, maxime quella de la Instituta, che nel vero è molto utile et de le più necessarie' (Mailand, Archivio di Stato, *Comuni*, 69).

[24] Franciscus de Curte und Lazarus Datalus. Beide waren aber zugleich mit der 'Lectura philosophie extraordinaria de Nonis' beauftragt und bezogen somit ein zusätzliches Gehalt in Höhe von 40 und 50 Gulden.

[25] Mariani, *Vita universitaria pavese*, 65; Trusen, 'Die Anfänge öffentlicher Banken und das Zinsproblem', 125; *Die lateinischen mittelalterlichen Handschriften der Universitätsbibliothek München*, 47; 49; Buzás, 'Die Bibliothek des Ingolstädter Professors Dr. Wolfgang Peysser', 83; Maffei, 'Manoscritti giuridici napoletani', 29; Denley, 'The Collegiate Movement', 91.

[26] *Ethik im Humanismus*; Kristeller, 'L'etica nel pensiero del Rinascimento'.

philosophie wie auch des Humanismus an einer traditionsreichen Universität wie Pavia sehr skeptisch.

Wenn Agricola nach Pavia kam, um Zivilrecht zu studieren, wird er wohl die Vorlesungen mindestens einiger der genannten Professoren besucht haben. Wir besitzen aber den Beweis, daß Agricola einige dieser Professoren gekannt und geschätzt hat. Man hat Agricolas *Panegyricus in laudem Papiae* ein kurzes, konventionelles Städtelobgedicht genannt.[27] Das Gedicht ist in der Tat nicht lang,[28] ob es auch konventionell ins Gefüge der pavesischen Literatur paßt, vermag ich nicht zu sagen. Ein Vergleich mit der Lobrede auf Pavia des Rhetorikprofessors Balthasar Rasinus scheint mir angebracht zu sein, bevor man das *Carmen* Agricolas für unbedeutend erklärt.[29] Wenn aber ein Literaturwissenschaftler bei der Analyse von Agricolas Gedicht zu einer negativen Schlußfolgerung kommt, so könnte das Urteil eines Universitätshistorikers doch anders ausfallen. Zwei Verse sind im *Panegyricus* Agricolas sehr wichtig: 'Nec mihi nunc Crassos nec raptum morte Catonem,/ non Puteos memorasse vacat, non artibus omnes/ omnibus excultis'. Diese Verse versetzen uns mitten in den pavesischen Universitätsbetrieb. Agricola beteuert, daß es ihm bei dieser Gelegenheit nicht möglich ist, die Professoren aus der Familie de Grassis, den verstorbenen Cato, die Professoren aus der Familie de Puteo und alle anderen Professoren und Studenten aufzuzählen, die sich in allen akademischen Fächern auszeichnen. Das Vorhandensein einer medizinisch-artistischen und einer theologischen Fakultät in Pavia war Agricola selbstverständlich bekannt.[30] Er erwähnt aber keine Professoren dieser Fakultäten, die unter dem allgemeinen Begriff 'Artes' subsumiert werden. Anders steht es mit der juristischen Fakultät. Die von Agricola namentlich aufgezählten Professoren sind nicht nur Juristen, sondern ausnahmslos Zivilrechtler. Meine Schlußfolgerung ist, daß wir damit die Namen der Juristen erfahren, deren Übungen von Agricola besucht wurden. Das gilt natürlich nicht für den seit einigen Jahren verstorbenen Cato Saccus (†1463),[31] den bekanntesten Vertreter der pavesischen Romanistik vor Jason de Maino.[32] Daß Agricola ihn erwähnt hat, wird wohl mehrere Gründe haben: zuerst der überschwengliche Ruhm, der Cato Saccus lebenslänglich auch als Pfleger der 'studia humanitatis' begleitet hat[33] und

---

[27] Leibenguth and Seidel, 'Die Korrespondenz Rudolf Agricolas', 248, Anm. 69.

[28] 17 Hexameter: Agricola, *Lucubrationes*, 309-10.

[29] Hammer, 'Balthasar Rasinus'; Zippel, 'Gli inizi dell'Umanesimo tedesco', 371.

[30] Belloni, 'Giovanni Dondi'; Sottili, 'Die theologische Fakultät der Universität Pavia'; Negruzzo, *Theologiam discere et docere*.

[31] Vgl. Sottili, 'Università e cultura a Pavia', 377, Anm. 149. Ferner: Zanetti, 'Il primo collegio pavese'; Cerrini, 'Libri e vicende di una famiglia di castellani'; Albertini Ottolenghi, 'La Biblioteca dei Visconti e degli Sforza', 19-21.

[32] Belloni, *Professori giuristi a Padova*, 412 s.v.

dann die Dankbarkeit, die die ausländischen Studenten der Universität Pavia Saccus schuldeten, da er in seinem Testament die Geldmittel zur Verfügung gestellt hatte, damit ein Studentenheim für Ausländer errichtet wurde.

Wenn die Professoren, die Agricola Crassos und Puteos nennt, seine Juralehrer gewesen sind, dann ist die Neugier verständlich, diese Juristen zu identifizieren, um eventuell zu versuchen, den *Panegyricus* zu datieren. Ich habe drei Namen, die in Frage kommen, schon genannt: Johannes de Grassis, Lucas de Grassis und Johannes de Puteo. Vielleicht kann ein vierter hinzu genannt werden: Petrus de Grassis, der aber gleich ausscheiden muß, denn er hat erst am 28. Mai 1474 *in utroque* promoviert[34] und ist am gleichen Tage ins juristische Doktorenkolleg aufgenommen worden.[35] Er hatte seine Lehrtätigkeit schon im akademischen Jahr 1471-72 als Professor für 'Institutiones' begonnen[36] und sie mit dem gleichen Lehrauftrag in den akademischen Jahren 1472-73,[37] 1473-74[38] und 1474-75[39] fortgesetzt. Während Agricolas Aufenthalt in Pavia hat Petrus de Grassis eine Professur innegehabt, die zwar als Einführungskurs wichtig war,[40] aber verhältnismäßig schlecht bezahlt[41] und manchmal von nicht promovierten Studenten vertreten wurde.[42] Zu Ehre und Geld kam Petrus de Grassis erst, nachdem Agri-

---

[33] Er ist einer der Gesprächsteilnehmer in der Beta-Fassung von Vallas *De vero falsoque bono* (xlvi-xlvii). Der pavesische Rhetorikprofessor Balthasar Rasinus hat Saccus 'Ytalie lux' und 'splendor Lombardie' genannt: Bertalot, Humanistisches Studienheft eines Nürnberger Scholaren aus Pavia (1460), in Bertalot, *Studien zum italienischen und deutschen Humanismus*, I 153.

[34] Sottili, *Lauree pavesi*, 318.

[35] Pavia, Museo dell'Università, *Statutenbuch und Matrikel des Juristenkollegs*, 39r: 'Dominus Petrus de Grassis Mediolanensis, iuris utriusque doctor, intravit collegium suprascriptum existente priore suprascripto Domino Iohanne Otone ut constat instrumento publico fieri rogato michi notario antedicto anno et indictione suprascriptis (1474, Indiktion 7a) die Sabati vigesimo octavo mensis Madii.'

[36] Mailand, Archivio di Stato, *Studi. Parte antica*, 390 (5) (Jahresgehalt: 20 Gulden). Hinweise auf Petrus de Grassis in Gabotto, *Miserie e suppliche di professori*, 7; *Ludovico il Moro*, 118. Am 10.3.1474 schlägt der Senat dem Herzog vor, das Gehalt des Petrus de Grassis zu erhöhen: Mailand, Archivio di Stato, *Comuni*, 69.

[37] Pavia, Archivio di Stato, *Acta Studii Ticinensis* 22, 155r.

[38] Mailand, Archivio di Stato, *Studi. Parte antica*, 390.

[39] Ibid., 390 (9).

[40] Vgl. Anm. 23.

[41] Im Vorlesungsverzeichnis für das akademische Jahr 1472-3 werden den zwei Professoren für 'Institutiones' Petrus de Grassis und Christoforus de Albaritiis 35 und 30 Gulden zugesprochen: Mailand, Archivio di Stato, *Studi. Parte antica*, 390. 1474-5 hat sich die Lage für diese Professoren verbessert, da sie mit jeweils 60 und 50 Gulden besoldet werden: ibid., 390 (15).

[42] Am 2.6.1441 wurde z.B. die 'Lectura Institutionum' 'Spinbertus de Treultio Iuris utriusque scholaris' zugesprochen: Maiocchi, *Codice diplomatico*, II ii 427. In der Regel mußte aber der Inhaber der 'Lectura Institutionum' promoviert haben. Im Vorlesungsverzeichnis für das akademische Jahr 1455-6 wird am 17.10.1455 ein Lehrauftrag für 'Institutiones' an Jacobus de Carcano unter der Bedingung verliehen, daß er vor Weihnachten promoviert: Pavia, Archivio di Stato, *Acta Studii Ticinensis* 22, 140r. Die Auszahlung des Gehaltes an Jacobus de Balsamo und Gualterellus Folpertus, die den Lehrauftrag für 'Institutiones' im akademischen Jahr 1467-8 innehaben, wird an die Bedingung geknüpft, daß sie promovieren: ibid., 151r.

cola Pavia verlassen hatte.[43] Er kann unmöglich zu den Mitgliedern der Familie de Grassis gehören, die nach Agricolas *Panegyricus* eine Zierde für Pavia waren.[44] Dagegen kann man sich wohl denken, daß Agricola als solche Johannes de Grassis und Lucas de Grassis betrachtet.

Wenn meine Vermutung stimmt, dann haben wir vielleicht einen Anhaltspunkt, um den *Panegyricus* zu datieren. Lucas de Grassis[45] hat während der ganzen Aufenthaltszeit Agricolas in Pavia doziert und sich an den Promotionen beteiligt.[46] Am 23. August 1475, also kurz vor der Abfahrt Agricolas, ist Lucas de Grassis 'promotor' bei Lizentiatur und Doktorat von Donatus de Pretis.[47] Im akademischen Jahr 1475-76, dem ersten akademischen Jahr nach Agricolas Abreise aus Pavia, wird Lucas de Grassis als erster Professor für Zivilrecht mit dem fabelhaften Gehalt von 900 Gulden verzeichnet.[48] Für die Datierung der *Laudes Papiae* Agricolas ist der 'cursus honorum' des Lucas de Grassis belanglos, nicht dagegen für Agricolas Stellung innerhalb der Universität. Der Humanist Agricola verkehrte unter Juristen: Johannes von Plieningen hat also die Wahrheit geschrieben, als er beteuert hat, daß Agricola einige Jahre Zivilrecht gehört hat.

Anders verhält es sich mit Johannes de Grassis. Das Vorlesungsverzeichnis für das akademische Jahr 1472-73[49] nennt ihn im Unterschied zu jenem für das akademische Jahr 1471-72 nicht mehr. Letzteres Vorlesungsverzeichnis ist ohne Angaben über die Gehälter der Professoren.[50] Im akademischen Jahr 1469-70 hatte Johannes de Grassis die erste Stelle unter den Zivilrechtlern inne und mit 950 Gulden das höchste Gehalt in der ganzen Universität.[51] Ein Student des Zivilrechts wie Agricola konnte unmöglich seine Ausstrahlung übersehen. Johannes de Grassis wird zum letztenmal am 24. November 1472 unter den Prüfern bei einer Promotion verzeichnet, und zwar an erster Stelle, was ein deutliches Zeichen für die Stellung ist, die ihm

---

[43] Im Vorlesungsverzeichnis des Jahres 1476-7 erhielt Petrus de Grassis die 'Lectura ordinaria iuris canonici' und ein Gehalt von 150 Gulden: Mailand, Archivio di Stato, *Studi. Parte antica*, 390 (17); 1477-8 wurde sein Gehalt erneut erhöht: Pavia, Archivio di Stato, *Acta Studii Ticinensis* 22, 163r. Im akademischen Jahr 1479-80 wurde Petrus de Grassis mit 300 Gulden besoldet: ibid., 165r.

[44] Es handelt sich um verschiedene Familien, die den gleichen Familiennamen führen.

[45] Vgl. Maiocchi, *Codice diplomatico*. Ferner u.a.: Gabotto und Badini Confalonieri, *Vita di Giorgio Merula*, 141; Bellone, 'Appunti su Battista Trovamala da Sale', 394; Vaccari, *Storia dell'Università di Pavia*, 63; Franceschini, *Inventari inediti di Biblioteche ferraresi*, 61; 128.

[46] Sottili, *Lauree pavesi*, 385 s.v.

[47] Ibid., 347.

[48] Pavia, Archivio di Stato, *Acta Studii Ticinensis* 22, 158v.

[49] Pavia, Archivio di Stato, *Acta Studii Ticinensis* 22, 155r-156r.

[50] Mailand, Archivio di Stato, *Studi. Parte antica*, 390 (5): 'Ad lecturam iuris civilis ordinariam de mane: Dominus Iohannes de Grassis, Dominus Iohannes de Putheo, Dominus Ambrosius de Oppizonibus'.

[51] Mailand, Archivio di Stato, *Studi. Parte antica*, 390 (2).

unter den pavesischen Juristen zukam.[52] Zu dieser Zeit lehrte er aber nicht
mehr, wie eben betont wurde. Am folgenden 3. Dezember fand erneut eine
Promotion statt. Der Notar Pietro Mombretto, der das entsprechende
'Instrumentum' angefertigt hat, hat zuerst Johannes de Grassis unter den
anwesenden Doktoren an zweiter Stelle verzeichnet, aber dann den Namen
des Johannes de Grassis durchgestrichen.[53] Da in den späteren Promotionsurkunden Johannes de Grassis nicht mehr erwähnt wird, glaube ich annehmen zu dürfen, daß er sich zwischen dem 24. November und dem 3. Dezember 1472 aus dem pavesischen akademischen Leben zurückgezogen hat.[54]
Wenn wir Agricola wörtlich deuten und somit annehmen, daß er mehrere
Professoren mit dem Familiennamen 'de Grassis' meint, als er in seinem
Panegyricus beteuert, er habe zur Zeit keine Möglichkeit, die 'Crassos', die
'Putheos' und 'Saccum' zu erwähnen, und wenn Petrus de Grassis nicht
berücksichtigt werden darf, weil er noch nicht bedeutend genug war, um in
einem solchen Gedicht erwähnt zu werden, da er nicht einmal promoviert
hatte, wenn ferner Johannes de Grassis Ende November 1472 von der akademischen Bühne verschwunden ist, dann ist der *Panegyricus* Agricolas vor
Ende November 1472 entstanden, wenn nicht schon früher, und zwar zu
einer Zeit, als Johannes de Grassis seine Lehrtätigkeit voll entfaltete.

Es ist ganz und gar nicht nebensächlich, ein Gedicht Agricolas zu
datieren. Diese ganze Konstruktion hat einen Haken oder sogar zwei davon.
Rufen wir uns die fraglichen Verse Agricolas in Erinnerung: 'Nec mihi nunc
Crassos [...] nec Puteos memorasse vacat'. 'Putei' ist ganz bestimmt ein Plural an Stelle eines Singulars, weil ein einziger Puteus in Pavia zur Zeit
Agricolas gelehrt hat, der schon erwähnte Zivilrechtler Johannes de Puteo,[55]
den wir in allen Vorlesungsverzeichnissen der Zeit von Agricolas Aufenthalt in Pavia verzeichnet finden: 1469-70 und 1471-73 mit 400 Gulden,[56]
1473-74 und 1474-75 mit 300.[57] Wenn 'Putei' ein Plural an Stelle eines
Singulars ist, könnte das gleiche für 'Crassi' gelten. In diesem Fall käme als
einziger Kandidat Lucas de Grassis in Frage, dessen Lehrtätigkeit sich auf
die ganze Zeit von Agricolas Aufenthalt in Pavia erstreckt, womit mein Da-
tierungsvorschlag für den *Panegyricus* vereitelt wird. Mein Datierungsver-
such des *Panegyricus* hat einen zweiten Haken. Agricola beteuert, daß Stu-

---

[52] Sottili, *Lauree pavesi*, 205.

[53] Ibid., 206. Die schon erwähnten Schede Marozzi enthalten viele Notizen zu Pietro Mombretto: Zaffignani, 'Lo schedario nobiliare Marozzi', 352.

[54] Johannes de Grassis starb in der Nacht zwischen dem 19. und dem 20. August 1473: Verde, *Lo Studio fiorentino*, 358-9.

[55] Gabotto, *Miserie e suppliche di professori*, 3-4; Mariani, *Vita universitaria pavese*, 70;
73; Kisch, *Die Anfänge der juristischen Fakultät*, 193; *Ludovico il Moro*, 42.

[56] Mailand, Archivio di Stato, *Studi. Parte antica*, 390 (2); Pavia, Archivio di Stato, *Acta
Studii Ticinensis* 22, 155v.

[57] Mailand, Archivio di Stato, *Studi. Parte antica*, 390 (8), 390 (9).

denten aus Spanien, Deutschland und Frankreich nach Pavia strömen. Die 1995 edierten pavesischen Promotionsurkunden weisen einen einzigen spanischen Studenten in Pavia nach,[58] der übrigens sehr ehrgeizig und den nicht italienischen Studenten der Juristenuniversität nicht genehm war. Von diesem Spanier hört man zum ersten Mal im Juli 1473: zu dieser Zeit war er noch nicht ein Jahr in Pavia und bewarb sich schon für den Rektorposten bei den Juristen.[59] Dies besagt aber nur, daß dieser Spanier nach dem 4. Juli 1472 in Pavia eingetroffen war.[60] Wenn Agricola in dem *Panegyricus* ihn meint, dann kann das Gedicht sehr wohl vor dem Juli 1473 entstanden sein, nämlich vor der Zeit, als der Spanier sich bei den ausländischen Studenten und somit bei Agricola unbeliebt gemacht hatte, und auch vor Ende November 1472, d. h. vor dem Rückzug des Johannes Crassus, aber nicht vor dem 4. Juli 1472, weil der Spanier zu diesem Datum noch nicht in Pavia weilte. Wenn die Erwähnung der Spanier, die studienhalber nach Pavia strömen, nicht zu den konventionellen Teilen des Gedichts gehört, dann ist dies die wahrscheinlichste Datierung. Der Friese ist also ein Hörer und Bewunderer des Johannes de Puteo gewesen und hat wahrscheinlich die Vorlesungen des Johannes de Grassis gehört, aber der Zivilrechtler, mit dem er am vertraulichsten verkehrt hat, ist Lucas de Grassis gewesen.

Als Agricola in Pavia studierte, war Lucas de Grassis höchstwahrscheinlich ein betagter Mann,[61] der eine sehr ehrenvolle Karriere als Jurist und Professor hinter sich hatte. Es ist keine verlorene Zeit, diesem Jura-Professor einige Worte zu widmen, den Agricola bestimmt gehört hat, weil er ihm ein 'carmen' gewidmet hat, das von Vertraulichkeit zeugt.[62] Nach Agricolas Weggang aus Pavia hat Lucas de Grassis seine Lehrtätigkeit fortgesetzt, da er im Vorlesungsverzeichnis für das akademische Jahr 1475-76 als Inhaber des ersten Lehrstuhls für Zivilrecht mit dem sehr hohen Gehalt von 900 Gulden verzeichnet wird.[63] Damit es klar sei, warum ich so insistent mit solchen Angaben über die Karriere der Professoren und ihre Gehälter bin, betone ich, daß es sich dabei um Notizen handelt, die noch nicht edierten Archivalien entnommen sind. Damit hat aber die Karriere des Lucas de Grassis ihren Höhepunkt erreicht. Der Mann ist alt und kann vielleicht seine Lehrverpflichtungen nicht mehr mit der üblichen Energie wahrnehmen, weil

---

[58] Ludovico Ala.

[59] Sottili, 'Le contestate elezioni rettorali', 274*; 300*; 301*.

[60] In der zweiten Hälfte des 15. Jahrhunderts fand die Wahl des Juristenrektors am 4. Juli statt: Sottili, 'Rettori e vicerettori', 246*.

[61] Im Vorlesungsverzeichnis für das akademische Jahr 1441-2 wird er als Beauftragter mit der 'Lectura extraordinaria Digesti Novi et Infortiati' erwähnt: Maiocchi, *Codice diplomatico*, II ii 431.

[62] Ad Lucam Crassum iuris utriusque doctorem: Agricola, *Lucubrationes*, 310.

[63] Pavia, Archivio di Stato, *Acta Studii Ticinensis* 22, 158v.

man ihm von den zugesprochenen 900 Gulden lediglich 700 auszahlt. Spätere Notizen über die Lehrtätigkeit des Lucas de Grassis sind mir nicht bekannt. Das Vorlesungsverzeichnis für das akademische Jahr 1479-80 erwähnt ihn nicht mehr,[64] weil er am 1. April 1478 schon tot war. In einem
Brief, der dieses Datum trägt, verfügt in der Tat der Herzog von Mailand,
daß der Stellvertretende Kanzler der Universität Pavia und der Juristenrektor
sich einschalten, damit ein Neffe des Lucas de Grassis in den Besitz des
Geldes und der Bücher kommt, die sein Onkel den Studenten geliehen
hatte.[65] Dieser Brief ist wichtig, weil er unsere Aufmerksamkeit auf eine für
die Universität Pavia gut belegte Gewohnheit richtet: die Professoren liehen
den Studenten mit oder ohne Zins die Bücher.[66] Zwischen Lucas de Grassis
und Agricola bestand eine derartige Vertraulichkeit, daß man vermuten darf,
daß Agricola von diesem Usus profitiert hat.

Wer aber war dieser Lucas de Grassis, der, wenn man den Versen
Agricolas Glauben schenken darf, eine genaue Kenntnis des ganzen Rechts
besaß?[67] Am 14. September 1435 ist er in Pavia als Student des römischen
Rechts nachgewiesen.[68] Im akademischen Jahr 1439-40 ist er als Professor
belegt und lehrt kanonisches Recht: den Liber Sextus.[69] Am 23. März 1453
wird ihm die Vertretung des Jakobus de Puteo vorläufig, d. h. bis zur
Fertigstellung des Vorlesungsverzeichnisses für das akademische Jahr 1453-
54, zugesprochen.[70] Es ist sehr wahrscheinlich, daß Lucas de Grassis in
diesen wenigen Monaten tatsächlich unterrichtet hat.[71] Nach einem Zwi-

---

[64] Pavia, Archivio di Stato, *Acta Studii Ticinensis* 22, 165r-166r. Die Notiz über die Vermin-
derung des Gehalts des Lucas de Grassis in: Mailand, Archivio di Stato, *Studi. Parte antica*,
390 (17).

[65] Mailand, Archivio di Stato, *Missive* 136, 154r: 'Vicecancellario nec non Rectori legista-
rum felicis Gimnasii. Expositum nobis est ab Iohanne Ludovico Grasso, nepote ac herede olim
preclari iurisconsulti Domini Luce itidem de Grassis, qui ius civile istic publice profitebatur
(Hs. 'profitentur') non nullos ibi scolares esse qui restituere ei negligant quasdam pecunias
librosque legales sibi mutuo concessos ab ipso Domino Luca dum adhuc in humanis ageret.
Quare equum ac iustum omnino censentes ut eiusmodi pecuniarum ac librorum restitutio fiat
(Hs. 'fit'), hortamur vos ac plurimum oneramus ut, si vobis constiterit de premissis, eam acco-
modare provisionem velitis que opportuna fuerit quo idem Iohannes Ludovicus omnis
assequatur pecunias et libros quos olim patruus suus istic studentibus mutuo concessisset nec
digne amplius ob id querendi causam habeat. Datum die primo aprilis 1478. Per Filippum'.
Juristenrektor im akademischen Jahr 1477-8 war Giovanni Guglielmo de Grassis: Sottili,
'Rettori e vicerettori', 261*. Als 'vicecancellarius' wird am 11.3. Antoninus de Malvicinis de
Fontana und am 28.4.1478 Antonius de Riciis erwähnt: Pavia, Archivio di Stato, *Archivio
Notarile di Pavia*, 95 c. 292r-v, Promotion in artibus des Antonius de Rusticis; ibid., c. 344r-v,
Promotion in Bürgerrecht des Filippus de Grassis.

[66] Pedralli, 'Il medico ducale milanese', 322-3.

[67] 'Crasse vir egregios pleno qui pectore mores/ Et ius omne tenes, sit tibi multa salus'.

[68] Maiocchi, *Codice diplomatico*, II i 350.

[69] Maiocchi, *Codice diplomatico*, II i 393.

[70] *Documenti per la storia dell'Università di Pavia*, 82-4.

[71] Er hat sich an einem Streik der Professoren nicht beteiligt: ibid., 131.

schenaufenthalt in Ferrara[72] ist Lucas de Grassis seit dem akademischen Jahr 1464-65 an der Universität Pavia festangestellt,[73] wo ihn Agricola kennengelernt und zu schätzen gewußt hat.[74] Die Verse an Lucas Crassus entwickeln sich um einen 'topos' des Freundschaftsgedichtes, des Geschenks von einem bißchen Obst, das die Kälte des Winters und die Raubgier der Kinder nicht wegraffen konnten.[75] Wenn der Herbst kommt, soll Lucas de Grassis einen Korb voller Trauben und sonstiges Obst bekommen, wobei wir erfahren, daß Agricola in Pavia ein Haus bewohnte, das einen kleinen Obstgarten, einen 'hortulus' hatte: 'Hortulus et quidquid fert meus ipse dabo', ich werde dir alles schenken, was mein kleiner Obstgarten aufbringen wird. Den Beweis, daß Agricola im Milieu der pavesischen Jurisprudenz völlig integriert war, halte ich damit für herbracht. Er hat die Zivilrechtler hochgepriesen, er hat berühmte verstorbene Vertreter der pavesischen Jura-Studien hochgelobt, er war mit einem der prominentesten Vertreter der Bürgerrechtswissenschaft befreundet: das, was sein Freund und Schüler Johannes von Plieningen überliefert hat, er habe einige Jahre lang Zivilrecht studiert, ist stichhaltig.

Zur Zeit Agricolas war Pavia in erster Linie eine große Juristenhochschule, wo aber das medizinisch-artistische Studium nicht vernachläßigt wurde und wo die Theologen nicht besonders hervortraten. Wie stand es mit den 'studia humanitatis', die im Lauf der Zeit zur Hauptbeschäftigung Agricolas wurden? Außer den zwei erwähnten *Carmina* hat Agricola in Pavia mit Sicherheit ein drittes Gedicht verfaßt, die Verse *Ad Cribellium Mediolanensem*, um ein Exemplar des *Panegyricus* des Plinius an Traian zu erhalten.[76] Daß es sich dabei um einen Einfluß von Catullus' Dichtungsart auf Agricola handelt, ist zu Recht hervorgehoben worden.[77] So weit ich weiß, hat sich aber niemand gefragt, wer dieser Cribellius war, der in Mailand wohnte und mit Agricola auf gutem Fuß stand. Es geht dabei keineswegs um die unheilbare Neugier eines überzeugten Positivisten, sondern um die Notwendigkeit, das Netz der Verflechtungen Agricolas mit der Welt der italienischen Humanisten zu verdeutlichen.

Die Crivellis sind eine sehr bedeutende Mailänder Familie gewesen, die dank jenem Lodrisius Cribellus, der sich auch als Gräzist ausgezeichnet hat,

---

[72] Franceschini, *Inventari inediti di Biblioteche ferraresi*, 61.

[73] 'Ad lecturam extraordinariam de sero: Dominus Lucas de Grassis, Floreni DC': Pavia, Archivio di Stato, *Acta Studii Ticinensis* 22, 145v.

[74] Ab 1459 beteiligt sich Lucas de Grassis regelmäßig an den Prüfungen: Sottili, *Lauree pavesi*, 385 s.v.

[75] Foresti, 'Per alcuni cestelli di pere ghiacciuole', 167-73. Dieser Aufsatz hat jedoch nichts gemeinsames mit dem 'carmen' Agricolas.

[76] 'Librum quo pariter duobus aevum/ Et longum dedit absque fine nomen/ Traiano atque sibi meus Secundus,/ Atque a morte tuetur ambos': Agricola, *Lucubrationes*, 294.

[77] Wiegand, 'Mentibus at vatum deus insidet', 267.

den Humanismusforschern gut bekannt ist.[78] Lodrisius Cribellus kommt jedoch als Empfänger der Verse Agricolas aus chronologischen Gründen nicht
in Frage. Ein in der Regel gut informiertes Werk belehrt uns, daß zur Zeit
von Agricolas Aufenthalt in Pavia ein Hieronymus Cribellus in Mailand
lebte, der sich zweifelsohne dem Humanismus verdingt hatte.[79] Ihm wurde
die Pflicht und die Ehre auferlegt, 1468 die Leichenrede für Bianca Maria
Visconti zu halten. Es wird von ihm tradiert, daß er Arzt war, obwohl diese
Notiz nicht gut belegt ist. Wenn wir die noch unedierten Vorlesungsverzeichnisse der Universität Pavia nachschlagen, finden wir dort auch einen
Hieronymus Cribellus, der durchaus als Empfänger der Elfsilber Agricolas
in Frage käme. Das Vorlesungsverzeichnis vom 18. Dezember 1475 für das
akademische Jahr 1475-76 verzeichnet als Rhetorikprofessoren in Mailand
'Dominus Hieronymus Cribellus canonicus Mediolanensis'[80] und 'Dominus
Albertus de Crescentino'. Im gleichen Vorlesungsverzeichnis lesen wir weiter, daß Hieronymus Cribellus in den Genuß eines Teiles des Gehalts gekommen war, das Cola Montanus[81] zugesprochen worden war. Wie hoch
das Gehalt des Hieronymus Cribellus war, erfahren wir aus einem herzoglichen Brief vom 7. Juli 1476 und aus einer Notiz, die sich auf das Jahr 1477
bezieht: ihm waren 110 Gulden zugesprochen worden, aber danach wurde
sein Gehalt um 5 Gulden heruntergesetzt, so daß er 105 Gulden verdiente.[82]
Wenn der erwähnte Verfasser der Leichenrede für Bianca Maria Visconti
tatsächlich Arzt und der Rhetorikprofessor Kanoniker in Mailand war, wie

---

[78] Petrucci, 'Lodrisio Crivelli'.
[79] Severi, 'Girolamo Crivelli'.
[80] *Camera apostolica*, 274-5.
[81] 'Sed salarium horum duorum (*scilicet Cole Montani et Ubertini de Crescentino*) ordina-
tum est partiatur inter Dominum Hieronymum Cribellum et eundem Albertinum vel aliter prout
per principem ordinabitur' (Pavia, Archivio di Stato, *Acta Studii Ticinensis* 22, 159r-v). Zu
Cola Montano: Garin, 'Orientamenti culturali milanesi e pavesi', 566-7; Ganda, 'Panfilo Castaldi', 15ff. Zu Ubertinus: *Bibliotheca Vadiana*, 39; Bellone, 'Note su Pietro Cara', 665; 667.
[82] Pavia, Archivio di Stato, *Acta Studii Ticinensis* 32, Faszikel 72: 'Pro magistro Hieronymo
Cribello. Dux Mediolani etc. Dilecti nostri. Quia magister Georgius Valla Placentinus qui depu-
tatus erat ad lecturam rethorice in rotulo istius nostri celebris Ticinensis Gymnasii usque die
duodecimo effluxi mensis Iunii a nobis licentiam impetravit, addidimus magistro Hieronymo
Cribello eam ad lecturam in Mediolano deputato, ultra florenos centum, illos decem florenos
quos antea addideramus eidem magistro Georgio, qui superabundabant ex summa illorum flore-
norum centum sexaginta quos habebat Cola Montanus Bononiensis, eius magistri Hieronymi
precessor, et septuaginta quinque quos prius habebat magister Ubertinus Crescentinus, eiusdem
Hieronymi concurrens. Ideo volumus quod ipso in rotulo huiusmodi additionem dicto Hieronymo poni et describi faciatis ac de pecuniis ipsis debitis ordinatisque temporibus responderi
atque opportunas bulletas et scripturas quascunque fieri. Datum Papie die quarto Iulii
MCCCC°LXXsexto. Christophorus'. A tergo: 'Prudentibus dilectis nostris .. Referendario et ..
Thesaurario'. Auf dem rechten Rand: 'Registrata'. Mailand, Archivio di Stato, *Studi. Parte
antica*, 390 (17): '1477. Additiones et renunciationes [...] Magistro Hieronymo Cribello ad
lecturam rethorice in Mediolano pro primo deputato qui habebat florenos 110 dempti sunt
floreni 5 ita quod nunc habebit nisi florenos 105'.

die Vorlesungsverzeichnisse behaupten, lebten in Mailand zur Zeit Agricolas zwei Cribelli namens Hieronymus, von denen einer Rhetorikprofessor und der andere Arzt und Höfling der Sforzas war. An wen hat sich Agricola gewandt, um das ersehnte Werk des Plinius zu bekommen? Vielleicht an den Schullehrer, wobei ich gleich betonen muß, daß mir jeglicher Beweis dafür fehlt, um diese Hypothese zu bekräftigen, um so mehr, da es nicht sicher ist, daß der Höfling der Sforzas wirklich Arzt war. Der Empfänger der Elfsilber Agricolas hat nun aber einen Taufnamen: Hieronymus.

Über die Rolle, die der Humanismus an der Universität Pavia spielte, sollten wir uns aber lieber keine Illusionen machen. Rhetorik wurde selbstverständlich unterrichtet, es handelte sich aber um ein Wahlfach, das die Studenten der zwei bzw. drei Fakultäten besuchten, wenn sie dazu Lust hatten. Rhetorik ist kein Prüfungsfach, niemand hat zu Agricolas Zeit in Rhetorik oder Grammatik promoviert und keiner der damaligen Rhetorikprofessoren hat als Prüfer an einer Promotion teilgenommen, wie die inzwischen veröffentlichten und von mir oft zitierten Promotionsurkunden beweisen. Wenn diese Urkunden für die Geschichte des Rhetorikunterrichts belanglos sind, so sind dagegen die unveröffentlichten und ebenfalls oft von mir erwähnten Vorlesungsverzeichnisse sehr aufschlußreich, weil sie uns die Namen und die Gehälter aller Rhetorikprofessoren überliefern, die an der Universität Pavia zu Agricolas Zeit gewirkt haben. 1467-68: Balthasar Rasinus, 425 Gulden; Franciscus Ocha, 160 Gulden; Georgius Valla, der auch Griechisch unterrichtete, 50 Gulden.[83] 1468-69: Franciscus Ocha, Georgius Valla, Ubertinus de Crescentino; das Vorlesungsverzeichnis überliefert keine Gehälter.[84] 1469-70: Franciscus Ocha, 165 Gulden; Georgius Valla, 140 Gulden; Ubertinus de Crescentino, 80 Gulden.[85] 1471-72: Franciscus Oca, Georgius Valla, Ubertinus de Crescentino, Basilius Aquilanus; für dieses akademische Jahr sind keine Gehälter überliefert.[86] 1472-73: Franciscus Ocha, 165 Gulden; Georgius Valla, 140 Gulden; Ubertinus de Crescentino, 80 Gulden; Basilius Aquilanus, 80 Gulden.[87] 1473-74: Franciscus Oca, 150 Gulden; Georgius Valla, 180 Gulden; Ubertinus de Crescentino, 70 Gulden; Basilius Aquilanus, 70 Gulden.[88] 1474-75: Franciscus Ocha, 125 Gulden; Georgius Valla, 130 Gulden; Ubertinus de Crescentino, 75 Gulden.[89]

---

[83] Pavia, Archivio di Stato, *Acta Studii Ticinensis* 22, 151r. Rasinus beteiligte sich an den Doktorprüfungen, weil er promovierter Zivilrechtler war.

[84] Ibid., 153r-v.

[85] Mailand Archivio di Stato, *Studi. Parte antica*, 390 (2).

[86] Ibid., 390 (3).

[87] Pavia, Archivio di Stato, *Acta Studii Ticinensis* 22, 156r.

[88] Mailand, Archivio di Stato, *Studi. Parte antica*, 390 (7).

[89] Ibid., 390 (14) und 390 (15).

Seit 1469 kehren drei Namen immer wieder: Georgius Valla, Francischus Ocha und Ubertinus de Crescentino. Ocha[90] war der Dienstälteste und sein Gehalt wird, zwar nur geringfügig, heruntergesetzt. Am Ende der berücksichtigten Zeitspanne ist Georgius Valla der bestbezahlte: das darf man sicher als Zeichen seines Erfolgs als Professor interpretieren.[91] Bekanntlich waren die Juristen, die Ärzte und die Artisten an die Lektüre und Interpretation bestimmter Lehrbücher gebunden, dem Rhetor stand dagegen frei, welche 'auctores' er zum Gegenstand seines Unterrichts wählen wollte. Agricola wird wohl die Übungen dieser Rhetores spätestens, nachdem er der Jurisprudenz den Rücken gekehrt hatte, besucht haben. Das ist Grund genug, um zu versuchen, herauszufinden, was die Rhetorikprofessoren während ihrer Übungen boten. Neuerdings hat man auf ein Werk Vallas aufmerksam gemacht, das bislang nicht beachtet wurde,[92] den Traktat *De recto scribendi modo,* der in einer Handschrift der Domkapitelbibliothek in Toledo und in einer anderen Handschrift der Stiftsbibliothek Schlägl überliefert ist. Bei dem Hinweis auf die Handschrift der Dombibliothek in Toledo ist die Frage aufgeworfen worden, ob das Datum (1469, V° Idus Decembris), das man auf dem letzten und sonst leeren Blatt des Kodex liest, sich auf die Abschrift der Handschrift oder auf die Entstehung des Werkes bezieht.[93] Ich würde den Vermerk eher auf die Abschrift des Kodex beziehen, da die zitierten Worte vom Werk getrennt sind, das von dem üblichen 'Telos' auf dem vorletzten Blatt abgeschlossen wird.

Die Beschäftigung mit diesem Werk setzt aber Griechischkenntnisse voraus, die sowohl der Schreiber der Toledo- wie auch derjenige der Schlägler Handschrift gehabt haben. In beiden Fällen stehen wir vor dem Stoff, den Valla in seinen Übungen bearbeitet hat. Ich habe absichtlich den Ausdruck 'in beiden Fällen' benutzt, weil es sich um zwei voneinander abweichende Fassungen des gleichen Werkes handelt, wie die Gegenüberstellung der Einführungsworte zum Kapitel über den Buchstaben 'Z' beweist. Der Toledo-Kodex enthält Hinweise auf die orthographischen Gepflogenheiten von Theocritus, die in der Schlägler Handschrift fehlen,[94] die sich lediglich über ein

---

[90] Speroni, 'Lorenzo Valla a Pavia'.

[91] Zu Georgius Valla: *Giorgio Valla tra scienza e sapienza.*

[92] Cerrini, 'Libri e vicende di una famiglia di castellani', 369-71.

[93] Ibidem.

[94] 'Ante huius litterae inventionem sd maiores ponebant, quod apud Theocritum spectare licet ubi saepenumero pro Z duplici sd positum comperimus quale est comasdo (III 1) pro comazo ab eo dictum. Quare nec recte patrizo matrizove aut tale aliud dicitur, sed patrisso matrissoque dicendum grammatici attestantur periti. Mutatur etiam, ut Diomedes reliquit, haec ipsa duplex in I in hac ditione: Iupiter. Nam Iupiter quasi Zeupater dici vult (Ars. II: *Grammatici Latini* I 422, 30-4)'.

Zitat des Grammatikers Diomedes ausläßt.[95] Wie dieses Werk beweist, hat Agricola von dem Besuch der Übungen Vallas wegen ihres philologischen, grammatikalischen und literarischen Reichtums nur profitieren können.

Wenn ich meine Ausführung damit abschließe, so geschieht das nicht, weil der Stoff zu Ende ist. Agricolas Italien-Aufenthalt bleibt ein weites und reiches Forschungsgebiet. Nun steht es jedoch fest, daß Agricola in Pavia tatsächlich Jura studiert hat, in Mailand einen Humanisten namens Hieronymus Cribellus zu seinen Freunden zählte, und daß in Pavia ein Grammatiker Übungen hielt, die Agricola mit Nutzen besuchen konnte.[96]

---

[95] 'a Latinis, ut refert Diomedes, quandoque invertitur, ut iugum pro zeugum a zogo scilicet deductum, et Zupiter pro Iupiter'.

[96] Dem in Groningen vorgetragenen Referat sind nur die Anmerkungen hinzugefügt worden.

A. TERVOORT

THE ITALIAN CONNECTION: THE *ITER ITALICUM* AND THE NORTHERN NETHERLANDS (1425-1575)[*]

There is almost general consensus about the important role of Italy as the cradle of humanism all over Europe. Various channels through which humanism was spread throughout Europe have been pointed out in the mass of literature on the subject: mobility to and from Italy, foreign correspondence of humanists, schools and universities and the diffusion of books and manuscripts, in which the invention of the printing press was a major agent of change.[1] Even the most recent survey on *Humanism and the Culture of Renaissance Europe* devotes most attention to the birth of humanism in Italy and its consecutive spread from Italy to other parts of Europe.[2]

The same survey states that the most obvious principal mechanism of the spread of humanism north of the Alps consisted in schools and universities.[3] And Italian universities, itinerant scholars and students who visited Italy figure prominently in this story. If it is generally assumed that Italy must be considered to be the cradle of humanism and the source of its spread over Europe, then the thousands of students who visited the several faculties of the different Italian universities in the fifteenth and sixteenth centuries must have played an important role in this cultural movement. This mobility to and from Italy, has been identified as the most direct and personal means of diffusing humanism.[4] Paul Oskar Kristeller stated that by far the most interesting group in the bulk of visitors to Italy consisted of the thousands of students who visited Italy for several years.[5]

There certainly is evidence for this statement. An interesting article devoted to the 'humanist challenge to medieval culture' states that Germans 'who lived and studied in Italy' played a pioneering role in the coming of humanism to Germany.[6] Two of the more interesting surveys on the coming

---

[*] This article, including its tables and graphs, is based on current research for my Ph.D. thesis entitled: *The iter italicum and the Northern Netherlands. The Dutch at Italian Universities and their Influence on the Netherlands Society* (1425-1575).
[1] Kristeller, *Concetti rinascimentali dell' uomo*, 140-56.
[2] Nauert, *Humanism and the Culture of Renaissance Europe*, 95.
[3] Ibid., 100.
[4] Burke, 'The Spread of Italian Humanism', 3.
[5] Kristeller, *Concetti rinascimentali dell' uomo*, 141.
[6] Nauert, 'The Humanist Challenge to Medieval German Culture'.

of humanism to the Netherlands[7] point to the fact that there was a – presumably – considerable number of students who visited Italy. Yet, these students are not awarded a paragraph of their own, although one of the authors claims that 'by 1500 a stay in Italy had become a 'must' for anyone who wished to be taken for a man of learning.'[8] The same elaborate article states that 'There were several other interesting Netherlanders in Italy, apart from the host of students *who left no trace in history*' [my italics: A.T].[9]

I would like to contest this last remark and try to show that these travellers did leave traces in history, not only in Italian university sources, but furthermore during their careers, and in their cultural contributions in various forms. I do not intend to single out only those outstanding humanists familiar to all and set them apart from the selection of students to which they belonged, namely the students who undertook the *iter italicum*. Rather than this I shall briefly sketch universities in Italy and make some remarks about students from the Northern Netherlands, more specifically those from the north-eastern regions, attending them. Furthermore I intend to show that an important part of this group of students was presupposed and able to make a contribution to the cause of humanism at various levels.

The basis for this is a prosopographical investigation into the lives of students from the Northern Netherlands – that is the present day Netherlands, without the provinces of Brabant and Limburg – who visited Italy from 1425 until 1575. Of an assembled population of 615 individuals I have gathered information about their academic curriculum, their careers after their studies, their cultural activities, etc. In this article I shall try to shed some light on the wider circle of students who came into contact with Italian universities and humanism and on the wider socio-cultural aspects of the spread of humanism to the Northern Netherlands through these students.

Humanism and Italian Universities

When confronted with the term 'humanism', the first thing that has to be said is that it is problematic.[10] It is not a term invented by the humanists themselves, but was coined by German scholars at the beginning of the nineteenth century. The term *humanista* was a contemporary term referring

---

[7] IJsewijn, 'The Coming of Humanism to the Low Countries'; Cameron, 'Humanism in the Low Countries'.

[8] IJsewijn, 'The Coming of Humanism to the Low Countries', 199-200.

[9] Op. cit., 230.

[10] Consider the reflections of Burke, 'The Spread of Italian Humanism', 1-3; and Rüegg, 'The Rise of Humanism'.

to men concerned with the teaching of the *studia humanitatis* (humanity and the human condition) inspired by the classics. While it is true that the original basis of 'humanism' lay in what we now refer to as the humanities, modern scholars tend to handle a wider definition.[11] It is now widely accepted that humanism had a serious impact on most scholarly disciplines in schools and universities.

The syllabus taught in the various European universities may have been quite similar up to the fifteenth century. Where the accents of teaching are concerned, Italian universities differed from their European counterparts in various ways. In the teaching of arts great emphasis was put on rhetoric. The fact that teaching and practice of law had such a prominent place in Italian university education and society in general was largely responsible for this situation. Similarly, logic and the natural sciences within the arts were regarded as instrumental to the teaching and practice of medicine, contrary to Paris, for instance, where the arts were considered to be the handmaiden of theology. The fact that arts and medicine were situated within the same faculty is surely noteworthy in this respect.

Until the discovery and rediscovery of important classical medical texts – often by Italian humanists – the *corpus* of texts in the teaching of medicine was roughly the same in Europe as a whole. The attention for practical medicine, however, was considerably more developed at especially Bologna and Padua. Anatomy had an important place within teaching. Public dissections were held in Bologna as early as 1316. Moreover, Italian *studia* could grant degrees in surgery, for which there was a special curriculum of texts to read. Again it is important to stress that the teaching of medicine in Italy was strongly influenced by the fact that the practice of medicine was well organised and well respected in the Italian cities. One should bear in mind that the colleges of doctors of medicine not only had strong ties with the *studium* – they after all examined the candidates for graduation – but that they had authority over all physicians practising within the city. In the sixteenth century medical teaching, especially at Padua, became even more elaborate. New text editions of the classics (by this time also in Greek), an intensified attention for anatomy and botany greatly enlarged medical knowledge of the day. Sixteenth century Padua can be considered as *the* medical centre of Europe.

The position of Bologna as the main centre of legal teaching made sure that developments in the teaching of law never bypassed Italy. The spread of the *mos italicus* – a legal school that claimed that reason should be the

---

[11] Grössing, *Humanistische Naturwissenschaft*, 12; Santing, *Geneeskunde en humanisme*, 15-18.

touchstone for law and its application – was very influential at Italian universities in the fifteenth and sixteenth centuries. Also, the *mos gallicus* – a school of legal humanists that considered Roman law no longer completely viable, but an object for historical and philological study – had strong roots in Italy in those same centuries.

It is justified to say that universities like Bologna and Padua were in the vanguard of intellectual development within university education. There are several factors that have to be taken into consideration when speaking of the intellectual innovation and the international popularity of Italian *studia*. First, Bologna and Padua were among the oldest and most respected universities in Europe. The fact that they had a primary position in the teaching of law had ever since their foundation ensured that large numbers of (foreign) students visited them. Second, the cities that harboured the universities were large and prosperous. Since part of this prosperity was brought in by foreign students, the authorities were willing to invest in education. They tried to attract numerous famous professors and paid them well.[12] Even the smaller universities in Italy profited from the huge attendance of foreign students at Bologna and Padua. The university of Ferrara offered special privileges to foreign students who would come there (e.g. low graduation rates).

It is also noteworthy that the method and contents of teaching altered in the course of the fifteenth and sixteenth centuries. The academic atmosphere at the university of Padua has been described as being primarily concerned with the practical and the secular. Physical demonstration and demonstrative proof of cause acquired primary position in methods of procedure, investigation and the way of teaching.[13]

The notion that humanism developed outside the universities and that the professors of especially the Italian universities 'were long the enemies of Humanism'[14] needs further revision. It is becoming increasingly clear that relations between these two were stronger than was thought in the past. University training (and often teaching) seems to have been a common biographical factor of most humanists in general and it has been justly claimed that the role universities played in the socio-professional context of humanism needs further examination.[15]

Not only this: whereas humanism was not a coherent philosophical system, it developed a certain method where the sanctity of sources played a key role. This philological approach enabled humanists to make a claim on

---

[12] In fifteenth-century Padua, professors earned 400 ducats a year on average. The income of a skilled artisan was about fifty ducats a year: Ohl, *The University of Padua*, 72.

[13] Ohl, *The University of Padua*, 114-5.

[14] Rashdall, *The Universities of Europe in the Middle Ages*, II 50-1.

[15] Denley, 'Recent Studies on Italian Universities', 194-5.

control over questions of authority and the original meaning of texts, which also had serious implications for the notions of historical, scientific and societal development. In this methodological sense humanism could and would challenge the traditional scholarly disciplines in the higher faculties – medicine, law and theology.[16] While traditional institutions, like universities, are not prone to immediate change, it has to be said that already at the end of the fourteenth century humanist learning began to make an impact on Italian universities. The Italian universities were the first in Europe where humanist thought figured in both informal and institutionalised ways. This was a gradual process. The new learning made a stronger impression on young students than on old professors, securely seated in their respective chairs. Eventually, some young students are bound to become professors themselves and in turn exert their influence in the adoption of humanist learning. We might say that in the fifteenth century humanist thought already had a firm position within the faculties of arts and medicine in Italy, and to some extent even in the faculties of law. The establishment of chairs for the study of Greek at the universities of Florence, Ferrara, Bologna and Padua can serve as a concrete example. The chairs for the reading of rhetoric and poetry are another. The appointment of humanists to university chairs – like Nicolò Leoncino, who taught medicine and philosophy at the university of Ferrara for sixty years beginning in 1464[17] – represents a more informal way in which humanist thought influenced and supplemented the contents of the university syllabus. The rediscovery of ancient sources and new translations of Greek texts further enhanced this development.

Students from the Northern Netherlands at Italian Universities (1425-1575)

Students from the Northern Netherlands had been visiting Italian universities since at least the thirteenth century, when several dozens of students who matriculated as *Phrisius* visited the university of Bologna. Ever since those days there had been a presence from the Northern Netherlands at the world's oldest university. Bologna was certainly not the only place frequented by Dutch students. From the fifteenth century onwards – since, university records have survived more often and more regularly[18] – attendance

---

[16] Nauert, 'The Humanist Challenge to Medieval German Culture', 302-3.

[17] *CE* II 323; Mugnai Carrara, *La biblioteca di Nicolò Leoniceno.*

[18] For an overview of administrative university sources, see Pacquet, *Les matricules universitaires*; and more specifically De Ridder-Symoens, 'Deutsche Studenten an italienischen Rechtsfakultäten'. Hardly any matriculation registers survive for the 15th and 16th centuries. For the Italian situation one has to resort to other complementary sources that give names of university students. Graduation records are among the most important. In recent decades we

of students from the Northern Netherlands can be certified for the universities of Bologna, Padua, Ferrara, Siena, Pisa, Florence, Pavia, Perugia, Turin, Naples, Rome and even Arezzo. My research population numbers 615 students, but in view of lack of sources for particular universities at certain times we might estimate that there may have been as many as 750 students from the Northern Netherlands visiting Italian universities in the period under consideration.

Two universities clearly stand out: Bologna and Padua. Both universities had more than 200 Dutch students attending in the period from 1425 until 1575. Ferrara and Siena were certainly the runners up.[19] The other universities follow at some distance. One has to make some reservations, however, about the popularity of Ferrara and Siena. A *peregrinatio academica* that might have started out at Louvain or Cologne frequently took the student to either Padua or Bologna, but often the actual act of graduation took place at Ferrara or Siena, often for reasons of economy, while still enjoying the prestige of an Italian doctorate. We might take as an example the *peregrinatio academica* of Aert van der Mijlen of Dordrecht. In October 1553 he went to Louvain to study arts at the age of fifteen. After a year he travelled to Heidelberg to continue his studies there. We lose track of his curriculum in the late fifties but in 1561 we find him again, in Padua where he matriculated in the German nation of the Law university. He stayed there for a year and a half – in 1562 he even occupied the post of proctor for a while – and then moved on to Siena where on the ninth of September 1562 'Hadrianus van der Mylen, filius Arnoldi Dordracenus Traiectensis diocesis Hollandus' graduated *in utroque iure*.[20]

Though there was an almost continuous presence of Dutch students in Italy, it was not evenly spread over the entire period. If we look at the numbers for the three most important universities, it becomes clear that the first three decades of the sixteenth century seem to have been a period of regression. This has no doubt to do with the political turmoil of the period, turmoil from which Bologna was comparatively exempt. In 1509 France with the help of both emperor and pope invaded the territory of the Republic of Venice. Both Padua and Ferrara were located within the *serenissima*. Padua in particular suffered from the winds of war. The city was sieged and conquered, liberated and sieged again. The *studium* in Padua almost ceased to exist. Foreign students fled and did not return until Padua had recovered.

---

have seen quite a few of them published, especially for Padua, Bologna and Siena. Some of the more important titles can be found in the bibliography.

[19] For all figures see the tables in the Appendix.

[20] *Matricule de l'Université de Louvain*, IV 483, 47; Den Tex, 'Nederlandse studenten in de rechten te Padua', 65, nr. 77; *Le lauree dello Studio senese nel 16. secolo*, 296-7.

Bologna on the other hand was hardly touched by this because of its safe location within the Papal State.[21]

In the second half of the sixteenth century Bologna lost out to Padua (and to a lesser extent to Siena) when Protestantism entered the stage. The lenient rule of Venice allowed students to study and graduate in Padua in considerable peace of mind. If a student wished to graduate, but wanted to avoid the bishop of Padua or his vicar, as representatives of the pope, and the oath to the Catholic faith, he could graduate after examination under the authority of the *comes palatinus*, a count palatine in Padua as representative of the emperor. When the religious question further polarised during and after the Council of Trent, particularly after Pius IV's bull *In Sacrosancta* of 1564 – which stated that every person obtaining a doctorate in theology, law or medicine, must swear allegiance to the Catholic faith and its doctrines before graduation – Venice continued to allow Protestant students to study and even graduate at Padua. The possibility to graduate under the authority of a count palatine ensured this. The Republic went even further in 1616 when it created the possibility to graduate in arts and medicine *auctoritate Veneta*, under authority of the Venetian College (1635 for lawyers). Bologna, located within the Papal State, was very strict in the enforcement of the papal bull and this had a negative impact on its popularity with students coming from regions where Protestantism had gained a foothold.[22] This is clearly visible in the numbers attending these universities. Student numbers from the Northern Netherlands declined in Bologna while they were booming in Padua.

We can make some clear observations about the subject of study that students chose. The two subjects that stand tall are law and medicine. Theology never really gained a foothold in the North-Italian universities and consequently it was not a popular subject for students who visited Italy – though the few that chose to *graduate* in theology are by no means unimportant people. We only have to mention the names of Erasmus, Johannes Vredewolt and Petrus Canisius to substantiate this claim. The assessment of the number of arts students is complicated by the fact that the study of arts took place in the *universitas artium et medicinarum*, so it is not always possible to differentiate between arts and medicine students. However, if we look at the number of students who visited a university closer to home at an earlier stage in their curriculum, nearly all studied arts. Moreover, if we look at the number of graduations in the faculties of arts and medicine in Italian universities, the number of graduations in arts is rather

---

[21] Lively account in Van Kessel, *Duitse studenten te Padua*, 10-15.
[22] Op. cit., 92-117.

small and can not be compared to the quite substantial number of graduations in medicine.[23]

If we look at the geographical origin of students from the Northern Netherlands, one thing becomes very clear: the preponderance of Holland in the total number of students. In relative terms the fact that Holland was the most populated part of the Northern Netherlands cannot explain this alone. There seems to be a clear relationship with its highly urbanised character. Dutch student mobility to Italian universities had an overwhelmingly urban character. Nine out of ten students registered mention one of the larger and more important towns in their respective regions. Further prosopographical research must reveal if the towns they mention were places of birth or of provenance.[24] It is obvious that highly urbanised regions had a greater need for university trained personnel. This relationship with urbanisation can be further ascertained by looking at the importance of the several towns in other parts of the Netherlands. The cities of Utrecht – seat of the bishop –, Groningen and the towns along the IJssel river all sent relatively high numbers of students for their respective regions.

Students from the northern parts of the Netherlands – the present day provinces of Friesland, Groningen, Drenthe and Overijssel – form a considerable part of the entire population. Out of 615 no less than 157 students (25.5%) came from these parts. Their numbers are not evenly divided over the period. Students from Friesland peaked in the first and third quarter of the sixteenth century. For Groningen and Ommelanden – including Drenthe[25] – the last quarter of the fifteenth and the third quarter of the sixteenth century seem to have been the periods when students were most keen to visit Italian universities. There might be a connection to political events. After 1500 the duke of Saxony secured his power over Friesland and in the last quarter of the fifteenth century Groningen established itself as a regional power that had its zenith around 1490. Both these developments would encourage demand for highly trained government personnel.[26] The numbers for the region of Overijssel seem to have had a contrary development to those for Friesland. Its peak was in the second quarter of the fifteenth century and not even 25% of all students from Overijssel who studied in Italy did so in the sixteenth century. Might it be argued that there is a connection between the decline in (economic) power of the towns along the IJssel river,

---

[23] Frijhoff, *La société néerlandaise et ses gradués*, 83-4, analyses this situation for the late 16th and 17th centuries.

[24] For discussion of problems involved here: Pacquet, *Les matricules universitaires*, 64-70.

[25] Drenthe sent only one student to Italy in the period under investigation.

[26] With some caution one might say that these figures correspond to the general trends that Zijlstra has identified in his important *Het geleerde Friesland*, 14-16.

ever since it started to silt up after 1400, and the need for specialised academics?

As for the subject of study chosen, law and medicine were definitely most popular for students from the north-east of the Netherlands. Between them law stands tall as the main attraction with 71.3% of students against 15.9% for students of medicine. Percentages for students of medicine for the north-east are substantially lower than for most other parts of the Northern Netherlands. This seems to indicate that career chances for learned physicians in the north-eastern regions of the Netherlands were worse than they were in the western parts.[27]

The study of law was the main reason to visit Italian universities for students from the north-eastern regions. At the university of Bologna – by far the most popular for students north of the IJssel – they account for almost 40% of law students from the Northern Netherlands. At Ferrara it was even as high as 40.4%. If we compare these figures with those for the famous, highly popular law university of Orléans, where they account for some 11% of the total of the Northern Netherlands,[28] there is a strong impression that the North-Italian universities were relatively more attractive for students from Friesland, Groningen and the IJssel-region than for students from Holland and Zeeland. The latter seem to be much more western oriented, to the university of Louvain and Orléans,[29] while students from the Utrecht-region seem to favour both university poles equally.[30] The north-eastern regions of the Netherlands seem to have been oriented more towards the neighbouring German lands and their universities, and also to the universities of northern Italy.

So, in Burke's terms of the most direct and personal means of diffusing humanism,[31] we have an important group here. In what way, then, could these students exert influence and contribute to the cause of humanism? A first level is, of course, to behave as a humanist, for instance in writing, publishing and keeping a learned correspondence. There is a tendency nowadays to view the emergence of especially northern humanism in terms of generations. It has to be said that students who visited Italy were in the vanguard

---

[27] Zijlstra, *Het geleerde Friesland*, 242-5 and 251-5, discusses this for Friesland and 'Stad en Lande' (=Groningen).
[28] De Ridder-Symoens, 'Studenten uit het bisdom Utrecht aan de rechtenuniversiteit van Orléans', 94.
[29] They account for 46.7% of law students from the Northern Netherlands at North-Italian universities, but for 68.1% in Orléans: ibidem.
[30] They account for 10.8% of law students from the Northern Netherlands at North-Italian universities and for 10.4% at Orléans: ibidem.
[31] Burke, 'The Spread of Italian Humanism', 3.

in propagating humanist ideas and forms. The first piece of what is called northern protohumanist rhetoric at the University of Louvain was performed by Johannes Snavel, a citizen of Zwolle who studied at the University of Padua and whose graduation – 'domini Iohannis Snavel de Zowolis magistri in artibus clerici traiectensis diocesis' – we find on June 21 1432,[32] before he started to teach law at Louvain in the thirties of the fifteenth century.

Nobody can dispute the enormous influence that Rodolphus Agricola, who had visited Pavia and Ferrara, exerted on the spread of humanism in the crucial last three decades of the fifteenth century. He was not however the only northerner at those universities. He is known to have had contacts with several other students there, attending their graduations[33] and staying in contact with them after their Italian experience. Johannes Vredewolt and Willem Frederiks are well-known examples of them and the latter was to become part of the Adwerth circle. But Agricola was also very well acquainted with Dirk Persijn, a native from Amsterdam, who studied with him in both Pavia and Ferrara[34] and who later became professor of law at the university of Louvain.

Especially since the last quarter of the fifteenth century this population of students who visited Italy yields a harvest of several dozens of people who considered themselves humanists. They adopted Latin names and made their contribution to humanism in writing, editing and in their behaviour. We can locate them in all humanist circles. One such circle is the Adwerth or Aduard circle, centred round the monastery in the province of Groningen. People like Gansfort, Agricola, Frederiks and Canter belonged to it. This circle set the standard for the discourse on humanist learning, and their members, who also came from the neighbouring German lands, managed to exert considerable influence on schools and their schoolmasters. The school at Deventer under Alexander Hegius is perhaps the most famous example. The young Erasmus visited this school and both he and some of his classmates sought contact with the learned men of the Aduard circle.

Erasmus, who received a degree from the university of Turin in 1506, is the most well-known humanist of them all. Though he desperately wanted to become part of a learned circle in his younger years, he later became the centre of a huge one himself. He corresponded with an incredible number of

---

[32] *Acta graduum academicorum gymnasii Patavini*, I 288-9, nr. 904.

[33] At the university of Ferrara he attended no less than seven graduations of students from the Netherlands in the period 1475-1478 (Wilhelmus Frederici, Jacobus Walteri van Ameyde, Henricus ex Palude, Theodoricus Persijn, Cornelius Florentii de Goes, Lambertus Vrylinck, Niclaus Gryp de Hagis): Pardi, *Titoli dottorali dallo studio di Ferrara*, 64-5 and 68-71. In Pavia, Agricola attended the graduation of Johannes Vredewolt together with Dirk Persijn in January 1473: Sottili, *Lauree Pavesi*, 216-8.

[34] Sottili, *Lauree Pavesi*, 216-8; Pardi, *Titoli dottorali dallo studio di Ferrara*, 68-9.

important people, both in the Netherlands and abroad. His fellow travellers to Italy were among them.

As mentioned before, humanists figure prominently in the student population that went to Italy. Several dozens of them published learned work. Some were well-known prolific writers whose pages passed the printing presses. The lesser gods may not have seen their thoughts in print, but there is no denying that even these humanists of second rank functioned as propagators of the phenomenon of humanism, since they frequently constituted a local elite. It would seem that current historiography takes a stronger interest in their life and work than the older historical writing has done.[35]

But there are also more indirect ways in which ideas may be diffused. For this we have to turn to other factors than immediate contributions to culture. Looking at the social background, the social status and the university curriculum of the population, one would be inclined to think that a substantial part was predisposed to attain rank and influence; especially law graduates, such as Cobelius, Viglius of Aytta and Johan van Oldenbarnevelt,[36] were destined for high places. In their capacity they could act as patrons to humanists and artists with less influence and money. In a wider sense students who went to Italy constituted a literate group of potentially successful and influential men on whom the culture of Renaissance Italy must have made an impression and who were likely to support or even propagate humanist culture, like Van Oldenbarnevelt who set aside a substantial sum for his sons to visit Venice, Florence, Rome, Bologna and Padua; or Erasmus whose fame attracted the attention of popes and princes.

For the north-eastern parts of the Netherlands specifically one could name several examples. The most obvious example would be Viglius of Aytta, who had studied in Padua and acquired the posts of *assessor* of the *Reichskammergericht* and member of the Secret Council. In these influential positions he was at the centre of a network that included several other law graduates from Italian universities. He was able to act as mentor and protector of lawyers from Friesland and Groningen: Johannes de Mepsche and Johannes Bogerman, both *assessores* of the *Reichskammergericht*. De Mepsche even became lord chancellor of Overijssel, Drenthe and Lingen as

---

[35] For example: Santing, *Geneeskunde en humanisme*; Bloccius, *Praecepta formandis puerorum moribus perutilia*.

[36] The publication of Den Tex, 'Nederlandse studenten in de rechten te Padua', is the unforeseen outcome of his investigation into the university curriculum of Johan van Oldenbarnevelt at Padua. Although Den Tex was unable to find the evidence that Van Oldenbarnevelt had actually studied in Padua, he was right in his presupposition. In the Archivio di Stato di Padova, *Archivio notarile* (Francesco Fabriani), inv. nr. 2335, f. 550-1, I have located the graduation *in utroque iure* of 'Ioannis ab Oldenbernevelt Flander Amersfordiensis'. I hope to give this discovery some more attention elsewhere.

well as lieutenant-governor of Groningen. To name two more: Hector van Hoxwier and Gisbertus Arentsma, both counsellors at the *Hof van Friesland*.[37]

One could, however, also present some less well-known cases. Ludolphus de Veno (or Van Veen) of Kampen graduated at the university of Bologna and subsequently became dean of the cathedral chapter in Utrecht. He was a counsellor to bishop David of Utrecht and held several other important posts in the diocese. He also had contacts with people from the Adwerth and Vollenhove circles and probably brought some of them to the attention of bishop David who had considerable interest in humanists and their works. Another example is the humanist Willem Frederiks, also an alumnus of the university of Bologna, who as *persona* of St. Martin's Church was in a position to exert considerable influence on the appointment of priests in St. Martin's Church and its schoolmaster. The same goes for his sixteenth century successor, Johannes Eelts, a graduate of Ferrara. At least three of the vicars of St. Martin's and Our Lady of der Aa Church in the late fifteenth and early sixteenth century had also studied in Italy.[38] Northerners who had studied in Italy supplied no less than eight counsellors, three lawyers and one master of accounts to the *Hof van Friesland* since it had been reformed in 1527.[39] It would seem that graduates from Italian universities were well able to secure influential positions in society.

We have mentioned schools. It has been stated earlier that schools and universities were the principal means of spreading humanism. When we turn to the careers of the population, we can see that the position of professor of law or medicine turns up frequently. Until the foundation of the University of Leiden, the Northern Netherlands did not have their proper university, but we can find students in the population teaching, not only at Italian *studia*, but also at the universities of Louvain, Cologne, Heidelberg, Ingolstadt, Basle, Copenhagen, Marburg and, only later, Leiden. It is significant that at the faculty of medicine of the university of Cologne – by far the smallest faculty – no less than seven teachers were Netherlanders from the North who graduated in Italy. In this respect it is also worthwhile to mention that the first four professors of medicine at the university of Leiden – two of them from the Northern Netherlands – had all studied in Padua, at that time *the* centre of medical humanist learning.[40]

---

[37] See, for example, Postma, *Viglius van Aytta,* 79; 86; and 102.
[38] Everhardus Jarges, Lubertus Koninck and Hermannus Abbringe.
[39] See a.o. Zijlstra, *Het geleerde Friesland*, 151-8.
[40] Luyendijk-Elshout, 'Der Einfluß der italienischen Universitäten auf die medizinische Fakultät Leiden'.

There is also a connection with schools; not only in governing them, as mentioned before, but also in teaching in them. From the career profile of the population it would appear that this did not happen all too often. Normally, a student with a degree from Italy could aspire to higher positions. There were however several men who had studied medicine in Italy that did serve as *rectores* of Latin schools in towns. Gerardus Listrius of Zwolle may serve as an example. The connection between teaching in a Latin school and the study of medicine is an obvious one. A student of medicine had to be well versed in the arts to follow the courses and so a medicine graduate became a wanted candidate for the position of *rector*.

It is worth noting that the function of *rector* of a Latin school was often closely tied up with the function of town physician. In several towns we find the construction that the *rector* of the school is town doctor as well. Hadrianus Junius combined these two positions in Haarlem in the fifties of the sixteenth century. Lambert Vrijling of Groningen, a graduate of Ferrara, was *rector* of the school in Rostock before he became town physician of Groningen in 1496. The position of town physician or personal physician we find more often. This is not very surprising when we take into consideration that the medical faculties north of the Alps were always the smallest and had comparatively few students and even fewer graduations. The relatively small population of 615 people alone gives us some 156 doctorates in medicine for the period. It is exactly in these two centuries that a more professional structure of health care starts to develop in the Northern Netherlands.[41] And it would seem that students of medicine who had visited Italy and who had seen the much more elaborate structure of health care in the Italian cities played a key role in this process. To give one more example: already in 1434 the town of Kampen appointed Gerardus Johannis Bentheim, born in Kampen and another graduate of Ferrara, as town physician. Numerous cases were to follow.

Looking at students who went to Italy and trying to pinpoint how they may have influenced discourse on humanism in the Northern Netherlands is one way of looking at the connection with Italy. There is another way of looking at this connection. In the first half of the sixteenth century humanism gained foothold in the Northern Netherlands. This was the result of the activities of both prolific protagonists and a greater number of powerful, but more passive propagators and patrons. Ever since, Italy came to be viewed as an eldorado of humanist culture that an educated man or a man who wanted to be educated had to visit. Indeed, the number of students attending Italian universities – especially Padua and Siena, partly for religious

---

[41] Van Herwaarden, 'Medici in de Nederlandse samenleving in de late Middeleeuwen'.

reasons – was clearly on the rise in the second half of the sixteenth century and continued to do so in the first half of the seventeenth.[42] The dissemination of humanism is not only visible in numbers. In the sixteenth century a lot of students proudly start bearing a Latin version of their surname (Bernardus ten Broecke becomes Paludanus)[43] and they designate their origin with a correct Latin adjective, even using the term *Batavus*, which originated in humanist discourse,[44] to indicate that they come from Holland.

Rising numbers of students from the Northern Netherlands visiting Italian universities are not an isolated phenomenon: the same can be said for the Southern Netherlands and other parts of Europe.[45] It is no wonder that Justus Lipsius, who had been to Italy himself, could understand so well the longing one of his young admirers had to go to Italy, a longing, he says, 'which is innate only in the best and noblest minds.'[46] For a visit to an Italian university should be part of the educational – not necessarily scholarly – upbringing of a young man of learning and/or standing (they are not necessarily the same). The trip to Italy became part of the *Grand Tour*. A visit to Italy was an opportunity to experience an important part of European culture, classic as well as humanist.

In these few pages I have tried to give an impression of what kind of traces this interesting group of students who visited Italy has left in history, and I tried to paint a picture of a direct and personal Italian connection to northern humanism. On the one hand, this brief sketch is asking for further attention for the wider circle of people who considered themselves humanists. For I believe that in-depth investigation of humanist networking – second and first rate scholars, authors and audience – can tell us much about the diffusion of humanism. On the other hand it argues that the relationship between universities, humanism and society in the fifteenth and sixteenth centuries is one that needs further exploration. In a specific international context I have tried to discuss the connection with Italy. It would seem that research into the relationship between students, humanism and society for

---

[42] Frijhoff, *La société néerlandaise et ses gradués*.
[43] Poelhekke, 'Nederlandse leden van de Natio Germanica Artistarum te Padua', 300.
[44] Tilmans, *Aurelius en de Divisiekroniek van 1517*.
[45] De Ridder-Symoens, 'Adel en universiteiten in de zestiende eeuw', 424; Sàrközy, 'Links to Europe'.
[46] 'In Italiam cogitare te audio, nobilissime iuvenum, et audio volens. Placet ea mens, quam agnatam scio non nisi optimae cuique menti.' Justus Lipsius to Philip Lannoy, in *Epistolae*, 198, letter nr. 90.

the more frequently visited universities closer to the Netherlands (Louvain and Cologne) might yield another rich harvest.[47]

---

[47] Zijlstra, *Het geleerde Friesland,* gives promising results. Similar research for other parts of the Northern Netherlands is desirable.

APPENDIX: TABLES[*]

Table 1: Total Population of Students from the Northern Netherlands Studying in Italy (615) according to Region

	H	Z	U	G	O	F	Gr.D	Un	T
1425-50	42	5	5	10	14	4	3	1	84
1451-75	81	25	4	4	7	4	5	9	139
1476-00	35	9	18	3	10	1	15	4	95
1501-25	20	2	6	3	3	18	9	1	62
1526-50	33	4	5	7	2	10	6	5	72
1551-75	61	14	19	21	5	27	14	2	163
Reg. T	272	59	57	48	41	64	52	22	615
Reg. %	44.2	9.6	9.3	7.8	6.7	10.4	8.5	3.6	100

Table 1a: Choice of Faculty in Italy of the Total Population (%)

Faculty	%
Law	52.1
Medicine	31.8
Arts	2.6
Theology	1.5
Unknown	12.1

[*] All tables and graphs deal with attendance and graduation of students from the Northern Netherlands only. The following abbreviations have been used in the tables: H = Holland; Z = Zeeland; U = Utrecht; G = Gelre; O = Overijssel; F = Friesland; Gr.D = Groningen including Drenthe.

L = Law; M = Medicine; A = Arts; Th = Theology; Un = Unknown; P = Graduation to *Doctor* or *Licenciatus*; R(eg) (%) = Region (as percentage of total); T = Total; Fa = Faculty; 15c = fifteenth century; 16c = sixteenth century.

Table 2: Graduation and Attendance according to Faculty at the University of Bologna (1425-1575)

	PL	PM	PTh	TP	L	M	Un	T
1425-50	7	-	1	8	10	1	-	12
1451-75	14	-	-	14	23	6	2	31
1476-00	17	5	-	22	50	9	1	60
1501-25	11	8	-	19	31	10	-	41
1526-50	5	19	1	25	11	23	-	35
1551-75	13	13	-	26	17	14	-	31
T	67	45	2	114	142	63	3	210

Table 3: Attendance at the University of Bologna according to Region (1425-1575)

	H	Z	U	G	O	F	Gr.	Un	T
1425-50	1	-	3	2	5	1	-	-	12
1451-75	17	5	3	3	2	-	-	1	31
1476-00	19	4	11	3	10	-	11	2	60
1501-25	11	1	2	3	2	16	5	1	41
1526-50	19	-	2	5	-	2	3	4	35
1551-75	13	4	3	2	1	2	4	2	31
Reg. T	80	14	24	18	20	21	23	10	210
Reg. %	38.1	6.7	11.3	8.6	9.5	10	10.9	4.8	100

Table 4: Choice of Faculty according to geographical origin at the University of Bologna (1425-1575)

	L15c	L16c	TL	M15c	M16c	TM	Th	FUn	T
H	26	18	44	9	25	34	-	2	80
Z	6	3	9	3	2	5	-	-	14
U	15	4	19	2	3	5	-	-	24
G	6	4	10	1	5	6	1	1	18
O	15	2	17	1	1	2	1	-	20
F	1	18	19	-	2	2	-	-	21
Gr.D	11	9	20	-	3	3	-	-	23
Un	3	1	4	-	6	6	-	-	10
T	83	59	142	16	47	63	2	3	210

Table 5: Graduation and attendance at the University of Padua (1425-1575)

	PL	PM	PA	PT	L	M	A	Un	T
1425-50	9	16	0	25	20	36	1	9	66
1451-75	3	8	0	11	18	21	1	19	59
1476-00	0	0	0	0	4	3	0	1	8
1501-25	1	1	1	3	2	1	1	0	4
1526-50	3	1	0	4	9	3	0	1	13
1551-75	7	13	0	20	62	25	0	2	89
T	23	39	1	63	115	89	3	32	239

Table 6: Attendance at the University of Padua according to region (1425-1575)

	H	Z	U	G	O	F	GrD	Un	T
1425-50	35	4	2	8	11	2	3	1	66
1451-75	41	9	1	1	0	0	2	4	58
1476-00	4	3	1	0	0	0	0	0	8
1501-25	3	0	0	0	1	0	0	0	4
1526-50	8	2	0	1	0	3	0	0	14
1551-75	39	9	10	6	2	14	7	0	87
Reg. T	130	27	14	16	14	19	12	5	237
Reg. %	54.9	11.4	5.9	6.7	5.9	8.0	5.1	2.1	100

Table 7: Choice of Faculty according to geographical origin at the University of Padua (1425-1575)

	L15c	L16c	TL	M15c	M16c	TM	A	FaUn	T
H	23	35	58	40	14	54	1	18	131
Z	5	9	14	8	2	10	0	3	27
U	1	7	8	1	3	4	1	1	14
G	2	5	7	5	2	7	0	3	17
O	6	2	8	3	1	4	0	2	14
F	1	12	13	1	3	4	0	2	19
GrD	4	3	7	0	4	4	0	1	12
RUn	0	0	0	2	0	2	0	3	5
T	42	73	115	60	29	89	2	33	239

Table 8: Graduations at the University of Ferrara (1425-1575)

	PL	PM	PA	PTh	TP
1425-50	1	10	0	0	11
1451-75	10	24	0	1	35
1476-00	7	15	1	0	23
1501-25	2	0	0	0	2
1526-50	7	3	0	0	10
1551-75	12	3	0	0	15
T	39	55	1	1	96

Table 9: Dutch Attendance at the University of Ferrara 1425-1575 (147 individuals)

	L	M	A	Th	Un	T
1425-50	4	13	0	0	1	18
1451-75	18	31	1	1	16	67
1476-00	8	15	1	0	8	32
1501-25	3	0	0	0	0	3
1526-50	7	5	0	0	3	15
1551-75	12	3	0	0	0	15
T	52	67	2	1	28	150

Table 10: Attendance according to geographical origin at the University of Ferrara (1425-1575)

	H	Z	U	G	O	F	GrD	Un	T
1425-50	12	1	0	0	4	0	1	0	18
1451-75	36	11	1	1	5	3	4	4	65
1476-00	19	5	1	0	0	1	5	0	31
1501-25	0	0	0	0	0	1	2	0	3
1526-50	5	1	2	0	2	3	2	0	15
1551-75	3	2	4	1	0	2	3	0	15
Reg. T	75	20	8	2	11	10	17	4	147
Reg. %	51.0	13.6	5.4	1.4	7.5	6.8	11.6	2.7	100

Table 11: Choice of Faculty according to geographical origin at the University of Ferrara (1425-1575)

	L15c	L16c	TL	M15c	M16c	TM	A+Th	FaUn	T
H	19	3	22	41	5	46	0	8	76
Z	1	3	4	11	0	11	0	5	20
U	0	4	4	0	2	2	0	2	8
G	0	1	1	0	0	0	0	1	2
O	4	0	4	4	0	4	1	2	11
F	1	5	6	1	0	1	0	3	10
GrD	5	6	11	2	1	3	2	3	19
RUn	0	0	0	0	0	0	0	4	4
T	30	22	52	59	8	67	3	28	150

M. VAN DER POEL

RUDOLPH AGRICOLA'S METHOD OF DIALECTICAL READING:
THE CASE OF CICERO'S DE LEGE MANILIA*

Among the minor works of Agricola there is a commentary on Cicero's
speech *De imperio Cn. Pompeii*, or *Pro lege Manilia* (*De lege Manilia*, as the
speech is commonly called today; henceforth referred to as DLM).[1] The commentary was written between 1479, the date of the completion of Agricola's
theory of argumentation, *De inventione dialectica* (henceforth referred to as
DID), and 1485, the year of Agricola's death. Agricola's commentary on DLM
is the first of a long series of Northern humanist commentaries on this Ciceronian speech.[2] It was published for the first time in 1539, and had a second,
better edition in 1541.[3]

Agricola manifestly wrote the commentary with an educational purpose in
mind, but it is not known whether he himself actually used it for this purpose,
for instance in his lectures at Heidelberg. The commentary illustrates three
specific goals with which classical authors, and orators specifically, were read
in the *trivium* curriculum of the humanists, namely to teach the student to
understand and use classical Latin, to instill the student with factual knowledge (ancient history, political science etc.), and to teach the skill of reasoning
and of expressing thought in the form of well-structured, elegant discourse
(grammar, dialectic, rhetoric). The first, shorter part of the commentary (1620
words) is devoted to linguistic and historical issues. It discusses on the one
hand matters of classical Latin in general and Ciceronian idiom and style in
particular,[4] and on the other hand historical *realia*.[5]

* The research for this article was made possible by a grant of the Dutch Royal Academy of
Sciences. I thank Professor Kenneth Lloyd-Jones (Trinity College, Hartford, CT) for help with my
English.
[1] See for a complete bibliography of the works of Agricola, *Rodolphus Agricola Phrisius*,
313-27; Claren and Huber, 'Rudolf Agricolas Scholien zu Ciceros Rede *De lege Manilia*'.
[2] Classen, *Recht, Rhetorik, Politik*, 270 n. 17. Agricola was influenced by the commentaries
of the Italian humanist Antonio Loschi; see Mack, 'Rudolph Agricola's Reading of Literature'.
[3] Modern edition: Van der Poel, 'Rudolph Agricola's *Scholia in Orationem pro lege Manilia*'. All references to the text of the commentary are to the line numbers in this edition.
[4] The following Latin words are briefly explained or discussed: 'industria', 'industrius' (section 1 of DLM; I have followed the text of the Oxford Classical Text series, edited by A.C.
Clark, 1905); 'privatus' (2); 'auctoritas' (2); 'honores' (2); 'facultas' (2); 'suscipere poenam'
vs. 'dare poenam' (7); 'calamitas' (Agricola refers to Donatus's definition of this word; 15);
'publicani' (Agricola quotes Ulpianus's definition of this word; 16), 'fructuosus' (16, but this
word does not occur in the modern text of DLM; Agricola mentions that some believe that this is
not a classical word, while others think it is because it occurs in this Ciceronian text); 'fides'

The second, larger part (3546 words) focuses on dialectic and rhetoric. In this part, Agricola analyzes DLM as a model of composition, following his theory of argumentation developed in DID. Agricola begins this part by giving some general rhetorical information concerning DLM. He explains that DLM is a deliberative speech, containing in the middle a section belonging to the demonstrative field (namely, the encomium of Pompey); he stresses that Cicero often included demonstrative sections in his deliberative or judicial speeches, and he refers to *Pro Archia poeta* as a noteworthy example of this combination. Next, Agricola observes that DLM is divided into four standard parts of the classical oration, namely *exordium* (introduction), *narratio* (statement of facts), *confirmatio* (argumentation, including the refutation of the opponents' arguments) and *epilogus* (peroration). He then proceeds to the analysis of each part in turn.

In this paper, we shall review those sections of the analysis in which Agricola puts into practice the three principles of dialectical reading set forth in DID, namely definition of the *quaestio* (question) and its subsidiary questions, the determination of the arguments, and the determination of the topics from which the arguments are drawn. Our discussion of Agricola's analysis is inspired by two motives. On the one hand, it sets out to show that Agricola's method constitutes an innovative and useful synthesis of traditional rhetoric and dialectic; his method indeed provides a very clear understanding of the argumentative structure of a speech such as DLM, and in some cases even a better understanding than that which is provided in standard rhetorical commentaries. On the other hand, our discussion will reveal the high degree of complexity of Agricola's method, and it will be pointed out in particular that his new systematization of the topics requires close study of DID before it can be put to use. These observations raise the question of whether Agricola's

(19; Agricola refers to the definition of this word in Nonius Marcellus, who cites Cicero, *On the Republic*); 'fanum' (23); 'sanctum' (24); '(con)certare' and 'confligere' (28); 'fortitudo' (29); 'deprecator' (35); 'obsides' (35); 'centuriatus' (37); 'ferre calamitatem' and 'accipere calamitatem' (38); 'hiberna'; 'excellere' with dative and with accusative (38); 'annona' (44); 'referre ad senatum' and 'intercedere' (58); 'extare' (Agricola discusses the different meanings of this verb; 68). Moreover, Agricola notes the following instances of Ciceronian idiom and style: use of 'tempora' for 'pericula' (2); use of the clausula 'esse videatur' (24; Agricola refers to Quintilian's remark on Cicero's use of this clausula); use of 'extrema pueritia' instead of 'extrema pars pueritiae' (28).

⁵ Agricola presents historical explanations and references to source texts (mainly Appianus, Plutarch, and Florus) concerning the following *realia*: the 'comitia' (section 2), the 'equites' (4), the identity of the envoy whose ill-treatment by the Corinthians caused the Achaean war, and the identity of the envoy who was treated badly by Mithridates (11), the 'ius legationis' (11), the 'Salinae fossae' (16), Lucullus's brave, but ultimately failed leadership in the war against Mithridates (20-1; 23; 25), Pompey's achievements (28-35); the promontory Misenum and the harbor Ostia (33). Agricola also interprets Cicero's citing of past maltreatment of Roman traders or ship-owners (11) as a reference to the war against Tarentum.

method might have hampered its own success on account of its complexity and inventiveness. For, while it is certain that Agricola's DID greatly influenced the discussion on methodology in the sixteenth century and inspired many of the great sixteenth-century theorists of the *trivium*, the degree of Agricola's influence on classroom practice at large has not yet been clearly demonstrated. The fact that Agricola's commentary went through only two editions, whereas commentaries by other humanists (also those influenced by Agricola) had many editions,[6] is perhaps a sign of the fact that the use of DID in the Renaissance classroom was not so common. Our analysis suggests that one of the factors explaining such a lack of success could be the fact that schoolmasters considered Agricola's method rather complicated and demanding, and therefore chose to adopt the traditional method of analyzing speeches on the familiar basis of classical rhetoric (e.g. Quintilian's *Institutio oratoria*).

We shall confine ourselves to Agricola's analysis of the *confirmatio* (sections 6-68 of DLM). Agricola's discussion of the *exordium* (sections 1-3 of DLM) and of the *narratio* (sections 4-5 of DLM) is brief and follows mostly Quintilian's classical handbook. His discussion of the *exordium* reflects DID 2, 24,[7] which is mainly inspired by Quintilian, *Institutio oratoria* 4, 1, 6 ff., and the discussion of the *narratio* is based on *Institutio oratoria* 4, 2, to which Agricola directly refers the reader in his commentary. Agricola's succinctness concerning the first two parts of the speech is plausibly motivated by the fact that these parts do not as such aim at convincing the audience, that is, do not develop arguments. In DID 2, 16 Agricola defines two basic forms of speech, namely *expositio* (exposition), which sets matters out for an audience which follows willingly, and *argumentatio* (argumentation), which is addressed to an audience which resists or which must be forced into assent.[8] Agricola defines the *narratio* of classical speeches explicitly as one of the forms of *expositio*, alongside non-argumentative sections in philosophical and learned writings, in poetry (which mainly aims at pleasing the audience), and in history and accounts of exemplary lives and deeds (which mainly aim at explaining the nature of some thing or person).[9] The *epilogus* (sections 69-71) is also dealt with in short by Agricola. He stresses that while perorations usually contain only *expositio*, the peroration of DLM combines *expositio* with *argumentatio*. More specifically, Cicero treats two questions, albeit very briefly and in a veiled and indistinct way.

---

[6] See statistical data in Classen, *Recht, Rhetorik, Politik*, 270 n. 17.

[7] Agricola, *De inventione dialectica*, ed. Mundt, 370-2, ll. 86-114 (hereafter referred to as 370-2, 86-114M).

[8] 302-6M; see on exposition and argumentation Mack, *Renaissance Argument*, 190-202.

[9] DID 2, 22-23 (344-64M). *Expositio* in poetry and historical writings is discussed in 2, 22; *expositio* in orations and in philosophical and learned writings is discussed in 2, 23.

We shall now proceed to our examination of Agricola's observations on the *argumentatio*, following the three steps distinguished in DID as indicated above, namely definition of the *quaestio* (question) and its subsidiary questions, the determination of the arguments, and the determination of the topics from which the arguments are drawn.

Main question and subsidiary questions

Agricola explains in DID 2, 8, that, if we are to define exactly the subject of a given text in prose or poetry, we must formulate it in the shape of a *quaestio* (question).[10] He discusses in detail how the *quaestio* of a given text can be determined. To this end, he distinguishes two classes of texts: non-argumentative texts on the one hand, such as poetry or history, and argumentative texts on the other hand, such as learned debates (*disputationes*) or juridical and deliberative speeches. In the second category, to which DLM belongs, the question coincides with the point concerning which the parties disagree.[11] Thus, the question of DLM is, according to Agricola, 'whether Pompey should be chosen by the Roman people to command in the war against Mithridates'.[12]

This question indicates the subject of the entire speech, and it is also a broad summing-up of the *confirmatio*. As such, the question can be subdivided into subsidiary questions, and Agricola therefore calls it the main question (*quaestio principalis*; l. 276). In DID 2, 14, Agricola explains how the question of a given discourse can be subdivided into subsidiary questions containing the key propositions which are to be treated in the main body of the discourse.[13] Agricola points out that Cicero has chosen, from the large number and wide variety of possible questions contained in the main question, to divide his main question into two subsidiary questions, by virtue of their utility.[14] The subsidiary questions concern two aspects of the element 'war against Mithridates', which occurs in the main question, namely (1) the necessity of this war, and (2) its size and danger, thus:

---

[10] See DID 2, 8 on the definition of the question; 2, 9-11 on the three ways to demarcate questions (244-72M). See Mack, *Renaisssance Argument,* 181-5.

[11] DID 2, 12 (274-8M). Agricola speaks in this case of the *status quaestionis,* a term borrowed from the ancient theory of juridical oratory. DID 2, 13 (280-4M) discusses the determination of the question in texts which do not deal with controversial issues, for instance demonstrative speeches. See Mack, *Renaissance Argument,* 185-9.

[12] 'An Cn. Pompeius sit a populo Romano ad Mithridaticum bellum deligendus' (l. 277-8).

[13] 284-296M; Mack, *Renaissance Argument,* 185-9.

[14] Agricola speaks of the 'mire utilis explicatio' of the two subsidiary questions (l. 284).

(1) if it were not certain that this war is necessary, there would be no
need to elect a general;
(2) if this war were not large-scale and therefore dangerous, it would not
be necessary to elect Pompey, since any general would do.[15]

The schematic representation of the *confirmatio* in two questions is very
efficient, because it shows that the three main points dealt with in the *confirmatio* are closely linked. These three points are, as Cicero himself indicates:
genus belli or *necessitas belli* (the kind of war; the danger of the war),
magnitudo belli (size of the war) and *imperator deligendus* (the choice of a
general) (sections 6 and 49). The advantage of Agricola's schematic arrangement is evident: it makes clear at a glance that the encomium of Pompey
(sections 26-59) fits well into the sequence of arguments developed in DLM.
This point is particularly important to Agricola, as is also clear from his
detailed analysis of section 27 and the beginning of 28, which serve as the
connection between Cicero's second point (the size of the war) and third point
(the choice of a general, that is, the eulogy of Pompey). As we shall see
below, Agricola's analysis of this passage explains by which sequence of
thoughts, represented in the form of three mutually connected syllogisms, the
praise of Pompey is logically connected with the necessity and magnitude of
the war. The advantage of Agricola's approach is that it reveals how Cicero,
through clever, logically correct reasoning, succeeds in disguising his political
reasons for praising Pompey. Agricola thus provides us with a very clear
understanding of Cicero's oratorical skill. It was indeed the fact that the outcome of the vote on the bill of Manilius was wholly settled at the time of
Cicero's speech, and it is widely accepted that Cicero used Manilius's invitation to address the assembly simply to gratify his powerful ally in political
terms, hoping thus to increase his chances of acquiring the consulship.[16]

In DID 2, 14, Agricola discerns two kinds of subsidiary questions, namely
those that are derived from the words of the main question ('ex verbis'), and
those that are derived from the content of the words of the main question ('ex
eis, quae verbis continentur'). The second category is subdivided into two
parts. Subsidiary questions either necessarily belong to the content of the
words from the main question ('necessario'), as a species is necessarily part of
the content of a genus, or they do not necessarily form part of the main question, but are part of it by virtue of a particular circumstance of time or place

[15] 'Nisi enim constitisset bellum hoc esse necessarium, nihil causae futurum erat, cur ad id
bellum ullus deligeretur imperator, et rursum, nisi magnum fuisset ac proinde periculosum, tum
necesse non fuisset Pompeium huic bello ducem creari, quum alius quivis ei bello sufficere potuisset' (l. 284-8).
[16] Gelzer, *Cicero*, 55-6.

('per conditionem', e.g. when a general question or *thesis* is turned into a particular question or *hypothesis*).[17] Agricola observes in his commentary that the two subsidiary questions of DLM belong to the second category. The first subsidiary question follows 'necessario' from the main question, the second subsidiary question follows 'per conditionem.' We observe, however, that in this particular case the distinction is not very clear, and this also appears from the fact that Agricola initially says that the first subsidiary question follows 'per conditionem' from the main question, but then changes this qualification to 'necessario.' Agricola's wavering suggests that this part of his dialectic is too theoretical to be immediately useful in practice.

The determination of the arguments

In DID 2, 26 and 27, Agricola explains in detail how the dialectical essence of complicated texts in prose or poetry can be found. This involves the determination of the topics (*loci argumentorum*) from which are drawn the individual arguments developed both in the course of the treatment of the questions, and in other argumentative passages (such as, in the case of DLM, the *peroratio*). In order to perform this task, the reader must have a command of two skills. First, he must know by heart the topics and understand their application, and secondly, he must be able to recognize the individual arguments. We shall now focus on Agricola's discussion of the second point.

Agricola explains that it is difficult to recognize the arguments used in an oration, because they are usually hidden beneath the orator's artifices and covered over with figures of speech. In order to uncover the arguments, it is useful to reduce the elaborate argumentations to the elementary forms of reasoning, namely syllogisms and enthymemes (deductions) on the one hand, and enumerations and examples (inductions) on the other hand.[18] In DID 2, 26 Agricola emphasizes that this technique is valuable for three reasons: first, it makes it possible to arrive at a well-founded judgment on the quality of a given author, in other words, it develops our literary taste; secondly, it provides a practical understanding of *inventio* and *elocutio* and specially of how the proper *elocutio* flows organically from the *inventio*; and finally, it furnishes the reader in the long run with a basic supply of arguments which may be used in any given case.[19]

Following his own rules set forth in DID, Agricola represents the content of the *confirmatio* of DLM by means of three series of mutually linked syllo-

---

[17] 286, 9-290, 99M.
[18] DID 2, 18 (314-22M).
[19] 386, 19-388, 48M.

gisms, enthymemes and enumerations; the first series comprehends the discussion of the first subsidiary question, the second series the discussion of the second subsidiary question, the third series the discussion of the *refutatio*. Through this reduction of large textual units to the basic forms of reasoning (syllogism, enthymeme, enumeration), Agricola adequately reveals the varying degree of complexity in Cicero's argumentations. For instance, it becomes clear that the rather long passage discussing the size and danger of the war (sections 20-26) contains only one consideration (one syllogism). On the other hand, we shall see that section 27 and the beginning of 28 contain as many as three considerations and hence require three syllogisms.

Moreover, Agricola's approach reveals the inner cohesion of the argumentation, which covers several sections of the speech. Take for instance the analysis of Pompey's talent in sections 29 through 42. The individual talents are discussed successively in two groups: first, skill of organization, courage, painstaking execution, prompt action, foresight in planning (section 29 ff.), then integrity, moderation, friendliness, trustworthiness, human feeling (section 36 ff.). Agricola brings these two series of talents together in one enthymeme, thus appropriately revealing the coherence between sections 29 ff. and sections 36 ff. Another example illustrating the strength of Agricola's approach is the definition of sections 52-58 as the refutation of the minor proposition of the second syllogism in the refutation. In these sections, Cicero gives a lengthy discussion of Pompey's recent exploits, which is for the most part factually beside the point.[20] Yet Agricola's analysis shows how it is nevertheless logically connected with the issue at hand, and thus reveals how it can indeed be seen as an effective passage in dialectical terms.

The following survey contains a full description of the argumentations which Agricola discerns in DLM.

First subsidiary question: the necessity of the war

The first subsidiary question covers sections 6-20 of DLM and consists, according to Agricola, of four sets of argumentation ('argumentationes principales', ll. 294-5; 318-9; 334-5; 345-6), which prove that the war against Mithridates must be waged. Each of the four sets of argumentation begins in the *partitio* (section 6), to be developed successively in sections 7-20.

---

[20] See Classen, *Recht, Rhetorik, Politik*, 296-8.

The first argumentation

Cicero formulates the first argumentation in the following proposition: 'Agitur salus sociorum atque amicorum, pro qua multa maiores vestri magna et gravia bella gesserunt' (The safety of our allies and friends is at stake, on whose behalf your ancestors fought so many wars; section 6).

In order to grasp the pertinence of this proposition, two steps must be taken. The first part of the sentence, 'the safety of our allies and friends is at stake', comprises the minor proposition of a syllogism which Agricola formulates as follows: (1)

> You must necessarily fight the war in which the safety of our allies is at stake;
> The safety of our allies is at stake in this war against Mithridates;
> Therefore you must necessarily fight this war.[21]

The second part of the sentence, 'on whose behalf your ancestors fought so many wars', contains the proof of the major proposition of the first syllogism. Agricola formulates this proof in the following enthymeme: our ancestors have waged many large-scale wars on behalf of their allies; therefore we must undertake a war, when the safety of our allies is in danger.[22]

Agricola observes next that one could deny the veracity of the proposition in the enthymeme. Therefore, Cicero has added in sections 12 (second sentence)-14 an enumeration of the various wars which the Romans have waged on behalf of their allies.

The second argumentation

The second argumentation is formulated by Cicero in the following proposition: 'Aguntur certissima populi Romani vectigalia et maxima, quibus amissis et pacis ornamenta et subsidia belli requiretis' (solid, substantial sources of national income are at stake; if you let these go, not only will the funds needed to pay for war be lost, but your own peace-time comforts will go as well;[23] section 6). As in the case of the first argumentation, two steps must be taken in order to grasp the pertinence of this argumentation. The first part of the

---

[21] 'Illud bellum necessario vobis gerendum est, in quo agitur salus sociorum; At in hoc bello Mithridatico salus sociorum agitur; Proinde hoc bellum necessario vobis suscipiendum atque gerendum est' (l. 296-9).

[22] 'Maiores nostri sociorum causa multa et magna bella gesserunt; Proinde ea nobis suscipienda, in quibus salus agitur sociorum' (l. 306-8).

[23] Translation by Grant, *Selected Political Speeches of Cicero*, 37-8.

sentence, 'solid, substantial sources of national income are at stake,' constitutes a paraphrase of the following syllogism: (2)

> Any war, in which solid, substantial sources of national income are at stake, must be fought by you;
> In this war, solid, substantial sources of national income are at stake;
> Therefore, this war must be fought by you.[24]

The second part of the sentence, 'if you let these go, not only will the funds needed to pay for war be lost, but your own peace-time comforts will go as well', hides a syllogism which constitutes the proof of the major proposition of the preceding syllogism, thus: (3)

> You must defend by means of war all those things which, if you let them go, will cause your peace-time comforts and the funds needed to pay for war to go as well;
> If you let go the sources of national income, your peace-time comforts and the funds needed to pay for war will go as well;
> Therefore, you must defend by means of war the sources of national income.[25]

The third argumentation

Cicero formulates the third argumentation as follows: 'Aguntur bona multorum civium, quibus est a vobis et ipsorum et rei publicae causa consulendum' (The personal property of many of our individual citizens is at stake, whom you are under an obligation to protect, both for their own sake and in the national interests of Rome)[26] (section 6). According to Agricola, this sentence constitutes a syllogism of which the major proposition has been deleted. He gives the complete syllogism: (4)

> You must undertake war to defend the personal property of those people, whose interests you and your generals must protect;
> You and your generals must protect the interests of the citizens;

---

[24] 'In quocunque bello aguntur maxima et certissima vectigalia populi Romani, id bellum vobis suscipiendum; Atqui in hoc bello aguntur maxima ac certissima populi Romani vectigalia; Proinde hoc bellum vobis suscipiendum atque gerendum' (l. 319-23).

[25] 'Quaecunque res sunt eiusmodi, ut eis amissis et ornamenta pacis et belli subsidia sitis requisituri, eae res vobis armis ac bello tutandae sunt; Atqui vectigalibus amissis ornamenta pacis et belli subsidia requiretis; Proinde vectigalia vobis armis ac bello defendenda sunt' (l. 326-9).

[26] Translation by Grant, *Selected Political Speeches of Cicero*, 38.

Therefore you must undertake war to defend the personal property of many citizens.[27]

The sections in which the personal property of these citizens is discussed (17-19) are considered by Agricola as the proof of the minor of the above syllogism (syllogism 4).

The fourth argumentation

Agricola's fourth argumentation commences in section 7, in which Cicero, after having mentioned the Romans' appetite for glory in section 6, starts his discussion of this point. Agricola reduces section 7 to the following syllogism: (5)

> You must certainly undertake any war in which you can acquire glory and expunge the memory of disgrace;
> You can acquire glory and expunge the memory of disgrace in this war;
> Therefore you must undertake this war.[28]

As Agricola sees it, Cicero then proves both the major proposition and the minor proposition of this syllogism. The proof of the major proposition is included in sections 11 and 12 (first sentence), and is represented by the following syllogism: (6)

> You must undertake war for the same reasons, whatever they are, for which your ancestors waged wars;
> Your ancestors waged many wars in order to acquire glory and expunge the memory of disgrace;
> Therefore you must also wage war in order to acquire glory and expunge the memory of disgrace.[29]

---

[27] 'Quoruncunque utilitati vos et imperatores vestri consulere debetis, propter eorum etiam bona defendenda bellum est vobis suscipiendum; Atqui civium utilitati vos et imperatores consulere debetis; Proinde ad defendenda bona multorum civium bellum est vobis suscipiendum' (l. 336-40).

[28] 'In quocunque bello gloria vobis quaerenda est et ignominia delenda, id bellum omnino suscipere debetis; Atqui in hoc bello et paranda est vobis gloria et ignominia delenda; Proinde hoc bellum vobis suscipiendum' (l. 346-9).

[29] 'Ob quascunque causas maiores vestri bella susceperunt ac gesserunt, ob easdem et vos bellum et suscipere et gerere debetis; Atqui maiores vestri plurima bella gesserunt ad parandam gloriam et ignominiam abolendam; Proinde vos quoque gloriae parandae et ignominiae abolendae causa bellum suscipere ac gerere debetis' (l. 354-9).

The proof of the minor proposition of the fifth syllogism is contained in the second part of section 7 through section 11, where Cicero reviews the acts through which Mithridates has caused the Romans to suffer disgrace, which has not yet been avenged.

Agricola observes about this argumentation that it seems stronger in appearance than in reality ('Habet haec argumentatio plus in specie quam re ipsa', l. 350). This observation explains why Agricola discusses the glory of the Romans as the fourth and last argument for the necessity of the war, whereas it manifestly counts for Cicero as the first and most important of the arguments. Agricola's remark suggests that the humanist is knowingly distorting the meaning of the text, probably in order to make it compatible with the teaching of Christian morality. In one other passage of his commentary, Agricola makes an observation which shows that his reading of Cicero aims at developing not only the student's cognition and linguistic skills, but also his sense of Christian values. The observation in question constitutes a comment on Cicero's proof of Pompey's integrity in sections 30-37. As we shall see, Agricola represents this proof in the form of an enthymeme, based on the topic of the opposites. To this, he adds that two key Christian tenets can be rendered in the same form:

> Similarly one should argue: The soul which sins will die, hence the soul which does not sin shall live; if one must do good to one's friends, then one must do evil to one's foes, yet Christ forbids this.[30]

Second subsidiary question: the size and danger of the war

Agricola explains that Cicero discusses the second subsidiary question in two steps, the first comprising sections 20-26, the second comprising sections 27-50. Section 22 occupies, according to Agricola, a separate place, because it contains an implied objection which might lead to the belief that the war against Mithridates is not large-scale and dangerous.

The sections 20-26 comprise an extended, but straightforward argumentation, which Agricola summarizes in the following syllogism: (1)

> Any war which is waged by two powerful kings and many belligerent nations must be large-scale and dangerous;
> This war is waged by the two most powerful kings, Mithridates and Tigranes, and extremely belligerent nations ally with them;

---

[30] 'Eodem modo argumentetur: Anima quae peccat morietur, ergo quae non peccat vivet; Si amicis benefaciendum, ergo inimicis male, verum hoc vetat Christus.' (l. 465-7)

Therefore this war must be large-scale.[31]

Next, the sections 27-50 are constructed as follows. The ratiocinative structure of sections 27 and the beginning of 28 is so complex that it requires no fewer than three syllogisms to understand its purport. Agricola takes the first sentence of section 28 as a starting point: 'Ego enim sic existimo, in summo imperatore quattuor has res inesse oportere: scientiam rei militaris, virtutem, auctoritatem, felicitatem' (The ideal general, I submit, should possess four qualities – military knowledge, talent, prestige and luck).[32] The first syllogism phrases the implicit thought which links the second subsidiary question with the first, namely the thought that a necessary and dangerous war asks for the best general. Agricola remarks that Cicero considered this thought to be widely accepted and hence left it unspoken. Agricola expresses it in the following syllogism: (2)

> The best general must be chosen to command in a necessary and dangerous war;
> This war against Mithridates is necessary and dangerous;
> Therefore the best general must be chosen to command in this war.[33]

The following syllogism picks up the conclusion of the preceding syllogism and leads to the conclusion that Pompey must be chosen as general: (3)

> He, then, who is the best general must be made the commander in this war;
> Pompey is the best general of our generation;
> Therefore Pompey alone must be made the commander in this war.[34]

The final syllogism proves the minor proposition of the preceding syllogism: (4)

---

[31] 'Quod enim bellum duo magni reges gerunt, quod multae ac bellicosae gentes suscipiunt, id magnum ac periculosum sit oportet; Atqui hoc bellum duo potentissimi reges Mithridates et Tigranes gerunt, similiter et bellicosissimae gentes eis sese adiungunt; Proinde hoc bellum magnum sit necesse est' (l. 369-74).

[32] Translation by Grant, *Selected Political Speeches of Cicero*, 48.

[33] 'Ad bellum necessarium ac periculosum deligendus est imperator optimus; Hoc autem bellum et necessarium et periculosum est; Proinde ad hoc bellum optimus imperator deligendus est' (l. 382-5).

[34] 'Is demum huic bello praeficiendus est, qui imperator sit optimus; Atqui Pompeius optimus nostro hoc aevo est imperator; Proinde solus Pompeius huic bello praeficiendus est' (l. 385-8).

He must be judged the best general, who chiefly has the following four
    qualities: military knowledge, talent, luck and prestige;
Pompey chiefly has these four qualities;
Therefore Pompey must be judged the best general.[35]

As we saw above, Agricola's analysis of these sections succeeds in showing
that the encomium of Pompey fits well into the argumentative pattern of the
speech.

The remaining part of the sections 28-50, covering the encomium of Pompey, comprises an extended series of arguments proving that Pompey possesses the qualities required to be hailed as the best general. Cicero discusses
each quality separately.

Military knowledge

Cicero discusses this quality in the latter part of section 28. Agricola distinguishes two parts in Cicero's argument. The first part comprises an enumeration of relevant facts from Pompey's biography, namely the fact that he
moved to the practical study of war at an early age, that in his youth he was a
soldier in the army of an outstanding general, and that in early adulthood he
commanded an immense army. The second part concerns the number of wars
which Pompey has fought; this point is presented in the following syllogism:
(5)

Whoever has experience in nearly every war must have outstanding mili-
    tary knowledge;
Pompey has experience in nearly every war;
Therefore Pompey must have outstanding military knowledge.[36]

The minor proposition of this syllogism has a separate proof, namely the
enumeration, in the latter part of section 28, of the wars which Pompey has
waged.

---

[35] 'Ille demum optimus imperator censeri debet, in quo haec quatuor potissimum insunt: rei
militaris scientia, virtus, felicitas, authoritas; Atqui haec quatuor potissimum insunt Pompeio;
Ergo Cn. Pompeius optimus censeri debet imperator' (l. 390-3).

[36] 'Quisquis in omnibus pene bellis exercitatus atque versatus est, huic praecipua quaedam
rei militaris scientia inest; Atqui Cn. Pompeius in omnibus pene bellis exercitatus atque versatus est; Proinde Cn. Pompeio necesse est praecipuam quandam rei militaris scientiam inesse' (l.
424-8).

Talent

This quality is discussed in sections 29-42. Cicero enumerates a number of aspects of Pompey's talent in sections 29 and 36, which Agricola summarizes in the following enthymeme:

> Pompey has the skill of meticulous organisation, courage in danger, painstaking execution, prompt action, foresight in planning (section 29), and furthermore integrity, moderation, friendliness, trustworthiness, human feeling (section 36);
> Therefore Pompey has, as general, every possible talent.[37]

Next, the different talents are discussed separately. In sections 30-35 ('per versus aliquot', as Agricola says, l. 451-2) Cicero enumerates some proofs of Pompey's meticulous organization, courage, painstaking execution and prompt action.

In sections 37-39, Pompey's integrity is discussed; Agricola summarizes Cicero's words in the following enthymeme:

> Those generals are dishonest, in whose army centurions' commissions are sold, who dole out money to the magistrates or leave it profitably invested in Rome (section 37), and who furthermore inflict more damage on our allies than on our enemies (section 38);
> Therefore Pompey, in whom we detect none of these things, is honorable.[38]

Pompey's moderation is discussed in section 40. Agricola explains how Cicero argues that Pompey's swiftness is a sign of his temperance. The rationale of the sentence 'Unde illam tantam celeritatem et tam incredibilem cursum inventum putatis?' (How do you suppose he managed to attain that extraordinary speed on this astonishing journey?)[39] is represented in the following syllogism: (6)

---

[37] 'In Cn. Pompeio inest labor in negociis, fortitudo in periculis, industria in agendo, celeritas in conficiendo, in providendo consilium, item in eodem est innocentia, temperantia, comitas, fides, humanitas; Proinde omnes virtutes in Cn. Pompeio imperatore inveniuntur' (l. 446-50). I have used Grant's translation of sections 29 and 36 (*Selected Political Speeches of Cicero*, 49 and 53).

[38] 'In quorum imperatorum exercitu centuriatus venduntur, qui pecuniam magistratibus dividunt vel Romae in quaestum relinquunt, item sociis plura damna quam hostibus inferunt, hi sunt nocentes; Ergo Pompeius, in quo nihil tale esse vidimus, est innocens' (l. 461-5).

[39] Translation by Grant, *Selected Political Speeches of Cicero*, 54.

Whoever attains utmost speed in bringing to conclusion wars must also
   possess absolute moderation;
Pompey attains utmost speed in bringing wars to conclusion;
Therefore Pompey must also possess absolute moderation.[40]

In the remaining part of section 40, Cicero sets out to prove this syllogism by
explaining that Pompey's swiftness must necessarily be a result of his moderation. To this end, he first denies that the swiftness was due to his exceptional
rowing power, a newly discovered method of navigation or a unique combination of winds. Secondly, Cicero argues that lack of moderation usually causes
generals to be slow; hence, Pompey's swiftness must be the result of moderation.

Finally, Pompey's friendliness is discussed in sections 41-42. Pompey's
possession of this talent is argued by showing that he was an easily accessible
person.

Prestige

Pompey's prestige is discussed in sections 43-46. In section 43, two points are
brought to the fore to prove that Pompey has prestige. The first point is the
fact that the enemy stands in awe of Pompey. The second point is summarized
by means of the following syllogism: (7)

Whoever has an illustrious name, great exploits and great marks of esteem conferred by your assembly, must have the greatest prestige;
Pompey's name is the most illustrious, his exploits are the greatest and
   your assembly has conferred great marks of esteem to him;
Therefore, Pompey has the greatest prestige.[41]

According to Agricola, sections 44-46 contain a further explanation of this
syllogism. More specifically, they constitute an explanation of either the
major or the minor proposition.

---

[40] 'In quocunque est summa quaedam bellorum conficiendorum celeritas, in eo et summam
temperantiam inesse necesse est; Atqui in Cn. Pompeio summa quaedam bellorum conficiendorum inest celeritas; Proinde in eodem Pompeio summam inesse temperantiam necesse est' (l.
472-6).
[41] 'Cuiuscunque hominis illustre nomen est et magnae res gestae et de quo vos magna ac
praeclara iudicia fecistis, in eo homine summa nimirum inest authoritas; Nomen Pompeii multo
est illustrissimum, res autem gestae maximae et de eodem vos magna et praeclara iudicia fecistis; Ergo in Pompeio summa nimirum inest authoritas' (l. 515-20). I have used Grant's translation of section 43 (*Selected Political Speeches of Cicero*, 55-6).

Luck

Pompey's last quality, his luck, is discussed in sections 47-48. In section 47, Cicero argues the relevance of this quality. Agricola formulates the rationale of this point in the following enthymeme:

> When Fabius Maximus, Marcellus, Scipio and Marius were chosen as generals, their luck was one of the reasons why they were chosen;
> Hence luck must be one of the reasons when every general is chosen.[42]

In section 48, Pompey's luck is shown by referring to his success, which is marked by four facts: the support of the Romans, the concurrence of the allies, the obedience of the enemies, and the cooperation of the winds and weather. This point is summarized by Cicero through the following reasoning: We consider many people lucky who hardly have the kind of luck that Pompey has; therefore we must not doubt that Pompey possesses the utmost luck.[43]

The refutation

Agricola deals with the refutation, comprising sections 51-68, in a much more limited way than the first part of the *confirmatio*. In DID 2, 21, Agricola discusses the *refutatio* in oratory.[44] He discerns two types of refutation: first, various 'actual' refutations ('verae solutiones'), which focus on the matter at hand and through which it is argued that the argumentation of the opponent is formally invalid for some reason, and secondly, various refutations 'of the man himself' ('solutiones ad hominem'), to which the orator will resort if he has no real arguments to refute his opponent. As it appears from the commentary, Agricola finds that Cicero used both kinds of refutation in DLM.

In the *refutatio* of DLM, Cicero sets out to refute the authoritative judgment of Catulus and Hortensius.[45] The refutation comprises two parts.

The first part comprises an 'actual' refutation. It begins with a general point. Cicero argues that in the case at hand, reason should weigh heavier than

---

[42] 'In Fabio Maximo, in Marcello, in Scipione, in Mario habita fuit ratio felicitatis; Proinde in omni imperatore deligendo felicitatis ratio habenda est' (l. 543-5).

[43] 'Multi alii sunt haudquaquam tam felices quam est Pompeius, et tamen hos felices iudicamus; Proinde nobis esse dubium non debet, quin in Pompeio summa quaedam felicitas insit' (l. 554-6).

[44] 336-344M.

[45] Agricola says that this comprises the 'prima obiectio' (l. 561), but this is a mistake, because the entire *refutatio* is taken up by Cicero's discussion of the opinions of Catulus and Hortensius.

authoritative opinions (section 51). This proposition is represented by Agricola in the following syllogism: (1)

> Authoritative opinions must only be resorted to, when there is no reason
>   strong enough to decide the matter either way;
> But in this case, the facts themselves provide adequate reason;
> Therefore, we must look here not at what many men assert, but at what
>   the facts of the case require.[46]

Cicero continues by discussing Hortensius's point that the supreme command ought not to be given to one man (section 52). Agricola explains that this point can be phrased in the form of a syllogism, whose major proposition comprises the unspoken supposition that Rome is a democracy, not a monarchy or an aristocracy. Agricola then formulates the minor proposition and conclusion as follows: (2)

> Wherever the people rules, power should not be given to one person;
> To give power to one person is to create a monarchy.[47]

According to Agricola, Cicero refutes Hortensius's point by opposing the minor proposition of the above syllogism (sections 52-58). In these sections Cicero argues, as Agricola points out, that the minor proposition in question is not always true, and specially that in critical times, democracies must hand over all power to one person, as many precedents show.

   Agricola continues his analysis of the first part of the refutation by discussing Cicero's resistance to Catulus's point. Agricola first analyzes Cicero's paraphrase of Catulus's clever interrogation of the audience, through which Catulus argues that the Roman people acts unwisely by setting all its hope on one person, because that person might die (section 59). Cicero refutes this point in two parts. First, he voices the audience's answer to Catulus's question: it says that the Romans will set their hope on Catulus, if something might befall Pompey. The second rebuttal of Catulus's point comprises the passage in which Cicero refutes the thought that there is no precedent for the proposal to give the supreme command to Pompey (sections 60-67). Agricola formulates Catulus's objection in the following syllogism: (3)

---

[46] 'Tunc demum recurrendum est ad authoritates, quum nulla ratio satis efficax in hanc vel illam partem adduci potest; At in hac causa satis aperta ratio est res ipsa; Proinde hic videndum non est quid multi dicant, sed quid res ipsa postulet' (l. 567-70).
[47] 'Ubicunque populi imperium est, ibi ad unum omnia referri non debent; Iam omnia deferre ad unum aliud non est, quam monarchiam quandam constituere' (l. 575-7).

It is not fitting that we do something which goes against the instructions of our forefathers;

To give the supreme command to one person goes against the instructions of our forefathers;

Therefore it is not fitting that we give the supreme command to one person.[48]

Agricola argues that Cicero shows both the major and the minor proposition of this syllogism to be false. The falseness of the minor proposition is demonstrated by the fact that the forefathers believed that the interest of the state must always prevail and therefore often, of necessity, they deviated from usual practice. The falseness of the major proposition is argued by pointing out that the forefathers indeed often deviated from usual practice, and that therefore the same thing must be done in this situation.

Agricola then points out that section 68 contains the conclusion of the first part of the refutation of the opinions of Hortensius and Catulus, as well as the beginning of its second part. In the second part, which comprises a refutation 'ad hominem', Cicero argues that many men hold a view contrary to that of Hortensius and Catulus.

Determination of the topics

In DID Agricola discerns 24 topics, subdivided into four groups, as follows.[49] The first ten topics constitute the internal topics (*loci interni*). (1) Definition of a thing, (2) its genus, (3) species, (4) property and *differentia* (specific difference), (5) whole, (6) parts and (7) conjugates. These topics relate to the inner substance of the thing, from which the thing receives what it is ('in substantia rei'). (8) Adjacents, (9) actions and (10) subject are inherent to the thing, but bring a certain manner or disposition to it ('circa substantiam rei'). The fourteen remaining topics constitute the external topics (*loci externi*). (11) Efficient cause, (12) final cause, (13) effects and (14) *destinata* (intended designs) are the cognates which share their origin. Agricola also uses the term *eventa* to denote the effects and *destinata* collectively. (15) Place, (16) time

---

[48] 'Nihil a nobis fieri decet quod sit contra instituta maiorum nostrorum; Atqui unum omnibus bellis praefici, est contra instituta maiorum; Proinde unum aliquem a nobis omnibus bellis praefici non decet' (l. 606-9).

[49] This survey reproduces the diagram of Agricola's topics in Alardus's edition (DID), 25; English translation in Mack, *Renaissance Argument*, 146. See also the diagram of Agricola's topics in Phrissemius's edition, Cologne 1528, 22.

and (17) *connexa*[50] are the *applicita*, which added to the thing from outside
provide it with a certain disposition and name. Both cognates and *applicita* are
necessarily joined to the thing. (18) Contingents, (19) name of a thing, (20)
opinions, (21) comparisons, (22) similars and dissimilars are accidents which
can exist with or without a thing. Finally, (23) opposites and (24) *distantia* (or
diversa, differentia) are repugnants (that is, the same thing cannot participate
in both). Accidents and repugnants are joined without necessity to the thing.

    According to Agricola, the topics constitute the essence of dialectic, as the
starting-point of both the definition of concepts and of the process of reasoning. The above definition and arrangement of the topics offers a critical synthesis of the topical system of ancient rhetoric, such as it had been discussed
in various forms, mainly by Cicero (*Topica*), Quintilian (*Institutio oratoria* V,
10, 20-125, on the *loci argumentorum* in the *confirmatio* of speeches) and
Boethius (*De differentiis topicis*, in which dialectical and rhetorical topics are
discussed separately). Agricola's division of the topics into internal and
external topics is inspired by the division in Cicero's *Topica*, which was also
used by Boethius. Agricola adopts most of the topics of Cicero (and Boethius), but changes the place of some topics within the system or adjusts the
explanation of their nature and function. Another noteworthy characteristic of
Agricola's topical system is that it abolishes the distinction between on the
one hand dialectical topics intended for use in general discussions, and on the
other hand the rhetorical topics such as they are discussed by Quintilian,
namely with the focus on the concrete circumstances (divided into *res* and
personae) of a given *causa*.

    Agricola discusses at length his division of the topics, their differences,
and the nature and practical application of each individual topic in DID 1, 4-
28.[51] Careful examination of these chapters is necessary if one wishes to
evaluate the particular merit of Agricola's system and to compare its practical
use in the analysis of a speech such as DLM with the practical use of the
classical topics. Such an evaluation and comparison is not possible in the
context of this paper, but a brief explanation concerning the role of the topics
in Agricola's art of reasoning is necessary to understand their function in the
commentary on DLM.

    Agricola defines the topics as the common headings containing everything
that can be said about any subject.[52] For instance, every object or concept has
a definition, denoting its genus and *differentia* (e.g. man is a living being

---

[50] These are elements which are necessarily linked to the thing, but not forming part of its
substance (e.g. 'wealth' is a *connexum* of 'rich man').
[51] 30-186M. Mack offers detailed observations on Agricola's topics in *Renaissance Argument*, 130-67, and in 'Agricola's Topics', in *Rodolphus Agricola Phrisius*, 257-69.
[52] DID 1, 2; 18, 89-20, 112M.

gifted with reason), and so on. Agricola's topics provide a detailed framework for the definition of concepts, which Agricola calls *descriptio rei*.[53] A topical description of two concepts results in a list of likenesses and differences, revealing in which respects the two concepts agree or differ. When the two concepts are joined in a proposition, the likenesses and differences revealed by the topical description will constitute the arguments pro or con the proposition.[54] This process of discovering arguments on the basis of topical description (*inventio*) is presented by Agricola as the foundation of reasoning.

In the case of topical reading the process goes in reverse. After the reduction of elaborate texts to the basic forms of deductive and inductive reasoning, the process of identifying the topics can begin. The topic of an inductive argumentation (comprising enumerations or examples) is by definition either species (topic 3) or part (topic 6).[55] In the case of deductive argumentations (i.e., syllogisms or enthymemes), the process of finding the topics is more complicated. The middle term of each syllogism must be compared with the major term on the one hand and the minor term on the other. This comparison reveals two topics, which function as the arguments of the syllogism. In order to illustrate this, let us take a look at the first syllogism which Agricola defines in the *confirmatio* of DLM:

> You must necessarily fight the war in which the safety of our allies is at stake;
> The safety of our allies is at stake in this war against Mithridates;
> Therefore you must necessarily fight this war.

The argument is the middle term of the syllogism, that is, the safety of our allies. The comparison of the middle term with the major and the minor term yields the topics of the argument; the topic then defines the way in which the middle term is connected with the two other terms. The comparison of 'the safety of our allies' with 'you' (i.e. the Romans) shows us that helping allies in danger is a *connexum* of the Romans, that is, helping allies in danger is something which is characteristic of the Romans (topic 17). The comparison of 'the safety of our allies' with 'this war' shows that the safety of our allies is a final cause to wage this war (topic 12).[56] The choice of these topics implies

---

[53] DID 2, 28; 404-12M. Mack, *Renaissance Argument*, 130-1.

[54] DID 2, 29; 412-24M.

[55] In DID 2, 18, Agricola defines the induction as an argumentation, through which the entirety of something is inferred on the basis of its parts or its species ('Est autem inductio vel (ut nos dicimus) enumeratio: argumentatio, qua ex pluribus vel partibus vel speciebus unum vel totum vel genus universaliter colligitur'; 316, 24-6M).

[56] Agricola explains this process of finding the argument and its topics in DID 2, 26; 390, 62-79M.

that the reader has made a topical description of the concepts concerning which the syllogism makes a statement, in other words, that he has made a rationalizing survey of everything he knows about the subject in question. For example, the choice of topic 17 presupposes the historical observation that the Romans usually came to the aid of their allies. Thus, it is clear that Agricola's method of analyzing stimulates thorough reflection on the subject matter at hand.

Moreover, Agricola's approach stimulates critical evaluation of the persuasive force of argumentations in the model text. We have already observed that it is possible to discern more than one topic in a syllogism. In DID 2, 26, Agricola suggests that in each case, it is easy to decide which topic it is best to consider as the source of the argument at hand on account of its force and efficacy, and he proposes that the argument must be named after that particular topic.[57] We notice, however, that in the commentary on DLM, this question is left undecided in some cases, as in the instance of the first syllogism. Moreover, Agricola mostly confines himself to simply mentioning one topic or both topics from which the argument is drawn, and in a few cases he completely refrains from mentioning a topic. One example in particular may illustrate how the choice of a topic can stimulate critical evaluation of the textual passage at hand. In section 28, Cicero mentions, among several other relevant facts from Pompey's biography, Pompey's early experience as a general as a proof of his military knowledge. Agricola proposes three different ways to define the relation between military knowledge and military experience, namely as contingent, as *destinatum* or as efficient cause. As we shall see below, the distinction between contingent and efficient cause seems, in this case, rather formal and inconsiderable, but the topic *destinatum* stresses Pompey's ambition and thus can be considered to add a dimension to the point Cicero is making.

So far, our discussion has involved almost exclusively those topics whose character is appropriate for use as sources of arguments. These topics include the internal topics (topics 1 trough 7), and the external topics which are necessarily joined with the thing (topics 8 through 17). The topics 18 through 24, defined as external topics which are not necessarily joined with the thing, occupy a separate place, in that they cannot be used to describe individual concepts or to discover arguments. The use of these topics seems restricted to describing the nature of a given argumentation or the relation between two argumentations.[58] Thus, Agricola notes that the *refutatio* of DLM is drawn from the topic 'opinions,' and this means that Cicero discusses the view of his opponents concerning the matter at hand. Figures of style and other rhetorical

---

[57] 390, 80-394, 115M.
[58] DID 2, 28; 410, 95-412, 138M.

techniques used to enhance clarity or expressiveness, such as comparisons and antithesis, are prominent in this group of topics. Agricola mentions a few of these topics in his commentary, as we shall see, but a more detailed analysis reveals that still others can be discerned.[59]

The survey below records the topics which Agricola distinguishes as well as the additional information concerning the topics such as he provides it.

First subsidiary question: the necessity of the war

Syllogism 1: *connexa* of the Romans; final cause of this war;[60] syllogisms 2 and 4: no statement of topics; syllogism 3: goal or final cause of sources of national income; syllogisms 5 and 6: comparisons.

The enthymeme proving the major proposition of the first syllogism: comparisons.

The enumeration of the various wars in sections 12-14 is drawn from the species. Similarly, the proof of the minor proposition of the sixth syllogism, namely the enumeration of the acts through which Mithridates has caused the Romans to suffer disgrace, is drawn from the species.

Second subsidiary question: the size and danger of the war

Syllogisms 1, 2, and 3: no statement of topics; syllogism 4: adjacents of Pompey and *destinata* or *secundaria efficientia*[61] of general; syllogism 6: contingents.

Agricola gives a full analysis of syllogism 5 (section 28), as follows. The major term is military knowledge, the minor term is Pompey, the middle term is 'to have experience in all wars.' The middle term is an *actus* of Pompey. The relation between the middle term and military skill can be defined in three different ways: as contingent (to have experience in all wars is a sign or token of military knowledge), as *destinatum* (Pompey accumulated war experience in order to acquire military knowledge), or as *efficiens* (to have war experien-

---

[59] For instance, Agricola mentions, in DID 1, 25, section 25 of DLM, where Cicero compares Lucullus's army with Medea, as an example of topic 21 (comparisons) or 22 (similar things); 162, 142-5M.

[60] I follow Agricola's method of defining the topics of argumentations, as given in DID 2, 26. In the commentary, he does not always follow this method strictly.

[61] Agricola means topic 11, efficient cause. It is not clear why he adds the adjective 'secundaria.'

ce is a kind of secondary cause of military knowledge).[62] Agricola likewise gives a detailed analysis of syllogism 7 (section 43). The major term is prestige, the minor term is Pompey, the middle term is great marks of esteem of the Roman people; the topic is cause of prestige.

The relevant facts from Pompey's biography, which are reviewed in section 28 as proof of Pompey's military knowledge can be drawn from various topics. The fact that Pompey moved to the practical study of war at an early age is an action of Pompey and a *destinatum* of military knowledge. The fact that in his youth he was a soldier in the army of an outstanding general is an action of Pompey; Agricola remarks that 'soldier' as such is a *connexum* of Pompey, and he stresses that the words 'of an outstanding general' are appropriate because 'general' is an efficient cause of 'soldier'. Finally, the fact that in early adulthood Pompey commanded an immense army is a *connexum* of Pompey; the relation between this fact and military knowledge can be defined in three ways: as an effect (military knowledge produces the best general), a *destinatum* (Pompey commanded an army at this early age in order to acquire military knowledge) or a contingent (the fact that Pompey commanded an army as a young adult is a certain sign of his military knowledge).

The enumeration of Pompey's wars, which proves the truth of the minor proposition of syllogism 5 (section 28) is drawn from the species of war. The proofs of Pompey's skill, namely meticulous organisation, courage in danger, painstaking execution, prompt action, and foresight in planning (sections 30-35) constitute contingents or *eventa*. The enthymeme proving Pompey's integrity (sections 37-39) is drawn from the opposites. The denial that Pompey's swiftness was due to his exceptional rowing power, a newly discovered method of navigation or a unique combination of winds (section 40) constitutes an argument drawn from the *differentia* (i.e. *distantia*). The reasoning which follows in section 40 is drawn from the opposites. The discussion of Pompey's friendliness (sections 41-42) is drawn from the effects of the notion friendliness. Finally, the fact that the enemy stands in awe of Pompey (section 43) is adequate proof of Pompey's prestige because it constitutes an effect of his prestige.

Sections 44-46 prove the veracity of either the minor or the major proposition of syllogism 7. Agricola explains that if it is considered as proof of the major proposition, then it is drawn from the species of prestige (Pompey's prestige had great influence in the course of the war, therefore the prestige of every general will have great influence in the course of the war). If it is considered as a proof of the minor proposition, then it is drawn from the effects of prestige (the reduction of grain prices, the checking of Mithridates, the surren-

---

[62] It is not clear why Agricola says 'tanquam causa secundaria' (a kind of secondary cause) instead of simply 'causa'.

der of the pirates, the sending of the Cretan deputation to Pompey, Mithridates's sending of an envoy to Pompey are the effects of Pompey's prestige) or the contingents of prestige (the above-mentioned things are signs of Pompey's prestige). Finally, the discussion of Pompey's luck (section 47) is drawn from the species of luck; the reasoning in section 48 embraces the definition of luck and its properties.

The refutation

Agricola states that the refutation as a whole is drawn from the opinions. Syllogism 1: no statement of topic; syllogism 2: comparison of the middle term and the major term reveals that the argument is drawn from the *differentia* (i.e. specific difference); in comparison with the Romans (in other words, with democracy), the argument is possibly drawn from the *connexa*. Finally, Cicero's remark that Catulus is the designated second man in case something happens to Pompey, is an argument drawn from the final cause. Syllogism 3: comparisons.

Conclusion

It will be apparent from the preceding discussion of Agricola's commentary on DLM that his method of dialectical reading follows closely the principles set forth in DID, Agricola's innovative theory of argumentation. Several characteristics of the commentary suggest the fine quality of Agricola's theory. First, the conceptual unity of the entire speech is clearly brought to light, secondly, the logical sequence of Cicero's argumentation throughout the speech becomes evident, and thirdly, the persuasive strength of each argument is well evaluated.

Simultaneously, it is clear that Agricola's approach is complex and that the practical use of some of his theoretical distinctions is not immediately evident. Moreover, Agricola's commentary presupposes a thorough knowledge of the method of invention set forth in DID. This last point is true specially for the topics, for which Agricola developed an entirely new system that was meant to compete with the system of Quintilian, who groups the topics around the persons and things involved in a particular *causa*. Our observation seems relevant with regard to the question of whether Agricola's method was integrally adopted in Renaissance schools. While it is beyond dispute that Agricola was a pioneer in the joint study of rhetoric and dialectic and the application of their principles to classical texts, testimonies of the integral use of his method in the Renaissance classroom do not abound. If this lack of evidence indicates that the actual use of DID was limited, then one explanation might very well be that schoolmasters preferred to follow the model of analyzing speeches proposed in classical manuals of rhetoric such as Quintilian's *Institutio oratoria*, and in particular Quintilian's treatment of topics.

VII. Portrait of Rudolph Agricola after Cranach from a private collection, courtesy Courtauld Institute of Art, London, through the good graces of Mr. K.T. Jansma, Baflo. See also R.E.O. Ekkart, 'The portraits of Rudolph Agricola', in *Rodolphus Agricola Phrisius*, 118-122.

Translation of the distich: 'Agricola! You were the first who dared lead the Muses from Latium to your fatherland, learned Rudolph!'

Z.R.W.M. VON MARTELS

BETWEEN OROSIUS AND UBBO EMMIUS: ON THE TRADITION OF GEOGRAPHICAL DESCRIPTIONS IN HISTORICAL WRITINGS[*]

> Groningen takes very good care of itself. It has trams, excellent shops and build-ings, a crowded inland harbour, and a spreading park where once were its forti-fications. The mounds in this park were the first hills I had seen since Laren. The church in the market square is immense, with a high tower of bells that kept me awake, but had none of the soothing charm of Long John at Middelburg [...]. The only rich thing in the whitewashed vastnesses of the church is the organ, built more than four hundred years ago by Rudolph Agricola of this province.[1]

Such was the impression of the English travel-writer E.V. Lucas, who visit-ed the town of Groningen at the beginning of this century. Though much has changed, the initial phrase – "Groningen takes very good care of itself" – is still valid today, and, it seems, has always been true: for the same notion was already at the heart of Ubbo Emmius's portrait of the same town in his *Rerum Frisicarum historia* (1596). The portrait forms an important part of a long, detailed, and accurate geographical description of all the lands in-habited by the proud and free people of 'Frisia'. Enthusiastically, Emmius praises its green meadows, fertile lands, the cows, horses, birds, the corn-fields, the lakes, and rivers, and the numerous little towns and hamlets.

Placed at the beginning of the work, and significantly opening with the words "Patriae meae", the lengthy and accurate description immediately at-tracts the attention of readers more accustomed to the short geographical paragraphs in the writings of classical historians.[2] It is clear that Emmius derived great pleasure from the composition of this section of his work, and that he himself regarded it an indispensable element of an historical work.

His writings contain three different types of description. In the first place there is the portrayal of historical events. Emmius was a story-teller and the study of history was his favourite subject. In addition to his *Rerum Frisica-rum historia*, Emmius produced a number of smaller studies.[3] Drawing his material from a great many sources he moulded it into an attractive form. Though much study has been made of the historical contents of Emmius's

---

[*] I am grateful to dr L.A.J.R. Houwen who corrected the English of this article and made valuable suggestions.

[1] Lucas, *A Wanderer in Holland*, 251-2.

[2] See pp. 266 and 272-4 of this article.

[3] For a list of Emmius's writings, see Huisman and Kingma, 'Werken van en over Ubbo Emmius', 226-8.

Rerum Frisicarum historia,[4] his narrative-technique and style have not received much attention.

A second group of descriptions in the works of Ubbo Emmius are the portraits of persons. Their role is less prominent and seems of secondary importance in the *Rerum Frisicarum historia*; yet an attractive example of this genre is Emmius's *Life of Willem Lodewijk*, in which biographical remarks alternate with descriptions of historical events.[5]

Finally, as I indicated, there are the many geographical descriptions in Emmius's works. Some of them cover entire chapters or are even small volumes. Their importance has been acknowledged,[6] but as is the case with the other descriptions, the style and vocabulary, the narrative technique, the use of sources, the interrelation of earlier sources and the emendations or changes in the various editions by the author have never been the subject of detailed philological study. Such research will certainly be rewarding because Emmius borrowed a great many ideas from earlier writers about Frisia, often placing them in a new context, or adapting the wording so as to suit his own style.

I shall not embark upon this huge task, but will concentrate on the geographical descriptions in his historical writings: the driving forces behind the custom to add such descriptions in historical writings will be discussed as well the extent to which Neolatin authors diverged from their classical models. Emmius's description of Groningen will serve as example and starting point for my further exposition of the geographical descriptions in his *Rerum Frisicarum historia*.[7]

Before I dwell a little longer on Emmius's characterization of Groningen in order to provide an impression of its character and its place within the *Historia*, it should be noted that this portrait of the town from 1596 was followed by a second more elaborate one in Emmius's *De agro Frisiae inter Amasum et Lavicam flumina. Deque urbe Groninga in eodem agro: et de jure utrius-*

---

[4] See the bibliography in *Ubbo Emmius. Een Oostfries geleerde in Groningen*, 234-7.

[5] Emmius, *Guilhelmus Ludovicus*. The work is translated by Schoonbeeg, *Willem Lodewijk* (with introductory essays by Waterbolk, 'Van Grafrede naar biografie', and Nonner-Hienkens, 'Willem Lodewijk in beeld: een portret-iconografie').

[6] Waterbolk, *Twee eeuwen Friese geschiedschrijving*, 147ff.

[7] I have been using the complete edition entitled *Rerum Frisicarum historia, autore Ubbone Emmio, Frisio; distincta in decades sex. Quarum postrema nunc primum prodit, prioribus ita recognitis et locupletatis, ut novae prorsus videri possint* (Leiden 1616). The first ten books of this history, which also included the description of Groningen, were published in 1596. The work gradually grew to sixty books (in six decades) published in 1616. For the list of editions, see Huisman and Kingma, 'Werken van en over Ubbo Emmius', 226-8. For some observations on changes made by the author in the editions of 1596 and 1616, see Appendix (at the end of this article).

que of 1605.[8] Both treatises unambiguously praise the prosperity, administration and beauty of Groningen. This is not what one would expect, for, according to modern scholarship, the works in which they appear were written
from two different perspectives. Emmius, namely, was born in Greetsiel
near Emden in 1547. Though distant from Groningen, Emden was not too
far away not to fear its power and influence. When in 1592 the historian
completed the first decade of his *Rerum Frisicarum historia*, which contains
his first description of the town of Groningen, he was the rector of the Latin
school in Leer. It is assumed that in those years he would have felt less
sympathy for the town of Groningen and particularly the ways in which the
town exercised control over the surrounding country. This is thought to have
influenced his treatment of the political and military actions in the earlier
and later parts of his *History*.[9] Though the laudatory character of the
description of Groningen makes this point controversial, it goes perhaps not
too far to conclude that after Emmius had become rector of the Latin School
in Groningen (1594) (and much later, in 1614, also the first Rector Magni-
ficus of the university in the same city), he was soon almost more patriotic
than the native inhabitants. It is from this later period that the second, more
elaborate description of Groningen dates.

In the oldest description the town, then, is described as at the northern
edge of a somewhat elevated stretch of land between the fields, and it is
situated at the very place where sand and heavier clay meet together. Immediately afterwards Emmius notes that "Groningen is not only the largest
town in the whole of Frisia, but also excels in name, power, deeds and by its
very beauty."[10] He then depicts in about thirty-five lines the half-aristo-
cratic, half-democratic bodies that govern and control life in the town itself
and the surrounding areas, the so called *Ommelanden*.

Emmius portrays the citizens of Groningen thus: The people of the town
are by character friendly, pleasant, witty, prudent, industrious and interested
in the culture and the understanding of literature. They have no low opinion
of themselves and are thus sumptuous in their dressing and eating habits.
They are very fond of power and for this they are prepared to undertake and

[8] The work was reprinted together with the *Rerum Frisicarum historia* in 1616; see Huisman and Kingma, 'Werken van en over Ubbo Emmius', 229-30.

[9] For important details about Emmius's early life, background, family, study and career, see
Feenstra, 'Ubbo Emmius, een Oostfries patriot in Groningen'. Rinzema notes that in the later
parts of the *Rerum Frisicarum historia* Emmius gave a more favourable judgment about Groningen's usurpation of the 'Ommelanden' than of the local aristocracy; see Rinzema, 'Ubbo
Emmius als historicus', esp. 58.

[10] The description starts with the following remark (p.18): "Atque hujus in solo, ubi arenis
gleba pinguior jungitur, editiore in dorso inter camporum humilia linguae instar se porrigente,
sedem habet GRONINGA, quam dixi, non maxima solùm inter urbes, quas Frisia amplectitur,
sed nomine etiam et potentiâ et rebus gestis, et specie quoque ipsâ antecellens."

endure everything. Still they are also most tenacious in protecting their rights and freedom against oppressors, and rather than be subject to slavery they will steadfastly endure everything.[11]

Hereafter in some forty lines, Emmius discusses the origin of the people living in the town, its impressive walls, bulwarks and other defensive works, its street plan, the beauty of its houses and market places. He devotes a paragraph to the twelve churches of Groningen and another that mentions the pleasant scenery of gardens and fruit trees scattered throughout the town. His final words praise Groningen as a flourishing market town and harbour, situated at the confluence of several busy water-ways leading in many directions.

When we read this description, Groningen of the sixteenth-century discloses itself before our eyes, presenting the reader as it were with a bird's eye view. Emmius's account is informative, but it concentrates on main points. It is clear that the author does not want to burden our mind with unnecessary details; statistical information is entirely absent. Besides, the characteristics of the description of Groningen correspond with the much longer description of the whole of Frisia, with which it forms the beginning of the *Rerum Frisicarum historia.*

Emmius's addition of long, detailed geographical descriptions at the beginning of an historical work is not an isolated phenomenon in Neolatin literature. It shows how Latin authors of this period attempted to grasp the surrounding world. This disposition was not limited to geography. Nearly every subject was thought worthy of description either in prose or in poetry.[12] This became a characteristic feature by which Neolatin authors distinguished themselves from classical authors. For as Otto Kluge, in an article entitled 'Die Neulateinische Kunstprosa', remarks: "Die Hauptstärke der Renaissance-Prosaisten ist die Schilderung der Gegenständlichkeit". He illustrates this with references to Petrarch, Poggio and Aeneas Silvius Piccolomini.[13] Indeed, reading, for instance, through Petrarch's letters, one cannot fail to experience this; one letter describes the poet's life in Vaucluse, another his journey to Aix la Chapelle and Cologne, a third deals with his famous ascent of Mont Ventoux. In short, the reader can almost tread in the

---

[11] *Rerum Frisicarum historia* (ed. 1616), 19 "Populus oppidanus moribus comis, blandus, dicax, solers, industrius, à literarum cultu et captu non abhorrens, neque abjectè de se sentiens, ideoque in veste et victu sumptuosus, imperii cumprimis avidus, ac ejusce gratiâ quidlibet suscipiens et perferens: pertinacissimus verò in tuendo jure suo et libertate contra oppressores, et cuncta potius quam servitutem perpetiens." Note that Emmius slightly revised this section (see Appendix).

[12] Didactic poetry is a good example; the genre lends itself admirably to the purpose of describing subjects never described before; it prospered in the hands of Neolatin authors.

[13] Kluge, 'Die neulateinische Kunstprosa', 60.

footsteps of the poet, almost see the places he visited, and feel the people he met and portrayed.[14] Many other authors can easily be found who shared with these Italians a strong inclination to observation and depiction of the world immediately surrounding them.

Since Burckhardt's *Kultur der Renaissance in Italien* (1860) the idea of "Die Entdeckung der Welt und des Menschen" by Renaissance men has become almost proverbial.[15] In the meantime, however, studies of the previous periods have made clear that the roots of this development went much deeper. What, one may ask, were the driving forces that urged Petrarch and other humanists to describe the world in such palpable terms, in opposition to the classical authors whom they claimed they were imitating?

Kluge wrote his article on Neolatin prose as a reaction to the almost general condemnation of Neolatin in the nineteenth and the first half of the twentieth centuries.[16] With his observation that Neolatin authors were strong in depicting the real world, he identified an important difference with classical literature. Here, of course, one must be wary of generalizations. Classical literature stretches from Homer till the period of the Church fathers and it offers beautiful examples of descriptions of the surrounding world. Yet it goes without saying that the authors of the classical period differed and that there are also differences between this period as a whole and the Middle Ages and the Renaissance.

Searching for topographical descriptions in general by Latin authors of the ancient world, we find that they are often more eloquent than informative. Though the need of adding information on the places, where particular events had taken place and where people had lived, is mentioned (or suggested) more than once, descriptions remain short.[17] The lack of information about military campaigns and battles in the writings of Caesar, Livy, Sallust and Tacitus, for instance, has made it very hard, often even impossible, to trace routes and places where armies fought and to reconstruct the precise circumstances under which such events took place.[18]

---

[14] Petrarca, *Epistolae Familiares*; see *Fam.* 1,4 and 1,5 for his journey to parts of the Netherlands and Germany; *Fam.* 4,1 for the ascent of Mont Ventoux; *Fam.* 8,3 and 13,8 about Vaucluse.

[15] Burckhardt, *Die Kultur der Renaissance in Italien*, 261-332.

[16] Burckhardt, too, belonged to the critics of the humanist Latin tradition, but the most outspoken negative judgment is to be found in Norden, *Die antike Kunstprosa*, II 773, and *passim*.

[17] Classen, 'Lodovico Guicciardini's *Descrittione*', 101 (note 8). Classen refers to Polybius 9, 13, 8. Also interesting is a short remark in Tacitus's *Annales* 4, 33, 3 from which it appears that descriptions of the living places of peoples are an inherent part of historical writing. Tacitus compares his own writings with those of more traditional historians: "Nam situs gentium, varietates proeliorum, clari ducum exitus retinent ac redintegrant legentium animum."

[18] This is not to say that these authors are misrepresenting the truth. Cf. Klotz, *Cäsarstudien*, 38: "Tacitus steht den kriegerischen Ereignissen, die er beschreibt, fremd gegenüber, daher will es nicht recht gelingen seine Schlachten und Märsche zu lokalisieren; Cäsar gibt das, was unbe-

Even where a longer, more elaborate description is found – such as Pliny the Younger's description of his villa in the seventeenth letter of the second book of his *Epistulae* – it is disappointing because it offers little factual information. From 1615 onwards scholars have made at least twelve attempts to reconstruct the plan of this house. All these reconstructions remain tentative, for as a commentator at the beginning of the twentieth century concludes: "Pliny's description is characterized by enthusiasm rather than clearness. He gives no description of the outside appearance of the house; he gives no actual dimension anywhere."[19] In the context of this article, this example is also interesting for another reason: it can be compared to Ubbo Emmius's remarkably detailed description of the church at Aduard in the middle of his *Rerum Frisicarum historia*:[20] it even contains exact measurements, thus helping modern archaeologists to establish a picture of the original building.[21] Furthermore it should be noted that the inclusion of such an accurate description would have been uncommon in an historical work of the classical era!

Concrete factual information is what modern readers really want. To them, the surrounding world is a reality and less a literary phenomenon to be described with detachment. It is hard to determine when the attitude towards the material world changed, but the effects of such a change are very well illustrated in late thirteenth-century descriptions of cities.[22] They reveal that authors from that period were concerned with the concrete and physical aspects of life within the city: its feasts and its events, its markets, its economy, and even its common citizens. Their interest in the material world received emphasis from the inclusion of much statistical information. The first example of such descriptions is Bonvesin da Riva's praise of Milan (*De magnalibus urbis Mediolani*), which dates from 1288.[23] This text treats a great variety of subjects in eight chapters: the location of the town, its habitation, the inhabitants, the fertility, the affluence of goods and so forth.

---

dingt nötig ist, nicht mehr, aber auch nicht weniger, so dass es in den allermeisten Fällen geglückt ist, die Felder seiner Taten wiederzufinden." A more positive judgment about Tacitus's accuracy in military matters and his honesty (contra Mommsen who had denounced the historian as the most unmilitary of historians) is given by Syme, *Tacitus*, I 156-75; 392-6; esp. 156 and 170.

[19] *Selected Letters of Pliny*, ed. G.B. Allen (Oxford 1915; repr. 1954), 108-12; 147ff.

[20] Emmius, *Rerum Frisicarum historia* (ed. 1616), 164.

[21] For the Latin text and its value as source for the reconstruction of the picture of the church, see Praamstra and Boersma, 'Die archäologischen Untersuchungen', esp. 183ff; 189ff; 199-200 (Latin text in note 18).

[22] There is much literature on this subject. See especially Hyde, 'Medieval Descriptions of Cities'; Classen, *Die Stadt im Spiegel der Descriptiones und Laudes urbium*; Schmidt, 'Mittelalterliches und humanistisches Städtelob'; Kugler, *Die Vorstellung der Stadt*; Classen, 'Lodovico Guicciardini's *Descrittione*'; for poetry, Slits, *Het Latijnse stededicht*.

[23] For the text, see Bonvesin da Riva, *Grandezze di Milano* and *De magnalibus Mediolani*.

In his article on medieval cities J.K. Hyde comments:

> While every *descriptio* had contained something about the fertility of the soil in
> general terms, Bonvesin developed this section of his book into a veritable cata-
> logue of grain, vegetable, fruit and nuts. [...] As he repeats over and over again,
> Bonvesin tried to find out all that he could by diligent enquiry, and most
> historians are now convinced that he made an honest attempt to be accurate.[24]

The realistic and detailed descriptions of this kind[25] can be regarded as proof
of the growing self-consciousness and self-assertiveness of the inhabitants
of late-medieval cities. This new attitude was the result of the dynamism,
expansion and successful competition of these cities, and this was passed on
to the individual citizens.

Self-consciousness finds expression in different modes: Bonvesin da
Riva was no less proud of his native country than Ubbo Emmius of his.
However, the latter's description of Groningen is very different in contents,
structure and style from Bonvesin da Riva's praise of Milan. The accurate
sense of detail and fondness of statistical information of the latter has become subservient to eloquence marked by a balanced structure and by the
removal of details that deflect the reader from the main points. This description in Emmius's *Historia* can be regarded as the amalgamation of two
developments: first, the gradually growing importance attached to individual
arts and intellectual disciplines in the Middle Ages which had stimulated the
production of concrete descriptions; secondly, the renewed interest in the
classical literary and rhetorical tradition as model for literature in the
Renaissance. As different kinds of literature grew out of these two developments, it is worthwhile to pay a little more attention to them.

The success of the individual arts and intellectual disciplines in the Middle Ages was the motor behind the rapid growth of European towns. There
was a tendency to specialisation and learning by experience and observation
combined with learning from literary sources which had been largely neglected for a long time.

Such a change to greater insight, criticism and usefulness can be observed in, for instance, natural philosophy, mathematics, and medicine.[26] The
great changes in the medical knowledge of the late Middle Ages are also reflected in its jargon, which developed into an instrument used all over
Europe; its language became more abstract and scientific, and an increasing

---

[24] Hyde, 'Medieval Descriptions of Cities', 327-8; Classen, *Die Stadt im Spiegel der Descriptiones und Laudes urbium*, 63-4.

[25] Examples of descriptions of cities are mentioned by Classen, 'Lodovico Guicciardini's
Descrittione', 112 (note 56).

[26] Kristeller, 'Salerno und die scholastische Wissenschaft', 89.

number of new words and concepts were introduced.[27] Similar developments took place in the less respectable, but influential art of alchemy, where the imitation of 'nature by nature' played an important role, and where practical experience and observation had become key notions.[28] Because of its great utility to mankind Roger Bacon became a fervent defender of its cause,[29] but soon prohibition and persecution thwarted its development. However, the 'scientific' curiosity of these experimenting early 'chemists' led to ever more detailed descriptions of substances, processes and discoveries. Geber's *Summa perfectionis* (*c*. 1300) is a good example of this.[30]

In the field of literary studies, this development went into the direction of greater practical usage as well. One aspect of this was the contribution of the study of Roman law to the rediscovery of classical authors in the late Middle Ages and early Renaissance. A number of pre- or early humanists were lawyers, notaries and judges.[31] One reason for this was that a better understanding of ancient law could be attained by a philological and historical study of classical authors. Through a better defined, purer language greater clarity of expression and accuracy could be achieved. It is indeed the precise use of words, ideas and eloquence that gives lawyers, judges and notaries the edge on their competitors. It is significant that as secretaries or chancellors to rulers or communes some humanists soon became effective instruments in the service to the state, and many others to the people in general by their predilection for teaching.

Likewise the explorations of merchants in search for new profits led to

---

[27] See Baader, 'Die Entwicklung der medizinischen Fachsprache'; Nutton, 'The Changing Language of Medicine'.

[28] This is part of a broad movement within alchemy which claimed that art can "equal or outdo the products of the natural world by altering the species of those products. It was first and most strongly defended by the alchemists of the thirteenth century." Cf. Newman, *The* Summa Perfectionis *of Pseudo Geber,* 40. After around 1300, fraudulent behaviour and excessive claims of its adepts had made alchemy a prohibited art, its positive contribution to the development of natural sciences was forgotten until it was gradually rediscovered in the 16th and 17th centuries.

[29] See the long quotation from Roger's *Opus tertium* in Newman, *The* Summa perfectionis *of Pseudo-Geber,* 21 (English transl.) and 44 (Latin).

[30] See, for instance, the detailed description of a metal like gold: "Dicimus ergo quoniam aurum est corpus metallicum, citrinum, ponderosum, mutum, fulgidum, equaliter in ventre terre digestum, aqua minerali diutissime lavatum, sub malleo extendibile, fusibile, examinationem cineritii et cementi tollerans. Ex hoc utique elicias quod aliquid non est aurum nisi causas diffinitionis et differentias omnes habeat auri. Quidquid tamen metallum radicitius citrinat, et ad equalitatem perducit, et mundat, ex omni genere metallorum facit aurum. Ideoque per opus nature perpendimus et artificio es in aurum mutari posse" and so it continues for another 22 lines in the edition of Newman, *The* Summa perfectionis *of Pseudo-Geber,* 337-8.

[31] Weiss, *The Dawn of Humanism in Italy,* 5-6; Ullmann, *Medieval Foundations of Renaissance Humanism,* 132; 161.

an ever more detailed, more precise picture of the earth, as is visually illustrated by the increased accuracy and level of detail of late medieval and
renaissance itineraries and maps. These sources in combination with geographical information from classical authors became a driving force in the
discovery of the New World and its treasures.[32] Soon geography became an
important part of the school curriculum.[33] Here Ubbo Emmius appears
again, for geography is on the list of subjects taught in the last class of the
grammar school at Groningen where he taught.[34]

In a similar way most other arts and intellectual disciplines developed,
becoming a source of new words and more precise definitions. This process
was often slow but at least there was some movement in the direction of as
yet undiscovered opportunities, and people became aware that they could
fashion and rule this earthly world as they saw fit. Though the origin of this
idea is in antiquity, it was more fully expressed in Giannozzo Manetti's *De
dignitate et excellentia hominis*, and Marsilio Ficino's praise of *homo faber*
in his *Theologia platonica*.[35]

All this warrants the conclusion that the increasing specialisation and
development of arts and disciplines in the late-Middle Ages left its mark on
the literature of the period. We must not be surprised that geographical and
topographical descriptions of cities, too, were influenced by this tendency.
One may even conclude that "Die Entdeckung der Welt und des Menschen"
by Petrarch and his contemporaries was not so much stimulated by their
contact with the admired classical authors as by the growing talent for observation of contemporaries and their immediate predecessors.

Before passing to the next point, it should be noted that a detailed work
such as Bonvesin da Riva's praise of Milan did not vanish with the arrival of
humanism. Similar observational faculties can be found in, for instance, a
short description of Vienna written by Aeneas Silvius Piccolomini (1405-
1464). The *descriptio* is only two pages long and it was originally intended

---

[32] Broc, *La géographie de la Renaissance*, passim. Day correctly observes in his *The Medieval Market Economy*, 167: "The ideal international merchant [...] thanks to a long apprentice-
ship in foreign lands, was a man of cosmopolitan interests and varied talents. He was sometimes also a man of culture, as is attested by the important literary figures like Villani, Boccac-
cio, Chaucer or Sacchetti, whose roots were in the merchant class, and by the great works of art
and literature created under the enlightened patronage of wealthy merchants."
[33] The growing importance of geography is also reflected in Erasmus's enormous knowledge of the subject; see the article of Schoeck in this volume.
[34] Emmius, *Programma bij de aanvaarding van het rectoraat*, 12. For the transformation of
geography to a school discipline in the course of the 16th and 17th centuries, see De Dainville,
La géographie des humanistes.
[35] See the quotations in Trinkaus, *In Our Image and Likeness*, I 482-4; II 784-6. A less
known eulogy of the prospering of the arts is to be found in Giovanni Aurelio Augurello's
poem on alchemy (*Chrysopoeia* 2,427-68, partly in imitation of Lucretius 1448-57).

to form the beginning of the *Historia Austrialis* (in its second redaction).[36] Some of the subjects that are briefly touched upon are: the strong walls of the town, its suburbs, the beautiful houses of the rich; the heated chambers against the cold winters; the glass windows and doors of iron; the birds kept in cages; the furniture; the stables; the wine cellars; the ugly protection of many roofs by wood instead of stone; the splendidly painted interior and exterior of the houses; the sturdy pavement used in busy places; the rich exterior and interior of churches; the priests; the prosperous living conditions of the four mendicant orders; and, last but not least, the converted whores in a monastery where they sang hymns in German day and night; Aeneas adds that should they return to their old habits they will be thrown into the Danube. Then follows a longer section on the state of education and knowledge and another on the great quantities of food imported into the city and the importance of wine. From wine the author easily passes on to quarrels and street fights between students, members of the various guilds and others. He relates how the Viennese indulged in food; and he cannot but mention the many whores and lasciviousness of its women in general. Finally there is a catalogue of names of the mighty Austrian barons, of the important cathedrals, and of the various bonds of barons and prelates with the dukes of Austria.

Like Bonvesin da Riva's praise of Milan, this rich, but rather unstructured, and not strictly rhetorical picture of Vienna is very different from Ubbo Emmius's description of Frisia and Groningen, where comparatively little attention is paid to private citizens and individual details and more to eloquence and a few important concepts. This, then, brings me to the second reason for the difference between late-medieval and late-renaissance descriptions: the renewed interest in the classical literary and rhetorical tradition as models for literature.

When exactly did the change from the late-medieval, detailed city-description to what we regard as that typical of the Renaissance occur? Leonardo Bruni's *Laudatio Florentinae urbis* is usually regarded as the turning point in the tradition of the *descriptio urbis*.[37] It dates from the end of the fourteenth century, thus antedating Aeneas Silvius a little. Here, instead of a rambling list of facts, the author chose a rhetorically structured, eloquent argumentation, concentrating not so much on facts but on specific

---

[36] Piccolomini, *Opera*, 718-20: "Descriptio urbis Viennensis per poetam Sylvium aedita, epist. CLXV"; the origin of this description is discussed by Voigt, *Die Briefe des Aeneas Silvius*, 110-3; cf. Worstbrock, 'Piccolomini, Aeneas Silvius', 641; 656-7.

[37] Hyde, 'Medieval Descriptions of Cities', 309-10; Schmidt, 'Mittelalterliches und humanistisches Städtelob', 123; Baron, *The Crisis of the Early Italian Renaissance* (1955), I 163ff. For the text of the *Laudatio Florentinae urbis*, see Baron, *From Petrarch to Leonardo Bruni*, 232-63; 151-71.

ideas. Bruni made an effort to correlate causes and effects and so created a
"first literary portrait of Florence's political and scenic position."[38] Here we
see certain elements which will later characterise Ubbo Emmius's style of
describing. The model of Bruni's *descriptio* was the *descriptio* of the Greek
orator Aelius Aristides of the second century.[39] For Emmius there was not
only a single model; he preferred to continue in the long tradition of humanists who culled what they needed from the styles, vocabulary and rhetorical
patterns of great classical authors.

As noted above, by far the most detailed descriptions in Emmius's
Rerum Frisicarum historia are the geographical ones. His geographical
interests were stimulated when he studied under David Chytraeus at the university of Rostock. Travelling to Switzerland a few years later to attend the
lectures of Beza in Geneva, he kept a diary in which he recorded his travel
experiences. Like many other travellers of this century, he diligently jotted
down the travel distances and the hours spent travelling, but he also added
short descriptive notes about buildings, churches and other places that he
visited.[40]

In the *Rerum Frisicarum historia* – Emmius's first official proof of his
great talent for descriptions – the first two books deal with the whole country of Frisia, all in all some thirty-seven folio pages. He considered this geographical introduction essential as background to the historical works that
were to follow. These occupied him for the next thirty years and ran to
another 925 folio pages. Though Emmius's descriptive prose constitutes only a small percentage of the total work it goes much deeper than any example from classical antiquity. Caesar's geographical explanation of Gaul at
the beginning of his *De bello Gallico* was restricted to only twenty-three
lines, nine of which are now believed to have been added by some medieval
author.[41] Also other Latin historians – Livy, Sallust and Tacitus, or later
Ammianus Marcellinus – offer little compared with the systematic geographical approach and the rich information Emmius is providing.[42] Even

---

[38] Baron, *The Crisis of the Early Italian Renaissance* (1966), 196-9. It is worth mentioning
that Aeneas Silvius was one of the imitators of Bruni's *Laudatio Florentinae urbis* when he
wrote a praise of the city of Basel in 1438; cf. Kugler, *Die Vorstellung der Stadt*, 195-210.

[39] Baron, *The Crisis of the Early Italian Renaissance* (1966), 192ff.

[40] Emmius, *Der Reisebericht.*

[41] This fact in itself is very interesting, because it suggests that in the Middle Ages Caesar's
geographical introduction was regarded as too meagre. A new attitude towards history was
born, perhaps in the tradition and wake of Orosius (see below). For the text, see Caesar, *De
bello Gallico* 1, 1; for comments on the passage, see Caesar, *De Bello Gallico*, 82; 347-8;
Klotz, *Cäsarstudien*, 26ff.

[42] Sallust, *Bellum Iugurtinum* 17-9; *Historiae* IV, fragm. 194 (ed. Gerlach); III, fragm. 61-80
("de situ Ponti"); Livy, *Periochae* 104 "prima pars libri situm Germaniae moresque continet";
Tacitus, *Agricola* 10-12 (description of England); the *Germania* offers very little on geography;
Bunbury, *A History of Ancient Geography*, II 173 (about Sallust); 492-502 (about geographical

the Greek Strabo (ca 64 BC-after 21 AD), who specialised both in geography and history, did not really combine the two disciplines in *one* work.[43] I found only one exception, namely Orosius's *Historiarum adversum paganos libri VII* (*The Seven Books of History Against the Pagans*, written around 417 AD). Orosius was the first to begin his work with a detailed geographical survey of the Ancient world (*Hist. adv. pag.* 1, 2, 1-106). He makes his intention clear in the following passage:[44]

> Therefore, I intend to speak of the period from the founding of the world to the founding of the City; then up to the principate of Caesar and the birth of Christ, from which time the control of the world has remained under the power of the City, down even to our own time. Insofar as I shall be able to recall them, I think it necessary to disclose the conflicts of the human race and the world, as it were, through its various parts, burning with evils, set afire with the torch of greed, viewing them as from a watchtower, so that first I shall describe the world itself which the human race inhabits, as it was divided by our ancestors into three parts and then established by regions and provinces, in order that when the locale of wars and the ravages of diseases are described, all interested may more easily obtain knowledge, not only of the events of their time, but also of their location.

Whereas the historical parts of Orosius's *History* were written in a difficult, literary style aimed at the essence, not the image of things, the geographical sections are dry, but praised for their clearness and intelligence. This is an original description of the world, not derived from Pliny or any other known source.[45] The large number of over two hundred preserved medieval Orosius-manuscripts proves that the author was widely read. As yet, little is known about his specific influence and we do not know to what extent this practice of adding a large geographical description at the beginning of an historical work found imitators.[46] What is clear, though, is that Renaissance

information offered by Tacitus); 679-80 (on Ammianus Marcellinus, who "takes occasion from time to time to give a general geographical sketch of the countries, which were the theatre of the wars that he is about to relate at occasions"). Syme, *Tacitus*, I 126 (referring to Pomponius Mela, *praefatio*) concludes: "Geography was held by Roman writers to be a difficult, abstruse, and rebellious subject. Germany or Britain, Tacitus shows little interest in it."

[43] His first publication was a work of history, the *Historical Commentaries*, which have not been preserved. His *Geography* was written over a long stretch of time. It is essentially "a compilation of details" without "any noticeable harmony of structure" (*The Cambridge History of Classical Literature*, 642-3). Literature on ancient geography is listed by Classen, 'Lodovico Guicciardini's *Descrittione*', 101 (note 10).

[44] Orosius, *The Seven Books of History against the Pagans*, 7; for the Latin edition, see Orosius, *Historiarum aduersum paganos libri VII* 1,1,4-17. For an introduction on Orosius, see Janvier, *La géographie d'Orose*.

[45] Orosius, *Historiarum adversum paganos libri VII* 1, 2, 1-106.

[46] Such a connection between Orosius and the historical work of authors such as Bede, Paulus Diaconus, Adam of Bremen, and Notker (to mention only a few) is suggested by Classen, 'Lodovico Guicciardini's *Descrittione*', 110 (note 53). Geography and topography, in general,

humanists were not aware of any such influence when they were writing
their historical works and that they, in general, preferred to regard the great
historians of the classical period as their models. We find an example of this
in Emmius's predecessor Cornelius Kempius. He justified his long geographical description at the beginning of his historical work not by reference
to what Orosius but to what Caesar or Sallust had done.[47]

The deeply rooted inclination to see Neolatin authors as pure imitators
(or emulators) of classical models easily blinds us to influences that made
their works so unusual. They themselves are partly to blame for this, because they ceaselessly emphasise their dependency on classical models. As a
consequence, their works are taken for bad imitations when they leave the
main stream of the classical tradition in matters of language, style and treatment of subject.

For the study and understanding of Emmius this means that we should
recognise that he is no mere imitator of Livy or any other classical author.
Others have reminded us that his style of writing, though modelled on classical authors, eventually developed its own personal character, and that in
this he was following the example of contemporary Latin authors. His Latin
is different from what we read in Caesar, Livy, Tacitus or Cicero.[48]

The same is true for the geographical description at the beginning of Emmius's *Rerum Frisicarum historia*, which is borne out by its length, its precise and detailed character, and its rhetorical structure. It has generally been
ignored that contemporary influences also left their mark on this work.
Moreover, it was only natural that these geographical introductions developed, for precise knowledge of the subject had increased enormously over
the centuries and proved to be of great use. Ubbo Emmius, like those before
him, felt the need to combine geography and history. It is significant that
when he wrote his *History of Greece (Vetus Graecia)* at the end of his life,
he divided it into three books: the first book of almost 200 pages is devoted
to an accurate geographical description of the regions, towns and islands

---

became important subjects for authors of the Middle Ages. The description of the shape of the
world and its geography becomes a part of medieval encyclopedic works. Isidore of Seville's
Etymologiae is an early example; Honorius Augustodunensis' *Imago mundi* (c. 1110-39), the
Lucidarius (c. 1190-95), Bartholomaeus Anglicus' *De rerum proprietatibus* (c. 1225) are late
ones. This tradition eventually resulted in detailed works such as Giraldus Cambrensis's *Topographia Hibernica*. On geographical descriptions in the Middle Ages, see Kaske, Groos and
Twomey, *Medieval Christian Literary Imagery*, 189; 191; 193; 202-3; 209.

[47] Kempius, *De origine, situ, qualitate et quantitate Frisiae, et rebus a Frisiis olim praeclare gestis*, 2. For Kempius, see Bolhuis van Zeeburgh, *Kritiek der Friesche Geschiedschrijving*,
130f.; Waterbolk, *Twee eeuwen Friese geschiedschrijving*, 147.

[48] Schoonbeeg and Akkerman, 'De Latijnse stijl van Ubbo Emmius', 70-1 (with regard to
his *Guilhelmus Ludovicus* from 1621, but the same can be said of his *Historia*): "Zijn stijl, een
leven lang gevormd door de voortdurende lectuur van Latijnse schrijvers en door voortdurend
zelf eigen gedachten schriftelijk in het Latijn uit te drukken, is vooral zijn eigen stijl."

that had played a part in the history of Greece; the second book deals with the history of Greece and the third book with its various institutions.

It is clear that geography was as important to Emmius as it was to his contemporaries Blaeu, Ortelius and Mercator. A discussion of his geographical descriptions should therefore take into account his great efforts to obtain or make accurate maps of Frisia by the very exact measurements that were made possible by new techniques.[49] I found several instances where his writing seems to follow the outlines of the map-drawer, like the description of the Dollard in his *De agro Frisiae*.[50] This literary account is so detailed that the windings of the coast and the creeks, and the marshes and places along the sea appear before our eyes.

As to the way the material was selected and presented, I have earlier referred to the method used by Bruni in his *Laudatio Florentinae urbis*. So as to dispel any notions that I am denying the classical authors their proper share in the honour, I will quote a passage from Strabo. His work was well-known to Emmius and it may have guided him in striking the right balance in his selections and descriptions of both his geographical and historical material. Strabo wrote:[51]

> After I had written my Historical Sketches, which have been useful, I suppose, for moral and political philosophy, I determined to write the present treatise [on Geography] also; for this work itself is based on the same plan, and is addressed to the same class of readers, and particularly to men of exalted stations in life. Furthermore, just as in my Historical Sketches only the incidents in the lives of distinguished men are recorded, while deeds that are petty and ignoble are omitted, so in this work also I must leave untouched what is petty and inconspicuous, and devote my attention to what is noble and great, and to what contains the practically useful or memorable, or entertaining. Now just as in judging of the merits of colossal statues we do not examine each individual part with minute care, but rather consider the general effect and endeavour to see if the statue as a whole is pleasing, so should this book of mine be judged. For it, too, is a colossal work, in that it deals with the facts about large things only, and wholes, except as some petty thing may stir the interest of the studious or the practical man.

Like Strabo, Emmius concentrated on points of general importance, illustrating each with some examples. Subjects of lesser interest were avoided because the author was constantly aware that readers can easily be lulled to sleep. Instead of providing dull statistical details or even numbers and

---

[49] See, for instance, Sonntag, 'Zur Ostfriesland-Karte des Ubbo Emmius'; Schumacher, 'Ubbo Emmius: Trigonometer, Topograph und Kartograph'. Other literature about Emmius's interest in cartography is listed in *Ubbo Emmius. Een Oostfries geleerde in Groningen*, 234-7.

[50] *De agro Frisiae* (1616), 5; Emmius, *Friesland tussen Eems en Lauwers*, 20.

[51] Strabo, *Geography* 1, 1, 23.

quantities, Emmius sought to win over his audience by useful information put into an eloquent form. In contrast to Strabo, the reader is struck by Emmius's great personal attachment to the country he describes, a country, moreover that he knew thoroughly. There is much pride in his voice when he speaks of these lands; his pleasure in relating about the richness of its soil, the abundance of its products such as milk and cheese, and the prospering hamlets, villages, towns and harbours is echoed in every sentence.[52] Small details betray where his heart beats faster, like his remark that all year long the fields resound with the singing of the lark.[53] And when he discusses the continuous threat of the sea in these provinces, he exclaims that without this threat Frisia would be one of the happiest parts of Europe.[54]

Ubbo Emmius takes thirty-seven pages to describe the whole of Frisia in his *Rerum Frisicarum historia*. Later, not content with the result, he repeated and added much. Within the space of this article only a few general questions could be discussed which arose from the study of this material. One conclusion is that the practice of adding really long and substantial geographical introductions to historical works did not have its origin in the classical models but rather in the historical works of Orosius and later authors of the Middle Ages and Renaissance. Such descriptions are proof that there was a growing need to describe as precisely as possible everything that could be observed. There are, I think, good reasons to believe that the increasing importance and specialisation of the arts and intellectual disciplines from the late Middle Ages onwards were the driving forces behind this process. The recovered classical tradition stimulated humanists to make the mass of details subservient to their desire to write eloquent descriptions. These eloquent humanists did not loose the old capacity for observation, nor their great love for the concrete and physical aspects of the world, and thus created descriptions which despite other influences are uniquely their own.

---

[52] For instance Emmius, *Rerum Frisicarum historia* (ed. 1616), 6: "Hinc lactis incredibilis illa abundantia, quo bis quotidie vaccarum ingentia distenduntur ubera, illa butyri et casei inde confecti vis, quae expletâ viciniâ in longinquas etiam regiones exportatur [...]. Tot enim oppidis, castellis, foris, vicis, pulcherrimis templis et villis ager totus obsitus est, ut multis in locis è longinquo spectans unam aliquam magnam civitatem te cernere arbitrere. Atque hanc ejus faelicitatem multum adauget portuum, quibus tota ora plena est, importandis et exportandis rebus per diversas regiones insignis commoditas: quorum nonnulli tales sunt, ut inter nobilissimos Europae, si situm spectes, censeri possint."

[53] Emmius, *Rerum Frisicarum historia* (ed. 1616), 8-9: "Nec culinis modò idoneae volucres, sed etiam, quae delectationi serviunt, alaudae praecipuè, quarum perpetuò concentu majore anni parte totus ager perstrepit, non sine singulari voluptate audientium."

[54] Emmius, *Rerum Frisicarum historia* (ed. 1616), p. 6: "Ingens sanè malum, quo luxuriante ejus orae faelicitatem coercere divino numini complacuit. Quo si careret, inter faelicissimas terrarum Europae haec ipsa numerari meritò posset."

APPENDIX

It proved to be rewarding to compare the description of Groningen in the first edition of the *Historia* (ed. 1596, pp. 36-38) with the one in the edition of 1616 (pp. 18-20).[55] Both works were printed with utmost care, so that hardly any errors can be found. What I did find were three small but significant differences for which the author must have been responsible. In order to inform future readers of Emmius about the character of his additions and changes, it is worthwhile evaluating these differences:

(a) On p. 38 of the first edition of 1596 Emmius characterised the people of the town of Groningen as "populus oppidanus moribus comis, blandus, solers, industrius, à literarum cultu et captu non abhorrens"; later he added the word *dicax* between *blandus* and *solers* (p. 19 of 1616-edition). The *Oxford Latin Dictionary* translates *dicax* as: "having a ready tongue, given to making clever remarks at another's expense". Because of its position, between a series of positive qualifications, the meaning of *dicax*, appears to be positive. Emmius's use of the word should, therefore, not be compared with Rudolph Agricola's negative judgment of the uncouth, ill-disposed and uncivilized people of Groningen, which Agricola qualified as *loquax* ('garrulous'), in a letter to Adolph Occo (d.d. 11 October 1482).[56]

(b) As to the number of churches in Groningen, Emmius writes on p. 39 of the 1596-edition: "fana in universum septem", whereas on p. 19 of the 1616-edition this is changed to: "fana in universum XII"; though here, one may think to have found a printing error for 'VII', this appears not to be the case: the 'twelve churches' return in the more elaborate description of Groningen in the *De agro Frisiae inter Amasum et Lavicam flumina. Deque urbe Groninga in agro eodem: et de iure utriusque. Cum serie magistratuum praecipuorum* (first printed in 1605); and on p. 15 of the description *De urbe Groninga* in the 1616-edition, the number is explained as follows: "Fana nunc in eâ sunt in universum XII, ex quibus tria sunt parochialia, uti vocant, quinque monastica, quatuor xenodocheis conjuncta."

(c) The last two words of the remark: "Ex caeteris [sc. fanis], quae monasticis familiis dicata sunt, duo quoque peregregia et splendida, Franciscanum in oppido ferè medio, et Dominicanum Iacobaei ordinis: reliqua minora" (p. 39 of 1596-edition) were, twenty years later, changed to: "reliqua ejus generis, et que cum ptochodocheis cohaerent, minora" (p. 19 of 1616-edition).

---

[55] Cf. note 7.
[56] Akkerman, 'Agricola and Groningen', 17.

A.E. WALTER

ZU DEN GELEHRTEN UND POLITISCHEN VERBINDUNGEN
ZWISCHEN DER KURPFALZ UND DEN VEREINIGTEN
NIEDERLANDEN IM KONFESSIONELLEN ZEITALTER – AM
BEISPIEL DER KORRESPONDENZ DES HEIDELBERGER OBERRATS
GEORG MICHAEL LINGELSHEIM (1558-1636)

Zwischen der Republik der Vereinigten Niederlande und der Kurpfalz, den
wichtigsten reformierten Mächten im alten Europa, bestanden im konfessionellen Zeitalter enge diplomatische und konfessionelle Kontakte.[1] Die habsburgischen Niederlande erlebten seit 1566 einen Aufstand gegen die spani-
sche Krone, der sich unter der politischen Führung der oranischen Statthalter und der wirtschaftlich mächtigsten Provinz Holland zu einem immer
weitere Teile der Bevölkerung erfassenden Kampf gegen die Inquisition und
die Katholiken ausweitete und schließlich zum staatlichen Zusammenschluß
der nördlichen Provinzen führte, deren Unabhängigkeit von Spanien und
politische Selbständigkeit im Waffenstillstand von 1609 erstmals anerkannt,
im Westfälischen Frieden schließlich endgültig besiegelt wurde. Entstanden
war ein föderalistischer Staatenverband, dessen *publieke kerk* zwar calvinistisch war, in dessen pluralistischer Glaubenslandschaft die Calvinisten jedoch nur eine Minderheit bildeten, die sich außerdem in eine gemäßigte und
eine orthodoxe Strömung, die sog. *rekkelijken* und *preciezen*, aufspaltete.
Aus dieser realen konfessionellen Konstellation resultierte zum einen eine
von den Zeitgenossen gepriesene religiöse Toleranz, von der lediglich die
Katholiken ausgeschlossen blieben, soweit sich bei ihnen konfessionelle
Interessen mit politischen Ambitionen Spaniens verbanden. Zum anderen
führte der multikonfessionelle status quo zu einer Distanz zwischen dem
Staat und der als Öffentlichkeitskirche konzipierten *publieke kerk*, die allerdings nicht als eine Säkularisierung des Staates mißverstanden werden darf.
Ämter standen ausschließlich Calvinisten offen. Diesen Widerspruch zwischen der untrennbaren Einheit von Glauben und Amt einerseits und der
Distanz von Staat und Kirche andererseits löste die Staatsrechtslehre auf,
welche die Träger der öffentlichen Ämter mit dem Volk, einen Teil also mit
dem Ganzen, gleichsetzte.[2] Wie schwierig die Wahrung dieser Distanz reali-
ter jedoch fiel, wenn herausragende Vertreter politischer Ämter persönliches

---

[1] Eine eingehende Untersuchung fehlt bisher. Einen ersten knappen Überblick entwirft Biundo,'Kurpfalz und Holland'.
[2] Grundlegend dazu Schilling, 'Religion und Gesellschaft'.

Machtstreben mit konfessionellen Interessen verwoben, wurde im Verlauf des Konflikts zwischen Remonstranten und Kontraremonstranten deutlich, als sich die beiden maßgeblichen politischen Persönlichkeiten der Republik in den Jahrzehnten um 1600, der Landesadvocat der Staaten von Holland, Johan van Oldenbarnevelt (1547-1619), und der Statthalter von Holland, Seeland und Utrecht und Generalkapitän der Generalstaaten, Moritz von Oranien (1567-1625), jeweils einer der beiden Parteien in eindeutig politischer Intention anschlossen. Die Synode von Dordrecht (1618/19), die gegen den Widerstand Oldenbarnevelts von Moritz von Oranien, der sich 1617 demonstrativ auf die Seite der Kontraremonstranten geschlagen hatte, einberufen wurde, führte schließlich zu einer Verurteilung der Remonstranten, deren führende Vertreter verhaftet, deren Anhänger in großer Zahl ihrer Ämter enthoben wurden. Oldenbarnevelt selbst wurde hingerichtet. Die Deputierten dieser Synode, die durch die Teilnahme von Vertretern aus Großbritannien, der Eidgenossenschaft, aus Genf, der Kurpfalz, der Wetterauischen Grafen, aus Hessen und Bremen zu einem internationalen calvinistischen Konvent geworden war, definierten in den sog. *canones* die strittige Frage der Prädestination, dieses zentralen Punktes der calvinistischen Theorie, im Sinne der Gomaristen und unterzeichneten den Heidelberger Katechismus wie die *Confessio Belgica* als verbindliche Grundlagen calvinistischer Lehre.

Die Kurpfalz hatte ihre calvinistischen Glaubensbrüder seit Beginn des *tachtigjarige oorlog* unterstützt. Kurfürst Friedrich III. (1559-1576), der 1563 mit dem Heidelberger Katechismus und einer neuen Kirchenordnung die Kurpfalz dem Calvinismus zugeführt hatte, erlaubte den vor der spanischen Inquisition geflohenen niederländischen Calvinisten die Ansiedlung in Frankenthal. Sein Sohn Johann Casimir führte als Landesherr von Pfalz-Lautern 1578 selbst ein Heer in den Kampf, um die Sache Wilhelms von Oranien zu unterstützen, konnte jedoch keine Erfolge erringen und überwarf sich zudem mit diesem.[3] Erst am Ende seiner Kuradministration für den minderjährigen Friedrich IV. entspannte sich das Verhältnis Johann Casimirs zum Hause Oranien wieder, nach dem Tod seines Oheims heiratete 1593 der junge Kurfürst mit Luise Juliane sogar eine Oranierin. Zur gleichen Zeit gewannen die Grafen von Nassau-Dillenburg, Verwandte des oranischen Hauses, Einfluß auf die kurpfälzische Politik.[4] Die auf diese Weise dynastisch fundierte Verbindung zu den Vereinigten Niederlanden sollte sich spätestens im Dreißigjährigen Krieg für die Kurpfalz auszahlen. Zwar unterstützten die Staaten Kurfürst Friedrich V. (1610-1619) bei seinem Griff

---

[3] Cf. zu diesem Feldzug und zur Politik Johann Casimirs: Krüger, *Die Beziehungen der Rheinischen Pfalz*; Kuhn, *Pfalzgraf Johann Casimir von Pfalz-Lautern*, 127-46.

[4] Cf. Press, *Calvinismus und Territorialstaat*, 390ss.

nach der böhmischen Krone nicht wie gewünscht – und fest einkalkuliert –
mit Geld und Truppen, weil ihre Kräfte durch den Konflikt zwischen Remonstranten und Kontraremonstranten gerade zu dieser Zeit gebunden
waren und kurz darauf der Krieg mit Spanien wieder aufflammte, doch
gewährten sie dem Winterkönig mit seiner Familie, seinem Hof und seinen
Beamten in Den Haag großzügig Asyl und duldeten die überaus regen Aktivitäten einer pfälzischen Exilregierung, die sich bis zur kurzzeitigen Restitution der kurpfälzischen Herrschaft unter schwedischer Protektion von dort
aus entfalteten.[5] Den Haag entwickelte sich gar 'zu einem Zentrum des internationalen protestantischen Widerstands',[6] England, Frankreich, Schweden und Venedig unterhielten hier Gesandtschaften, die Vereinigten Niederlande ihrerseits investierten bedeutende Summen in die Allianzbemühungen
und Feldzüge dieser Mächte.

Die junge Republik der Vereinigten Niederlande gewann durch diese
Konzentration der europäischen Diplomatie auf ihrem Territorium eine
politische Nähe zu den Großmächten, die in dem seit 1621 fortgesetzten
Unabhängigkeitskampf gegen das katholische Spanien eine Stärkung der
Position der Staaten im europäischen Ringen garantierte. Bereits das Auf-
treten als glanzvolle Gastgeberin der Dordrechter Synode hatte ihre internationale Stellung gestärkt. Diese festigte sich in Folge einer ökonomischen
Prosperität, die v.a. dem Seehandel, der bis in die Neue Welt expandierte, zu
verdanken war und die auch durch das Kriegsgeschehen nicht unterbrochen
wurde. Die Vereinigten Niederlande durchlebten ihr goldenes Zeitalter. Mit
der wirtschaftlichen ging eine kulturelle Blüte einher, die in besonderem
Maße in der zeitgenössischen niederländischen Malerei sichtbar wurde, die
sich aber auch in der Dichtung widerspiegelte, die auf die deutsche
Dichtung so maßgeblichen Einfluß gewinnen sollte. Eine herausragende
Bedeutung für das europäische Geistesleben gewannen außerdem die
späthumanistischen Gelehrten. Einen hervorragenden Ruf konnte besonders
die Universität Leiden erwerben, die 1575 mit eindeutig konfessionspoliti-
scher Intention – nämlich den Calvinisten humanistische Bildung zu ermög-
lichen und so Beamte für die Aufgaben des Staates und Priester für die
Kirche heranzuziehen – gegründet worden war und sich neben Paris zu *dem*
Zentrum des europäischen Späthumanismus entwickelte. Sofort nach ihrer
Gründung übte die Universität eine große Anziehungskraft auf Studenten
und Gelehrte des protestantischen Europa aus, wirkten an ihr doch einige
der größten Geister der Zeit.[7]

---

[5] Zu den Aktivitäten und zur personellen Zusammensetzung dieser Exilregierung cf. Schubert, 'Die pfälzische Exilregierung im Dreißigjährigen Krieg'.
[6] Lademacher, *Geschichte der Niederlande*, 502.
[7] Zur Geschichte der Leidener Universität cf. den zum vierhundertjährigen Jubiläum

Parallel zu diesen politischen Beziehungen zwischen den Vereinigten Niederlanden und der Kurpfalz entwickelten sich auch zahlreiche persönliche Kontakte. Diese wurden nicht nur über niederländische Glaubensflüchtlinge, von denen einige wie der Hofprediger Petrus Dathenus (†1588) oder der Professor für Geschichte und Bibliothekar der Palatina Janus Gruter (1560-1627) in einflußreiche Ämter in Heidelberg aufsteigen konnten, gepflegt, sondern ganz wesentlich durch Korrespondenzen geknüpft. Der Brief war das zentrale Kommunikationsmedium der europäischen Humanisten. Hier wurde der gelehrte Austausch gepflegt, hier wurden die politischen und konfessionellen Ereignisse diskutiert, hier wurde aber auch das persönliche Wort gesucht. Geschöpft aus dem reichen Wissenskosmos humanistischer Bildung, ausformuliert auch immer mit dem Blick auf eine spätere Publikation, sind diese Briefe eine der wichtigsten, bisher bei weitem noch nicht ausgeschöpften Quellen jeder kulturgeschichtlichen Forschung.[8]

Zu den großen Epistolographen der späthumanistischen *res publica litteraria* gehörte Georg Michael Lingelsheim. Seine Korrespondenz teilt das Schicksal zehntausender von Briefen aus dieser Epoche, die als ungehobene Schätze in den Archiven und Bibliotheken Europas und Amerikas liegen, soweit sie nicht den Zeitläuften unwiderruflich zum Opfer gefallen sind. Die internationale Wissenschaft hat mit der Verzeichnung der erhaltenen Briefbestände eine ihrer größten Herausforderungen noch vor sich, obwohl mit der Einrichtung und organisierten Führung nationaler Autographenkataloge oder zahlreichen auf einzelne Epistolographen, Korrespondentenkreise oder Korrespondenzgruppen konzentrierten Forschungen eine große Zahl dieser Briefe bereits bekannt geworden ist. Eine mehrjährige akribische Recherche hat mehr als 2.300 Briefe der Korrespondenz Lingelsheims aus sechs Jahrzehnten zwischen 1579 und 1636 in deutschen, niederländischen, französischen, schweizerischen, österreichischen, polnischen, dänischen und englischen Archiven und Bibliotheken entdecken lassen, von denen nur ein Teil bisher durch Editionen seit dem 17. Jahrhundert zugänglich oder durch

---

(1975) erschienenen Sammelband *Leiden University in the Seventeenth Century. An Exchange of Learning*. Die Bedeutung der Universität für und ihre Stellung in der europäischen *res publica litteraria* untersuchen Dibon, 'L'université de Leyde'; und – für die deutschen Beziehungen grundlegend – Schneppen, *Niederländische Universitäten und deutsches Geistesleben*.

[8] Zum Brief der Renaissance und des deutschen Barock liegen zwei Tagungsbände vor, die die wesentlichen Aspekte der Epistolographie wie der Brieftheorie behandeln: *Der Brief im Zeitalter der Renaissance* und *Briefe deutscher Barockautoren*. Darüberhinaus ist für die humanistische/späthumanistische Brieftheorie äußerst wichtig: Fumaroli, 'Genèse de l'épistolographie classique'. Maßgeblich für die späthumanistische Briefkultur bleiben nach wie vor die Ausführungen von Trunz, 'Der deutsche Späthumanismus um 1600 als Standeskultur'. Dieser Aufsatz, der 1931 erstmals erschien, ist jetzt wieder ganz leicht zugänglich und um überaus wertvolle bibliographische Hinweise und Materialien reich ergänzt; zum Brief und zur Freundschaftsdichtung sp. 36ss.

verschiedene Bestandskataloge bekannt war. Diese Korrespondenz umfaßte einen Kreis von nahezu einhundert Korrespondenten, wobei sich Einzelbriefe ebenso finden wie langjährige regelmäßig geführte Briefwechsel. Der Korrespondentenkreis beschränkte sich geographisch ausnahmslos auf die Regionen des Heiligen Römischen Reiches deutscher Nation und Europas, mit denen im konfessionellen Zeitalter die Kurpfalz, deren Kurfürsten Lingelsheim über fast vierzig Jahre diente, diplomatische Verbindungen suchte. D.h. Lingelsheims Korrespondenz bewegte sich in der antipapistisch-antihabsburgischen Sphäre des – mit der einzigen Ausnahme Frankreichs, wo aber gerade die Humanisten zu den *politiques* gehörten – nichtkatholischen Westeuropa.[9] So zählten auch einige der herausragenden niederländischen Späthumanisten zu Lingelsheims Korrespondenten. Der Schwerpunkt dieser Korrespondenzen, von denen heute noch 79 Briefe existieren, die sich unregelmäßig auf fünf Personen verteilen, lag in den eineinhalb Jahrzehnten zwischen 1604 und 1619, also in der Zeit zwischen dem Beginn der Waffenstillstandsverhandlungen und der Dordrechter Synode. Die Markierung dieser beiden für die konfessionelle Entwicklung in den Niederlanden entscheidenden historischen Eckpunkte legt die Fragestellung nahe, inwieweit sich die Ereignisse dieser Zeitspanne in einer späthumanistischen Korrespondenz, deren Korrespondenten sämtlich dem reformierten Bekenntnis angehörten, reflektierte, welche Spuren die konfessionellen und politischen Entscheidungen also in einer Korrespondenz des konfessionellen Zeitalters hinterließen, und wie sich persönliches Schicksal, offizielles Amt und humanistisch-irenische Positionen vor diesem Horizont miteinander verknüpften. Diesen Fragen soll hier nachgegangen werden. Vorher jedoch scheint es angebracht, die Biographie Georg Michael Lingelsheims zu skizzieren, dessen Name zu seiner Zeit so bekannt war wie er heutzutage in Vergessenheit geraten ist. Er hat in der deutschen und europäischen historischen, literaturgeschichtlichen und neulateinischen Forschung zwar verschiedentlich als wichtige Figur in der Nebenrolle eines geistigen Mentors beispielsweise eines Jean Hotman oder eines Martin Opitz seinen Auftritt, stand jedoch noch niemals sozusagen als Hauptdarsteller im Zentrum wissenschaftlicher Aufmerksamkeit. Angesichts der zahlreichen, immer weiter tradierten Fehler und der großen Lücken der bisherigen Darstellungen, möge der folgenden Biographie deshalb eine korrigierende und ergänzende Ausführlichkeit erlaubt sein.[10]

[9] Eine kulturgeschichtliche Auswertung der Korrespondenz und des Korrespondentenkreises nimmt der Vf. in seiner soeben an der Univ. Osnabrück eingereichten Dissertation vor. Sie wird im nächsten Jahr in der Reihe 'Frühe Neuzeit' (Niemeyer-Verlag Tübingen) erscheinen.

[10] Cf. als ersten umfangreichen biographischen Versuch Walter, 'Georg Michael Lingelsheim'. Dort auch die relevante Forschungsliteratur, die an dieser Stelle nicht titularisch wiederholt werden soll.

Georg Michael Lingelsheim wurde am 9. Dezember 1558 geboren.[11] Der Geburtsort ist unbekannt, lag aber auf keinen Fall in Straßburg,[12] wenngleich er die Reichsstadt in seinen Briefen mehrmals als seine 'patria' bezeichnete. Sein Vater Diebolt (um 1528-1609) war Lehrer am Straßburger Gymnasium, das 1566 als Akademie privilegiert wurde, und es ist anzunehmen, daß der junge Lingelsheim diese Schule besuchte. Sichere Nachricht über seinen Bildungsweg können wir erst ab dem Jahre 1579 gewinnen, als sich Lingelsheim an der Heidelberger Universität immatrikulierte,[13] diese aber bereits ein Jahr später wieder verließ. Wahrscheinlich zeichnete für diesen Schritt die Änderung der Universitätsstatuten durch den lutherischen Kurfürsten Ludwig VI. (1576-1583) verantwortlich, entstammte doch Lingelsheim der reformierten Minderheit Straßburgs. Durch Vermittlung Hubert Languets, der mit Philipp Sidney in freundschaftlichem Kontakt stand, erhielt Lingelsheim noch 1579 die Stelle als *praeceptor* des damals gerade seine *peregrinatio academica* absolvierenden jüngeren Bruders des englischen Adligen,[14] trennte sich von diesem jedoch bereits ein Jahr später und kehrte nach Straßburg zurück, um an der dortigen Akademie bei Obertus Giphanius (Hubrecht van Giffen, 1534-1604) die Jurisprudenz zu studieren.[15] Für das Studienjahr 1582/83 immatrikulierte sich Lingelsheim an der Universität Basel, wo er am 25. Juli 1583 von Simon Grynäus zum *doctor iuris utriusque* promoviert wurde.[16] Mitte des Jahres 1584 trat er in

[11] Bisher wurde – basierend auf der Angabe bei Johannes Gualterius Belga (d.i. Janus Gruter), *Chronicon chronicorum ecclesiastico-politicum, Chronici chronicorum ecclesiastici lib. II* (1614), 1105 – stets das Jahr 1556 als Geburtsjahr angegeben. Lingelsheim bezeichnete aber selbst in einem Brief an Jacques Bongars vom 9.12.1605 sein Geburtsdatum: 'Vellem te praesenti nos hodie saltem frui posse, eo quod annum aetatis XLVIII hodie ingredior' (Autograph in der Burgerbibliothek Bern, cod. 141, no. 74, 102v). Rechnerisch ergibt sich daraus das Geburtsjahr 1558. Da über seine Geburt keinerlei offizielle Dokumente zu existieren scheinen, sehe ich bis auf weiteres keinen Grund, an dieser Selbstaussage zu zweifeln.

[12] Die Taufbücher dieser Zeit sind komplett im Archive municipale de Strasbourg erhalten, der Name Georg Michael Lingelsheim findet sich nirgends.

[13] Cf. *Die Matrikel der Universität Heidelberg*, 2. Teil (1554-1662), 86.

14 Dies geht aus zwei Briefen Languets an Lingelsheim vom 5.3.1580 bzw. vom 28.1.1581 (Abschriften in der Bibliothèque National de Paris, Col. Dupuy 797, f. 364 bzw. f. 362). Cf. auch Nicollier-de Weck, *Hubert Languet*, 295, Anm. 92; und 411, Anm. 119.

[15] Davon berichtete Lingelsheim in einem Brief an den Wiener Hofbibliothekar Hugo Blotius vom 15.1.1582: 'Hic igitur ad studia mea redij, quae peregrinatione illa interrupta fuerunt: et remotis omnibus alijs curis et occupationibus illis solis vaco, praesertim vero Iurisprudentiae, in qua auctorem habeo benevolentissimum dominum Giphanium tuarum laudum et virtutis conscium et praeconem.' (Autograph in der Österreichischen Nationalbibliothek Wien, cod. 9737 Z16, 216r)

[16] Cf. *Die Matrikel der Universität Basel*, 312. Zwei Exemplare der Dissertation mit dem Titel *Theses De Solvtionibvs eas pro consequendis in V.I. Docturae Codicilis in inclyta Basiliensi Academia propositas D.O.M.A. publicè disputando propugnabit Georgivs Michael Lingelshemivs Argentorat. A.D. XI. Kal. August. MDXXCIII.* (Basel 1583) haben sich in der Öffentlichen Bibliothek der Universität Basel erhalten (Signaturen: Diss. 204 no 52 [mit handschriftlicher Widmung Lingelsheims]; Diss. 230 no 76), ebenso die Einladung zur Promotion

kurpfälzische Dienste als 'praeceptor und Zuchtmeister' des Kurprinzen, der nach dem Willen seines Oheims, des Administrators Johann Casimir, eine calvinistische Erziehung erhalten sollte.[17] Für Lingelsheims weiteres Leben war diese Bestallung entscheidend: 1592 mit dem Regierungsantritt seines Zöglings Friedrich IV. in den Oberrat, das entscheidende politische Gremium der Kurpfalz, aufgestiegen, verblieb er bis zu seiner Flucht aus Heidelberg im November 1621 in Diensten des aktivsten protestantischen Reichsstandes auf dem Boden des Heiligen Römischen Reiches deutscher Nation in dieser einflußreichen politischen Position. In der kurpfälzischen Politik verbanden sich um 1600 konfessionelle mit machtpolitischen und dynastischen Interessen, die reichspolitisch auf die Zusammenführung der protestantischen Stände zu einer Fraktion unter kurpfälzischer Führung gegen die katholischen Kaiser aus dem Hause Habsburg zielten, die aber zugleich eine europäische Dimension besaßen, denn die pfälzischen Kurfürsten unterstützten den westeuropäischen Calvinismus in seinem Existenzkampf in Frankreich und den Niederlanden militärisch und suchten enge diplomatische Verbindungen zu Heinrich IV. ebenso wie zu Bethlen Gabor. Sie knüpften außerdem dynastische Verbindungen mit den Häusern Oranien und Stuart – auch hier war die Stoßrichtung also stets antihabsburgisch und antikatholisch.[18] Lingelsheim gehörte im Heidelberger Oberrat nicht zu den forcierenden, letztendlich einen Krieg zwischen den Religionsparteien einkalkulierenden Kräften, die sich um Christian von Anhalt sammelten, er zählte ebensowenig zu den Räten, die einer Annahme der böhmischen Königskrone, wodurch dieser Krieg schließlich ausgelöst wurde, zurieten. Lingelsheim vertrat vielmehr eine gemäßigte, irenische Position, die allerdings eindeutig politische Intentionen im Sinne calvinistischer Interessen verfolgte und somit den Grundzügen kurpfälzischer Politik entsprach, indem er – wie auch David Pareus mit seinem *Irenicum sive de unione et synodo Evangelicorum concilianda* (Heidelberg 1614) – die Einheit der Protestanten einforderte, zugleich aber den römischen Antichristen und das katholische Haus

---

Lingelsheims und dreier weiterer Promovenden (ibid., Signatur: Mscr. O 11a, f. 693).

[17] Obwohl ihn die kurpfälzischen Dienerbücher erst unter dem 1.1.1587 als 'praeceptor vnd Zuchtmeister' des Kurprinzen (Generallandesarchiv Karlsruhe, 67/928, 82v) führten, lassen verschiedene Briefe an Lingelsheim aus dem Jahre 1584 keinen Zweifel, daß er bereits Mitte des Jahres dieses Amt übernommen hatte (so der Brief des Petrus Denaisius an ihn vom 18.6.1584 [Abschrift in der Staats- und Universitätsbibliothek Hamburg, Sup. ep. 4°34, 1r] und von Obertus Giphanius vom 16.8.1584 [Abschriften in der Kongelige Bibliotek København, u.a.: Gl. kgl. S. 4°2133, no. 220, abgedruckt in: Reifferscheid, *Briefe G.M. Lingelsheims*, 1s.]). Giphanius teilte außerdem Freunden in zwei Briefen vom Oktober bzw. Dezember des Jahres die Berufung Lingelsheims zum praeceptor des jungen Fürsten mit (cf. die entsprechenden Briefauszüge ibid., 684).

[18] Dazu im einzelnen – und zu Lingelsheims Funktion in der kurpfälzischen Politik dieser Zeit – stets heranzuziehen die großartige Untersuchung von Press, *Calvinismus und Territorialstaat*.

Habsburg als Feindbilder aus der *res publica christiana* ausgrenzte.[19] So vermochte er auch trotz seiner vorsichtigen Haltung in einem Brief an Pierre Dupuy (1582-1651) die Annahme der böhmischen Königskrone durch Friedrich V. als eine notwendige Entscheidung für die Sicherheit der christlichen Sache und des Reiches vorbehaltlos zu verteidigen:

> Princeps Elector noster tandem persuaderi sibi passus est, ut delatum Regnum Bohemicum accipiat, eo quod si ipse recusaret porro, ad extrema redacti Bohemi perduci possent ad consilia rei Christianae exitiosa atque eo deuentura res esset, ut limitem Turcicum habituri essemus in ipsa ditione nostra Superioris Palatinatus.[20]

Diese Entscheidung des seine politischen und finanziellen Möglichkeiten maßlos überschätzenden pfälzischen Kurfürsten führte geradewegs in die Katastrophe des Dreißigjährigen Krieges. Lingelsheim floh in seine *patria* Straßburg und zog sich aus der aktiven Politik zurück, hielt allerdings über seine Korrespondenz mit Ludwig Camerarius Verbindung mit der pfälzischen Exilregierung in Den Haag und blieb ein genauer Beobachter der politischen Ereignisse im Reich, die seiner – keinesfalls ungerechtfertigten – Meinung nach auf die völlige Ausrottung der Calvinisten zielten, die er im Jahre 1629 verwirklicht sah mit dem Restitutionsedikt, das er gegenüber Grotius entsprechend kommentierte: 'Omnis libertas apud nos periit. [...] Ita Calvinistae miseri profligantur ex Imperio.'[21] Das Eingreifen Schwedens kehrte diese Entwicklung allerdings noch einmal um und ermöglichte Lingelsheim nach der Restitution der Kurpfalz unter Ägide Gustav Adolfs 1633 sogar die Rückkehr nach Heidelberg, wo er sich um den Wiederaufbau der Universität bemühte.[22] Doch die letzten Lebensjahre Lingelsheims besitzen eine ganz besondere Tragik, denn bereits ein Jahr später – nach der Schlacht von Nördlingen – mußte er erneut aus Heidelberg fliehen, diesmal in die Festung Frankenthal. Nachdem auch diese erobert worden war, geriet er, der von der katholischen Partei im Reich als einer der führenden kurpfälzischen Räte in der 'Rebellion' gegen den Kaiser betrachtet wurde, in mehrwöchige

---

[19] Zur kurpfälzischen Irenik cf. Holtmann, *Die pfälzische Irenik*, sowie Brinkmann, *Die Irenik des David Pareus*.

[20] Lingelsheim an Dupuy, 15./25.10.1619 (Autograph in der Bibliothèque Nationale de Paris, Col. Dupuy 699, 253r).

[21] Lingelsheim an Grotius, 17.4.1629 (Autograph in der Bibliotheek der Universiteit van Amsterdam, R 31, c).

[22] Dies geht aus einem Brief Lingelsheims an Johannes Buxtorf d.J. vom 7.10.1633 (Autograph in der Öffentlichen Bibliothek der Universität Basel, G I 60, 16r) sowie aus seiner Korrespondenz der Jahre 1633/34 mit Matthias Bernegger hervor, den Lingelsheim massiv drängte, eine Professur in Heidelberg anzunehmen, die dieser jedoch unter dem Eindruck des sich wendenden Kriegsglücks in seinem Brief an Lingelsheim vom 7.9.1634 ausschlug (Abschrift in der Staats- und Universitätsbibliothek Hamburg, Sup. ep. 4°32, 127).

Festungshaft.[23] Kurz nach seiner Freilassung, Lingelsheims letzter Brief datiert vom 26. Juli 1636,[24] verstarb er im tausendfachen Morden des Krieges unbeachtet.

Als Politiker blieb Lingelsheim bis zu seinem Lebensende ein vehementer Verfechter der calvinistischen Sache und bei aller humanistisch-irenischen Zurückhaltung ein überzeugter Verteidiger der kurpfälzischen Ambitionen. Dieses Bild machten sich auch die Zeitgenossen und spätere Generationen von Lingelsheim, dem wiederholt verschiedene scharfe satirische und sogar kontroverstheologische Schriften zugeschrieben wurden. Scaliger beispielsweise vermutete ihn als Autoren der gegen Justus Lipsius gerichteten Polemik *Dissertatio de Idolo Hallensi Iusti Lipsii mangonio et phaleris exornato atque producto* aus dem Jahre 1605.[25] Doch er verfaßte, soweit wir es heute sehen können, überhaupt kein einziges selbständiges Werk außer seiner Dissertation und trat ansonsten nur mit einer anonym erschienenen lateinischen Übersetzung der englischen Ausgabe der *Militia Romana* von Henry Savile hervor.[26] Seine bedeutendste editorische Leistung war die erste vollständige Ausgabe der *Historiarum sui temporis, ab anno Domini 1543 usque ad annum 1607, libri CXXXVIII* des Jacques-Auguste de Thou,[27] die in der prokatholischen Atmosphäre Frankreichs nach der Ermordung Heinrichs IV. nicht mehr zu veröffentlichen war und wegen ihrer Verfechtung der Gedanken staatlicher Souveränität und religiöser Toleranz auf dem

---

[23] In einer Proskriptionsliste aus dem Jahre 1625 tauchte Lingelsheims Name an erster Stelle der von der kurbayerischen Regierung gesuchten Heidelberger Politiker auf: '1. Dr. Lingelsheimber Vice Cantzler vnndt geheimber Rath, hat sich viel brauchen laßen in dem Rebellions weesen wie dannch, helt sich zue Straßburg auf, hat sich uff die außgangene Citation nicht endtschuldiget noch erschienen; dießer hat ein Haus allhier vnndt Gärtten.' (Manuskript im Bayerischen Haupt-Staatsarchiv München, Kasten blau 122/4a, 3'; mit Transkribierungsfehlern abgedruckt in Von Lingelsheim, *Familien-Chronik*, 25).

[24] In diesem an Josias Glaser in Straßburg gerichteten Brief berichtete Lingelsheim sogleich in den ersten Sätzen von seiner Einkerkerung und von einer durch diese verursachten schweren Erkrankung: 'Miseriae nostrae diuturnae, ad quas accessit pro cumulo carcer quinquaginta dierum et ex illo squalore contractus morbus gravissimus, impediverunt omnem scriptionem. Iam respirare datum est aliquantulum, sed tenemur adhuc inclusi septo huius urbis.' (mehrere Abschriften in der Kongeligen Bibliotek København, ich zitiere nach: Böll. Brevs. U. 4°, no. 551.)

[25] Cf. Scaligers Brief vom 25.5.1605 (Abschrift in der Bibliothèque Nationale et Universitaire de Strasbourg, Ms 155, 39r-v). Lingelsheim antwortete Scaliger am 28.6.1605, daß nicht er, sondern vielmehr Petrus Denaisius der Verfasser wäre: 'Verum non satis notus tibi ego, si me talem foetum edere posse putasti, ac quamuis auctoris maximè intersit nomen suum caelari, cum viuendum ipsi sit inter Jesuitas et homines a vera fide alienissimos, tamen apud te dissimulandum non putaui, auctorem scripsi esse Petrum Denaisium, Argentorati, quae et mihi patria [...]' (Autograph in der Bibliotheek der Universiteit Utrecht, ms 987, 233r).

[26] *Henrici Savilis Angli Commentarius De Militia Romana Ex Anglico Latinus factus* (Heidelberg 1601). – Wie verworren die Situation im Hinblick auf eine sichere Zuweisung von Werken an den Verfasser Georg Michael Lingelsheim ist, zeigt sich auch bei dieser Schrift, die in verschiedenen Bibliothekskatalogen Marquard Freher und in der Staatsbibliothek zu Berlin sogar Friedrich Lingelsheim (Sign.: Rn 6802; das Exemplar ist verloren) zugewiesen wird.

[27] Sie erschien unter dem fingierten Druckort Genf 1620.

päpstlichen Index stand.[28] Die Publikation dieser Zeitgeschichte, zumal in dem brisanten Jahre 1620, erhielt somit einen eminenten konfessionspolitischen Charakter und paßt sich in das Bild ein, das wir und die Zeitgenossen von Lingelsheim gewonnen haben und das durch weitere Zeugnisse gesichert werden kann, so durch die Edition einer bisher nicht bekannten Schrift des Jacques Bongars gegen den Kardinal Bellarminus[29] oder durch die Publikation eines Briefes an Marc Antonio de Dominis, dessen Konversion eindeutig begrüßt wird.[30]

Nichtsdestotrotz sollten wir uns davor hüten, Lingelsheim als Politiker über- und als späthumanistischen Gelehrten abzuwerten. Die Zeitgenossen schätzten an Lingelsheim gerade seine humanistische Bildung, und seine Briefe sind ein beredtes Zeugnis dafür, wie sehr Lingelsheim an der gelehrten Kommunikation der *res publica litteraria* partizipierte und welchen Stellenwert er in der Gelehrtenrepublik besaß. Zwar trat er nicht durch eigene Werke hervor, aber er war ein unermüdlicher Förderer und Anreger der philologischen und historischen Forschungen anderer. Ob er auswärtigen Gelehrten den Zugang zu den Beständen der Palatina ermöglichte, ob er sich um einen Drucker für die Schriften seiner Freunde bemühte, ob er an Ausgaben des Heliodor oder des Apollodor maßgeblich mitwirkte,[31] oder ob er sich an der Suche nach Scaliger-Briefen für deren Edition beteiligte[32] –

---

[28] Zu diesem Werk liegt eine ausgezeichnete Studie vor von Kinser, *The Works of Jacques-Auguste de Thou*; zur Edition Lingelsheims dort 26-38 et passim.

[29] Diese bisher von der Forschung übersehene Schrift trägt den Titel: *Ad Roberti Cardinalis Bellarmini librum De temporali potestate Papae commentatio [...]* (Heidelberg 1612) und befindet sich heute unter den Bongarsiana der Burgerbibliothek Bern (Sign.: Bong. I. 212 [2]). Daß Bongars der Verfasser und Lingelsheim derjenige war, der sie in Heidelberg zum Druck gebracht hatte, entdeckte Lingelsheim selbst in seinem Brief an Jean Hotman vom 5.2.1613: 'J'ay estè bien aise d'entendre le iugement de Padre Paolo, de l'Antibellarmin de feu mons de Bongars, que i'ay fait imprimer icy sans y mettre son nom. Car il voulait que personne ne le scent, depuis son deces i'ay trouvè raisonable, qu'on es scent l'auteur. Je vous enuoye vn exemplaire, que i'ay en d'un de mes a qui ie l'auois donnè, veu que nuls exemplaires se trouuent plus icy et que i'ay distribuè tout ce qu'i'auois.' Lingelsheim an Hotman, 5.2.1613 (Autograph in der Bibliothèque de la Sociéte du Protestantisme français Paris, Mss. 10, V, 13r). Lingelsheim hatte das Manuskript von Bongars Ende des Jahres 1611 erhalten und gab es mit einigen Überarbeitungen an den Drucker weiter. Der Druck verzögerte sich jedoch, erst Anfang April des folgenden Jahres konnte Lingelsheim die ersten Exemplare an seinen Freund senden. Die Edition dieser Schrift zieht sich durch die Korrespondenz zwischen Lingelsheim und Bongars von Januar bis April 1612.

[30] Dieser Brief ist in lateinischer und englisch übersetzter Version einer Verteidigungsschrift de Dominis' angehängt: *A manifestation of the motives whereupon [...] M.A. Marcvs Antonius de Dominis, Archbishop of Spalato [...] vndertook his departure thence, Englished out of his latine copy* (London 1616), M2r-M3v. (British Library London, 477.a.26 (1))

[31] Den bei Hieronymus Commelinus in Heidelberg erscheinenden Ausgaben des Heliodor (1596) und des Apollodor (1599) gehen Widmungsreden an Lingelsheim voran, die auf seine maßgebliche Beteiligung an diesen Werken hindeuten. Cf. Port, *Hieronymus Commelinus*, 36; 40. Die an Lingelsheim gerichteten Widmungsvorreden beider Werke ibid., 106s. und 123s.

[32] In der Korrespondenz zwischen Lingelsheim und Ludwig Camerarius ging es in den

Lingelsheim befand sich stets auf der Höhe der gelehrten Diskussionen seiner Zeit, sein Rat wurde von vielen Seiten gesucht, seine Hilfe gewährte er gern und uneigennützig. Seine Teilnahme an der internationalen Kommunikation der *res publica litteraria* sicherte sich Lingelsheim durch seine umfangreiche Korrespondenz. Halboffizielle diplomatische, aber immer wieder auch in gelehrte Diskurse abschweifende Briefe standen neben gelehrten, ihrerseits wiederum mit politischen Nachrichten durchsetzten. So wie Amtspflicht und Gelehrsamkeit im Leben Lingelsheims nebeneinander existierten, waren beide Bereiche auch in seiner Korrespondenz nicht voneinander zu trennen. Das trifft im besonderen Maße auch für Lingelsheims niederländische Korrespondenzen und ihren biographischen Ausgangspunkt zu, knüpfte er doch während einer seiner seltenen diplomatischen Missionen persönliche Kontakte zu den niederländischen Gelehrten, mit denen er später in Briefwechsel eintrat.

Mitte des Jahres 1602 befand sich der pfälzische Kurfürst Friedrich IV., obwohl noch jung an Jahren, in einem besorgniserregenden Gesundheitszustand aufgrund seines exzessiven Lebenswandels und rang für einige Tage sogar mit dem Tode. Da sein Sohn zu diesem Zeitpunkt gerade erst sechs Jahre alt war, die Regierung jedoch erst im Alter von 18 Jahren antreten durfte, drohte der Kurpfalz bei einem frühzeitigen Ableben des Kurfürsten eine langjährige Administration, die nach geltendem Reichsrecht dem Fürsten Philipp Ludwig von Pfalz-Neuburg zugefallen wäre. Dieser jedoch war ein orthodoxer Lutheraner, seine Vormundschaft hätte eine ernste Bedrohung für das reformierte Bekenntnis in der Kurpfalz bedeutet. Schon einmal hatte die Kurpfalz unter dem lutherischen Kurfürsten Ludwig VI. einen Konfessionswechsel erlebt, der zu einem großen Aderlaß der Beamten und Professoren geführt hatte. Erst unter der Administration Johann Casimirs, endgültig jedoch mit der Übertragung der Kurwürde auf Friedrich IV. konnte der Calvinismus gesichert werden. Der kurpfälzische Oberrat als zentrale weltliche Behörde versuchte natürlich, diese neuerliche Gefahr abzuwenden: In einem Testament Friedrichs IV. wurde Ende des Jahres unter Verletzung der Reichsgesetze die Administration auf den calvinistischen Pfalzgrafen Johann I. von Zweibrücken übertragen, der die Sicherung des reformierten Bekenntnisses in der Kurpfalz garantierte und sämtliche bestehenden Landesordnungen anerkannte. Zu Kontutoren bestimmte das

Jahren 1624 und 1625 immer wieder um die Edition der Scaliger-Briefe, für die Lingelsheim nach Zeugnissen suchte. Diese Edition, Ausdruck des von der europäischen res publica besonders eifrig gepflegten Anliegens, die Briefe großer Gelehrter zu edieren, erschien unter dem Titel *Illustriss. viri Iosephi Scaligeri [...] epistolae, omnes quae reperiri potuerunt, nunc primum collectae ac editae* im Jahre 1628 in Frankfurt.

Testament u.a. neben der Kurfürstin Louise Juliane und Graf Johann VII. von Nassau-Dillenburg auch Moritz von Oranien. Dessen Zustimmung zu dieser Vormundschaftsregelung mußte jedoch erst noch eingeholt werden. Mit diesem Auftrag wurde Lingelsheim betraut, der Anfang März 1603 in die Vereinigten Niederlande aufbrach.[33]

Den Verlauf der Reise und seiner Verhandlungen schilderte Lingelsheim ausführlich in mehreren Briefen zwischen dem 26. März und 14. Mai 1603 an seinen Schwiegervater und Kollegen im Heidelberger Oberrat Michael Loefen (um 1550-1620).[34] Lingelsheim und sein Begleiter, der Heidelberger Hofrichter Johann Gernand (um 1545-1615) nutzten ihre diplomatische Mission zu einem längeren Besuch in Leiden. Dort wurden sie von Daniel Heinsius, der im vorangegangenen Jahr seine erste öffentliche Vorlesung gehalten hatte, im philosophischen Hörsaal mit einer *Oratio cum Theocritvm auspicaretur*[35] ehrenvoll begrüßt. Der – und das verdeutlicht nicht zuletzt die akademische Lobrede Heinsius' – in der europäischen *res publica litteraria* bereits berühmte Lingelsheim gewann während dieses Aufenthaltes Zugang zu Joseph Justus Scaliger und seinem Schülerkreis. Aus dieser ersten und einzigen persönlichen Begegnung entstanden teilweise langjährige Korrespondenzen, die fortan den Heidelberger Politiker und Gelehrten mit diesem holländischen Zentrum des europäischen Späthumanismus und zugleich des europäischen Calvinismus verbanden. So wirkten sämtliche niederländischen Korrespondenten Lingelsheims in Leiden als Professoren bzw. hatten die dortige Universität absolviert.

Einen ganz offensichtlich singulären Brief richtete Lingelsheim am 31. März 1604 an den Professor für Griechisch Bonaventura Vulcanius (1538-1614), der in religiösen Fragen zeit seines Lebens jede persönliche Parteinahme konsequent vermied.[36] Lingelsheim bedankte sich hier für die freundliche Aufnahme, die ihm Vulcanius im vorangehenden Jahr in Leiden gewährt hatte und empfahl einen jungen Studenten, der an der damals berühmten medizinischen Fakultät der Universität studieren wollte, der

---

[33] Zu dieser Situation cf. Press, *Calvinismus und Territorialstaat*, 420-9; zu Lingelsheims Mission ibidem, 428s.

[34] Die Autographen dieser Briefe befinden sich in der Staats- und Universitätsbibliothek Hamburg, Sup. ep., 251-6.

[35] Diese Rede ist der *Dan. Heinsii Poematvm nova editio auctior emendatiorque: Quorum seriem aversa statim pagina indicabit* (Leiden 1606) beigefügt (302-17). Ihr geht eine Widmung 'NOBILISS. AMPLISS. | VV. | GEORGIO MICHAELI | LINGELSHEMIO | IOANNI GERNANDO, | Ser. Electoris consiliarijs. | D.D.D. | DAN. HEINSIVS' voran (301).

[36] Eine Biographie ist ein dringendes Desiderat. Sie besitzt mit seiner umfangreichen Manuskriptsammlung eine wunderbare Ausgangssituation, cf. dazu den Katalog von Molhuysen, *Codices Vulcaniani*. Vorerst bleiben wir auf die biographischen Artikel in den bekannten Nachschlagewerken angewiesen, am ausführlichsten hier Ter Horst, 'Vulcanius'; Roulez, 'Vulcanius'; jeweils mit Hinweisen auf die ältere Literatur.

Obhut des Professors. Es gehörte zu den üblichen Kommunikationsprozes-
sen der Gelehrtenrepublik, daß berühmte Gelehrte junge Studierende mit
Empfehlungsschreiben an ebenso berühmte Gelehrte des Ortes, den der
Empfohlene im Rahmen seiner *peregrinatio academica* besuchen wollte,
ausstatteten.[37] Diese Briefe blieben durchaus Einzelstücke und entstanden
nicht unweigerlich aus einer bereits bestehenden oder in der Folge entstehenden umfangreicheren Korrespondenz heraus. Davon ist auch in diesem
Falle auszugehen, denn Andeutungen auf einen weiteren Briefwechsel zwischen Lingelsheim und Vulcanius sind Lingelsheims übriger Korrespondenz
nicht zu entnehmen.

Mit dem herausragenden Vertreter der älteren Generation der Leidener
Späthumanisten, mit Joseph Justus Scaliger (1540-1609),[38] entspann sich
jedoch zwischen 1605 und 1608 eine zwar spärliche, dennoch kontinuierliche Korrespondenz. Insgesamt entstanden in diesem Zeitraum sieben Briefe,
vier von der Hand Lingelsheims, drei aus der Feder Scaligers. Hinweise auf
weitere Briefe konnten wir bisher nicht aufspüren, so daß wir davon ausge-
hen müssen, mit diesem Bestand die komplette Korrespondenz der beiden
heute noch vorliegen zu haben. Der im französischen Agen geborene Sohn
des weitberühmten Verfassers der *Poetices libri septem* hatte nach einem
unsteten Wanderleben und einer durch einen französischen Adligen finan-
zierten freien Gelehrtenexistenz 1593 einen Ruf an die Leidener Universität
gegen die Aussicht auf eine großzügige Entlohnung und das Versprechen,
keinen Lehrverpflichtungen nachkommen zu müssen, angenommen. Nach
dem abrupten Ausscheiden des Justus Lipsius (1547-1606) konnte die Universität somit den neben jenem wohl bedeutendsten Gelehrten seiner Zeit
gewinnen. Obwohl der 'aquila in nubibus'[39] nicht an der Universität lehrte,
zog alleine sein Ruf Studenten nach Leiden, wo er einen großen Schülerkreis um sich versammelte, dem u.a. Daniel Heinsius, Hugo Grotius und
Johannes Meursius angehörten, die später selbst in der europäischen Gelehrtenrepublik Ruhm erwerben sollten. Scaligers philologisches Interesse galt
in seiner zweiten Lebensphase vorwiegend der historischen Chronologie,
wodurch er im Zuge des Kalenderstreits zunehmender jesuitischer Kritik
ausgesetzt wurde, die sich im Stile der Zeit zu Invektiven gegen seine Herkunft und Person steigerte und die besonders Kaspar Schoppe in verschiedenen Polemiken führte.[40] In der Korrespondenz zwischen Lingelsheim und
Scaliger bildeten die publizistischen Fehden zwischen Calvinisten und

---

[37] Cf. auch den Brief Lingelsheims an Meursius vom 29.3.1618 (Autograph in der Universitätsbibliothek Leipzig, MS 0355, 54r).
[38] Zu ihm jetzt grundlegend die zweibändige Monographie von Grafton, *Joseph Scaliger*.
[39] Zu diesem Ehrentitel cf. Bernays, *Joseph Justus Scaliger*, 19s.
[40] Zu diesem boshaften, weite Kreise ziehenden Angriffen Schoppes cf. Hausmann, 'Schoppe, Scaliger und die Carmina Priapea'.

Jesuiten und in diesem Zusammenhang natürlich die persönlich gegen Scaliger gerichteten Angriffe folglich einen Schwerpunkt neben Nachrichten über die neuesten Forschungen Scaligers. Aber auch die politischen Ereignisse, in den vier Briefen zwischen dem 1. November 1607 und dem 11. Juli 1608 insbesondere die Waffenstillstandsverhandlungen zwischen den aufständischen Niederländern und Spanien, wurden von beiden ausführlich kommentiert. Scaliger zeigte sich hier, ganz deutlich in seinem letzten Brief vom 11. Juli 1608, zutiefst mißtrauisch gegen die Absichten der Spanier – 'Hispana vaferrima' – denen er echten Friedenswillen absprach und von deren geheimen Absprachen mit Rom – 'inter fratres collusionem' – er zu berichten wußte.[41] Auch für ihn standen in seiner insgesamt moderaten Beurteilung die Jesuiten als treibende Kraft im Hintergrund, er bediente sich also des Feindbildes, welches damals das calvinistische Europa teilte:

> Negari tamen non potest coniurationem diu meditatam fuisse, cui explicandae nihil praeter honestam occasionem defuit. An in hoc mimo Iesuitae primas habuerint, nescio. Certe vel primas vel omnes.[42]

Die europäische Dimension des niederländischen Aufstands erkannte Scaliger ebenso wie Lingelsheim. Ersterer orakelte angesichts des schleppenden Fortgangs der Waffenstillstandsverhandlungen bereits am 26. Februar 1608 in seinem Brief an Lingelsheim:

> Sane res eodem loco est, quo, antequam ullus legatus huc veniret, fuit. Quo evadet, nescio. Hoc unum scio, hunc annum aliquod monstrum pariturum. Ita res ad magnam mutationem spectare videtur, quae non ad unum anglum Europae, sed ad totam Europam prope pertinebit. Ego rempublicam non tracto, sed video, quae fortasse peritiores fugiunt, qui mentes iam diviserunt.[43]

Wenige Wochen zuvor hatte Lingelsheim ebenfalls das europäische Interesse an einer friedlichen Lösung in den Niederlanden in einem Brief an Hugo Grotius vom 3. Februar 1608 betont und jenen aufgefordert, daran mitzuwirken:

> Omnis Europa oculos iam coniectos habet in catastrophen, qua de apud vos laboratur. Tot annis tanquam palaestra fuit, in qua pro Europae libertate certatum: inde iam quies reliquae Europae pendere videtur. Ego infidam illam gentem nihil sincere agere persuasum habeo; itaque nil nisi insidias metuendas puto: sed votum tuum ad Pacem praeclarum.[44]

---

[41] Zitiert nach Scaliger, *Epistolae omnes*, 576s.

[42] Op. cit., 577.

[43] Op. cit., 573s.

[44] Zitiert nach der ausgezeichneten Gesamtausgabe: *Briefwisseling van Hugo Grotius*, I 96s.

Den als Sohn einer calvinistischen Patrizierfamilie in Delft geborenen Hugo
Grotius (1583-1645)[45] lobten seine Zeitgenossen als ein wahres Wunder-
kind. Bereits 1598 wurde er, als er Oldenbarnevelt auf einer Gesandtschaft
zum französischen König Heinrich IV. begleitete, in Orléans zum *doctor
iuris utriusque* promoviert. Seit 1599 in Den Haag als Anwalt tätig, erlebte
er den Höhepunkt seiner öffentlichen Karriere, als er 1613 zum Pensionär
des Rotterdamer Magistrats ernannt und dadurch Mitglied in den Generalstaaten wurde. Grotius war der wichtigste niederländische Korrespondent
Lingelsheims, insgesamt existieren heute noch 55 Briefe, die jedoch nicht
den ursprünglichen Umfang dieses Briefwechsels wiedergeben – mehrfach
rekurrierten beide in den erhaltenen Briefen auf inzwischen verlorene bzw.
bisher nicht wiederentdeckte Schreiben. Der erste Brief von Grotius an Lingelsheim datierte auf den 25. Januar 1604, den heutzutage als letztes zu
ermittelnden Brief verfaßte ebenfalls Grotius am 25. September 1631.[46] Soweit die Anschlußbriefwechsel beider diesen Schluß zulassen, brach ihre
Korrespondenz danach ab.

Nach der Zahl der gewechselten Briefe lag der Schwerpunkt dieser Korrespondenz in den Jahren zwischen 1613 und 1618, also zwischen dem Jahr,
in welchem Grotius als Pensionär des Rotterdamer Magistrats großen politischen Einfluß gewann, und dem Jahr seiner Inhaftierung als Anhänger
Oldenbarnevelts. In dieser Zeit dominierten konfessionspolitische Themen
die Korrespondenz,[47] was angesichts der politischen Tätigkeiten und vor
dem Hintergrund der sich zunehmend dramatisierenden Ereignisse in den
Vereinigten Niederlanden zu erwarten stand. Es wird deutlich, in welchem
Maße Grotius in die konfessionellen und politischen Auseinandersetzungen
involviert war und inwieweit er sich selber um Lösungen bemühte. Beispielsweise erbat er in seinem Brief vom 21. Juni 1613 von Lingelsheim die
Zusendung eines Exemplars der Pfälzischen Kirchenordnung, um dort zu
erfahren, 'qua potestate ac mandatis utatur ecclesiasticus senatus, a quibus et
ex quibus constituatur.'[48] Dahinter stand der Gedanke des *ius circa sacra*,
das die Remonstranten mit ihrer Anrufung der Generalstaaten eingefordert
hatten und das Grotius als entschiedener Erastianer vertrat. Lingelsheim

---

[45] Hugo Grotius gehört zweifellos zu den am besten erforschten Gestalten des europäischen
Späthumanismus, seine Korrespondenz und seine Werke gehören zu den wenigen Schriften
dieser Epoche, um deren Edition sich die Wissenschaft heute intensiv bemüht. Aus der Fülle
der Literatur soll gar nicht erst eine Auswahl versucht werden; als wohl kompetenteste, die
wichtigsten übergeordneten Aspekte seines Werkes behandelnde Einführung sei auf den
Tagungsband *The World of Hugo Grotius* verwiesen.
[46] Dieser Brief war zwar an Lingelsheim adressiert, richtete sich aber an diesen und Bernegger. Letzterer verfaßte auch das Antwortschreiben.
[47] Dies gilt insgesamt für die Korrespondenz Grotius' in diesen Jahren, wie Nellen, *Hugo
Grotius*, 7 feststellte.
[48] Zitiert nach *Briefwisseling van Hugo Grotius*, I 247.

sandte ihm umgehend ein Exemplar zu und bot an, daß Abraham Scultetus und er jederzeit für weitere Fragen zur Verfügung ständen.[49] Ein führender Politiker der Kurpfalz unterbreitete also einem führenden Politiker der Vereinigten Niederlande ein inoffizielles Hilfsangebot, die öffentliche Tätigkeit zweier Späthumanisten wirkte in diesem konkreten Beispiel, das aus Briefen anderer Korrespondenzen dieser Jahre um ein Vielfaches zu ergänzen wäre, massiv in ihre private Korrespondenz und drängte alle anderen Themen weitgehend zur Seite. Grotius berichtete regelmäßig vom Verlauf der Auseinandersetzung zwischen Arminianern und Gomaristen, an denen er selber maßgeblich beteiligt war und in die er mit verschiedenen Schriften eingriff, u.a. mit dem Traktat *Ordinum Hollandiae ac Westfrisiae Pietas* (Leiden 1613), das in den Niederlanden allerdings auf heftigen Widerstand stieß und Grotius zu einer Reizfigur für die Kontraremonstranten werden ließ. Lingelsheim, dem Grotius jede seiner neuen Schriften zusandte, dagegen fand ein sehr lobendes Urteil über dieses Traktat und befürwortete es explizit:

> Sum[m]a cum voluptate iterum atque iterum relegi Scriptum, in quo multa praeclara didici ac video te aptè et decorè caussam agere. Et quamvis dolendum sit lacerari Ecclesiam, tamen intemperies istorum hominum extorsit hanc necessariam Apologiam.[50]

Lingelsheim stand in diesem Konfessionsstreit den irenisch gesinnten Arminianern näher, er sah jedoch in der Kurpfalz eine Mehrheit gegen diese – zu recht, trugen doch die kurpfälzischen Gesandten auf der Dordrechter Synode sämtliche gegen die Remonstranten gerichteten Beschlüsse mit und beteiligten sich in der Person des Hofpredigers Abraham Scultetus (1566-1624) sogar an der Redaktion der *canones*. Er hoffte aber zugleich auf einen Ausgleich der beiden Parteien im Sinne einer protestantischen Irenik:

> Nostros plerosque animatos video in Arminianos; sed ii non satis considerare mihi videntur, quid factione utrimque firmis subnixa subsidiis obtineri possit. Ego censeo in istis libertatem quidlibet sentiendi permittendam; ita tamen, ne pax turbetur et in concionibus hae non neccessariae subtilitates agitentur. Deus vos respiciat et reddat pacem Ecclesiae vestrae.[51]

---

[49] '[...] mitto tibi Constitutionem Senatus nostri Ecclesiastici, qua vtimur. Si quid in ea dubij tibi occurrerit, lubentes Scultetus et ego tibi satisfaciemus.' Lingelsheim an Grotius, 24.7.1613 (Autograph in der Bibliotheek der Rijksuniversiteit Leiden, PAP 2, recto).
[50] Lingelsheim an Grotius, 12.12.1613 (Autograph in der Koninklijke Bibliotheek Den Haag, HS 135 D 23, recto).
[51] Lingelsheim an Grotius, 4.1.1618, zitiert nach *Briefwisseling van Hugo Grotius*, I 606s.

Zwar zeitigte die Dordrechter Synode eine Wiederherstellung des kirchlichen Friedens in den Vereinigten Niederlanden, doch nur um den hohen Preis einer Verfolgung der Remonstranten. Grotius, der zu den engsten Vertrauten Oldenbarnevelts gehört hatte, wurde zu einer lebenslangen Festungshaft verurteilt, seine sämtlichen Güter wurden eingezogen. Als Lingelsheim von der Verhaftung Oldenbarnevelts und Grotius' erfahren hatte, reagierte er in einem Brief an Johannes Meursius vom 12. September 1618 sehr betroffen, hoffte aber auf ihre baldige Freilassung:

> Vehementissimè adficior gravissimo casu Grotii nostri. Spe tamen sustentor, fore, ut ejus et magni patroni tui Barnefeldii innotescat innocentia. Deus eripiat eos ex ista calamitate et det porrò bene mereri de Republica.[52]

Doch erst im Sommer 1621 konnten die beiden Gelehrten ihre Korrespondenz wieder aufnehmen, nachdem Grotius eine abenteuerliche Flucht gelungen war, und er sich in Paris niedergelassen hatte.[53] Dort pflegte er intensiven Kontakt zum Cabinet Dupuy, mit deren Mitgliedern Lingelsheim ebenfalls brieflichen Kontakt hielt.[54] Die Intensität ihrer Korrespondenz nahm ab, doch blieben die politischen Ereignisse, die beide zu Flüchtlingen hatten werden lassen, sowie die gelehrten Arbeiten Grotius' die hauptsächlichen Themen ihrer Briefe. Grotius sah und fand in Lingelsheim nach wie vor einen begeisterten Leser und Förderer seiner Werke. So sandte er 1622 seinen soeben in Paris veröffentlichten *Apologeticus*, mit dem er sich für sein Verhalten in den Niederlanden rechtfertigte und gegen seine Verurteilung durch die Dordrechter Synode verteidigte, unverzüglich nach Straßburg in der Hoffnung, daß Lingelsheim in Deutschland einen Nachdruck beförderte:

> Qui librum meum hic excudi curavit, maiorem compendii sui quam mei honoris habuit rationem. Nam exemplaria excudit non plura septingentis, cum cen-

---

[52] Autograph in der Universitätsbibliothek Leipzig, MS 0355, 55r.

[53] Die Wiederbelebung ihrer Korrespondenz vermittelte maßgeblich der französische Diplomat Etienne de Sainte Cathérine, ein enger Korrespondent Lingelsheims und selbst ein Gast in den gelehrten Kreisen der französischen Hauptstadt. Cf. Lingelsheims Brief an Grotius vom 17 Juli 1621 (Autograph in der Bibliotheek der Universiteit van Amsterdam, R 31, b). Noch am gleichen Tag schrieb Lingelsheim an Sainte Cathérine, den er der Freundschaft des Flüchtlings empfahl (Autograph in der Bibliothèque Nationale de Paris, Fr. 4122, 76v). Sainte Cathérine scheint dieser Bitte gefolgt zu sein, denn Grotius berichtete kurze Zeit später an Lingelsheim: 'Sancatharinum pro merito amo atque amplector' (9.9.1621; zitiert nach *Briefwisseling van Hugo Grotius*, II 130). Zum Verhältnis von Grotius und Sainte Cathérine cf. auch die Briefe Lingelsheims an Sainte Cathérine vom 3./13.10.1622 und 2./12.11.1622 (Autographen in der Bibliothèque Nationale de Paris, Fr. 4122, 110 und 112) sowie Grotius' an Lingelsheim vom 10.5.1623 (Druck u.a. in *Briefwisseling van Hugo Grotius*, II 291).

[54] Zu diesem einflußreichen privaten Gelehrtenkreis cf. Garber, 'A propos de la politisation' (erweiterte deutsche Fassung: Garber, 'Paris, die Hauptstadt des europäischen Späthumanismus').

tena aliquot iam patria nostra consumserit, tum vero singula care vendit, ses-
quifloreno. Si quis in Germania typographus editionem novam in tempus Fran-
cofurtensis mercatus adornet, puto rem facturum. In Anglia liber hic benigne
exceptus fuit, quod mihi summae dignitatis ac pietatis viri significarunt.[55]

Dieser befand sich dazu auch bereit, wurde jedoch von Janus Gruter und
dem Straßburger Geschichtsprofessor Matthias Bernegger mehrfach davon
abgebracht, da beide Bedenken gegen diese einseitige Rechtfertigungsschrift
hegten.[56] Deshalb konnte erst 1629 der erhoffte Nachdruck der Apologie
erscheinen.[57] Eine andere Bitte des Grotius jedoch unterstützte Bernegger
ganz aktiv, nämlich die Herausgabe des *Syllabus* von Jean Hotman,[58] für die
er unter dem Pseudonym Theodosius Irenaeus das Vorwort verfaßte. Dieses
kleine Werk war ein ganz entscheidender Beitrag für das jenseits der
konfessionspolitischen Konflikte des Zeitalters unter den späthumanistischen Gelehrten lebendige irenische Denken. Hotman trug hier die Titel von
175 Werken aus den Jahren 1522 bis 1627 zusammen, die von Autoren aller
Konfessionen und aller Nationen stammen und auf einen Ausgleich der
Konfessionen, auf die Wiedererrichtung einer *res publica christiana* hin-
zielen. Der Einsatz von Lingelsheim und Bernegger für die Publikation
dieser Schrift, deren Veröffentlichung angesichts ihres hochbrisanten Inhalts
zur damaligen Zeit in Frankreich kaum möglich schien,[59] war ein eindeutig
konfessionspolitisches Fanal dieser beiden Späthumanisten in einer Zeit, als
der Krieg der Religionsparteien mit unverminderter Heftigkeit in Deutschland wütete.

[55] Grotius an Lingelsheim, 19.11.1622 (zit. nach *Briefwisseling van Hugo Grotius*, II 259).
[56] Cf. mit den entsprechenden Nachweisen Reifferscheid, *Briefe G.M. Lingelsheims*, 761.
[57] Grotius, *Apologeticus*.
[58] Bereits der Titel des Werkes verdeutlicht seine Intention: *Syllabus aliquot synodorum et colloquiorum, quae auctoritate et mandato caesarum et regum super negotio religionis ad controversias conciliandas indicta sunt: doctorum item aliquot ac piorum virorum utriusque religionis, tam Catholicae Romanae quam Protestantium, libri et epistolae, vel ex iis excerpta; ex quibus videri potest, quam non sit difficilis controversiarum in religione conciliato, si pugnandi vincendique animus absit, veritatis vero studium cum pacis studio conjungatur* [Straßburg] 1628 (Druckort ist fingiert als Aurelia angegeben). Die Veröffentlichung wurde von Hugo Grotius, der damals in seinem Pariser Exil in der Umgebung des Verfassers lebte, an Lingelsheim und Bernegger herangetragen. Cf. Grotius an Lingelsheim vom 9.5.1627 (Druck u.a. in *Briefwisseling van Hugo Grotius*, III 129) und 8.9.1627 (Druck u.a. op. cit., 167). Zu diesem Werk und der Beteiligung Lingelsheims und Berneggers an seiner Herausgabe erstmals Schiff, 'Zur Literaturgeschichte der kirchlichen Einigungsbestrebungen'. Sehr viel ausführlicher auf das Werk und seine Entstehung geht ein: Posthumus Meyjes, 'Jean Hotman's Syllabus of eirenical literature' (frz. Übersetzung: idem, 'Autour d'une liste de Jean Hotman'). Hier wird auch die Korrespondenz Lingelsheims, soweit sie diese Edition betrifft, ausgewertet.
[59] So Grotius an Lingelsheim am 9.5.1627 (zitiert nach *Briefwisseling van Hugo Grotius*, III 129): 'Is, quem dixi, index non satis commode in Gallia nunc quidem vulgari potest, sed nec in Batavia nostra rerum potientibus iis, qui nihil probant non in extimo positum. Quare censeo deligendam huic obstetricatui Germaniam. Si putes Argentorati edi posse, mittetur eo exemplum. Si ibi non potest, forte tuo indicio typographum reperiemus Francofurti.'

Wie Hugo Grotius wurde auch Johannes Meursius (1579-1639) ein Opfer der konfessionellen Konflikte in den Niederlanden.[60] Nach Abschluß
seiner Studien in Leiden hatte er zunächst als *praeceptor* im Hause Oldenbarnevelts gedient, bevor er – 1608 in Orléans zum Doktor beider Rechte
promoviert – 1610 einen Ruf nach Leiden erhielt, um dort Geschichte und
Griechisch zu lehren. Ein Jahr später wurde er außerdem zum Historiogra-
phen der Staaten von Holland ernannt. In dieser Funktion verfaßte er eine
zunächst ganz die Interessen seiner Auftraggeber an einer legitimierenden
Geschichtsschreibung erfüllende historische Darstellung des niederländischen Freiheitskampfes (*Rerum Belgicarum Liber unus*, Leiden 1612), die
er wenig später allerdings überarbeitete und in einer sich – erfolgreich – um
mehr Objektivität bemühenden Version seiner Geschichte der Statthalter-
schaft des Herzogs von Alba hinzufügte (1567-1573).[61] Lingelsheim äußerte
sich in seinem Brief an Meursius vom 9. Oktober 1614 äußerst wohlwollend
über dieses Werk und verglich seinen Verfasser mit Jacques-Auguste de
Thou, dessen große Zeitgeschichte Lingelsheim von Anfang an mit begei-
stertem Wohlwollen begleitet hatte – ein deutliches Zeichen, daß Meursius
seine Überarbeitung gelungen war. Ich möchte die entsprechende Passage
ausführlich zitieren, weil sie uns zeigt, wie die Argumentationslinie in
diesem Brief über eine allgemeine Klage über den Verlust glanzvoller
Geister sofort wieder antihabsburgisch-antikatholisch gewendet wird, hier
durch die Hervorhebung der Universität Groningen als geistiges Bollwerk
gegen die gottlosen Jesuiten:

> Legi tua maxima cum voluptate, et pro iudicio, quod a me postulas, acclamati-
> ones adfero, ut porrò pergas reipublicae et literis plurimum prodesse. Exemplo
> magni Thuani id video te exactè praestare, ut veritatem ipsam sine studio
> partium proponas, neque insimulari possis affectibus te quidquam tribuisse,
> adeò ut hostis egregia facta saepius extollas, prae καθορθώμασι pro patria et
> libertate praestitis. Quod deploras erepta tam exiguò tempore, lumina litera-
> rum, eundem tibi sensum nobiscum esse animaduerto. Deo gratiae agendae,
> qui tam insignes viros dederit. Laudabile hoc institutum vestratium, quod Gro-
> ningae nouam sedem Musarum collocarunt. Sic debet barbariem expugnare ir-
> ruentem per impetum blasphemae illius Societatis, quae bellum indixit praecla-
> ris ingenijs et bonis literis ipsis. Tu verò, vir magne, in proposito perseuera, et
> perge prodesse publicè.[62]

Die konfessionspolitische Implikation Lingelsheims wird an dieser Stelle
ganz deutlich und seine Aufforderung an Meursius, weiterhin der öffentli-

---

[60] Auch zu seiner Person fehlt eine wissenschaftliche Biographie. Die einzige mir bekannte
Einführung in sein Werk und Leben stammt von Heesakkers, 'Te weinig koren'.
[61] Meursius, *Rervm Belgicarvm Libri Quatuor*.
[62] Autograph in der Staats- und Universitätsbibliothek Hamburg, Sup. ep. 94, 16r.

chen Sache nützlich zu sein, zeigt uns erneut, wie auch die Späthumanisten selber ihre öffentliche Geltung im frühabsolutistischen Staat beanspruchten.

Dieser letzte Wunsch Lingelsheims erledigte sich jedoch bald durch die Ereignisse im Zuge der Auseinandersetzungen zwischen Remonstranten und Kontraremonstranten. Meursius, der zu den Vertrauten Oldenbarnevelts gehörte und – wie große Teile der späthumanistischen Gelehrten – den Arminianern zuneigte, sah sich nach der Synode von Dordrecht Repressalien der Akademie ausgesetzt und mußte die Lehre ruhen lassen. In dieser Situation sann er ernsthaft darüber nach, Leiden zu verlassen; Lingelsheim bot ihm sofort seine Hilfe an, eine neue Stellung zu finden,

> vel in hac nostra Universitate, vel in antiqvissima Bohemica, qvae, ut facultatibus prae aliis insigniter instructa, ita Viris industriis et doctrina claris aliqvamdiu caruit.[63]

Dieser Plan gedieh jedoch ob der Kriegsereignisse nicht über eine vage Überlegung hinaus, Meursius blieb in Leiden und berichtete Lingelsheim am 10. September 1621, wie er sich inzwischen in seine Situation gefügt hatte:

> Mihi, si privata quaeris, reddita Professio et Senatus; sed non munus Historiae scribendae, quod differtur: sive ea, quod ego existimo, quaedam quasi est negatio. Cuperem tamen, si hoc vellent, ut apertè potius facerent. Sed et istud tolerandum. Interim vivo et tranquillo animo contemno inimicorum meorum malevolentiam ac Museo me includo, ubi scripsi [...]. Quibus puto satis me declaraturum animum mihi supra fortunam omnem positum neque facile à statu suo deturbari.[64]

Dieser Brief ist gleichzeitig das letzte überlieferte Schreiben der Korrespondenz zwischen Lingelsheim und Meursius. Insgesamt haben sich seit 1607 vierzehn Briefe erhalten, die jedoch nicht die komplette Korrespondenz darstellen, wieder sind im Laufe der Jahrhunderte schmerzliche Lücken in die Überlieferung gerissen worden. Spätestens mit Meursius' Umzug nach Dänemark, wohin ihn 1625 endlich der ersehnte Ruf ins Ausland als Professor für Geschichte und Staatswissenschaft an die gerade gegründete Universität Sørø lockte, brach ihre Verbindung endgültig ab.

---

[63] Lingelsheim an Meursius, 2.10.1619 (zitiert nach der Abschrift ebda., Sup. ep. 60, 104v-105r). Meursius bekräftigte in seinem Antwortschreiben seinen Wunsch, Leiden zu verlassen, '[...] honestam mihi aliquam vocationem procurari, vt ingrata patria sciat aestimari me ab exteris, et me ipsa aestimare etiam discat.' (1.11.1619; Autograph in der Staats- und Universitätsbibliothek Hamburg, Sup. ep. 13, 117r).

[64] Meursius an Lingelsheim, 10.9.1621 (zitiert nach der Abschrift Kongelige Bibliotek København, Böll. Brevs. D., 647v-648r).

In seinen Briefen an Meursius erkundigte sich Lingelsheim verschiedentlich nach Daniel Heinsius (1580-1655) und seinen philologischen Studien.[65] So fragte er in seinem Brief vom 5. Juli 1617 nach dem Stand der von Heinsius vorbereiteten Edition der aristotelischen Politik. Seit 1612 bekleidete der aus Gent stammende Heinsius in Leiden die Professur für Politik und Geschichte und legte einen Schwerpunkt seiner Lehre auf dieses Werk,[66] das aber erst im Jahre 1621 mit ausführlichen Kommentaren in Leiden veröffentlicht wurde:[67]

> Sed quid Heinsius noster? Iam dudum nihil ejus monumentorum vidimus. Spes nobis facta fuerat insignis operis Politici, quo Aristotelis observationes ad nostrum saeculum accommodabat. Iubetne nos porrò sperare an aliud aliqvid adgreditur? Scio non torpere ingenium tam vegetum.[68]

Die Zeugnisse einer direkten Korrespondenz zwischen Lingelsheim und dem wohl vertrautesten Scaliger-Schüler, der als späthumanistischer Gelehrter ebenso weitberühmt war wie als neulateinischer und niederländischer Dichter, sind jedoch spärlich. Lediglich zwei Briefe von Heinsius aus den Jahren 1624 und 1626 lassen sich heute noch auffinden, doch schrieb auch Lingelsheim zumindest in dieser Zeit an Heinsius.[69] Diese Briefe behandelten jedoch weitgehend persönliche Angelegenheiten und reflektierten nicht die politischen Ereignisse in den Niederlanden, in die Heinsius aufgrund seiner engen Beziehungen zu Schweden und seiner vertrauten Verbindung zu Moritz von Oranien genaue Einblicke hatte.

Das Paradigma der niederländischen Korrespondenzen Georg Michael Lingelsheims, und d.h. bereits eine im Verhältnis zu der unüberschaubaren Zahl von Briefen der noch lange nicht hinreichend erforschten Korrespondenzen der späthumanistischen *res publica litteraria* Europas schmale Textbasis, verdeutlicht unzweifelhaft, in welchem Umfang die Späthumanisten der calvinistischen Sphäre in die Ereignisse ihrer Zeit involviert waren, zugleich aber auch, inwieweit es Unterschiede geben konnte, die davon abhingen, in welcher Funktion diese Späthumanisten dem Staate bzw. Fürsten verbunden waren. Scaliger, der über allem schwebende 'aquila in nubibus', brüskierte sich über die gegen ihn gerichteten persönlichen Angriffe der Jesuiten,

---

[65] Biographien von Ter Horst, *Daniel Heinsius*; Becker-Cantarino, *Daniel Heinsius*.
[66] Cf. Meter, *The literary theories of Daniel Heinsius*, 30.
[67] Heinsius, *Aristotelis Politicorvm libri VIII*.
[68] Lingelsheim an Meursius, 5.7.1617 (zitiert nach der Abschrift Kongelige Bibliotek København, Gl. kgl. S. 4°3072, 305v).
[69] Das geht aus der Einleitung zu Heinsius' Brief vom 30.1.1626 eindeutig hervor: 'Praeter expectationem hanc scribendi occasionem nactus, non potui, quin tribus ad tuas responderem.' (zitiert nach der Abschrift Kongelige Bibliotek København, Böll. Brevs. U., 163r).

agierte aber nicht jenseits seiner gelehrten Studien. Grotius, der aktiv als Politiker und Publizist in den Konflikt zwischen Remonstranten und Kontraremonstranten eingegriffen hatte, gelang es schließlich im Exil ganz, sich von den Schlacken unversöhnlichen konfessionellen Denkens zu befreien und konsequent eine Irenik im erasmischen Sinne weiterzuentwickeln. Seine Irenik, die Grotius im Kontakt mit den französischen *politiques* um den Cercle Dupuy in seinen späten Schriften entwickelte und die den Gedanken von der Einheit der *res publica christiana*, von der *pax Dei*, die nach dem Worte Gottes allen Christen, also auch den Katholiken gegeben sein sollte und somit die von den Reformierten unverrückbar vertretene Gleichsetzung von Papst und Antichrist auflöste, fand unter den Politikern, Theologen und Gelehrten Europas jedoch kaum Gehör.[70] Meursius erduldete sein Schicksal mit der unerschütterlichen *constantia* des Neostoizismus als einer *philosophia practica*,[71] nachdem ihm als Remonstranten die Lehre verboten worden war und er sein Amt als Historiograph verloren hatte, und arbeitete an unpolitischen Werken, bis er 1625 endlich den ersehnten Ruf ins Ausland erhielt. Heinsius dagegen, ein orthodoxer Calvinist, der als Anhänger der Kontraremonstranten dem Hause Oranien nahestand und als Sekretär der Laiendeputierten an der Dordrechter Synode, deren Beschlüsse er auch für die Publikation redigierte, teilnahm, absolvierte eine glänzende universitäre Karriere. So manifestierte sich der konfessionelle Konflikt in den Vereinigten Niederlanden sogar in diesem kleinen auserwählten Schülerkreis Scaligers. Während überall in Europa Glaubenskämpfe tobten, konnten die späthumanistischen Gelehrten, die ihrem Selbstverständnis nach auf öffentliche Wirksamkeit zielten und weitgehend in Diensten frühabsolutistischer Fürsten aktiv in die konfessionellen Konflikte ihrer Zeit involviert waren, ihre irenischen Grundpositionen nur noch schwer behaupten und kaum durchsetzen. Lingelsheim, der als kurpfälzischer Oberrat ein politisches Amt ausfüllte, blieb Zeit seines Lebens ein Verfechter einer protestantischen Irenik, die gegen die *pestem Loioliticam*[72] und den päpstlichen Antichristen eine Allianz des

---

[70] Die Grundzüge der Grotius'schen Irenik bei Wolf, *Die Irenik des Hugo Grotius*.

[71] Gerade der niederländische Späthumanismus war, v.a. durch die Schriften Justus Lipsius', von einem Neostoizismus geprägt, der als *philosophia practica* als alternativer Lebensentwurf der intellektuellen Elite gerade in der Zeit der konfessionellen Bürgerkriege gesehen werden muß, war er doch 'durchaus auf eine umfassende Wissenschaft und Wirksamkeit aus, auf ein festes weltanschauliches Leitbild als Grundlage zur Lebensbewältigung, auf politisch-militärische Gestaltung, auf Erziehung zum öffentlichen Handeln, auf Selbstbeherrschung und Tat.' So formulierte Oestreich, 'Justus Lipsius als Theoretiker', 39, und entwickelte davon ausgehend in seinen Lipsius-Forschungen eine politische Dimension des europäischen Späthumanismus, die bei Trunz, 'Der deutsche Späthumanismus um 1600 als Standeskultur', noch nicht gesehen wurde. Cf. auch die Dissertation von Oestreich, *Antiker Geist und moderner Staat bei Justus Lipsius*, die seit kurzem vorliegt.

[72] Diese Bezeichnung benutzt er in seinem Brief an Pierre Dupuy vom 21.7.1614 (Autograph in der Bibliothèque Nationale de Paris, Col. Dupuy 699, 261r).

internationalen Protestantismus errichten wollte. Wie durch die europäische Politik verliefen auch durch die Gelehrtenrepublik konfessionelle Gräben, die sich in den turbulenten Zeitläuften vertieften und von immer weniger Gelehrten überwunden wurden. Die Verbindung des Späthumanismus mit der Konfessionspolitik war im konfessionellen Zeitalter nicht zu trennen.

A.G. WEILER

THE DUTCH BRETHREN OF THE COMMON LIFE, CRITICAL THEOLOGY, NORTHERN HUMANISM AND REFORMATION

Thirty years ago professor Post in his book *The Modern Devotion*[1] confronted the *devotio moderna* with the intentions of humanists and reformist theologians in the Low Countries. He asked himself these questions: Were those humanists and theologians themselves Brethren of the Common Life or closely connected to them? Were they spiritually moulded by the Brethren, and did they in their turn influence the opinions of the Brothers? Were the Brethren innovators of the schoolsystem, and did they introduce humanist requirements in teaching and education? This paper proposes to re-examine these questions, considering the facts that have been brought forward as results of my recent research.[2] I will confine myself mostly to the fifteenth century.

A Characteristic of the Brethren

The Brethren meant to remodel their way of life on that of the early Christians. Allusions to *Acts* 2, 44 and 4, 32 (*habebant omnia communia; cor unum et anima una*) recur time and again in documents relating to the foundation of a house or in their chronicles. For instance in Zwolle, the local parish priest Henri of Compostelle recognized that the Brethren intended to live *secundum primitivae ecclesiae normam* (December 20, 1418). The Utrecht brothers, founding the last house of the Common Life (November 28, 1475), in their charter referred to the same text from Acts. Nonetheless, this effort of the Brethren to bring about a renaissance of early Christian life[3] met with fierce opposition, especially from the mendicant orders. In answer to this reaction, adjustments were made but the simple form of life

---

[1] Post, *The Modern Devotion*.

[2] The present author is preparing the publication of *Monasticon Fratrum Vitae Communis. III. Niederlande*. An abridged edition is published under the title *Volgens de norm van de vroege kerk*. All details concerning Houses given in this paper, will be fully accounted for in the forthcoming *Monasticon* or in *Volgens de norm*.

[3] The Renaissance-metaphor e.g in Johannes Busch, *Liber de viris illustribus*, 12 and 14: 'vita communis [...] post successu temporis reabolita per patres de Windeshem iterum refloruit et revixit [...] regularem vitam et ordinis disciplinam refloruisse repullulasseque cognovimus.' Quoted by Staubach, 'Das Wunder der Devotio Moderna'; Oberman, *The Dawn of the Reformation* I 17, esp. 14-17.

inaugurated by Geert Grote and Florens Radewijnsz. in Deventer survived. Finally the way of life of the Brethren was forbidden by pope Pius V in 1568. The Reformation quickly swept all the Houses away although the St.-Gregoriushuis at 's-Hertogenbosch survived until 1629, when the city was taken by the protestant prince Frederik Hendrik.

The Brethren were concerned with spiritual renewal,[4] for themselves, for the communities of Sisters of the Common Life entrusted to their care, for lay people in the towns, and above all for adolescents. In their convicts, and in some cases even in their own schools (Deventer (c. 1480?-1534), Groningen (c. 1511-1578), Utrecht (1475-1578) and incidentally in Gouda (c. 1457-1460) and Harderwijk), they imbued schoolboys with Christian morality and spirituality. By their *collationes* they presented these young men with examples of virtuous living.[5] Moral education went together with learning in (town-)schools. In some cases, as in Amersfoort and 's-Hertogenbosch and very briefly in Zwolle, Brothers were involved in teaching in the town school, but this was exceptional. In Deventer, for instance, teachers left their activities at the local school behind on becoming a *frater*. Thus Post rightly concludes that the influence of the Brethren on the youth did not pass mainly through the channels of school-education in the proper sense of the word, without however denying their influence within the context of the convicts.

There were virtually no relations with academic education even though some Brethren had studied at universities before becoming a *frater*. They were not interested in theological or philosophical disputations but had the highest regard for the sound learning required for their roles as spiritual guides, confessors or *collationatores*. Wisdom of this kind was largely developed through self-study. In this connection it is interesting to note that Arnold Geilhoven of Rotterdam, a regular canon of the monastery of Groenendaal, wrote a *Speculum conscientiae (Parvum Gnotosolitos)*[6] specifically (c. 1423) for clerical students in Deventer and Louvain. This was the first big book to be printed by the Brethren of the House at Brussels in 1477 in an enlarged editon called *Magnum Gnotosolitos*.

---

[4] For a characteristic of the Modern Devotion as spiritual movement see Debongnie, 'Dévotion moderne'; and Van Dijk, 'Windesheim'.

[5] Van Engen, 'The Virtues, the Brothers and the Schools'; Mertens, 'Collatio und Codex'.

[6] Edition in preparation by the present author, 'La systématique de la théologie morale selon Arnold Geilhoven', Table I, gives the categories that were used by Geilhoven as an organizing principle of his work. Van Engen, 'The Virtues, the Brothers and the Schools', speaking of the excerpts of the *Vitasfratrum* in ms. Anholt, Museum Wasserburg, 45, says: 'The exemplar for this particular set of spiritual topics has not yet been found, or was particular to this house and has been lost.' Such an exemplar could have been the *Parvum Gnotosolitos* of Arnold of Geilhoven.

The Brethren were not as such opposed to monasticism. On the contrary, their houses and convicts often served as seminaries for future monks. The transition to the Third Order of St. Francis and to the Rule of St. Augustine, in one form or another, was a normal phenomenon in the spiritual policy of the Brethren. The houses at Delft and Amersfoort present good examples of different attempts of such transitions. Strong and successful opposition to these ideas came from the rector of Deventer, Egbert ter Beek, as is shown in the case of the *fratres* of Doesburg, who in 1465 intended to accomplish a transition in vain. The Regular Canons of the Congregation of Windesheim and the Regular Canonesses were especially strong defenders of the communities of devout men and women. Still, the transformation of a House into a *collegium* of secular canons observing common life, as in Amersfoort and 's-Hertogenbosch in 1469, was not easily accepted. Egbert ter Beek strongly opposed such a change-over for the Deventer community. The community in Berlikum which from its foundation had been conceived of as such a *collegium* was unsuccessful (1483-1491).

The Brethren and Critical Theology

The nascent new theology in the Low Countries found voice in men such as Wessel Gansfort (c. 1419-1489), who was closely associated with the Brethren and the Regular canons of the monastery of St. Agnietenberg near Zwolle. Mention must also be made of John Pupper of Goch (†1475), who was *frater* in Amersfoort, rector of the House at Gouda, and finally rector of a nunnery in Malines, and of John Hinne Rode, who was rector of the Brotherhouse in Utrecht (1520-1522).[7]

With respect to the relations between the Brethren and critical, reformist theologians, we may summarize the theses of professor Post as follows.[8] He sharply distinguished between persons who in fact were Brethren of the Common Life and those who were not. Only by such a distinction, he supposed correctly, can a fair judgement be made of the relations between the Brethren and the reformist theologians in the Low Countries of the fifteenth century. Post points out that Wessel Gansfort was not a member of the Brotherhood and he dissociates his theological positions from those of the Brethren: Wessel's ideas can not be ascribed to the Brethren as such.

---

[7] Post, *The Modern Devotion*, 470-85; 574-5.
[8] Weiler, 'Het werk van professor Post', esp. 233-4.

Wessel Gansfort

Professor Post was right, but it cannot be denied that Wessel during some periods of his life was closely associated with the Brethren. While studying at the city-school at Zwolle (from c. 1432 onwards), he probably lived in one of the three convicts of the Brethren in the town, although Albert Rizaeus Hardenberg in his *Vita Wesseli Groningensis* asserts that he was placed in the monastery of St. Agnietenberg, which is highly unlikely.[9] As a *convictor* he was subjected to the regime of the students (*regimen scolarium*) along with the other pupils. After completing his studies in the second and the first classes of the townschool, he was appointed a lecturer in that same school for the pupils of the third class. During that time he lived in the convict for wealthy clerics, which was run by the Brethren: the *domus parva/ vicina/ proxima clericorum/ fratrum* (Kleine or Naaste huis). He wore the clerical garb of the Brethren, just as the other boys in the house were dressed according to their status. He went with them to church and to the *collationes* that the *procurator* of the house held in the evening. In Wessel's times the function of procurator was held by Rutger of Doetinchem (†1478), the former cook of the house. This man, who at that time was not yet a full member of the community, cast an eagle's eye on the progress of the youngsters in virtue and learning. Not excluding the whip, he rebuked those who committed excesses against custom and good manners, and during his regime the house flourished in good discipline. Wessel assisted Rutger in the evening admonitions (*collationes*), and together they urged the boys to embrace virtues and to hate vices. Rutger's collations were devout and eloquent, he was well versed in the Bible and a good interpreter and moralisator of Scripture.

This information about Wessel's years in Zwolle with the Brethren is provided by *frater* Jacob de Voecht, writing c. 1500, in his chronicle of the House in Zwolle.[10] He also mentions the fact that Wessel gave medical assistance to the rector of the House in Zwolle, Albert Paep of Kalkar, who died on May 4, 1482.[11] Furthermore, we know that Gansfort, after wandering about in the academic worlds of Cologne and perhaps of Louvain, Paris, Heidelberg, Angers and Rome, lived in more pious circles like that of the monastery of St. Agnietenberg and with the Cistercians at Aduard near Groningen (c. 1475-1489). In his later years he was thus again in close contact with people who adhered to or sympathized with the *Devotio Moderna*.

---

[9] Hardenberg, 'Vita Wesseli Groningensis', **1.
[10] Traiecti, *Narratio de inchoatione domus clericorum in Zwollis*, 153-8.
[11] Op. cit., 169.

It may therefore be concluded that Wessel's spiritual life as a young man took shape in Zwolle, and that vice versa in his later years he himself influenced his auditors by discussing theological and ecclesiastical problems and expounding his particular views. Of course his works were printed only in 1522, but the eager disputant, the *Magister contradictionis* that he was,[12] proposed his ideas for discussion wherever there was an interested audience. Erika Rummel recently rightly wrote: 'In his lifetime, Gansfort may have influenced more minds through his teaching and homiletic activity than through his writings. He taught and acted as spiritual adviser to the boys of the city-school and at the convict [not as Rummel has it: *school*] of the Brethren of the Common Life in Zwolle. He was in close contact with the Canons Regular of St. Agnietenberg near Zwolle, and often read and discussed Scripture with the Tertiaries [not as Rummel has it: *the Poor Clares*] of Groningen, where he lodged in his old age.'[13] His critical opinions were present on the intellectual and spiritual forum of the fifteenth century, not only in academic disputations but also in private colloquies and lectures in smaller circles such as that of Aduard. Let us examine some aspects of his theological positions.[14]

The Gospel as the first and only rule of faith

Wessel begins his treatise *On ecclesiastical dignity and power*[15] with the thesis that the faithful are not obliged to believe what the Pope says unless he believes rightly.

> The pope should – nay must – have his convictions, even as all the faithful must have theirs. When he believes what he should, the faithful are bound to assent to it, not simply because he believes it, but because it is what he should believe. If however, the belief of another is better than that of the pope, the pope himself ought to concur in it, even if it be that of a layman or a woman, not because it is a layman or woman that entertains this belief, but because he or she walks uprightly according to the truth of the gospel. [...] Although it may be assumed that the pope and the prelates, in view of the high station of dignity to which they have been raised, walk in the truth of the gospel more nearly than all others, and that therefore, other things being equal, they should be believed rather than any of those subject to them, nevertheless their subjects are not bound to believe them without reserve (*simpliciter*). To deny this is so

---

[12] Oberman, 'Wessel Gansfort: *Magister contradictionis*'.

[13] Rummel, 'Voices of Reform from Hus to Erasmus', 73.

[14] Cf. Post, *De via antiqua en de via moderna*, 11-15; Post, *The Modern Devotion*, 476-85; Oberman, *The Harvest of Medieval Theology*, 408-12.

[15] Gansfort, 'De dignitate et potestate ecclesiastica', 748; the quoted English translation is from *Wessel Gansfort. Life and Writings*, 151-2.

> unreasonable, so full of blasphemy, that it is actually more pernicious than any
> heresy whatever. For a prelate – even the highest prelate – may err.

Wessel continues that belief is an obligation towards the Holy Spirit, not towards a human being. Faith is dependent solely upon God, in Whom alone the just lives through faith (*iustus ex fide vivit*: *Rom.* 1,17; *Hebr.* 10,38; *Galat.* 3,11). The life of a believer would be endangered if it were to depend on the life of a pope. Look how popes like Benedict XIII (pope at Avignon, 1394-1417), Boniface IX (1389-1404) and John XXIII (pope of the council, 1410-1415) have done much harm to faith, as recently became clear during the Council of Constance. Even the first pope, Peter, erred, and Paul resisted and rebuked him.

Arguing in this way, Wessel sets up the Gospel as the first and only rule of faith for everybody, popes as well as common believers. Faith is guided primarily by the Gospel, not by the pope and his authority. The mandates of ecclesiastical prelates should not to be accepted as if they were mandates of God. In that case, the yoke of the Gospel would be even heavier than the yoke of the Law (p. 750). The flock that is entrusted to the shepherd disposes of reason and free will; therefore it is not totally given into the power of the shepherd who can demand obedience. Any sheep has to determine itself by whom it is tended, by whom damage is inflicted, and it must by all means avoid a contagious infection, even when it is brought along by the shepherd. When it follows the shepherd with blind eyes, it is not therefore and as such excused (p. 752-3).

Wessel takes great pains to show that ecclesiastical mandates must be obeyed only in as far as they stem from God and are wise and just. Wessel calles upon the conscience and power of judgment of the individual believer, even of a monk in the cloister, to be active in judging commandments and not to obey slavishly. Obeying without discretion is itself an indiscretion (p. 757). God and the Gospel are the points of reference for faith and conscience; any preaching must be judged by these standards. We are obliged to believe the Gospel because of God; we have to believe the Church and the pope because of the Gospel; we are not obliged to believe the Gospel because of the Church (p. 759). The believer has therefore to seek out the truth and understanding of the Gospel.

Well then, Wessel argues, doctors in theology often are more learned and better at home in the truths of Scripture than prelates (p. 758). Certainly, a single person may more easily err than a whole church of learned men, although a situation of common error amongst the learned is not impossible. However, no power is given against Wisdom and Truth. Therefore, when a wise man disagrees with the pope, one has to side and to consent with the wise man, more than with the pope. In matters of conflict, the pope is obligated to hear and to follow the opinion of the wise man. And the wise man must stand firm. In matters in which he believes the word of the true Wisdom according to the immaculate Law of God, he must not step back from his opinion and comply with papal authority. The entire community of the faithful has to adhere to the wise man as well. So it was done during the Council of Constance, when the community of believers disagreed with pope John XXIII and consented with the theologian Jean Gerson (1363-1429). Wessel also calls to mind the example of Bernard of Clairvaux (c. 1090-1153) who in his treatise *De consideratione* clearly opposed pope Eugenius III (1149-1153) upon which the pope accepted his rebukes and warnings with all his heart. It is the task of the wise theologian to determine to what extent papal mandates are obligatory. The Church is more preserved in unity by the consensus of the wise men than by the government of prelates, because the consensus of the wise is guided effectively by God (p. 767). One has to side with those who are closest to the Gospel. At the top of his voice Wessel shouts: 'We are the servants of God, not of the pope.'[16] We are not obliged to accept all ecclesiastical sentences on the grounds of their legal status (p. 760). According to Gansfort every prelate who scandalizes the little ones in the Church is an Antichrist (p. 763). He finally calls upon all Christians, including the very humblest peasants, to resist those who corrupt the Church, that is to say: the corrupt clergy (p. 769), in the same way that resistance is allowed against wicked rulers (p. 766). Where the wickedness of prelates and princes stems from the foolishness and wickedness of the people, the people have to be educated in order to learn how to distinguish good from evil.

Here Wessel is with the Brethren of the Common Life and their constant attention for spiritual and moral education. However, he adds to this more than a little mistrust of authority as such. The education of a critical intellect that can form a critical judgment even in matters of faith and the rules of Christian life greatly affects the way in which people see their position in the Church. Obedience presented in the way of the docility and tractability of sheep is not good enough for a Christian. There is here a roll-call for the people's well-formed conscience. Authority alone does not suffice.

Gansfort's *De dignitate et potestate ecclesiastica* comes very close to the position of William of Ockham (c. 1285-1347). Ockham in his *Octo Quaestiones de Potestate Papae* opposed the position that the pope possesses the plenitude of power in temporal and spiritual matters in such a way that he can do anything that is not against divine law, natural law, Holy Scripture,

---

[16] 'Dei enim servi sumus, non Papae; cui utique serviremus, si ad omnia ejus qualiacumque obligaremur. Dictum est autem: *Dominum Deum tuum adorabis, et illi soli servies*' (Gansfort, 'De dignitate et potestate ecclesiastica', 760).

positive law and the evidence of reason. For Ockham, the law of the Gospel is a law of freedom – with regard to Mosaic law – and the pope cannot simply impose slavery on the community of the faithful. The pope has no power over matters that are not necessary for eternal life and the reasonable rights and freedom of people cannot be affected by his power.[17] Ockham does not even think it necessary that all believers without exception should obey the pope in those matters which are fundamental to the community of the faithful. The intelligent judgment of what is necessary in these cases is incumbent on theologians and expert scholars, regardless of their rank and status. If the pope errs in his judgment of power, every Christian, according to his rank and status, has the obligation to withstand him. The idea of the evangelical freedom of the Christian person prevents any form of absolutism be it either in lay or in spiritual power.[18]

Clearly the source of Gansfort's position is Ockham's political theology. As in matters of faith the ultimate decision lies with the believer, so it is with regard to the mandates of prelates. Submission to a prelate must always be voluntary and spontaneous, and therefore it must not be assented to without deliberation. For this reason the spiritual formation of the people must include a strengthening of the power of judgment, built upon a thorough knowledge of Scripture and the theology of the early Fathers of the Church.

'I believe with the Holy Church'

We can elaborate Wessel's position a little further, examining his position with regard to indulgences. Gansfort wrote to Jacob Hoeck, then dean of Naaldwijk:

> Let me speak more openly: as long as it seems to me that the pope or theologians or any school assert a position contradicting the truth of Scripture, my concern for scriptural truth obliges me to give it the first place, and after that I am bound to examine the evidence on both sides of the question, since it is unlikely that the majority would err. But in every case I owe more respect to canonical Scripture than to human assertions, regardless of who holds them.[19]

It is interesting to note, that Gansfort in this letter refers to his mental attitude, his sheer commitment to truth when he was still a boy. As a boy, he was educated in Zwolle, living with the Brethren of the Common Life:

---

[17] Weiler, 'The foundations of the superior secular and spiritual powers', 148.
[18] Op. cit., 149; 151.
[19] Gansfort, *Opera,* 879. English translation by Nyhus in Oberman, *Forerunners of the Reformation,* 99-100.

For from boyhood it seemed to me absurd and unbefitting to believe that the mere appearance and intervention of a human decree could change the value of a good act in God's eyes. [...] Since boyhood I have sought this truth above all things, and now more than ever I seek it, because only via truth does one come to life.

With the same ardour, he says, he had proposed his opinion thirty-three years earlier among Parisian doctors, of whom he mentions quite a few.[20] The Brethren could not have wished for better compliments with regard to their educational activities. Wessel's statements clearly mark his position in the spiritual context of the Modern Devotion at Zwolle during his youth.

Gansfort did not build his position with regard to indulgences on the mere fact that Scripture contains nothing on the subject. He made it quite clear to Jacob Hoeck:

I know very well that Scripture alone is not a sufficient rule of faith. I know that some things which were not written, were handed down by the Apostles, and that all these teachings ought to be received into the rule of faith just like Scripture. These two, together with what can be logically deduced from them, constitute the only rule of faith, and this is the only rule of faith to which I hold so strictly, that I believe that no one can deviate from it without destroying his salvation [...] I agree, therefore, that regarding this rule of faith I ought to depend on the authority of the Church *with* which – not *in* which – I believe [...] I believe *with* the Holy Church, I believe *according* to the teachings of the Holy Church, but I do not believe *in* the Church, because believing is an act of worship, a sacrifice of theological virtue which ought to be offered to God alone.[21]

The spiritual church

Wessel's concept of the spiritual Church is expressed in his work *De sacramento poenitentiae*. Explaining his ideas concerning the real communion of the saints, he states that all saints communicate in a true and essential unity, as long as they adhere to Christ in one faith, one hope, one love, regardless which prelates they have, wherever in the world, however much distant in time. The diversity of prelates distracts nothing from this unity and union of the saints nor does their identity promote it. 'The unity of the Church under one pope is therefore only accidental, and even so much, that this unity is not necessary, although it brings much to the communion of the saints.' Similarly he states: 'There is a double priesthood, one of the sacramental order, the other of a rational nature, which is common to everybody. The sec-

---

[20] Gansfort, *Opera*, 878; 887; Oberman, *Forerunners of the Reformation*, 99; 104.
[21] Gansfort, *Opera*, 887-8; Oberman, *Forerunners of the Reformation*, 105; Oberman, *The Dawn of the Reformation*, 280-3.

ond is sufficient without the first. The first one is defective without the second.'[22]

The wording of these statements strongly resembles a letter of Geert Grote (1340-1384) to his friend and teacher, William of Sarvavilla, cantor of the church of Paris, archdeacon of Brabant in the church of Liège, written in the summer of 1381. Grote writes in this *Epistola de scismate*:

> Truly, the head of the Church is Christ, and the truly life-giving ordering of the members is according to the construction of the Church upon this head; therefore firstly Christ is the head; and after Him, those who are higher in sainthood in the militant Church and more spiritual, are the neck and the arms etcetera of the body. The true order is the interior one, the living one, and therefore the unity of the Church proceeds from one life, viz. the Lord Christ, and from the unity of the Spirit. [...] But the pope can be outside the immaculate Church; he may not even belong to the Church, nor be her head or even a member; the pope is only the head of the congregation with regard to the judicial presidency and the exterior government. And that unity is less principal than the true unity of the Church.[23]

Earlier in the same letter he wrote:

> Happy the pope who is pope according to the divine law. For if according to divine law all things belong to the just, then it seems that, according to the same law, to have everything in power or even in fullness of power, belongs only to the most outstanding or saint person.[24]

The issue of the construction of the spiritual Church was Grote's deepest concern. More than once we find in his letters the terms *constructio corporis [Christi] mistici, Ecclesiae sanctae constructionem, realis Ecclesiae spiritualis constructio*.[25] For the edification of that spiritual Church to the fullness of age in Christ, he required knowledge and books, as he wrote to the school rector at Zwolle, his good friend John Cele: 'unum est nobis necessarium, si simul currere debemus in edificacionem Ecclesie in plenitudinem etatis Christi. Ad edificacionem enim querimus et scienciam et libros, ut habundemus.'[26] Constructing the spiritual Church was a work of education of the faithful, the 'saints'. The Brethren of the Common Life took exactly that line in their educational work with the lay people, especially the young.

One cannot deny that in the wordings of Geert Grote and of Wessel Gansfort with regard to the communion of the saints, there is some resem-

---

[22] Gansfort, *Opera*, 809-10; 775.

[23] Translated from the Latin original in Grote, *Epistolae*, 91.

[24] Op cit., 88.

[25] Op. cit., 47; 66; 69.

[26] Op. cit., 42.

blance to the theses of John Wycliffe and Jan Hus that were condemned at the Council of Constance. Another Dutch theologian, Henry of Gorkum (†1431), lectured on the matter of these theses at the University of Cologne around 1430. Wycliffe considered the papacy as an interstice (*intersticium*) that stood in the way of a direct infusion of grace, the direct communication between God and the believers. Wycliffe also believed, that nobody who lived outside grace had any right to temporal or spiritual goods, to dominion or to dignity.[27] Still neither Grote nor Gansfort advocated a form of spiritualistic extremism, but they have in common with many spiritual writers of the late Middle Ages their aversion to corrupt clergy and prelates and their rejection of doubtful ecclesiastical ordinances. Heiko Oberman thus rightly qualifies Wessel's ecclesiology as 'spiritualizing'.[28]

John Pupper of Goch

Post also denied any connection between the Brethren of the Common Life and another famous critical theologian, John Pupper of Goch.[29] Research in the archives of the city of Amersfoort by C.A. Kalveen in the late 1970s has shown, however, that John Pupper was a member of the community of the Brethren in Amersfoort.[30] In a document of October 9, 1442 he is mentioned with his full name, as a cleric, who, together with six other clerics and two priests and the rector of the House, Godfried van Hemert, stipulated that they intended to live in communion of property, promising not to alter their way of life but with consent obtained from the rectors of the Houses in Deventer and Zwolle and the majority of the Amersfoort fraternity. This agreement was confirmed before the court of aldermen of Amersfoort on December 29, 1442. He was ordained a priest before 1447.

The next step in his biography brings us to Gouda. A certain *frater* John of Goch from the House at Amersfoort was appointed rector of the House at Gouda after his predecessor Hendrik Herp had left for Rome to become a mendicant friar in the monastery Ara Coeli. This person must be the same man as John Pupper of Goch. There is no other *frater* 'Van Goch' known in the Amersfoort fraternity. Though often ill, John Pupper held this function

---

[27] Weiler, *Heinrich von Gorkum*, 196-241, esp. 208-9; 219; Oberman, *Forerunners of the Reformation*, 205; 208; 236.

[28] Oberman, *Forerunners of the Reformation*, 22; Ogilvie, 'Wessel Gansfort's Theology of Church Government'. For the general context cf. Van Engen, 'The Church in the Fifteenth Century'.

[29] Post, 'Johann Pupper van Goch'; Post, *The Modern Devotion*, 469-76; 480-6; 489; Post, *De via antiqua en de via moderna*, 15-18.

[30] Van Kalveen, 'Johan Pupper van Goch'.

from 1451 to 1454. The House in Gouda did not prosper and at a given time
there were only two priests to present collations to the public. The house had
been expressly established for that purpose in 1425 and it was re-established
as a House of the Brethren in 1445. It was properly called *domus collacionis*
(St.-Pauluscollatiehuis). At long last, John of Goch was the only person left
in the House. His collations irritated the clergy of the town and he had to
leave the House around June 24, 1454. The Brothers of Amersfoort did not
give him any help or assistance. He also probably left the brotherhood but
remained a priest.[31]

On December 15, 1454, John Pupper immatriculated in the university of
Cologne to study law. Afterwards he was for a time rector of a house of
Tertiaries in Sluis (Zeeland). In 1459 he went to Malines (Belgium), and
founded a nunnery following the rule of St. Augustine according to the regulations of Cardinal Nicholas of Kues. He died there on March 6, 1475. His
name is found in the *Memoriale van Sanct Agnieten 't Amersfoert*, a list of
the defunct Brethren of Amersfoort.[32]

John of Goch's works were published in 1522, together with the works
of Wessel Gansfort. We have seen that as rector of the House in Gouda his
collations did not please the Gouda clergy. We may assume that John of
Goch ventured some of the critical opinions we find in these printed works
in his sermons to the public at Gouda in the years 1451-1454. Surely he can
therefore be called a forerunner of the Reformation, especially if we note
Luther's praise of his theology.[33]

In an introductory letter to the printed edition of John Pupper's *Fragmenta* (1522 or 1523),[34] Luther expressed his joy that in Germany there had
been found examples of a more honest theology than what the scholastics
had produced. He mentions John Tauler (whose works had appeared in print
in 1521 in Basel), the *Theologia teutonica* (an ascetic and mystical treatise
in Eckhardian orientation, stemming from the circles of the *Gottesfreunde*
[first, incomplete edition 1516]),[35] Wessel Gansfort,[36] whom he extolls

---

[31] Details concerning the Gouda house are given by Hendrik van Arnhem, fifth rector of the
House, in his Chronicle, written c. 1483, over the years 1419-56 (ed. by Hensen, 'Henric van
Arnhem's kronijk van het Fraterhuis te Gouda').

[32] Van Kalveen, 'Johan Pupper van Gogh', 113 and n. 49, referring to ms The Hague, Royal
Libr. 75 H 18, 71r-v. Pupper did not die in Amersfoort, as I mistakenly put it in my *'Het werk
van professor Post'*, 236.

[33] Benrath, *Reformtheologen des 15. Jahrhunderts;* Oberman, *Forerunners of the Reformation*, 1-50 (chapter one: 'The Case of the Forerunner').

[34] Benrath, *Reformtheologen des 15. Jahrhunderts*, 9-10; Pupper von Goch, *Fragmenta*,
283-4.

[35] Luther, *WA* 1, 153; second, complete edition 1518 (*WA* 1, 375-9); Oberman, *The Dawn of
the Reformation*, 140-1.

[36] Cf. Luther's preface to Gansfort's *Epistolae, WA* 10/II, 311-7.

above Rudolph Agricola with regard to the purity of theology, and finally John Pupper of Goch from Malines, whose works were now available in print. Luther hoped that through the influence of these theologians there would soon be no more Thomists, Albertists, Scotists or Ockhamists, but only simple children of God and true Christians. According to Luther one should not look in theology for eloquence or ingenuity – hard to be found in the works of our Dutch theologians – because the wisdom of God makes even the tongues of children eloquent.[37]

Evangelical freedom

Let us now examine Van Goch's letter on the dignity and unbreakable authority of Holy Scripture and the way he thinks the writings of theologians and philosophers of the school should be read.[38] In the introduction of his letter he refers to a booklet written by the Dominican Engelbert Messemaker, lector in Zutphen and prior in Zwolle, who had attacked Pupper's main work *De libertate christiana*.[39] Engelbert had referred to the authority of Thomas Aquinas's opinion, but for John of Goch the truth of the canonical Scripture comes first. Modern philosophers, following Aristotle, try to understand the created things. For him, this is not enough. The light of truth leads to the knowledge and love of God, Who in His Son and eternal Word incarnate created everything. Philosophers and schoolmen present only opinions, but Scripture gives the solid foundation of the truth. John prefers to follow Peter, Paul and John the Evangelist above Albertus, Thomas or Scotus (p. 13). Abundantly he quotes St. Augustine (from the *Decretum Gratiani*), who had stressed the precedence of canonical Scripture over mere opinions. Even pope Urban[40] held that a pope can establish new laws, but never against the teachings of Christ and the Apostles. According to John, Engelbert, who tried to enclose evangelical freedom under the necessity arising from the obligation of monastic vows, absolutely contradicts Scripture. Paul and James state clearly that the law of the Gospel is the law of perfect freedom, because it is free from any slavery and servitude (*Gal.* 5,

---

[37] Benrath, *Reformtheologen des 15. Jahrhunderts*, 9-10; Oberman, *Forerunners of the Reformation,* 17-19, delineates Luther's own understanding of 'reformation' with reference to, among others, Gansfort and Pupper. 'Luther's reformation is precisely *not* the intensification of individual or monastic reform but rather the radical criticism of this 'man-made road to reformation''; ibidem, 10 and n. 14.

[38] Benrath, *Reformtheologen des 15. Jahrhunderts*, 10-19.

[39] Pupper von Goch, *De libertate christiana*; Pupper von Goch, *Fragmenta*.

[40] *Decretum Gratiani*, c. 25, q. 1, c. 6: 'In quibus liceat Romano Pontifici novas condere leges'; Friedberg I, 1008 n. 57: 'non est inter epp. Urbani neque I, neque II'.

13; *1 Cor.* 7,17-22; *Jac.* 1,25). Also in the Acts of the Apostles evangelical freedom leads the way (*Acts* 15). The law of the Gospel has been instilled from the beginning in the freedom of the spirit and therefore man does not derive any merit from the obligation of a vow as such but only because he does the good things he has obliged himself to do in the freedom of the spirit. The law of the Gospel is a law of love, yet no one can love but by his free will. Nobody can be forced to love. By the virtuous works which are done under human mandates by force of obligation no-one will be justified; he will not share in the freedom of the glory of God's children (*Rom.* 8, 21).

John's conclusion is that under the law of the Gospel nothing is meritorious and agreeable to God that is done under the necessity of an obligation, but everything has to be done by the love of freedom, *by which freedom Christ has liberated us* (*Gal.* 4, 31; 3, 26; *Rom.* 8, 15 and 29). Arguing in this way, he does not deny the value of vows but he only opposes the idea that their efficacy is in the obligation as such. Good works of faith spring from the freedom of the will and from grace.

It is important to realize, that Geert Grote in Kampen opposed the adherents of the movement of the Free Spirit, as it was called.[41] Here, with John of Goch, the Pauline terminology of the freedom of the spirit returns but now in an attack on the idea, that the obligation of a vow in itself would be effective in making good works meritorious. One must remember that the Brethren and Sisters of the Common Life in their communities did not take vows. On the firm basis of a voluntary communion of goods, they gave themselves voluntarily in an obedience of love under the guidance of the rector of the House.[42] Knowing now that John of Goch was a member of the Brotherhood, his defence of evangelical freedom does not astonish us. It is more surprising to find this *defensor evangelicae libertatis*, after he had left the House in Gouda, as the rector of a convent of Regular Canonesses in Malines. Yet, he held these theses to be valid even for the nuns who had taken vows.

---

[41] Grote, *Epistolae*, 133-7; Wormgoor, 'De vervolging van de Vrijen van Geest'.

[42] Cf. Gansfort, *Scala Meditationis*, 337, who distinguishes as a separate 'grade' of Christians those 'qui regularis professionis et obedientiae magistrum veriti, Christiana libertate contenti, sobrie, juste, pie, caste vivunt in seculo', clearly meaning the Brethren and Sisters of the Common Life. I fail to understand why Oberman ('Wessel Gansfort: *Magister Contradictionis*', 111) interprets this qualification as ranking the Devouts under the monks. In my opinion the translation of this sentence should read: 'they are the ones who content themselves with Christian liberty, shying away from any teacher of monastic profession and obedience.' Cf. Oberman, *Werden und Wertung der Reformation*, 8-9, on Gabriel Biel's position concerning the Common Life, which is in line with Wessel's statement.

On the merits of vows and other good works for eternal salvation

In another *Fragment* (p. 22), John opposes those who ascribe the justification of man and the eternal reward not exclusively to grace but partly also to the works of justice done out of love. He now proceeds somewhat further, arguing that it is Christ Himself, Who, dwelling in us, operates the good works. To believe in the force of works as such is Judaism. In using this term he refers forward to the criticism of Erasmus on this particular point.[43]

Christ incarnate is the complete cause of our salvation, as He is of our creation, another *Fragment* states (p. 25). In the light of this thesis, John explains the dictum of Augustine 'He who created you without you, will not justify you without you.' This is taken to mean that just as God created man without his will and without his cooperation He will justify man without his cooperation but not without his will. As is well-known, the problem of human cooperation with grace is a theme that was frequently dealt with in nominalist theology. It was also widely distributed in spiritual writings of Franciscan origin that repeated time and again that 'to those who do what is in their power, God will not deny his grace' *(facientibus quod in se est, Deus non denegat gratiam)*.[44] This formula is even found in Thomas a Kempis's *De imitatione Christi*.[45] John comes very close to this theology when he writes that God does not give us the kingdom of heaven because of our deeds. He only fulfills His promise because He has promised to give the kingdom to them who follow Him. There is no question of God remunerating human works with merited reward for in that case the free gift of grace would be lost (p. 27).

It should not come as a surprise to find Luther applauding John's critical theology of the merits of vows and other good works. It is somewhat strange, however, to find an adherent of the Brotherhood of the Common Life arguing in this way in setting the spiritual practice of the Modern Devotion.[46] The Brethren put much store by *exercitia* in obedience, humility, poverty, discipline and the like. Of course Geert Grote, Gerard Zerbolt of Zutphen, Gerlach Peeters and Thomas a Kempis knew about the necessity of cooperating grace, but their strong emphasis lies on the practice of virtue. The rectors of several houses for Brothers or Sisters of the Common Life are praised by their biographers as strong *exercitatores* of the young men and women entrusted to their spiritual care. Did no-one ever think that he or she

---

[43] Godin, 'L'antijudaïsme d'Erasme'.
[44] Bange, '"Laat-middeleeuwse" moralistisch-didactische traktaten'.
[45] Thomas a Kempis, *De Imitatione Christi*, 1,7; cf. 3,7; 4,10 and 12. Cf. Weiler, 'Christelijke identiteit en tolerantie volgens Geert Grote en Thomas van Kempen', esp. 39-40.
[46] Weiler, 'Over de geestelijke praktijk van de Moderne Devotie'.

was 'meriting' or earning eternal salvation through the exercise of the humility, obedience, poverty and discipline that had been imposed by a superior? John of Goch made it quite clear to his audiences that so-called meritorious works did not oblige God to give the expected reward. For the Devouts as for the laity who heard his collations in Gouda, this message must have been disturbing. What was to be the use of individual good deeds if there were no reciprocity in the relations between men and God? If love is sufficient, why then exercise yourself and others in works of virtue? Small wonder that the Brethren of Amersfoort did not come to rescue their former companion when he found himself in trouble in Gouda!

The Brethren and Northern Humanism

The Brethren as humanists

According to Professor Post, the influence of the Brethren on the incoming tide of Northern Humanism was very small and indeed restricted to three men. The first is *frater* John Synthen († before 1493) in Deventer. He was a teacher of Greek at the chapterschool of St.-Lebuinus and also at the school of the Brethren that only existed from about his time onward until 1534. We might add, however, that under rector Alexander Hegius († December 27, 1498) other brothers such as James of Gouda and Henry of Amersfoort shared in the teaching activities of the chapterschool. Post, however, seems to have ignored the fact that the circle of humanists at Deventer is wider than the inner circle of the House. John Butzbach, who began his studies at Deventer in August 1498, names as his teachers one Geoffrey (fifth form), John of Venray (fourth form) and Bartholomew of Cologne (third form). These men were not brothers, no more than rector John Oostendorp was. Erasmus praised Hegius and Bartholomew of Cologne in a letter of 1489 (?) to Cornelius Gerard of Gouda.[47] In this letter and elsewhere, he mentions that at the age of twelve he once saw the humanist Rudolph Agricola in Deventer.[48]

In this context special mention must be made of Gerard Listrius. This humanist taught at Deventer after 1505 until 1514; from 1516 to 1522 he was rector of the school at Zwolle. Erasmus praised him for his knowledge of

---

[47] Erasmus, *Opus epistolarum*, I 103-9 (ep. 23).
[48] Erasmus, *Opus epistolarum*, epp. 1 and 2; *Adagia* 339 *Quid cani et balneo* (*ASD* II-1, 438-42); Waterbolk, *Een hond in het bad.*

Latin, Greek and Hebrew.[49] He wrote some schoolbooks, among others *Commentarioli in dialecticen Petri Hispani* (1520), which he dedicated to Goswinus of Halen (see below), and a commentary on Erasmus's *Encomium Moriae*.[50] In Deventer and in Zwolle he kept close contact with the Brethren but he was also affected by the new critical theology. He defended justification by faith and other theses of Luther, with whom he corresponded (1520). In a letter to Goswinus on February 3, 1520 he says that he has been accused of having a low opinion of the sacrament of penance and of ecclesiastical ceremonies. His explanation of Erasmus's *Enchiridion* may have been the cause of these accusations.[51] After he became rector of the Latin school at Amersfoort in 1522 nothing more is known of his life.[52]

Secondly, Post mentions the *frater*-humanist Goswinus of Halen, a pupil of Hegius at Deventer. As a young man, he became *famulus* of Wessel Gansfort during his days at Aduard.[53] He was present at some of Wessel's conversations with Rudolph Agricola. He entered the House of the Brethren at Groningen on June 25, 1489, and from 1507 onwards he was the rector of the Groningen House (not of the townschool, as Allen has it) until his death in 1530. He visited Erasmus in April 1521,[54] bringing a gilt goblet as a gift from Willem Frederiks, the *persona* of Groningen. He was also in contact with Martinus Dorpius, Gerard Listrius and Philip Melanchthon.[55] He wrote a *Vita Wesseli Gansfort*,[56] a biography of Rudolph Agricola in the form of a

---

[49] Erasmus, *Opus epistolarum,* II 22 (ep. 305, 184-6) 'item Giraerdus Listrius, medicae rei non vulgariter peritus, ad hec Latinae, Graecae, et Hebraicae literaturae pulchre gnarus, denique iuuenis ad me amandum natus.'

[50] Biographical notes on Listrius in Erasmus, *Opus epistolarum*, II 407 n.; I 19, 12-13; IV 483 introd.; IX 449; *CE* II 335-6. He was accused of having poisoned John Murmell († 2 October 1517): III 122, 1-17; 297, 9; 308, 1-11; on Murmellius see 308, n. 2.

[51] Hoefer, 'Een onuitgegeven brief van Dr. Maarten Luther' (with edition of the text of this letter to Listrius); in his biography of Listrius, Rogge mistakenly says that the school at Zwolle was founded by the Brethren. In an *Oratio ad scholasticos Swollanos* (1516), Listrius praises the Brethren at Zwolle for having constructed a new convict for poor students that could admit 200 students (*domus pauperum scolarium*); Rogge, 'Gerardus Listrius', 210, n. 2, quoting from J. Lindeborn, *Historia sive notitia episcopatus Daventriensis* (Cologne 1670), 382; Van Rhijn, *Studiën,* 151.

[52] *CE* II 335-6.

[53] Biographical note on Goswinus in Erasmus, *Opus epistolarum*, III 309, n. 11; Van Rhijn, *Studiën,* 137-59.

[54] Erasmus, *Opus epistolarum,* IV 482-5; esp. 483, 6-9; cf. III 308. Biographical note on Frederiks in Erasmus, *Opus epistolarum,* IV 482-3. Erasmus praises Willem that he had adorned the church with a library, containing the works of Origen, Chrysostom, Cyprian, Ambrose, Augustine, Jerome, 'quorum scripta spirant Euangelicam charitatem' (484, 33-36 and n. 33). Willem donated his library to the Brethren in Groningen, but there is no trace of these books.

[55] Van Rhijn, *Wessel Gansfort,* Bijlage I, viii-xi; Van Rhijn, *Studiën,* 152-4.

[56] Kan, 'Wesseli, Agricolae, Erasmi Vitae', 9; Van Rhijn, *Wessel Gansfort*, Bijlage A, iii-vi.

letter,[57] and two letters to Albert Rizaeus Hardenberg, then living at Aduard. In the first letter (1528) he extolls the Aduard Academy and its visitors.[58] The second letter (1529) included a list of classical and Christian authors that he recommended for reading. This list is comparable to the non-comprehensive list given by Erasmus in his *De ratione studii*.[59] Goswinus is mentioned as a possible author of the *Disputatio Groningensis*, a report of a discussion between the Dominican friars of Groningen and reformists in 1523.[60]

Here also some other persons may be mentioned. Herman Torrentinus (van Beek) of Zwolle († c. 1520), a member of the fraternity, was a teacher in the fifth form of the fraterschool at Groningen.[61] He was influenced by Wessel Gansfort. Later he became rector of the school at Zwolle, where Gerard Listrius became his successor in 1516. He produced many books, most of which were printed in Deventer. His commentary on the first book of Alexander de Villa Dei's *Doctrinale* was printed in Zwolle. He also published *Scholia in Evangelia et Epistolas* (Cologne 1499). His *Orationes familiares ex omnibus P. Ovidii libris formate* (without date), was printed in 's-Hertogenbosch by Laurentius Hayen. After Laurentius's death the Brethren in that town set up their own press and publishing house in 1525.[62]

As related but further removed from the Brethren mention might be made of Reinier Praedinius of Winsum (1510-1559), a teacher and rector of the St.-Maartenschool in Groningen, and Albertus Rizaeus Hardenberg (1510-1574), a teacher at the same school after 1528, then a monk at Aduard, but subsequently married and a propagator of the Reformation in Emden. As boys, the two men had shared room and bed in the Groningen convict of the Brethren (*domus pauperum*).

Frater Georgius Macropedius (†1556) is Post's third example. He was a teacher at and rector of the townschool in 's-Hertogenbosch and at the frater school in Utrecht. His literary works include schoolbooks such as the well-known *Epistolica* (Antwerp, 1543), also called *Methodus de conscribendis*

---

[57] Agricola, *Lucubrationes*, *2r. According to Visser, 'Among the good teachers', 143 n. 5 and 7, Goswin's letter will be included in the final volume of the *Briefwechsel* of Melanchthon.

[58] In Gansfort, *Opera*, **4-4v; Van Rhijn, *Studiën*, 141-3.

[59] In Gansfort, *Opera*, **5-5v; Elsmann, 'Hardenberg und Molanus in Bremen', esp. 198-9; Erasmus, *Ratio studii*, *ASD* I-2, esp. 121, 1-3; *CWE* 24, esp. 673, 8-14.

[60] *Disputatio habita Gruningae;* Wolfs, *Das Groninger Religionsgespräch.* Van Rhijn, *Wessel Gansfort*, 149, says that Goswinus was not involved in this disputation.

[61] Postma, 'Praedinius', 294 n. 13, states, without sufficient reason, that there was no frater school in Groningen. This question has been re-examined by Weiler, *Volgens de norm*, s.v. Groningen, concluding that indeed there was a school of the fraters, from c. 1511 to 1578.

[62] Nijhoff and Kronenberg, *Nederlandsche bibliographie van 1500-1540*, nrs 2026, 2063, 2064, 2066, 4406; Van den Oord, *Twee eeuwen Bosch' Boekbedrijf*, 83-84; 94-100. The Brethren at Gouda started printing c. 1486 (?) until 1521; first print 1492/3 (*IDL* II 52-53 lists the production between 1492/3 and 1497; those in Brussels in 1475 until 1485/7).

epistolis (Dillingen, 1561), schooldramas, letters and dedications of works to the pupils of the Utrecht St.-Hieronymusschool, *cantilenae* for the same boys, addresses to benefactors, magistrates, his Antwerp printer John Hillen of Hoochstraten and to the auxiliary bishop of Utrecht, Nicolaas of Nieuwland.[63] In conclusion, mention must be made of another humanist, *frater* Petrus of Vladeracken (†1618), member of the St.-Gregoriushuis in 's-Hertogenbosch. He is the author of *Tobias comoedia sacra* (1595), a *Carmen scholasticum [...] pro anno iubilaei 1600*, and other works.[64]

This complete listing of Brethren whose works had any significance on the humanist forum is certainly not impressive. Now we must turn to the wider circle of humanists who felt the influence of the Brethren.

Humanists in relation with the Brethren

A very early example of the humanist connections between the Low Countries and Italy is the the Regular Canon and canonist Arnold Geilhoven of Rotterdam († August 31, 1442), mentioned above as the author of the *Parvum Gnotosolitos*, which was composed as a handbook for clerics studying for the priesthood in the House of the Brethren in Deventer and in the *paedagogium* of Henry Wellens in Louvain. Geilhoven studied at the universities of Bologna, Padua and Vienna. Around 1399 he lectured at the university of Bologna under the patronage of his master Gaspar de Calderinis. In Padua he stayed in the house of his master Francesco Zabarella, where Pier Paolo Vergerio also lived. In the library of Zabarella he found the works of Petrarch, whose son-in-law Francescuolo and his son and daughter were among Arnold's acquintances. In his works he quotes many texts of Petrarch and for this reason he earned the qualification 'an early disciple of Petrarch in the Low Countries.'[65]

The most eminent humanist who must be discussed in relation with the Brethren is obviously Desiderius Erasmus. Professor Post and more recently professor Augustijn denied any influence of the Modern Devotion on Erasmus.[66] We have to take seriously, however, the facts that Erasmus knew the Brethren of his native town Gouda (he generally calls them by their specific Gouda name of *fratres collationarii*)[67] and that he was brought up by the

---

[63] A complete list of his works in chronological order in Puttiger, *Georgius Macropedius' Asotus,* 11-22; Weiler, *Volgens de norm,* s.v. Utrecht.

[64] Weiler, *Volgens de norm,* s.v. 's-Hertogenbosch 1; to be revised in *Monasticon III* (n. 2).

[65] Mann, 'Arnold Geilhoven'; Weiler, 'La systématique de la théologie morale selon Arnold Geilhoven'.

[66] Augustijn, 'Erasmus en de Moderne Devotie'.

[67] Erasmus, *Opus epistolarum,* II 295, 101-2 (ep. 447); V 428, 29 (ep. 1436).

Brethren in Deventer and 's-Hertogenbosch. If we accept Vredeveld's recent reconstruction of Erasmus's youth as a convincing argument to put his birthdate in 1466,[68] Erasmus lived in the convict (*domus pauperum*) of the Brethren in Deventer from Autumn 1477 or around Easter 1478 until the Summer of 1484, following classes in the chapterschool up into the third form. There is no evidence that he was a pupil of the Brethren in their own school, which was held in the public attic (*in solario publico*) of their House. That institution was brought over to them from the Cusanus-convict (founded in 1469).[69] Unfortunately we do not know the exact year of this transfer. We do know for certain, however, that the school of the Brethren was suppressed by the town magistrates in 1534.[70] 'Educabar apud hos Deventurii, nondum egressus annum decimum quintum', Erasmus wrote in *De recta Latini Graecique pronuntiatione* (ed. Froben, Basel 1528).[71] The prefect of the congregation (*eius sodalitii prefectus*: does Erasmus mean the (unknown) rector of the House, the procurator of the convict, or the *rector scolarium* of the convict?) did his utmost to bring the young man to the decision to join their institute; Erasmus was indeed, as he himself says, a child inclined to piety. The scene between the *frater* and the pupil was sketched vividly by Erasmus fifty years later. He was at that time not very impressed by the standards of learning of the Brethren, who knew nearly nothing about the pagan, classical authors he thought necessary for the knowledge of antiquity and eloquence. They were nearly all of them *autodidaktoi*, not having received a liberal education themselves. Erasmus considered their morose manners most depressing, especially as they were applied to children with candid characters, whom they tried to bring into their fraternity (as in his personal case), or, when they did not succeed, into another monastic fold.

Erasmus had been from boyhood attracted to literature, as he puts it, 'by a kind of secret natural force', but in Deventer he found little of the *bonae litterae* that had begun to flourish in Italy. At Deventer he had seen Rudolph Agricola, who brought some little breeze of better literature from Italy. He drew from the books at his disposal whatever he could, and exercised his

---

[68] Vredeveld, 'The Ages of Erasmus'; see, however, Weiler, *Erasmus*, 51, n. 1.

[69] Post, *The Modern Devotion*, 251.

[70] Van Engen, 'The Virtues, the Brothers and the Schools', 190 and n. 34-5, says: 'In 1482 [...] the Brothers [of the House] in Emmerich resolved to establish a school similar to that in Deventer.' There was in Emmerich, however, not a school, but only a convict established for the students of the townschool; see *Monasticon Fratrum Vitae Communis II*, 66-7. The rector of the House in Herford (Germany), Gerhard Wiskamp, correctly states in a letter of October 9, 1534, that the *fratres* in Deventer had [at that moment] no school: 'alsth kentlyck tho Deventer, Swoll, Embrick, dar de fraters der schole nycht heben'; Stupperich, 'Luther und das Fraterhaus in Herford', esp. 238.

[71] *ASD* I-4, 29, 507-8.

pen, making notes and composing texts.[72] The school in Deventer was judged by him rather severely in his *Compendium Vitae*: 'Ea schola tunc adhuc
erat barbara [...] nisi quod Alexander Hegius et Zinthius coeperant aliquid
melioris litteraturae invehere.' His schoolmates from the higher classes told
him about the better doctrine put forward by *frater* Synthen. This literate
man delighted in Erasmus's progress, and predicted him that he would reach
the summit of learning one day, embracing the boy and kissing him. In later
years Erasmus listend to Hegius as that rector lectured for all the boys on
festival days.[73] He gives a list of the schoolbooks and exercises that were
used at Deventer and which he abhorred.[74]

After his years in Deventer, he was sent by his tutor to the Brethren at 's-
Hertogenbosch. There he lived in the *domus divitum scolarium* from Summer 1484 to 1487, before joining the Canons Regular in the monastery of
Stein near Gouda. The *frater instructor* or *repetitor* was a certain Rombol-
dus, who tried to bring him into the fraternity. Erasmus could not learn very
much at 's-Hertogenbosch. There was no reason to visit the city-school
because the school lacked the second and first classes. Thus Erasmus had
three years free for self-study. The large library of the Brethren was at his
disposition and the statutes of the House gave him the express permission to
use it.[75]

Erasmus says that he spent or rather 'lost' three years in the buildings of
the *fratres* at 's-Hertogenbosch.[76] In a way this is true. He might have had
more profit by going directly to a university, but his uncle and tutor, the
Gouda schoolmaster Peter Winckel, would not allow him to go abroad. We
must not underestimate the fruits his studies in 's-Hertogenbosch brought
him. Where else than in the library of the Brethren (and later in that of the
Canons in Stein)[77] would Erasmus have acquired the knowledge shown in

---

[72] Erasmus to John Botzheim (Basel, 30.1.1523): 'tamen velut occulta naturae vi rapiebar ad
bonas literas'; Erasmus, *Opus epistolarum*, I 2, 20-34, esp. 30ff. (ep. 1); cf. I 104, 37-42 (ep.
23): 'Is enim mihi est atque a puero fuit literarum amor', and IV 278, 1-9 (ep. 1110): 'quod
cum me puero prorsus exularent ludis literariis bonae literae, cum deessent librorum ac prae-
ceptorum subsidia [...] naturae sensus quidam ad Musarum sacra velut afflatum rapiebat.' This
statement refers to the 'schrijfschool' in Gouda and maybe also the cathedral school in Utrecht;
Compendium Vitae, in Erasmus, *Opus epistolarum*, I 48, 30-1; I 56, 8-9 (ep. 4); I 579-80
(Appendix II: Erasmus' early life); Schoeck, 'Agricola and Erasmus'.
[73] *Compendium Vitae*, in Erasmus, *Opus epistolarum*, I 48, 30-42; on the appreciation of
Hegius and *frater* Synthen, see the sketch of Erasmus's life by Beatus Rhenanus to Charles V
(1540), in Erasmus, *Opus epistolarum*, I 57, 11-32.
[74] Weiler, 'Erasmus of Rotterdam's *Institutum hominis christiani*'.
[75] 'Ex statutis domus fratrum S. Gregorii, quae erecta est anno 1425'. XVII. De librario: 'et
ne habeat quotidie accessus scholarium petentium studia, statuat eis certam horam festivis die-
bus, qua vacet circa eos expediendos' (*Analecta Gijsberti Coeverincx*, II 106).
[76] *Compendium Vitae*, in Erasmus, *Opus epistolarum*, I 49, 52-7.
[77] Erasmus mentions twice the *copia librorum* in the monastery at Stein: *Opus epistolarum*,
I 50, 84-6 (*Compendium vitae*); II 300, 315 (ep. 447); see also I 564-573 (ep. 296), esp. 566,

his *De Contemptu Mundi*, written at the end of 1489 or 1490/91? In this treatise he refers to the sources of Christian knowledge, to the works of Jerome, Augustine, Ambrose, Cyprian, Lactantius, Thomas Aquinas and Albertus Magnus, that a well-trained man could read or transcribe.[78] As Erika Rummel has shown, he himself used a letter by bishop Eucherius of Lyon for the composition of this treatise;[79] in a letter to Alard of Amsterdam (Louvain <1517>) he writes that 'he had read and enjoyed [it] when still a child.' Yet, it was exactly as a child that he had been with the Brethren.[80]

Again, in the *Antibarbari*-version of 1494-5, which he began as early as 1488 and possibly even earlier[81] and which has been preserved in the Gouda manuscript, he attacked the medieval grammarians Alexander de Villa Dei, Graecista, Ebrardus, Mammetrectus and Catholicon, Michael the Modist, encyclopedists like John Balbi (*Catholicon*) and John de Mera (*Breviloquium*), and the rhymed cathechism *Floretus*. He brought in examples of people who were both educated and saints: Moses, Paul, the Prophets, Clement of Alexandria, Origen, Gregory of Nazianze, Lactantius, Cyprian, Jerome, Bede and Thomas Aquinas. These references again show that by this time, Erasmus knew the works of these authors.[82]

Already in these early years, Erasmus's ideal is clearly expressed: 'What I recommend is that you should reflect the moral virtues of the apostles and at the same time the learning of Jerome' (*ut moribus apostolos exprimas, eruditione Hieronymum*).[83] He will repeat this program several times in other works and letters.[84] In this statement the objectives of the Brethren of the Common Life and of the Northern Humanists come together. It is not correct to deny that Erasmus was profoundly imbued with the ideals of moral education as presented by the Brethren. Even when later in his life he showed himself no great admirer of their intellectual level, the propensity to piety and literature in his character was strongly enhanced by his years with the Brethren and, of course, with the Canons of Stein.

Obviously it cannot be said that the Modern Devotion lay at the roots of Christian Humanism north of the Alps in all its respects, but with regard to

---

34-6: 'Quasi quis postulet ut puer anno decimo septimo, maxime in litteris educatus, norit seipsum'; Demolen, 'Erasmus' Commitment to the Canons Regular of St. Augustine'.

[78] *ASD* V-1, 80, 96-103. Cf. Weiler, 'Christelijke identiteit, morele vorming en laat-middeleeuws onderwijs', esp. 193-5.

[79] Rummel, 'Quoting poetry instead of Scripture'.

[80] Erasmus, *Opus epistolarum*, III 98-9, 1-3 (ep. 676): 'Libellus quem misisti [...] quod olim puero mihi et lectitatum esse et placuisse memini.'

[81] *CWE* 23, xix.

[82] *ASD* I-1, 1-138 (esp. 19); in the second version of the *Antibarbari* (1520), he added Basil and Chrysostomus, Hilary and Gregory (ibidem, 22-3).

[83] *ASD* I-1, 129, 28-9.

[84] Schottenloher, *Erasmus im Ringen um die humanistische Bildungsreform.*

the ideal of Christian and moral education along the maxims and adhortations of the Gospel there is a close relationship. A single line can be drawn from Jean Gerson[85] to the rector of the House in Zwolle, Dirk of Herxen, who wrote a large number of treatises about bringing children and adolescents to Christ: *Tractatus de iuvenibus trahendis ad Christum; Libellus de parvulis trahendis ad Christum; Libellus de laudabili studio eorum trahentium parvulos ad Christum.*[86] This line goes directly forward into Erasmus's program 'that the spirits of youngsters should be formed to virtues and their tongues to right speech.'[87]

The Brethren and the Reformation

Professor Post is correct in saying that only few of the Brethren went over to the Reformation. Assembling the facts, we find that in 1545 the rector of the House in Deventer, in his quality of general visitator of the Houses in the Netherlands, sought the support of emperor Charles V. The emperor was asked to force those Brethren, who had left their communal Houses, taking with them the properties they had before brought into the House, to restore these goods. A similar request was made by the rector of Deventer, Simon of Doesburg, but in 1561 he was deposed from his office as was rector Andreas N.N. in 1569; both were also dismissed from the brotherhood. With regard to the Brethren in Zwolle there is no evidence of any kind about any influence of the Reformation. In Amersfoort the bishop in 1529 suspected some brothers of heresy. The community was placed under the surveillance of the prior of the Regular Canons of Vredendaal near Utrecht. Those of the Brethren who did not submit to the discipline were expelled. Afterwards the House was converted into a monastery of the Canons Regular. In 1525 the inhabitants of the House of Hulsbergen were accused of reformist sympathies upon which the House was temporarily transformed into a Benedictine monastery against the mind of most of the brothers. Some ten *fratres* departed.

More detailed information is found in the *Chronicle* of the House at Doesburg.[88] From 1520 onwards the chronicler frequently mentions Lutheranism. It spread rapidly and also reached the Houses of the Brethren. He relates that at Utrecht rector John Hinne Rode was deposed in 1522 and that

---

[85] Glorieux, 'Le chancelier Gerson et la réforme de l'enseignement'; Glorieux, 'L'enseignement universitaire de Gerson'.

[86] Knierim, *Dirc van Herxen*; Weiler, *Volgens de norm*, s.v. Zwolle.

[87] Erasmus, *Opus epistolarum*, II 3, 44-5 (298); Weiler, 'Christelijke identiteit, morele vorming en laat-middeleeuws onderwijs', 193; Oberman, *Forerunners of the Reformation*, 309-11.

[88] Weiler, *Necrologie, kroniek en cartularium c.a. van het fraterhuis te Doesburg*.

there were internal problems at Deventer. In Doesburg the younger brothers began adhering to Lutheran doctrine and they opposed the customary tonsure. Nine religious persons who had been pupils of the town-school at Doesburg (and who possibly had lived in the convict of the Brethren) were expelled from their monasteries; others fled from the city. Some *fratres* left the House: one lay-brother, three clerics and one priest, the procurator of the House, Johannes Heusden. In 1529 duke Charles of Guelders came to Doesburg in person to examine complaints about heresy that had reached him. The homes of the schoolmaster and of a monk were searched. Johannes Heusden and Jacob Bislick, a former procurator of the House, escaped from town. The schoolmaster Arnold of Cuyk was imprisoned and burnt in Arnhem, together with a Carthusian priest. There is no mention of reformist influences on the Brethren at Groningen, Harderwijk, Gouda and Nijmegen.

In Utrecht rector John Hinne Rode was deposed from his office in 1522. He was the bearer of the well-known letter by Cornelis Hoen, lawyer at the Court of Holland, on the spiritual significance of the presence of Christ in the Eucharist, to Martin Luther in order to seek his approval. Luther did not accept Hoen's opinion. Rode also brought as many of the books of Wessel Gansfort as could be had at that time to Luther. He visited Oecolampadius at Basel, Zwingli at Zurich, and Martin Bucer at Strasbourg.[89]

Hoen believed that the theological elimination of the real presence of Christ in the sacrament of the Eucharist would cause the entire 'religion of the pope' to collapse (p. 275). Rode clearly sympathised with the new theological ideas of his times. Luther wrote to him the letter that was printed as an introduction to the works of Wessel Gansfort, adding to it a letter to Oecolampadius on the Eucharist, seeking Rode's opinion on it, and asking that Wessel's *Opera* be printed at Basel. Rode left Wessel's works in Zurich. They were consequently printed by Adam Petri in Basel; an edition was also published at Zwolle by Simon Corver (*De sacramento eucharistiae*, 1521; *Farrago*, 1522). Rode was also involved in the edition of the New Testament in Dutch that was printed by Doen Pietersz. at Amsterdam in 1522. Most probably he helped edit the Deventer New Testament, published by Albert Pafraet (October 20, 1525). The enterprise of translating Luther's *Dat Ganz Neuw Testament* (ed. Adam Petri, Basel 1522) in 'Nederlands Duytsch' was conceived of and executed by a group of reformist Christians in Deventer among whom Hinne Rode, Johan Oostendorp and Gerard Geldenhauer. Already on December 3, 1525 the magistrate of Kam-

---

[89] Cornelisz. Hoen, 'A Most Christian Letter', in Oberman, *Forerunners of the Reformation*, 268-76; Gansfort, *Opera*, **6v-7v; Spruyt, 'Wessel Gansfort and Cornelis Hoen's *Epistola christiana*'. On the so-called 'sacramentarian movement', see op. cit., 124 and n. 13-15, with recent literature.

pen censured this publication. Rode went to Norden (Ostfriesland, Germany) and was accepted there as a Lutheran minister. Finally he lived at Wolthusen near Emden († c. 1550).[90]

Hendrik van Bommel (1490? 1500?-1570) was not a member of the Brethren's House at Utrecht. He may have been a vicar in Wesel, Germany. He is thought to be the author of the *Summa der godliker scrifturen*, an adaptation of the anonymous *Oeconomica christiana*. This was the first book in the Netherlands to be condemned as heretical by emperor Charles V.[91]

This is all there is to say with regard to the effects of the Reformation on the Brotherhouses. No Dutch House as such went over to the Reformation in the way for example of the House of Herford in Germany.[92] The Doesburg chronicle does make clear, however, that especially the young inmates of the Houses were affected by the new theology and that the House of Doesburg was in trouble. This might have been the case for other Houses as well, but we cannot be sure. There are no chronicles which inform us about the situation in other fraternities during the times of the Reformation.

Conclusion

It can be argued that the program of Northern Humanism as the furtherance of the *bonae litterae* in close connection with moral education, owed a great deal to the Brethren of the Common Life with regard to the latter component. Through spiritual guidance, hearing confessions, by treatises and *collationes,* they promoted a typical form of the Christian self that was also

---

[90] Van Toorenenbergen, 'Hinne Rode'; *Nieuw Nederlands Biografisch Woordenboek,* VII 822; Frédéricq, *Corpus Inquisitionis,* 4, 71-2; Post, *De Moderne Devotie,* 106; De Bruin, 'Hinne Rode'.

[91] Van Toorenenbergen, *Het oudste Nederlandsche verboden boek.* Van Bommel's authorship has been doubted. The former opinion is found by Brugmans in *Nieuw Nederlandsch Biografisch Woordenboek,* I 397-8, and Knipscheer, *Hendrik van Bommel*; Trapman, *De Summa der godliker scrifturen,* 52-6, however, doubts the authorship of the *Summa* as well as of the *Oeconomica,* which work was at the base of the *Summa.* De Jong, in his review in *Bijdragen en Mededelingen,* does not accept Trapman's thesis without questions; cf. Huisman and Santing, *Wessel Gansfort,* nr. 86. Post, *The Modern Devotion,* 571-2, disputes his being a *frater.* There was, in fact, another Hendrik van Bommel, who was indeed a *frater* and also rector of the Magdalenaconvent in Utrecht (in popular speech called 'de bekeerde susteren'); Dodt van Flensburg, *Archief voor de kerkelijke en wereldsche geschiedenissen,* III 154; 156. If an ordination-letter from 1502 (Muller, *Catalogussen van de bij het stads-archief bewaarde archieven,* inv. nr. 754*) bears on the same person as this *frater* Henry of Bommel, the year of his birth might be c. 1482. He died in 1542.

[92] *Monasticon Fratrum Vitae Communis II,* 69-76; in general Hinz, *Die Brüder vom gemeinsamen Leben.*

valid for lay people.[93] This spiritual type was adopted by northern humanists and consequently introduced to the Latin schools, where the joint exigencies of humanist learning and moral education dictated the programs.[94] Of course it cannot be said that the Devouts influenced nearly every humanist to bring about a personal interiorisation of piety, connected with self-knowledge and Christian practice. Neither can it be argued that their spiritualistic emphasis on piety and their nearly stoical ethical norms and maxims induced them and others to minimalize the effectivity of the sacraments as means of grace, and of the Church as an instrument of salvation. No such causal connexion can be proven.

The Brethren lived in a climate of criticism and renewal, in matters of the church and religion as well as in education. Humanist activities and the ideas alive in circles of the Modern Devotion approached each other. The spiritual leaders of that movement in its later phases joined with the new forces on the field of spiritual and cultural formation.[95] The influence of this joint spiritual and educational effort was widely felt in the Europe of modern times as well as in New England, in Protestant as well as in Catholic areas.[96]

---

[93] Weiler, 'Soziale und sozial-psychologische Aspekte der Devotio Moderna'; Weiler, 'De betekenis van de Moderne Devotie voor de Europese cultuur'.

[94] Oberman, *Werden und Wertung der Reformation*.

[95] Mokrosch, 'Devotio Moderna und Verhältnis zu Humanismus und Reformation', 612.

[96] *Renaissance Humanism: Foundations, Forms, and Legacy* (review by O'Malley in *RQ*, 43 (1990), 158-61); *Education in the Renaissance and Reformation* (with extensive bibliography). For the spiritual practice of puritan selfconstitution, see Furlong, *Puritans' Progress*. Todd, *Christian Humanism and the Puritan Social Order*, has recently shown the impact of Erasmus on Puritan social thought in England; the book was, however, severely criticized by Bouwsma in *RQ*, 42 (1989), 568-70. Orme, *Education and Society in Medieval and Renaissance England*; Oberman, 'Die *Gelehrten die Verkehrten*'.

BIBLIOGRAPHY

Abendländische Mystik im Mittelalter. Symposion Kloster Engelberg 1984, ed. K. Ruh (Stuttgart 1986)

Acta graduum academicorum gymnasii Patavini ab anno 1406 ad annum 1450, eds. G. Zonta and G. Brotto (new edition, Padua 1970) (3 vols)

Adams, H. M., *Catalogue of Books Printed on the Continent of Europe, 1501-1600, in Cambridge Libraries* (Cambridge 1967) (2 vols)

Adelmann, F., *Dietrich von Plieningen, Humanist und Staatsmann* (Munich 1981)

Agricola, Rodolphus, *De inventione dialectica libri tres, cum scholiis Ioannis Matthaei Phrissemii* (Cologne 1528; repr. Hildesheim 1976)

–, *De inventione dialectica libri omnes*, ed. Alardus Aemstelredamus (Cologne 1539; repr. Nieuwkoop 1967)

–, *Lucubrationes aliquot*, ed. Alardus Aemstelredamus (Cologne 1539; repr. Nieuwkoop 1967)

–, *De inventione dialectica libri tres. Drei Bücher über die Inventio dialectica. Auf der Grundlage der Edition von Alardus von Amsterdam (1539) kritisch herausgegeben, übersetzt und kommentiert von Lothar Mundt* (Tübingen 1992)

Ahsmann, M., *Collegia en colleges. Juridisch onderwijs aan de Leidse universiteit 1575-1630 in het bijzonder het disputeren* (Groningen 1990)

Akkerman, F., 'Rudolf Agricola, een humanistenleven', in *Algemeen Nederlands Tijdschrift voor Wijsbegeerte*, 75 (1983), 25-43

–, 'De Neolatijnse epistolografie–Rudolf Agricola', in *Lampas*, 18/5 (1985), 321-337

–, 'Agricola and Groningen. A Humanist on his Origin', in *Rodolphus Agricola Phrisius*, 3-20

Alain de Lille. Textes Inédits, ed. M.-Th. d'Alverny (Paris 1965)

Albertini Ottolenghi, M.G., 'La Biblioteca dei Visconti e degli Sforza: gli inventari del 1488 e del 1490', in *Studi petrarcheschi*, 8 (1991), 1-238

Albertus Magnus, *De natura et origine animae*, ed. B. Geyer (Opera omnia, 12) (Münster 1955)

Allegri, R., *La feudalità tortonese: i Rati Opizzoni* (Alessandria 1973)

Allen, P.S., 'Letters of Arnold Bostius', in *The English Historical Review*, 34 (1919), 225-236

Amama, Sixtus, *Anti-Barbarus biblicus* (Amsterdam 1628)

Ambt en avondmaalsmijding. Herderlijk schrijven van de generale synode der Nederlandse Hervormde Kerk ten aanzien van avondmaalsmijding door gemeenteleden en ambtsdragers (The Hague 1986)

Analecta Gijsberti Coeverincx, eds. G. van den Elzen and W. Hoevenaars ('s-Hertogenbosch 1907) (2 vols)

Andreas, V., *Bibliotheca Belgica* (Louvain 1643)

Angelelli, I., 'The Techniques of Disputation in the History of Logic', in *Journal of Philosophy*, 67 (1970), 800-815

Angenent, M., 'Het Gentse Boethiuscommentaar en Reinier van Sint-Truiden', in *Tijdschrift voor Nederlandse Taal- en Letterkunde*, 107 (1991), 274-310

ASD: v. Erasmus, *Opera Omnia*

Ashworth, E.J., 'Traditional Logic', in *The Cambridge History of Renaissance Philosophy*, 143-172

–, *Language and Logic in the Post-Mediaeval Period* (Dordrecht 1974)

–, 'Changes in Logic Textbooks from 1500 to 1650: The New Aristotelianism', in *Aristotelismus und Renaissance*, eds. E. Keßler, Ch.H. Lohr and Ch.B. Schmitt (Wiesbaden 1988), 75-88

Auctarium in secundum Topicorum Aristotelis, complectens absolutam Inventionis dialecticae methodum, quae aperit locorum usum, in quaerenda omni quaestioni tractandae materia, in tractandis affectibus, denique in omnibus iis, quae vel a Rhetore, vel a Philosopho, vel etiam a quocunque differente ex artis praescripto observantur, ut hinc lector studiosus facile promptus evadat ad iudicandum de scriptis autorum, simul ad instituendam orationem de omni themate, in quacunque versetur disciplina (Louvain, S. Zassenus, 1537)

Auer, P.A., *Johannes von Dambach und die Trostbücher vom 11. bis zum 16. Jahrhundert* (Münster

1928)

Aufbruch, Wandel, Erneuerung. Beiträge zur 'Renaissance' des 12. Jahrhunderts, ed. G. Wieland (Stuttgart 1995)

Augustijn, C., 'Humanisten auf dem Scheideweg zwischen Luther und Erasmus,' in *Humanismus und Reformation: Martin Luther und Erasmus von Rotterdam in den Konflikten ihrer Zeit*, ed. O. Pesch (Freiburg 1985), 119-134

–, *Erasmus* (Baarn 1986)

–, 'Erasmus en de Moderne Devotie', in *De doorwerking van de Moderne Devotie*, 71-80

–, 'Calvin und der Humanismus', in *Calvinus servus Christi. Die Referate des Internationalen Kongresses für Calvinforschung vom 25. bis 28. August 1986 in Debrecen*, ed. W.H. Neuser (Budapest 1988), 127-142

–, *Erasmus: His Life, Works, and Influence* (Toronto 1991)

–, 'Wessel Gansfort's rise to celebrity', in *Wessel Gansfort (1419-1489) and Northern Humanism*, 3-22

–, 'Humanisten auf dem Scheideweg zwischen Luther und Erasmus,' in idem, *Erasmus. Der Humanist als Theologe und Kirchenreformer* (Leiden 1996), 154-167

Augustinus, *In Iohannis Evangelium Tractatus 124*, ed. R. Willems (Turnhout 1954)

–, *Confessionum libri XIII*, ed. L. Verheijen (Turnhout 1981)

Autenrieth, J., *Die Handschriften der ehemaligen Hofbibliothek Stuttgart* (Wiesbaden 1963)

Axters, S., *Geschiedenis van de vroomheid in de Nederlanden, III* (Antwerp 1956)

Baader, G., 'Die Entwicklung der medizinischen Fachsprache im hohen und späten Mittelalter', in *Fachprosaforschung. Acht Vorträge zur mittelalterlichen Artesliteratur*, eds. G. Keil and P. Assion (Berlin 1974), 88-123

Badius Ascensius, Jodocus, *Commentum duplex in Boetium de Consolatione Philosophiae* (Lyon 1498; [1]1495)

Bakker, F.J., 'Handschriften en boeken in Groningse Archiefstukken tot 1597', in *Driemaandelijkse bladen 1987-1988*, 93-117 (I) and 1-26 (II)

Bange, P., '"Laat-middeleeuwse" moralistisch-didactische traktaten in de zestiende eeuw: invloed van de Moderne Devotie?', in *De doorwerking van de Moderne Devotie*, 233-252

Barbet, J., *François de Meyronnes–Pierre Roger. Disputatio (1320-1321)* (Paris 1961)

Barger, H.H., *Ons Kerkboek* (Rotterdam [2]1907)

Barlaeus, Caspar, *Mercator sapiens*, ed. S. van der Woude (Amsterdam 1967)

Barner, W., *Barockrhetorik. Untersuchungen zu ihren geschichtlichen Grundlagen* (Tübingen 1970)

Baron, H., *The Crisis of the Early Italian Renaissance* (Princeton 1955)

–, *The Crisis of the Early Italian Renaissance. Civic Humanism and Republican Liberty in an Age of Classicism and Tyranny* (revised one-volume edition with an epilogue) (Princeton 1966)

–, *From Petrarch to Leonardo Bruni. Studies in Humanistic and Political Literature* (Chicago 1968)

Bartels, P., *Abriss einer Geschichte des Schulwesens in Ostfriesland* (Aurich 1870)

Becker-Cantarino, B., *Daniel Heinsius* (Boston 1978)

Beckschäfer, B., 'Alexander Hegius', in *Festschrift des staatlichen Gymnasiums zu Emmerich* (Emmerich 1932), 67-71

Bedaux, J.C., *Hegius poeta. Het leven en de Latijnse gedichten van Alexander Hegius* (Deventer 1998) (diss. Leiden)

Bejczy, I., 'Erasmus Becomes a Netherlander', in *The Sixteenth-Century Journal*, 28 (1997), 387-399

Bellone, E., 'Appunti su Battista Trovamala da Sale O.F.M. e la sua "Summa casuum"', in *Studi francescani*, 74 (1977)

–, 'Note su Pietro Cara, giurista e umanista piemontese della seconda metà del Quattrocento', in *Bollettino Storico-Bibliografico Subalpino*, 86 (1988)

Belloni, A., 'Giovanni Dondi, Albertino da Salso e le origini dello Studio pavese', in *Bollettino della Società Pavese di Storia Patria*, 82 (n.s. 34) (1982), 17-47

–, *Professori giuristi a Padova nel secolo XV. Profili bio-bibliografici e cattedre* (Frankfurt 1986)

Benrath, G.A., *Reformtheologen des 15. Jahrhunderts. Johann Pupper von Goch, Johann Ruchrath von Wesel, Wessel Gansfort* (Texte zur Kirchen- und Theologiegeschichte, 17) (Gütersloh 1968)

Bernays, J., *Joseph Justus Scaliger* (Berlin 1855)

Bertalot, L., *Studien zum italienischen und deutschen Humanismus*, ed. P.O. Kristeller (Rome 1975) (2 vols)

Berthold of Moosburg, *Expositio super Elementationem theologicam Procli, 184-211: De animabus*, ed. L. Sturlese (Rome 1974)

–, *Expositio super Elementationem theologicam Procli. Prologus. Propositiones 1-13*, eds. M.R. Pagnoni-Sturlese and L. Sturlese (Hamburg 1984)

Bibliotheca Calviniana I, eds. R. Peter and J.-F. Gilmont (Geneva 1991)

Bibliotheca Vadiana. Die Bibliothek des Humanisten Joachim von Watt nach dem Katalog des Josua Kessler von 1553 unter Mitwirkung von H. Fehrlin und H. Thurnheer bearbeitet von V. Schenker-Frei (St. Gallen 1973)

Biundo, G., 'Kurpfalz und Holland. Ihre gegenseitigen Beziehungen während des Reformationszeitalters und die daraus entstehenden Einwirkungen auf den Fortgang der Reformation in beiden Ländern', in *Blätter für pfälzische Kirchengeschichte und religiöse Volkskunde*, 23 (1956), 59-65

Blanckaert, Nikolaus, *Die Bibel/ we//derom met grooter nersti//cheit ouersien ende gecorrigeert/ meer dan // in seß hondert plaetzen/ ende Collacioneert // met den ouden Latinschen/ ongefalßten Biblien. Duer B. Alexander Blanckart/ Carmelit. Geprent toe Coelen by Jaspar van Gennep [...] M.D.XLVIII.* (Colophon: 1547)

–, *Iudicium Iohannis Calvini de Sanctorum reliquiis: collatum cum Orthodoxorum sanctae Ecclesiae Catholicae Patrum sententia.* (f. A2r-D7v) Printed with: *Item Oratio [prima: f. D8v] de Retributione Iustorum statim a morte.* (f. D8r-G4v)

Bloccius, Petrus, *Praecepta formandis puerorum moribus perutilia*, ed. A.M. Coebergh-Van den Braak (Louvain 1991)

Bock, J.P., *Die Brotbitte des Vaterunsers. Ein Beitrag zum Verständnis dieses Universalgebetes und einschlägiger patristisch-liturgischer Fragen* (Paderborn 1911)

Böhme, G., *Wirkungsgeschichte des Humanismus im Zeitalter des Rationalismus* (Darmstadt 1988)

Boeles, W.B.S., 'Levensschetsen der Groninger hoogleeraren', in *Gedenkboek der Hoogeschool te Groningen*, ed. W.J.A. Jonckbloet (Groningen 1864)

–, 'Iets over de St. Maartens en der A scholen te Groningen 1562-1595', in *Bijdragen tot de Geschiedenis en Oudheidkunde, inzonderheid van de Provincie Groningen. Eerste deel* (Groningen 1864), 144-152

Bömer, A., 'Alexander Hegius', in *Westfälische Lebensbilder, Hauptreihe, III* (Münster 1934), 345-362

Böse, A., 'R.P. Mag. Alexander Blanckaert', in *Archief voor de geschiedenis van het Aartsbisdom Utrecht*, 37 (1911), 262-272

Boethius, Manlius Severinus, *The Theological Tractates; The Consolation of Philosophy*, eds. H.F. Stewart and E.K. Rand, transl. S.J. Tester (Loeb) (Cambridge, MA 1973)

Boethius: His Life, Thought, and Influence, ed. M.T. Gibson (Oxford 1981)

Boethius in the Middle Ages. Latin and Vernacular Traditions of the 'Consolatio Philosophiae', eds. M.J.F.M. Hoenen and L. Nauta (Leiden 1997)

Bolhuis van Zeeburgh, J., *Kritiek der Friesche Geschiedschrijving* (Amsterdam 1962)

Bonvesin da Riva, *Grandezze di Milano*, ed. A. Paredi (Fontes Ambrosiani, 38) (Milan 1967)

–, *De magnalibus Mediolani/ Le meraviglie di Milano*, ed. M. Corti (Milan 1974)

Bot, P.N.M., *Humanisme en onderwijs in Nederland* (Utrecht 1955)

Boyle, M. O'Rourke, *Rhetoric and Reform: Erasmus' Civil Dispute with Luther* (Cambridge, MA 1983)

Braakhuis, H.A.G. and M.J.F.M. Hoenen, 'Marsilius of Inghen: a Dutch Philosopher and Theologian', in *Marsilius of Inghen. Acts of the International Marsilius of Inghen Symposium organized by the Nijmegen Centre for Medieval Studies (Nijmegen, 18-20 December 1986)*, eds. H.A.G. Braakhuis and M.J.F.M. Hoenen (Nijmegen 1992), 1-11

Brecht, M., *Martin Luther. Shaping and Defining the Reformation, 1521-1532* (Minneapolis 1990)

Der Brief im Zeitalter der Renaissance, ed. F.J. Worstbrock (Weinheim 1983)

Briefe deutscher Barockautoren. Probleme ihrer Erfassung und Erschließung. Arbeitsgespräch in der Herzog August Bibliothek Wolfenbüttel, 10. und 11. März 1977. Vorträge und Berichte, ed. H.-H. Krummacher (Hamburg 1978)

Briefwisseling van Hugo Grotius, eds. P.C. Molhuysen, B.L. Meulenbroek, P.P. Witkam, H.J.M. Nellen and C.M. Ridderikhoff (The Hague 1928-)

Brink, L., 'Thomas en Calvijn tezamen ter communie', in *Tijdschrift voor theologie*, 29 (1989), 232-249

Brinkmann, G., *Die Irenik des David Pareus. Frieden und Einheit in ihrer Relevanz zur Wahrheitsfrage* (Hildesheim 1972)

Broadie, A., *The Circle of John Mair. Logic and Logicians in Pre-Reformation Scotland* (Oxford 1985)

Broc, N., *La géographie de la Renaissance (1420-1620)* (Mémoires de la section de Géographie, 9) (Paris 1980)

Browe, P., *Die häufige Kommunion im Mittelalter* (Münster 1938)

Bucer, Martin, *Correspondance de Martin Bucer*, ed. J. Rott (Leiden 1979)

Bunbury, E.H., *A History of Ancient Geography* (London 1879)

Burckhardt, J., *Die Kultur der Renaissance in Italien. Ein Versuch* (Kröners Taschenausgabe, 53) (Stuttgart 1976)

Burger, C., 'Der Kölner Karmelit Nikolaus Blanckaert verteidigt die Verehrung der Reliquien gegen Calvin (1551)', in *Auctoritas Patrum II. New Contributions on the Reception of the Church Fathers in the 15th and 16th Century*, eds. L. Grane, A. Schindler and M. Wriedt (Mainz 1997), 27-49

Burie, L., 'Proeve tot inventarisatie van de in handschrift of in druk bewaarde werken van de Leuvense theologieprofessoren uit de XVe eeuw', in *Facultas S. Theologiae Lovaniensis 1432-1797*, ed. E.J.M. van Eijl (Louvain 1977), 215-272

Burke, P., *Montaigne* (Oxford 1981)

–, 'The Spread of Italian Humanism', in *The Impact of Humanism on Western Europe*, eds. A. Goodman and A. MacKay (London 1990), 1-22

Burr, D., *Eucharistic Presence and Conversion in Late Thirteenth-Century Franciscan Thought* (Philadelphia 1984)

Busch, Johannes, 'Liber de viris illustribus', in *Des Augustiner Propstes Iohannes Busch Chronicon Windeshemense und Liber de reformatione monasteriorum*, ed. K. Grube (Geschichtsquellen der Provinz Sachsen 19) (Halle 1886)

Butzbach, Johannes, *Odeporicon*, ed. A. Beriger (Weinheim 1991)

Buzás, L., 'Die Bibliothek des Ingolstädter Professors Dr.Wolfgang Peysser in der Universitätsbibliothek München', in *Sammelblatt des Historischen Vereins Ingolstadt*, 71 (1962)

Caesar, Gaius Iulius, *Commentarii De Bello Gallico*, eds. F. Kraner, W. Dittenberger and H. Meusel (Berlin 1913-1920; repr. Dublin 1960) (2 vols)

Caesarius Heisterbacensis, *Dialogus Miraculorum II*, ed. J. Strange (Cologne 1851)

Calvinus, Johannes, 'Traité des reliques', in *Jean Calvin. Three French Treatises edited by F.M. Higman* (London 1970), 12-16; 47-97

–, *Ioannis Calvini admonitio, qua ostenditur quam e re Christianae reip.[ublicae] foret sanctorum corpora et reliquias velut inuentarium redigi [...] E Gallico per Nicolaum Gallasium in sermonem Latinum conuersa* (Geneva 1548) (Bibliotheca Calviniana I, nr 48/4)

The Cambridge Companion to Renaissance Humanism, ed. J. Kraye (Cambridge 1996)

The Cambridge History of Classical Literature, eds. P.E. Easterling and B.M.W. Knox (Cambridge 1985)

The Cambridge History of Later Medieval Philosophy, from the Rediscovery of Aristotle to the Disintegration of Scholasticism 1100-1600, eds. N. Kretzmann, A. Kenny and J. Pinborg (Cambridge [5]1992)

The Cambridge History of Renaissance Philosophy, eds. C.B. Schmitt and Q. Skinner (Cambridge 1990)

Camera apostolica. Documenti relativi alle diocesi del ducato di Milano (1458-1471). I "libri annatarum" di Pio II e Paolo II, ed. M. Ansani (Milan 1994)

Cameron, J.K., 'Humanism in the Low Countries', in *The Impact of Humanism on Western*

Europe, eds. A. Goodman and A. MacKay (London 1990), 137-163

Canter, Jacobus, *Dialogus de solitudine*, ed. B. Ebels-Hoving (Munich 1981)

–, *Dialogus de solitudine*: see Enenkel 1995

Caspers, C.M.A., *De eucharistische vroomheid en het feest van Sacramentsdag in de Nederlanden tijdens de Late Middeleeuwen* (Leuven 1992)

–, 'Het laatmiddeleeuwse passiebeeld. Een interpretatie vanuit de theologie- en vroomheidsgeschiedenis', in *Nederlands kunsthistorisch jaarboek*, 45 (1994), 161-175

–, 'The Western Church during the late Middle Ages: Augenkommunion or popular mysticism?', in *Bread of Heaven. Customs and Practices Surrounding Holy Communion. Essays in the History of Liturgy and Culture*, eds. C.M.A. Caspers and G. Lukken (Kampen 1995), 83-97

Catalogus van de bibliotheek van Jan de Hondt (1486-1571), ed. C. Coppens (Kortrijk 1990)

Catechismus Romanus seu catechismus ex decreto Concilii Tridentini ad parochos Pii Quinti Pont. Max. iussu editus, editio critica, ed. P. Rodriguez (Vatican City 1989)

Catto, J.I., 'Wyclif and Wycliffism at Oxford 1356-1430', in *The History of the University of Oxford, Vol. 2: Late Medieval Oxford*, eds. J.I. Catto and R. Evans (Oxford 1992), 175-261

–, 'Theology after Wycliffism', in *The History of the University of Oxford, Vol. 2: Late Medieval Oxford*, eds. J.I. Catto and R. Evans (Oxford 1992), 263-280

Cavagna, A.G., '"Questo mondo è pien di vento". Il mondo librario del Quattrocento pavese tra produzione e consumo', in *Storia di Pavia, terzo volume: Dal libero comune alla fine del principato indipendente, 1024-1535, tomo secondo: La battaglia di Pavia del 24 febbraio 1525 nella storia, nella letteratura e nell'arte. Università e cultura* (Milan 1990), 267-357

CE: v. *Contemporaries of Erasmus*

Celtis, Konrad, *Der Briefwechsel*, ed. H. Rupprich (Munich 1934)

Cerrini, S., 'Libri e vicende di una famiglia di castellani nella seconda metà del Quattrocento', in *Studi petrarcheschi*, n.s. 7 (1990), 345-348

–, 'Libri dei Visconti-Sforza. Schede per una nuova edizione degli inventari', in *Studi petrarcheschi*, 8 (1991), 239-281

Chadwick, H., *Boethius, The Consolations of Music, Logic, Theology, and Philosophy* (Oxford 1981)

Chartularium Universitatis Parisiensis, I, eds. H. Denifle and E. Chatelain (Paris 1899)

Claren, L. and J. Huber, 'Rudolf Agricolas Scholien zu Ciceros Rede *De lege Manilia*–Zu Typologie und Verfahren des humanistischen Autorenkommentars', in *Rudolf Agricola 1444-1485*, 147-180

Classen, C.J., *Die Stadt im Spiegel der Descriptiones und Laudes urbium in der antiken und mittelalterlichen Literatur bis zum Ende des zwölften Jahrhunderts* (Beiträge zur Altertumswissenschaft 2) (Hildesheim 1980)

–, *Recht, Rhetorik, Politik. Untersuchungen zu Ciceros rhetorischer Strategie* (Darmstadt 1985)

–, 'Lodovico Guicciardini's *Descrittione* and the Tradition of the *Laudes* and *Descriptiones Urbium*', in *Lodovico Guicciardini (1521-1589). Actes du Colloque international des 28, 29 et 30 mars 1990*, ed. P. Jodogne (Travaux de l'Institut Interuniversitaire pour l'étude de la Renaissance et de l'Humanisme, 10) (Louvain 1991), 99-117

Clemen, O., 'Die Lamentationes Petri', in *Zeitschrift für Kirchengeschichte*, 19 (1899), 431-48

Codices Boethiani. A Conspectus of Manuscripts of the Works of Boethius I, eds. M.T. Gibson, L. Smith and J. Zeigler (Warburg Institute Surveys and Texts, 25) (London 1995)

Colish, M.L., 'From the Sentence Collection to the Sentence Commentary and the Summa: Parisian Scholastic Theology 1130-1215', in *Manuels, programmes de cours et techniques d'enseignement dans les universités médiévales*, ed. J. Hamesse (Louvain-La-Neuve 1994), 9-29

Colish, M.L., *Peter Lombard* (Leiden 1994) (2 vols)

Colomer, E., *Nikolaus von Kues und Raimund Llull aus Handschriften der Kueser Bibliothek* (Berlin 1961)

Commentarii Lovanienses = Commentaria in Isagogen Porphyrii, et in omnes libros de dialectica Aristotelis summi in omni genere disciplinae Philosophorum. Nunc recenter maturo consilio, et gravissimis sumptibus venerandae Facultatis Artium in inclyta Academia Lovaniensi, per Dialecticae ac totius Philosophiae peritissimos viros composita [...] (Louvain, S. Zassenus, 1535)

Contemporaries of Erasmus. A Biographical Register of the Renaissance and Reformation, eds.

P.G. Bietenholz and Th.B. Deutscher (Toronto 1985-1987) (3 vols) (=*CE*)

Copenhaver, B.P. and C.B. Schmitt, *Renaissance Philosophy* (Oxford 1992)

Correspondance des Réformateurs dans les pays de langue française, ed. A.-L. Herminjard (Geneva 1866-97)

Courcelle, P., *La Consolation de Philosophie dans la tradition littéraire. Antécédents et postérité de Boèce* (Paris 1967)

Courtenay, W.J., *Schools and Scholars in Fourteenth-Century England* (Princeton 1987)

Cranz, F.E. and C.B. Schmitt, *A Bibliography of Aristotle Editions, 1501-1600* (Baden-Baden ²1984)

CWE: v. Erasmus, *Collected Works*

Danaeus, Lambertus, *In Petri Lombardi librum primum Sententiarum* (Geneva 1580)

Day, J., *The Medieval Market Economy* (Oxford 1987)

Debongnie, P., 'Dévotion moderne', in *Dictionnaire de Spiritualité*, 3 (1957), 743-744

De Bruin, C.C., *De Statenbijbel en zijn voorgangers. Nederlandse bijbelvertalingen vanaf de Reformatie tot 1637* (Leiden 1937; new edition Haarlem 1993)

–, 'Hinne Rode', in *Jaarboek Oud-Utrecht*, 1981, 191-208

De Chandieu, A., *Locus de verbo Dei scripto adversus humanas traditiones* (London 1592)

Decrees of the Ecumenical Councils. I. Nicaea to Lateran V, ed. P. Tanner (London 1990)

De Dainville, F., *La géographie des humanistes* (Paris 1940)

De deelname aan het Avondmaal. Overwegingen van de generale synode der Nederlandse Hervormde Kerk ten aanzien van de avondmaalsmijding (The Hague 1960)

De Enzinas, Francisco, *Epistolario*, ed. I.J. García Pinilla (Geneva 1995)

De Haan, A.A.M., 'Geschiedenis van het wijsgerig onderwijs te Deventer', in *Deventer denkers*, 29-122

De Jong, O.J., review of Trapman, *Summa der godliker scrifturen*, in *Bijdragen en Mededelingen betreffende de Geschiedenis der Nederlanden*, 96 (1981), 97-99

D'Elia, F., 'Il commento di Giovanni Murmellius al carme Boeziano "O qui perpetua ..."', in *Miscellanea Francescana*, 83 (1983), 450-454

De Libera, A., *Albert le Grand et la philosophie* (Paris 1990)

–, *La philosophie médiévale* (Paris 1993)

–, *La querelle des universaux de Platon à la fin du Moyen Age* (Paris 1996)

Demolen, R.L., 'Erasmus' Commitment to the Canons Regular of St. Augustine', in *Renaissance Quarterly*, 26 (1973), 437-443

Denley, P., 'Recent Studies on Italian Universities of the Middle Ages and the Renaissance', in *History of Universities*, 1 (1981), 193-205

–, 'The Collegiate Movement in Italian Universities in the Late Middle Ages', in *History of Universities*, 10 (1991), 29-91

Den Tex, J., 'Nederlandse studenten in de rechten te Padua (1545-1700)', in *Mededelingen van het Nederlands Historisch Instituut te Rome*, 3rd s. 10 (1954)

De Ridder-Symoens, H., 'Adel en universiteiten in de zestiende eeuw. Humanistisch ideaal of bittere noodzaak?', in *Tijdschrift voor Geschiedenis*, 93 (1980), 410-432

–, 'Deutsche Studenten an italienischen Rechtsfakultäten. Ein Bericht über unveröffentlichtes Quellen- und Archivmaterial', in *Ius Commune*, 12 (1984), 287-315

–, 'Studenten uit het bisdom Utrecht aan de rechtenuniversiteit van Orléans 1444-1546. Een overzicht', in *Mensen van de Nieuwe Tijd. Een liber amicorum voor A.Th. van Deursen*, ed. M. Bruggeman (Amsterdam 1996), 70-97

De Rijk, L.M., *Middeleeuwse wijsbegeerte* (Assen 1977)

–, *La philosophie au Moyen Age* (Leiden 1985)

De Smet, A., 'Érasme et la cartographie', in *Scrinium Erasmianum*, ed. J. Coppens (Leiden 1969), I 277-291

De Smet, I.A.R., 'A Sixteenth-Century Carmelite at Louvain: Adrianus Hecquetius and his friendship with Petrus Nannius', in *Lias*, 22 (1995), 1-17

Die deutsche Literatur des Mittelalters. Verfasserlexikon, ed. K. Ruh (Berlin 1978-) (9 vols)

Deventer denkers. De geschiedenis van het wijsgerig onderwijs te Deventer, eds. H.W. Blom, H.A. Krop and M.R. Wielema (Hilversum 1993)

De Vocht, H., *Monumenta Humanistica Lovaniensia. Texts and Studies about Louvain Humanists*

in the first half of the XVIth Century. Erasmus-Vives-Dorpius-Clenardus-Goes-Moringus (Louvain 1934)
–, *History of the Foundation and the Rise of the Collegium trilingue Lovaniense, 1517-1550* (Louvain 1951-1955) (4 vols)
Devote samenspraak over de veelvuldige Communie, geschreven rond de jaren 1435, ed. D.A. Stracke (Antwerp 1912)
De Wulf, M., *Histoire de la philosophie scolastique dans les Pays-Bas et de la Principauté de Liége jusqu'à la Révolution française* (Louvain 1895)
Dibon, P., *L'Enseignement philosophique dans les universités néerlandaises à l'époque pré-cartésienne (1575-1650)* (Amsterdam 1954)
–, *La Philosophie néerlandaise au siècle d'or* (Paris 1954)
–, 'L'université de Leyde et la République des Lettres au 17e siècle', in *Quaerendo*, 5 (1975), 5-38
Dickens, A.G., *Erasmus the Reformer* (London 1994)
Dicks, M., *Die Abtei Camp am Niederrhein. Geschichte des ersten Cistercienserklosters in Deutschland (1123-1802). Nach archivalischen Quellen* (Moers 1913; repr. 1978)
Dietrich of Freiberg, *Opera omnia*, ed. K. Flasch (Hamburg 1977-1985)
Dionysius Carthusiensis, *Opera omnia* (Tournai 1896-1913) (44 vols)
–, *Opera Selecta*, ed. K. Emery jr (Turnhout 1991) (2 vols)
Dirc of Delft, *Tafel van den Kersten Ghelove, III B*, ed. L.M.F. Daniëls (Antwerp 1938)
Disputatio habita Gruningae, ed. F. Pijper, in *Bibliotheca Reformatoria Neerlandica. Geschriften uit den tijd der Hervorming in de Nederlanden*, VI (The Hague 1910), 549-575
Documenti per la storia dell'Università di Pavia nella seconda metà del '400, I (1450-1455), ed. A. Sottili (Milan 1994)
Dodt van Flensburg, J.J., *Archief voor de kerkelijke en wereldsche geschiedenissen, inzonderheid van Utrecht* (Utrecht 1838-1848) (7 vols)
De doorwerking van de Moderne Devotie. Windesheim 1387-1987. Voordrachten gehouden tijdens het Windesheim Symposium Zwolle/Windesheim 15-17 okober 1987, eds. P. Bange a.o. (Hilversum 1988)
Downs, R.M. and D. Stea, *Maps in Minds. Reflections on Cognitive Mapping* (New York 1977)
Drees, C., *Der Christenspiegel des Dietrich Kolde von Münster* (Werl 1954)
Duke, A.C., 'Building Heaven in Hell's Despite: The Early History of the Reformation in the Towns of the Low Countries', in *Britain and the Netherlands*, vol. VII: *Church and State since the Reformation*, eds. A.C. Duke and C.A. Tamse (The Hague 1981), 45-75
–, 'The Face of Popular Religious Dissent in the Low Countries, 1520-1530', in *Journal of Ecclesiastical History*, 26 (1975), 41-67
Eckert, W.P., 'Köln II. Universität', in *Theologische Realenzyklopädie Bd. 19* (Berlin s.a.), 301-5
Eckhart, *Traktate*, ed. J. Quint (Stuttgart 1963)
–, *Parisian Questions and Prologues*, transl. A.A. Maurer (Toronto 1974)
–, *Sermons and Treatises*, ed. M.O'C. Walshe (London 1981)
Edskes, C.H., 'Rudolph Agricola and the organ of the *Martinikerk* in Groningen', in *Rodolphus Agricola Phrisius*, 112-117
Education in the Renaissance and Reformation, ed. P.F. Grendler (Papers presented at the plenary session of the annual meeting of the Renaissance Society of America) (Toronto 1990)
Edwards, M.U., 'Catholic Controversial Literature, 1518-1555: Some Statistics', in *ARG*, 79 (1988), 189-205
Effigies et vitae professorum academiae Groningae et Omlandiae (Groningen 1654; repr. with Dutch transl. Groningen 1968)
Ellinger, G., *Geschichte der neulateinischen Literatur Deutschlands im sechzehnten Jahrhundert I: Italien und der deutsche Humanismus in der neulateinischen Lyrik* (Berlin 1929)
Elm, K., 'Mendikanten und Humanisten im Florenz des Tre- und Quattrocento. Zum Problem der Legitimierung humanistischer Studien in den Bettelorden', in *Kaspar Elm, Vitasfratrum. Beiträge zur Geschichte der Eremiten- und Mendikantenorden des zwölften und dreizehnten Jahrhunderts*, ed. D. Berg (Werl 1994), 263-284
Elsmann, T., 'Humanismus in Bremen. Christoph Pezel, Philipp Melanchthon und die *Institutio*

Traiani', in *1200 Jahre St. Petri-Dom in Bremen* (Bremen 1989), 77-112

–, 'Reformierte Stadt und humanistische Schule. Nathan Chytraeus in Bremen (1593-1598)', in *Nathan Chytraeus 1543-1598. Ein Humanist in Rostock und Bremen*, eds. T. Elsmann a.o. (Bremen 1991), 71-93

–, 'Albert Rizäus Hardenberg und Johannes Molanus in Bremen: zwei Humanisten im konfessionellen Zeitalter', in *Wessel Gansfort (1419-1489) and Northern Humanism*, 195-211

–, 'Ubbo Emmius: Inhalt und Ziel des Unterrichts. Eine Analyse auf dem Hintergrund seiner Bildungsbiographie', in *Ubbo Emmius. Een Oostfries geleerde in Groningen*, 186-202

–, 'Ein unbekannter *Ordo lectionum et horarum* der Universität Franeker (1647)', in *De Vrije Fries*, 76 (1996), 27-34

–, 'Humanismus, Schule, Buchdruck und Antikenrezeption. Anmerkungen zur Bremer Entwicklung bis 1648', in *Stadt und Literatur in deutschen Sprachraum der Frühen Neuzeit. Vol. I*, eds. K. Garber, S. Anders and T. Elsmann (Tübingen 1998), 203-238

Emmius, Ubbo, *De agro Frisiae inter Amasum et Lavicam flumina. Deque urbe Groninga in eodem agro: et de jure utriusque* (1605)

–, *Rerum Frisicarum historia, autore Ubbone Emmio, Frisio; distincta in decades sex. Quarum postrema nunc primum prodit, prioribus ita recognitis et locupletatis, ut novae prorsus videri possint* (Leiden 1616)

–, *Guilhelmus Ludovicus comes Nassovius, id est ΛΟΓΟΣ ΕΠΙΤΑΦΙΟΣ [...]* (Groningen 1621)

–, *Briefwechsel*, eds. H. Brugmans and F. Wachter (Aurich 1911/ The Hague 1923) (2 vols)

–, *Programma bij de aanvaarding van het rectoraat der Latijnse school*, ed. and transl. A.G. Roos (Groningen 1951)

–, *Der Reisebericht/Itinerarium des Ubbo Emmius*, eds. E.H. Waterbolk and W. Bergsma, transl. E. von Reeken (Groningen 1980)

–, *Friesland tussen Eems en Lauwers en de stad Groningen*, transl. P. Schoonbeeg (Groningen 1981)

Enenkel, K.A.E., *Kulturoptimismus und Kulturpessimismus in der Renaissance. Studie zu Jacobus Canters* Dyalogus de solitudine *mit kritischer Textausgabe und deutsche Übersetzung* (Frankfurt 1995)

Epistolae aliquot eruditorum virorum (Basle 1520)

Erasmus, Desiderius, *Opera Omnia*, ed. J. Leclerc (Leiden 1703-1706) (=*LB*)

–, *Opera Omnia* (Amsterdam 1969-) (=*ASD*)

–, *The Collected Works of Erasmus* (Toronto 1974-) (=*CWE*)

–, *Opus Epistolarum*, ed. P.S. Allen (Oxford 1906-1958)

Ethik im Humanismus, eds. W. Rüegg and D. Wuttke (Boppard 1979)

Evans, R.J.W., *The Wechel Presses: Humanism and Calvinism in Central Europe 1572-1627* (Oxford 1975)

On the Eve of the Reformation: 'Letters of Obscure Men', transl. F.G. Stokes (New York 1964)

Faber, Jacobus, *Panegijricon in Jesu Christi triumphum* (Deventer 1506)

Fabisch, P., 'Eberhard Billick OCarm (1499/1500-1557)', in *Katholische Theologen der Reformationszeit, Bd. 5*, ed. E. Iserloh (Münster 1988), 96-116

Farge, J.K., *Biographical Register of Paris Doctors of Theology, 1500-1536* (Toronto 1980)

Fatio, O., *Méthode et théologie. Lambert Daneau et les débuts de la scolastique réformée* (Geneva 1977)

Feenstra, H., 'Ubbo Emmius, een Oostfries patriot in Groningen. Enige aspecten van de betrekkingen tussen Oost-Friesland en Groningen in de tijd rond 1600', in *Ubbo Emmius. Een Oostfries geleerde in Groningen*, 11-30

Feith, J.A., 'Jacob Canter', in *Groningsche Volksalmanak*, 1891, 1-25

Foresti, A., 'Per alcuni cestelli di pere ghiacciuole', in A. Foresti, *Aneddoti della vita di Francesco Petrarca. Nuova edizione curata e ampliata dall'autore a cura di A. Tissoni Benvenuti con una premessa di G. Billanovich* (Padova 1977)

Fraenkel, P., *De l'écriture à la dispute. Le cas de l'academie de Genève sous Théodore de Bèze* (Lausanne 1977)

Franceschini, A., *Inventari inediti di Biblioteche ferraresi del sec. XV, B–La biblioteca del Capitolo dei canonici della Cattedrale* (Ferrara 1982)

Franz, A., *Die Messe im deutschen Mittelalter. Beiträge zur Geschichte der Liturgie und des religiösen Volkslebens* (Freiburg 1902)

Frédéricq, P., *Corpus Inquisitionis Pravitatis Haereticae Neerlandicae* (The Hague 1900)

Freedman, J.S., 'Philosophy Instruction within the Institutional Framework of Central European Schools and Universities during the Reformation Era', in *History of Universities*, 5 (1985), 117-166

–, *European Academic Philosophy in the Late Sixteenth and Early Seventeenth Centuries. The Life, Significance, and Philosophy of Clemens Timpler (1563/4-1624)* (Hildesheim 1988) (2 vols)

–, 'Aristotle and the Content of Philosophy Instruction at Central European Schools and Universities during the Reformation Era (1500-1650)', in *Transactions of the American Philosophical Society*, 137 (1993), 213-253

–, 'The Diffusion of the Writings of Petrus Ramus in Central Europe, c. 1570-c. 1630', in *Renaissance Quarterly*, 46 (1993), 98-152

Frijhoff, W.Th.M., *La société néerlandaise et ses gradués, 1575-1814. Une recherche sérielle sur le statut des intellectuels à partir des registres universitaires* (Amsterdam 1981)

Fumaroli, M., 'Genèse de l'épistolographie classique: rhétorique humaniste de la lettre, de Pétrarque à Juste Lipse', in *Revue d'histoire littéraire de la France*, 78 (1978), 886-905

Furlong, M., *Puritans' Progress* (New York 1975)

Gabotto, F., *Miserie e suppliche di professori* (Alessandria 1891)

–, and A. Badini Confalonieri, *Vita di Giorgio Merula* (Alessandria 1893)

Gaeta, F., *Lorenzo Valla: Filologia e storia nell' umanesimo italiano* (Naples 1955)

Ganda, A., 'Panfilo Castaldi e le origini della tipografia milanese (1471-1472). Nuovi documenti', in *La Bibliofilia*, 83 (1981), 1-24

–, 'Origini della Biblioteca dei Giureconsulti Milanesi (1486-1502)', in *La Bibliofilia*, 84 (1982), 209-235

Gansfort, Wessel, *Tractatus de oratione et modo orandi cum luculentissima Dominicae orationis explanatione* (Zwolle, Simon Corver, c. 1520-1522)

–, *Opera quae inveniri potuerunt omnia*, ed. P. Pappus à Tratzberg (Groningen 1614)

–, 'Scala meditationis', in Gansfort, *Opera* (Groningen 1614), 193-412

–, 'De dignitate et potestate ecclesiastica', in Gansfort, *Opera* (Groningen 1614), 748-771

–, 'Epistola ad M. Engelbertum Leydensem', in Gansfort, *Opera* (Groningen 1614), 865-912

– : see also Wessel Gansfort

Garber, K., 'A propos de la politisation de l'humanisme tardif europeen. Jacques Auguste de Thou et le "Cabinet Dupuy" à Paris', in *Le juste et l'injuste à la Renaissance et à l'âge classique. Actes du colloque international tenu à Saint-Etienne du 21 au 23 avril 1983*, eds. C. Lauvergnat-Gagnière and B. Yon (Saint-Etienne 1986), 157-177

–, 'Paris, die Hauptstadt des europäischen Späthumanismus. Jacques Auguste de Thou und das Cabinet Dupuy', in *Res Publica Litteraria. Die Institutionen der Gelehrsamkeit in der frühen Neuzeit*, eds. S. Neumeister and C. Wiedemann (Wiesbaden 1987), 71-92

Garin, E., 'Aux origines de la scolastique', in *De la philosophie et l'histoire de la philosophie*, ed. E. Castelli (Paris 1956), 169-183

–, 'Orientamenti culturali milanesi e pavesi. La cultura milanese nella seconda metà del XV secolo', in *Storia di Milano*, 7 (1956), 566-567

–, *Geschichte und Dokumente der abendländischen Pädagogik. Vol. II: Humanismus* (Reinbek 1966)

Geiselmann, J., *Die Eucharistielehre der Vorscholastiker* (Paderborn 1926)

Gelzer, M., *Cicero. Ein biographischer Versuch* (Wiesbaden 1969)

Les genres littéraires dans les sources théologiques et philosophiques médiévales (Publications de l'Institut d'Études Médiévales, 2/5) (Louvain-La-Neuve 1982)

Gerl, H.-B., *Einführung in die Philosophie der Renaissance* (Darmstadt 1989)

Gerrits, G.H., *Inter Timorem et Spem. A Study of the Theological Thought of Gerard Zerbolt of Zutphen (1367-1398)* (Leiden 1986)

Gerritsen, W.P., 'Dese fabule es elken toegescreven ... De Gentse Boethiusvertaler en de mythe van Orpheus', in *De Nieuwe Taalgids*, 73 (1980), 471-491

–, 'Coornhert and Boethius. A sidelight on the genesis of Dutch renaissance vers', in *From Wolfram and Petrarch to Goethe and Grass. Studies in literature in honour of Leonard Foster*, eds. D.H.

Green a.o. (Baden-Baden 1982), 307-322

Gerson, Jean, *Oeuvres complètes*, ed. P. Glorieux (Paris 1960-1973)

Geulincx, A., 'Tractatus de officio disputantium', in *Opera philosophica II*, ed. J.P.N. Land (The Hague 1892), 112-122

Gilman, D., 'From Dialectics to Poetics: Johann Sturm's Definition of Dialogue', in *Acta Conventus Neo-Latini Hafniensis. Proceedings of the Eighth International Congress of Neo-Latin Studies, Copenhagen 12 August to 17 August 1991*, eds. R. Schnur and A. Moss (New York 1994), 419-427

Gilmont, J.-F., 'Deux traductions concurrentes de l'Ecriture Sainte. Les Bibles flamandes de 1548', in idem, *Palaestra typographica. Aspects de la production du livre humaniste et religieux au XVIe siècle* (Aubel 1984), 131-148

Gilson, E., *La philosophie au Moyen Age des origines patristiques à la fin du XIVe siècle* (Paris ²1947)

Giorgio Valla tra scienza e sapienza. Studi a cura di G. Cardenal, P. Landucci Ruffo, C. Vasoli, ed. V. Branca (Florence 1981)

Giraldus Cambrensis, *Topographia Hibernica*, in *Giraldi Cambrensis opera*, ed. J.F. Dimock (London 1867; repr. 1964), V 3-204

Glorieux, P., 'L'enseignement universitaire de Gerson', in *Recherches de Théologie ancienne et médiévale*, 23 (1956), 88-113

–, 'Le chancelier Gerson et la réforme de l'enseignement', in *Mélanges E. Gilson* (Toronto 1959), 285-298

Godin, A., 'L'antijudaïsme d'Erasme: Équivoques d'un modèle théologique', in *Bibliothèque d'Humanisme et Renaissance*, 48 (1986), 537-553

Goichon, A.M., *Lexique de la langue philosophique d'Ibn Sina (Avicenne)* (Paris 1938)

González y González, E., *Joan Lluís Vives. De la Escolastica al Humanismo* (Valencia 1987)

Goris, M., 'Het metrum in de gedichten van de Gentse Boethiusvertaling van 1485. Een evaluatie van een methode', in *Tijdschrift voor Nederlandse Taal- en Letterkunde*, 110 (1994), 115-128

–, 'Boethius' *De consolatione philosophiae*: twee Middelnederlandse vertalingen en hun bronnen', in *Verraders en bruggenbouwers. Verkenningen naar de relatie tussen Latinitas en Middel-nederlandse letterkunde*, ed. P. Wackers (Amsterdam 1996), 112-132

Grafton, A., *Joseph Scaliger. A Study in the History of Classical Scholarship. Vol. I: Textual Criticism and Exegesis. Vol. II: Historical Chronology* (Oxford 1983-1993)

Grafton, A. and L. Jardine, *From Humanism to the Humanities. Education and the Liberal Arts in Fifteenth- and Sixteenth-century Europe* (Cambridge, MA 1986)

Grant, M., *Selected Political Speeches of Cicero* (Harmondsworth 1969)

The Greek Commentaries on Plato's Phaedo, Vol. 1: Olympiodorus, ed. L.G. Westerink (Amsterdam 1976)

Green, V.H.H., *Bishop Reginald Recock. A Study in Ecclesiastical History and Thought* (Cambridge 1945)

Green-Pedersen, N.J., *The Tradition of the Topics in the Middle Ages. The Commentaries on Aristotle's and Boethius' "Topics"* (Munich 1984)

Grössing, H., *Humanistische Naturwissenschaft: zur Geschichte der Wiener mathematischen Schulen des 15. und 16. Jahrhunderts* (Baden Baden 1983)

Grosheide, D., review of Wolfs, *Das Groninger 'Religionsgespräch'*, in *Bijdragen voor de geschiedenis der Nederlanden*, 15 (1960), 118-121

Grote, Geert, *Epistolae*, ed. W. Mulder (Antwerp 1933)

Grotius, Hugo, *Apologeticus eorum qui Hollandiae Westfrisiaeque et vicinis quibusdam natio-nibus ex legibus praefuerunt ante mutationem quae evenit anno MDCXVIII* (Heidelberg 1629)

Grün, H., 'Die theologische Fakultät der Hohen Schule Herborn 1584-1817', in *Jahrbuch der hessischen kirchengeschichtlichen Vereinigung*, 14 (1968), 57-144

Guerlac, R., *Juan Luis Vives against the Pseudodialecticians. A Humanist Attack on Medieval Logic* (Dordrecht 1979)

Hamelmann, Herman, *Geschichtliche Werke. Band I: Schriften zur niedersächsisch-westfälischen Gelehrtengeschichte*, eds. H. Detmer, K. Hosius and K. Löffler (Münster 1908)

Hammer, W., 'Balthasar Rasinus and his Praise of Studies at the University of Pavia', in

Studies in Philology, 37 (1940), 133-148

Handbook of European History, 1400-1600. Late Middle Ages, Renaissance and Reformation, eds. Th.A. Brady jr and H.A. Oberman (Leiden 1994-1995) (2 vols)

Hankins, J., *Plato in the Italian Renaissance* (Leiden 1990) (2 vols)

Hardenberg, Albertus Rizaeus, 'Vita Wesseli Groningensis', in Gansfort, *Opera* (Groningen 1614)

Haude, S., review of *Humanismus in Köln*, in *Sixteenth Century Journal*, 26/2 (1995), 449-451

Hausmann, F.-R., 'Kaspar Schoppe, Joseph Justus Scaliger und die Carmina Priapea oder wie man mit Büchern Rufmord betreibt', in *Landesgeschichte und Geistesgeschichte. Festschrift für Otto Herding zum 65. Geburtstag*, eds. K. Elm, E. Gönner and E. Hillenbrand (Stuttgart 1977), 382-395

Hautz, J.F., *Geschichte der Universität Heidelberg* (Mannheim 1864) (2 vols)

Heath, T., 'Logical Grammar, grammatical Logic and Humanism in three German Universities', in *Studies in the Renaissance*, 18 (1971), 9-64

Heereboord, Adrianus, *Meletemata* (Amsterdam 1665)

Heesakkers, C.L., 'Te weinig koren of alleen te veel kaf? Leiden's eerste Noordnederlandse filoloog Johannes Meursius ‹1579-1639›', in *Miro Fervore. Een bundel lezingen & artikelen over de beoefening van de klassieke wetenschappen in de zeventiende & achttiende eeuw. Uitgegeven ter gelegenheid van het zestiende Lustrum van het Collegium Classicum* (Leiden 1994), 13-26

Hegius, Alexander, *Carmina* (Deventer, R. Pafraet, 1503)

–, *Dialogi* (Deventer, R. Pafraet, 1503)

Heinsius, Daniel, *Aristotelis Politicorvm libri VIII, cum perpetua Danielis Heinsii in omnes libros paraphrasi, accedit accuratus rerum index* (Leiden 1621)

Hensen, A.H.L., 'Henric van Arnhem's kronijk van het Fraterhuis te Gouda', in *Bijdragen en Mededeelingen van het Historisch Genootschap*, 20 (1899), 1-46

Herding, O., 'Probleme des frühen Humanismus in Deutschland', in *Archiv für Kulturgeschichte*, 38 (1956), 344-389

Hermans, Jos.M.M., *Laatmiddeleeuwse boeken in Zwolle* (forthcoming)

Herrmann, M., *Albrecht von Eyb und die Frühzeit des deutschen Humanismus* (Berlin 1893)

Hessus, Eobanus, *Dialogi tres* (Erfurt 1524)

Heymericus de Campo, *Problemata inter Albertum Magnum et Sanctum Thomam* (Cologne, J. Landen, 1496)

Hinz, U., *Die Brüder vom gemeinsamen Leben im Jahrhundert der Reformation. Das münstersche Kolloquium* (Tübingen 1997)

Historie van Groningen: Stad en Land, eds. W.J. Formsma a.o. (Groningen 1976; repr. with updated bibliography Groningen 1981)

Historisches Wörterbuch der Rhetorik, eds. G. Ueding and W. Jens (Tübingen 1992-)

A History of Twelfth-Century Western Philosophy, ed. P. Dronke (Cambridge 1988)

Hoefer, F.A., 'Een onuitgegeven brief van Dr. Maarten Luther', in *Archief voor Nederlandsche Kerkgeschiedenis*, 7 (1898), 203-206

Hoek, J.M., *De Middelnederlandse vertalingen van Boethius' «De consolatione philosophiae». Met een overzicht van de andere Nederlandse en niet-Nederlandse vertalingen* (Harderwijk 1943)

Hoenen, M.J.F.M., *Marsilius of Inghen. Divine Knowledge in Late Medieval Thought* (Leiden 1993)

–, 'Albertistae, Thomistae und Nominales: Die philosophisch-historischen Hintergründe der Intellektlehre des Wessel Gansfort (†1489)', in *Wessel Gansfort (1419-1489) and Northern Humanism*, 71-96

–, 'Denys the Carthusian and Heymeric de Campo on the Pilgrimages of Children to Mont-Saint-Michel in France (1458)', in *Archives d'Histoire Doctrinale et Littéraire du Moyen Age*, 61 (1994), 387-418

–, 'Academics and Intellectual Life in the Low Countries. The University Career of Heymeric de Campo (†1460)', in *Recherches de Théologie Ancienne et Médiévale*, 61 (1994), 173-209

–, 'Heymeric van de Velde (†1460) und die Geschichte des Albertismus: Auf der Suche nach den Quellen der albertistischen Intellektlehre des Tractatus Problematicus', in *Albertus Magnus und der Albertismus. Deutsche philosophische Kultur des Mittelalters*, eds. M.J.F.M. Hoenen and A.

de Libera (Leiden 1995), 303-331

–, 'Tradition and Renewal. The Philosophical Setting of Fifteenth-Century Christology. Heymericus de Campo, Nicolaus Cusanus, and the Cologne *Quaestiones vacantiales* (1465)', in *Christ among the Medieval Dominicans*, eds. K. Emery jr and J. Wawrykow (forthcoming)

Holcot, Robert, *In quatuor libros Sententiarum quaestiones* (Lyon 1518; repr. Frankfurt 1967)

Hollerbach, M., *Das Religionsgespräch als Mittel der konfessionellen und politischen Auseinandersetzung im Deutschland des 16. Jahrhunderts* (Frankfurt 1982)

Hollweg, W., 'Calvins Beziehungen zu den Rheinlanden', in *Calvinstudien. Festschrift zum 400. Geburtstage Johann Calvins* (Leipzig 1909), 129-187

Holtmann, W., *Die pfälzische Irenik im Zeitalter der Gegenreformation* (diss. Göttingen 1960) (unpublished)

Honnefelder, L., *Scientia transcendens. Die formale Bestimmung der Seindheit und Realität in der Metaphysik des Mittelalters und der Neuzeit* (Hamburg 1990)

Hooykaas, R., *Humanisme, science et réforme. Pierre de la Ramée (1515-1572)* (Leiden 1958)

Hornius, Georgius, *Historiae philosophicae libri VII* (Leiden 1655)

Huisman, G.C. and J. Kingma, 'Werken van en over Ubbo Emmius', in *Ubbo Emmius. Een Oostfries geleerde in Groningen*, 224-237

Huisman, G.C. and C.G. Santing, *Wessel Gansfort en het Noordelijk Humanisme* (Groningen 1989)

Huizinga, K., *Groningen en de Ommelanden onder de heerschappij van Karel van Gelder (1514-1536)* (Groningen 1925)

Humanismus in Köln. Studien zur Geschichte der Üniversität zu Köln, Bd. 10, ed. J. Mehl (Cologne 1991)

Humanistische Buchkultur. Deutsch-Niederländische Kontakte im Spätmittelalter (1450-1520), eds. Jos.M.M. Hermans and R. Peters (Münster 1997)

Hyde, J.K., 'Medieval Descriptions of Cities', in *Bulletin of the John Rylands Library Manchester*, 48 (1965-1966), 308-340

IJsewijn, J., 'The coming of humanism to the Low Countries', in *Itinerarium Italicum. The profile of the Italian Renaissance in the mirror of its European Transformations. Dedicated to Paul Oskar Kristeller on the occasion of his 70th birthday*, eds. H.A. Oberman and T.A. Brady jr (Leiden 1975), 193-301

–, 'Gli studi greci di Rodolfo Agricola', in *Umanesimo Ferrarese*, ed. A. Antonioni (Ferrara 1990), 25-45

–, with D. Sacré, *Companion to Neo-Latin Studies. Part II* (Louvain 1998)

Imbach, R., *'Deus est intelligere'. Das Verhältnis von Sein und Denken in seiner Bedeutung für das Gottesverständnis bei Thomas von Aquin und in der Pariser Questionen Meister Eckharts* (Freiburg 1976)

Die indices librorum prohibitorum des sechzehnten Jahrhunderts, ed. H. Reusch (Tübingen 1886; repr. Nieuwkoop 1961)

Janse, W., *Albert Hardenberg als Theologe. Profil eines Bucer-Schülers* (Leiden 1994)

Janvier, Y., *La géographie d'Orose* (Paris 1982)

Jardine, L., 'The Place of dialectic teaching in sixteenth-century Cambridge', in *Studies in the Renaissance*, 21 (1974), 31-62

–, 'Humanism and Dialectic in sixteenth-century Cambridge: a preliminary Investigation', in *Classical Influences on European Culture A.D. 1500-1700. Proceedings of an International Conference King's College Cambridge april 1974*, ed. R.R. Bolgar (Cambridge 1976), 141-154

–, 'Lorenzo Valla and the intellectual origins of humanist dialectic', in *Journal of the History of Philosophy*, 15 (1977), 143-164

–, 'Humanist Logic', in *The Cambridge History of Renaissance Philosophy*, 173-98

–, 'Humanism and the Teaching of Logic', in *The Cambridge History of Later Medieval Philosophy*, 797-807

Jedin, H., 'Die deutschen Teilnehmer am Trienter Konzil', in *Theologische Quartalschrift*, 122 (1941), 238-261

Jelsma, A.J., 'Doorwerking van de Moderne Devotie', in *De doorwerking van de Moderne Devotie*, 9-28

Jensen, K., 'The Humanist Reform of Latin and Latin Teaching', in *The Cambridge Companion to*

Renaissance Humanism, 63-81

John of Salisbury, *Policraticus*, ed. C.I. Webb (Oxford 1909)

Kaluza, Z., *Les querelles doctrinales à Paris. Nominalistes et realistes aux confins du XIVe et du XVe siècles* (Bergamo 1988)

–, 'La voix creatrice de dieu. Remarques sur l'*Alphabetum* de Heimeric de Campo', in *From Athens to Chartres. Neoplatonism and Medieval Thought. Studies in Honour of E. Jeauneau*, ed. H.J. Westra (Leiden 1992), 439-468

–, 'Les sciences et leurs langages. Note sur le statut du 29 Décembre 1340 et le prétendu statut perdu contra Ockham', in *Filosofia e teologia nel trecento. Studi in ricordo di Eugenio Randi*, ed. L. Bianchi (Louvain-la-Neuve 1994), 197-258

–, 'La crise des années 1474-1482: L'interdiction du Nominalisme par Louis XI', in *Philosophy and Learning. Universities in the Middle Ages*, 293-327

Kan, J.B. (ed.), 'Wesseli Groningensis, Rodolphi Agricolae, Erasmi Roterodami Vitae ex Codice Vindobonensi typis descriptae', in *Erasmiani Gymnasii Programma Litterarium* (Rotterdam 1894), 3-13

Karagiannis, E., *De functionarissen bij de Raad van Vlaanderen (1477-1542). Een onderzoek naar de sociale invloeden bij de samenstelling van de Raad* (Verhandeling ingediend met het oog op het behalen van de graad van licenciaat in de Geschiedenis, richting Middeleeuwen, Rijksuniversiteit Gent, Academiejaar 1991-1992) (unpublished)

Kaske, R.E., A. Groos and M.W. Twomey, *Medieval Christian Literary Imagery. A Guide to Interpretation* (Toronto Medieval Bibliographies, 11) (Toronto 1988)

Katechismus der katholischen Kirche (Munich 1993)

Kaylor jr, N.H., *The Medieval Consolation of Philosophy. An Annotated Bibliography* (New York 1992)

Kempius, Cornelius, *De origine, situ, qualitate et quantitate Frisiae, et rebus a Frisiis olim praeclare gestis* (Cologne 1588)

Kenny, A. and J. Pinborg, 'Medieval Philosophical Literature', in *The Cambridge History of Later Medieval Philosophy*, 11-42

Kerckhoffs-De Hey, A.J.M., *De Grote Raad en zijn functionarissen 1477-1531: biografieën van raadsheren* (Amsterdam 1980)

Kinn, J.W., *The Pre-Eminence of the Eucharist among the Sacraments according to Alexander of Hales, St. Albert the Great, St. Bonaventura and St. Thomas Aquinas* (Mundelein 1960)

Kinser, S., *The Works of Jacques-Auguste de Thou* (The Hague 1966)

Kisch, G., *Die Anfänge der juristischen Fakultät der Universität Basel 1459-1529* (Basle 1962)

Kist, N.C., 'Nog iets over den Nederlandschen oorsprong der zoogenaamde Zwingliaansche Avondmaalsleer', in *Nederlandsch Archief voor Kerkelijke Geschiedenis*, 3 (1843), 385-402

Klotz, A., *Cäsarstudien. Nebst einer Analyse der Strabonischen Beschreibung von Gallien und Brittanien* (Leipzig 1910)

Kluge, O., 'Die neulateinische Kunstprosa', in *Glotta. Zeitschrift für griechische und lateinische Sprache*, 23 (1935), 18-80

Knierim, P., *Dirc van Herxen (1381-1457), rector van het Zwolse fraterhuis* (Amsterdam 1926)

Knipscheer, F., *Hendrik van Bommel, 1490?-1570, kerkhervormer in Nederland en de Rijnlanden* (Meppel 1955)

Koch, A.C.F., *The year of Erasmus' birth and other contributions to the chronology of his life* (Utrecht 1969)

–, *Zwarte kunst in de Bisschopstraat* (Deventer 1977)

Kölker, A.J., *Alardus Aemstelredamus en Cornelius Crocus. Twee Amsterdamse priesterhumanisten. Hun leven, werken en theologische opvattingen. Bijdrage tot de kennis van het Humanisme in Noord-Nederland in de eerste helft van de zestiende eeuw* (Nijmegen 1963)

Der Kommentar in der Renaissance, eds. A. Buck and O. Herding (Boppard 1975)

Kooiman, P., 'The letters of Rodolphus Agricola to Jacobus Barbirianus', in *Rodolphus Agricola Phrisius*, 136-146

–, 'The biography of Jacob Barbireau (1455-1491) reviewed', in *Tijdschrift van de Vereniging voor Nederlandse Muziekgeschiedenis*, 38 (1988), 36-58

Kottler, B., 'The Vulgate Tradition of the *Consolatio Philosophiae* in the Fourteenth Century', in

Mediaeval Studies, 17 (1955), 209-214

Krafft, K. and W. Crecelius, 'Mittheilungen über Alexander Hegius und seine Schüler, sowie andere gleichzeitige Gelehrte, aus den Werken des Johannes Butzbach, Priors des Benedictinerklosters am Laacher See', in *Zeitschrift des Bergischen Geschichtsvereins*, 7 (1871), 213-288

–, 'Beiträge zur Geschichte des Humanismus in Rheinland und Westfalen', in *Zeitschrift des Bergischen Geschichtsvereins*, 11 (1876), 1-68

Kristeller, P.O., *Renaissance Thought: The Classic, Scholastic, and Humanist Strains* (New York 1955)

–, 'Salerno und die scholastische Wissenschaft', in *Artes Liberales. Von der antiken Bildung zur Wissenschaft des Mittelalters*, ed. J. Koch (Studien und Texte zur Geistesgeschichte des Mittelalters, 5) (Leiden 1959), 84-90

–, *Medieval Aspects of Renaissance Learning: Three Essays*, ed. E.P. Mahoney (Durham NC 1974)

–, 'The contribution of religious orders to Renaissance thought and learning', in idem, *Medieval Aspects of Renaissance Learning: Three Essays*, 95-114

–, 'The scholar and his public in the late Middle Ages and the Renaissance', in idem, *Medieval Aspects of Renaissance Learning: Three Essays*

–, *Concetti rinascimentali dell'uomo e altri saggi* (Florence 1978)

–, 'L'etica nel pensiero del Rinascimento', in *Il Veltro*, 24 (1980), 245-259

Krop, H.A., 'Georg Hornius als historicus van de filosofie. Een 17e-eeuwse visie op de middeleeuwen', in *Geschiedenis van de wijsbegeerte in Nederland*, 1 (1990), 74-88

Krüger, P., *Die Beziehungen der Rheinischen Pfalz zu Westeuropa 1576-1582. Die auswärtigen Beziehungen des Pfalzgrafen Johann Casimir 1576-1582* (diss. Munich 1964)

Kugler, H., *Die Vorstellung der Stadt in der Literatur des deutschen Mittelalters* (Munich 1986)

Kuhn, M., *Pfalzgraf Johann Casimir von Pfalz-Lautern 1576-1583* (Otterbach 1961)

Lademacher, H., *Geschichte der Niederlande. Politik-Verfassung-Wirtschaft* (Darmstadt 1983)

Lamentationes Petri autore Esdra Scriba, Ioannes Andreas (s.l., s.a.) [Zwolle, Simon Corver, 1521]

Lansink, H.G.J., O.Carm., *Studie en onderwijs in de Nederduitse provincie van de Karmelieten gedurende de Middeleeuwen* (Nijmegen 1967)

Die lateinischen mittelalterlichen Handschriften der Universitätsbibliothek München. Die Handschriften aus der Folioreihe. Zweite Hälfte, eds. N. Daniel, G. Schott and P. Zahn (Wiesbaden 1979)

Le lauree dello Studio senese nel 16. secolo: regesti degli atti dal 1516 al 1573, eds. G. Minnucci and P.G. Morelli (Siena 1992)

Lawn, B., *The Rise and Decline of the scholastic 'Quaestio Disputata'. With special Emphasis on its Use in the Teaching of Medicine and Science* (Leiden 1993)

LB: v. Erasmus, *Opera Omnia*

Leibenguth, E. and R. Seidel, 'Die Korrespondenz Rudolf Agricolas mit den süddeutschen Humanisten', in *Rudolf Agricola 1444-1485*, 181-259

Leiden University in the Seventeenth Century. An Exchange of Learning, eds. Th.H. Lunsingh Scheurleer and G.H.M. Posthumus Meyjes (Leiden 1975)

Leinsle, U.G., *Einführung in die scholastische Theologie* (Paderborn 1995)

Lickteig, F.-B., *The German Carmelites at the medieval universities* (Rome 1981)

Lindeboom, J., *Het Bijbelsch Humanisme in Nederland* (Leiden 1913)

Lipsius, Justus, *Epistolae*, eds. A. Gerlo, M.A. Nauwelaerts, H.D.L. Vervliet, S. Sue, H. Peeters and J. de Landtsheer (Brussels 1978-)

Listrius, Gerardus, *Epistola theologica*: see Spruyt 1991

–, *Commentarioli Listrii in Dialecticen Petri Hispani* (Zwolle, Simon Corver, 1520)

–, *Oratiuncula habita in coetu Scholasticorum Suollensium* (s.l., s.a.)

Lockwood, L., *Music in Renaissance Ferrara 1400-1505* (Oxford 1984)

Löhr, G.M., *Die theologischen Disputationen an der Universität Köln im ausgehenden 15. Jahrhundert nach den Angaben des P. Servatius Fanckel OP* (Leipzig 1926)

Lohr, C.H., 'Renaissance Latin Aristotle Commentaries: Authors L-M', in *Renaissance Quarterly*, 31 (1978), 532-603

–, 'Latin Aristotle Commentaries: Supplementary Renaissance Authors', in *Freiburger Zeitschrift für Philosophie und Theologie*, 40/1 (1993), 161-168

Lombardus, Petrus, *Sententiae in IV libris distinctae*, vol. 1/2 (Grottaferrata 1971)

Lorgion, J.J. Diest, *Verhandeling over Regnerus Praedinius* (Groningen 1862)

Lucas, E.V., *A Wanderer in Holland* (London 1905)

Ludovico il Moro, la sua città e la sua corte (1489-1499) (Como 1983)

Luth, J., 'Communion in the Churches of the Dutch Reformation to the Present Day', in *Bread of Heaven. Customs and Practices Surrounding Holy Communion. Essays in the History of Liturgy and Culture*, eds. C.M.A. Caspers and G. Lukken (Kampen 1995), 99-117

Luther, Martin, 'The Bondage of the Will', in *Luther and Erasmus: Free Will and Salvation*, transl. E. Gordon Rupp (Philadelphia 1969)

–, *Martin Luthers Werke. Kritische Gesamtausgabe: Briefwechsel* (Weimar 1930-85)

Luyendijk-Elshout, A.M., 'Der Einfluß der italienischen Universitäten auf die medizinische Fakultät Leiden (1575-1620)', in *Die Renaissance im Blick der Nationen Europas*, ed. G. Kauffmann (Wiesbaden 1991), 339-353

Machiels, J., *Meester Arend de Keysere 1480-1490* (Gent 1973)

–, *De boekdrukkunst te Gent tot 1560* (Gent 1994)

Mack, P., 'Rudolph Agricola's Reading of Literature', in *Journal of the Warburg and Courtauld Institutes,* 48 (1985), 23-41

–, *Renaissance Argument. Valla and Agricola in the Traditions of Rhetoric and Dialectic* (Leiden 1993)

–, 'Humanist Rhetoric and Dialectic', in *The Cambridge Companion to Renaissance Humanism*, 82-99

Macy, G., *The Theologies of the Eucharist in the Early Scholastic Period. A Study of the Salvific Function of the Sacrament according to the Theologians c. 1080-c. 1220* (Oxford 1984)

Maffei, D., 'Manoscritti giuridici napoletani del Collegio di Spagna e loro vicende fra Quattro e Cinquecento', in *Scuole diritto e società nel Mezzogiorno medievale d'Italia, I* (Catania 1985)

Maiocchi, R., *La Chiesa e il Convento di San Tommaso in Pavia* (Pavia 1895)

–, *Ticinensia. Noterelle di storia pavese nei secoli XV e XVI* (Pavia 1900)

–, *Codice diplomatico dell'Università di Pavia* (Pavia 1915; repr. Bologna 1971)

Makdowell, William, *Oratio habita* [...], *cum ornatissimi nonnulli iuvenes* [...] *disputationes philosophicas auspicarentur, de quadruplici nodo philosophico* (Groningen 1616)

Malusa, I.L., 'Introduzione, sezione prima', in *Storia delle storie generali della filosofia*, ed. G. Santinello (Bari 1982), 14-25

Mann, N., 'Arnold Geilhoven: an early disciple of Petrarch in the Low Countries', in *Journal of the Warburg and Courtauld Institutes*, 32 (1969), 454-468

Manns, P., 'Luther und die Heiligen', in *Reformatio Ecclesiae. Festgabe Erwin Iserloh* (Paderborn 1980), 535-580

Marchi, R., 'La cultura letteraria a Pavia nei secoli XIV e XV', in *Storia di Pavia, terzo volume: Dal libero comune alla fine del principato indipendente, 1024-1535, tomo secondo: La battaglia di Pavia del 24 febbraio 1525 nella storia, nella letteratura e nell'arte. Università e cultura* (Milan 1990), 157-203

Mariani, M., *Vita universitaria pavese del sec. XV* (Pavia 1899)

–, 'La laurea in leggi di Giason del Mayno', in *Bollettino della Società Pavese di Storia Patria*, 3 (1903), 241

Marsh, D., *The Quattrocento Dialogue. Classical Tradition and Humanist Innovation* (Harvard 1980)

Marshall, P., 'Parisian Psychology in the Mid-Fourteenth Century', in *Archives d'Histoire Doctrinale et Littéraire du Moyen Age*, 58 (1983), 101-193

Massaut, J.-P., *Josse Clichtove, l'humanisme et la réforme du clergé, tome I* (Paris 1968)

Massetto, G.P., 'La cultura giuridica civilista', in *Storia di Pavia, terzo volume: Dal libero comune alla fine del principato indipendente, 1024-1535, tomo secondo: La battaglia di Pavia del 24 febbraio 1525 nella storia, nella letteratura e nell'arte. Università e cultura* (Milan 1990), 475-531

Matricule de l'Université de Louvain, eds. E. Reusens, J. Wils and A. Schillings (Brussels 1903-1974) (10 vols)

Die Matrikel der Universität Basel. Im Auftrage der Universität Basel, II. Band, 1532/33-1600/01, ed. H.G. Wackernagel (Basle 1956)

Die Matrikel der Universität Heidelberg von 1386-1662, ed. G. Toepke (Heidelberg 1886)

Matrikel der Universität Köln, ed. H. Keussen (Bonn 1919; repr. Düsseldorf 1979)

Maurer, A., '*Ens Diminutum*: a Note on its Origin and Meaning', in *Medieval Studies*, 12 (1950), 216-222

Maurer, W., 'Melanchthon als Humanist', in *Philip Melanchthon*, ed. W. Ellinger (Göttingen 1961), 116-132

Mazzacane, A., 'Lancellotto Decio', in *Dizionario Biografico degli Italiani*, 33 (Rome 1987), 560-561

The Medieval Boethius: Studies in the Vernacular Translations of 'De Consolatione Philosophiæ', ed. A.J. Minnis (Cambridge 1987)

Meersseman, G., *Geschichte des Albertismus. Heft 2: Die ersten Kölner Kontroversen* (Rome 1935)

Melanchthon, Philippus, *Opera quae supersunt omnia*, in *Corpus Reformatorum*, I-XXVIII (Halle 1834-60)

–, 'Oratio de vita Rodolphi Agricolae', in *Corp. Ref.* XI (1843), ed. C.G. Brettschneider, 438-446

–, 'Epistola Alardo Aemstelredamo', in Agricola, *Lucubrationes*, ed. Alardus Aemstelredamus (Cologne 1539), †3r-†4r; also in *Corp. Ref.* III (1836), ed. C.G. Brettschneider, 673-676

Mellink, A.F., 'Uit de voorgeschiedenis van de Reformatie te Groningen', in *Historisch bewogen. Bundel opstellen voor Prof. Dr. A.F. Mellink* (Groningen 1984)

Menk, G., 'Kalvinismus und Pädagogik. Matthias Martinius (1572-1639) und der Einfluß der Hohen Schule Herborn auf Johann Amos Comenius', in *Nassauische Annalen*, 91 (1980), 77-104

–, *Die Hohe Schule Herborn in ihrer Frühzeit (1584-1660). Ein Beitrag zum Hochschulwesen des deutschen Kalvinismus im Zeitalter der Gegenreformation* (Wiesbaden 1981)

–, 'Johann Amos Comenius und die Hohe Schule Herborn', in *Acta Comeniana*, 8 (1989), 41-60

Mertens, Th., 'Collatio und Codex im Bereich der Devotio moderna', in *Der Codex im Gebrauch*, eds. C. Meier, D. Hüpper and H. Keller (Munich 1996), 163-182

–, 'Ter Inleiding', in *Boeken voor de eeuwigheid. Middelnederlands geestelijk proza*, ed. Th. Mertens (Amsterdam 1993), 8-35

Mesters, G., 'Candidus, Alexander (Nikolaus Blanckaert), O.Carm.', in *LThK Bd. 2* (Freiburg ²1958), 915

Meter, J.H., *The literary theories of Daniel Heinsius. A study of the development and background of his views on literary theory and criticism during the period from 1602-1612* (Assen 1984)

Meursius, Johannes, *Rervm Belgicarvm Libri Quatuor, In Quibus Ferdinandi Albani Sexennium, belli Belgici principium, additvr qvintvs, seorsim antea excusus, in quo indvciarvm historia; et eiusdem belli finis* (Leiden 1614)

Meuthen, E., *Das 15. Jahrhundert* (Munich 1984)

–, *Kölner Universitätsgeschichte. Band I: Die alte Universität* (Cologne 1988)

–, 'Die Artesfakultät der alten Kölner Universität', in *Die Kölner Universität im Mittelalter. Geistige Wurzeln und soziale Wirklichkeit*, ed. A. Zimmermann (Berlin 1989), 366-393

Middeleeuwsche Glose op het Pater en Ave, XIVe eeuw, ed. D.A. Stracke (Antwerp 1936)

Minnis, A.J., *Chaucer's "Boece" and the Medieval Tradition of Boethius* (Chaucer Studies, 18) (Cambridge 1993)

Moffitt Watts, P., *Nicolaus Cusanus. A Fifteenth-Century Vision of Man* (Leiden 1982)

Mojsisch, B., *Die Theorie des Intellekts bei Dietrich von Freiberg* (Hamburg 1977)

Mokrosch, R., 'Devotio Moderna und Verhältnis zu Humanismus und Reformation', in *Theologische Realenzyklopädie*, 8 (1981), 605-616

J. Molanus. Les quatorze livres sur l'histoire de la ville de Louvain, ed. P. de Ram (Brussels 1861)

Molenaar, M., *Werken van de Heilige Geertruid van Helfta, I* (Bussum 1951)

Molhuysen, P.C., 'Alexander Hegius', in *Overijsselsche almanak voor oudheid en letteren*, 1852, 37-66

–, *Codices Vulcaniani* (Codices manuscripti/ Bibliotheca Universitatis Leidensis, 1) (Leiden 1910)

Molland, G., 'Addressing Ancient Authority', in *Annals of Science*, 53 (1996), 213-234

Moltmann, J., 'Zur Bedeutung des Petrus Ramus für Philosophie und Theologie des Calvinismus', in *Zeitschrift für Kirchengeschichte*, 68 (1957), 295-318

–, *Christoph Pezel (1539-1604) und der Calvinismus in Bremen* (Bremen 1958)

Monasticon Fratrum Vitae Communis II: Deutschland, eds. W. Leesch, E. Persoons and A.G. Weiler (Brussels 1979)

Mugnai Carrara, D., *La biblioteca di Nicolò Leoniceno. Tra Aristotele e Galeno: cultura e libri di un medico umanista* (Florence 1991)

Muller Fzn., S., *Catalogussen van de bij het stads-archief bewaarde archieven. Eerste afdeling. De aan de stad Utrecht behoorende archieven* (Utrecht 1913)

Mundt, L., 'Rudolf Agricolas *De inventione dialectica*–Konzeption, historische Bedeutung und Wirkung', in *Rudolf Agricola 1444-1485*, 83-146

Murdoch, J.E., 'From the medieval to the Renaissance Aristotle', in *New Perspectives on Renaissance Thought: essays in the history of science, education and philosophy*, eds. J. Henry and S. Hutton (London 1990), 163-176

Murphy, J.J., *Renaissance Eloquence. Studies in the Theory and Practice of Renaissance Rhetorics* (Berkeley 1983)

Nauert, Ch.G., 'The Humanist Challenge to Medieval German Culture', in *Daphnis*, 15 (1986), 277-306

–, *Humanism and the Culture of Renaissance Europe* (Cambridge 1995)

Nauta, L., 'The Preexistence of the Soul in Medieval Thought', in *Recherches de Théologie ancienne et médiévale*, 63 (1996), 83-125

–, 'Platonic and Cartesian Philosophy in the Commentary on Boethius' *Consolatio Philosophiae*', in *British Journal for the History of Philosophy*, 4/1 (1996), 79-100

Nauwelaerts, M.A., 'Johannes Murmellius. Roermond 1480-Deventer 1517', in *Historische Opstellen over Roermond en omgeving*, eds. A. van Rijswijck, M.K.J. Smeets and B.A. Vermaseren (Roermond 1951), 201-234

Negruzzo, S., *Theologiam discere et docere. La Facoltà teologica di Pavia nel XVI secolo* (Milan 1995)

Nellen, H.J.M., *Hugo Grotius 1583-1645. Geschichte seines Lebens basierend auf seiner Korrespondenz* (Bonn 1983)

Newman, W.R., *The* Summa Perfectionis *of Pseudo-Geber. A Critical Edition, Translation and Study* (Collection de Travaux de l'Académie Internationale d'Histoire des Sciences, 35) (Leiden 1991)

Nicollier-de Weck, B., *Hubert Languet (1518-1581). Un réseau politique international de Melanchthon à Guillaume d'Orange* (Geneva 1995)

Nijhoff, W. and M.E. Kronenberg, *Nederlandsche bibliographie van 1500-1540* (The Hague 1923-1971) (3 vols)

Norden, E., *Die antike Kunstprosa vom VI. Jahrhundert v. Chr. bis in die Zeit der Renaissance* (Stuttgart 1958; [1]1898) (2 vols)

Noreña, C.G., 'Agricola, Vives and the Low Countries', in *Erasmus in Hispania, Vives in Belgio. Acta Colloquii Brugensis 23-26 IX 1985*, eds. J. IJsewijn and A. Losada (Louvain 1986)

Nouwens, J., *De veelvuldige H. Communie in de geestelijke literatuur der Nederlanden vanaf het midden van de 16e eeuw tot in de eerste helft van de 18e eeuw* (Bilthoven 1952)

Nutton, V., 'The Changing Language of Medicine, 1450-1550', in *Vocabulary of Teaching and Research between Middle Ages and Renaissance. Proceedings of the Colloquium. London, Warburg Institute, 11-12 March 1994*, ed. O. Weijers (Etudes sur le vocabulaire intellectuel du Moyen Age, 8) (Turnhout 1995), 184-198

Oberman, H.A., *The Harvest of Medieval Theology. Gabriel Biel and Late Medieval Nominalism* (Cambridge, MA 1963)

–, *Forerunners of the Reformation. The Shape of late Medieval Thought Illustrated by Key Documents* (New York 1966)

–, *Werden und Wertung der Reformation. Vom Wegestreit zum Glaubenskampf* (Tübingen [2]1979)

–, 'Die *Gelehrten die Verkehrten:* Popular Response to Learned Culture in the Renaissance and Reformation', in *Religion and Culture in Renaissance and Reformation. Papers from a Symposium held at Harvard University, November 1987*, ed. S.E. Ozment (Sixteenth Century Essays and Studies, 11) (Kirksville 1989), 43-63

–, *The Dawn of the Reformation. Essays in Late Medieval and Early Reformation Thought. Vol. I: Fourteenth-Century Religious Thought: A Premature Profile* (Grand Rapids MI 1992)

–, 'The Pursuit of Happiness: Calvin between Humanism and Reformation', in *Humanity and Divinity in Renaissance and Reformation. Esssays in honor of Charles Trinkaus*, eds. J.W. O'Malley, Th.M. Izbicki and G. Christianson (Leiden 1993)

–, 'Wessel Gansfort: *Magister contradictionis*', in *Wessel Gansfort (1419-1489) and Northern Humanism*, 97-121

Obertello, L., *Severino Boezio* (Genova 1974) (2 vols)

Oestreich, G., 'Justus Lipsius als Theoretiker des neuzeitlichen Machtstaates', in idem, *Geist und Gestalt des frühmodernen Staates. Ausgewählte Aufsätze* (Berlin 1969), 35-79

–, *Antiker Geist und moderner Staat bei Justus Lipsius (1547-1606). Der Neostoizismus als politische Bewegung* (diss. Berlin 1954; unpublished), ed. N. Mout (Göttingen 1989)

Ogilvie, M.H., 'Wessel Gansfort's Theology of Church Government', in *Nederlands Archief voor Kerkgeschiedenis*, 55 (1975), 125-50

Ohl, R., *The University of Padua 1405-1509: an International Community of Students and Professors* (unpublished diss.; Univ. of Pennsylvania 1980)

Ong, W.J., *Ramus. Method, and the Decay of Dialogue. From the Art of Discourse to the Art of Reason* (Cambridge, MA 1983; [1]1958)

–, *Ramus and Talon Inventory* (Cambridge, MA 1958)

–, 'Ramus, Peter', in *The Encyclopedia of Philosophy*, VII, 66-68

Orationes ad inaugurationem academiae illustrium ordinum Groningae et Omlandiae habitae (Groningen 1614)

Orme, N., *Education and Society in Medieval and Renaissance England* (London 1989)

Orosius, Paulus, *Historiarum aduersum paganos libri VII*, ed. K. Zangemeister (CSEL 5) (Vienna 1882; repr. New York 1966)

–, *The Seven Books of History against the Pagans*, transl. R.J. Deferrari (Washington 1964)

Overfield, J.H., *Humanism and Scholasticism in Late Medieval Germany* (Princeton 1984)

Pabel, H., 'The Peaceful People of Christ: The Irenic Ecclesiology of Erasmus of Rotterdam', in *Erasmus' Vision of the Church*, ed. H. Pabel (Ann Arbor 1996), 57-94

Panofsky, E., *Renaissance and Renascences in Western Art* (New York 1960)

Paquet, J.N., 'Statuts de la Faculté des Arts de Louvain (1567-1568)', in *Bulletin de la Commission royale d'Histoire*, 136 (1970), 179-271

–, *Les matricules universitaires* (Typologie des sources du moyen âge occidental, 65) (Turnhout 1992)

Paquot, J., *Mémoires pour servir à l'histoire littéraire des dix-sept Provinces des Pays-Bas, de la Principauté de Liège et de quelques contrées voisines* (Louvain 1763-1770) (18 vols)

Pardi, G., *Titoli dottorali conferiti dallo studio di Ferrara nei sec. XV e XVI* (Lucca 1901; repr. Bologna [2]1970)

Pathuis, A., *Groninger gedenkwaardigheden. Teksten, wapens en huismerken van 1298-1814* (Assen 1977)

Pattin, A., 'Le Liber de causis. Édition établie à l'aide de 90 manuscripts avec introduction et notes', in *Tijdschrift voor Filosofie*, 28 (1966), 90-203

Paulus, N., *Geschichte des Ablasses am Ausgange des Mittelalters* (Paderborn 1923)

Pecock, Reginald, *The Repressor of Overmuch Blaming of the Clergy*, ed. C. Babington (London 1860; repr. New York 1964) (2 vols)

Pedralli, M., 'Il medico ducale milanese Antonio Bernareggi e i suoi libri', in *Aevum*, 70 (1996), 307-350

Pellegrin, E., *La biliothèque des Visconti et des Sforza ducs de Milan au XVe siècle* (Paris 1955)

Persijn, A.J., *Wessel Gansfort: De oratione dominica in een dietse bewerking* (Assen 1964)

Peterse, H., *Jacobus Hoogstraeten gegen Johannes Reuchlin. Ein Beitrag zur Geschichte des Antijudaismus im 16. Jahrhundert* (Mainz 1995)

Petrarca, Franciscus, *Epistolae Familiares*, ed. V. Rossi (Florence 1933-42) (4 vols)

Petrucci, F., 'Lodrisio Crivelli', in *Dizionario Biografico degli Italiani*, 31 (Rome 1985), 146-152

Petrus, Suffridus, *De scriptoribus Frisiae decades XVI et semis* (Cologne 1593)

Philoponus, *Against Aristotle. On the Eternity of the World*, transl. Ch. Wildberg (Ithaca, NY 1987)

Philosophy and Learning. Universities in the Middle Ages, eds. M.J.F.M. Hoenen and J.H.J. Schneider (Leiden 1995)

Piacente, L., 'Battista Guarini: l'uomo e il letterato', in *"In supreme dignitatis...". Per la storia dell'Università di Ferrara 1391-1991*, ed. P. Castelli (Florence 1995), 195-206

Piccolomini, Aeneas Silvius, *Opera* (Basle 1551; repr. Frankfurt 1965)

PL = *Patrologia Latina*

Pleij, H., *Nederlandse literatuur van de late middeleeuwen* (Utrecht 1990)

Poelhekke, J.J., 'Nederlandse leden van de Inclyta Natio Germanica Artistarum te Padua 1553-1700', in *Mededelingen van het Nederlands Historisch Instituut te Rome*, 31 (1961), 263-373

Popkin, R.H., 'Theories of knowledge', in *The Cambridge History of Renaissance Philosophy*, 678-684

Port, W., *Hieronymus Commelinus, 1550-1597. Leben und Werk eines Heidelberger Drucker-Verlegers* (Leipzig 1938)

Post, R.R., *De Moderne Devotie* (Amsterdam ²1950)

–, *De via antiqua en de via moderna bij vijftiende-eeuwse Nederlandse theologen* (Nijmegen 1964)

–, 'Johann Pupper van Goch', in *Nederlands Archief voor Kerkgeschiedenis*, n.s. 47 (1965-66), 71-97

–, *The Modern Devotion. Confrontation with Reformation and Humanism* (Leiden 1968)

Posthumus Meyjes, G.H.M., 'Jean Hotman's Syllabus of eirenical literature', in *Reform and Reformation. England and the Continent, c 1500-c 1750. Dedicated and presented to Clifford W. Dugmore to mark his seventieth birthday*, ed. D. Baker (Oxford 1979), 175-193

–, 'Autour d'une liste de Jean Hotman', in *La controverse religieuse [XVIe-XIXe siècles]. Actes du 1er Colloque Jean Boisset, VIeme Colloque du Centre d'Histoire de la Réforme et du Protestantisme*, ed. M. Péronnet (Montpellier 1980) (2 vols), I 43-56

Postina, A., *Der Karmelit Eberhard Billick. Ein Lebensbild aus dem 16. Jahrhundert* (Freiburg 1901)

Postma, F., *Viglius van Aytta als humanist en diplomaat (1507-1549)* (Zutphen 1983)

–, 'Regnerus Praedinius (c. 1510-1559), seine Schule und sein Einfluss', in *Wessel Gansfort (1419-1489) and Northern Humanism*, 291-324

Praamstra, H., and J.W. Boersma, 'Die archäologischen Untersuchungen der Zisterzienserabteien Clarus Campus (Klaarkamp) bei Rinsumageest (Fr.) und St. Bernardus in Aduard (Gr.)', in *Palaeohistoria*, 19 (1977), 173-259

Praedinius, Regnerus, *Opera quae supersunt omnia* [...] (Basle 1563)

–, *Commentationes: De fidei antecessionibus* [...] (Geneva, Jean Crespin, 1568)

Prantl, C., *Geschichte der Logik im Abendlande* (Leipzig 1855-1870) (4 vols)

Press, V., *Calvinismus und Territorialstaat. Regierung und Zentralbehörden der Kurpfalz 1559-1619* (Stuttgart 1970)

Pupper von Goch, Johannes, *De libertate christiana*, ed. F. Pijper, in *Bibliotheca Reformatoria Neerlandica. Geschriften uit den tijd der Hervorming in de Nederlanden*, VI (The Hague 1910), 33-255

–, *Fragmenta*, ed. F. Pijper, in *Bibliotheca Reformatoria Neerlandica. Geschriften uit den tijd der Hervorming in de Nederlanden*, VI (The Hague 1910), 279-344

Puttiger, H.P.H., *Georgius Macropedius' Asotus. Een Neolatijns drama over de verloren zoon door Joris van Lanckvelt* (Nieuwkoop 1988)

Raczek, K., 'Candidus (Blanckart), Alexander, OCarm', in *LThK Bd. 2* (Freiburg ³1994), 921

Rashdall, H., *The Universities of Europe in the Middle Ages*, eds. F.M. Powicke and A.B. Emden (Oxford 1936)

Reedijk, C., *The Poems of Desiderius Erasmus* (Leiden 1956)

Reeve, M.D., 'Classical Scholarship', in *The Cambridge Companion to Renaissance Humanism*,

20-46

Reichling, D., 'Beiträge zur Charakteristik der Humanisten Alexander Hegius, Joseph Horlenius, Jacob Montanus und Johannes Murmellius', in *Monatsschrift für rheinisch-westfälische Geschichtsforschung und Alterthumskunde*, 3 (1877), 294-5

–, *Johannes Murmellius: sein Leben und seine Werke* (Freiburg 1880)

Reifferscheid, A. (ed.), *Briefe G.M. Lingelsheims, M. Berneggers und ihrer Freunde, Nach Handschriften [...]* (Heilbronn 1889)

Renaissance Humanism: Foundations, Forms, and Legacy. Vol. I: Humanism in Italy. Vol. II: Humanism beyond Italy. Vol. III: Humanism and the Disciplines, ed. A. Rabil jr (Philadelphia 1988)

Renaudet, A., *Préréforme et Humanisme à Paris pendant les premières guerres d'Italie (1494-1517)* (Paris 1953)

Renouard, Ph., *Bibliographie des éditions de Simon de Colines 1520-1546* (Paris 1894)

Reusens, E., 'Statuts primitifs de la Faculté des Arts de Louvain', in *Bulletin de la Commission royale d'Histoire*, 9 (1867), 147-206

Reynolds, L.D. and N.G. Wilson, *Scribes and Scholars. A Guide to the Transmission of Greek and Latin Literature* (Oxford ³1991)

Reypens, L., 'Oude mystieke teksten I. Gheraert Appelmans' glose op het Vaderons', in *Ons Geestelijk Erf*, 1 (1927), 80-107

Rinzema, A.J., 'Ubbo Emmius als historicus', in *Ubbo Emmius. Een Oostfries geleerde in Groningen*, 49-62

Ripelin of Stratsburg, Hugo, *Compendium totius theologicae veritatis*, ed. J. de Combis (Freiburg 1880)

Risse, W., *Die Logik der Neuzeit. I: 1500-1640* (Stuttgart 1964)

–, *Bibliographia Logica. Verzeichnis der Druckschriften zur Logik mit Angabe ihrer Fundorte. Band I: 1472-1800* (Hildesheim 1965)

Robb, N.A., *Neoplatonism of the Italian Renaissance* (New York 1968)

Robson, J.A., *Wyclif and the Oxford Schools* (Cambridge 1961)

Rodolphe Agricola, Ecrits sur la dialectique et l'humanisme, ed. M. van der Poel (Paris 1997)

Rodolphus Agricola Phrisius 1444-1485. Proceedings of the International Conference at the University of Groningen, 28-30 October 1985, eds. F. Akkerman and A.J. Vanderjagt (Leiden 1988)

Rogge, H.C., 'Gerardus Listrius', in *Archief voor Nederlandsche Kerkgeschiedenis*, 7 (1899), 207-220

Rosier, I., O.Carm., *Biographisch en bibliographisch overzicht van de vroomheid in de nederlandse Carmel van 1235 tot het midden der achttiende eeuw* (Tielt 1950)

Rotermund, H.W., *Lexikon aller Gelehrten, die seit der Reformation in Bremen gelebt haben [...]* (Bremen 1818) (2 vols)

Roulez, J., 'Vulcanius', in *Biographie nationale de Belgique*, 5 (1876), 753-759

Rudolf Agricola 1444-1485. Protagonist des nordeuropäischen Humanismus zum 550. Geburtstag, ed. W. Kühlmann (Bern 1994)

Rüegg, W., 'The Rise of Humanism', in *A History of the University in Europe. I. Universities in the Middle Ages*, ed. H. de Ridder-Symoens (Cambridge 1992), 442-448

Rummel, E., 'Quoting poetry instead of Scripture: Erasmus and Eucherius on *Contemptus mundi*', in *Bibliothèque d'Humanisme et Renaissance*, 45 (1983), 503-509

–, *Erasmus and His Catholic Critics* (Nieuwkoop 1989)

–, '*Et cum theologo bella poeta gerit*. The Conflict between Humanists and Scholastics Revisited', in *Sixteenth Century Journal*, 23/4 (1992), 713-726

–, *Scheming Papists and Lutheran Fools* (New York 1993)

–, 'Voices of Reform from Hus to Erasmus', in *Handbook of European History, 1400-1600*, II 61-91

–, *The Humanist-Scholastic Debate in the Renaissance and Reformation* (Cambridge, MA 1995)

Saccaro, A.P., *Französischer Humanismus des 14. und 15. Jahrhunderts. Studien und Berichte* (Munich 1975)

Santing, C.G., *Geneeskunde en humanisme: een intellectuele biografie van Theodericus Ulsenius (c. 1460-1508)* (Rotterdam 1992)

Sàrközy, P., 'Links to Europe: Hungarian Students at Italian Universities in the 13-18th Centuries', in *Hungarian Studies Review*, 17 (1990), 47-55

Sassen, F., *Henricus Renerius, de eerste 'Cartesiaansche' hoogleeraar te Utrecht* (Amsterdam 1941)

–, '350 jaren wijsgerig onderwijs te Groningen', in *Groninger Universiteitsblad*, 15 (1965), 69-81

Satiren und Pasquillen aus der Reformationszeit, ed. O. Schade (Hannover 1863)

Scaliger, Josephus Justus, *Epistolae omnes quae reperiri potuerunt, nunc primum collectae ac editae* (Frankfurt 1628)

Schiff, O., 'Zur Literaturgeschichte der kirchlichen Einigungsbestrebungen. Eine Bibliographie von 1628', in *Nederlandsch Archief voor Kerkgeschiedenis*, 30 (1938), 35-39

Schillebeeckx, E., 'Sacrament', in *Theologisch Woordenboek III* (Roermond 1958), 4185-4231

–, *De sacramentele heilseconomie. Theologische bezinning op S. Thomas' sacramentenleer in het licht van de traditie en van de hedendaagse sacramentsproblematiek* (Antwerp 1952)

Schilling, H., 'Religion und Gesellschaft in der calvinistischen Republik der Vereinigten Niederlande. "Öffentlichkeitskirche" und Säkularisation, Ehe und Hebammenwesen, Presbyterien und politische Partizipation', in *Kirche und gesellschaftlicher Wandel in deutschen und niederländischen Städten der werdenden Neuzeit*, ed. F. Petri (Städteforschung. Reihe A, 10) (Cologne 1980), 197-250

Schindling, A., *Humanistische Hochschule und freie Reichsstadt. Gymnasium und Akademie in Straßburg 1538-1621* (Wiesbaden 1977)

Schlette, H.R., *Die Lehre von der geistlichen Kommunion bei Bonaventura, Albert dem Großen und Thomas von Aquin* (Munich 1959)

Schmidt, P.G., 'Iodocus Badius Ascensius als Kommentator', in *Der Kommentar in der Renaissance*, 63-71

–, 'Mittelalterliches und humanistisches Städtelob', in *Die Rezeption der Antike. Zum Problem der Kontinuität zwischen Mittelalter und Renaissance. Vorträge gehalten anlässlich des ersten Kongresses des Wolfenbütteler Arbeitskreises für Renaissanceforschung in der Herzog August Bibliothek Wolfenbüttel vom 2. bis 5. September 1978*, ed. A. Buck (Wolfenbütteler Abhandlungen zur Renaissanceforschung, 1) (Hamburg 1981), 119-128

Schneppen, H., *Niederländische Universitäten und deutsches Geistesleben. Von der Gründung der Universität Leiden bis ins späte 18. Jahrhundert* (Münster 1960)

Schoeck, R.J., 'Agricola and Erasmus: Erasmus' Inheritance of Northern Humanism', in *Rodolphus Agricola Phrisius 1444-1485*, 181-188

–, *Erasmus of Europe. Vol. II: The Prince of Humanists, 1501-1536* (Edinburgh 1993)

Schönberger, R., *Was ist Scholastik* (Hildesheim 1991)

De scholastieke Voetius, eds. W.J. van Asselt and E. Dekker (Zoetermeer 1995)

Schoonbeeg, P., 'Friderici Mauri carmina', in *Wessel Gansfort (1419-1489) and Northern Humanism*, 325-386

–, *Willem Lodewijk, graaf van Nassau (1560-1620). Stadhouder van Friesland, Groningen en Drenthe* (Hilversum 1994)

Schoonbeeg, P. and F. Akkerman, 'De Latijnse stijl van Ubbo Emmius', in *Ubbo Emmius. Een Oostfries geleerde in Groningen*, 63-80

Schottenloher, O., *Erasmus im Ringen um die humanistische Bildungsreform. Ein Beitrag zum Verständnis seiner geistigen Entwicklung* (Reformationsgeschichtliche Studien und Texte, 61) (Münster 1933)

Schubert, H., 'Die pfälzische Exilregierung im Dreißigjährigen Krieg. Ein Beitrag zur Geschichte des politischen Protestantismus', in *Zeitschrift für die Geschichte des Oberrheins*, 102 (1954), 575-680

Schuitema Meijer, A.T., *Historie van het archief der stad Groningen* (Groningen 1977)

Schumacher, H., 'Ubbo Emmius: Trigonometer, Topograph und Kartograph–unter besonderer Berücksichtigung neuer Forschungsergebnisse–', in *Ubbo Emmius. Een Oostfries geleerde in Groningen*, 146-165

Seeing the Future Clearly. Questions on Future Contingents by Robert Holcot, eds. P.A. Streveler and K.H. Tachau (Toronto 1995)

Senguerd, A., *De vero philosopho* (Amsterdam 1648)

Severi, P., 'Girolamo Crivelli', in *Dizionario Biografico degli Italiani*, 31 (Rome 1985), 141-2

Shank, M.H., *'Unless You Believe You Shall Not Understand'. Logic, University, and Society in Late Medieval Vienna* (Princeton 1988)

Slits, F.P.Th., *Het Latijnse stededicht. Oorsprong en ontwikkeling tot de zeventiende eeuw* (Amsterdam 1990)

Smits van Waesberghe, M., 'Iets over leer en praktijk van de Geestelijke Communie in de Middeleeuwen, voornamelijk in het licht van de vaderlandse devotie-literatuur', in *Studia Catholica*, 19 (1943), 129-140 and 172-187

Sonntag, R., 'Zur Ostfriesland-Karte des Ubbo Emmius und ihrer Zustandsfolge–Bekanntes und neue Erkenntnisse–', in *Ubbo Emmius. Een Oostfries geleerde in Groningen*, 130-145

Sottili, A., 'Notizie per il soggiorno in Italia di Rodolfo Agricola', in *Rodolphus Agricola Phrisius 1444-1485*, 79-95

–, 'Università e cultura a Pavia in età visconteo-sforzesca', in *Storia di Pavia, terzo volume: Dal libero comune alla fine del principato indipendente, 1024-1535, tomo secondo: La battaglia di Pavia del 24 febbraio 1525 nella storia, nella letteratura e nell'arte. Università e cultura* (Milan 1990)

–, 'Rettori e vicerettori dell'Università legista pavese nella seconda metà del Quattrocento', in *Università e cultura. Studi sui rapporti italo-tedeschi nell'età dell'Umanesimo*, ed. A. Sottili (Goldbach 1993), 246-271

–, 'Le contestate elezioni rettorali di Paul van Baenst e Johannes von Dalberg all'Università di Pavia', in *Università e cultura. Studi sui rapporti italo-tedeschi nell'età dell'Umanesimo*, ed. A. Sottili (Goldbach 1993), 272-318

–, 'Die theologische Fakultät der Universität Pavia in der zweiten Hälfte des 15. Jahrhunderts. Die gescheiterte Berufung des Theologen Thomas Penketh und die Einrichtung der "Lectura Thomae"', in *Studien zum 15. Jahrhundert. Festschrift für Erich Meuthen*, eds. J. Helmrath, H. Müller and H. Wolff (Munich 1994), I 541-564

–, *Lauree pavesi nella seconda metà del Quattrocento, I (1450-1475)* (Milan 1995)

Speroni, M., 'Lorenzo Valla a Pavia: Il Libellus contro Bartolo', in *Quellen und Forschungen aus italienischen Archiven und Bibliotheken*, 59 (1979), 453-467

Spruyt, B.J., 'Gerardus Listrius' Epistola theologica adversus Dominicanos Suollenses', in *NAKG/DRCH*, 71-72 (1991), 224-244

–, 'Listrius lutherizans: His Epistola theologica adversus Dominicanos Suollenses (1520)', in *Sixteenth Century Journal*, 22/4 (1991), 727-751

–, 'Humanisme, Evangelisme en Reformatie in de Nederlanden, 1520-1530', in *Reformatie in meervoud. Congresbundel 1990*, eds. M. van Campen and W. de Greef (Kampen 1991)

–, 'Verdacht van Lutherse sympathieën. Maria van Hongarije en de religieuze controversen van haar tijd', in *Maria van Hongarije (1505-1558). Koningin tussen keizers en kunstenaars*, eds. W.P. Blockmans, J. Bruyn and A.M. Koldeweij (Zwolle 1993), 87-103

–, 'Wessel Gansfort and Cornelis Hoen's *Epistola christiana*: "The ring as a pledge of my love"', in *Wessel Gansfort (1419-1489) and Northern Humanism*, 122-141

–, 'Laat-middeleeuwse ketterijen en de vroege hervorming in de Nederlanden. Cornelis Henrixz. Hoen en zijn *Epistola christiana* (1525)', in *Doopsgezinde bijdragen*, n.r. 19 (1993), 15-28

–, '"En bruit d'estre bonne luteriene": Mary of Hungary (1505-58) and Religious Reform', in *The English Historical Review*, 109 (1994), 275-307

–, *Cornelius Henrici Hoen [Honius] and his Epistle on the Eucharist [1525]* (Leiden 1996)

Starin, A., OCarm, 'Candidus (Blankaert), Nikolaus, kath. Theologe, Karmeliter, * Gent, † 31.12.1555 Köln', in *Neue deutsche Biographie, 3. Bd.* (Berlin 1957), 122a/b

Statuta et Leges Fundamentales Academiae Frisiorum (Franeker 1638)

Les statuts synodaux français du XIIIe siècle. IV. Les statuts synodaux de l'ancienne province de Reims (Cambrai, Arras, Noyon, Soissons et Tournai), ed. J. Avril (Paris 1995)

Staubach, N., 'Das Wunder der Devotio Moderna. Neue Aspekte im Werk des Windesheimer Geschichtsschreiber Johannes Busch', in *Windesheim 1395-1995. Kloosters, teksten, invloeden. Voordrachten gehouden tijdens het internationale congres '600 jaar Kapittel van Windesheim', 27 mei 1995 te Zwolle*, eds. A.J. Hendrikman, P. Bange a.o. (Middeleeuwse Studies, XII) (Nijmegen 1996), 170-185

Stegmüller, F., *Repertorium commentariorum in Sententias Petri Lombardi* (Würzburg 1947) (2 vols)

Strabo, *Geography,* transl. H.L. Jones (Cambridge, MA 1939; repr. 1989)

Straube, W., 'Die Agricola-Biographie des Johannes von Plieningen', in *Rudolf Agricola 1444-1485,* 11-48

Stupperich, R., 'Luther und das Fraterhaus in Herford', in *Geist und Geschichte der Reformation. Festgabe Hanns Rückert zum 65. Geburtstag* (Arbeiten zur Kirchengeschichte, 30) (Berlin 1966), 219-238

Sturlese, L., 'Proclo ed Ermete in Germania da Alberto Magno a Bertoldo di Moosburg. Per una prospettiva di ricerca sulla cultura filosofica tedesca nel secolo delle sue origini (1250-1350)', in *Von Meister Dietrich zu Meister Eckhart,* ed. K. Flasch (Hamburg 1984), 22-33

Syme, R., *Tacitus* (Oxford 1958) (2 vols)

Taylor, L.J., 'The Influence of Humanism on Post-Reformation Catholic Preachers in France', in *Renaissance Quarterly,* 50/1 (1997), 119-135

Ter Horst, D.J.H., *Daniel Heinsius ‹1580-1655›* (Utrecht (1934)

–, 'Vulcanius', in *Nieuw Nederlandsch biografisch woordenboek,* 10 (1937), 1143-1145

Tewes, G.R., *Die Bursen der Kölner Artisten-Fakultät bis zur Mitte des 16. Jahrhunderts* (Cologne 1993)

Tholuck, A., *Das akademische Leben* (Halle 1853)

Thomas Aquinas, *Summa Theologica XXIX. Die Sakramente. Taufe und Firmung (III 60-72)* (Salzburg 1935)

– , *Summa Theologica XXX. Das Geheimnis der Eucharistie (III 73-83)* (Salzburg 1938)

Thomas of Sutton, *Quodlibeta,* eds. M. Schmaus and M.González-Haba (Munich 1969)

Tilmans, C.P.H.M., *Aurelius en de Divisiekroniek van 1517. Historiografie en humanisme in Holland in de tijd van Erasmus* (Hilversum 1988)

Titelmans, Franciscus, *Collationes quinque super epistolam ad Romanos* (Antwerp 1529)

Todd, M., *Christian Humanism and the Puritan Social Order* (New York 1987)

Traiecti (alias De Voecht), Jacobus, *Narratio de inchoatione domus clericorum in Zwollis,* met akten en bescheiden betreffende dit fraterhuis uitgegeven door M. Schoengen (Werken Historisch Genootschap, s. 3, nr 13) (Amsterdam 1908)

Trapman, J., *De summa der godliker scrifturen (1523)* (Leiden 1978)

Trapp, D., 'Peter Ceffons of Clairvaux', in *Recherches de Théologie ancienne en médiévale,* 24 (1957), 101-154

Trinkaus, C., *In Our Image and Likeness. Humanity and Divinity in Italian Humanist Thought* (Chicago 1970; 2 vols)

Troelstra, A., *Stof en methode der catechese in Nederland vóór de Reformatie* (Groningen 1903)

Troncarelli, F., *Boethiana Aetas. Modelli grafici e fortuna manoscritta della 'Consolatio Philosophiae' tra IX e XII secolo* (Alessandria 1987)

Troß, L., 'Alexander Hegius', in *Zeitschrift für vaterländische Geschichte und Alterthumskunde,* 21 (1861), 339-59

Trunz, E., 'Der deutsche Späthumanismus um 1600 als Standeskultur', in E. Trunz, *Deutsche Literatur zwischen Späthumanismus und Barock. Acht Studien* (Munich 1995), 7-82

Trusen, W., 'Die Anfänge öffentlicher Banken und das Zinsproblem. Kontroversen im Spätmittelalter', in *Recht und Wirtschaft in Geschichte und Gegenwart. Festschrift für Johannes Bärmann zum 70. Geburtstag,* eds. M. Lutter, H. Kollhosser and W. Trusen (Munich 1975), 113-131

Ubbo Emmius. Een Oostfries geleerde in Groningen–Ubbo Emmius. Ein Ostfriesischer Gelehrter in Groningen, ed. W.J. Kuppers (Groningen 1994)

Ullmann, W., *Medieval Foundations of Renaissance Humanism* (Ithaca, NY 1977)

Vaccari, P., *Storia dell'Università di Pavia* (Pavia [3]1982)

Valla, Lorenzo, *De vero falsoque bono,* ed. M. de Panizza Lorch (Bari 1970)

Van Beelen, J., *Doet dit tot Mijn Gedachtenis. Een onderzoek naar de relaties tussen avondmaal en ambt: over avondmaalsmijding van ambtsdragers en het probleem van de bediening* (Leiden 1996)

Van Belle, A., *De Fakulteit van de Artes te Leuven. Haar vroegste organisatie 1426-1441*

(unpublished diss., Louvain 1959)

Van Berkel, K., 'Franeker als centrum van ramisme', in *Universiteit te Franeker 1585-1811*, eds. G.T. Jensma, F.R.H. Smit and F. Westra (Leeuwarden 1985), 424-437

Van den Oord, C.J.A., *Twee eeuwen Bosch' Boekbedrijf, 1450 -1650. Een onderzoek naar de betekenis van de Bossche boekdrukkers, uitgevers en librariërs voor het regionale socioculturele leven* (Tilburg 1984)

Vanderjagt, A.J., 'Filosofie tussen humanisme en eclecticisme', in *'Om niet aan onwetendheid en barbarij te bezwijken.' Groningse geleerden 1614-1989*, eds. G.A. van Gemert, J. Schuller tot Peursum-Meijer and A.J. Vanderjagt (Hilversum 1989), 31-49

Van der Laan, A.H., *Anatomie van een Taal. Rodolphus Agricola en Antonius Liber aan de wieg van het humanistische Latijn in de Lage Landen (1469-1485)* (diss. Groningen 1998)

Van der Poel, M., 'The "Scholia in Orationem pro lege Manilia" of Rudolph Agricola (1444-1485). Edition of the Text with Introduction and Explanatory Notes', in *Lias*, 24 (1997), 1-35

Vander Straeten, E., *La musique aux Pays-Bas avant le XIXe siècle. Documents inédits et annotés* (Brussels 1885)

Van Deursen, A.T., *Bavianen en slijkgeuzen. Kerk en kerkvolk ten tijde van Maurits en Oldebarnevelt* (Assen 1974)

Van Dijk, R.Th.M., 'Windesheim (chanoines réguliers de –; Frères de la Vie commune)', in *Dictionnaire de Spiritualité*, 16 (1994), 1457-1478

Van Engen, J., 'The Virtues, the Brothers and the Schools', in *Revue Bénédictine*, 98 (1988), 178-217

–, 'The Church in the Fifteenth Century', in *Handbook of European History, 1400-1600*, I 305-330

Van Gelder, H.E., *Geschiedenis der Latijnsche School te Alkmaar I* (Alkmaar 1905)

Van Herwaarden, J., 'Medici in de Nederlandse samenleving in de late Middeleeuwen (veertiende-zestiende eeuw)', in *Tijdschrift voor Geschiedenis*, 96 (1983), 348-378

Van Iseghem, A.F., *Biographie de Thierry Martens d'Alost, premier imprimeur de la Belgique, suivie de la bibliographie de ses éditions* (Malines 1852)

Van Kalveen, C.A., 'Johan Pupper van Goch en de broeders des Gemenen Levens', in *Archief voor de Geschiedenis van de Katholieke Kerk in Nederland*, 20 (1978), 103-113

Van Kessel, P.J., *Duitse studenten te Padua. De controverse Rome-Venetië en het Protestantisme in de tijd der Contra-Reformatie* (Assen 1963)

Van Leijenhorst, G.C., 'Alexander Hegius of Heek, d. 27 December 1498', in *CE* II 173

Van Pamel, G., *Echo's van een wetenschappelijke revolutie. De mechanistische natuurwetenschap aan de Leuvense Artes-faculteit (1650-1797)* (Brussels 1986)

Van Rhijn, M., *Wessel Gansfort* (The Hague 1917)

–, *Impugnatorium M. Antonii de Castro contra epistolam M. Wesseli Groningensis ad M. Jacobum Hoeck, de indulgentiis* (The Hague 1919)

–, 'Goswinus van Halen', in *NAKG*, 18 (1925), 1-23

–, *Studiën over Wessel Gansfort en zijn tijd* (Utrecht 1933)

Van Rooden, P.T., *Constantijn L'Empereur (1591-1648), professor Hebreeuws en theologie te Leiden* (Leiden 1985)

Van Schelven, A.A., 'Een brief van Praedinius', in *NAKG*, 21 (1928), 54-56

Van Sluis, J., 'Bibliografie van Deventer disputaties 1630-1815', in *Deventer denkers*, 213-226

Van Toorenbergen, J.J., *Het oudste Nederlandsche verboden boek. 1523. Oeconomica christiana. Summa der godliker scrifturen* (Leiden 1882)

–, 'Hinne Rode (Joh. Rodius), rector der Hiëronymusschool te Utrecht (-1522), predikant te Norden (-1530) in betrekking tot de Anabaptisten', in *Nederlands Archief voor Kerkgeschiedenis*, 3 (1888/9), 90-101

Van Veen, H., *Carmelieten en humanisten: de geschiedenis van een verwijdering* (Groningen 1977; unpublished)

Van Vicus Artium tot nieuwbouw: 550 jaar Faculteitsgeschiedenis. Catalogus van de tentoonstelling 13 november-19 december (Louvain 1975)

Vasoli, C., *La dialettica e la retorica dell'Umanesimo. "Invenzione" e "Metodo" nella cultura del XV e XVI secolo* (Milan 1968)

Verbeek, Th., 'Tradition and Novelty: Descartes and Some Cartesians', in *The Rise of Modern*

Philosophy. The Tension between the New and Traditional Philosophies from Machiavelli to Leibniz, ed. T. Sorell (Oxford 1993), 167-196

Verde, A.F., *Lo Studio fiorentino 1473-1503. Ricerche e documenti, II: Docenti, Dottorati* (Florence 1973)

Vermaseren, B.A., *De katholieke Nederlandse geschiedschrijving in de 16e en 17e eeuw over de opstand* (Leeuwarden 1981)

Vernulaeus, N., *Academia Lovaniensiss libri III. Ejus origo, incrementum, forma, magistratus, facultates, privilegia, scholae, collegia, viri illustres, res gestae* (Louvain 1667)

Visser, D., 'Among the good teachers: Melanchthon on Wessel Gansfort', in *Wessel Gansfort (1419-1489) and Northern Humanism*, 142-153

Vives, Juan Luis, *In pseudodialecticos. A Critical Edition, Introduction, Translation and Commentary by C. Fantazzi* (Leiden 1979)

Voetius, Gisbertus, *Illustris gymnasii Ultrajectini inauguratio, una cum orationibus inauguralibus* (Utrecht 1634), [e2]r-[l3]v

–, 'De scholastica theologia', in idem, *Selectarum disputationum theologicarum I* (Utrecht 1648), 12-29

Vogel, P.H., *Europäische Bibeldrucke des 15. und 16. Jahrhunderts in den Volkssprachen: ein Beitrag zur Bibliographie des Bibeldrucks* (Baden Baden 1962)

Voigt, G., *Die Briefe des Aeneas Silvius von seiner Erhebung auf dem päpstliche Stuhl* (Vienna 1856)

Von Bundschuh, B., *Das Wormser Religionsgespräch von 1557* (Münster 1988)

Von Lingelsheim, W., *Familien-Chronik derer von Lingelsheim* (Mengeringhausen 1922)

Voolstra, S., *Het woord is vlees geworden. De melchioritisch-menniste incarnatieleer* (Kampen 1982)

'La vraie piété'. Divers traités de Jean Calvin et Confession de foi de Guillaume Farel, eds. I. Backus and C. Chimelli (Geneva 1986)

Vredeveld, H., 'The Ages of Erasmus and the Year of His Birth', in *Renaissance Quarterly*, 46/4 (1993), 754-809

Waddington, C., *Pierre Ramus (1515-1572). Sa vie et ses écrits* (Paris 1855)

Walter, A.E., 'Georg Michael Lingelsheim. Esquisse biographique d'un humaniste politique dans la région du Rhin supérieur (1558-1636)', in *Revue d'Alsace*, 124 (1998), 35-54

Walter, P., 'Johannes von Dalberg und der Humanismus', in *1495–Kaiser Reich Reformen. Der Reichstag zu Worms. Ausstellung des Landeshauptarchivs Koblenz in Verbindung mit der Stadt Worms zum 500-jährigen Jubiläum des Wormser Reichstags von 1495* (Koblenz 1995), 139-171

Walz, D., 'Marsilius von Inghen als Schreiber und Büchersammler', in *Marsilius von Inghen. Werk und Wirkung*, ed. S. Wielgus (Lublin 1993), 31-71

Waterbolk, E.H., *Twee eeuwen Friese geschiedschrijving. Opkomst, bloei en verval van de Friese historiografie in de zestiende en zeventiende eeuw* (Groningen 1952)

–, *Een hond in het bad. Enige aspecten van de verhouding tussen Erasmus en Agricola* (Groningen 1966)

Weijers, O., 'L'enseignement du *trivium* à la Faculté des arts de Paris: la *questio*', in *Manuels, programmes de cours et techniques d'enseignement dans les universités médiévales*, ed. J. Hamesse (Louvain-La-Neuve 1994), 57-74

Weiler, A.G., *Heinrich von Gorkum (†1431). Seine Stellung in der Philosophie und Theologie des Spätmittelalters* (Hilversum 1962)

–, *Necrologie, kroniek en cartularium c.a. van het fraterhuis te Doesburg (1432-1559) met een inleiding. Voorzien van paleografische en boek-archeologische aantekeningen door A. Gruijs* (Leiden 1974)

–, 'Les relations entre l'Université de Louvain et l'Université de Cologne au XVe siècle', in *The Universities in the Late Middle Ages*, eds. J. IJsewijn and J. Paquet (Louvain 1978), 49-81

–, 'The foundations of the superior secular and spiritual powers according to William of Ockham's *Octo Quaestiones de Potestate Papae*', in *Ockham and Ockhamists*, eds. E.P Bos and H.A. Krop (Acts of the Symposium organized by the Dutch Society for Medieval Philosophy *Medium Aevum* on the occasion of its 10th anniversary, Leiden, 10-12 september 1986) (Artistarium Supplementa, 4) (Nijmegen 1987), 145-152

–, 'La systématique de la théologie morale selon Arnold Geilhoven', in *Actes du colloque Terminologie de la vie intellectuelle au moyen âge (Leyde/La Haye 20-21 septembre 1985)* (Turnhout 1988), 11-18

–, 'Over de geestelijke praktijk van de Moderne Devotie', in *De doorwerking van de Moderne Devotie*, 29-45

–, 'Soziale und sozial-psychologische Aspekte der Devotio Moderna', in *Laienfrömmigkeit im späten Mittelalter. Formen, Funktionen, politisch-soziale Zusammenhänge*, ed. K. Schreiner (Schriften des Historischen Kollegs. Kolloquien, 20) (Munich 1992), 191-201

–, 'De betekenis van de Moderne Devotie voor de Europese cultuur', in *Trajecta*, 1 (1992), 33-48

–, 'Christelijke identiteit, morele vorming en laat-middeleeuws onderwijs', in *Geloof, moraal en intellect in de middeleeuwen. Voordrachten gehouden tijdens het symposium t.g.v. het tien-jarig bestaan van het Nijmeegs Centrum voor Middeleeuwse Studies, 10 en 11 december 1993*, ed. P. Bange (Middeleeuwse Studies, 10) (Nijmegen 1995), 177-198

–, 'Het werk van professor Post. Een historische plaatsbepaling van het laatmiddeleeuwse Nederlandse katholicisme tussen protestantisme en humanisme', in *Trajecta*, 4 (1995), 226-40

–, 'Christelijke identiteit en tolerantie volgens Geert Grote en Thomas van Kempen', in *Identiteit en tolerantie. Nederlandse filosofen aan het begin van de nieuwe tijd*, ed. H.E.S. Woldring (Baarn 1995), 30-46

–, *Volgens de norm van de vroege kerk. De geschiedenis van de huizen van de Broeders van het Gemene Leven in Nederland* (Middeleeuwse Studies, 13) (Nijmegen 1996)

–, 'Erasmus of Rotterdam's *Institutum hominis christiani*, a substitute for the mediaeval *Liber Floretus*', in *Media Latinitas. A collection of essays to mark the occasion of the retirement of L.J. Engels*, eds. R.I.A. Nip a.o. (Steenbrugge 1996), 359-363

–, *Desiderius Erasmus. De spiritualiteit van een christen-humanist* (Nijmegen 1997)

Weiss, R., *The Dawn of Humanism in Italy. An Inaugural Lecture Delivered at University College London on 28th May 1947* (London 1947)

Wessel Gansfort (1419-1489) and Northern Humanism, eds. F. Akkerman, G.C. Huisman and A.J. Vanderjagt (Leiden 1993)

Wessel Gansfort. Life and Writings. Principal Works Translated, eds. E.W. Scudder and J.W. Miller (New York 1917) (2 vols)

Wiegand, H., '*Mentibus at vatum deus insidet...* Zu Rudolf Agricolas lateinischer Dichtung', in *Rudolf Agricola 1444-1485*, 261-291

Wierda, L., *De Sarijs-handschriften. Laat-middeleeuwse handschriften uit de IJsselstreek* (Zwolle 1995)

Wiese, J., *Der Pädagoge Alexander Hegius und seine Schüler* (Berlin 1892)

William of St.-Thierry, *Meditativae orationes*, in *PL* 180, 205-248

–, *Meditaties* (Bonheiden 1978)

Wind, E., *Pagan Mysteries in the Renaissance* (London 1968)

Wissink, W., 'Dolinghe der consciencien. Adviezen voor een gerust geweten in de *Gentse Boethius*', in *Wat is wijsheid? Lekenethiek in de Middelnederlandse letterkunde*, ed. J. Reynaert (Amsterdam 1994), 337-352

Wolf, D., *Die Irenik des Hugo Grotius nach ihren Prinzipien und biographisch-geistesgeschichtlichen Perspektiven* (Marburg 1969)

Wolfs, S.P., *Das Groninger 'Religionsgespräch' (1523) und seine Hintergründe* (Nijmegen 1959)

The World of Hugo Grotius ‹1583-1645›. Proceedings of the International Colloquium organized by the Grotius Committee of the Royal Netherlands Academy of Arts and Sciences, Rotterdam 6-9 april 1983 (Amsterdam 1984)

Wormgoor, I., 'De vervolging van de Vrijen van Geest, de begijnen en begarden', in *Nederlands Archief voor Kerkgeschiedenis*, 65 (1985), 107-130

Worstbrock, F.J., 'Hegius, Alexander', in *Die deutsche Literatur des Mittelalters. Verfasserlexikon*, III 572-577

–, 'Liber, Antonius', in *Die deutsche Literatur des Mittelalters. Verfasserlexikon*, V 747-751

–, 'Piccolomini, Aeneas Silvius', in *Die deutsche Literatur des Mittelalters. Verfasserlexikon*, VII 634-669

–, 'Zur Biographie des Alexander Hegius', in *Humanistica Lovaniensia,* 29 (1980), 161-165
Wyclif, John, 'Determinatio contra Kylingham Carmelitam', in *Fasciculi Zizaniorum magistri Johannis Wyclif cum tritico,* ed. W. Waddington Shirley (London 1858), 453-476
–, *De veritate Sacrae Scripturae,* ed. R. Buddensieg (London 1905-1907; repr. New York 1966) (3 vols)
–, *On Universals (Tractatus de universalibus),* transl. A. Kenny (Oxford 1985)
Zaffignani, G., 'Lo schedario nobiliare Marozzi', in *Bollettino della società Pavese di Storia Patria,* 93 (1993)
Zanetti, D., 'Il primo collegio pavese per studenti stranieri', in *Studi in memoria di Marco Abrate, II* (Turin 1986), 789-812
Zijlstra, S., *Het geleerde Friesland–een mythe? Universiteit en maatschappij in Friesland en Stad en Lande ca. 1380-1650* (Leeuwarden 1996)
Zimmerman, 'Les Carmes Humanistes (Environ 1465 jusque 1525)', in *Etudes Carmélitaines,* 20/2 (1935), 19-93
Zippel, G., 'Gli inizi dell'Umanesimo tedesco e l'Umanesimo italiano nel XV secolo', in *Bullettino dell'Istituto Storico Italiano per il Medioevo e Archivio Muratoriano,* 75 (1963)
Zuidema, W., *Wilhelmus Frederici, Persona van Sint Maarten te Groningen (1489-1525) en de Groninger Staatkunde van zijn tijd* (Groningen 1888)
Zwingli, Huldreich, *Sämtliche Werke. III. Werke 1524-März 1525* (Leipzig 1914; repr. Zürich 1982)
–, 'Von der Anrufung der Verstorbenen, die im Himmel sind', in *Zwingli. Hauptschriften, Band X: Der Theologe* (Zürich 1963), II 157-169

INDEX OF PERSONAL NAMES

BRILL'S STUDIES
IN
INTELLECTUAL HISTORY

1. POPKIN, R.H. *Isaac la Peyrère (1596-1676)*. His Life, Work and Influence. 1987. ISBN 90 04 08157 7
2. THOMSON, A. *Barbary and Enlightenment*. European Attitudes towards the Maghreb in the 18th Century. 1987. ISBN 90 04 08273 5
3. DUHEM, P. *Prémices Philosophiques*. With an Introduction in English by S.L. Jaki. 1987. ISBN 90 04 08117 8
4. OUDEMANS, TH.C.W. & A.P.M.H. LARDINOIS. *Tragic Ambiguity*. Anthropology, Philosophy and Sophocles' *Antigone*. 1987. ISBN 90 04 08417 7
5. FRIEDMAN, J.B. (ed.). *John de Foxton's Liber Cosmographiae (1408)*. An Edition and Codicological Study. 1988. ISBN 90 04 08528 9
6. AKKERMAN, F. & A. J. VANDERJAGT (eds.). *Rodolphus Agricola Phrisius, 1444-1485*. Proceedings of the International Conference at the University of Groningen, 28-30 October 1985. 1988. ISBN 90 04 08599 8
7. CRAIG, W.L. *The Problem of Divine Foreknowledge and Future Contingents from Aristotle to Suarez*. 1988. ISBN 90 04 08516 5
8. STROLL, M. *The Jewish Pope*. Ideology and Politics in the Papal Schism of 1130. 1987. ISBN 90 04 08590 4
9. STANESCO, M. *Jeux d'errance du chevalier médiéval*. Aspects ludiques de la fonction guerrière dans la littérature du Moyen Age flamboyant. 1988. ISBN 90 04 08684 6
10. KATZ, D. *Sabbath and Sectarianism in Seventeenth-Century England*. 1988. ISBN 90 04 08754 0
11. LERMOND, L. *The Form of Man*. Human Essence in Spinoza's *Ethic*. 1988. ISBN 90 04 08829 6
12. JONG, M. DE. *In Samuel's Image*. Child Oblation in the Early Medieval West. 1996. ISBN 90 04 10483 6
13. PYENSON, L. *Empire of Reason*. Exact Sciences in Indonesia, 1840-1940. 1989. ISBN 90 04 08984 5
14. CURLEY, E. & P.-F. MOREAU (eds.). *Spinoza. Issues and Directions*. The Proceedings of the Chicago Spinoza Conference. 1990. ISBN 90 04 09334 6
15. KAPLAN, Y., H. MÉCHOULAN & R.H. POPKIN (eds.). *Menasseh Ben Israel and His World*. 1989. ISBN 90 04 09114 9
16. BOS, A.P. *Cosmic and Meta-Cosmic Theology in Aristotle's Lost Dialogues*. 1989. ISBN 90 04 09155 6
17. KATZ, D.S. & J.I. ISRAEL (eds.). *Sceptics, Millenarians and Jews*. 1990. ISBN 90 04 09160 2
18. DALES, R.C. *Medieval Discussions of the Eternity of the World*. 1990. ISBN 90 04 09215 3
19. CRAIG, W.L. *Divine Foreknowledge and Human Freedom*. The Coherence of Theism: Omniscience. 1991. ISBN 90 04 09250 1
20. OTTEN, W. *The Anthropology of Johannes Scottus Eriugena*. 1991. ISBN 90 04 09302 8
21. ÅKERMAN, S. *Queen Christina of Sweden and Her Circle*. The Transformation of a Seventeenth-Century Philosophical Libertine. 1991. ISBN 90 04 09310 9
22. POPKIN, R.H. *The Third Force in Seventeenth-Century Thought*. 1992. ISBN 90 04 09324 9
23. DALES, R.C & O. ARGERAMI (eds.). *Medieval Latin Texts on the Eternity of the World*. 1990. ISBN 90 04 09376 1
24. STROLL, M. *Symbols as Power*. The Papacy Following the Investiture Contest. 1991. ISBN 90 04 09374 5
25. FARAGO, C.J. *Leonardo da Vinci's 'Paragone'*. A Critical Interpretation with a New Edition of the Text in the *Codex Urbinas*. 1992. ISBN 90 04 09415 6

26. JONES, R. *Learning Arabic in Renaissance Europe*. Forthcoming. ISBN 90 04 09451 2
27. DRIJVERS, J.W. *Helena Augusta*. The Mother of Constantine the Great and the Legend of Her Finding of the True Cross. 1992. ISBN 90 04 09435 0
28. BOUCHER, W.I. *Spinoza in English*. A Bibliography from the Seventeenth-Century to the Present. 1991. ISBN 90 04 09499 7
29. McINTOSH, C. *The Rose Cross and the Age of Reason*. Eighteenth-Century Rosicrucianism in Central Europe and its Relationship to the Enlightenment. 1992. ISBN 90 04 09502 0
30. CRAVEN, K. *Jonathan Swift and the Millennium of Madness*. The Information Age in Swift's *A Tale of a Tub*. 1992. ISBN 90 04 09524 1
31. BERKVENS-STEVELINCK, C., H. BOTS, P.G. HOFTIJZER & O.S. LANKHORST (eds.). *Le Magasin de l'Univers. The Dutch Republic as the Centre of the European Book Trade*. Papers Presented at the International Colloquium, held at Wassenaar, 5-7 July 1990. 1992. ISBN 90 04 09493 8
32. GRIFFIN, JR., M.I.J. *Latitudinarianism in the Seventeenth-Century Church of England*. Annotated by R.H. Popkin. Edited by L. Freedman. 1992. ISBN 90 04 09653 1
33. WES, M.A. *Classics in Russia 1700-1855*. Between two Bronze Horsemen. 1992. ISBN 90 04 09664 7
34. BULHOF, I.N. *The Language of Science*. A Study in the Relationship between Literature and Science in the Perspective of a Hermeneutical Ontology. With a Case Study in Darwin's *The Origin of Species*. 1992. ISBN 90 04 09644 2
35. LAURSEN, J.C. *The Politics of Skepticism in the Ancients, Montaigne, Hume and Kant*. 1992. ISBN 90 04 09459 8
36. COHEN, E. *The Crossroads of Justice*. Law and Culture in Late Medieval France. 1993. ISBN 90 04 09569 1
37. POPKIN, R.H. & A.J. VANDERJAGT (eds.). *Scepticism and Irreligion in the Seventeenth and Eighteenth Centuries*. 1993. ISBN 90 04 09596 9
38. MAZZOCCO, A. *Linguistic Theories in Dante and the Humanists*. Studies of Language and Intellectual History in Late Medieval and Early Renaissance Italy. 1993. ISBN 90 04 09702 3
39. KROOK, D. *John Sergeant and His Circle*. A Study of Three Seventeenth-Century English Aristotelians. Edited with an Introduction by B.C. Southgate. 1993. ISBN 90 04 09756 2
40. AKKERMAN, F., G.C. HUISMAN & A.J. VANDERJAGT (eds.). *Wessel Gansfort (1419-1489) and Northern Humanism*. 1993. ISBN 90 04 09857 7
41. COLISH, M.L. *Peter Lombard*. 2 volumes. 1994. ISBN 90 04 09859 3 (Vol. 1), ISBN 90 04 09860 7 (Vol. 2), ISBN 90 04 09861 5 (Set)
42. VAN STRIEN, C.D. *British Travellers in Holland During the Stuart Period*. Edward Browne and John Locke as Tourists in the United Provinces. 1993. ISBN 90 04 09482 2
43. MACK, P. *Renaissance Argument*. Valla and Agricola in the Traditions of Rhetoric and Dialectic. 1993. ISBN 90 04 09879 8
44. DA COSTA, U. *Examination of Pharisaic Traditions*. Supplemented by SEMUEL DA SILVA's *Treatise on the Immortality of the Soul*. Tratado da immortalidade da alma. Translation, Notes and Introduction by H.P. Salomon & I.S.D. Sassoon. 1993. ISBN 90 04 09923 9
45. MANNS, J.W. *Reid and His French Disciples*. Aesthetics and Metaphysics. 1994. ISBN 90 04 09942 5
46. SPRUNGER, K.L. *Trumpets from the Tower*. English Puritan Printing in the Netherlands, 1600-1640. 1994. ISBN 90 04 09935 2
47. RUSSELL, G.A. (ed.). *The 'Arabick' Interest of the Natural Philosophers in Seventeenth-Century England*. 1994. ISBN 90 04 09888 7
48. SPRUIT, L. Species intelligibilis: *From Perception to Knowledge*. Volume I: Classical Roots and Medieval Discussions. 1994. ISBN 90 04 09883 6
49. SPRUIT, L. Species intelligibilis: *From Perception to Knowledge*. Volume II: Renaissance Controversies, Later Scholasticism, and the Elimination of the Intelligible Species in Modern Philosophy. 1995. ISBN 90 04 10396 1
50. HYATTE, R. *The Arts of Friendship*. The Idealization of Friendship in Medieval and Early Renaissance Literature. 1994. ISBN 90 04 10018 0
51. CARRÉ, J. (ed.). *The Crisis of Courtesy*. Studies in the Conduct-Book in Britain, 1600-1900. 1994. ISBN 90 04 10005 9

52. BURMAN, T.E. *Religious Polemic and the Intellectual History of the Mozarabs, 1050-1200.* 1994. ISBN 90 04 09910 7
53. HORLICK, A.S. *Patricians, Professors, and Public Schools.* The Origins of Modern Educational Thought in America. 1994. ISBN 90 04 10054 7
54. MacDONALD, A.A., M. LYNCH & I.B. COWAN (eds.). *The Renaissance in Scotland.* Studies in Literature, Religion, History and Culture Offered to John Durkan. 1994. ISBN 90 04 10097 0
55. VON MARTELS, Z. (ed.). *Travel Fact and Travel Fiction.* Studies on Fiction, Literary Tradition, Scholarly Discovery and Observation in Travel Writing. 1994. ISBN 90 04 10112 8
56. PRANGER, M.B. *Bernard of Clairvaux and the Shape of Monastic Thought.* Broken Dreams. 1994. ISBN 90 04 10055 5
57. VAN DEUSEN, N. *Theology and Music at the Early University.* The Case of Robert Grosseteste and Anonymous IV. 1994. ISBN 90 04 10059 8
58. WARNEKE, S. *Images of the Educational Traveller in Early Modern England.* 1994. ISBN 90 04 10126 8
59. BIETENHOLZ, P.G. *Historia and Fabula.* Myths and Legends in Historical Thought from Antiquity to the Modern Age. 1994. ISBN 90 04 10063 6
60. LAURSEN, J.C. (ed.). *New Essays on the Political Thought of the Huguenots of the Refuge.* 1995. ISBN 90 04 09986 7
61. DRIJVERS, J.W. & A.A. MacDONALD (eds.). *Centres of Learning.* Learning and Location in Pre-Modern Europe and the Near East. 1995. ISBN 90 04 10193 4
62. JAUMANN, H. *Critica.* Untersuchungen zur Geschichte der Literaturkritik zwischen Quintilian und Thomasius. 1995. ISBN 90 04 10276 0
63. HEYD, M. *"Be Sober and Reasonable."* The Critique of Enthusiasm in the Seventeenth and Early Eighteenth Centuries. 1995. ISBN 90 04 10118 7
64. OKENFUSS, M.J. *The Rise and Fall of Latin Humanism in Early-Modern Russia.* Pagan Authors, Ukrainians, and the Resiliency of Muscovy. 1995. ISBN 90 04 10331 7
65. DALES, R.C. *The Problem of the Rational Soul in the Thirteenth Century.* 1995. ISBN 90 04 10296 5
66. VAN RULER, J.A. *The Crisis of Causality.* Voetius and Descartes on God, Nature and Change. 1995. ISBN 90 04 10371 6
67. SHEHADI, F. *Philosophies of Music in Medieval Islam.* 1995. ISBN 90 04 10128 4
68. GROSS-DIAZ, T. *The Psalms Commentary of Gilbert of Poitiers.* From *Lectio Divina* to the Lecture Room. 1996. ISBN 90 04 10211 6
69. VAN BUNGE, W. & W. KLEVER (eds.). *Disguised and Overt Spinozism around 1700.* Papers Presented at the International Colloquium, held at Rotterdam, 5-8 October, 1994. 1996. ISBN 90 04 10307 4
70. FLORIDI, L. *Scepticism and the Foundation of Epistemology.* A Study in the Meta-logical Fallacies. 1996. ISBN 90 04 10533 6
71. FOUKE, D. *The Enthusiastical Concerns of Dr. Henry More.* Religious Meaning and the Psychology of Delusion. 1997. ISBN 90 04 10600 6
72. RAMELOW, T. *Gott, Freiheit, Weltenwahl.* Der Ursprung des Begriffes der besten aller möglichen Welten in der Metaphysik der Willensfreiheit zwischen Antonio Perez S.J. (1599-1649) und G.W. Leibniz (1646-1716). 1997. ISBN 90 04 10641 3
73. STONE, H.S. *Vico's Cultural History.* The Production and Transmission of Ideas in Naples, 1685-1750. 1997. ISBN 90 04 10650 2
74. STROLL, M. *The Medieval Abbey of Farfa.* Target of Papal and Imperial Ambitions. 1997. ISBN 90 04 10704 5
75. HYATTE, R. *The Prophet of Islam in Old French:* The Romance of Muhammad *(1258) and* The Book of Muhammad's Ladder *(1264).* English Translations, With an Introduction. 1997. ISBN 90 04 10709 2
76. JESTICE, P.G. *Wayward Monks and the Religious Revolution of the Eleventh Century.* 1997. ISBN 90 04 10722 3
77. VAN DER POEL, M. *Cornelius Agrippa, The Humanist Theologian and His Declamations.* 1997. ISBN 90 04 10756 8
78. SYLLA, E. & M. McVAUGH (eds.). *Texts and Contexts in Ancient and Medieval Science.* Studies on the Occasion of John E. Murdoch's Seventieth Birthday. 1997. ISBN 90 04 10823 8

79. BINKLEY, P. (ed.). *Pre-Modern Encyclopaedic Texts.* Proceedings of the Second COMERS Congress, Groningen, 1-4 July 1996. 1997. ISBN 90 04 10830 0
80. KLAVER, J.M.I. *Geology and Religious Sentiment.* The Effect of Geological Discoveries on English Society and Literature between 1829 and 1859. 1997. ISBN 90 04 10882 3
81. INGLIS, J. *Spheres of Philosophical Inquiry and the Historiography of Medieval Philosophy.* 1998. ISBN 90 04 10843 2
82. McCALLA, A. *A Romantic Historiosophy.* The Philosophy of History of Pierre-Simon Ballanche. 1998. ISBN 90 04 10967 6
83. VEENSTRA, J.R. *Magic and Divination at the Courts of Burgundy and France.* Text and Context of Laurens Pignon's *Contre les devineurs* (1411). 1998. ISBN 90 04 10925 0
84. WESTERMAN, P.C. *The Disintegration of Natural Law Theory.* Aquinas to Finnis. 1998. ISBN 90 04 10999 4
85. GOUWENS, K. *Remembering the Renaissance.* Humanist Narratives of the Sack of Rome. 1998. ISBN 90 04 10969 2
86. SCHOTT, H. & J. ZINGUER (Hrsg.). *Paracelsus und seine internationale Rezeption in der frühen Neuzeit.* Beiträge zur Geschichte des Paracelsismus. 1998. ISBN 90 04 10974 9
87. ÅKERMAN, S. *Rose Cross over the Baltic.* The Spread of Rosicrucianism in Northern Europe. 1998. ISBN 90 04 11030 5
88. DICKSON, D.R. *The Tessera of Antilia.* Utopian Brotherhoods & Secret Societies in the Early Seventeenth Century. 1998. ISBN 90 04 11032 1
89. NOUHUYS, T. VAN. *The Two-Faced Janus.* The Comets of 1577 and 1618 and the Decline of the Aristotelian World View in the Netherlands. 1998. ISBN 90 04 11204 9
90. MUESSIG, C. (ed.). *Medieval Monastic Preaching.* 1998. ISBN 90 04 10883 1
91. FORCE, J.E. & D.S. KATZ (eds.). *"Everything Connects": In Conference with Richard H. Popkin.* Essays in His Honor. 1999. ISBN 90 04 110984
92. DEKKER, K. *The Origins of Old Germanic Studies in the Low Countries.* 1999. ISBN 90 04 11031 3
93. ROUHI, L. *Mediation and Love.* A Study of the Medieval Go-Between in Key Romance and Near Eastern Texts. 1999. ISBN 90 04 11268 5
94. AKKERMAN, F., A. VANDERJAGT & A. VAN DER LAAN (eds.). *Northern Humanism between 1469 and 1625.* 1999. ISBN 90 04 11314 2